W9-CZM-522

BRADFORD
COLLEGE
LIBRARY

HUMAN EXPERIMENTAL PSYCHOLOGY

HUMAN EXPERIMENTAL PSYCHOLOGY

Joan Gay Snodgrass
Gail Levy-Berger
Martin Haydon

New York Oxford
OXFORD UNIVERSITY PRESS
1985

Oxford University Press
Oxford New York Toronto
Delhi Bombay Calcutta Madras Karachi
Kuala Lumpur Singapore Hong Kong Tokyo
Nairobi Dar es Salaam Cape Town
Melbourne Auckland

and associated companies in
Beirut Berlin Ibadan Mexico City Nicosia

Published by Oxford University Press, Inc.,
200 Madison Avenue, New York, New York 10016

Library of Congress Cataloging in Publication Data

Snodgrass, Joan Gay.
Human experimental psychology.

Bibliography: p.
Includes index.
1. Psychology, Experimental. 2. Human experimentation in psychology. I. Levy-Berger, Gail. II. Haydon, Martin. III. Title. [DNLM: 1. Psychology, Experimental. 2. Research Design. BF 181 S673h]
BF181.S66 1985 150′.724 84-29463
ISBN 0-19-503574-7
ISBN 0-19-504942-X (pbk.)

Printing (last digit): 9 8 7 6 5 4 3 2

Printed in the United States of America

To today's students who will become
tomorrow's experimental psychologists

Preface

This textbook is designed to be used in an undergraduate or graduate laboratory course in human experimental psychology, in which students obtain hands-on experience in designing experiments, setting up apparatus, running subjects, analyzing and interpreting data, and writing up the results as a research report. This text can also be adapted for use in a one-semester survey course in either research methods or content.

Orientation. This textbook effectively integrates the content of experimental psychology with its methods. This not only allows the student to understand what psychologists have learned about mental processes, but also to appreciate how they have made their discoveries. It is the nature of experimentation that "facts" will constantly be revised. Therefore, it is important to know how facts are gathered and how they are interpreted. For this reason, we have incorporated experimental methods into the content chapters. For the course that requires more detailed coverage of methods or procedures, special chapters have been provided. In particular, Part III, procedural methodology, is a reference to be used as experiments are designed, run, and analyzed. For a one-semester course covering research methods or content, Part III can be eliminated and appropriate chapters from Parts I and II selected accordingly. One of the many strengths of this book is that each chapter is self-contained and one or more chapters may be deleted without loss of continuity.

Organization. The book is organized into three sections. Part I, design methodology, describes what experiments are (Chapter 1), how to design them (Chapter 2), and how to avoid pitfalls in carrying them out (Chapter 3). The next two chapters in Part I describe general types of procedures, including psychophysical methods (Chapter 4) and the use of reaction time in mental chronometry (Chapter 5).

Part II of the book describes content areas in experimental psychology. The five chapters in this section cover the major areas of research in experimental psychology by specifically concentrating on particular problems in each area and describing ways in which experimental methods have been used to investigate these problems. The areas covered are perception and attention (Chapter 6); conditioning, learning, and motivation (Chapter 7); episodic memory (Chapter 8); semantic memory (Chapter 9); and thinking and problem solving (Chapter 10). The section ends with a chapter describing how experimental methodology has been used in other areas of psychology (Chapter 11).

Part III of the book covers procedural methodology—the nuts and bolts of experimentation. It describes, chapter by chapter, the ingredients that make up the Methods section of a research report. Part III covers subjects (Chapter 12); apparatus (Chapter 13); materials (Chapter 14); descriptive statistics (Chapter 15); and inferential statistics (Chapter 16). Although students are expected to have some background in statistics, Chapters 15 and 16 provide a brief review of statistical concepts along with complete recipes for computing descriptive and inferential statistics. An appendix containing statistical tables complements

Chapter 16. Chapter 17 describes both the form and style of the research report, based on the American Psychological Association's 1983 Publication Manual. Examples from our files of student research reports are used to illustrate what not to do, and their corrections are shown to illustrate what to do.

Designing good experiments to discover principles of human functioning is exciting and challenging. We hope we have succeeded in capturing some of the excitement and intellectual challenge in this book.

Acknowledgments

I wish to offer thanks to my parents, for providing the necessary conditions for this book to be written; to my significant other, Timothy, for his encouragement and devotion; and to an all-but-forgotten colleague for challenging me to go out and get a Ph.D. if I thought I knew more than my bosses. Without his challenge, I never would have entered the field of experimental psychology. Without the help and guidance of my mentors at University of Pennsylvania—most importantly Frank Irwin and Duncan Luce—I would never have fulfilled the challenge. And without the support and encouragement of the Department of Psychology at New York University, this book would never have emerged from a dark corner in our common file cabinets.

J.G.S.

I wish to thank those whose support and encouragement made this task seem manageable and possible during those times that I perceived it as unmanageable and impossible. Principal among my support group is my husband, Israel Berger, my parents, Dr. Bernice Levy and Stanley Levy, my sister, Karen Lane, and my brother, Paul Levy. In addition, I am grateful to my children, Jonathan and Judith, for the joy they have brought me that often provided the essential emotional counterpoint to the task of writing this book

G.L.B.

When I consider what it took to get me to the point where I could contribute to such a work, I recognize my immense debt to a company of dedicated teachers at New York University who showed me how to look at old learning in new ways, to think critically about emerging knowledge, and above all, to find what is concealed behind the obvious. They know who they are, so I will acknowledge them all by naming those with whom I was most involved: Murray Glanzer, Stanley Lehmann, Gay Snodgrass, Doris Aaronson, Martin Braine, George Sperling, and of course, *et al.* I think that helping to produce this text for teaching is an appropriate way to express my thanks.

M.H.

Finally, we acknowledge one another's indispensable contribution to this work. Without our collective cooperation, energy, good will and sense of humor, we would never have brought this book to publication.

New York
June 1985

J.G.S.
G.L.B.
M.H.

Contents

HUMAN EXPERIMENTAL PSYCHOLOGY

I

Design Methodology: Understanding and Planning Experiments

This section introduces and explores issues that arise when planning and designing experiments. To ensure meaningful, purposeful research we must know how to formulate answerable questions (Chapter 1), how to design appropriate experiments (Chapter 2), and how to avoid design problems that could yield misleading or erroneous results (Chapter 3). Once our questions have been asked and our experiment designed, we must choose appropriate measures for our data. We discuss the important relationship between the physical world and the psychological world and the appropriate psychophysical methods for quantifying this relationship (Chapter 4). Next we discuss the methods of mental chronometry with the use of reaction time (Chapter 5).

Upon completing Part I of this text, the student will have a clear understanding of how questions are asked and how they are answered. This background (amplified by the procedural details in Part III) provides the framework to understand and explore areas of interest in experimental psychology (Part II).

1

Introduction to Human Experimental Psychology

What is *human experimental psychology?* Human experimental psychology is that branch of psychology that uses experimentation to gather knowledge about how we select, perceive, interpret, store, and respond to the barrage of stimuli in our environment. It is the branch of science that studies how we learn, remember, think, and act.

The province of the special discipline we call "human experimental psychology," which is the subject and title of this book, does not comprise every kind of experiment in all of human behavior. The study of experimental psychology (which deals with both human and animal behavior) is concerned with *basic* mental processes. Although the distinction between basic and applied science is not always clearly defined, we can say that human experimental psychology centers on such internal processes as sensory and perceptual responses, thinking and reasoning, memory storage and retrieval, speech, motivation, and learning. Experimental psychologists are not primarily interested in investigating problems in personality development, clinical psychopathology, social and industrial behavior, except when such study may bear on the underlying basic processes that play their roles in the more complex behaviors of daily life.

The first challenge we meet as we approach the study of human psychology is How can we learn what goes on in that most complex of mechanisms, the human mind? This question is so formidable that it defied meaningful research in psychology until just a little more than 100 years ago. Experimental psychology has the shortest history of experimentation among all the sciences—in contrast to the physical and life sciences, psychological research is still in its infancy. Of course, we benefit from the methods and experiences of the other sciences. But the nature of the mind calls for special techniques that deal with the relative inaccessibility of mental processes to direct observation. How do these techniques fit the demands of scientific study?

Our understanding can come from various sources, including observations and intuitions that seem to "make sense." However, casual observations and unsupported intuitions are not reliable and can lead to faulty conclusions. What we need for a valid and useful understanding of behavior is a methodical and consistent procedure for making and evaluating observations of human responses. Only then can we explain and predict human behavior. Such methodical study and predictable results are the principal characteristics of scientific experimentation.

THE EXPERIMENTAL METHOD

Experimentation is a formal process through which we gather and analyze the necessary information to understand human behavior. This information is gathered in the form of systematic observation of behavioral responses to manipulated factors applied under controlled conditions. This operational definition allows us to distinguish the kinds of experiments that constitute the work of experimental psychology from the methods of observing and collecting behavioral data that are used in other areas of psychology.

Let us first consider what makes an experiment, according to our definition. We specified that the experimenter engages in a *formal process* of making *systematic observations* of *responses* to *manipulated* factors under *controlled* conditions. The key criteria that determine whether a procedure is really an experiment are the *italicized* concepts. They are all essential components of an experiment. However, we recognize that a formal experiment may not be the only way to obtain useful data about behavior. Research of various sorts (e.g., correlational studies) can and often does yield valuable data. However, research in experimental psychology relies on experimentation.

One of the areas of psychological study in which controlled laboratory experimentation is not always feasible is research on child behavior. For example, in order to develop theories about the acquisition of native language by children, studies are made of progressive additions to children's vocabularies and of the elaboration of their sentences from single-word statements (e.g., "Ball!" accompanied by a pointing finger) to full sentences with complete subject-predicate syntax. The data are obtained through tallying various aspects of the speech content of children. Useful conclusions can be drawn from such observations, but are these studies experiments? Not according to our definition. What is missing is the manipulation and control of the variables.

Useful information can be obtained without direct observation, often by inspecting and analyzing available data. For example, we might wish to study the relationship between the national employment rate and the birth rate. To do this the employment and birth rates for a 20-year period could be correlated. Although data are collected and analyzed, there is no manipulation or control. We call such a procedure a correlational study, not an experiment. Again, although meaningful data have been analyzed and hypotheses have been investigated, no experiment was conducted.

In another example, we might want to determine whether right- or left-handed people are more verbally oriented by testing their respective performances in a recognition memory test of pictures and words. The handedness of the individual is a subject variable selected by the experimenter. The type of stimulus materials (pictures or words) is a variable manipulated by the experimenter. Here, we satisfy the criteria for an experiment because one of the independent variables was manipulated by the experimenter. The ability to experimentally manipulate variables is a major factor that distinguishes an experiment from such nonexperimental research as correlational studies or surveys.

In experimental research, the process of data collection is really detective work—we even refer to it as "investigation." The experimental psychologist plays the role of a Sherlock Holmes in digging for the facts of the case in order to solve a mystery. In human experimental psychology, the mysteries arise out of the complex mental processes that govern the way we deal with our daily lives.

The first step in solving any mystery is to clearly state the problem or question. Only a clearly stated question can be answered by sensible interpretation of available information or data. In scientific research, this is done by formulating a hypothesis. If the hypothesis is not to remain just an interesting guess, it must be testable; that is, it must be stated in such a way that it can be either accepted as true or rejected as false on the basis of the evidence, consisting of clearly defined observations.

The next step is designing a way to get the facts, or data, with which to test the hypothesis. This involves the techniques that make up the experimental design. Following the specified design, the data are collected, organized, described, and interpreted, using the appropriate data-analytic techniques. Finally, the interpreted results are used to understand and predict the behavior of similar groups of people in related situations. This is usually accomplished by using the techniques and formulas of inferential statistics. Here, we see the operation of predictability that we spoke of earlier.

OVERVIEW OF THIS BOOK

This book is about the *why, how,* and *what* of human experimental psychology. It explains to the student who is being introduced to experimental psychology in a laboratory setting *why* experimental psychologists study certain topics, *how* they perform experiments, and *what* they discover. The *what* comprises the content areas of experimental psychology.

The structure of the book is built on these three questions. This introductory chapter explains *why* certain questions and issues are selected and explored by experimental psychologists. The remaining chapters in Part I describe the substantive details that constitute the *how* of experimentation. These chapters describe the principles of experimentation, which lead to different types of experimental designs with their associated statistical tests (Chapter 2); some of the common pitfalls, or procedural errors, in experimentation that can make the obtained results dubious (Chapter 3); and the techniques employed for measuring behavior and collecting data (Chapters 4 and 5).

Although there are many different ways of classifying experiments—for example, by topic area or methodology—one useful way of partitioning experiments is according to the type of response and its corresponding measure. We consider first, in Chapter 4, experimental methods that fall within the subdivision of psychology called *psychophysics*. As the term suggests, experiments in this area probe the psychological effects of what are mainly physical stimuli. We want to measure relationships between sensations and the stimuli that evoke them as the basis for explaining the underlying perceptual processes involved in our sense functions. The objective behind many of these experiments is to measure and quantify the sensations that humans experience when exposed to comparatively simple physical stimuli, such as light and sound. The measure most often used in psychophysical experimentation is response probability—the probability that the critical response will be made to a stimulus of specified characteristics. Although most psychophysical research has centered on sensory phenomena, we will show in later chapters how these methods have been productively applied to other types of behavior, such as memory processing.

A second type of response measure is the time subjects require to perform a task, generally referred to as *reaction time*. The pattern of reaction times on particular tasks is studied to infer the nature and sequence of the mental operations subjects must have performed to complete a task. The use of reaction time measurement in psychological experiments is called *mental chronometry*, and its techniques are described in Chapter 5.

Part II of this book develops a number of content areas that represent the *what* of experimental psychology. These are the areas in which topics of interest to researchers are found. We have selected key areas in which extensive investigative activity occurs. Each chapter focuses on several crucial models and theories, which are discussed in terms of certain landmark experiments. These experiments illuminate the significant problems and illustrate different ways to study the issues.

Chapters 6 through 10 discuss the various mental processes involved in the acquisition and practical use of information from the environment. These processes are related to the broad function of cognition; that is, thinking in all of its modes and purposes. The treatment of cognition begins in Chapter 6 with the first stages in the processing of information: *perception* and *attention*, using a modern, information-processing approach to perception.

Because the acquisition of knowledge implies learning, Chapter 7 follows with a review of relationships that link *conditioning, learning*, and *motivation*. Landmark experiments trace the development of learning theory from the earlier, classical models, based on study of lower animals, through the more advanced theories of human learning and motivation.

Chapters 8 and 9 divide the fundamental function of memory into two structural and operational modes: episodic and semantic memory. The first of these, *episodic memory*, contains representations of events experienced by the individual as part of his or her personal history. These episodic events are stored with their associations to the situational context in which each one was experienced. Episodic memory research is reviewed in Chapter 8.

Our basic source of stored knowledge is *semantic memory,* and several theoretical models of semantic memory are described in Chapter 9. Semantic memory stores in organized fashion the common knowledge an individual shares with other members of the same cultural group. This includes words and their meanings, and rules that must be used to formulate meaningful sentences.

Chapter 10 applies acquired and remembered knowledge to the requirements of *thinking* and *problem solving.* Here, the increased complexities and uncertainties in designing research to probe these commonplace processes are explored.

The final chapter in Part II, Chapter 11, points up the problems and progress in applying experimental psychology techniques and findings to research in other areas of human behavior. These include research in social psychology, industrial organizations, clinical issues, and parapsychology. By describing the ways in which techniques from experimental psychology have been applied in these areas, the review demonstrates the continuity between the basic research of experimental psychology and the applied research of other areas of psychology. Although the purpose of Chapter 11 is to show how techniques of experimental psychology have been *applied* to other areas, it is important to recognize that basic research (i.e., studies of fundamental psychological processes) has been conducted in these other areas.

A classic example of such basic research was the study of schizophrenic thought processes by Kent and Rosanoff (1910), which led to the development of norms of word association, an invaluable contribution by basic research in clinical psychology to subsequent memory research in experimental psychology. Postman and Keppel (1970) present a number of word association norms based on the Kent-Rosanoff work.

In our treatment of the content areas of experimental psychology, we do not propose to review each one exhaustively. To do so in one comprehensive book would be impossible. Indeed, entire books have been devoted to each of the chapter topics and subtopics. Rather, we have selected certain salient issues and have sampled the more interesting and illuminating lines of research dealing with these issues. In this way, the discussion of the content of experimental psychology gives the student a practical sense of how questions are framed in terms of meaningful concepts. It also provides a clear view of how experimental techniques are used to investigate these questions and how such designs establish the paradigms (the basic experimental models) that determine the patterns of research performed in each topic area.

Part III returns to the business of *how* to conduct an experiment. This section is concerned with the implementation, rather than the planning, of the experiment.

The object of this research—the human subject—is the center of interest in Chapter 12. Here we describe the proper way to treat human subjects. This chapter discusses how to prepare task instructions, how to protect the subject's rights in the experimental situation, and how to give the subject a sense of personal importance as a member of the research enterprise. Chapter 13 describes the design and operation of the various types of apparatus used in performing the experiments described in Part II. Stimulus materials (especially verbal and pictorial) are described in Chapter 14, along with guidance in finding or developing them, and in using them effectively.

Chapter 15 and 16 focus on critical features of statistical analysis—first, the use of descriptive statistics to present the data clearly and understandably (Chapter 15) and, second, procedures for applying inferential statistical tests to determine the significance of the data (Chapter 16). We assume that most students who take a laboratory course in experimental psychology have taken an introductory statistics course. Therefore, Chapters 15 and 16 are designed to refresh forgotten knowledge and are not intended to constitute a course in statistics.

Finally, in Chapter 17, we reach the end product of an experiment—the research report. Here, we provide direction on both the appropriate *form* of a research report, following guidelines established by the American Psychological Association, and the appropriate *style* in which such reports should be written.

Designing and running an experiment can be fun; analyzing the results can be carried out relatively easily with a little help from your computer; and even interpreting unexpected results can be a challenge. However, the process of conveying what you did and what you found in written form is usually a painful and frustrating task. This is true not only for beginning students in a laboratory course but for veteran researchers as well. Chapter 17 will make writing the research report a little less mysterious and a little less painful.

WHY DO EXPERIMENTAL PSYCHOLOGISTS STUDY WHAT THEY DO?

In teaching a laboratory course in experimental psychology for many years, the senior author has found that students frequently question the apparent triviality of the problems researchers study. As you will see when you read about the *what* of experimentation, the questions that are the focus of much research concern very ordinary human behaviors that most of us take for granted. For example, how do we distinguish one object from another in our environment? Why is it easier to recall a familiar object than an unfamiliar one? How do we solve simple problems in logic?

We do these mental acts so effortlessly that we hardly give them a second thought. After all, why study the obvious behavior of everyday life when there are so many more interesting and complicated issues to explore? What useful purpose can be served with such basic information?

Curiously, issues of triviality and usefulness are almost never raised in the physical sciences. Why would Newton ponder such a commonplace thing as a falling apple? Of course you know the important consequences of his study of that "trivial" event. And why should physicists strive to prove that the speed of light is finite? After all, at a rate of 186,000 miles per second, light gets to us almost instantaneously from any source we are interested in. But that simple fact did not satisfy Einstein, and so he questioned us right into the Nuclear Age.

Can answers to the obvious and the trivial in psychology produce such momentous results? Experimental psychologists believe the answer is Yes. For example, what we have learned about the structures of memory storage and the dynamics of semantic retrieval (see Chapters 8 and 9) has served as the basis for a better understanding of the effects of organic brain dysfunctions of various kinds and for the development of batteries of verbal and pictorial tests used in the diagnosis of neurological disorders. A great deal of experimental work in lateralization of brain function (see Chapter 6) has contributed to an increased understanding of the effects of brain injuries such as strokes.

As another example, basic research in categorization has revealed the important role played by prototypes (those objects that are most typical of a category) in classifying new objects (see Chapter 9). This research has been related to the process by which people form stereotyped perceptions of others. Thus, experimental psychology contributes to social psychology experimentation (Tajfel, 1982).

Even when there is no apparent application of basic research to real life problems, we, as experimental psychologists, stand in awe of what ordinary people do everyday. We seek first to understand these ordinary, everyday behaviors before studying behaviors that are more unusual. This attitude—that the everyday and commonplace is worthy of study—is well described in a recent book on picture perception:

What could be interesting about a sketch that anyone can recognize? The answer is almost paradoxical and is a lesson for every generation of psychologists; *in psychology we study the ordinary.* To understand the commonplace is one of the main aims of psychology. If we are to understand human activity, we must study that which occurs most of the time and that is, naturally, the ordinary. Psychologists must describe and explain whatever is normal, straightforward, and obvious to the man in the street. For our subject matter is people in the streets—their skills, their commonplace activities, and how they become that way, able to do what they do effortlessly and casually without a second's thought. If something is easy for an ordinary man to understand, and does not require his serious study, then we have to take this as a sign of a well-practiced skill that we should try to describe, not as evidence that the something is obvious and not worthy of study.

(Kennedy, 1974, p. 5)

Although Kennedy is referring to the mysteries of line drawings as depictions of real objects, similar mysteries occur in the area of speech perception (Chapter 6), the nature of memory and how it is accessed (Chapters 8 and 9), and the rules by which we solve problems (Chapter 10).

Experimental psychology is a basic science. It is the function of experimental psychology to discover, describe, and delineate the basic laws of human behavior. The goal of this research is to learn how and why humans think, perceive, act, and react the way they do. The gathering of this knowledge is a goal unto itself. For those who need a more concrete rationale (and many do), learning the basic principles of human mental functioning will ultimately lead to an understanding and improvement of the human condition.

SOURCES OF HYPOTHESES

The first step in experimentation is stating the question, or hypothesis, that your experiment will be designed to answer or test. Without the question, there can be no answer. To paraphrase a famous exchange between Gertrude Stein and her long-time companion, Alice B. Toklas, when Gertrude was on her deathbed: "Alice, what is the answer?" When no response was forthcoming, Gertrude then asked, "Well, then, what is the question?"

The source of questions in experimental psychology seems to be one of life's great mysteries to the beginning student of the field. And, indeed, hypothesis formulation *is* perhaps the most mysterious and least understood aspect of experimentation. We can write down rules and procedures for designing the experiment, collecting the data, analyzing the results, and even interpreting them. But it is much more difficult to describe how to come up with a good hypothesis and, more important, how to recognize a good hypothesis when you find one.

First, a hypothesis must ask a question about general principles governing human behavior. To do this, it must ask a fundamental question so that an answer can be meaningfully generalized to other situations, people, and stimuli. On the other hand, it cannot be so generally or vaguely stated as to be untestable. An example of an untestable question is How much of what we hear do we remember? There are a number of answers to the question depending on the type and amount of material being presented, the subjects being tested, the time between study and testing, and the way we measure remembering.

To make the question testable, we might ask: Does interest in a topic improve recall of spoken material? The following experiment would be appropriate to test this hypothesis. Subjects would listen to six five-minute speeches on various topics. After the presentations are completed, subjects would be asked to rate their interest in each topic, and then to recall as much information as possible. Subsequent analysis of the relationship between interest and recall would be used to evaluate this hypothesis.

So hypotheses must be specific enough to be testable, yet general enough to be meaningful. Where do they come from? We shall consider a number of sources.

A common source of hypotheses is an existing theory. A good theory makes testable predictions about behavior, and thereby generates good hypotheses. For example, a two-store theory of memory postulates two different types of storage systems—short-term and long-term stores—which have different characteristics and thus are influenced by different experimental manipulations. Short-term store holds items for only short periods of time, is of limited capacity, and seems to be predominantely acoustic in nature. Long-term store holds items for indefinitely long periods of time, is of apparently unlimited capacity, and stores information primarily by meaning and significance. Glanzer and Cunitz (1966) tested the two-store theory by separately manipulating two independent variables, one of which was predicted to affect short-term store and one, long-term store. They found evidence for independent effects of the two variables (see Chapter 8).

As another example, Quillian (1968, 1969) wrote a computer program to answer questions about both superset/subset relationships (like *animal/dog* or *furniture/chair*) and properties of real world objects. The program used a hierarchical organization to store and retrieve relevant information. In order to test whether the human memory system was organized in a similar hierarchical fashion—that is, whether the computer program was an adequate simulation of a human memory system—Collins and Quillian (1969) tested certain predictions of the model on human subjects answering questions and found support for the organization proposed (see Chapter 9).

As still another example, Broadbent's (1958) original theory of attention hypothesized that an unattended channel was filtered at the perceptual level. Broadbent's model predicts that information presented to an unattended ear will not be analyzed for meaning. However, several experiments showed that high-priority, meaningful material got through this perceptual filter. As a result of these experiments, the concept of an early, all-or-none filtering device had to be revised (see Chapter 6).

A second source of hypotheses is the search for functional relationships between some characteristic of a set of stimuli and a human subject's responses to these stimuli. Many such functional relationships exist in the sensory literature. These include the relationship between threshold responses and simple characteristics of stimuli such as the wavelength of lights (colors) and the frequency of sounds (tones). One important psychophysical law discovered as a result of testing these functional relationships is called Weber's law. Weber's law states that the relationship between the discriminability of two stimuli and their intensities is approximately a constant—that is, the difference in intensity of two stimuli necessary for them to be distinguished bears a constant ratio to the average intensity of the two stimuli (see Chapter 4 on Psychophysical Methods). The functional relationship between arousal and performance provides another example. The Yerkes-Dodson law states that performance is greatest at some intermediate level of arousal (the functional relationship is an inverted U-shaped function). Arousal at either extreme (very high or very low) leads to poor performance. The peak of the relationship shifts toward lower levels of arousal when the difficulty of a task is increased (see Chapter 7).

Interesting and potentially powerful hypotheses often arise from two competing theories or laws that predict different outcomes from an experiment. Indeed, in order to declare one theory a competitor with another, the two theories must make different predictions about the results of one or more experimental manipulations.

For example, there are two competing laws proposed for the psychophysical function—the function that relates psychological sensation to stimulus intensity. Fechner's law states that sensation grows with the logarithm of stimulus intensity, whereas Steven's law proposes that psychological sensation grows with some power of stimulus intensity. Much of the research on unidimensional scaling described in Chapter 4 has been devoted to testing these competing hypotheses.

Another example is the competition between the dual-code and single-code theories of mental representation (see Chapter 8). Paivio's (1971) dual-coding theory proposes that there are two separate systems of mental representation, one visual and one verbal. Dual-coding theory predicts that there will be specific interactions between certain experimental manipulations and the type of material—pictorial or verbal—being learned. The competing theory to dual-coding theory, single-coding or propositional theory, claims that both surface forms of stimuli (pictures and the words that name them) will show similar effects of these experimental manipulations. The competition between these theories has yielded many interesting and testable hypotheses.

Although hypotheses generated by two competing theories have the potential to support one theory and disprove another, experimental results are rarely that definitive. It often happens that one set of results will support the first theory and another set will support the second theory. The history of science shows us that existing theories never die out for lack of evidence; rather they are replaced by better theories.

A source of many hypotheses is simple observation. For example, we might observe that we fail to remember certain events that we experienced while in an unusual state, such as alcohol or drug intoxication. Yet these memories are sometimes retrieved when we take another drink or take the same drug. This phenomenon is known as *state-dependent learning*. Hypotheses based on this phenomenon have been tested extensively. Another observation is our failure to recognize a person's face in a strange environment. We might not recognize our psychology professor, for example, if we saw him in a tuxedo or her in an evening gown at a Las Vegas gaming table. These observations can lead to hypotheses that test which states of mind or environmental cues provide a helpful context for recall and recognition.

When formulating a hypothesis from an observation, we must be careful to be specific enough that the hypothesis will be testable. For example, the observation that context affects memory raises many questions. We may well ask: What kinds of context conditions influence recall? Do the same conditions affect recognition? Which factors operate in these effects? Does the nature of the material to be remembered interact with the state or context? Does the relevance of the original context or state enhance or weaken the effect? How does familiarity of the central figure (the psychology professor versus the President of the United States) affect state- or context-dependent memory? As you can see, the questions can quickly multiply. And each question can be translated into one or more hypotheses.

Another source of hypotheses is simple curiosity. Many hypotheses are generated with no particular theoretical or observational basis—or more accurately, none that an experimenter can put his or her finger on. Often an experimenter may play a hunch in designing an experiment, asking the question "What would happen if . . . ?," and thereby discover an important phenomenon. In fact, some of these "What would happen if . . . ?" hypotheses were motivated by necessity or convenience as well as curiosity.

B. F. Skinner (1956) describes how he discovered the use of the partial reinforcement schedule (a schedule that does not reinforce every response; e.g., food is not given to the rat for every bar press). It seems that Skinner was reluctant to continue spending the rest of a beautiful Saturday afternoon making food pellets by hand. In order to conserve the number of reinforcers needed, he wondered what would happen to the animal's behavior if he did not reinforce every positive response. Testing this idea led to the discovery that lower animals would work persistently under partial reinforcement schedules and that their behavior was highly resistant to extinction. The behavior of organisms to partial reinforcement, particularly their high resistance to extinction, has provided many clues to the persistent behavior of humans in the absence of any observable positive reinforcement.

Wondering "what would happen if ..." led Eleanor Gibson to embark on a program of research on whether the fear of heights is innate or learned. The source of the question was a disagreement with her husband about the wisdom of letting their children walk to the edge of the Grand Canyon. Gibson and Walk (1960) invented the visual cliff—an optical illusion of a sheer drop-off—which can be used to determine whether baby animals and baby humans have an innate fear of heights. Gibson and her co-workers discovered that we are indeed born with fear of heights, and thus with a powerful fear of falling.

There is an old saying that a discovery is an accident waiting to find a prepared mind. "What would happen if ..." hypotheses often lead to interesting and exciting research findings and, ultimately, to new theories. But this can happen only to researchers who are prepared for them.

MANY QUESTIONS—FEW ANSWERS

In the preceding examples, we showed how hypotheses are developed from questions. In this book, we will focus on the kinds of questions experimental psychologists have investigated, the ways they have collected relevant information, and the answers they have discovered to these questions. But we must keep in mind that these answers are rarely the last word on an issue. What we are most interested in is the way each answer evokes another set of questions that rely on experimental designs to answer them.

In this book, we seldom present experimental findings as final, definitive answers to the questions posed in the various areas covered. Rather, our goal is to describe methods through which the answers might be obtained. Even if certain experimental lines of attack on a problem turn out to be blind alleys, we will have learned which false leads to avoid, and we will also identify situation-specific conditions that might yield different results. That knowledge will sharpen our judgment, so that we can proceed on a more productive course. In the long run, a single right answer may be less informative than a series of failures. (This is particularly true in problem-solving experiments, as described in Chapter 10.) After all, discovering which situations do not support hypotheses also provides important information. It is how you use the information that gives it value. Our main purpose is to exercise the student's critical faculties in the study and practice of experimental psychology and to teach the student to profit from both positive and negative experimental results. We will have achieved our objective if students learn to evaluate appropriately all data and never to accept any result as final nor any theory as *The Answer.*

SUMMARY

This chapter first presented an overview of this book and its purpose—to teach the student the whys, hows, and whats of human experimental psychology. Simply stated, the purpose of human experimental psychology is to solve the fundamental mystery of how we, as humans, meaningfully deal with the world.

The second part of this chapter was devoted to exploring ways in which hypotheses are generated. Hypotheses are the questions that experimentation is designed to answer. Among the sources of hypotheses discussed here are theory testing, functional relationships, comparison of theories, observations, and simple curiosity (What would happen if ... ?).

Without meaningful questions, there are no meaningful answers. In many senses, the most critical aspect of an answer is the question itself. Every science relies on appropriate questions for the gathering of knowledge. Human experimental psychology is no exception.

2

Designing the Experiment

Pat McGuire had a hangover three mornings in a row. The first night he drank five scotches with water, the second night he drank five ryes with water, and the third night he drank five vodkas with water. After this experience, he vowed to give up water.

The fallacy of Pat McGuire's conclusion is apparent to most of us. Because we know that the agent that produces a hangover is the alcohol in scotch, rye, or vodka, we know that Pat's conclusion that the other common element in all of the drinks—water—was the causative agent is fallacious.

This simple example, however, will provide a springboard for our discussion of experimental design. First, Pat's three-day experience is an example of an experiment, even though it is a poorly designed one. He administered three types (or *levels*) of treatment (the three types of alcoholic beverages) and observed their effect the next morning. The variable of types of alcoholic beverages we call the *independent variable,* because it was manipulated by the experimenter and is independent of the subject's behavior. The variable of whether or not a hangover occurred (and perhaps its severity) we call the *dependent variable,* because the question of interest is whether the behavior we measure is dependent on the variable we manipulated. You can think of the independent variable as the cause of behavior, and the dependent variable as its effect.

How could Pat have improved his experiment? One way would have been to include a fourth night, during which he drank only water. If a hangover resulted from a water-alone drinking night, his conclusion that water was the responsible agent would have more support.

THE EXPERIMENTAL APPROACH

As we pointed out in Chapter 1, the seeds of psychological research can come from observation. We observe that overindulgence in alcohol leads to hangovers, that coffee in the morning makes us more alert, that close attention to a task makes us less aware of other events in our environment, that many children with behavior problems in school come from broken homes, and that many stroke patients with paralysis on the right side have speech problems. At first, these observations are made unsystematically on a few people (perhaps only on ourselves). Each of them, however, contains the germ of an idea, or *hypothesis,* which could be tested by an experiment.

Experiments vary along a continuum from *true experiments* at one end to *correlational* or *observational studies* at the other end. As in any other human endeavor in which people try to classify complex activities into the pigeonholes required by language, the borderline between a true experiment and a correlational study is a fuzzy one. Here we give two criteria for a true experiment, and then show how relaxation of these criteria can move us along the continuum from the experimental to the correlational method.

The two criteria for a true experiment are, first, that there be at least two conditions or groups, and, second, that the independent variable whose values define the two groups be manipulated by the experimenter. The requirement that at least two groups be included in an experiment comes from the logic of the experimental method. In order to determine that a particular independent variable has some effect, we must demonstrate that it has an effect over and above the effect we would observe by measuring subjects' behavior in the absence of the independent variable. So, if we are interested in determining the effect of a new drug on subjects' behavior, we need to compare the behavior of an experimental group of subjects who were given the drug to that of a comparable group of subjects who were not given the drug, but were otherwise treated identically. Thus, many experiments involve the comparison of an experimental group, receiving a particular value (or level) of the independent variable, with a control group, receiving a zero level of the independent variable. In cases in which it is impossible to administer a zero level of the independent variable (as in studying the effect of meaningfulness of prose material on learning), at least two levels of the independent variable (such as high and low meaningfulness) are used.

Consider some examples of studies that violate the two-groups criterion. One example is the way in which "clinical trials" of a new drug were once conducted by doctors. Doctors would give their patients the new drug and solicit patient reports of its effectiveness. But to truly measure the effectiveness of a new drug, it was found necessary to measure the drug's effectiveness against that of a "placebo"—an inert substance, such as a sugar pill, administered to patients who have the same disease. Otherwise, the results of "the placebo effect" (the reaction of a patient to something he believes will cure him, in the absence of any specific activity) and spontaneous remission from disease cannot be separated from the effects of the drug itself.

As a second example, consider the widely reported "experiment" on the effectiveness of the subliminal message "EAT POPCORN" when flashed on a screen of a drive-in movie in New Jersey several years ago. It was reported in the popular press that sales of popcorn skyrocketed among the audience attending the movie. But this was not a true experiment, because it lacked a control evening, during which the message was not shown, to serve as a baseline for popcorn-buying behavior.

The second criterion for a true experiment is that the independent variable be manipulated by the experimenter rather than merely selected by him. Whenever possible, we prefer to test hypotheses by manipulating the independent variable. The more control an experimenter has over the independent variable, the more he or she will be able to attribute the results of the experiment to the independent variable alone rather than to other extraneous variables that accompany the independent variable of interest and cannot be controlled.

There are situations, however, in which it is unethical or impractical for the experimenter to manipulate the independent variable. If we were interested in studying drug abuse, for example, we could not create drug abusers of various degrees because of ethical considerations. Instead, we would take advantage of "naturally" occurring groups and resort to an observational or correlational paradigm.

Let us take the simplest possible experiment, that in which we observe some behavior of two groups of subjects. Consider two hypothetical experiments that are derived from two common observations. In the first experiment, we hypothesize that caffeine increases alertness. To test this, we give caffeine to one group of subjects (the experimental group) and nothing to a second group of subjects (the control group), and then compare the two groups on some measure of alertness. We could decide to measure it by two-choice reaction time—a procedure in which one of two stimuli is presented randomly on each trial, and the subject responds to a stimulus by pressing one of two designated response keys as quickly as possible. Subjects who are more alert should respond faster than those who are less alert. The experimental group receives caffeine in the form of a pill prior to the experiment and the control group receives a pill containing a nonactive ingredient (placebo).

In this example, we as experimenters are free to assign a subject to the experimental and control group in any way we choose. We may do this by randomly assigning subjects to the two groups or by matching the subjects on some criterion (such as the amount of coffee they normally drink). A variety of considerations dictate whether randomization or matching should be used.

In the second experiment, we hypothesize that stroke patients with paralysis on the right side of their bodies are more likely to have speech problems than patients with left-side paralysis. (In fact, we know this to be true. The left side of the brain controls the motor function of the right side of the body and is the language center for most people. Therefore, damage to the left side of the brain would result in both a right-side paralysis and a speech deficit.) To test this hypothesis, we select a group of patients with paralysis on the right side (experimental group), and test their language abilities, and then select a group of patients with left-side paralysis (control group), and test their language abilities. This time it is important to match the two groups of patients for any characteristics we know are related to performance on language tests. This might include native language, IQ, and age.

In this second example, the experimenter is no longer free to decide which treatment (or group) a patient belongs to. The patient has either right- or left-side paralysis—the independent variable has already been manipulated by nature (the word is meant to include both genetic and environmental influences), and the psychologist's job is simply to select, rather than create, the two groups of subjects.

Because we wish to call both types of procedures experiments, we define the first type, in which the experimenter has complete control over which subject is given which treatment, an *artificial experiment* and the second type, in which the experimenter has no control over which subject is given which treatment, a *natural experiment.* The term *artificial* is not meant pejoratively but rather is used to capture the fact that more control is possible over both the manipulated variable (the independent variable) and the variables kept constant (the control variables) than in the *natural* experiment. Natural experiments use independent variables that are properties of the subject, and therefore these independent variables are sometimes called subject variables. In the stroke patient example, whether the paralysis occurs on the right or left side of the body is a patient characteristic or variable and is defined by experimenter selection rather than by manipulation. Sometimes these "natural" or subject variable experiments are described as correlational, rather than manipulation, experiments. However, there is an important distinction between a truly correlational study and one in which a variable is defined by nature's selection of subject characteristics rather than the experimenter's selection. We clarify this difference in the next section on experimental versus correlational methods.

Generally, there is a natural experiment for every artificial experiment, although the reverse is not true. If we wanted to study the effect of caffeine on alertness "naturally," we could ask people coming from lunch whether they had coffee with lunch or not, accumulate one group of subjects who claim to have drunk coffee and another group who claim to have had none, and compare both groups in the choice reaction-time task. The problem with this procedure is that people who have coffee with lunch may be different in many other respects from people who have an alternative beverage such as milk, wine, or beer, so that our groups could differ in ways other than whether or not they ingested caffeine.

Experimenters will generally choose an artificial experiment over a natural experiment if given a choice. The reason is that results from natural experiments can often be caused by confounded variables rather than the independent variable of interest. A *confounded variable* is one that is correlated with the independent variable and thus can be responsible for the effect in question. We will return to the question of confounding later in the chapter.

Experimental Versus Correlational Methods

The distinction between artificial and natural experiments captures to a degree what we mean by the distinction between experimental and correlational methods. In a natural experiment, the variable in question is divided into two or more categories. These categories may be truly dichotomous, as in comparing males and females or left-handers versus right-handers, or may lie along a continuum but be divided into groups by the experimenter (as in whether the person drank coffee for lunch or not). However, when the independent or subject variable actually lies along a continuum, there is no particular reason to categorize subjects into discrete groups. Rather, we could measure the amount of caffeine drunk or the degree of paralysis of right- or left sides on a more-or-less continuous scale, and look at the relationship between this independent variable and the dependent variable of interest. When we measure the degree of relationship between two continuous or quasi-continuous variables, we use a truly correlational method.

For example, correlational techniques could be used to test the hypothesis that caffeine increases alertness, or more precisely, that increases in caffeine consumption are related to increases in alertness. Here we could take a single group of subjects, ask them how much caffeine (coffee, tea, cola) they have had in the last 2 hours, and then measure their alertness by two-choice reaction time. The experimenter would then correlate the inferred amount of caffeine with the measured alertness to determine if there is a relationship between the two. It is easy to see, however, that in this second experiment the researcher has much less control. For example, if no one drank a beverage with caffeine or failed to report it, the results would be meaningless. Or it is possible that voluntary consumption of caffeine is related to another factor—perhaps a personality trait—that in turn is related to alertness. This illustrates only two of the possible problems with the correlational method.

In the stroke patient's case, the experimenter might choose to test the hypothesis by determining from medical histories the degree of right-side paralysis and the degree of language deficits for a large number of patients with right-side paralysis. These two measures could then be correlated and the relationship between these two variables determined.

Thus, as there are two hallmarks of a truly experimental method, there are also two hallmarks of a truly correlational method. First, both variables whose relationships are sought can take on a number of different values, and second, one variable does not necessarily have to depend on, or be caused by, the second variable. That is, we can use the correlational method when neither variable is clearly independent (and thus neither is clearly dependent). In the caffeine example, we expect alertness to depend on caffeine (and not the other way around), whereas in the stroke patient case, both right-side paralysis and language deficit depend on (in the sense of being caused by), a third variable—namely, damage to the left hemisphere. It is for this reason that the slogan "Correlation is not causation" resounds from the ceilings of so many classes in statistics and experimental design.

In contrast, true experiments are usually designed so that the independent variable is thought to truly cause the dependent variable, so that the latter can be considered to depend on the former. Because the experimental techniques we describe here are based on the latter philosophy, we emphasize the experimental rather than the correlational approach in this book.

INDEPENDENT, CONTROL, AND DEPENDENT VARIABLES

A *variable* is anything that can take on a number of values. The weights of a group of children are variables because each child will differ somewhat from each of the others in weight. Three classes of variables are important in experimental psychology: independent, control, and dependent variables. Independent variables are those that are either *manipulated* or *selected* by the experimenter; control variables are those *held constant* by the experimenter across the conditions of an experiment; and dependent variables are those *measured* by the experimenter as some selected behavior of the subjects.

Independent Variables

An *independent variable* is manipulated or selected by a psychologist in an experiment. Some independent variables are easily manipulated by the experimenter. These include the specific dose of an administered drug, or the type of instructions given to subjects. Other independent variables must be selected by the experimenter rather than manipulated. These include such subject variables as sex, eye color, and diagnostic category for patient groups. When we manipulate the independent variable, we can randomly assign subjects to groups defined by the different levels of the variable. In contrast, when we select for levels of the independent variable, subjects are assigned to groups by nature, rather than by the experimenter. Despite the fact that these subject variables are not actually manipulated by the experimenter, they function in every way (conceptually and statistically) as independent variables. As discussed earlier, the experimenter has less control with selected variables.

An independent variable can take on any number of values (called *levels*), but the minimum number is two. One of the levels is often the control condition in which nothing is manipulated. In the caffeine example, the independent variable, caffeine intake, has two levels. One is a specific dose of caffeine, and the other is a nonactive substance (a placebo). It would be possible to increase the number of levels in this experiment by having different doses of caffeine, in addition to a placebo (zero dose). In the stroke experiment, the independent variable, side of paralysis, is selected rather than manipulated by the experimenter. Here subjects for the experiment are selected for membership in one of the two levels of the independent variable according to the side of paralysis. An independent variable may be quantitative, as in the caffeine dosage sample, or qualitative, as in the experiment comparing speech in patients with right- and left-side paralysis.

Control Variables

A *control variable* is a characteristic of the subjects or of the environment that is kept constant across all levels of the independent variable. A variable is controlled when it is believed to affect the behavior of interest. If this variable were linked with the independent variable, then any results that occurred could be attributed to the independent variable, to the control variable, or to both.

There are many potential control variables, and which of them are controlled and which are not depend both on the problem being studied and on the difficulty of controlling the variable. Some control variables are characteristics of the subjects who are being studied, and some are characteristics of the environment in which the experiment is conducted. Among the possible important subject variables are sex, intelligence, age, socioeconomic status, family history, and whether subjects have volunteered or not. Among the possible important environmental variables are the room in which the experiment is conducted, the sex and attitude of the experimenter, the time of day, and the time of year. Any of these may or may not be important, depending on the problem being studied.

Environmental variables are usually easier to control than subject variables and for that reason often serve as control variables, even if they are sometimes not identified as such. It is obvious that instructions read to the placebo and experimental groups in the caffeine experiment should be identical, as should the reaction-time apparatuses on which the reaction times are measured. It is harder to control time of day or time of year, so these are generally left to vary. However, these factors may be of subtle importance; college student subjects may be more anxious during midterm examination periods, and subjects from the introductory psychology pool who wait until the end of the term to volunteer for experiments may be less motivated to perform well than those who volunteer at the beginning of the term.

Any variable that has not been controlled, and that also varies systematically with the levels of the independent variable, is known as a *confounded variable.* To return to the caffeine experiment, suppose that subjects in the caffeine group were informed that they were receiving caffeine and those in the placebo group were informed that they were receiving a placebo. Information about the drug being given is perfectly confounded with the substance that is actually being given, so that it is impossible to determine if superior performance under the caffeine condition is due to caffeine itself, knowledge that caffeine was being given, or both. Similarly, if a cold, hostile experimenter has tested all subjects given anxiety-producing instructions but a warm, friendly experimenter has tested all those given neutral instructions, the effect of this manipulation on performance could be caused by the instructions, the experimenter, or both, because instructions and experimenter are perfectly confounded.

Dependent Variables

A *dependent variable* is a characteristic of a subject's behavior that is observed and measured as a result of the manipulation or selection of the independent variable. It is the data produced by the subject. The reaction times of subjects in the caffeine experiment and the language performance of paralyzed patients are both dependent variables.

Like the independent variable, the dependent variable may be quantitative or qualitative. Quantitative dependent variables include reaction time, number of correctly recalled words, rating of the degree to which another is liked, or the electrical activity of the skin (GSR). Qualitative dependent variables include the type of behavior exhibited by a group of nursery school children, the types of responses given on the Thematic Apperception Test (TAT), or the types of confusions made on a multiple-choice memory test.

In most experiments, subjects are perfectly aware that their behavior is being measured. Measurement of the dependent variable is what we call obtrusive, because it is obvious to subjects that certain behaviors are being measured. Obtrusive measures include presses on a key in a reaction time experiment, description of an ambiguous figure in a perception experiment, or responses to a questionnaire in an experiment on personality and attitude change.

In certain areas of psychology, such as attitude change, personality, and social psychology, the obtrusiveness of the dependent variable may affect the behavior of interest, and so a more subtle way of measuring behavior is desired. In an influential book entitled *Unobtrusive Measures,* Webb, Campbell, Schwartz, and Sechrest (1966) discuss the use of a variety of unobtrusive measures that leave subjects unaware that their behavior is being measured. Such measures include physical traces, archival records, and physical interpersonal distance, among others. Physical traces may provide a more valid record of the popularity of everything from museum exhibits to advertisements. The frequency with which tiles around a particular exhibit need to be replaced has been used to measure the number of people stopping at an exhibit in a museum, and the number of fingerprints on a page has been used to measure the number of people who have glanced at that page (and thus presumably read the advertisement on the page). Archival records, such as library withdrawals, have been used to measure the effect of television on a community. In one such study, withdrawal of fiction books declined when television became available, whereas the number of nonfiction books withdrawn remained the same. The physical locations of people in crowds have been used to measure racial attitudes. In one study, the investigators observed different degrees of clustering of blacks and whites in the lecture halls of two different colleges.

Milgram (1972) used a "lost letter" technique to unobtrusively measure attitudes toward organizations. Milgram planted letters in a random sample of locations so that they appeared to be lost. The independent variable was the political organization to which the letter was addressed (Republican, Democratic, or Communist parties, or the John Birch Society) and the dependent variable was the proportion of lost letters that were mailed by their finders. Because the finders were expected to be a random sample of the population, this technique provided an unobtrusive measure of the population's attitudes toward these organizations.

Dependent and Independent Variables Compared

Independent and dependent variables are distinguished not by what the variable is, but by the way in which it is used. An independent variable is something that is manipulated or selected by an experimenter. A dependent variable is some characteristic of a subject that is observed and measured by an experimenter. Many students are confused when they try to distinguish between the two types of variables, partly because the same variable may serve as the independent variable in one experiment and the dependent variable in another. Nothing in the variable itself identifies it as one or the other.

Following are examples of two variables that can serve as either the independent or dependent variables. The first is weight and the second is light intensity. We will present four hypothetical experiments, one that uses weight as the independent variable, a second that uses weight as the dependent variable, a third that uses light intensity as the independent variable, and a fourth that uses light intensity as the dependent variable.

Weight can be used as an independent variable. A psychologist may hypothesize that overweight people are more sensitive to external stimuli than normal-weight people. To test this hypothesis, she first *selects* two groups of subjects, one overweight and the other of normal weight. Their sensitivity to sound is then measured to determine whether subjects of different weights show different sensitivities. In this experiment, weight is the independent variable because it is selected by the psychologist, and sensitivity to sound is the dependent variable, because the psychologist measures these sensitivities and uses them to compare the two weight groups.

Weight may also serve as a dependent variable. Another psychologist might hypothesize that a lesion (damage) in the satiety center of the brain will cause a group of rats to gain more weight than an unlesioned control group. To test this, he makes lesions in the brains of one group of rats and does nothing to a second group. This manipulation (lesions versus nothing) is his independent variable. He then measures the weights of the two groups of animals to determine if the lesioned animals gain more weight than the controls. Weight, or weight gain, of the rats is thus his dependent variable, which he measures in response to the manipulation of his independent variable.

Intensity of light may serve as an independent or dependent variable. A psychologist is interested in determining how intensity of a light source affects reaction time. Light intensity is the independent variable, which is manipulated over several levels from barely visible to very bright during the experiment. The time of the subject's reaction to each of the light intensities is the dependent variable, because that is what the experimenter measures in response to each of the different light intensities.

In another experiment, light intensity is a dependent variable. An investigator is interested in determining how bright different intensities of light appear to a subject. One way to measure brightness is to present the subject with two light intensities of different brightness and ask him or her to adjust the intensity of a third light until it appears to be halfway between the other two in brightness. The subject's adjustment is known as a half-brightness judgment. The independent variable is the pair of light intensities presented to the subject, and the dependent variable is the light intensity set by the subject for the half-brightness judgment.

TYPES OF EXPERIMENTAL DESIGNS

We can classify experimental designs along at least three dimensions. The first is the number of independent variables that are manipulated. The second is the number of levels of the independent variable or variables that are used. The third is whether the same subjects receive all conditions or different subjects are randomly assigned to the different conditions.

Number of Independent Variables

We may wish to manipulate only a single independent variable, or we may want to manipulate jointly two or more independent variables. For simplicity, we consider no more than two independent variables.

Number of Levels of the Independent Variable(s)

Levels are the values of the independent variable that are used in the experiment. Each value or level is also called a *condition.* The conditions may vary quantitatively, as when manipulating levels of the reward (e.g., number of points) in a learning situation, or qualitatively, as in the type of learning material (e.g., pronounceable compared with nonpronounceable trigrams such as *gax* versus *gbx)* in a memory experiment.

Randomized Versus Repeated Measures Designs

When different subjects are assigned at random to the different conditions of an experiment, we call the experiment a *randomized design* or *random groups design,* and when the same subjects participate in all conditions of an experiment or different subjects are matched on some basis across conditions, we call it a *repeated measures* or *matched groups design.*

If the number of conditions or levels is small (usually only two) subjects may be paired on some set of criteria related to the dependent variable, and this is called a *matched groups design.* In the caffeine experiment, we could match subjects on intelligence and then randomly assign one member of the pair to the caffeine condition and the other member to the control condition. In the experiment on stroke patients, we could match each patient with right-side paralysis with a patient with left-side paralysis on the basis of intelligence, age, and native language before measuring the language ability of each patient. When there are two independent variables, one may be randomized and one may be matched. This is called a *mixed design.*

Randomized designs are appropriate whenever the subject's behavior is differentially altered by exposure to two different experimental conditions. For example, when studying brain function in animals by lesioning particular brain structures, the effect of a lesion in one location can be compared with the effect of a lesion in another location. The same animal cannot serve in both lesion conditions, and so a randomized design is used. Examples from the human experimental literature include memory studies in which retention for studied material is tested at different delays. Here the effect of the testing itself affects retention scores for future tests. For this reason, separate groups of subjects must be used at the different retention intervals to avoid repeated testing of the same subjects.

Matched or repeated measures designs are appropriate any time exposure to one condition can be assumed not to affect behavior in subsequent conditions (that is, when we expect no carry-over effects across conditions). Generally, matched designs are preferred to randomized designs because the former are more sensitive—that is, when there is a real difference between conditions, the experimenter will be more likely to detect it with a matched design than with a randomized design. In matched or repeated measures experiments, the same subject or pair of subjects functions as their own controls, automatically controlling for the potentially confounding effects of variables such as IQ, genetic history, and environment. We will return to this point in more detail later.

Scale of Measurement of the Dependent Variable

The vast majority of dependent variables observed in psychological experiments are quantitative in nature or, in technical terms, are measured on an interval scale of measurement. On an *interval scale,* differences between scores on the dependent variable can be treated as equal units, and thus scores can be meaningfully averaged. Examples of such dependent variables are number of correct responses, reaction time, galvanic skin response magnitude, and response on a seven-point rating scale on a questionnaire. Whenever data are on an interval scale, it is legitimate to compute averages (arithmetic means) on the data.

The statistical tests we consider are appropriate for a quantitative dependent variable on an interval scale of measurement or higher. Three aspects of the experimental design determine the appropriate statistical test: the number of independent variables; the number of levels of each variable; and whether the design is matched (repeated measures), randomized, or mixed.

A SINGLE INDEPENDENT VARIABLE

In many experiments, there is only a single independent variable (also called a *factor*). For example, we may wish to compare recognition difficulty for words of high and low frequency in print (determined by counting words in published material). The independent variable here is word frequency and there are two *levels* of frequency, high and low. The dependent variable is visual recognition threshold, usually measured as the shortest time the word must be exposed for correct recognition. We could extend the independent variable to cover more levels of frequency: high, medium, and low. We still have only one independent variable, but now it has three rather than two levels. As we shall see, whether there are two or more than two levels of a single independent variable partly determines which statistical test is used.

Another important distinction is whether separate unrelated groups of subjects are assigned to different conditions, in a random groups design, or whether subjects are matched across conditions of the experiment by either matching subjects on some relevant variable or running the same subject repeatedly, in a matched groups or repeated measures design. Generally, repeated measures designs are more sensitive than randomized designs and are to be preferred as long as exposure to one condition of the experiment is not expected to affect performance under another condition of the experiment. Repeated measures designs are more sensitive because there are usually large individual differences among people in any dependent measure the experimenter wishes to study. People differ widely in their reaction times, their tachistoscopic recognition thresholds, and their recall performances. Students who have never run an experiment before are often surprised (and sometimes frustrated) to discover that their subjects show such large individual differences. With repeated measures designs, subjects serve as their own controls. When comparing the behavior of the same subject in many conditions, the effects of numerous subject variables (e.g., IQ, age, and sensitivity) can be controlled. The statistical analysis of repeated measures designs takes into account these individual differences, and hence is more likely to detect true effects of the independent variable.

On the other hand, if there is any suspicion that exposure to one condition will affect a subject's performance during another condition of the experiment, different subjects should be used in each condition in a completely randomized design. Each experimenter must decide for himself

Table 2-1 Experimental Designs and Their Appropriate Statistical Tests for One Independent Variable

Design	Number of levels	
	Two	More than two
Random groups	*t* test (independent)	analysis of variance (one-way randomized)
Matched or repeated measures	*t* test (matched groups)	analysis of variance (one-way, repeated measures)

whether subjects will be affected by previous conditions, using as guidelines common sense and any experimental literature available—there is no simple rule for making this decision. Greenwald (1976) and Poulton (1973) summarize the arguments for and against within-subject designs in more detail.

Table 2-1 shows the four possible combinations of two or more levels, and random or repeated designs, along with their appropriate statistical tests. All four are called "one-factor" designs because there is only one independent variable. We will consider each of the four combinations in detail.

Random Groups Design with Two Levels

In a random groups design with two levels there are two levels of a single independent variable and two independent groups of subjects. Examples of this design are as follows: comparing reaction time performance of neurotic and normal subjects; comparing ease of identifying words for a group of subjects who have been shown the words prior to the experiment and a group who have not; and comparing the speed with which bystanders come to the aid of a victim for subjects alone in a situation and subjects in groups of three. The independent variable for these three examples are subject status (neurotic versus normal), exposure status (preexposed versus nonpreexposed), and group size (one versus three). In each case, there are two levels, or conditions, of the independent variable, but a single subject participates in only one condition. The appropriate statistical test is an *independent groups* t *test.*

Matched or Repeated Measures Design with Two Levels

In a matched or repeated measures design with two levels, there are still two levels of a single independent variable, but a single subject participates in both conditions or each of two subjects paired on some criterion participates in one condition. In both cases, there is some basis on which to pair scores. In the first, scores are paired because a single subject generated both of them, and in the second, scores are paired because subjects have been matched on some criterion. Statistically, members of a matched pair are treated as though they were the same person.

In a matched or repeated measures design, we have the advantage of statistically controlling some of the variance resulting from individual differences. If the same patient is tested before and after therapy, subject variables such as sex, intelligence, socioeconomic status, and disease are automatically controlled. If, however, exposure to one condition is likely to alter the subject's performance in another condition, such as in a deception experiment, then the same subject cannot be used twice, although matched subjects can sometimes be used.

Two examples of experiments in which the same subject participates in both conditions are comparing the speed of learning a list of words for the same subject under alcohol and no-alcohol conditions, and comparing the visual recognition thresholds for frequent and infrequent words seen by the same subject. The two independent variables are alcohol consumption and word frequency. Three examples of experiments in which subjects are paired or matched are comparing the IQs of the first and second-born children from the same families, comparing school performances of two groups of children matched on school grades after one group is exposed to a novel teaching method, and comparing personality test scores of wives and their husbands. In these examples, subjects are matched on family membership, school grades, and marital unit, respectively. The three independent variables are birth order, teaching method, and sex. The same statistical test is used regardless of whether the same subject is used in both conditions or subjects are matched on some criterion. In both designs, the appropriate statistical test is a *matched pairs* t *test.*

Random Groups Design with More than Two Levels

In a random groups design with more than two levels, there are more than two conditions of an independent variable and a different group of subjects is run in each condition. Some examples are comparing school performance of students in four different educational programs (e.g., open classroom, individualized studies, etc.); measuring how long subjects take to help a victim when subjects are alone, with two confederates who make no attempt to help, and with two friends; and comparing memory performance of mental patients from four diagnostic classifications. The independent variables are the educational program, the situation in which a victim requests help, and the diagnostic category of each patient. In each case, there are more than two levels of a single independent variable, but a single subject participates in only one condition. The appropriate statistical test is a *one-way randomized analysis of variance (ANOVA).*

Repeated Measures Design with More than Two Levels

In a repeated measures design with more than two levels, there are more than two conditions of a single independent variable, and each subject participates in all conditions. Although possible, it is impracticable to *match* subjects across more than two conditions, so in the typical experiment the same subject participates in all conditions. That is why we refer to a *matched pairs t* test but a *repeated measures* analysis of variance. The former test can be appropriate for matched pairs of subjects whereas the latter is typically used when the same subjects are measured repeatedly.

Some examples of single-factor repeated measures designs are comparison of recognition thresholds for high-, medium-, and low-frequency words given to all subjects; comparison of choice reaction times to pairs of stimuli of various probabilities (frequencies of occurrence) presented to the same subjects; and comparison of patients on a memory task before, during, and after therapy. The independent variables are word frequency, stimulus probability, and status in therapy. The appropriate statistical test is a *one-way repeated measures analysis of variance.*

TWO INDEPENDENT VARIABLES

So far we have discussed designs in which there is only a single independent variable, such as psychiatric classifications of patients, frequency of words in print, type of drug, dosage of drug, and whether a subject is alone or with others. Often, however, we have two independent variables, or two factors, and we wish to test all possible combinations of the two factors, as well as their interaction. We call this a *factorial* design.

Suppose we are interested in both type of drug and drug dosage: we might want to test four types of drugs at each of three dosage levels—low, medium, and high—in all possible combinations. This results in a total of twelve ($4 \times 3 = 12$) conditions. Or we might be interested in recognition thresholds for high-, medium-, and low-frequency words when one group of subjects is familiar with the word lists and the other group is not. Frequency, with three levels, is the first independent varia-

Table 2-2 Experimental Designs and Their Appropriate Statistical Tests for Two Independent Variables, Either of Which May Be Random (Between Subjects) or Repeated (Within Subjects) Variables

	Factor A	
Factor B	Random groups (between subjects)	Repeated measures (within subjects)
Random groups (between subjects)	two-way ANOVA, completely randomized	two-way ANOVA mixed
Repeated measures (within subjects)	two-way ANOVA mixed	two-way ANOVA, completely repeated measures

ble, and familiarity, with two levels, is the second independent variable. Their factorial combination results in six (3 × 2 = 6) conditions.

When there are two independent variables, both may be random, both may have repeated measures, or one may be random and one may have repeated measures. The appropriate statistical test for data gathered in these experiments is an ANOVA. Table 2-2 presents the possible combinations of the two types of independent variables with the appropriate analyses of variance for each combination.

In two-factor experiments, random groups variables are sometimes referred to as *between-subjects variables* and repeated measures variables as *within-subjects variables.* Two of the cells in Table 2-2 are identical—the combination of one within-subjects with one between-subjects variable. These are known as *mixed* designs. We will adopt the convention of calling the between-subjects variable factor A, and the within-subjects variable factor B in mixed designs.

Regardless of whether one or both factors have repeated measures, each may vary on any number of levels. If we let *a* refer to the number of levels of factor A and *b* refer to the number of levels of factor B, then the total number of different conditions in a two-factor experiment is equal to the product of $a \times b$.

The simplest possible case of a factorial design is one in which A has two levels and B has two levels, so the total number of conditions is 2 × 2, or 4. The two-way ANOVA that results is called a 2 × 2 (2 by 2) ANOVA. Note that the "two-way" refers to the two independent variables, and "2 × 2" refers to the number of levels of each variable. If one variable had three levels and another four, then the two-way ANOVA would be referred to as a 3 × 4 ANOVA, where "3 × 4" again refers to the number of levels of each variable.

We consider next the three possible types of two-factor designs—completely randomized, completely repeated measures, and mixed. In all cases, analysis of variance is the appropriate statistical test.

The reason that we use analysis of variance for all experiments with more than two groups is that it is inappropriate to conduct multiple *t* tests between all pairs of conditions. Thus, we would never analyze the results of a 2 × 2 design with *t* tests between each of the six possible pairs of conditions. Using the *t* test for this purpose is both statistically and conceptually incorrect.

Using multiple *t* tests on all pairs of means is prohibited by the logic of statistics because such comparisons must necessarily use redundant, overlapping information. The consequence of this would be a complicated interdependence among the test results. The *t* distribution, to which the calculated *t* statistics are compared, assumes independence between any two *t* values. If the *t*s are dependent on one another, as they would be with multiple *t* tests on the same set of means, the interpretation of the significance levels would be impossible. As we increase the number of comparisons on the same data, we increase the risk of a Type I error (falsely rejecting a true null hypothesis).

Even if multiple *t* tests were allowable, they would be undesirable because the *t* test, unlike the analysis of variance, does not permit us to evaluate interactions. The ability to evaluate interactions, one of the strengths of the analysis of variance, is discussed in a later section on interaction in two-factor experiments.

Completely Randomized Design

In a completely randomized design, separate groups of subjects are run in each of the conditions. Two examples of two-factor randomized designs are described below.

In the first example, subjects are asked to learn a set of material and then are tested for recall at one of three retention intervals—immediately, one hour later, and 24 hours later. The investigator also manipulates the meaningfulness of the material, using both sentences and nonsense syllables. Each subject is tested with only one retention interval and one type of material, so this is a completely randomized 3 × 2 design.

In the second example, a field experiment is conducted to evaluate the relationship between the sex of the experimenter and the sex of the subject on willingness to help. Male and female experimenters stood in a crowded shopping center asking randomly chosen passersby for change. (Do you have two nickels for a dime?) Subjects were either male or female. Subjects' willingness to look for change was analyzed as a function of their sex and the sex of the experimenter. Thus, there were two levels of experimenter (male versus female) and two levels of subject (male versus female) for a 2 × 2 completely randomized design.

Completely Repeated Measures Design

In a completely repeated measures or within-subjects design, each subject receives each combination of levels of the two independent variables. Two examples of completely repeated measures designs are described next.

In the first experiment, recall of words as a function of both their imagery and their frequency in print is measured, in which two levels of imagery (high and low) and three levels of frequency (high, medium, and low) are factorially combined in a 2 × 3 design. Each subject is tested on his or her ability to memorize words from all six categories; therefore, this is a completely within-subjects design.

In the second experiment, tachistoscopic recognition thresholds (TRTs) for four types of words (nouns, verbs, adjectives, and adverbs) are studied as a function of five trial blocks (each experimental session has been divided into five equal segments) to determine the effect of practice on the TRTs to the various stimuli. One factor is type of stimulus, with four levels and the other factor is trial block, with five levels. Because subjects participate in all conditions, this experiment has a repeated measures 4 × 5 design.

Mixed Design

A mixed design, in which there is one random-groups independent variable and one repeated-measures independent variable, is often used when one of the variables is nature's own, such as sex, race, birth order, or some personality characteristic. These naturally occurring independent variables can be selected but not manipulated by the experimenter. The selected natural variable becomes the random-groups independent variable. Subjects are assigned to separate groups according to nature's whim, not the experimenter's, and no subject can belong to more than one selected level (that is, subjects are either male *or* female, left- *or* right-handed, and so on). Here are some examples.

We want to measure the ease of identifying taboo (obscene) words compared with neutral words for male and female subjects. Type of word has two levels (taboo and neutral) and is the repeated-measures independent variable because every subject is exposed to both types of word. Sex of the subject also has two levels (male and female) and is the randomized independent variable selected by the experimenter because each subject is of only one sex. A mixed 2 × 2 ANOVA is the appropriate statistical test.

We measure the acuity of sensory discrimination for five sense modalities (vision, hearing, touch, taste, and smell), comparing subjects high in rigidity with those low in rigidity (as measured by a questionnaire). Here the repeated-measures independent variable is sense modality with five levels because each subject is administered all five sensory tests. The random-groups independent variable is subject rigidity having the two levels, high versus low, because a subject can be either high or low in rigidity, but not both. A mixed 2 × 5 ANOVA is the appropriate statistical test.

We wish to compare the reactions of men and women to fear situations versus anxiety situations. The two types of subjects are exposed to a fear-producing and an anxiety-producing experience, and the investigator measures how much each subject wants to be alone or with others (the dependent variable). Sex is the random-groups independent variable, because each subject can have only one sex, and exposure to a fear-producing and an anxiety-producing experience is the repeated-measures independent variable, because all subjects are exposed to both conditions. This is a mixed 2 × 2 design.

In some experiments, the random-groups independent variable is not nature's own but a manipulation that the experimenter believes could not be repeated on the same subject. Consider the following modification of the experiment, which compares recognition thresholds for taboo versus neutral words. Suppose we hypothesize that alcohol will remove inhibitions that keep us from either seeing or saying taboo words. In order to test our hypothesis, we want to compare recognition thresholds for taboo and neutral words for subjects who are intoxicated with those who are sober. However, if the same subject is tested twice, once sober and once intoxicated, his or her inhibitions concerning taboo words may change between the two testing sessions. A person who has already received the alcohol condition might behave differently under the sober (control) condition than a naive sober subject. Therefore, we must use separate groups of subjects for the alcohol and control conditions, although each subject will be shown both taboo and neutral words. Here the alcohol versus control condition is the randomized independent variable, and the taboo versus neutral word condition is the repeated-measures independent variable. This is also a mixed 2 × 2 design, but now the randomized independent variable is under the experimenter's rather than nature's control because the experimenter is free to assign subjects to either the alcohol or control group.

As another example, consider a modification of the experiment comparing sensory discrimination of rigid and nonrigid subjects. An investigator might attempt to create a rigid subject experimentally (as opposed to selecting him) by rewarding all statements that agreed with previously stated positions taken by the subject. Conversely, the experimenter might attempt to create a nonrigid subject by rewarding all statements that disagreed with previously stated positions. Sensory discrimination for the five senses could be measured and performance of the two groups compared. The rigid/nonrigid independent variable is still random but the experimenter is free to assign subjects to the two groups at will. The same mixed 2 × 5 analysis of variance is appropriate although the random independent variable is now under the experimenter's rather than nature's control.

Interaction in Two-Factor Experiments

One of the major purposes of manipulating two independent variables is to determine whether they interact. By *interaction,* we mean that the effect of moving

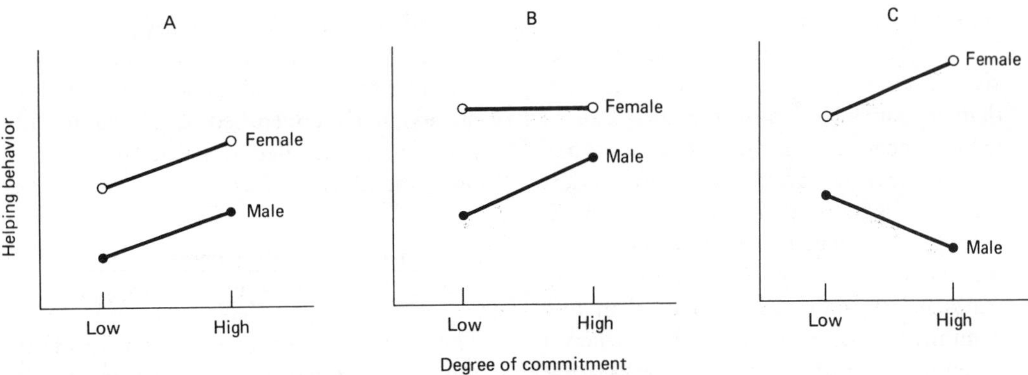

Fig. 2-1 Some possible outcomes in the bystander intervention experiment when sex of victim and degree of commitment are jointly manipulated.

from one level to another in the first factor is not the same for each level of the second factor. For example, adding salt to unsalted pork roast usually increases taste preference, whereas adding salt to unsalted ice cream usually decreases taste preference. In this case, salt interacts with food type because adding salt to meats increases preference, whereas adding it to desserts decreases preference.

We will discuss a completely randomized 2 × 2 design to illustrate interaction. In a field experiment, the effect of a bystander's commitment and the sex of the victim (who was a confederate of the experimenter) on willingness to help the victim is evaluated. Commitment is manipulated by having the bogus victim at a beach either ask the bystander for a match (low commitment) or ask the bystander to watch the victim's portable radio while the victim is absent (high commitment). Following this, the subject witnesses someone trying to steal the victim's radio. Whether the subject is willing to help the victim is then evaluated as a function of both degree of commitment (high versus low) and the sex of the victim (male versus female). A subject (the bystander) is assigned to a single level of commitment and sex, so this is a completely randomized 2 × 2 design.

We might predict several different outcomes for this experiment. In general, we might expect more helping behavior when the victim is a female than a male and when the commitment is high than when it is low. The question, however, is whether bystanders will be affected by both variables in an additive fashion—that is, whether they will be more eager to help females than males in the low commitment condition to the same degree as they were in the high commitment condition.

Figure 2-1 presents several possible outcomes for this 2 × 2 experiment. The dependent variable, helping behavior, is plotted along the ordinate (y-axis) against degree of commitment along the abscissa (x-axis). Sex of the victim is represented by the two separate lines in each panel. Panel A demonstrates a lack of interaction between the two factors, whereas panels B and C each show interaction between the two factors.

In panel A, helping behavior increases in an *additive* fashion, as commitment is changed from low to high and as the sex of the victim is varied from male to female. The additivity is indicated by the fact that the two lines are parallel. Bystanders are equally more likely to help as commitment is increased from low to high for both male and female victims, even though they are uniformly more likely to help females.

Panels B and C both show interaction, because the lines are not parallel, although the *form* of the interaction varies. In panel B, bystanders are equally likely to help females, regardless of commitment, whereas they are more likely to help males when commitment is high than when it is low. Panel C shows yet another type of interaction. Here the interaction is stronger than in panel B because the *direction* of helping changes for the two sexes when commitment is varied. Now, bystanders are more likely to help females under high commitment than low commitment conditions, but they are *less likely* to help males under high commitment than low commitment conditions. That is, when a potential victim who is a male asks a bystander to watch his radio, the bystander is less likely to intervene when it is stolen than when the male victim simply asks for a match.

This outcome might be understood in a variety of ways, including societal expectations that males should be more sophisticated about the probabilities of theft at beaches, and we will leave it to our readers to generate reasonable hypotheses. The point we wish to highlight here is the power of manipulating two variables to look for interactions—there are so many more possible and interesting outcomes that can occur when two variables are manipulated jointly than when only a single variable is manipulated. (Statistical analysis of interaction is described in Chapter 16.)

ROLE OF RANDOMIZATION AND CONTROL IN EXPERIMENTS

An experiment is a sample of behavior of a sample of subjects exposed to a sample of stimuli. We conduct an experiment, however, not to learn about this sample of subjects on this sample of occasions responding to this sample of stimuli but to learn about populations—of subjects, occasions, and stimuli. We would like our experiment, based on samples, to generalize to populations. To do this, we must ensure that the samples are representative of their respective populations.

There are two general schemes of selecting samples from populations. The first is *random sampling,* defined as selection from a population so that each member has an equal chance of being selected. The second is *controlled sampling,* in which characteristics of the population that are thought to affect the dependent variable are explicitly controlled. (See Chapter 12 for a more detailed description of sampling methods.)

SELECTING SUBJECTS FROM SUBJECT POPULATIONS

The lore of experimentation insists that subjects be randomly sampled from the populations to which they belong. In a random sample every potential subject has an equal probability of being chosen. Why might we want a random sample? Normally, we do an experiment to test some idea or hypothesis about how the human mind works (or, alternatively, what factors control human behavior). Whatever results our experiment yields should be generalizable to the population in question. The population is not limited to all students enrolled in the introductory psychology class at University X but should extend beyond that to all human beings, or more modestly, to all normal adults in Western civilization. In fact, however, subjects in most psychology experiments are not randomly selected at all. Instead, they are almost overwhelmingly chosen from the population of college undergraduates, and usually from the population of students taking Introduction to Psychology, who are usually required to participate in experiments as part of the course requirement.

The importance of a truly random sampling of subjects from a subject population is dependent on two factors: (1) how general or universal the phenomenon in question is believed to be and (2) whether the investigator is interested in what an organism *does* do or what that organism *can* do.

How General or Universal Is the Phenomenon?

People may differ from one another in crucial ways on certain dependent variables, depending on their backgrounds, and be remarkably similar on other dependent variables. Political views are markedly affected by race, socioeconomic status, and geographical location whereas such sensory abilities as discrimination between tones of different frequencies are, as far as we know, remarkably free of effects of such background variables for subjects with normal hearing.

A political pollster, for example, might be interested in how people will vote next November or how they feel about an issue. However, since voting patterns are very dependent on socioeconomic and ethnic factors, groups of people will cast their votes very differently. Hence, it is incumbent on the pollster to select a representative sample of the electorate to properly predict an election or adequately represent views on an issue.

Perhaps the most famous case of a biased voting sample is the *Literary Digest* poll of 1936, which was conducted to predict the outcome of the presidential election. The *Digest* poll, based on over 2 million responses, predicted that Republican candidate Landon would win over Democrat Roosevelt. In actuality, Roosevelt won a landslide victory over Landon. The source of this bias in the *Digest's* sample was the use of telephone directories and lists of *Digest* subscribers to select the "random" sample. In 1936, the poor (who tended to vote Democratic) could not afford either telephones or magazine subscriptions, and so the *Digest* poll included too many wealthy Republicans and too few poor Democrats.

Most polls today are conducted by means of *stratified sampling,* in which proportions of people from relevant subsectors of the populace are polled in proportion to their representation in the population. It is important to note that only relevant factors are taken into consideration; because it has never been noted that height makes a difference in political behavior, height has never been made a criterion for stratified sampling in voting polls.

Most psychological experiments (70–80% of those published in psychological journals) use college students, often students enrolled in introductory psychology classes, as subjects. How representative of the population at large are college students? It depends on what the manipulation is and what the dependent variable is.

For example, volunteer subjects have been shown to differ from nonvolunteers in their degree of susceptibility to persuasion, with the former being more susceptible than the latter (Adair, 1973). Thus, in any between-groups experiment manipulating persuasion, the volunteer status of subjects should become a control variable. This can be accomplished by using volunteers or nonvolunteers exclusively, by equating the numbers of volunteers in the various conditions, or by using volunteer status as another independent variable. The sex of the subject has been shown to be a factor when personality variables have been manipulated; therefore, sex should be controlled and reported in such experiments (Schwabacker, 1972).

Sex of the subject may or may not be an important control variable for cognitive tasks. In recent years, it has become common practice among experimenters studying basic perceptual and memorial tasks to ignore differences in sex, either by simply not reporting the number of male and female subjects in an experiment or, in between-groups experiments, by not equating numbers of male and female subjects. The rationale for this practice is that there is no basis on which to assume that women differ from men in basic cognitive capacities.

There is, however, strong evidence that women do better than men on tests of verbal ability, whereas men do better than women on tests of spatial and mathematical ability (Very, 1967). Although these differences are small and there is substantial overlap between the two groups in performance scores, it is important for the experimenter to carefully equate for the numbers of male and female subjects in between-groups experiments studying these tasks or to report their numbers in within-subjects experiments. Failing to do so may bias the results in unknown ways, or it may make the results from one study incomparable with those of another using the same task. In fact, recent results have shown that females and males may differ in some very simple visual tasks (Brabyn & McGuinness, 1979; McGuinness, 1976), and a rather impressive set of data has accumulated that females are less lateralized for verbal and spatial tasks than males (McGlone, 1980). (Chapter 6 discusses hemispheric differences in more detail.) Given that sex differences in cognitive processing may be subtle *and* that sex is a very easy subject variable to control, it seems wisest to equate the number of males and females in between-groups designs and to report the number of males and females in within-subjects experiments.

In some basic human abilities, it may be that the overall level of college students may differ from that of the population in general but that the manipulation in question makes the same relative difference in performance, regardless of differences in absolute level. For example, the use of mnemonic strategies improves memory; this has been shown both in classes for the general public on memory improvement and in laboratory experiments using college students as subjects. Therefore, the phenomenon is truly general, and with respect to it, college students are probably a representative sample.

Some human performances, particularly sensory performances, are assumed to behave in exactly the same way from subject to subject, for subjects without deficiencies in that sensory modality. For these simple sensory tasks, a single subject should, in theory, be sufficient to reveal the phenomenon in question (see Dukes, 1965, for a discussion of single-subject designs).

Are We Interested in Ideal or Average Performance?

Often, the psychologist is interested in the limits of the performance of a human subject rather than the subject's performance in a naive, unpracticed, and perhaps unmotivated state. This is particularly true for sensory ability and for the broad class of experimentation that is known as human information processing. We might take investigations of physical abilities as an analogy to mental abilities. On the one hand, we might be interested in how fast the average human adult could run the mile; this would be a question of what people *usually* do, not what they *can* do. To carry out such an experiment, we would carefully sample the population, paying particular attention to those characteristics that affect running speed, such as sex, height, age, and physical fitness, to name just a few. On the other hand, if we are interested in what people can do, we would search track records for winners of mile races, and determine the fastest speed.

Similarly, if we were interested in how the average human adult usually performs a sensory or information processing task, we would carefully sample the population, paying particular attention to those characteristics that would be likely to affect these tasks, such as sex, intelligence, and level of education. On the other hand, if we are interested in how well subjects can do, we would select highly motivated subjects and train them for some time before measuring their responses. The data on these highly practiced and well-motivated subjects would reveal the upper limits of performance of subjects, not the average performance of a typical subject selected randomly from the population. In short, it may or may not be necessary to obtain a truly random sample of subjects from the population—it depends on the purpose of the experiment.

SELECTING STIMULI FROM STIMULUS POPULATIONS

Although random or controlled selection of subjects from subject populations may be impossible to achieve, and at the same time not necessary, there is little question that random or controlled sampling from stimulus populations is very important. Here we give examples of both random and controlled sampling from a stimulus population.

One of the largest and most variegated stimulus populations from which psychologists draw samples is the population of all

English words. Words can be selected from such a population either randomly, or in a controlled manner subject to some restrictions. Consider, for example, an experiment comparing ease of seeing high-frequency (common) compared to low-frequency (rare) words. A number of sources list the frequency with which words in the English language appear in various kinds of printed material. One of the oldest is the Thorndike-Lorge count (1944), based on a corpus (total sample size) of more than 4½ million words. Although many current investigators still rely on the Thorndike-Lorge counts, they are somewhat out of date. The most complete up-to-date count is that of Kučera and Francis (1967), whose counts are based on a corpus of 1 million words. Brown (1976) has provided a catalog of scaled verbal material that lists sources of a variety of measures for words in the English language, such as frequency in print, judged frequency, and judged pleasantness.

For an experiment comparing ease of recognition of high- and low-frequency words, we would select the samples of words either randomly or with some restrictions. To select the two samples randomly, we would first select appropriate ranges of frequencies, one in the high end and one in the low end of the frequency range. All English words in either of these two frequency ranges would constitute the two populations of high- and low-frequency words. We could then randomly select samples from these populations using an appropriate method, such as a random number generator or a random number table.

An alternative to random sampling is to select the two samples of words so that they are equated on those characteristics known to affect ease of reading. These could include number of letters, number of syllables, first letter, conceptual category, and so forth. It may be important to equate the two samples of high- and low-frequency words for factors such as length rather than leave this factor to chance. In this way, we can be reasonably sure that any differences we observe between the two types of words cannot be attributable to chance differences between lengths of words arising from random sampling. Even though we equate the two sets of words for word length, number of syllables, and so forth, there still may be a confounding variable that covaries with frequency and that may be responsible for any effects on the recognition thresholds we observe. For example, high-frequency words are also judged more pleasant than low-frequency words (Matlin & Stang, 1978), so lower thresholds may be a result either of frequency, pleasantness, or both. The only way to test this is to manipulate both variables independently.

In general, it is better to select samples of stimuli in a controlled way, so that the two or more samples are equated for those characteristics that could affect the dependent variable that interests us. Which characteristics are controlled will depend on the problem we are studying. (Characteristics of words that are often considered when designing experiments are discussed in Chapter 14 on materials.)

SELECTING CONDITIONS FOR TRIALS OR TRIAL BLOCKS

When at least one independent variable has a matched or within-subjects design, so that a single subject participates in more than one condition of the experiment, it is necessary to present these repeated conditions in some order. However, across a series of trials performance may improve as a result of practice or get worse as a result of fatigue simply because of exposure to the situation. For this reason, it is important to arrange conditions so that they are equally distributed over the sequence of trials.

There are two methods of distributing conditions across a sequence of trials in an experiment: randomization and counterbalancing. In *randomization,* trials representing each of the n conditions are selected at random for the sequence, so that each possible condition has an equal chance of being presented at each temporal location. (Note the similarity of this definition of randomization of trial types or conditions to the procedure for random sampling of subjects discussed in the preceding section.)

Randomization, on the average, will produce sequences of trials in which each condition will be equally distributed across the sequence. However, this only holds across a large number of random sequences. By chance, any particular random sequence may have all the trials for one condition at the beginning of the sequence and all the trials for another condition at the end. Thus, it is important to use a different randomization for each subject. (The types of randomization possible will depend, in part, on the limitations of the particular apparatus being used.)

Randomized Sequences

Randomization of conditions is used whenever it is important for the subject not to anticipate which condition or stimulus will be presented on the next trial. Here we give two extreme examples of randomization. In the first, two stimuli are presented repeatedly over a long series of trials, and in the second each of a number of stimuli is presented exactly once over the same number of trials.

Randomization with Repeated Stimuli. Suppose we are conducting a choice reaction time experiment in which subjects are to press one key when a red light is presented and a second when a green light is presented. Our dependent variable is the time between stimulus onset and the subject's response. For this experiment, we will want to use a random sequence of the two stimuli, so that a subject cannot anticipate which of the two stimuli will be presented on the next trial. To construct a random sequence for *n* trials, we need to know the presentation probabilities of the two stimuli. One possibility is to make them equally probable (.50/.50). One way of constructing a .50/.50 sequence is to toss a coin *n* times and present the red light whenever heads occurs and the green light whenever tails occurs. A faster means of accomplishing this is to use the table of random digits in the Appendix (Table A-1). In tables of random digits, each of the ten digits, 0 through 9, has an equal probability, .10, of occurrence in any position in the table. Thus, to construct a .50/.50 sequence of binary events, we divide the set of digits into two equal groups such as 0 to 4 and 5 to 9, or odd and even. A random starting place is selected, and we proceed in any direction from there, selecting the presentation of one stimulus when any one of the digits 0 through 4 occurs, and the other stimulus when any one of the digits 5 through 9 occurs, or we may select one stimulus for the odd digits and the other for the even digits.

If we wanted probabilities other than .50/.50, we would simply modify the assignment of digits to events. For a binary sequence of .30/.70, we could use the digits 0 through 2 for the lower probability event and the digits 3 through 9 for the higher probability event. An alternative to a table of random digits is to use the random number generator programmed into many computers.

Randomization with Nonrepeated Stimuli. Consider the experiment described earlier comparing frequent with infrequent words. We might conduct this experiment by selecting ten frequent words and ten infrequent words and present each word once to each subject. To randomize the sequence of twenty words, we could number them and then select a permutation of twenty numbers from Table A-3 in the Appendix. A permutation of *n* items is a sequence of shuffled numbers in which the same number is never repeated; that is, digit order is important. For example, there are six permutations of the first three digits: 123, 132, 231, 213, 312, and 321.

When we permute the order of the unique stimulus words, we also randomize the order of the two conditions of word frequency. In a typical permutation, the frequent and infrequent words will tend to be well mixed throughout the sequence, although an occasional permutation could be quite imbalanced. A different permutation should be used for every subject because a single permutation can show imbalances in the distribution of conditions over trials by chance. On the other hand, a counterbalanced sequence of conditions, as described next, guarantees a balanced distribution of conditions over trials.

Counterbalancing is a method of arranging sequences of trials to ensure that the conditions will have the identical average position within any particular sequence of trials. A counterbalanced sequence is deterministic, instead of random, in that once a scheme of counterbalancing is selected, the condition that will appear on a particular trial is determined. Whether randomization or counterbalancing is used depends on how important it is for the subject to be unaware of the condition on the next trial.

Counterbalanced Sequences

When it is not important that the occurrence of one type of event be unpredictable, or when the various conditions are difficult or impossible for the subject to distinguish, and therefore to predict, we might want to use a counterbalanced sequence. A counterbalanced sequence is one in which the ordinal position of conditions is carefully controlled so that the average position of any condition equals (or nearly equals) that of all others. Counterbalancing can take place over single trials or over blocks of trials. Often it is done in situations in which each of the conditions consists of several stimuli. Although the order of the conditions is counterbalanced, the order of the particular stimuli that constitute instances of that condition are usually randomized.

Counterbalancing by Trials. Suppose we wish to determine subjects' memory spans for four types of material. The four types of material might be words, letters, digits, and shapes. Suppose, further, that we wish to present ten trials of each type of stimulus. Our experiment, therefore, would consist of 40 trials.

We will want to control for practice and fatigue effects by evenly distributing the four types of trials across the session. To do this, we can use repeated permutations of the four trial types, so that each trial type appears once within each block of four trials.

There are a total of 4! (4 factorial) or 24 ($4! = 4 \times 3 \times 2 \times 1 = 24$) distinct permutations of four conditions (e.g., 1234, 2134, 4321, etc.). One way to construct a sequence of 40 trials in a counterbalanced way is to select 10 different permutations from the possible set of 24 and assign trials to conditions within blocks of four trials so that each condition occurs in each trial block. In other words, every block will consist of four trials in which each of the four stimulus types (words, letters, digits, and shapes) is represented.

As another example, suppose we wish to counterbalance the sequence of high- and low-frequency words in a word recognition experiment to control more carefully the order in which high- and low-frequency words occur. One way of doing this is to use strict alternation of the two types of trials so that on even-numbered trials, high-frequency words are presented, and on odd-numbered trials, low-frequency words are presented. Strict alternation has the slight disadvantage that the condition presented on the odd-numbered trials has an average position that is slightly earlier than the condition presented on the even-numbered trials. In order to absolutely equate the average position of the two conditions, we could alternate the alternations by repeating the sequence high-low-low-high (or low-high-high-low) across blocks of four trials (this scheme is called the ABBA method).

The goal of any counterbalancing scheme is to assign conditions to trials in a deterministic fashion. (That is, given that you know the scheme, you also know which condition will be presented on a given trial.) However, which high- or low-frequency word appears on which trial is determined randomly and may be accomplished by choosing two random permutations of 10 digits from Table A-2 in the Appendix.

Counterbalancing by Trial Blocks. For some experiments, it will not be advisable or even possible to change conditions on every trial. Any time an investigator feels that switching conditions from trial to trial will lead to a decrement or bias in performance, it is advisable to run all the trials of a condition in a single block (or in several blocks). For the memory example, it may be better to present all the trials for a given type of material together so that the subject may learn the most efficient strategy for remembering that type of material. In this method, a particular condition will appear in only a single block of trials.

We will still use permutations to counterbalance the four conditions, but the permutations will be of trial *blocks* rather than of successive trials. However, because each subject is exposed to only a single block of each condition, each subject will receive only a single permutation of the four conditions. Thus, it is necessary to control for order effects *across* subjects rather than within a single subject.

A device for counterbalancing the order of conditions across subjects is known as a *latin square.* A latin square is a set of n permutations of n conditions having the property that across the n permutations each condition appears once in each position. A standard latin square for four conditions is shown in Table 2-3.

Table 2-3 Standard and Rearranged Latin Square for Four Conditions

	Standard trial block			
Subject	(1)	(2)	(3)	(4)
(a)	A	B	C	D
(b)	B	C	D	A
(c)	C	D	A	B
(d)	D	A	B	C
	Rearranged trial block			
Subject	(1)	(2)	(3)	(4)
(a)	B	A	C	D
(b)	C	B	D	A
(c)	D	C	A	B
(d)	A	D	B	C

The columns represent trial blocks, and the rows represent subjects. Across subjects, each condition appears exactly once in each position, although in this square, each condition does not follow every other condition an equal number of times (for example, condition B is always followed by C except when it is the last condition). By rearranging the latin square, as shown at the bottom of Table 2-3, we can equate both the ordinal positions of each condition and the number of times one condition follows another (now B is followed once by A, once by C, and once by D). Note that this rearrangement was accomplished by transposing columns 1 and 2 of the standard square.

Once a latin square has been constructed, subjects are randomly assigned to rows of the latin square, subject to the restriction that an equal number of subjects be assigned to each row. Thus, when n conditions are counterbalanced for position by the use of a latin square, it is necessary to use integral multiples of n subjects. For the present example, we could use 4, 8, 12, 16, or 20 subjects in the memory span experiment.

When a condition appears in two blocks of trials for each subject, it is possible to counterbalance the order of presentation within a subject so that the average position of all conditions is the same. This is the ABBA method. For example, if we have two conditions, A and B, and present them in two blocks, we can present them in the order ABBA. Note that the average position of both conditions within the sequence is the same. If either practice or fatigue effects, or both, act uniformly throughout the sequence, the ABBA method should equalize them between the two conditions. It is usually considered desirable to use the order ABBA with half the subjects and the complementary order BAAB with the other half to equate actual (in addition to average) position of conditions across subjects.

The ABBA method can be extended to more than two conditions. For example, three conditions, A, B, and C, can be run in the order ABCCBA. Such a counterbalancing has two complementary orders:

BCAACB, and CABBAC, and, as with the ABBA method, all three orders should be used equally across subjects.

SUMMARY

An experiment in psychology is defined as any procedure in which a manipulated (independent) variable is applied to two or more samples drawn from their corresponding populations and some dependent variable is measured on the samples. In an experiment, the independent variable can be manipulated by the experimenter or can be manipulated by nature and selected by the experimenter. Designing an experiment consists of making a series of decisions about various dimensions of an experiment. The particular decisions that are made depend on the nature of the problem being studied. Both knowledge and good judgment about the problem are required to design a good experiment.

There are three types of variables in an experiment—independent variables, those manipulated or selected by the experimenter; control variables, those kept constant across different conditions by the experimenter; and dependent variables, those characteristics of behavior measured by an experimenter in response to manipulations of the independent variables.

The particular statistical test used to analyze the dependent variable will depend on (a) the number of independent variables that are manipulated or selected, (b) the number of levels each independent variable can assume, and (c) whether the experiment has a randomized, repeated measures, or mixed design. For dependent variables on a quantitative scale of measurement, the appropriate statistical tests are t test or analysis of variance. A t test is used for a single, independent variable with two levels. A one-way analysis of variance (ANOVA) is performed when there are more than two levels of a single independent variable, and a two-way analysis of variance is performed when there are two independent variables whose levels are factorially combined.

Although the formal design determines the type of statistical analysis to be performed, there are many other considerations in designing the experiment that are important. These are concerned with selecting subjects, selecting stimuli, and selecting or ordering conditions in a sequence for within-subject independent variables. We want the results of our experiment to generalize from this sample of subjects to some defined population of subjects, from this sample of stimuli to a population of stimuli, and from this sample of situations to a population of situations. Accordingly, it is important to define the populations to which our results should generalize. This will determine the scheme we adopt to sample from these populations. Two types of sampling schemes are used: random sampling, in which each member of the population has an equal chance of being included, and controlled sampling, in which subjects, stimuli, and situations are selected according to some constraints.

In most experiments studying basic human processes, subjects are not randomly sampled at all but rather are selected on the basis of their being members of an available pool (e.g., volunteers from the Introductory Psychology pool or from a paid subject pool). In most cases, this lack of random sampling is not a problem. In contrast to subject selection, whether stimuli are selected using random or controlled sampling is more important. In scheduling conditions for ordering across sessions or days, random or counterbalanced sampling is very important. Whether randomization or counterbalancing is used for ordering conditions depends primarily on how difficult it is for subjects to distinguish the condition, and whether their knowledge of the order of conditions will affect their behavior.

Thus, we see that designing an experiment requires consideration of many factors. These include type and number of variables and selections of subjects, stimuli, and conditions. Careful consideration of these factors, in light of the problem being studied, is essential for meaningful, well-designed experiments.

3

Pitfalls in Experimentation

After carefully conditioning a flea to jump out of a box on an appropriate auditory signal, the "experimenter" removed the first pair of legs to see what effect this had. Observing that the flea was still able to perform his task, the second pair of legs were removed. Once again noting no difference in performance, the researcher removed the final pair of legs and found that the jumping behavior no longer occurred. Thus, the investigator wrote in his notebook, "When all the legs of the flea have been removed, it will no longer be able to hear."

(From Huck & Sandler, 1979, p. xiii)

This fictional anecdote (original source unknown) illustrates one of the fallacies experimental psychologists can commit. It illustrates the experimenter's neglect of what Huck and Sandler call *rival hypotheses.* The flea's failure to respond to the auditory signal could be due *either* to the possibility that the flea has its hearing receptors on its back legs *or* to the likelihood that the response of jumping has been made impossible.

In the last chapter, we described some of the "do's" of experimentation. These included how to design the experiment; how to select the subjects, stimulus materials, and orders of conditions; and how to select the appropriate statistical tests for data analysis. In this chapter, we describe the other side of the coin—namely, errors in design, errors in running the experiment, errors in selecting the appropriate dependent variable, errors in analyzing the data, and errors in drawing the appropriate conclusions. We will point out the flaws most commonly found in each step of the experiment, so that you can be aware of where the hazards lie and how to avoid them.

PITFALLS IN DESIGNING THE EXPERIMENT

Choosing, Combining, and Controlling the Independent Variables

In designing an experiment, it is important to choose levels of the independent variable that will demonstrate the effects you are interested in, to combine two or more independent variables appropriately, and to control for factors that may confound or obscure the effects of the independent variable.

Choosing Levels of the Independent Variable. There are two pitfalls in choosing levels of the independent variable. The first is the danger of not sampling enough levels, or a sufficient range of levels, to reveal the true functional relationship between your independent variable and the dependent variable. For example, the Yerkes-Dodson law of behavior (see Chapter 7) states that the relationship between drive (e.g., anxiety) and performance is an inverted U-shape. That is, both low and high levels of drive produce low levels of performance, whereas some intermediate or optimum level produces the highest performance.

Suppose you are interested in the effect of anxiety (the independent variable) on performance in a memory task (the dependent variable). First, it is obvious that if you use only two levels of anxiety in your experiment, you will not find the U-shaped function predicted by the theory. If your two levels are chosen below the optimum point, performance will increase with anxiety level. If the two levels are chosen above the optimum point, performance will decrease with anxiety level. And if two levels that straddle the optimum point are chosen, performance may not change with anxiety level. Accordingly, it is necessary to choose at least three levels to determine the shape of the function relating your independent and dependent variables, although even with three levels, they must be chosen judiciously to cover the full range of possible values.

A second pitfall in sampling levels of the independent variable is choosing levels that are too close together to show an effect. To return to the example of the effect of anxiety on memory, if your manipulation has no discernible effect on anxiety, you will find no effect on performance. Suppose you try to manipulate anxiety by instructions. The control group might be given the standard memory instructions, and the experimental (anxiety) group might be given the same instructions with the added sentence: "Performance on this memory task is a good indication of intelligence." By linking performance with intelligence, the experimenter hopes to elicit more anxiety in the experimental than in the control group. But has this manipulation been successful? Perhaps the college student subjects are so sophisticated that they do not believe rote memory has anything to do with intelligence, or they may believe it but could not care less (or they may even have read this chapter!). In any case, the manipulation could be so weak as to produce no discernible effect on anxiety (and hence no effect on performance).

Experimenters who attempt to manipulate some internal emotional state, like anxiety, often check to see whether their manipulation has been successful by a *manipulation check.* The manipulation check is usually a questionnaire given after the experiment in which subjects are asked to evaluate their state during the experiment. If the experimental and control groups show no difference on their ratings of anxiety, the experimenter may conclude that the manipulation has not worked, and thus that the experiment has not tested the hypothesis.

As another example, word frequency has been shown to have effects on the ease of perception of words (Chapter 6) and on their memorability (Chapter 8). When the independent variable of word frequency is manipulated, investigators usually try to choose subsets of words that differ widely in frequency-in-print. If the frequency levels are too closely spaced, the experimenter may find no significant effect of frequency on either perceptual or memory performance, even though numerous studies in the literature have demonstrated that frequency is an important variable.

Combining Levels of Two Independent Variables to Avoid Incomplete or Unbalanced Designs. A common problem in faulty designs is the use of an incomplete or unbalanced design, in which every combination of levels of the independent variables is not used. For example, suppose you are interested in comparing the effect of imagery instructions with verbal rehearsal instructions on learning two types of materials—words and the pictures that depict them. In this case, every combination of the two types of instructions and the two types of materials should be used. (This is called a 2 × 2 factorial design because there are two independent variables with two levels on each.)

Now suppose you want to save time or subjects and decide that it would be wasteful to use imagery instructions with pictures (because the image is already available in the stimulus itself) and verbal rehearsal instructions with words (because subjects generally name verbal materials). By eliminating these two conditions, you are left with only the two conditions: imagery instruction with words and verbal rehearsal instructions with pictures. The problem with this design is that it will not permit you to evaluate the extra advantage of imagery instructions with words over the baseline condition of verbal rehearsal alone and the extra advantage of verbal encoding instructions with pictures over the baseline condition of imagery encoding alone. This is an example of an incomplete design, as shown in Table 3-1, in which two of the cells of the design are missing. With this design, it is impossible to evaluate the effect of the two types of independent variables separately.

A second reason that an investigator might eliminate some conditions of a factorial design is that data already exist in the literature that provide the relevant baseline conditions. For example, suppose you are interested in comparing recognition thresholds (minimum exposure duration needed for identification) for real English words presented tachistoscopically with recognition thresholds for nonwords that are orthographically regular (that is, that follow the spelling patterns of English, e.g., *derk*). You might argue that

Table 3-1 An Incomplete 2 × 2 Factorial Design

	Instructions	
Material	Imagery	Verbal rehearsal
Words	X	0 (Missing)
Pictures	0 (Missing)	X

since the literature abounds with data on tachistoscopic recognition thresholds for words, you could simply use those thresholds as baseline data and measure the thresholds for nonwords only. However, this is a terrible idea for several reasons.

First, there is a host of factors known to affect thresholds for any type of stimulus, including words. These include the apparatus on which the thresholds are measured, the amount of light illuminating the stimulus, the size of the stimuli, their type font, and the particular sample of subjects who participate in the experiment and their level of practice. There are also other, less obvious factors that might affect performance. These include such things as the time of day, time of year, temperature of the room, attitude of the experimenter, number of people present. Thus, it is essential to measure the baseline thresholds for words using your equipment, you as experimenter, your sample of subjects, and so on. In fact, given the large individual differences observed in tasks of this kind, you would want to use a within-subjects rather than between-subjects design so that each subject will be measured on both levels of the independent variable—words and orthographically regular nonwords.

Confounding of Independent Variables

Confounding means that some uncontrolled variable changes with the independent variable so that the effects of this uncontrolled variable on the dependent variable cannot be disentangled from the effects of the experimenter's independent variable. The confounding may be inherent in the design, the environmental events that accompany the independent variable, characteristics of the subjects that covary with manipulated subject characteristics, and errors in subject selection and assignment.

Perhaps the most insidious confounding variable is the simple passage of time. Many studies employ pre- and posttreatment designs, in which subjects' behavior is evaluated before some experimental treatment (pretreatment) and then after the treatment (posttreatment). Any difference between the pre- and posttreatment measures is considered evidence that the treatment has been effective in changing the behavior. The treatment could be a new teaching method, a new drug for some medical or psychological condition, or a new therapy for psychiatric patients. Regardless of which type of treatment is being evaluated, it is necessary to unconfound the effects of passage of time alone from those of the treatment. Therefore, in pre- and posttreatment designs, it is necessary to have a control group given the same pre- and posttests, but without the intervening treatment, to see whether or not they show improvements comparable to those of the experimental groups.

Psychotherapy research has been criticized for failing to include such control groups. In 1952, Hans Eysenck published a paper in which he reviewed a large number of therapy-outcome studies. Eysenck amassed data from published sources for over seven thousand patients to establish the rate of "spontaneous remission" from neuroses. The spontaneous remission rate is the rate of recovery without benefit of psychotherapy; that is, with no treatment. Eysenck found that roughly two thirds of neurotic patients recover within 2 years of the onset of their illness when given no therapy. When Eysenck compared this spontaneous remission rate with the rate of recovery for patients given various forms of therapy, the patients in therapy did no better than the spontaneous remission rate, and for some forms of therapy—

notably, psychoanalysis—they did more poorly. Eysenck described the apparently damaging effects of some types of therapy as *iatrogenic* (illness caused by medical care). While the debate about the efficacy of therapy for neurotics understandably rages on (see Bergin & Lambert, 1978, for a more favorable view and Fisher & Greenberg, 1977, for a review of the effectiveness of psychoanalytic therapy), the important point of Eysenck's critique for our purposes is clear. It is necessary to include a control group that does not receive a treatment in order to evaluate the effect of the passage of time alone on the behavior of interest.

Environmental Confounding. In environmental confounding, a manipulation of the independent variable is accompanied by another event in the environment, so that the effect of the first cannot be separated from that of the second.

A classic example comes from a famous experiment conducted at the Hawthorne plant of the Western Electric Company (Roethlisberger & Dickson, 1939), in which a number of different environmental manipulations, such as changes in lighting, temperature, number and scheduling of coffee breaks, and work hours were administered to determine which, if any, contributed to greater productivity. The experiment was conducted on a specially selected group of women, who were regularly asked for their opinions about the new changes (and also about their reaction when conditions were changed back to their original states). In fact, each time a change was made, productivity increased, including a change that consisted in reinstating the original conditions. It seems apparent that the increases in productivity resulted in part from worker participation in the study. The beneficial effects of subject involvement in a study has come to be known as "the Hawthorne effect." The specific confounding effects are discussed in detail in a critique of this study in Chapter 11.

Another example is the famous Pepsi-Cola/Coca-Cola taste comparison conducted by the Pepsi-Cola Company. The Pepsi investigators recruited a group of Coke lovers, who indicated their preference between Pepsi and Coke in a "blind" taste test. To identify the two drinks to the experimenters, Pepsi was served in a glass marked "M" and Coke was served in a glass marked "Q." Most of the Coke lovers showed a preference for the Pepsi. However, as the Coca-Cola Company was quick to point out, the two glasses differed in both the drink they contained and the letter by which they were identified. Thus, the "neutral" identifying label on the glass and the drink it contained were confounded. When another group of subjects, tested by the Coca-Cola Company, was presented with identical drinks (this time Coke) in two glasses marked "Q" and "M," subjects still preferred the glass marked "M," presumably because of such verbal associations as *mother, marvelous, mmm,* and so on. To conduct taste tests fairly (rather than to conduct them with a biased intent to show one product is superior), there should be no distinguishing characteristics between the two products except their different tastes, order of tasting should be counterbalanced across and/or within subjects, and experimenters themselves, as well as the subjects, should be "blind" to which liquid or other substance is which.

Confounding of Subject Characteristics. In the last chapter we discussed those subject characteristics that should be controlled, either by equalizing the number of subjects in the various conditions having that characteristic or by treating a characteristic such as sex as another independent variable. Sex of subjects might be an important variable to control when tasks are related to cultural stereotypes, such as reactions to frustration or hostility or measurement of the need for achievement. Although it was formerly standard practice to control for sex differences in most experiments by equalizing the proportions of males and females in each group, many experimenters are now inclined to ignore sex differences as insignificant in today's liberated society. The decision about whether to control for sex or not should usually be made in the context of common practice and known effects from the literature.

Experimental experience on the part of the subject is another potential confounding variable. Naive subjects are essential to most learning tests. In many cases, the subject should be unfamiliar with the particular stimuli that are to be used, such as lists of words, pictures, texts, and so on. It may also be advisable to insist that they have no previous exposure to the particular type of task under study. The latter requirement may be impracticable, however, given that most subjects are college students, and many of them have course requirements to participate in a number of experiments. In addition, pretests or practice trials are often conducted before the formal experiment to give subjects some familiarity with the procedure and the required task. It is absolutely necessary that all subjects, both treatment and control groups, be given identical pretests or practice trials.

Differential motivation is one of the many possible confounding variables that are important to assess whenever two or more different groups of subjects are compared on some task. For example, are older people less motivated to perform well on a memory test than younger people? Or, alternatively, are older people less likely to guess a word or the name of a picture on a recall test than younger people because of a more conservative *response bias*? (Response bias is a general term to indicate a differential tendency to be conservative or liberal in strategies. Guessing when unsure is an example of a liberal strategy.) Such differences in motivation could produce apparently poorer performance in elderly than in younger subjects when no actual memory differences exist. Similarly, do particular rewards that satisfy the needs of some subjects fail to stimulate others? Solving certain kinds of problems may in itself be rewarding to some students but leave other subjects cold. Or a male subject might react differently from a female subject to electrical shocks because he considers the ability to withstand pain a test of his masculinity.

Other differences between subjects are organically determined. These include right- or left-handedness and -eyedness, right or left ear preference, color blindness, and visual or auditory acuity. Whenever such differences might affect the task at hand, subjects should be evaluated for these characteristics and either assigned in equal numbers to the different conditions or eliminated if the difference affects performance.

Confounding in Subject Selection and Assignment. Whenever a between-subjects design is used, in which separate subjects participate in the various conditions, it is important to make sure that subjects are randomly assigned to the various conditions. As we pointed out in Chapter 2, random assignment means that every subject has an equal chance of being assigned to each condition. Random assignment can be violated in some obvious and some not-so-obvious ways.

One extreme example of bias in subject assignment occurred in the Lanarkshire milk experiment, conducted on 20,000 school children in the spring of 1930 in the county of Lanarkshire, Scotland. The health department wished to determine the effectiveness of a supplementary daily milk ration on growth (measured by both height and weight) of school children. Half of the children (the experimental group) were given the milk ration (half of this sample in raw form and half in pasteurized form) and the other half, matched for age and physical health with the experimental subjects, served as controls and were given no milk.

As expected, there was a significant increase in height and weight gain at all ages over the four-month trial period for the experimental subjects compared with the controls, although there was no difference between raw and pasteurized milk groups.

Unaccountably, however, the control subjects at the start of the experiment were significantly heavier and taller than the experimental subjects, so that the spectacular improvements shown by the experimental subjects *could have been* because they had more room for improvement.

W. S. Gosset, an employee of the Guiness brewery who published under the pen name "Student" (and who developed "Student's" *t* test), analyzed the possible reasons for the inadequate matching of the two groups (Gosset, 1971). Because teachers in the schools participating in the study were given a certain amount of latitude in assigning schoolchildren to groups, Gosset speculated that teachers probably had a bias toward selecting just those children—the short, puny ones—who seemed most in need of milk for the experimental condition and assigned their taller and more robust classmates to the control condition. Thus, this large-scale and expensive study was probably compromised by an all too human tendency on the part of teachers to favor the poor and undernourished in preference to the well-fed.

A more subtle effect can occur if volunteer subjects from a subject pool are assigned to conditions in the order in which they sign up. Suppose, for example, you plan to run four between-subjects conditions, that each condition takes some time to set up, and that you plan to run the first during the first quarter of the semester, the second during the second quarter, and so on. In fact, conditions are perfectly confounded with time during the semester. It seems likely that subjects who volunteer for experiments late in the semester are less highly motivated than those who volunteer early, and thus will do more poorly on the task. The difference in motivation will be confounded with the four conditions, because the four conditions are confounded with time of testing. Weigel, Weigel, and Hebert (1971) have reported differences in study habits and attitude between subjects who sign up for an experiment early in the term and those who sign up late in the term.

Choosing Dependent Variables

Every danger we pointed out for independent variables also applies to dependent variables. In selecting and measuring the dependent variable, there are three issues that are important: appropriateness or validity, reliability, and sensitivity.

Appropriateness. The appropriateness of a dependent variable is also known as its *construct validity.* We ask that the dependent variable measure that aspect of performance we want to study. However, because most of the constructs we use in human experimentation are unobservable—what we call *intervening variables* (such as memory, perception, intelligence, thinking)—most constructs are defined *operationally,* that is, by the operations that are used to measure them. According to operational definitions, intelligence is what intelligence tests measure, memory is what memory tests measure, comprehension is what comprehension tests measure, and perception is what perception tests measure. However, as we shall see, there are many different ways of measuring each construct, and all of them will not point to the same conclusions. Thus, whichever dependent variable is selected must be justified on the basis of previous literature, your own theoretical orientation, and general practice in the field.

To take comprehension as an example, suppose we want to test the ability of children of different ages to comprehend words of various degrees of meaningfulness, presented in sentence contexts. Our hypothesis is that comprehension increases with meaningfulness and age. Here, the two independent variables are meaningfulness and age, and our dependent variable is some measure of comprehension. In this experiment, we might present children of various ages with a set of sentences, whose meaningfulness also varies. At some later time, we would give them a test of memory for the gist of the sentences, to measure their comprehension.

But how shall we measure comprehension? There are several alternatives. First, we might prepare modified versions of the original sentences that preserve their meaning, and ask the children whether they recognize the meaning of the sentences, in a paradigm first introduced by Bransford and Franks (1971). Second, we could use homonyms in the original sentences, and vary the sentence context to bias one or the other meaning (e.g., "She went to the *bank* for money" versus "He sat on the *bank* fishing"). In the comprehension test, the children would be asked to pick out the meaning they remember among several alternatives. Or, third, and apparently most simply, we could ask them to recall as many of the sentences as they could, assuming that the words they remembered must have been understood first.

The last alternative, recall of the sentences, turns out to be the most complicated of the three alternatives because, in addition to testing sentence comprehension, it also tests recall memory, and memory performance as measured by recall shows a steady increase with age for children. Both the recognition test, which is an easier memory task than recall, and the multiple-choice test are preferable methods of measuring pure comprehension independent of memory. (Note, however, that both rely on memory because they are given after the children have studied the sentences.)

Another example of a dependent variable that is affected by factors other than that supposedly measured occurred in some experiments by George Sperling (1960), who sought to measure the span of apprehension, or capacity, of the visual system. He discovered that the number of unrelated consonants or digits that subjects could see in a brief tachistoscopic presentation were underestimated when subjects were asked to report as many items as they had seen in the whole array. The number they could report was limited, not by what they could see, but rather by what they could remember from the display. Introducing a partial report procedure, in which subjects had only to report a selected portion of the display, showed the visual capacity to be much larger than originally estimated from the full report procedure (see Chapter 6).

Reliability. Reliability refers to the degree to which a constant value for the dependent measure is obtained for the same subject from one set of trials to the next. Obviously, a test or procedure that was low on reliability would be as misleading as a weight scale that showed widely different values each time it weighed the same object.

Most discussions of reliability are concerned with standardized tests of various kinds of abilities or tendencies, such as intelligence, extroversion, and authoritarianism. When such tests are widely used, data on their reliability are available, and as long as the conditions of the testing are adhered to, the reliability reported for that test can be assumed. For the dependent measures most often used by human experimental psychologists, reliability is ensured primarily by keeping environmental conditions constant from trial to trial or condition to condition, by making sure the equipment is properly calibrated, and by being consistent in recording data.

Often, a dependent measure is based on classification or judgment by an experimenter or rater. Examples of such measures are incidents of aggressive behavior among children, classification of a subject's recall response as a synonym of a word on the list that was learned, or classification of an association to a target word in a word association task along several hierarchical dimensions such as superordinate, coordinate, subordinate, or sensory quality. In many of these cases, the classification is fuzzy and subject to bias, so it is common practice to use at least two raters, working independently, and report interrater reliability as measured by a correlation coefficient showing degree of agreement between raters' scores.

Sensitivity. Sensitivity of a dependent variable refers to its ability to reflect changes in the independent variable. There are two important constraints on the sensitivity of a dependent variable—floor and ceiling effects. A *floor effect* occurs when performance is so poor that no discrimination is possible among conditions that should produce differences. A *ceiling effect* occurs when performance is so good that no discrimination is possible among conditions that should produce differences.

Consider, for example, an experiment that manipulates the length of lists of words to be memorized from 100 to 350 words (the independent variable) and assesses the effect of list length by giving subjects a two-alternative, forced-choice recognition test in which one alternative is "old" (that is, had appeared on the list) and the other alternative is "new" (was not on the list). In a two-alternative, forced-choice recognition test, the subject is expected to be correct by chance on 50% of the trials. This means that if several conditions yield performance at about the 50% level, there can be no discrimination among these conditions because of floor effects.

Table 3-2 shows some hypothetical data from a memory experiment using the forced-choice recognition test. In this experiment, the two independent variables of list length and cueing condition were factorially combined. On cued trials, subjects were presented with a cue word paired with the word to be remembered on the study list, and the cue word is assumed to serve as an aid to recall of the target word. Up to a list length of 200, it is apparent that the dependent variable is sensitive to both the effects of list length and cueing condition, since performance deteriorates with increases in list length, and cued trials are better than uncued trials. Beyond a list length of 200, however, the memory load is so overwhelming that performance is at the chance or floor level, so the dependent variable has no chance to exhibit effects of either independent variable even though we expect effects. In order to show a decrement in performance for list-length effects beyond a list of 200 items, we would have to make the task easier by some manipulation such as increasing the presentation time or presentation frequency or changing the nature of the materials to make them more memorable.

Table 3-2 Percentage of Correct Responses in a Two-Alternative Forced-Choice Recognition Test from an Experiment in which List Length and Cueing Were Manipulated Factorially (Hypothetical Data)

	List length (words)					
Response	100	150	200	250	300	350
Cued	92	76	63	50	51	49
Uncued	88	71	59	50	49	50

Ceiling effects are obtained whenever the task is so easy that manipulations of conditions that should improve performance cannot be observed. In memory experiments, for example, if lists that are too short are used, subjects may be near 100% accuracy regardless of whether they are asked to remember abstract or concrete words, or to remember concrete words or pictures (in both cases, the second type of material usually shows an advantage). Or in perception experiments in which subjects must perceive a visually presented letter string in as short an exposure as possible, the exposure conditions might be so optimal that no differences can be observed regardless of whether the words are presented to the right visual field (which projects directly to the left hemisphere), or to the left visual field (which projects directly to the right hemisphere), even though the first condition is usually better than the second because of the special language abilities of the left brain hemisphere.

PITFALLS IN RUNNING THE EXPERIMENT

No matter how well we design an experiment in terms of appropriate independent and dependent variables, suitable stimuli, and discriminating conditions, there is always the possibility of unforeseen trouble during the conduct of the experiment. To test for such bugs in the procedure, one or more pilot studies should be run to detect these problems. To underscore that recommendation, we point out several of the varied troubles that can disrupt the integrity of the experiment while it is in progress.

Loss of Subjects

It is not uncommon for some subjects to drop out of an experiment that is run in several stages on different occasions. There may also be a loss when subjects find the task difficult or frustrating and fail to complete it, sometimes handing in blank response sheets. Furthermore, differential attrition from different groups of subjects can affect the conclusions that can be drawn about the different conditions, as illustrated in the following example.

Johnson, Smith, and Myers (1968) studied the effects of different degrees of sensory deprivation on a vigilance task, in which subjects had to respond to a randomly presented signal over a long period of time. They hypothesized that sensory deprivation would increase alertness and minimize interference with efforts to focus attention on an expected signal. In the severe sensory deprivation condition, subjects were isolated in cubicles that were sound-reducing and darkened, thereby reducing visual and auditory stimulation to a bare minimum. In the mild sensory deprivation condition, subjects were housed in well-lighted cubicles equipped with radio, television, and a means of communicating with each other. Both groups were to spend seven consecutive days in their respective cubicles.

At three points during the seven-day trial, all the subjects were given a test of vigilance. A series of short beeps was transmitted through a loudspeaker in every cubicle at randomly spaced intervals ranging from ½ to 2½ minutes during a 90-minute testing period. The subjects were required to pull a lever after hearing each beep. Responses made within 2 seconds of a beep were scored as correct, and a statistical analysis showed that the subjects in the severe sensory deprivation condition made significantly higher scores on the vigilance tests than those in the mild deprivation condition, a result that is consistent with the experimenters' original hypothesis. Should they conclude that extreme sensory deprivation increases vigilance performance?

Unfortunately, another explanation is just as likely. During the course of the experiment, 19 of the 40 subjects in the severe sensory deprivation condition defected from the experiment, whereas none of the 20 subjects in the mild sensory deprivation condition quit. For various other reasons, the numbers in each group were reduced to 15 before the final statistical comparison. Although the numbers were now equal between groups, any conclusion drawn from the data would be dubious. In view of the numerous defections from the severe deprivation group, it seems likely that the seven-day ordeal without light or sound may have eliminated the less able, competent, and motivated subjects. Those who remained probably had abilities that enabled them to stay alert and attentive during the long silent vigil, and those abilities would serve well in the task. In other words, the survivors were not a representative group but a specially qualified group, screened and selected by the conditions of the experiment. The results could certainly not be generalized to the normal population.

Similar to the problem of lost subjects is the matter of missing data in certain cells because of subjects' failure to answer all questions or to respond to all stimuli. Fortunately, unlike the case of lost subjects, this is a reparable defect, which will be discussed in the subsequent section on data analysis.

Experimenter Effects on Subjects

Most experimenters are aware of their influence on subjects' behavior but may not be sensitive to all the ways in which their influence can be communicated. A classic example of how subtle yet effective such communication can be is the notorious case of Clever Hans. Hans was a horse who could apparently add, subtract, multiply, divide, and spell, and communicated his answers by tapping with his hoof.

Hans had been trained by a retired mathematics teacher, Mr. von Osten, using methods developed at the end of the nineteenth century for teaching deaf-mute children. These methods had spectacular success, particularly in the case of Helen Keller. Many had wondered whether animals might not have the same reasoning powers as people but, like deaf-mute children, were unable to express them. Von Osten trained Hans to respond to questions by tapping his forefoot and moving his head. Numbers were counted out by repeated taps, and letters were coded by pairs of numbers. At the end of several years of training, Hans could spell words spoken to him, written on a slate, or presented as pictures. He could solve complicated numerical problems, recognize musical tones, and recognize people from photographs. Furthermore, he was as good at answering questions posed by strangers as those posed by his owner.

Hans's performance, which seemed to defy explanation except as an expression of intelligence, was considered so important to the theory of animal intelligence that a special commission of scientists, educators, and public officials was set up in 1904 to examine the horse, and Hans passed with flying colors. A psychologist member of the commission, von Pfungst, who wrote a book about his experiences with Hans (Pfungst, 1911), noted that Hans always faced his questioner, and wondered whether the questioner, or other members of the audience, might be inadvertently cuing Hans when the correct answer was reached.

To test this conjecture, Pfungst carried out a very simple experiment. He showed Hans cards with numbers on them to count out; however, half of the cards had been seen by the questioner (Pfungst) and the other half had not. Hans scored remarkably well on "reading" the numbers on the cards the experimenter had seen, but failed miserably on those the experimenter had not seen. Therefore, von Pfungst concluded, Hans must be responding to some unintended cues given by the questioner, and these were presumably visual. The cues were certainly unintentional, because Hans could answer questions correctly from the most skeptical of experimenters, as long as they themselves knew what the question was (and thus, presumably, what the answer was).

Several more years of research by von Pfungst were needed to determine exactly what cues were used by Hans to start and stop tapping. He discovered that the horse responded to slight movements of the questioner's head, eyebrows, body, and even nostrils. For example, some questioners would lean forward when the horse was expected to start tapping out the answer with his hoof, and then straighten up when the proper count had been reached. As a double-check, Pfungst found that Hans would start and stop tapping at such signals even when no question had been asked. In short, Hans was clever, not because he could spell, count, and do arithmetic, but because he was an expert at reading faces and body movements.

The important thing to note is that when Hans's trick was still secret, unaware questioners were making the signals spontaneously. If a "dumb" animal could detect and react appropriately to such barely perceptible signs, how much more effective will the experimenter's unwittingly signaled expectations be with human subjects?

The case of Hans has been resurrected in the recent debate about whether chimpanzees can really be taught to use language (Wade, 1980). Although considerable evidence has been marshaled to support the language capabilities of the great apes, the recent work of Terrace and his colleagues (1979) with their chimpanzee "Nim Chimpsky" (named for the famous linguist, Noam Chomsky), convinced these researchers that the ape's use of sign language is more similar to performances of clever animals like Hans than to the way people use language (Terrace, 1979; Terrace, Petitto, Sanders, & Bever, 1979).

Intentional experimenter effects are communicated by instructions or feedback. Except for the care that must be taken in phrasing and manner, to achieve the desired effect, these present no special problems. Far more dangerous is the unintended projection of experimenter bias, knowledge, or personality, as well as the effect of situational influences and *demand characteristics* of the experimental task. (The nature and effects of task demands are discussed at length in Chapter 12.)

When we speak of experimenter bias, the more notorious cases of Kammerer (MacDougall, 1940) and Burt (Kamin, 1974) spring to mind. In his eagerness to demonstrate inheritance of acquired characteristics, Kammerer blackened his laboratory toads' foot pads with India ink. Cyril Burt appears to have doctored his data to prove the heritability of intelligence. These were deliberate acts of distortion. More common are the unintentional effects of experimenter bias. How insidious they can be is evidenced in counting and observation errors made by experimenters. These errors include miscounting of repeated events and biased characterization of subjects' behaviors. The direction of the miscount and classification of behaviors, of course, tends to favor the experimenter/observer's hypothesis. As early as 1885, Ebbinghaus pointed to the effects of experimenter expectancy. He acknowledged that the data he obtained often reflected his expectations and that awareness of the biased effect alone was not enough to control it.

The experimenter bent on proving a pet thesis may unintentionally "stack the cards" in his favor by focusing on experimental designs that are likely to show the effect he predicts. He can also manipulate the subjects to perform in a desired way. If good performance is wanted, the experimenter may project a friendly, encouraging attitude, coloring his instructions with assurances of an easy task. If poor performance would support the theoretical argument, he may (very likely without being aware) make his subjects nervous and diffident by adopting a brusque, authoritarian manner. The effects are sometimes surprising. For example, in a digit-span test (Young, 1959), subjects performed better with experimenters who were judged "poorly adjusted" than with experimenters judged "well adjusted."

Even laboratory rats can be conditioned by differential treatment. Studies have shown that the way rats are handled in maze-learning experiments has significant positive or negative effects on their performance (Rosenthal & Fode, 1963). How much the different treatment of human subjects by advocates and challengers of a hypothesis contributes to replication successes or failures we can only surmise.

Subjects are also responsive to the experimenter's sex. Most notable here is the force of society's expectations. The culturally conditioned disposition of women to submit to the authority of men and the socially approved model of masculine behavior toward women must be taken into account in anticipating the possibility of sex-oriented responses to experimental tasks in the presence of an opposite-sex experimenter.

One of the most pervasive conditions caused by experimenter expectancy is the reverse *placebo* effect. In medical research, a placebo is an inert substance, traditionally administered as a pill, which a patient believes will relieve his or her symptoms. The literal translation of the word *placebo* is "I shall please," which usually describes the physician's intention to make the subject feel that he or she is getting an effective drug. In psychological research, the effect describes the subject's motivation to do what seems to be expected. The subject is usually disposed to give the experimenter the responses the subject thinks are wanted. This can distort the results, especially when the responses involve judgment or introspective report. Thus, the subject may say he or she is relaxed or anxious or in whatever emotional state the experimenter is trying to induce (as a preconditioning for some task) when the subject is really experiencing little or nothing of that emotion. Some independent measure of the state is necessary.

If biased expectancy does not affect the design or conduct of the experiment, the experimenter has one more chance to influence the results—by misinterpreting them. In 1929, Pavlov rejected a previously claimed experimental success in inducing the heritability of an acquired ability to learn in successive generations of mice (contrary to Darwinian theory). Pavlov showed that what had been interpreted as an improvement in *learning* ability was actually the result of an improvement in the *teaching* ability of the experimenter (Gruenberg, 1929).

Considerable discussion has been devoted to the confounding effects of experimenter bias and expectancy because many of the gross defects that invalidate experiments are consequences of such confoundings. In valiant efforts to avoid the costly loss in rejected experimental results, researchers take pains to guard against biasing effects. The *double-blind* experiment, in which neither the experimenter nor the subject knows which of the treatment conditions is being tested, is used to prevent the experimenter's influence on the subject's performance.

Double-Blind Method. Most experiments with drug treatments use the double-blind method. In a study of the effect of caffeine on alertness, (Elkins, et al., 1981) each of the subjects was run in three conditions: (1) a low dose of caffeine, (2) a high dose of caffeine, and (3) an inert placebo were administered alternately on three successive days. Each dose was followed within an hour by a reaction time task consisting of 20 trials in which the subject was to release a telegraph key at a tone signal. The response latency after the signal was the criterion measure of alertness (or "vigilance," as the experimenters called it). The order of the conditions was varied randomly among the subjects. The high caffeine dose significantly improved reaction time performance above the no-effect placebo, whereas the low caffeine dose showed no effect above the placebo.

The validity of the caffeine experiment was safeguarded by three precautions. First, the placebo provided a control, or no-effect baseline for each subject, against which that subject's caffeine effect could be measured. Second, the randomly varied order protected against the "blind" experimenter's guessing by noting sequential effect patterns and also against the biasing effect of task practice. And finally, the double-blind method prevented the experimenter from inadvertently giving the subjects any cue to which dose they were getting. If the subjects in either of the two caffeine conditions had suspected that they were getting an effective dose, it is likely they would have exerted some effort to achieve a good performance. This alone would have enhanced their alertness, thereby compromising the results of the treatment. But because this experiment was run as a double-blind, we can be confident that the effects of caffeine dosage were not confounded by subjects' or experimenters' expectations.

Misinterpreted Instructions

One of the strongest arguments for pilot runs is provided by the high frequency of misunderstood instructions. Some experimenters, who choose the short-cut of omitting the pilot experiment, attempt to compensate by trying out the instructions for comprehension on a separate group of subjects or on several colleagues.

Unfortunately, this procedure does not test the instructions against the task itself. Understanding the language and objective of an instruction is not the same as being able to perform the task exactly as specified. A naive subject may know what the instruction seems to be saying, yet experience confusion when attempting to do what is required. Not only the subjects' questions, but the errors they make in following the instructions during the pilot trials will enable the experimenter to revise the instructions before running the experiment proper. It is certainly questionable practice to modify instructions for a portion of the subjects after the others have completed their tests.

PITFALLS IN DATA ANALYSIS

We will consider problems in data analysis in two parts: (1) the quality of, and defects in, the data and (2) the hazards of inappropriate statistical methods.

Defective Data

Although it is possible to prevent some cases of inadequate or erroneous data by good design and the use of pilot trials, some of the accidents that damage the data cannot be avoided. Because there is nothing more devastating than discovering data defects after the experiment has been run and the subjects are no longer available, it is helpful to know some honest, professionally approved techniques for making the data usable.

Two of the most likely difficulties are missing data and extreme values. Both can be treated by various procedures suited to the characteristics of the data.

Missing Data. Missing data are generally replaced by a variety of estimating methods based on an averaging process. Winer (1971) describes a formula that fits the computed value to both row and column means in the whole data matrix of a factorial experiment. In this way, he ensures the consistency of the computed replacements with the pattern of all the experimental data. Winer's method is described in Chapter 15.

Other methods average only the cells adjacent to the empty one. More elaborate methods are available that take account of the shape of the profiles and trends at the appropriate levels. Of course, certain assumptions are associated with each method, and the experimenter must decide how to make the trade-off between advantages and constraints. Federer (1955) presents a comprehensive review of such methods. Because the estimated data take on the reality of actual observations once their computed values are entered in the tabulation, their synthetic quality must be kept in mind when the analysis of variance is of only borderline significance.

Extreme Scores or Outliers. Extreme values appear in the data as either isolated events or individual subjects whose entire performance deviates sharply from the range of the rest. In the latter cases, should the subjects who exhibit extreme performance be discarded as anomalies—"misfits"? In psychological experiments, it is possible that individual subjects will respond excessively to the stress of the task, the environmental situation, or some extraneous experience outside of the laboratory.

Deviant subjects may be discarded if their abnormal performance is due to factors other than the variables under study. Such factors might include poor motivation, low or deficient ability to perform the task, or failure to understand the instructions. (For an extended discussion of subject performance, see Chapter 12.) If an analysis is made with a curtailed sample, the fact should be noted in the report and the basis for discarding subjects reported. Subjects who fail to meet required criteria for learning the stimuli cannot, of course, be used on subsequent tasks.

When isolated extreme scores, or *outliers,* are found in the data of individual subjects, again there is a temptation to discard the outlying values. Professional opinions differ markedly on this issue. Should you be obliged to retain data that was produced during a momentary disturbance or resulted from some recognized malfunction—human or instrument—during the proceedings? Obviously not, if you are certain this is how the outliers were produced. We want to minimize, if not eliminate, their effect on the analysis.

First, we must determine whether the

outlying values are indeed intruders from another population. A rule-of-thumb used by many investigators, particularly with reaction time data, is to discard reaction times (RTs) that are more than three standard deviations from the mean for that subject. Another technique, the Dixon test, is more sophisticated statistically (Dixon, 1953; Dixon & Massey, 1957, pp. 275ff). The Dixon test is based on the statistical fact that the larger the number of observations in a sample, the more likely one is to observe a value that is large or small in relation to the mean. Thus, the criterion for rejecting an outlier by the Dixon test depends on the number of observations in the sample. As sample size increases, we become more tolerant in accepting extreme values as reasonable. Dixon's method for rejecting outliers is fully described in Chapter 15.

To this point, we have talked about eliminating outliers when we find them, thus reducing our sample size. This is known as *trimming* in the statistical literature. However, an alternative technique is called *Winsorizing*. This involves replacing the outlier with the next smaller or larger value that is not an outlier. Whether to trim, Winsorize, or leave well enough alone is a complex topic that is covered more fully elsewhere (Tukey, 1977; Wike, 1971).

Statistical Pitfalls

The availability of so many different statistical testing methods at once aids and challenges the experimenter. There is a temptation to use a method that shows significance favorable to the desired hypothesis. This is the last point of impact at which the experimenter can bias the results. However, the researcher who is concerned with validity in the interests of genuine scientific progress will look to the assumptions that must be satisfied and the constraints that must be applied in using each of the various methods.

Inappropriate Methods. The cardinal question is whether or not the form of the distribution is normal. Because so many characteristics, such as height and intelligence, are normally distributed, it is tempting (and sometimes misleading) to assume that all human characteristics are normally distributed. Larson and Stroup (1976) describe the error this can lead to when applied to human gestation.

Mean human gestation is generally agreed to be 268 days. The shortest full-term pregnancy on record was 214 days and the longest was 365 days. Thus, the shortest was 54 days less than the mean, and the longest was 97 days more than the mean. A common estimate for the standard deviation for this distribution is 16. Would a 308-day pregnancy be part of a normal gestation? (The decision might have social significance in establishing paternity!) Here is the result of a z test to determine whether the 308-day pregnancy is likely within a normal distribution with a mean of 268 and a standard deviation of 16:

$$z = \frac{308 - 268}{16} = 2.50$$

According to the normal distribution table (Table A-4 in the Appendix), the area above a z score of 2.50 is .0062, a probability of only 6.2 times in 1000, sufficient to lead to rejection of the null hypothesis. In other words, the claimed data of conception is judged highly unlikely at the .01 confidence level. (We say, the z of 2.50 is *significant.*) But does that settle the matter? Not without a closer look at the basic distribution.

We see that it must be positively skewed, since the minus tail reaches a minimum at 54 days less than the mean, whereas the positive tail goes to 97. The probability of a long gestation period is greater in such a skewed distribution. So in spite of our expectation that a large population (all child-bearing women) would represent a normal distribution of gestation periods, it appears that it is not necessarily so. We are accordingly obliged to use a nonparametric method or apply a transformation such as a log normal one to the data. A log normal transformation will make a positively skewed distribution, such as that for human gestation period, more normal so that a z test is appropriate. With a log normal transform, the z for a 308-day pregnancy is only 1.12, which is *not* significant. The lesson here is that the experimenter must examine his or her population and sample distributions closely and know their shape and other characteristics before carrying out parametric (normal distribution) statistical tests.

PITFALLS IN INTERPRETING THE RESULTS

The possible errors and excesses that the experimenter can fall victim to in the final stage of the study, when he or she must find meaning in the results, are of three kinds: (1) faulty reading of the implications of the results for the null hypothesis, (2) unreasonable or unsupported explanation of the results, (3) unwarranted generalization to other populations.

Flaws in Hypothesis Testing

Null hypothesis testing, as practiced by researchers in the social sciences, has been a target for criticism since Ronald Fisher, of Cambridge University, described the experimental design and statistical analysis methods he had developed and applied to his agricultural experiments in the 1950s. The essential instrument of Fisher's methods was the *analysis of variance* used to determine acceptance or rejection of the null hypothesis. In Fisher's research on the effect of fertilizer treatments on plant growth, there were only two possible outcomes: either the yields were higher and plants grew faster, or no significant change was observed. If growth was increased, there was nothing else to account for it but the treatment (Fisher, 1951).

Since then, social scientists have developed an elaborate statistical technology, but null hypothesis testing is still the keystone in the foundation. The common theme of the critics is the difference between psychology and agriculture. In psychology, treatment effects are not an open-and-shut, either-or case. Rozeboom (1960) argues that null hypothesis testing unrealistically limits the significance of an experimental outcome to a mere two alternatives, confirmation or disconfirmation of the null hypothesis. Further, he finds the arbitrary setting of a go/no-go limit at 95% or 99% untenable. If yes at 95%, why not at 94%? How much more certainty does 95% give than 94%? Rozeboom proposes that the rejection or acceptance of the null hypothesis be a matter of *degree* and that it trigger a reexamination of the hypothesis in light of the statistical support certain effects earned in the analysis. The objective of the analysis is not merely to decide the fate of a hypothesis but to contribute knowledge that can lead to further discovery. (The principles of null hypothesis testing and statistical significance are discussed in Chapter 16.)

Yeaton and Sechrest (1981) offer an illuminating example of the importance of a modest although statistically insignificant effect. They were interested in determining whether subjects categorized as Type A individuals differed from those categorized as Type B individuals in a behavior as simple as getting to an appointment on time. Type A individuals are more likely to exhibit coronary heart diseases than Type B individuals. The coronary-prone behavior pattern is characterized as competitive and hard-driving with an exaggerated sense of time urgency and an overinvolvement in one's job and professional responsibilities (Friedman, 1969; Friedman & Rosenman, 1959; Jenkins, 1975). In contrast, Type B people live a relatively unhurried, relaxed, satisfied, serene style of life.

College students were given a Type A scale and divided into two groups on the basis of high (Type A) versus low (Type B) scores. When their mean arrival time at an assigned event was measured, the Type A students arrived 3.85 minutes earlier than the Type B students. Nonetheless, the correlation between Type A scores and arrival time was only an insignificant +.13. However, Yeaton and Sechrest point to the relative importance of such an average time differential if consistently maintained by Type A people. With that effect in mind, we might want to look at larger numbers of subjects and more strongly motivating objectives. For example, would the correlation be greater if the subjects were ambulance drivers or firefighters en route to a life-threatening emergency? Indeed, further research might demonstrate the advantage in employing Type A people for such critical functions. The point is, an experimenter must not be hasty in discarding a hypothesis completely when the observed effect is not large enough to reject the null hypothesis.

The dangers of hasty acceptance of the null hypothesis are matched only by the horrors of accepting a trivially true alternative hypothesis. Meehl (1978) states it this way: "... if you have enough cases and your measures are not altogether unreliable, the null hypothesis will always be falsified, regardless of the truth of the substantive theory." This refers to the concept of statistical power (see Chapter 16). No matter how small the true difference is between two levels of an independent variable, if you use a large enough sample size, you are likely to find the difference significant statistically, even if it is insignificant practically.

Another statistical artifact occurs when analyses of numerous effects in an experiment are conducted. Given enough different conditions, you can find some set of them that will yield a significant statistical result. After all, one out of twenty comparisons of two or more conditions that really do not differ will be significant at the .05 level *by chance*. This is because .05 is the usual significance level adopted in psychological research, and significance level is the probability that you will reject the null hypothesis when the true differences are zero. That is why multiple comparisons in experiments require special methods that discount the increase in chance significance when many conditions or groups are contrasted.

To replace raw guesswork in determining alpha levels and sample sizes, Welkowitz, Ewen, and Cohen (1982) strongly recommend a *power-of-test* analysis as part of the design stage. This analysis permits computation of reasonable confidence limits and sample sizes according to appropriate degrees of experimental precision and reliability.

Unreasonable Explanations

Given valid data and appropriate analyses, experimenters are frequently challenged on the inferences they draw from the statistics. One such erroneous error occurs from a phenomenon known as *regression to the mean*.

More than a century ago, Francis Galton, the eminent British researcher who studied inherited characteristics, coined the term *regression to the mean*, which he called "regression to mediocrity." He described it as the tendency of values and measurements to move toward the average for their kind. Thus, tall fathers tend to have sons who are not quite as tall, whereas the sons of below-average fathers are likely to be taller than their fathers. Both sets of sons regress toward the mean height for all men. This phenomenon appears in many kinds of mental performance. A group of fourth graders may happen to surpass a group of fifth graders on one part of an achievement test, but on the whole test, each group's scores will tend toward their respective means.

This pattern of regression-to-the-mean is reflected in the regression formula $\hat{z}_y = r \cdot z_x$, where $\hat{z}_y$ is the predicted z score, r is the correlation coefficient, and z_x is the score that is the basis for the prediction. As the formula indicates, when the correlation is less than perfect ($r < 1.0$)—which is generally the case—the predicted new value will be less than the z_x value for every pair of scores, and hence, closer to the mean of all the z_y scores than the z_x value is to the mean of all the z_x scores.

Even in the case of a perfect correlation ($r = 1.0$) the new score can do no better than equal the old score.

This, of course, is a statement of mathematical certainty, based on a well-defined statistical relation. When it fails to hold true in general, the conclusion is that a change has occurred in the basic relationship—a genetic mutation or environmental change, perhaps. If developing conditions produce a persistent up or down trend, then no regression coefficient can be used as a basis for prediction. We see this in the steady improvement in life expectancy at various ages. The increased longevity resulting from improved nutrition and health care cannot be calculated by ordinary, linear regression formulas but requires more complex probabilistic (i.e., actuarial) formulas. However, most predictions that relate to psychological behavior in experimental situations are based on linear regression. Therefore, the regression-to-the-mean tendency should be kept in mind when explaining experimental effects, because it can account for substantial changes when correlations are in the moderate (.25–.50) range.

Kahneman and Tversky (1973) found the failure to take regression into account to be pervasive. In a psychological test, flight instructors praised trainees for each good performance and verbally punished poor performers. Contrary to expectations, the good performers did worse on the trial following the praise, and the poor performers did better following their punishment. Does this result contradict behavioristic theories about the benefits of positive reinforcement? No. It demonstrates the powerful effect of regression to the mean. Just as water tends to seek its level, the performance of a group tends toward its established mean. Individuals in the group may do better or worse than their previous result. Those who were fortunate enough to surpass their previous level will tend to drop back, reducing the mean of the superior group, while those in the group who fell lower than their usual performance will tend to improve up to their average level. The overall result is that groups that do well tend to slip down, while those that do poorly will move up to their regular mean, regardless of (or in addition to the effects of) experimental treatment.

Unwarranted Generalizations

Generalization to Subject Populations. The ultimate objective of experimentation is to discover some law or principle of behavior that is a property of some larger population from which the subject sample was drawn. This directs us to the first question that must be answered before the conclusions can be generalized: Does the sample of subjects indeed represent the larger population? Although the method of subject selection may have ostensibly conformed with the rules, the actual procedure may have failed to fulfill one or more requirements as a result of difficulties in finding, or gaining the cooperation of, the desired subjects. It is no secret that many, if not most, experiments in psychology are conducted with college students as subjects. And even then, most of the student subjects are not volunteers but compulsory recruits. The practice has been generally sanctioned on the assumption that the mental processes under investigation are not affected by intellectual prowess or vocation. Nevertheless, the experimenters who follow this common practice cannot claim to have made a truly random selection from the population to which the conclusions will be generalized. (Problems in subject selection are discussed further in Chapter 12.)

Certainly, the experimenter must consider the degree of risk involved according to the nature of his or her procedure. If complete naiveté is a requisite and the subject's awareness of what the experimenter is really trying to do would affect the performance, there is a strong possibility that psychology students familiar with psychological research will guess the purpose of the experiment whereas a group of factory workers or electrical engineers would not.

Such hazards suggest that sampling procedures prevalent in academic research centers should not be followed routinely, without regard for the special requirements of each experiment.

Replication is an important means of establishing the generality of hypotheses. If the same result can be obtained with different subjects in another environment, the applicability of the effect to the larger population is given strong confirmation. However, Meehl (1950) warns that statistical results are dependent on the setting and the subject population on which the observations are made. Although a close approximation of results on replication may be taken as confirmation of the original findings, we have no way of determining the mathematical changes that should be expected when a different population is used for a replication. Meehl calls this *context-dependency.* Although you may never be involved in performing replications, it is useful to recognize their problems and limitations.

Generalization to Stimulus Populations. We have been considering the effects of subject sampling on generalizing conclusions. An equally disturbing issue is that of stimulus selection. Here we normally select stimuli because of their special properties rather than by random methods. This is particularly true of verbal stimuli such as words. The matter of valid generalization of verbal stimuli to the whole language population is particularly serious in view of the vast number of experiments in verbal learning.

Clark (1973) discusses the question at length and proposes several statistical formulations that can be used to deal with such verbal stimuli as words, nonsense syllables, and sentences as random effects, just as we treat subject samples statistically as random effects. He protests the assumption that any arbitrary choice of verbal stimuli we take to suit the objectives of an experiment will automatically be representative of the whole language population. Certainly, we must question the representativeness of a sample that is selected for characteristics whose dimensions are carefully rated to eliminate unsuitable examples. And the constraints are even more restrictive in composing sentences that answer experimental requirements. Imagine a random sample of words from the language population that would yield nouns of similar frequencies, concreteness ratings, and number of letters! Yet we freely generalize conclusions based on the use of such lists to the whole population without applying appropriate statistical methods, such as those suggested by Clark.

In his 1973 paper, Clark amplifies and combines several formulas for *F* ratio tests in which words are treated as a random variable just as conditions (or treatments) and subjects are conventionally handled. In one *F* formula, he tests the effect of the same list of words on a different sample of subjects. In a second *F* formula, he tests the effect of a different random sample of words on the same subjects. Finally, he combines the two formulas to test the combined effect of new words on a new sample of subjects. Clark's procedure enables the experimenter to base the generalization of results on a combination of tests of selected words on both the same subjects and different sets of subjects. This allows him to get an approximate measure of the differences that might be expected if a random list of words were presented to a random sample of the population. Approximate as the procedure is, it provides a reasonable means of dealing with a serious defect in much verbal research that uses fixed-effect designs.

SUMMARY

Pitfalls in experimentation can occur in any of four phases: design, running, data analysis, and conclusions. In designing the experiment, it is important to choose levels of the independent variable so that they will reveal the shape of the underlying function relating the dependent variable to the independent variable. If such a function is complex, testing only two levels will misrepresent and distort its shape. It is also important to choose levels that are far enough apart so that, if your independent variable does have an effect on the behavior in question, the experiment will be able to show it.

When levels of two or more independent variables are combined, in a factorial experiment, it is important to use all combinations of the various levels. Omitting one or more combinations will produce an incomplete or unbalanced design, and will not permit you to evaluate the effects of all independent variables and their interactions.

Confounding occurs whenever one uncontrolled variable accompanies the manipulation of the independent variable so that the effects of this uncontrolled variable cannot be disentangled from the effects of your independent variable. An insidious form of confounding is simple passage of time. Any experiment that studies the effect of an intervention or treatment on behavior should use a control group that can be compared to the experimental group in pre- and postevaluations. Other factors in the environment can also affect the behavior of interest, including subjects' perceptions that they are part of an important research enterprise (the Hawthorne effect). Subject confounding can occur in a number of ways: by the fact that other characteristics of subjects can covary with the characteristics being studied, and by errors or biases in assigning subjects to conditions in between-groups designs.

In choosing dependent variables, it is important to choose those that are appropriate (i.e., actually measure the variable being studied). This is a particular problem in psychological research, because so many of our variables are unobservable intervening variables such as intelligence, memory, and comprehension. Often, a number of dependent variables are used that measure different aspects of the mental trait or state of interest. Dependent variables should also be reliable (be replicable from one trial to another for the same subject and conditions), and sensitive. Sensitivity refers to the ability of a dependent variable to reflect changes in the independent variable when such changes are expected. A variable is not sensitive when it exhibits floor effects (the worst possible performance) or ceiling effects (the best possible performance).

Pitfalls in running the experiment can occur when subjects are lost because of stress or difficulty that varies between conditions or when subjects' behaviors are affected by the experimenter's knowledge and expectations. An antidote to the dangers of both experimenter and subject expectancies is provided by the double-blind design, in which both experimenter and subject are blind to the conditions of testing. Finally, experimenters should be sure that subjects understand the instructions given to them prior to the experiment. Many pitfalls in both design and running can be avoided by carrying out pilot runs before the experiment proper.

Some of the pitfalls in data analysis occur when data are missing from cells of the experiment or when extreme observations (outliers) can distort the results. Fortunately, there are acceptable statistical remedies for these problems. Once the data are complete, other pitfalls await the investigator in choosing the appropriate statistical test. Several of these pitfalls and their remedies have been described.

Finally, there are many hazards in interpreting the results. These include logical flaws in inferring support for a hypothesis from a set of results, questions about the shortcomings of the null hypothesis testing procedure, and the pitfalls in overgeneralizing the results from a single experiment to other populations of subjects or stimuli.

4

Psychophysical Methods

A graduate student attending his first convention happened to find himself next to a distinguished-looking psychologist at a cocktail party. After a strained silence, the student asked the psychologist what his research field was. The psychologist replied, "I'm in reaction time." After a pause, the psychologist, returning the compliment, asked the student what his field of research was. "Oh," replied the student, "I'm in probability correct."

This anecdote contrasts the two major dependent measures used in experimental research—probability correct and reaction time. The reason the story is amusing is precisely because both measures act as dependent variables rather than independent variables. Probability correct and reaction time are usually not considered topics in and of themselves, but rather are used as indices of the effects of some independent variable.

In this chapter and the next one on mental chronometry, we consider in turn these two basic dependent measures—response probability and response time—as they are used to study various questions in psychology. Because of a long historical tradition, psychophysical methods are based on response probability rather than response time, whereas attempts to analyze the processes involved in mental operations are based on response time rather than response probability.

Psychophysics means the relationship of the sensation (psychological effect) to the physical stimulus. The field of psychophysics was founded by Gustav Fechner in 1860 with the publication of his book *Elemente der Psychophysik.* The important problem of psychophysics, as seen by Fechner, was to discover the *psychophysical function*—the relationship between the physical intensity of a stimulus and its perceived intensity. However, Fechner did not measure sensation (perceived intensity) directly. Instead, he used the indirect method of measuring the ability of subjects to *discriminate* between two physical intensities as a way of constructing such a function. The psychophysical function was discovered by indirect scaling to be the logarithmic function, and this function, called *Fechner's law,* has been the subject of intense debate among psychophysicists ever since.

Psychophysical methods developed as ways of understanding sensory experience. For this reason, the classical psychophysical methods will be introduced as they are applied to the senses, particularly vision and audition. However, later in this chapter we will describe how more recent psychophysical methods, particularly signal detection and scaling methods, can be applied to other domains of experience.

QUESTIONS ABOUT THE SENSES

Whatever we know about the world comes to us through our senses. The limitations of our sense organs limit what we can know of the world directly, and bias our view of the world. Accordingly, the study of sensory limits is extremely important. Although we are limited to sensing only certain ranges of physical energies, the variety and form of sensory experience is truly impressive. Observe your sensory world at the present moment. Your visual system is processing the flux of environmental sights produced by changes in lightness and darkness, in colors, in shapes, and in distances. You are aware of the sight of parts of your body, views of the objects in the room where you are sitting, and the change of illumination and shadows on these objects when a passing cloud obscures the sun. Similarly, your auditory system is processing the flux of environmental sounds—the rock and roll record in the next apartment, the sound of traffic, or the conversation of your partner.

The two questions about the senses important in psychophysics are (1) their limits and (2) their growth function, that is, the way increases in stimulus intensity are transformed by the human nervous system to produce increases in sensory experience. These are the psychophysical questions, and they are answered by psychophysical methods. These psychophysical questions may be divided into three areas—detection, discrimination, and scaling.

DETECTION AND DISCRIMINATION

Our sense organs have obvious limitations. Our eyes are insensitive to X-rays, our ears are insensitive to sounds that a bat can hear, and our tongues are insensitive to the taste of certain poisons. Experiments in *detection* study the question—What is the minimal amount of physical energy required to detect a stimulus? Experiments in *discrimination* study the question—What is the minimal difference in physical energies required to discriminate between two stimuli? Sensitivity is measured by the threshold—the *absolute threshold* for detection, and the *difference threshold*, or *just-noticeable-difference*, for discrimination.

The Concept of Threshold

A dictionary definition of *threshold* is "the limit below which a given stimulus, or the difference between two stimuli, ceases to be perceptible." This definition is somewhat misleading, however, because it suggests that we could find some point along a physical continuum below which a particular observer would *never* detect a stimulus and above which the observer would *always* detect a stimulus. But nothing could be further from the truth. Even under the best-controlled conditions and with the most highly motivated subjects, a particular subject will show *variability* in response to stimulus intensities near threshold. A subject shown repeated presentations of stimuli that bracket the limits of perceptibility might produce the data shown in Table 4-1.

Table 4-1 Hypothetical Data Showing How the Percentage of Detections of a Weak Stimulus Increases as a Function of Stimulus Intensity, Expressed in Arbitrary Units.

Intensity of stimulus	Percentage of detections
7	100
6	90
5	75
4	50
3	25
2	10
1	0

As shown in Table 4-1, our subject always detects the most intense stimulus and never detects the least intense stimulus. However, the intermediate intensities are sometimes detected and sometimes not. This variability in response to near-threshold stimuli is characteristic of all subjects and all sensory domains and is usually attributed to variability in the state of the subject produced by momentary changes in attention or changes in sensitivity of the sense organ. These changes produce variability in responsiveness to a constant stimulus.

Because responses to the same stimulus are variable, the subject's threshold must be defined statistically rather than absolutely. We define the threshold of an observer as that stimulus intensity which is detected 50% of the time in detection experiments or as the difference between two stimuli which is detected either 50% or 75% of the time (depending on the number of response categories) in discrimination experiments.

We will describe two classic methods and one modern method for measuring thresholds. The classical methods are the *method of limits* and the *method of constant stimuli*, and the modern method is the *method of signal detection*. We will consider the application of the two classic methods separately for *detection* and *discrimination*.

DETECTION

In stimulus detection experiments, we measure the subject's absolute threshold for a stimulus as a function either of some physical attribute of the stimulus, some state of the observer, or both. In vision we might be interested in a subject's detection threshold for spots of light when the wavelength is varied over the visible range (a stimulus variable), or for a spot of light of fixed wavelength when the subject's degree of *dark adaptation* is varied (a subject state variable). *Dark adaptation* is the process by which the eye increases in sensitivity to weak visual stimuli as a result of the amount of time in the dark. This process primarily occurs with the rod (scotopic) system.

In a typical experiment, stimuli are presented singly against a null background (e.g., darkness for vision or silence for audition) and the observer merely reports whether the stimulus is present. The absolute threshold is that stimulus intensity (for a particular wavelength or state of dark adaptation) that is "just" detectable; that is, to which the observer responds "Yes" 50% of the time. The difference between the two classic methods we consider—limits and constant stimuli—lies in whether the stimulus presentation schedule is systematic, as in limits, or random, as in constant stimuli.

The Method of Limits

In the *method of limits,* the stimulus intensity is either increased or decreased in small steps. On an ascending trial, the intensity is set below the subject's threshold and is increased by small amounts until the subject reports sensing the stimulus. On a descending trial, the intensity is set above the subject's threshold and is decreased until the subject reports he or she can no longer sense the stimulus. A threshold on any trial is the midpoint intensity between a detection and a nondetection, and the average threshold across trials is taken as the subject's threshold. Usually, ascending and descending trials are alternated, although tachistoscopic recognition thresholds (see Chapter 6) are usually measured using only the ascending method. (A *tachistoscopic recognition threshold* is the shortest duration at which a visually presented letter-string, such as a word, must be exposed to be recognized.)

Because of the systematic nature of the method of limits, the subject knows that the stimulus intensity will either increase or decrease on every trial. Although some investigators feel this is an advantage, others have criticized the method on exactly that ground. By knowing the stimulus-presentation schedule, the subject may commit one of two errors: the *error of habituation,* a tendency to continue reporting perception of the stimulus in a descending series (or nonperception in an ascending series), or the *error of expectation,* a tendency to change the response from perception to nonperception (or vice versa) after a certain number of stimulus presentations.

The Method of Constant Stimuli

The *method of constant stimuli* differs from the method of limits in that stimulus intensities are presented in a random rather than regular order. Several stimulus intensities are selected to bracket the absolute threshold, so that the stimulus at the lowest intensity is never detected and the stimulus at the highest intensity is always detected. The stimuli are presented a number of times at each intensity, but in a random order so that the subject cannot anticipate which intensity will be presented on the next trial. The relevant data from such an experiment are the proportions of trials (p) on which the subject reported detecting the stimulus at each intensity. The *psychometric function,* a plot of p against stimulus intensity, summarizes the data from such an experiment.

Figure 4-1 represents a hypothetical psychometric function for visual detection, in which a normal ogive (the cumulative of the normal distribution) has been fitted to the data points. The absolute threshold is that stimulus intensity for which $p = .50$, and in this example it is approximately 9.4. Usually, there is no intensity that is detected on exactly 50% of the trials. In these cases, the threshold can be located by linear interpolation between the closest point below 50% and the closest one above 50%.

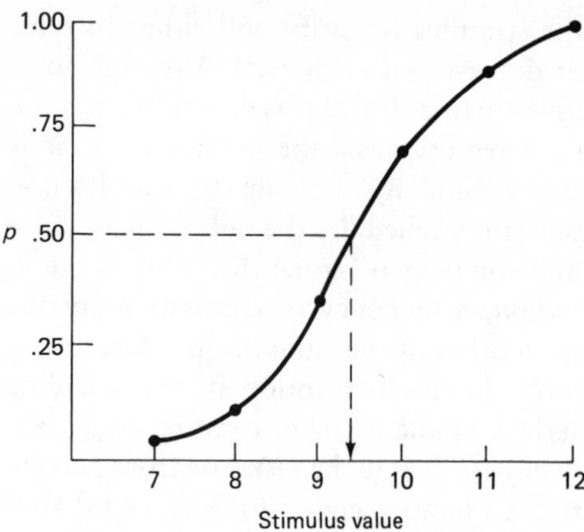

Fig. 4-1 A hypothetical psychometric function for absolute visual detection. The value of the absolute threshold, indicated by the arrow, is found graphically to be approximately 9.4.

DISCRIMINATION

In stimulus discrimination experiments, we measure the subject's difference threshold for a *pair* of stimuli rather than the absolute threshold for a *single* stimulus. The *difference threshold* is defined as that difference between two stimuli that is large enough to be detected 50% or 75% of the time. Because two stimuli are presented, there are a number of different ways to present the stimuli and a number of ways for the subject to respond. First, the two stimuli need to be distinguished, by being presented either successively in two time intervals or simultaneously in two spatial positions. Generally, auditory stimuli are presented successively, and visual stimuli are presented simultaneously.

Three-Category versus Two-Category (Forced-Choice) Method

A difference threshold is always defined with respect to a standard, or reference, stimulus. The standard is thus always presented on a trial along with a comparison stimulus, which may be less than, equal to, or greater than, the standard stimulus. Often the standard is presented first and the comparison second. In the *three-category method,* the subject is instructed to respond with three responses by deciding whether the comparison stimulus is larger than, equal to, or smaller than the standard; in the *two-category method,* the subject is forced to choose between two responses by deciding whether the comparison stimulus is larger or smaller than the standard. The two-category method is also called the *forced-choice method.* Figure 4-2 shows the sequence of events on a trial in a forced-choice discrimination experiment.

There are two statistics calculated from discrimination experiments: the *difference threshold* or *just-noticeable-difference (jnd),* and the *point of subjective equality (PSE).* The *jnd* is the minimum amount of physical change needed to yield a perceived change. It is defined as the physical difference between two stimuli that is correctly detected 50% of the time in the three-category method, and 75% of the time in the forced-choice method. The *PSE* is that physical value of the comparison stimulus that is perceived as equal to the standard. Interestingly, this value is not always *physically* equal to the standard. When two stimuli are presented suc-

Fig. 4-2 Sequence of events on a trial in a forced-choice discrimination experiment. The standard is presented first, the comparison is presented second, and the subject's response is signaled by a key press or a vocal response.

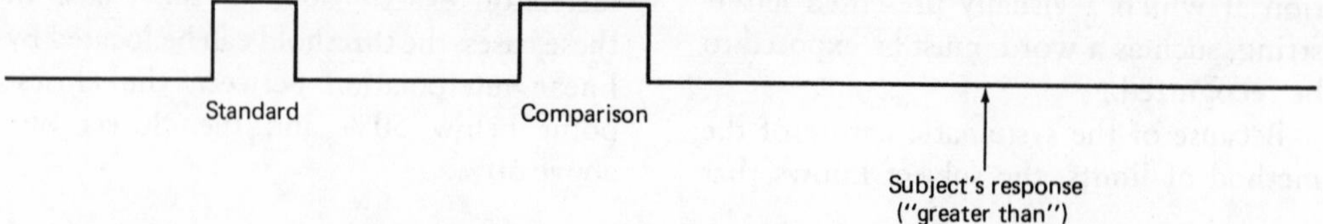

cessively in time, there is a general tendency for the second stimulus to appear somewhat more intense than the first. This is particularly true of loudness judgments. Perceptual errors that depend on the order of stimulus presentation are known as *time order errors.*

The three-category method of measuring discrimination thresholds is less optimal than the two-category method because it permits (indeed, encourages) the "equal" response category. Because it seems unlikely that any two sensations will be *exactly* equal, subjects must set some criterion for determining when two stimuli (or the sensations produced by them) are to be judged equal and when they are to be judged unequal. There is no guarantee that different subjects will adopt the same criterion or that the same subject will use the same criterion from one trial to the next. This instability of the equal response is of particular concern because the number of equal judgments can affect the size of the *jnd.* In general, increasing the number of equal judgments will increase the *jnd.*

Because of this problem with the three-category method, most present-day psychophysical experiments are run using the two-category, or forced-choice method. In this method, the subject is forced to choose between the two responses, larger and smaller. When he or she is uncertain (as when the two stimuli appear equal), the subject is assumed to choose equally between the two responses. Use of the method of constant stimuli to measure the difference threshold with the two-category method is described next.

The Method of Constant Stimuli—Two-Category Method

In the method of constant stimuli for discrimination, pairs of stimuli—the comparison and the standard—are presented in a random order, so that the subject has no cue about whether the comparison will be larger or smaller than the standard on any trial. Because there are only two responses, a single psychometric function, which plots the proportion of "larger" responses against the value of the comparison stimulus, summarizes the data.

Two representative psychometric functions are shown in Figure 4-3. The value of the comparison that is judged larger

Fig. 4-3 Two psychometric functions from a forced-choice discrimination experiment. Stimulus values increase from left to right. The function on the left, obtained with a small standard, also has a small *jnd,* while the one on the right, obtained with a large standard, also has a large *jnd.* $S_{.25}$ is the stimulus judged larger than the standard 25% of the time, $S_{.75}$ is the stimulus judged larger than the standard 75% of the time, and the *PSE* is the stimulus judged larger than the standard 50% of the time.

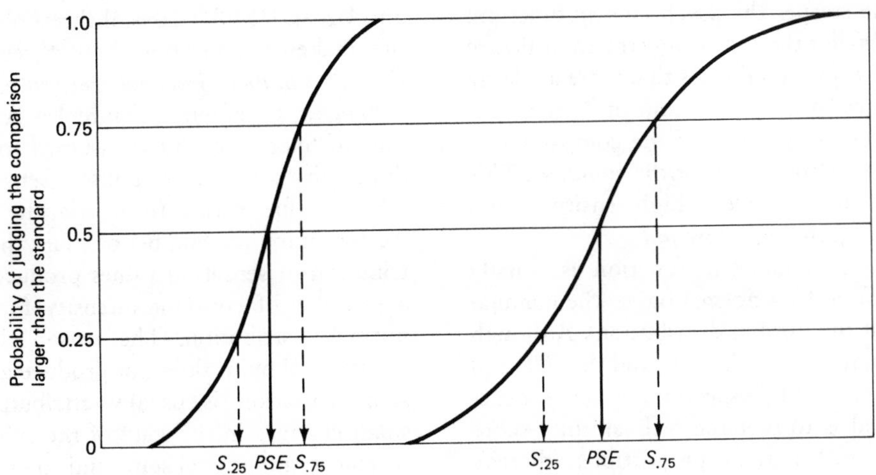

50% of the time (indicated by the solid line) is defined as the *PSE*. The *PSE* is the 50% point, because we assume that when the comparison stimulus appears equal to the standard, the subject will call it larger 50% of the time (and smaller 50% of the time).

The upper difference threshold is the difference between the *PSE* and the stimulus judged larger than the standard 75% of the time ($S_{.75} - PSE$), and the lower difference threshold is the difference between the *PSE* and the stimulus judged larger than the standard 25% of the time ($PSE - S_{.25}$). The *jnd* is the average of the upper and lower difference thresholds.

The rationale for using the 75% and 25% points to define the *jnd* is as follows. Recall that we defined the difference threshold as that difference between two stimuli that is detected 50% of the time. In the forced-choice method, however, chance performance is 50% since the subject must choose between two responses even when the two stimuli appear equal. Accordingly, the subject can only be said to detect a (threshold) difference in the appropriate direction when he or she is correct 75% of the time. The 75% figure includes the 50% of responses that are correct by chance, and the half of the remaining 50% responses that are correct by true detections. Thus, the subject is truly detecting a difference only 50% of the time when he or she is correct 75% of the time.

The steeper the psychometric function, the smaller the *jnd*, as illustrated in Figure 4-3. Steepness indicates that there are large changes in the proportion of "larger" responses as the value of the comparison is increased above that of the standard. This rapid increase reflects high sensitivity and a correspondingly low *jnd*.

The psychometric function is usually well fitted by a normal ogive (the cumulative of the normal distribution). Although this may be done by eye, and the *PSE* and *jnd* found by inspection, a more exact method is to plot the ordinate in *z*-score units, rather than proportions, thereby producing a straight-line psychometric function. This function can then be fitted by standard linear regression techniques. (More details may be found in Gescheider, 1976.)

THEORETICAL VIEWS OF THRESHOLDS

As we noted earlier, the threshold must be defined statistically because subjects are not consistent in their responses to identical stimuli at threshold level. A subject presented with several trials of the same stimulus or pair of stimuli will sometimes successfully detect or discriminate them and will sometimes fail. Theories of thresholds have attempted to identify the bases for these inconsistencies in detection or discrimination responses, and thereby prescribe the methods by which sensitivity should be measured. Here we consider two threshold theories: the classical theory and signal detection theory. Each theory makes at least two assumptions. The first concerns the way stimulus energy is transformed into an internal sensation or observation, and the second concerns the way in which the sensation is transformed into an observable judgment or response.

Classical (High Threshold) Theory

Classical threshold theory was originally developed by Fechner (1860) and further refined by Cattell (1893), Jastrow (1888), and Urban (1910). Classical threshold theory makes assumptions about three continua: *stimulus, internal response,* and *judgment,* as shown in Figure 4-4. A stimulus of fixed intensity is assumed to produce an internal response (sensation) whose value varies from trial to trial. Across an infinite number of trials, the distribution of sensation values produced by a stimulus of constant intensity forms a normal distribution. The reason that a constant stimulus does not produce a constant sensation is usually attributed to small changes in the state of the subject's receptors, attentional state, and so on. The

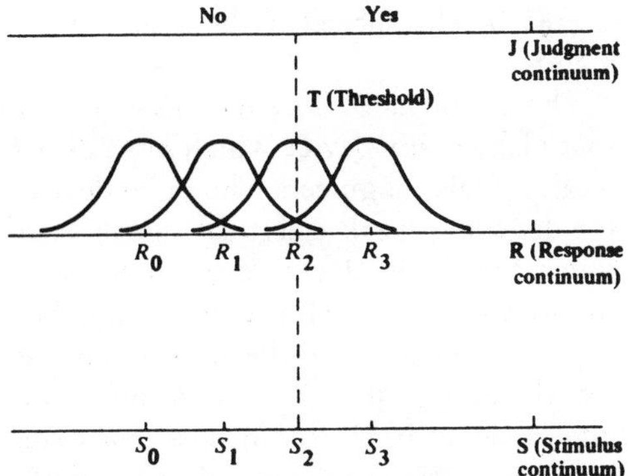

Fig. 4-4 The three continua—stimulus (S), internal response (R), and judgment (J)—proposed by the classical theory of thresholds. Stimulus S_2 is the absolute threshold because half of the time it is presented, it exceeds the subject's absolute threshold (T) and thus elicits a YES response 50% of the time.

classical theory also assumes that the threshold is a fixed point within this internal response continuum. Theoretically, the subject is conscious of all sensations above the threshold and not conscious of any sensations below the threshold. This means that the subject can only detect a stimulus when it produces a sensation above the threshold and will fail to detect a stimulus when it produces a sensation below the threshold. Under normal circumstances, subjects are assumed to judge the stimulus as present whenever a sensation is above threshold, and not present whenever a sensation is below threshold.

According to the classical definition of the threshold, stimulus S_2 in Figure 4-4 is the value of the absolute threshold for this subject. The mean of its response distribution exactly coincides with the subject's threshold, so the subject will detect S_2 on 50% of the trials it is presented (because it will produce a sensation that exceeds his or her threshold) and will fail to detect it on the remaining 50% of the trials (because the sensation will fall below his or her threshold). S_1 will be detected less than 50% of the time and S_3 will be detected more than 50% of the time. For stimuli spaced closely enough along the stimulus continuum, a plot of stimulus intensity against detection probability will produce a psychometric function corresponding to the cumulative of the normal distribution (normal ogive). Thus the classical theory accounts for the variability in judgments of a constant stimulus, the ogival form of the psychometric function, and the statistical definition of the threshold.

Still another assumption of the classical theory, as shown in Figure 4-4, is that presentation of the zero-level stimulus, S_0 (called a *catch trial*), will never produce a sensation in the subject strong enough to cross the threshold. In other words, the "threshold of awareness" is high enough so that the background against which a stimulus is presented, if presented alone, will never be taken for a stimulus presentation. Because the threshold is assumed "high," classical theory is also known as *high-threshold theory.*

The assumptions of a theory often dictate the method by which data should be collected, and classical threshold theory is no exception. Because of the high threshold assumption, classical theory prescribes that when catch trials are presented, subjects should never respond "Yes" to them. Subjects who make such *false alarms* are assumed to be judging the presence of the stimulus on grounds other than their sensations (e.g., by guessing) and may be eliminated from the experiment. Furthermore, the notion that the threshold is "all-or-none" leads experimenters to devise situations, such as the method of limits, in which the subject is quite aware of what the stimulus presentation is, and needs only to concentrate on the resulting sensation.

Although classical psychophysical data for the senses have typically been based on the two classical methods for detection or discrimination—limits and constant stimuli—in recent years the method of signal detection has supplanted these earlier methods. Signal detection methodology, like the classical methods, is based on a *theoretical* view of the nature of thresholds. Accordingly, before presenting signal detection methods, we review the theory behind the methods.

Signal Detection (No Threshold) Theory

Signal detection theory (SDT) takes as its starting point the observation that the sensitivity of many human sensory abilities seems limited primarily by the existence of intrinsic "neural noise" that provides a background against which the observer must detect the existence of an external signal. The problem for an observer in a signal detection experiment is one of distinguishing the signal itself from such internal noise. Signal detection theory, contrary to classical theory, assumes that the human observer is aware of a continuum of sensations or observations, ranging from very low levels that are very likely due to noise in the nervous system up to very high levels that are very likely due to an external signal, the stimulus. There is no "threshold of awareness" as such, but rather a continuum of sensations. According to this theory, the observer will have to establish some criterion for deciding in favor of or against the presence of an external signal. Such a criterion might be termed a *response threshold*. It differs from a "stimulus threshold" in that it is an arbitrary point along the sensation continuum rather than one fixed by the observer's sensory system. The observer is as aware of stimuli below the response criterion as of those above it. Because it is an arbitrarily defined point, it can easily be shifted by the subject if the situation demands it.

The problem of internal noise is one that plagues any device which must detect weak signals. Engineers who build devices for detecting weak electrical signals have found that if the device is set to go off at too low a signal level, it will also misclassify some occurrences of electrical noise as signal, whereas if it is set to go off at too high a signal level, it will miss many signals. The setting of the device corresponds to its criterion. A common example of the problem is setting the "sensitivity level" of a smoke detector. If it is set too low, broiling a steak can set it off, but if it is set too high, it will fail to go off when there is real danger from a fire. In the attempt to deal with the problem of detecting weak signals by electrical devices, the field of engineering has developed many of the concepts of SDT.

Although there is ample physiological evidence for neural noise in the absence of stimulation, for reasons of experimental control most signal detection experiments introduce a noise background against which a signal may be presented. In many auditory experiments, the noise background is white noise consisting of all frequencies in equal amplitude, and the signal is either a pure tone or an increment to the noise intensity. In visual experiments, the noise background is usually white light and the signal is an increment in intensity of a small patch.

Figure 4-5 presents the underlying as-

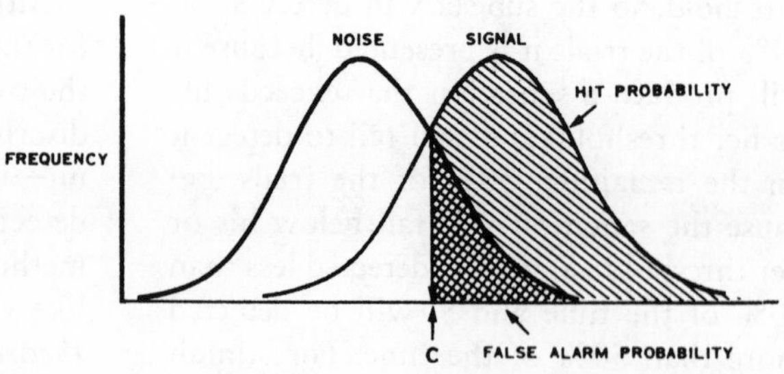

Fig. 4-5 The sensation continuum proposed by signal detection theory. The observer's criterion is placed at the criterion point (c), and the hatched portion of the noise distribution to the right of the criterion represents the false alarm probability, while the striped portion of the signal distribution to the right of the criterion represents the hit probability.

sumptions of SDT. Repeated presentations of "noise alone" are assumed to produce a normal distribution of sensations whose mean is μ_n and whose standard deviation is σ_n. Repeated presentations of "signal + noise" are assumed to produce a normal distribution of sensations whose mean, μ_s, is above that of μ_n, and whose standard deviation is σ_s.

A particular value of a subject's criterion, *c*, is shown along the sensation continuum. Whenever a sensation produced by one of the presentations falls above the criterion, the subject says "Yes, the signal is present" by pressing a key or producing a vocal response. Whenever the sensation falls below the criterion, the subject responds "No." Because the theory requires that a large number of observations be obtained under the "noise alone" condition, SDT experiments are run with a relatively large number of catch or noise-alone trials, on which the signal is omitted. The proportion of noise-alone trials may vary from 0.10 to 0.90. Thus, there are two types of trials, signal (*s*) and noise (*n*) trials, and two types of unconditional responses, YES, and NO. This results in the four types of conditional responses shown in Table 4-2.

Table 4-2 The Four Types of Conditional Responses Possible in a Signal Detection Experiment

Stimulus presentation	Response: Yes	Response: No	Sum of probabilities
Signal (*s*)	Hit	Miss	1.0
Noise (*n*)	False alarm	Correct rejection	1.0

Note. The probabilities of a "hit" and "miss" sum to 1.0, as do the probabilities of a "false alarm" and "correct rejection."

A *hit* occurs when the subject says YES to a signal presentation, and a *false alarm* occurs when the subject says YES to a noise presentation. A *miss* occurs when the subject says NO to a signal presentation, and a *correct rejection* occurs when the subject says NO to a noise presentation. Therefore, there are two types of correct responses, hits and correct rejections, and two types of errors, misses and false alarms. The hit rate is the conditional probability of saying YES when a signal has been presented, $P(Y/s)$. The miss rate is the complementary probability, $P(N/s)$. Because there are only two possible responses on signal trials, YES or NO, the two conditional response probabilities are mutually exclusive and exhaustive and must sum to a probability of 1.0. Because the hit and miss rates sum to 1.0, the hit rate is sufficient to describe what has happened on signal trials (the miss rate is 1.0 minus the hit rate). Similarly, the false alarm rate is the conditional probability of a YES response when noise has been presented, $P(Y/n)$, and the correct rejection rate is the complementary probability $P(N/n)$. Because these two probabilities must also sum to 1.0, the false alarm rate is sufficient to describe what has happened on noise trials (the correct rejection rate is 1.0 minus the false alarm rate). The pair of probabilities corresponding to hit and false alarm rates are sufficient to summarize the data from a particular condition in a YES/NO signal-detection experiment.

There are two theoretical values of interest in signal detection theory—the measure of sensitivity, called d' (*d* prime), and the measure of bias, called β (Greek beta). The sensitivity measure, d', is defined theoretically as the difference between the means of the signal and noise distributions measured in units of the standard deviation of the noise distribution.

This theoretical definition of d' can be expressed as follows:

$$d' = \frac{\mu_s - \mu_n}{\sigma_n}$$

Of course, it is not possible to measure directly the mean of the signal distribution (μ_s), the mean of the noise distribution (μ_n), or the standard deviation of the noise distribution (σ_n). Instead, we can only measure the *difference* between them. But if we measure the difference between the mean of the signal and noise distributions in z score units, this means we are measuring the difference in units of the standard deviations of one of the two distributions. (Recall that we assumed a normal distribution form for both distributions.)

We can calculate d' from a single hit and false alarm probability if we assume that the signal standard deviation, σ_s, equals the noise standard deviation, σ_n. The hit probability corresponds, in Figure 4-5, to the area to the right of the criterion in the signal distribution (the striped area), and the false alarm probability corresponds to the area to the right of the criterion in the noise distribution (the hatched area). To calculate d', we need to find the distance that c (the criterion point) is from the mean of the signal distribution and add to it the distance that c is from the mean of the noise distribution.

By its definition, d' is measured in units of the noise standard deviation, and thus d' tells us how many standard deviation units apart the means of the two distributions are. From tables of the normal distribution (Table A-4 in the Appendix), we find a z score, z_n, such that the area above it equals the false alarm rate. Similarly, we find a z score, z_s, such that the area above it equals the hit probability. Then d' is equal to the sum of the absolute values of z_n and z_s.

Actually, there is a very simple rule for calculating d' which works for any criterion placement:

$$d' = z_n - z_s$$

so d' is equal to the z score of noise minus the z score of signal at the criterion point. When the criterion is located between the means of the two distributions, as in Figure 4-5, z_n will be positive and z_s will be negative, so the formula has the effect of adding their absolute values.

The measure of bias, β, describes the location of the subject's criterion. It is measured by the ratio of the ordinate of the signal distribution to the ordinate of the noise distribution at the criterion, c, or

$$\beta = \frac{f_s(c)}{f_n(c)}$$

where $f_s(c)$ represents the ordinate of the signal distribution at the abscissa value of c and $f_n(c)$ represents the ordinate of the noise distribution at the abscissa value of c. (Table A-4 in the Appendix shows the ordinate values for various z score values.) β is known as the criterion likelihood ratio because it represents the ratio of the likelihood that a particular observation, x, was selected from the signal distribution to the likelihood that it was selected from the noise distribution. As the value of the sensation increases (moves to the right in Figure 4-5), its likelihood of being a signal rather than noise increases because the ordinate of s increases in relation to the ordinate of n. For any observation, x, the subject is assumed to compute its likelihood ratio, $l(x)$, and respond YES if the likelihood ratio is greater than or equal to the criterion, β, and respond NO if it is less than β.

Because the criterion is arbitrarily selected, it should be easily moved. In sensory experiments, the criterion is moved by varying signal probabilities or payoffs. For example, if signals are presented often, or if hits are highly valued, subjects should adopt a liberal criterion by moving c to the left in Figure 4-5, thereby decreasing β, the likelihood ratio. This means that even weak sensations will be classified as signals. If, on the other hand, noise trials are more probable or correct rejections are more valued, subjects should adopt a conservative criterion by moving c to the right, thereby increasing β. In this case only very strong sensations will be classified as signals.

Even when the experimenter does not explicitly manipulate a subject's criterion, individual subjects will differ in their "natural" criteria. A subject with a liberal criterion may decide that the best way to do well in a signal detection experiment is by making as many hits as possible, which

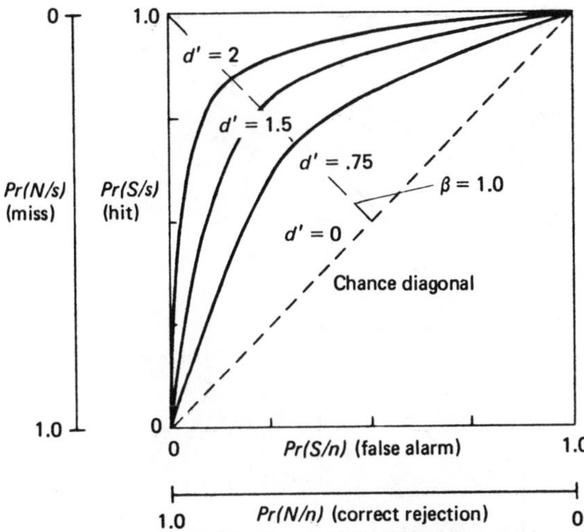

Fig. 4-6 Some theoretical ROC curves for various values of d', under the equal-variance assumption for signal and noise distributions. Movement along any ROC curve reflects equal discrimination but differing bias. The $\beta = 1.0$ line represents no bias toward YES or NO responses. (From "Psychophysics" by J. G. Snodgrass. In B. Scharf (Ed.), *Experimental Sensory Psychology.* Copyright 1975 by Scott, Foresman. Reprinted by permission.)

will also increase his or her false alarm rate and decrease the correct rejection rate. Another, more conservative subject, may try to avoid making false alarms, thereby decreasing his or her hit rate but increasing the correct rejection rate. The first subject, with a liberal criterion, is like the "eager beaver" student in your class who raises his or her hand every time the professor asks a question. The student may answer many questions correctly (make many hits) but also may make many false alarms to questions for which he or she does not really know the answer. The second subject, with a conservative criterion, is like the "shrinking violet" student in your class who never volunteers to answer a question unless he or she is positive of the answer. By having a conservative bias, this student misses many questions he or she knows the answer to but at the same time makes few false alarms.

Criterion bias differences have been used to distinguish patient groups from normal groups. For example, Clark and his associates (Clark, 1966; Clark, Brown, & Rutschmann, 1967) found that psychiatric patients had a conservative bias in classifying a flickering stimulus as nonflickering at high intermittency rates. Their flicker fusion thresholds, usually found to be higher than normals, did not indicate a neurological deficit, as had been thought, but rather reflected their bias against classifying a stimulus that they knew was flickering as appearing steady.

The ROC Curve

The results of a signal detection experiment are often summarized by plotting the probability of a hit against the probability of a false alarm in what is known as a *receiver operating characteristic curve (ROC curve).* For a fixed stimulus, an ROC curve can be plotted by systematically varying the probability of the signal presentation or by varying the relative payoffs for correct responses and errors.

Figure 4-6 presents some examples of ROC curves for different values of d' and different criteria. High-intensity signals or a highly sensitive subject will generate a curve that lies in the upper-left-hand corner and has a large d'. Conversely, low-intensity signals or an insensitive subject will generate ROC curves that are closer to the main diagonal and have small d's. The larger the d', the greater the difference between the signal and noise distributions or the greater the sensitivity of the subject. The main diagonal, shown in the figure by the dotted line from (0, 0) to (1.00, 1.00), represents chance performance (and a d' of 0) since the hit and false alarm rates are equal. Movement along any particular

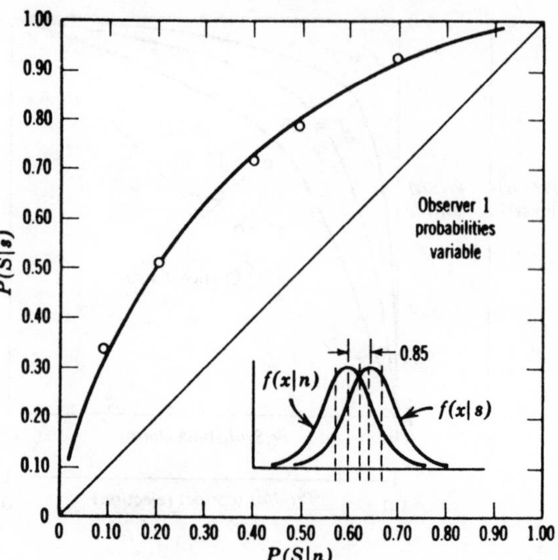

Fig. 4-7 ROC curve for detection of an auditory signal in noise. The empirical data points were obtained by varying the signal presentation probabilities, and the theoretical curve is for $d' = 0.85$ and equal-variance noise and signal distributions. (From *Signal Detection Theory and Psychophysics* by D. M. Green and J. A. Swets. Copyright 1974 by Krieger Publishing. Reprinted by permission.)

ROC curve indicates changes in bias without changes in sensitivity.

The minor diagonal, marked $\beta = 1.0$, shows performance that varies in sensitivity but has no bias. A *liberal criterion,* which leads the subject to respond YES on a large proportion of trials, produce points above this no-bias line, whereas a *conservative criterion,* which leads the subject to respond NO on a large proportion of trials, produces points below the no bias line.

Figure 4-7 shows an ROC curve in an auditory detection experiment that was produced by varying signal probability. Each point on the graph was obtained with a different signal probability: .1, .3, .5, .7, and .9. The estimated d' was constant at 0.85. This means that the subject's sensitivity remained constant with changes in signal probability, and only the subject's bias changed. The insert shows the theoretical distributions of signal and noise distributions for the ROC curve drawn through the data points. Each dashed line in the insert represents one of the five criteria used by the subject under each of the signal probabilities.

Figure 4-8 shows an ROC curve from the same auditory detection experiment that was produced by varying only payoffs with five payoff matrices designed to manipulate the subject's criterion from conservative to liberal. Three of the five payoff matrices are shown in Table 4-3. Signal intensity was constant and the signal presentation probability was fixed at 0.5. The payoff matrix shows the reward or cost, in points or money, for each of the four types of responses.

Payoff matrix A is designed to produce a conservative criterion—the subject should report the signal as present only when very sure it is there. The subject should show a bias toward saying "No," because under payoff matrix A, he or she wins only one point for a hit but wins nine points for a correct rejection, and loses nine points for a false alarm but loses only one point for a miss. In contrast, payoff matrix C is designed to produce a liberal criterion—the subject should report the signal as present whenever there is the slightest evidence it was there. Here, the subject wins nine points for a hit and only one for a correct rejection, whereas he or she loses only one point for a false alarm but loses nine points for a miss. Thus, it is to the subject's advantage to show a bias toward saying "Yes." Although the five schedules of payoffs should have produced exactly the same criteria as the five signal

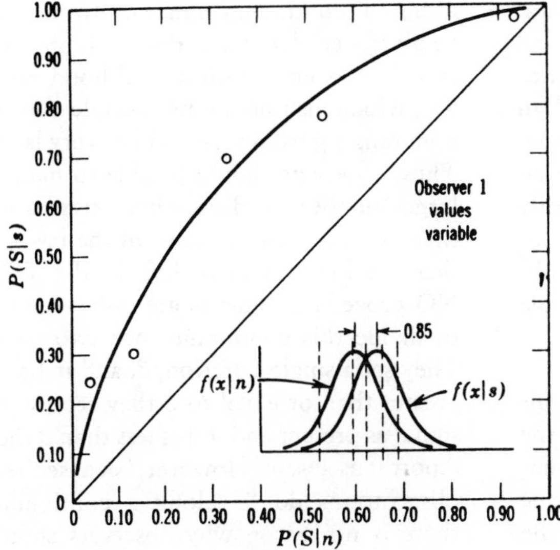

Fig. 4-8 ROC curve obtained by varying payoffs rather than presentation probabilities, for the same observer as in Figure 4.7. (From *Signal Detection Theory and Psychophysics* by D. M. Green and J. A. Swets. Copyright 1974 by Krieger Publishing. Reprinted by permission.)

probabilities, extreme payoffs were more effective than extreme signal probabilities in inducing the observer to adopt extreme criteria, as can be seen by comparing Figure 4-8 with Figure 4-7.

The Three Procedures of SDT

There are three experimental procedures for collecting data within signal detection theory: The *YES/NO procedure,* the *forced-choice procedure,* and the *rating scale procedure.* We have already used the YES/NO procedure to discuss the assumptions of SDT, so we will review that very briefly.

YES/NO Procedure. Subjects are given many signal trials randomly mixed with noise trials. During a given experimental session, a number of trials (from as few as 100 to as many as 1000) are run using a single signal intensity, a single presentation probability, and a single payoff matrix. This is done so that during this session the subject can be considered to have a single sensitivity value and a single criterion. Data from one session are plotted as a single point on an ROC-curve. To generate an entire ROC curve for a particular subject and a signal intensity, we must run several sessions with different payoffs or signal probabilities. The subject is told as much as possible about the experimental

Table 4-3 Three Payoff Matrices Designed to Vary the Subject's Criterion from Conservative (A) through Moderate (B) to Liberal (C).[a]

	A Response		B Response		C Response	
	Yes	No	Yes	No	Yes	No
Signal (*s*)	1	−1	1	−1	9	−9
Noise (*n*)	−9	9	−1	1	−1	1

[a]These were three of the five payoff matrices used by Green and Swets (1974) to produce the ROC function shown in Figure 4-8.

conditions, including the signal presentation probability and the payoff matrix, and is usually given trial-by-trial performance feedback. Since payoffs are considered an important aspect of the subject's criterion, subjects are usually paid for their participation. In sensory experiments, highly trained subjects are used repeatedly to obtain stable results. In certain other applications of SDT, however, it is not possible to use the same subject repeatedly.

Forced-Choice Procedure. In the two-alternative, forced-choice experiment, the subject is presented with a pair of presentations, one of which is the signal and one the noise. If the stimuli are auditory, the presentations usually occur in different temporal intervals, and the subject's task is to report in which interval, the first or the second, the auditory signal occurred. Or auditory stimuli could be presented simultaneously to the two ears, in a dichotic presentation. Here the subject would have to report which ear heard the stimulus. If the stimuli are visual, the presentations usually occur in two different spatial locations, and the subject's task is to report in which location, left or right, the visual signal occurred.

The forced-choice procedure is ideal for exploring the effect of sensory, as opposed to motivational, variables on detection performance, since subjects in a forced-choice experiment do not usually show a bias toward one or the other interval.

The Rating Scale Procedure. The rating scale procedure is a method for obtaining an entire ROC curve in a single session. You will recall that SDT assumes that the magnitude of internal observations lies along a continuum ranging from very small to very large and that each observation is converted into a likelihood ratio, $l(x)$, which also lies along a single continuum ranging from very small to very large. Thus, observers should be able to make a large number of discriminations among their internal observations on the basis of these various values of $l(x)$. In the YES/NO procedure, subjects are only required to divide this continuum into two parts. They set a single criterion, β, and if $l(x)$ is greater than or equal to β they report the signal as present and if it is less than β they report it as absent. However, because these observations do lie along a continuum, there is no reason why observers should not be able to grade their observations into more than just the two categories of YES and NO, and they are asked to do exactly that in the rating scale procedure.

In a five-category rating scale experiment, subjects are presented with a signal or noise presentation on each trial and are asked to rate their observation along a five-point scale, where 5 means "Sure it's signal," 4 means "Fairly sure it's signal," 3 means "Unsure whether signal or noise," 2 means "Fairly sure it's noise," and 1 means "Sure it's noise." In order to place their responses into one of n categories, subjects are assumed to set up $n - 1$ criteria placements. For a five-point rating scale, they are assumed to set up the four criterion placements, c_1, c_2, c_3, and c_4, as shown in Figure 4-9, and respond with the ratings 1 through 5 depending where on the sensation continuum their observations lies (e.g., a 1 if below c_1, a 3 if between c_2 and c_3, and a 5 if above c_4).

An ROC curve may be generated by computing the proportion of signal trials

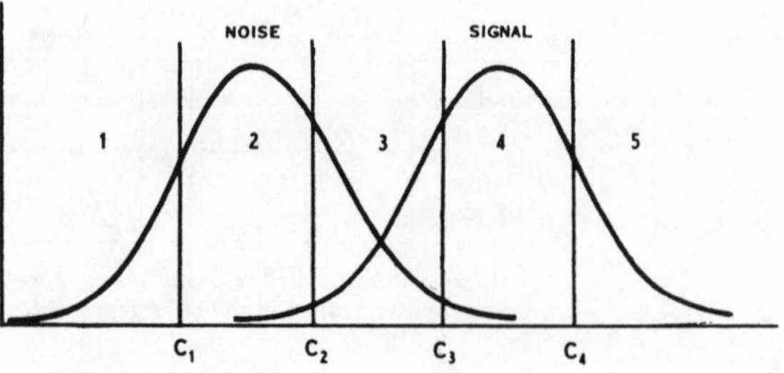

Fig. 4-9 Some hypothetical placements of criteria for a five-category rating scale procedure.

Table 4-4 Hypothetical Frequency Data from a Five-Category Rating Experiment, in which "5" Indicates the Subject Is Sure the Presentation Was a Signal and "1" Indicates the Subject Is Sure The Presentation Was Noise.

	Response					
	1	2	3	4	5	
Signal	73	138	206	254	329	1000
Noise	325	255	205	151	64	1000
	398	393	411	405	393	2000

exceeding each criterion and plotting these against the proportion of noise trials exceeding each criterion. To do this, we compute *P* (5/signal), *P* (4 + 5/signal), *P* (3 + 4 + 5/signal), and *P* (2 + 3 + 4 + 5/signal), and plot these against the corresponding proportions conditionalized on noise.

Table 4-4 presents some hypothetical data from a five-category rating scale experiment. These were generated in order to represent a d' of approximately 1.0 and so that each category would be used approximately equally often. In order to plot these data in an ROC curve, the frequencies are cumulated from the right and then converted to proportions by dividing by the total number of signal and noise trials. The frequencies have been cumulated in Table 4-5, and the proportions of hit and false alarm rates associated with each category (and lower) are shown in Table 4-6, along with the z scores and d' values. The d' values calculated from the individual data points are all very close to 1.0, not a surprising result since these data are hypothetical rather than real.

An n category rating scale experiment generates $n - 1$ points on an ROC curve, so the data from this five-category rating scale experiment generated a four-point ROC curve. The same four-point ROC curve could be obtained with four experimental sessions using four different signal probabilities or four different payoff schedules. With the rating scale procedure, however, all four points can be obtained in a single experimental session.

The ROC curve obtained from the rating scale experiment has been plotted in Figure 4-10 on linear coordinates and in Figure 4-11 on double probability coordinates. The straight line fitted to the data points in Figure 4-11 has a slope of 1.0, indicating $\sigma_s = \sigma_n$, and the difference between the z_s and z_n coordinates is 1.0, indicating that $d' = 1.0$.

Table 4-5 Cumulated Frequency Data, Indicating the Frequency of a Response *k* or Higher

	Response				
	1+2+3+4+5	2+3+4+5	3+4+5	4+5	5
Signal	1000	927	789	583	329
Noise	1000	675	420	215	64

Table 4-6 Cumulative Proportions of a Response *k* or Higher, z_s and z_n, and the d' Estimated from each Pair of Hit and False Alarm Proportions

	k			
	2	3	4	5
Pr (*k* or higher/signal)	.927	.789	.583	.329
Pr (*k* or higher/noise	.675	.420	.215	.064
z_s	−1.454	−0.802	−0.209	0.442
z_n	−0.453	0.201	0.789	1.522
$d' = z_n - z_s$	1.001	1.003	0.998	1.080

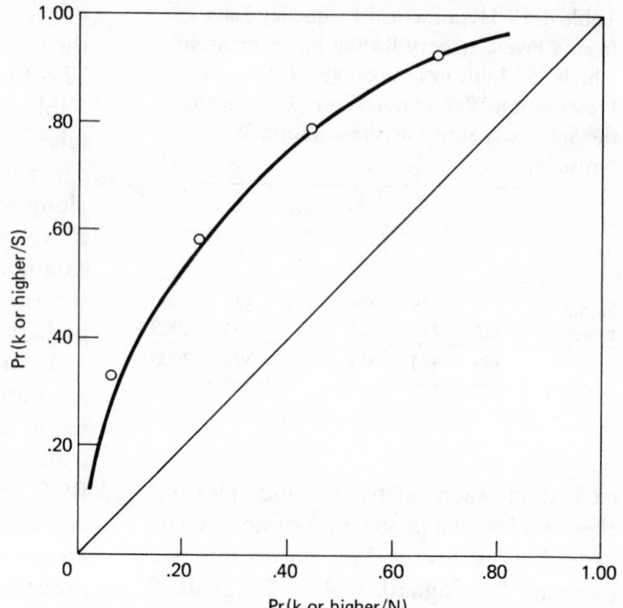

Fig. 4.10 ROC curve constructed from the rating scale data presented in Table 4-5. The theoretical curve is for $d' = 1.0$ and equal-variance signal and noise distributions.

Fig. 4-11 ROC curve from Figure 4.10 plotted in double probability coordinates.

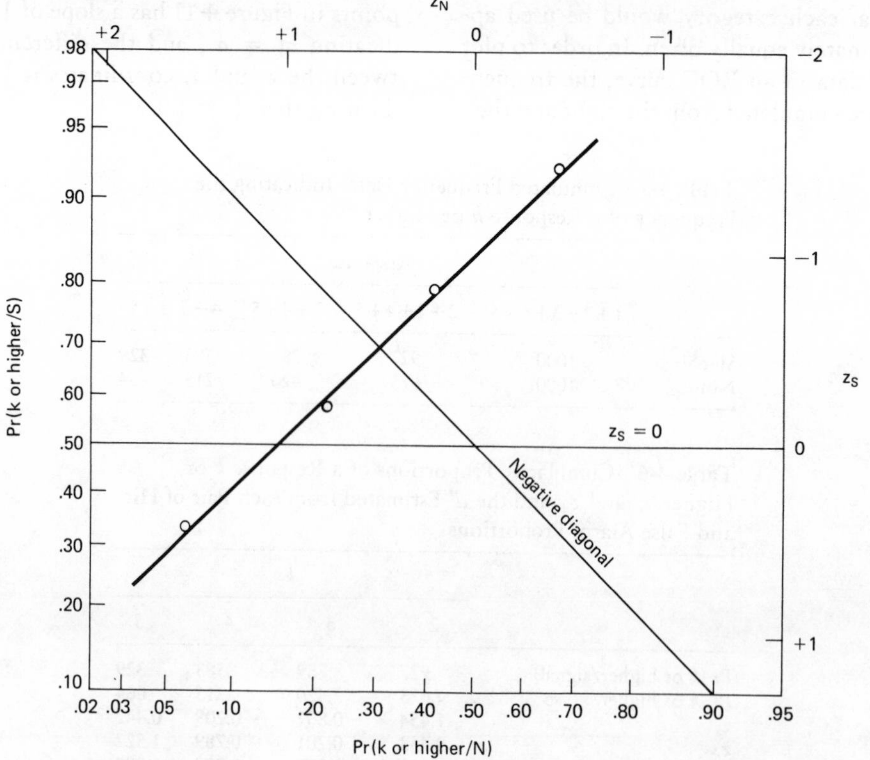

In summary, the YES/NO procedure is a good one for estimating the degree of response bias, as well as for obtaining sensitivity estimates. It has the disadvantage of being time-consuming, because several sessions must be run under different signal probabilities or payoffs in order to generate an ROC curve. The two-alternative, forced-choice procedure is the method *par excellence* for measuring sensitivity alone, either by the probability of a correct response or d', since there is typically little response bias toward one or the other interval. The rating scale procedure is a very economical one, because the experimenter can generate an entire ROC curve from the data of a single subject in a single session. Not only is it possible to estimate the subject's sensitivity from the resulting ROC curve, but the shape of the ROC curve provides evidence for or against SDT as opposed to other theories of thresholds. An ROC function of curved shape is evidence for SDT whereas other shapes, such as straight lines, are evidence for other threshold theories.

Finally, we note that in almost all sensory experiments employing SDT methodology, data from individual subjects are analyzed separately—that is, an ROC curve represents a single subject's performance, not that of a group of subjects. However, in many nonsensory applications of SDT, it is not practicable to obtain sufficient data from individual subjects, so ROC curves for grouped data must be constructed. An example of grouped data from a recognition memory study may be found in Appendix B.

Comparison of Classical and Signal Detection Theories

There is strong evidence that classical or high-threshold theory is incorrect. Subjects can detect supposedly subthreshold, weak stimuli at better than chance levels. This finding contradicts the classical theory, which predicts that detections of below-threshold stimuli are the result of chance alone. Signal detection theory predicts this result directly, because it assumes that sensations lie along a continuum, and correct detections result from the strength of the stimulus surpassing the subject's criterion (not threshold). Accordingly, an investigator who measures thresholds should always include a fair proportion of catch trials on which no signal is presented.

Most classical threshold data have been obtained using classical methods, in which catch trials were rarely used. How do we interpret such data, given that the evidence indicates there is either no, or a low, threshold? The answer that most investigators accept is that classical threshold data reveal the general functional relationship between sensitivity and either stimulus or subject-state variables. However, absolute threshold values are probably overestimated by the classical methods—that is, subjects are *more* sensitive to external stimuli than we have given them credit for!

SCALING

Historically, the goal of scaling was to discover the form of the psychophysical function—that is, the relationship between the physical intensity of such simple stimuli as lights, tones, and temperature and their corresponding psychological intensities. By psychological intensity we mean the phenomenological experience described by such terms as brightness, loudness, warmth, cold, and pain. Each of these experiences can be produced by varying the physical intensity of a light or a tone, or by varying the physical temperature or voltage of a metal object touching the skin. We seek to discover how varying the physical parameters of the stimulus affects the psychological parameters.

Traditional scaling procedures investigated the way sensation varied when a single dimension of a simple stimulus was varied. Accordingly, in the first part of this section, we discuss *unidimensional scaling*. These are situations in which all other dimensions of a stimulus are kept fixed while the dimension of interest is varied.

Later in this chapter, we consider more complex scaling techniques, in which we seek to discover the psychological difference between two stimuli that differ on a number of dimensions. We refer to this second type of scaling as *multidimensional scaling*.

UNIDIMENSIONAL SCALING

Within unidimensional scaling, it is important to distinguish between two different types of dimensions—*prothetic* and *metathetic*. This distinction, first introduced by Stevens and Galanter in 1957, distinguishes dimensions of quantity (*prothetic*) from dimensions of quality (*metathetic*). Imagine, for example, all the ways a spot of light can be altered. One could vary its intensity (and hence its brightness), its wavelength (and hence its hue), its diameter (and hence its perceived size), its horizontal position (and hence its perceived position), its saturation (and hence its perceived saturation), and so forth. All of these variations in physical dimensions produce corresponding changes in psychological dimensions, which are either prothetic or metathetic.

Prothetic continua are defined by Stevens and Galanter as attributes "for which discrimination appears to be based on an additive mechanism by which excitation is added to excitation at the physiological level" (p. 377). These attributes are exemplified by brightness, size, and saturation for visual stimuli, loudness for auditory stimuli, and warmth, cold, and pain for tactile stimuli. *Metathetic continua* are defined as attributes "for which discrimination behaves as though based on a substitutive mechanism at the physiological level" (p. 377). They are exemplified by hue and position for visual stimuli and by pitch for auditory stimuli. Only the prothetic or quantitative dimensions are relevant in discovering the form of the psychophysical function, because such a function relates a quantitative physical dimension to a quantitative psychological dimension.

The founder of psychophysics, Gustav Fechner, developed and systematized the various methods for measuring thresholds. However, his ultimate goal was not the thresholds themselves, but their use in discovering the form of the psychophysical function. A central question at the time Fechner was developing his ideas was the relationship between the size of the difference threshold and the size of the standard—how big does a difference need to be when two large things are being compared as opposed to when two small things are being compared? Intuitively, it would seem that a small change is more noticeable against a small-magnitude background than against a large-magnitude background. For example, lighting a candle in a completely dark room can have a blinding effect, but it will make no noticeable difference in a brilliantly lit room. A person's whisper is audible in silence but completely masked at a jet airfield. Similarly, a small difference between stimuli of small magnitude is more noticeable than that same difference between stimuli of large magnitude. It is easier to tell that two lemons are of unequal weight than two melons when the inequality is the same.

Over 100 years ago, E. H. Weber reported a remarkable relationship between the size of the *jnd* and the size of the standard for lifted weights. This relationship, known as *Weber's law*, states that the ratio of the *jnd* to the standard is a constant over a wide range of standards. We can describe Weber's law by the formula:

$$jnd/\text{standard} = K$$

where K is a constant known as Weber's constant. Weber's law means that there must be an equal *percentage* increase in the comparison stimulus over the standard for it to be discriminated to the same criterion. For example, if the Weber constant for weight is 1/30, the *jnd* will be 1 g for a standard of 30 g, 2 g for a standard of 60 g, and 10 g for a standard of 300 g.

In present-day notation, the *jnd* is called ΔI and the standard is called I. As shown in Figure 4-12, Weber's law is supported if a plot of $\Delta I/I$ against I is flat, as in A, or if

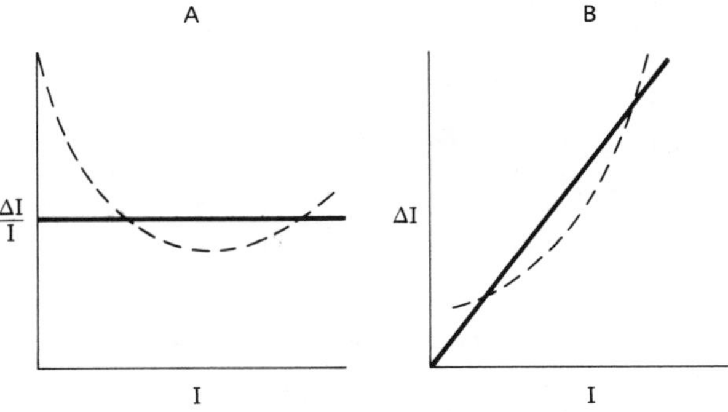

Fig. 4-12 Idealized Weber functions *(solid line)* and Weber functions as they are usually observed *(dotted line).* A and B show two ways of plotting Weber's law.

a plot of ΔI against I is a straight line with a positive slope which passes through the origin, as in B. A large body of data in intensity discrimination shows that Weber's law is approximately true over an intermediate range of stimulus intensities, although it breaks down at the extremes. This is shown in Figure 4-12 by the dotted functions which are above the solid functions near threshold and also for high values of I.

Weber's law is a way of quantifying discrimination ability. But Fechner saw a way of extending Weber's law from its role as a description of the *discriminability* of stimuli to one of describing the *subjective intensity* of stimuli. In Fechner's method of indirect scaling, Weber's law provides the unit of sensation magnitude.

Indirect Scaling

Fechner firmly believed that it was impossible to measure sensation directly. He believed that subjects are not capable of assessing the *magnitude* of their sensation, but only whether one stimulus produces a stronger or weaker sensation than another stimulus. Accordingly, he sought a way to use data from discrimination experiments to infer the form of the psychophysical function.

Fechner was also aware of the work of the mathematician Daniel Bernouilli, who was led through some paradoxes in betting to propose that the utility (subjective value) of money increased more slowly than its monetary value. Bernouilli proposed that the form of the function relating the objective value of money to its subjective value was logarithmic, the same function that Fechner came to propose for the relationship between stimulus intensity and sensation intensity. Bernouilli's function predicts that equal *percentage increases* in money (rather than equal absolute increases), will produce equal increases in utility (satisfaction or happiness). To apply Bernouilli's law to salary raises, it is necessary to raise salaries by equal percentages of income to give equal satisfaction to two employees earning different amounts. So, someone who is earning $10,000 a year will be as happy with a $1000 raise as someone earning $20,000 is with a $2000 raise. If they were both given a $1500 raise, the higher-paid employee would be disappointed compared to the lower-paid employee.

Fechner's assumptions in deriving his logarithmic law are as follows. First, he assumed that a difference that is just detected by a subject (e.g., a difference detected 50% of the time) is subjectively equal regardless of whether it is a small physical difference between two weak stimuli or a large physical difference between two strong stimuli. Therefore, if two lemons are just noticeably different in weight and differ by 1 g, and if two melons are also just noticeably different in weight and differ by 5 g, the subjective difference in weight at the low end of the scale for lemons will be equal to the subjective difference at the high end of the scale for melons. Second, he assumed that Weber's law is true across the entire

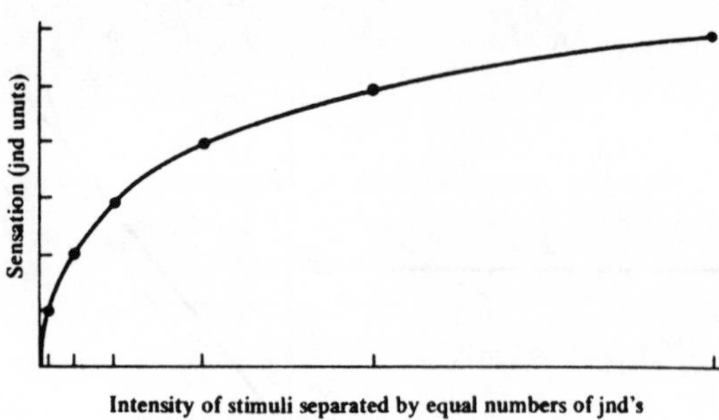

Fig. 4-13 Logarithmic relationship between sensation and stimulus intensity proposed by Fechner. (From "Psychophysics" by J. G. Snodgrass. In B. Scharf (Ed.), *Experimental Sensory Psychology.* Copyright 1975 by Scott, Foresman. Reprinted by permission.)

stimulus intensity range. (This is somewhat inaccurate because Weber's law has been shown to break down near threshold.) Third, he assumed that equally often noticed differences are also subjectively equal, unless they are always or never noticed. Thus, differences that are detected 75% of the time are also equal to one another.

Given these three assumptions, Fechner was able to deduce that the form of the psychophysical function was logarithmic, as shown in Figure 4-13. In this figure, sensation begins at the absolute threshold. Stimulus intensity is measured in units of the absolute threshold, and stimuli differing by equal numbers of *jnd*s are marked off along the abscissa. Note that because *jnd*s increase in physical size as stimulus intensity increases (because of Weber's law), stimuli differing by equal numbers of *jnd*s become more widely spaced as we move to the right along the stimulus scale (abscissa). However, because *jnd*s are assumed to be subjectively equal, these stimuli are equally spaced as we move upward along the sensation scale (ordinate).

Now we are ready to formalize some of these laws.

Weber's law states

$$\frac{\Delta I}{I} = K$$

The discrimination threshold, ΔI, is a constant proportion, K, of the background or standard stimulus, I, against which the comparison stimuli are judged. Weber's law is true for prothetic continua, but not usually for metathetic continua.

Fechner's law states

$$S = C \log I$$

The sensation, S, produced by a stimulus is related to the log of the stimulus magnitude, I, by a constant C (a different constant from the K constant in Weber's law).

Fechner derived his law from Weber's law by use of his fundamental formula:

$$\Delta S = K\left(\frac{\Delta I}{I}\right)$$

The change in sensation, ΔS, is proportional to the ratio of the change in the physical intensity of the stimulus, ΔI, to the intensity of the standard, I, times a constant, K. When ΔI represents the *jnd*, this fundamental formula represents both Weber's law and the assumption of subjective equality of *jnd*s. By treating the fundamental formula as a differential equation and integrating it, Fechner derived the logarithmic law.

Logarithmic Versus Power Law. For well over 100 years, Fechner's law dominated the field of psychophysics. For example, the intensity of acoustic stimuli has long been measured in logarithmic units, called decibel scales, in conformity with the way their loudness was thought to be perceived. However, when investigators began to measure sensation magnitude directly, they found differences between Fechner's logarithmic function and the observed data.

In 1961, S. S. Stevens, the most prolific and vociferous of Fechner's critics, published a paper entitled "To Honor Fechner and Repeal His Law" in which he argued that the correct form of the psychophysical function was not a logarithmic function, but a power function (Stevens, 1961b). Before describing Steven's power law, we first describe the direct methods he introduced for measuring sensation, of which the best-known is the *method of magnitude estimation.*

Direct Scaling—Magnitude Estimation

Stevens's solution to the problem of measuring sensation was simple and direct. He merely asked subjects to report directly, with numbers, how intense various stimuli appear. In a typical *magnitude estimation* experiment, subjects are given a standard, or modulus, to which they are to assign some easily remembered number, like 10. Stimuli that appear twice as intense (e.g., twice as loud, bright, heavy, or long) are to be called 20, those that appear half as intense, 5, and so on. From the method of magnitude estimation, or one of several related methods, Stevens found that for prothetic continua, the psychophysical function is a *power function* rather than a *logarithmic function.* The equation for the power law is

$$S = aI^b$$

where S is sensation magnitude, I is stimulus magnitude, and a and b are constants.

The important quantity in the *power law* is the value of the exponent, b, because its value tells us whether sensation grows linearly with stimulus intensity (which would be true if $b = 1$), more slowly (for $b < 1$) or more quickly (for $b > 1$). The value of the constant a merely reflects the particular number the subject gave to the modulus. Instructions to call the modulus 20 instead of 10 would double the value of a, and instructions to call the modulus 5 instead of 10 would halve a.

Figure 4-14 presents three representative psychophysical functions for three prothetic continua. Power functions that are

Fig. 4-14 The psychophysical functions for electric shock, apparent length, and brightness. The curve for electric shock is concave upward because its power law exponent is 3.5, while the curve for brightness is concave downward because its exponent is 0.33. The power function for apparent length is almost straight in these linear coordinates because its exponent is close to 1.0. (From "The Psychophysics of Sensory Function" by S. S. Stevens. In W. A. Rosenblith (Ed.), *Sensory Communication.* Copyright 1961 by MIT Press. Reprinted by permission.)

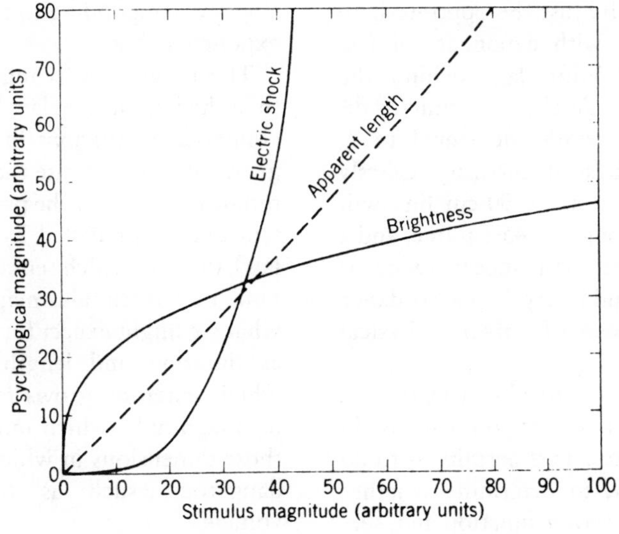

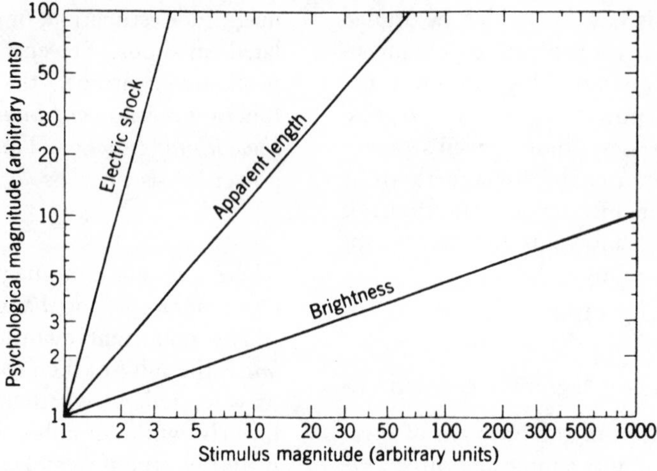

Fig. 4-15 When the curves in Figure 4.14 are plotted against logarithmic coordinates, they become straight lines. The slope of the line corresponds to the exponent of the power function. (From "The Psychophysics of Sensory Function" by S. S. Stevens. In W. A. Rosenblith (Ed.), *Sensory Communication.* Copyright 1961 by MIT Press. Reprinted by permission.)

concave upward, like the one for electric shock, indicate an exponent greater than 1; those that are approximately straight lines, like the one for length, indicate an exponent equal to 1; and those that are concave downward, like the one for brightness, indicate an exponent less than 1.

An exponent greater than 1 means that as the physical intensity of a stimulus is doubled, the sensation is more than doubled. So increasing shock intensity in a continuous and linear fashion will lead to a sensation that grows slowly at first and then more quickly. Just the opposite happens for stimuli with exponents of less than 1—the sensation lags behind the physical intensity. Finally, for stimulus dimensions having exponents equal to 1, doubling the physical intensity exactly doubles the sensation—a 90-cm line will appear twice as long as a 45-cm line, and a 20-second interval will appear twice as long as a 10-second interval, in accordance with the ratios of their physical dimensions.

A convenient way to plot data from a magnitude estimation experiment is in log-log coordinates. This permits us to do two things—first, to determine whether the data follow a power function and, second, to estimate the two constants for the power law. The reason for plotting the data in log-log coordinates is that if we take logarithms of both sides of the equation for a power function, we obtain the following equation for a straight line:

$$\log S = b \log I + \log a$$

in which the exponent b is the slope of the function on log-log coordinates, and $\log a$ is its intercept.

The same three power functions from Figure 4-14 are plotted on log-log coordinates in Figure 4-15, where it can be seen that they each form straight lines with slopes corresponding to the values of their exponents.

The power law is much more flexible than the logarithmic law because it can accommodate situations in which sensation grows at a slower rate than stimulus magnitude (a feature of the psychophysical system *always* predicted by the logarithmic law), those in which sensation grows at the same rate as stimulus magnitude (which is what we might expect for such dimensions as duration and length), and those in which sensation grows faster than stimulus magnitude (which might be useful for those dimensions in which high levels are dangerous, such as temperature and voltage).

Table 4-7 presents representative exponents from different stimulus modalities obtained from magnitude estimation studies. As can be seen, a number of them have exponents that are equal to or greater than 1. These data contradict the logarithmic law. (It should be noted that a power function with an exponent less than 1 is *not* identical to a logarithmic function; however, it is often difficult to tell them apart on the basis of data from direct scaling.)

A number of other direct scaling methods have been used to corroborate and extend the results from magnitude estimation. These include *cross-modality matching,* in which subjects adjust the intensity of one modality, such as the brightness of a light, to match the intensity of another modality, such as the loudness of a tone. The results of cross-modality matching experiments should be predictable from a knowledge of each of the magnitude estimation exponents alone, and they usually are. Another method is *magnitude production,* in which subjects are given a number and asked to produce a stimulus magnitude that matches the number. The exponent should be about the same in both production and estimation, which it generally is. Finally, subjects may be asked to do *inverse scaling,* in which they give estimates of the magnitude of the inverse sensation, such as softness (as opposed to loudness) and darkness (as opposed to brightness). Here the exponent should be the negative of the exponent for positive scaling, which it usually is.

Although the direct scaling methods, and the power law that results from them,

Table 4-7 Representative Exponents of the Power Functions Relating Subjective Magnitude to Stimulus Magnitude

Continuum	Measured exponent	Stimulus condition
Loudness	0.67	Sound pressure of 3000-hertz tone
Vibration	0.95	Amplitude of 60 hertz on finger
Vibration	0.6	Amplitude of 250 hertz on finger
Brightness	0.33	5° Target in dark
Brightness	0.5	Point source
Brightness	0.5	Brief flash
Brightness	1.0	Point source briefly flashed
Lightness	1.2	Reflectance of gray papers
Visual length	1.0	Projected line
Visual area	0.7	Projected square
Redness (saturation)	1.7	Red-gray mixture
Taste	1.3	Sucrose
Taste	1.4	Salt
Taste	0.8	Saccharine
Smell	0.6	Heptane
Cold	1.0	Metal contact on arm
Warmth	1.6	Metal contact on arm
Warmth	1.3	Irradiation of skin, small area
Warmth	0.7	Irradiation of skin, large area
Discomfort, cold	1.7	Whole body irradiation
Discomfort, warm	0.7	Whole body irradiation
Thermal pain	1.0	Radiant heat on skin
Tactual roughness	1.5	Rubbing emery cloths
Tactual hardness	0.8	Squeezing rubber
Finger span	1.3	Thickness of blocks
Pressure on palm	1.1	Static force on skin
Muscle force	1.7	Static contractions
Heaviness	1.45	Lifted weights
Viscosity	0.42	Stirring silicone fluids
Electric shock	3.5	Current through fingers
Vocal effort	1.1	Vocal sound pressure
Angular acceleration	1.4	5-Second rotation
Duration	1.1	White noise stimuli

(From *Psychophysics* by S. S. Stevens © 1975 by John Wiley and Sons. Reprinted by permission.)

are not without their critics (see, e.g., Baird & Noma, 1978; Savage, 1966), most present-day psychophysicists would opt for some more direct method of measuring the psychophysical function than the indirect method used by Fechner. Fechner's assumptions seem to have been wrong in at least one very fundamental respect: namely, that *jnd*s of different physical size have the same subjective size. To take just one counterexample, it is more difficult to tell the difference between 45 and 50 minutes than it is to tell the difference between 5 and 10 minutes. This does not mean, however, that our perception of the passage of time lags behind physical time. In fact, subject's *estimates* of time duration are fairly accurate: however, the longer the duration of time to be estimated, the more variance subjects show in their response. Thus, high variance of estimations (lack of discrimination) does not produce underestimation.

Other Scaling Methods: Category and Rating Scales. In magnitude estimation, subjects are asked to assign numbers to stimuli so that ratios among their sensations are preserved. Any numbers the subjects choose to use are permissible (although, in fact, they tend to choose whole, round numbers). In *category scaling,* in contrast, the subject is given a small set of numbers, such as the numbers 1 through 5, to use to assign stimuli to categories. Usually, subjects are instructed to make the subjective width of their categories equal, so that the difference between stimuli categorized as 1 and 2 is equal to the difference between stimuli categorized as 4 and 5. *Rating scales* are similar to category scales, except that their use does not emphasize equal subjective differences among the numbers.

The psychophysical function obtained from category scaling is usually not identical to the psychophysical function obtained from magnitude estimation, especially for prothetic (quantitative) dimensions. Category scaling often produces the logarithmic function of Fechner rather than the power law function of Stevens. Stevens and Galanter (1957) have analyzed these differences at some length and conclude that category scaling is not a desirable technique for scaling prothetic continua, although it may be for metathetic continua, in which the differences between category and magnitude scales are much less.

MULTIDIMENSIONAL SCALING

The previous section on unidimensional scaling describes methods that have been developed for scaling a single dimension of relatively simple stimuli. Such direct methods as magnitude estimation have sometimes been used for single dimensions of more complex, and not physically measurable, dimensions, such as the severity of crimes or the socioeconomic status of occupations (see Stevens, 1975). Here, the subject is instructed to attend to a single dimension (e.g., severity or degree of status) when making judgments.

In some cases, however, we want to investigate all the ways in which one complex object or event differs from another. In fact, our aim is often to discover how many types of differences might exist among a set of stimuli that account for how similar or different they appear.

In this section, we briefly describe techniques for scaling sets of stimuli in which all possible sources of difference are to be considered. For convenience, we entitle this section Multidimensional Scaling, to distinguish it from the unidimensional scaling techniques described earlier. By this term, we simply mean the various scaling methods that permit us to investigate the ways in which a set of stimuli can differ simultaneously along many different dimensions.

However, there is also a method for analyzing how complex stimuli differ from one another on a variety of dimensions, and this method is also called *multidimensional scaling*. To avoid confusion, we will try to be clear when we are talking about the specific method.

Multidimensional scaling methods are

concerned with the analysis of similarities among all possible pairs of a set of stimuli. Such stimuli might be fairly simple, like the letters of the alphabet, or more complex, like sets of nations, animals, or personality types. Similarity data are collected with a variety of methods. For the letters of the alphabet, similarity might be measured by observing how often subjects mistake a briefly presented letter for another. If the presentation mode is auditory, auditory similarities usually predominate: so, E is more often reported as G than as F, but J is more often reported as A than as T. Alternatively, subjects might be asked to rate the degree of acoustic similarity between pairs of letters or the conceptual similarity between pairs of animals or nations. The basic data consist of a similarity matrix showing the average rated similarity among all possible pairs of stimuli.

Multidimensional Scaling: The Method

The goal of multidimensional scaling is to construct a psychological Euclidean space within which stimuli may be located. Distances within this spatial representation should represent degree of psychological similarity, so that pairs of stimuli that are close together are more similar than those that are far apart.

To take a simple example, imagine that you have obtained similarity ratings for rectangles varying in height-to-width ratio (e.g., from those that are short and wide to those that are tall and narrow). Also imagine that you have varied the area of the rectangles from small to large. When subjects are asked to judge the similarity of a pair of these rectangles, they will presumably consider both factors (height-to-width ratio and area) in making their judgments. When multidimensional scaling techniques are applied to subjects' similarity judgments, we should retrieve the two dimensions that the experimenter introduced into the stimuli, namely, height-to-width ratio and area.

However, if this were all that multidimensional scaling could accomplish, it would be fairly uninteresting, because the dimensions obtained were prefigured in the stimulus generation process. It becomes of much greater interest when some preexisting category of stimuli is used, in which the dimensions along which the concepts vary is not clear. In this case, the use of multidimensional scaling can sometimes reveal which dimensions of difference subjects use in perceiving, remembering, or clustering them. It should be emphasized, however, that practical use of multidimensional scaling is based on two assumptions; first, that the ways in which stimuli differ are along *dimensions* that vary quantitatively (or at least have more than two levels) rather than *features* (which are either present or absent) and, second, that the number of dimensions is not too large.

To illustrate the distinction between dimension (more than two ordered values), and feature (presence or absence of a characteristic), consider one category of objects—animals. Imagine how many different ways animals may vary from one another: by size, by ferocity, by having fur or not, by being native to Africa or not, by laying eggs or not, and by level of intelligence. Some of these differences are dimensional in the sense we described: that is, size, ferocity, and intelligence all can be considered to have more than two ordered values, and in fact to be fairly continuous. Others have a featural quality—the animal either has fur, is native to Africa, lays eggs, or not. The feature differences, which can take on only two values, are unlikely to appear as dimensions in a multidimensional solution.

Figure 4-16 presents the results of a multidimensional scaling solution for rated dissimilarities among a group of 30 mammals (Henley, 1969). A three-dimensional solution was judged to give adequate fit to the similarity data (the more dimensions there are, the better the fit), although Figure 4-16 presents the results for only the best two of the three dimensions that were obtained. By inspecting the locations of the animals with regard to each dimen-

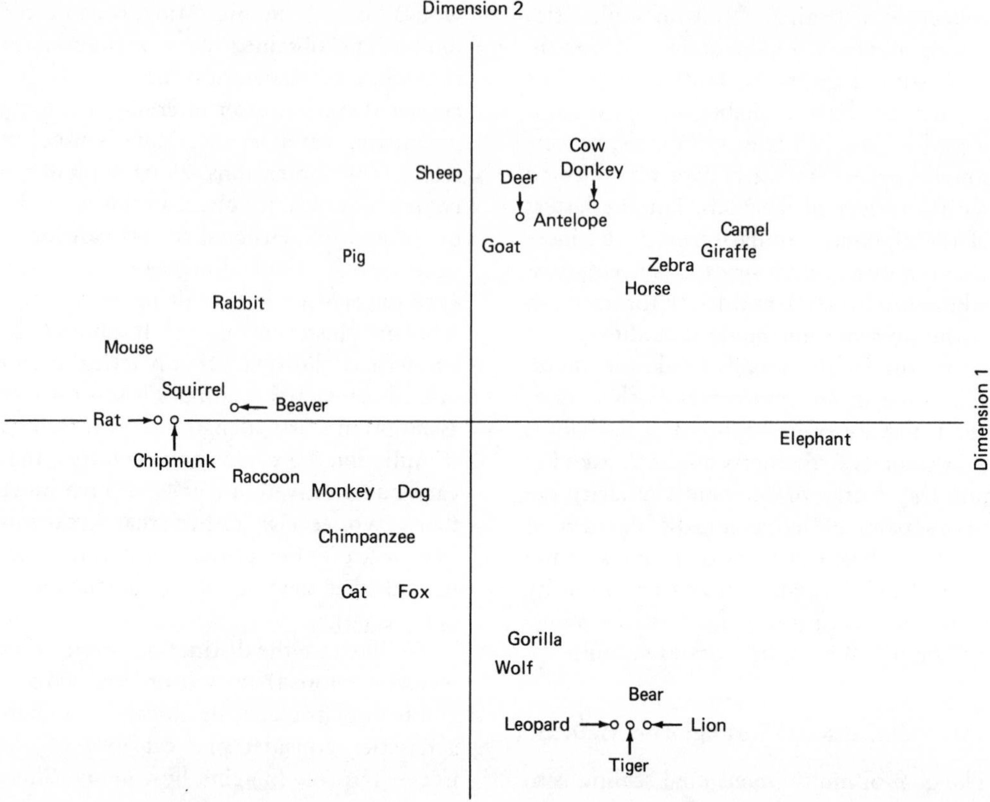

Fig. 4-16 The results of a multidimensional scaling analysis on subjects' ratings of similarity among 30 animals. The plot shows dimensions 1 and 2 of a 3-dimensional solution. Dimension 1 appears to correspond to size, while dimension 2 corresponds to ferocity or predacity. (From "A Psychological Study of the Semantics of Animal Terms," by N. M. Henley. In *Journal of Verbal Learning and Verbal Behavior,* 1969, *8,* 176–184. Copyright 1969 by Academic Press. Reprinted by permission.)

sion, and determining what seems to differentiate those with high values on a dimension from those with low values, it is usually possible to infer what the dimension might be.

On this two-dimensional plot, the closer together two animals are, the more similar they are judged to be, and the further apart they are, the more dissimilar they are judged to be. One dimension of this configuration is the horizontal one. To identify what this dimension represents psychologically, we need to ignore differences in the vertical dimension and try to infer what distinguishes animals at the left of the plot from those at the right. In this case, the dimension would appear to be size—animals on the left (e.g., mouse and rat) are small and those on the right (e.g., elephant, camel, and giraffe) are large.

The second dimension is identified by ignoring differences along the horizontal dimension and attempting to determine what differentiates animals along the vertical dimension. In this case, the dimension appears to be ferocity or predacity. Animals low on the plot (e.g., leopard, bear, lion, and tiger) are ferocious, found in the wild, carnivorous, and prey on other animals, whereas those high on the plot (e.g., cow, donkey, deer, and sheep) are domesticated, timid, nonpredatory, and herbivorous.

More information about the mathematical techniques of multidimensional scaling and some applications may be found in

Baird and Noma (1978), Kruskal and Wish (1978), and Shepard, Romney, and Nerlove (1972).

Cluster Analysis

Cluster analysis is an alternative method to analyze similarities among a set of stimuli that differ in several ways. Cluster analysis, like multidimensional scaling, uses a matrix of similarities as input. The output of such an analysis is a series of segregations of stimuli into tighter and tighter clusters with maximum similarity and separations into disparate clusters with maximum dissimilarity. When the results of a cluster analysis are compared to the results of multidimensional scaling for the same similarity matrix, the same pattern of results is not always obtained. For example, Sattath and Tversky (1977) applied cluster analysis to Henley's similarity ratings of mammals, with the results shown in Figure 4-17. Here, the size dimension emerges as an ordering of the clusters from top to bottom, while the ferocity or predacity dimension emerges as the difference between the two major clusters of herbivores and carnivores. The closer to the right any pair of animals is joined, the more similar they appear to be. Thus, giraffe and camel (at the top) are less similar to one another, even though in the smallest cluster among the tall herbivores, than rat and mouse (at the bottom), who are the most closely related of the rodents. Clustering techniques

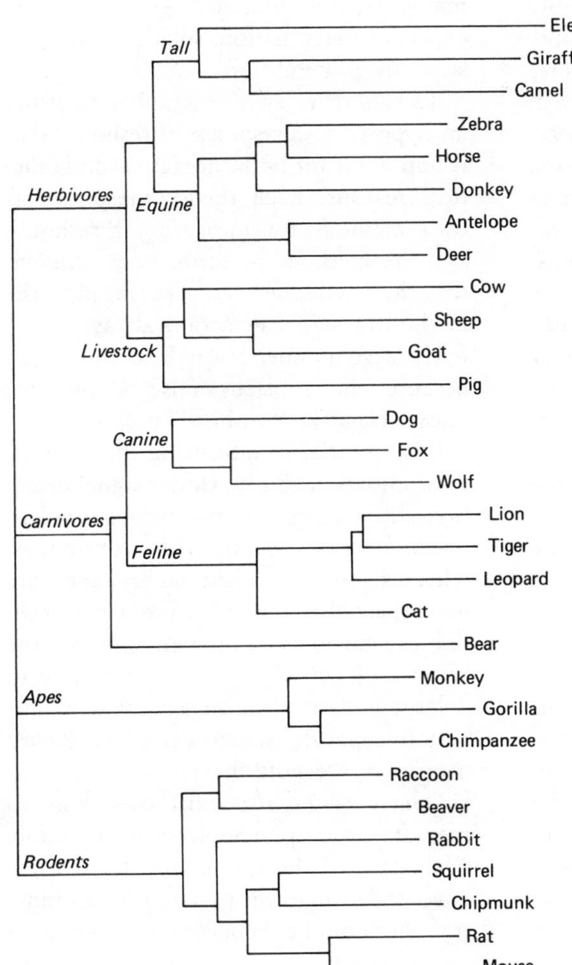

Fig. 4-17 The results of a hierarchical cluster analysis on the same similarity data analyzed in Figure 4-16. Note that the size dimension from the multidimensional scaling emerges as an ordering of the clusters from top to bottom, while the ferocity dimension emerges as the difference between the two major clusters of herbivores and carnivores. (From "Additive Similarity Trees" by S. Sattath and A. Tversky. In *Psychometrika,* 1977, 42, 319–345. Copyright 1977 by the Psychometric Society. Reprinted by permission.)

may be more appropriate when objects differ by features than when they differ along quantitative dimensions. Baird and Noma (1978) discuss clustering methods in more detail.

SUMMARY

The main purpose of psychophysics is to describe the psychophysical function that relates the subjective world to the physical world—that is, the function that relates psychological magnitude to physical magnitude. Two aspects of the psychophysical function are of interest: the point at which the function begins (the absolute threshold of sensation), and the manner in which psychological magnitude increases with physical magnitude (the scaling function).

Determination of the absolute threshold gives the starting point of the function—the amount of physical intensity that is required for awareness. In absolute detection, we measure the amount of energy required by the subject to detect the difference between a threshold amount of stimulation and the absence of such stimulation. In difference detection, we measure the amount of energy required by the subject to detect the difference between two levels of energy, and vary the energy levels to determine the relationship between the difference threshold and the energy level of a background or standard stimulus. Weber's law is a statement of the relationship between the size of the difference threshold, or *jnd*, and the size of the background stimulus. Weber's law states that the difference threshold is a constant fraction of the background stimulus.

The classical theory of thresholds assumes that a barrier within the nervous system must be overcome in order for the subject to detect either the difference between a stimulus and its absence, for the absolute threshold, or the difference between a stimulus increment and its background intensity, for the difference threshold. The classical theory proposes that the threshold is real and can be found within the subject's nervous system.

In contrast, signal detection theory maintains that no true threshold exists as a barrier between the observer and the external stimulus or stimulus increment, but rather humans are sensitive to continuous changes in intensity, whether those changes occur against a silent or noise background. According to signal detection theory, the subject does not show perfect discrimination because there is noise in the system, generated both from within by the nervous system and from without by the experimenter. Such noise forces the subject to adopt a response criterion for deciding whether a particular sensation was the result of signal or noise. However, such a response criterion is not a threshold in the classical sense, because its location is easily manipulated by nonsensory aspects of the experimental situation, such as payoffs or stimulus probabilities.

The controversy over whether a sensory (as opposed to a response) threshold exists is important for both theoretical and practical reasons. Each theory prescribes its own methods for measuring thresholds, and the methods prescribed are different for the two theories. Specifically, the method of signal detection always uses a fairly large number of catch or noise trials because the subject's false alarm rate (falsely classifying a noise stimulus as a signal) is essential in measuring the subject's discrimination ability. Under signal detection theory, false alarms are expected to occur because sensation is continuous, whereas under classical theory, they are not expected to occur because the threshold is assumed to be high enough that the absence of a stimulus could never cross it. A large body of data on sensory discrimination supports signal detection theory over high threshold theory.

Controversies also exist over how to measure the psychophysical function. Fechner used discrimination data to discover the form of the psychophysical function because he believed that sensation could not be measured directly. He constructed the psychophysical function by using the difference threshold as the unit of measurement along the sensation scale. By taking Weber's law as a given (i.e., that the *jnd* is a constant proportion of the background), and by assuming that the subjective size of the difference threshold was identical regardless of its physical size, he derived the law bearing his name. Fechner's law states that sensation grows as the logarithm of physical intensity, expressed by the equation $S = a \log I$.

Stevens introduced the direct method of magnitude estimation to measure sensation magnitude. When subjects directly estimated the magnitude of their sensations by assigning numbers to them, the resulting psychophysical function was not found to conform to Fechner's logarithmic function. Instead, Stevens found it was a power function, expressed by the equation $S = aI^b$, in which the exponent b describes the rate at which sensation magnitude grows with stimulus magnitude. The power function is more versatile than the logarithmic function because it can accommodate situations in which sensation grows at the same rate as stimulus magnitude (when the exponent is equal to 1.0) as well as those in which sensation grows more quickly than stimulus magnitude (when the exponent is greater than 1.0).

Both Fechner and Stevens were concerned with unidimensional scaling—with discovering the relationship between a single dimension of a stimulus, such as its intensity or area, and its perceived intensity or area. In contrast, the techniques of multidimensional scaling seek to determine all the possible ways that two stimuli can differ from one another. The results of multidimensional scaling can help to determine the number of dimensions along which stimuli differ as well as the psychological nature of these dimensions.

Psychophysical methods were developed to answer questions about the senses—questions about detection, discrimination, and scaling. However, these methods have been found useful in many other areas of research in human psychology and will continue to be applied in new and as yet undreamt of ways.

5

Mental Chronometry: Measuring the Speed of Mental Events

> Would thought also not have the infinite speed usually associated with it, and would it not be possible to determine the time required for shaping a concept or expressing one's will? For years this question has intrigued me.
>
> (Donders, 1868/1969, p. 417)

With this comment, F. C. Donders, a professor of physiology at the University of Utrecht, introduced the field of mental chronometry to psychology in a paper published in 1868 entitled "On the Speed of Mental Processes."

Donders' method of measuring the speed of mental processes, usually referred to as the *subtraction method,* fell into disfavor around the turn of the century until it was revived 60 years later, in a different form, by a group of modern-day psychologists. The most influential of these has been Saul Sternberg, whose revision of the subtraction method, called the *additive factors method,* we describe in detail later in this chapter. However, it is important to understand the history of these early attempts to measure the duration of mental processes, why these initial attempts failed, and why modern attempts to use the subtraction method have succeeded.

DONDERS' SUBTRACTION METHOD

Donders was influenced in his attempts to measure the speed of mental processes by the work of Helmholtz. In 1850, Helmholtz attempted to measure the speed of nerve transmission in the frog by measuring the time between the stimulation of a part of the frog's body and the resulting muscular contraction. He later applied this technique to humans by measuring the time to respond to a mild electric shock delivered at points of varying distance from the brain. Helmholtz used the method of subtraction to do this: He measured the difference in time between stimulation of the elbow and stimulation of the hand. Then, knowing the approximate length of nerve fibers between the hand and elbow, he was able to use the difference in reaction time as a measure of nerve transmission time.

Donders sought to measure processes vastly more complex than nerve transmission time, namely, the sum of all the processes that must intervene between presentation of a stimulus and activation of a voluntary response. When there is a single stimulus to which the subject makes a single simple response, such as moving the hand or foot, the time elapsing between stimulus presentation and completion of the motor response is known as the *simple reaction time.* Donders lists no fewer than 12 mental events that must take place between presentation of a stimulus and its motor response in simple reaction time. Present-day reaction-time theorists have whittled the number down to three subprocesses: stimulus input time, central processing or decision time, and motor response time.

Donders saw no way to disentangle the three processes and separately measure each component—in fact, we are in much the same state today. However, he proposed that by complicating the simple reaction time to make it what we now call *choice reaction time,* he could "insert" one or more steps in the simple reaction time mental process chain and, by subtraction, measure the time of those added steps.

In *choice reaction time,* two or more stimuli are presented, and the subject must indicate which stimulus has been presented by producing one of two or more responses, a different response for each stimulus. The choice reaction time must include both the time to discriminate one stimulus from another *(discrimination time)* and the time to select one of the several motor responses *(motor choice time).* Thus, Donders reasoned that the difference between simple reaction time (which he called the *a-reaction*) and choice reaction time (which he called the *b-reaction*) must represent the sum of discrimination time and motor choice time.

Next, to get rid of motor choice time, he invented the *c-reaction.* (Today, we call it

Donders' c-reaction.) In the c-reaction, the subject is presented with two or more stimuli, just as in the b-reaction, but makes only a single response, to one of the stimuli, and omits that response to all others. The c-reaction might be called a go/no-go response: the subject responds by making a single motor response to one stimulus (the go response) but omits the response to all others (no-go). This procedure, Donders reasoned, should eliminate motor-choice time and leave only discrimination time. The responses thus increase in complexity from a to c to b (the order of the letters reflects the order in which they were developed rather than their complexity). By subtracting c from b, Donders was able to measure motor-choice time, and by subtracting a from c, he measured discrimination time.

To summarize:

a-reaction = stimulus input time
+ decision time
+ motor-response time
b-reaction = stimulus input time
+ decision time
+ *discrimination time*
+ *motor-choice time*
+ motor-response time
c-reaction = stimulus input time
+ decision time
+ *discrimination time*
+ motor-response time

Therefore

c − a = *discrimination time,*

and

b − c = *motor-choice time.*

Donders used a variety of methods to test the subtraction method, but the one he reports on most fully in his paper (1868/1969) used the experimenter's pronunciation of one of the syllables* *koo, ko, kah, cay, key, queue* as the stimulus and the subject's repetition of that syllable as the response. In the a-reaction, only one syllable is presented, and the subject always repeats just that syllable. In the b-reaction, any of two or any of six of the syllables are spoken and the subject repeats whichever syllable has been spoken. In the c-reaction, one of the syllables is designated beforehand as the target, or to-be-responded-to stimulus, and the subject repeats that syllable when it is presented and remains silent for all others.

From this experiment, Donders found that c − a, the discrimination time, was about 36 ms (millisecond or 1/1000 of a second) whereas b − c, motor-choice time, was 47 ms. These times, even by today's standards, are exceedingly short, and, as Donders points out, probably represent the minimum values for these mental processes, since repeating what someone says is a highly overlearned task (or, as we would describe it today, there is high stimulus-response compatibility). For other, less well-learned stimulus-response links, such as pressing a right key to a red light and a left key to a white light, the differences are much larger and represent the time of those processes when no strong compatibility exists.

The subtraction method was soon adopted in other psychological laboratories of the day, but with disappointing results. First, the c-reaction was not always found to be shorter than the b-reaction, which it must be if the method is to be valid. Recall that in the c-reaction, the subject responds to one stimulus and refrains from responding to a second. This reaction was developed by Donders to eliminate the stage of motor choice, which is assumed to be included in the b or choice reaction. However, experimental psychologists of that day, Wundt among them, pointed out that the c-reaction *does* involve a motor choice—a choice between making and not making a response. To eliminate motor choice entirely, Wundt invented an alternative reaction-time response, the *d-reaction,* or "discrimination" reaction. Wundt's d-reaction is like Donders' b-reaction in that several different stimuli are presented. It is like the a-reaction in that only a single motor response is made, and it is made to all of the

*Approximate English translation as given by Koster (Donders, 1868/1969, p. 410).

stimuli. The difference between the d- and a-reaction is that for the d-reaction, the subject is instructed to recognize or identify the stimulus before responding—in short, to discriminate it from other possible stimuli. Wundt thus assumed that discrimination time could be measured by subtracting a- from d-reaction times.

As with the c-reaction, however, d-reaction times were unreliable, sometimes being as fast as a-reactions, and sometimes slower than b-reactions. The problem is that there is no way for the experimenter (or, for that matter, the subject) to know that the stimulus has been identified before the response is made, since the same response is made to all of the stimuli.

Another criticism of the method came from introspections of the subjects (who were usually the experimenters themselves). Subjects observed that their internal mental operations differed in the simple and choice reaction-time tasks. For simple reactions, the response was evoked by the stimulus as if it were a prepared reflex, with little in the way of voluntary decision involved. For choice reactions, in contrast, the subjects were aware of a variety of cognitive processes that intervened between stimulus and response. In addition, motor readiness seemed to be much higher in the simple than in the choice reaction time situation, so the motor response time component of both was unlikely to be equal. This is a particularly devastating criticism because the subtraction method is based on the assumption that inserting the processes of discrimination and motor choice into the a-reaction to produce the b-reaction does not affect the common stages of stimulus input and motor-response time. If this assumption is not true, the whole method is invalidated. Because of these problems, the subtraction method was abandoned as a way of timing mental events (although the use of reaction time as a dependent measure in a variety of tasks continued).

In the next section, we consider a reinterpretation and restatement of Donders' position proposed by Saul Sternberg. Sternberg's contribution was to reinstate the study of timing of mental processes by showing how substages of mental processes could be studied by subtraction. Sternberg's subtraction method differs from Donders' in that it does not involve inserting or deleting a whole stage of processing, but rather is based on manipulating variables to affect the amount of time each stage requires. This method is called the *additive factors method.*

After discussing Sternberg's theoretical contribution, we consider a number of different questions about the mind's functioning that have been asked using the additive factors method, and finally we discuss some methodological issues on the use of reaction time as a dependent variable.

STERNBERG'S ADDITIVE FACTORS METHOD

The approach of the additive factors method is to manipulate the task of the subject in such a way that a complete stage (such as discrimination or motor choice) is not deleted but rather is simply affected—either lengthened or shortened—by the experimenter's manipulation. Use of the method can indicate how many stages there are, how long a particular stage, or combination of stages, must take, and which variables affect which stages.

The best way to illustrate the additive factors method is with a concrete example, but before we describe the particular example, we need to introduce some new terminology. All of the experiments that test the additive factors method use a binary or two-choice reaction time paradigm. By that, we mean that the subject chooses one of two responses (usually the press of one of two keys) in response to the presentation of a stimulus. In *binary classification* experiments, there are more stimuli than responses, and the subject's task is to partition the set of stimuli into two exhaustive and mutually exclusive categories by responding to one set with one response and to the second set with the second response.

In binary classification experiments, then, there is a many-to-one relationship between stimuli and responses.

Memory-Scanning Experiments

The particular experiment we use to illustrate the additive factors method is known as a *memory-scanning* experiment or paradigm (sometimes also referred to as the Sternberg paradigm). In this paradigm, subjects are given a short list of items, such as digits, letters, or words, to memorize. The length of the list is varied within the limits of short-term memory (see Chapter 8), so that no more than five or six items are presented for memorization. The length of the memory list is called the *memory set size,* and the memory set is either varied from trial to trial, in what is called the *varied-set procedure,* or remains constant across a blocked series of trials, in what is known as the *fixed-set procedure.* The results from both procedures are quite similar, and in a laboratory that is not fully automated, the fixed-set procedure is more convenient. However, for purposes of illustration, we will use the varied-set procedure as a model.

After the memory set has been presented to the subject (usually with a visual display), a trial begins with the presentation of the test item, or *probe.* The probe can be selected from either the memory or *positive set* or its complement, the *negative set.* If the item is from the positive set, the subject responds by pressing a YES button, and if it is not, the subject responds by pressing a NO button.

Results from some typical trials in a memory-scanning experiment are shown in Table 5-1. The first column in Table 5-1 gives the trial number; the second column shows the actual memory set presented; the third column shows the set size (the number of items in the memory set); the fourth column shows the probe; the fifth column shows the correct response; and the sixth column shows a typical reaction time.

It is apparent that the memory demands on the subject are not great (that is, forget-

Table 5-1 Typical Trials in a Memory-Scanning Experiment with a Varied Set Procedure, Showing the Memory Set in Use on Each Trial, the Probe Presented, the Correct Response, and a Typical Reaction Time

Trial number	Memory set (visually displayed)	Set size (n)	Stimulus probe	Correct response	Reaction time (RT)
1	4,6,1	3	1	YES	470
2	2	1	6	NO	440
3	5	1	5	YES	390
4	7,2,8,9	4	0	NO	560
5	1,3,2,9,7,4	6	9	YES	590
6	4,5	2	9	NO	480
7	9,5,0	3	0	YES	470
8	0,4,2	3	3	NO	520
9	0,7,9,6	4	8	NO	560
10	4,2,0,6,8	5	7	NO	600
11	4,0,3	3	3	YES	470
12	0,3	2	8	NO	480
13	1,0,3,7,4	5	1	YES	550
14	3,7,1,8,0,4	6	0	YES	590
15	2,1,9,3	4	2	YES	510
16	6,2,1,8,3	5	7	NO	600

Note. The RTs are predicted by the following equations:

$$\text{RT (YES)} = 350 + 40n$$

$$\text{RT (NO)} = 400 + 40n$$

The RT depends on both the set size and the response types.

ting which items are in the positive set is unlikely), so few errors occur in this task and the major variable of interest is response time. The substantive question of interest in this experiment is how the subject accesses items in short-term memory (that limited-capacity memory system holding information we are immediately aware of) to make the yes/no decision. Two questions are relevant to asking how a subject searches short-term memory. First, does it take longer to decide an item is in short-term memory if there are more items to choose from (that is, when the memory set size is increased)? And second, if reaction times do increase with memory set size, does the way they increase tell us anything about how the subject searches his or her memory? The answer to both of these questions is "Yes." The larger the memory set, the longer it takes the subject to make both positive and negative decisions. Furthermore, positive and negative reaction times increase linearly, and at the same rate, with memory set size. This second result provides us with a way of determining how the subject searches short-term memory.

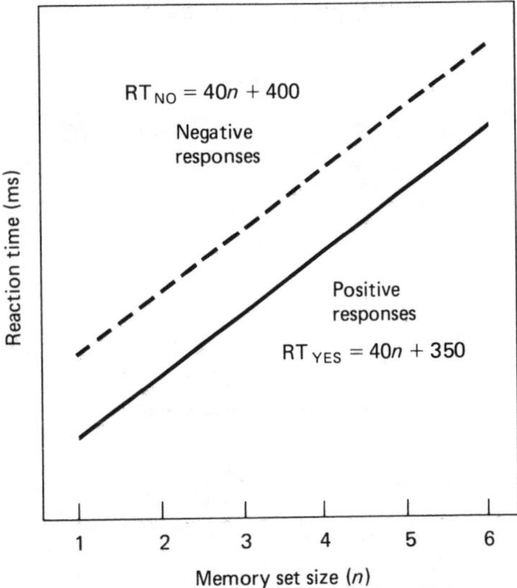

Fig. 5-1 Hypothetical data from a memory-scanning experiment.

Figure 5-1 shows some hypothetical data from an experiment in which memory set size was varied from one to six items, positive and negative items were presented equally often, and the RT functions for positive and negative responses are plotted as a function of memory set size. The positive and negative responses are indicated by different lines, and memory set size increases along the abscissa. The equations of the best-fitting straight lines (using the linear regression techniques described in Chapter 15) are shown on the graph.

Before we reveal the secret of how we can discover the subject's search strategy by the way his or her reaction times increase with memory set size, let us consider some possible strategies subjects might use in this task. First, to determine that a stimulus probe item *is* a member of the positive set, the subject need only find the item in the memory set that matches the probe. Logically, subjects could terminate their search as soon as they had located the positive item in the set, so we call the positive decision a logically self-terminating one. As an analogy, imagine looking for a book of matches in your purse or pocket. Once you find the matches, you could terminate the search.

Consider, however, the problem of determining that a probe item *is not* a member of the positive set. In order to do this, the subject needs to search through the entire set of items in memory in order to verify that the item is not there. The analogy to a missing book of matches in purse or pocket should be clear. Logically, the negative decision is exhaustive in that all items must be checked before deciding the probe is not among the set. With this in mind, let us consider some possible strategies that might be used in this task, and what they predict about the relationship between RT and set size. These are shown symbolically in Figure 5-2.

Parallel Self-Terminating Search. In parallel self-terminating search, subjects search the items in their short-term memory by considering all of them simultaneously, and terminating the search once

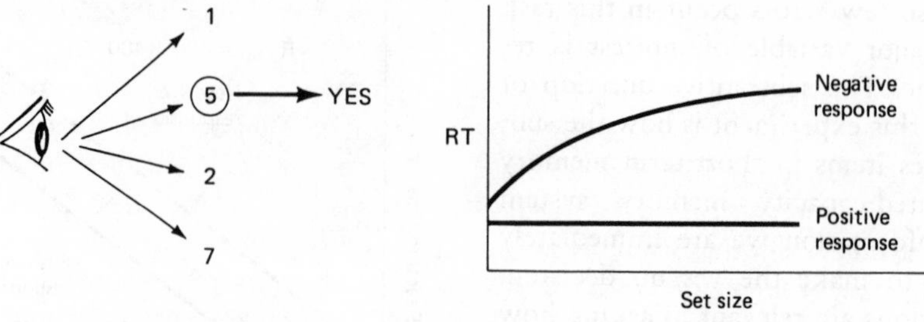

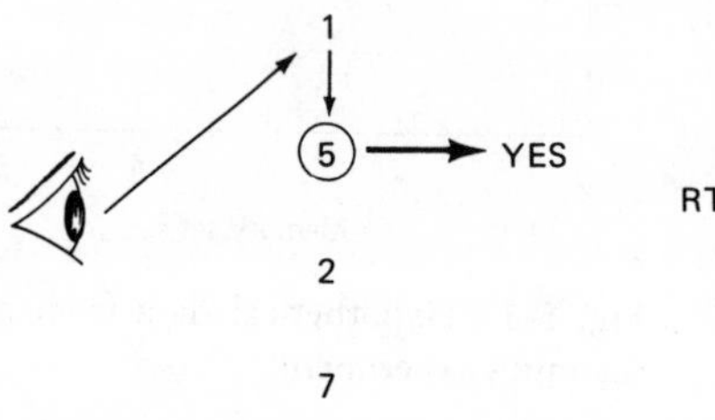

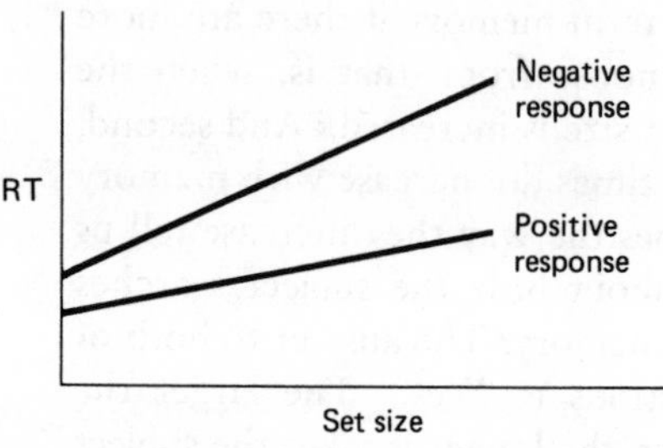

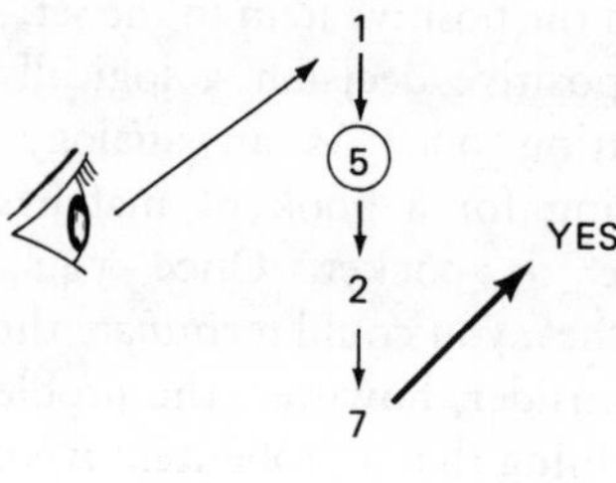

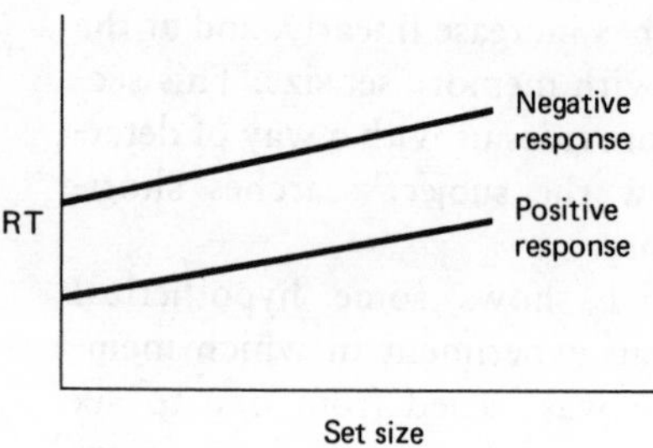

Fig. 5-2 Some possible strategies, and their predicted RT functions, for the memory-scanning task. The memory set consists of the four items (1,5,2,7), and on the trial illustrated, the probe is 5 so a positive response is correct.

the probe item is found. This process is illustrated in Figure 5-2A by the arrows from the mental eye pointing to each member of the entire set simultaneously. If subjects could do this with no loss of efficiency as memory set size increases, then YES responses should be unaffected by how many items are in the positive set. Thus, the function relating positive responses to memory set size should be flat, as shown in the graph to the right.

For negative decisions, the situation is somewhat different. Even though subjects can access all items simultaneously, if there is some variability in access times across items *and* if they need to wait until all have been accessed before they can decide NO (the logically exhaustive criterion for negative decisions), then the more items there are, the longer it should take for NO responses.

If this is not clear, think of a horse race in which we vary the number of horses running in the race. The number of horses corresponds to memory set size. You, the observer, are seated at the finish line and can only tell a particular horse ran the race by whether or not the horse crosses the finish line. A positive decision that a particular horse was in the race can be made whenever that horse crosses the finish line, and that horse's speed will be unaffected by how many other horses are running in the race (disregarding all the obvious limiting physical and psychological factors). On the other hand, a negative decision can only be made when the *slowest* horse has crossed the finish line. The more horses there are in the race, the slower the slowest one will be, on the average. Another example is illustrated by the problem of collecting a group of people for a committee meeting or for dinner at a restaurant. The larger the group of people who must assemble together before the event can begin, the longer it takes for the last person to arrive. Both of these are examples of the general rule that the larger the sample, the more likely it is, on purely statistical grounds, to have a very large or small value in that sample.

Although the way in which the largest or maximum value in a distribution increases with n depends on the theoretical distribution assumed (see Gumbel, 1958), the value of the maximum generally increased more slowly than n. Thus, the parallel self-terminating search model predicts that negative responses will increase with set size, but at a negatively accelerated rate, as shown in the negative response function of Figure 5-2A. Because we observe a very different pattern of experimental results, we will have to conclude that this *parallel self-terminating model* is not a good description of a subject's strategy in this task. (Here we consider only a simple parallel model for this task. There are more complex parallel models that give other patterns of results, but their discussion lies beyond the scope of this chapter. These models are discussed in Snodgrass & Townsend, 1980.)

Serial Self-Terminating Search. A second possibility is that subjects search the items in their short-term memory by considering the items one by one. This is known as *serial processing* or *serial search.* Suppose that they follow a self-terminating rule and on positive trials search through the list of memory items until they find the one that matches the probe. On some trials, the matching item will be found immediately, with the first comparison; on other trials, it will be found with the second comparison; and on still others, it will be found on the last comparison. On the average, subjects will need to search through $(n + 1)/2$ items to find the matching item on positive trials. So for a memory set of three, they will need to search through an average of two, for a memory set size of five, they will need to search through an average of three, and so on.

The way this works is as follows: Imagine there are three items in memory, and the subject searches them in the order they were presented on a trial. Because items are probed across serial positions an equal number of times, on one third of the trials, the target will be found with the first comparison; on one third of the trials the target will be found with the second comparison; and on one third of the trials the target will be found with the third comparison. The average number of comparisons needed for a memory set size of three is $(1 + 2 + 3)/3$, or an average of two. In general, the average number of comparisons that need to be carried out for a memory set size of n is given by summing the digits $1 \ldots n$ and dividing by n. This formula can be simplified to the form $(n + 1)/2$ given above.

On negative trials, on the other hand, the subject will need to search through all the memory list items before concluding that the probe item is not a member of the positive set. Therefore, the subject always needs to search through n items before deciding the item was not there. The combination of these two strategies—a terminating rule on positive trials and an exhaustive rule on negative trials—is called a *serial self-terminating search.*

The crucial prediction for this type of search is that the time for positive responses will increase at a *slower* rate than the time for negative responses as memory set size is increased. Increasing the memory set size by two items, from three to five, will only increase the average number of items searched by one (from two to three) for positive trials, but will increase the number of items searched by two (from three to five) for negative trials. In fact, the slope of the positive response function should be half the slope of the negative response function, as shown in Figure 5-2B. Because the experimental RT functions do not show this pattern, we also reject the serial self-terminating strategy as a reasonable description of what subjects do in this experiment.

Serial Exhaustive Search. A third possibility, which is consistent with the pattern of empirical results, is that on both positive and negative trials subjects search through the entire list of items. This is termed *serial exhaustive search* because on positive trials, the subject exhaustively examines all items in the set, even though an exhaustive search is not logically required. In serial exhaustive search, increasing the number of items in the memory set will have exactly the same effects on both positive and negative reaction times (RTs), so the two RT functions will be parallel, as shown in Figure 5-2C. This is consistent with the pattern of observed data, so we conclude the subject must be using the serial exhaustive search strategy for this task.

Later we consider why subjects might adopt the strategy of serial exhaustive search, which, on the surface, appears to be inefficient. However, for now, let us introduce the stages that Sternberg has inferred must exist in this task (Sternberg, 1966, 1969a, 1969b, 1975). These are shown in Figure 5-3.

Figure 5-3 shows the four stages that are hypothesized to intervene between the presentation of the stimulus (probe item) and the recording of the response (key press). Stage 1 is *stimulus encoding,* by which is meant the process of perceiving the stimulus and representing it in some way so that it can be compared with the items in memory. The nature of this representation is unclear, although it is probably not in an acoustic or articulatory form. Stage 2 is *serial comparison* of the encoded representation of the probe with the items in memory. As noted previously, this is assumed to be a serial exhaustive search, so the number of comparisons for both positive and negative probes is identical and equal to *n.* Stage 3 is *binary decision*—the decision about whether or not the probe was in the memory set. This decision is fed to Stage 4, which is *response organization and execution.*

It should be noted that these stages themselves are serial and additive, in that one stage does not begin until the previous one has finished. Also, no stages are ever experimentally deleted in the additive factors method. Rather, variables are manipulated which are assumed to selectively affect one or more stages.

Let us now try to interpret the data graphed in Figure 5-1 in terms of the stages shown in Figure 5-3. First, note that for this hypothetical experiment, there were only two independent variables: (1) the number of items in the memory set, which varies from one to six, and (2) whether the probe was a member of the positive set or not, which occurred with equal probability.

Disregarding for the moment the distinction between positive and negative responses, the increase in RT with set size is assumed to occur entirely in stage 2, the serial comparison stage. As the number of items is varied from one to six, the number of serial comparisons that are required increases from one to six. Therefore, it is

Fig. 5-3 The four stages proposed by Sternberg for the memory-scanning task.

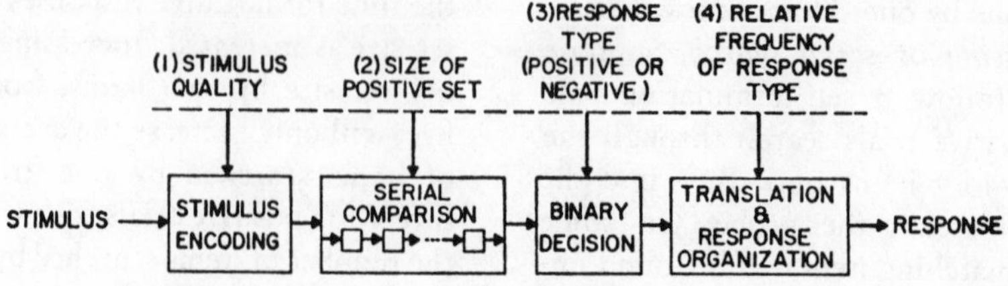

possible to use the *slopes* of the RT functions to estimate the time for each serial comparison (recall that the slope of a straight line represents the increase in the *Y* variable, or RT, for each unit increase in the *X* variable, or set size). For the data in Figure 5-1, we conclude that the time it takes to compare the encoded version of the probe to a single item in memory takes approximately 40 ms, because the slopes for both RT functions are 40 ms. Stated another way, the number of comparisons that can be made in a second is equal to 1000/40 or 25.

This is an extremely rapid rate of search, and its very rapidity gives us clues to two puzzles that we were unable to resolve earlier in the chapter: (1) why should the search be exhaustive and (2) what is the form of the encoded probe? The search is apparently exhaustive because the comparison process itself is so fast that it is more efficient to complete the search through all the items and then determine whether the probe item has matched any of the items than to stop after each comparison and make a decision. That is, taking the time to decide whether or not the probe matches each item may take much longer than making the comparison on which the decision is based (see Sternberg, 1975).

Before leaving the topic of the exhaustiveness of the short-term memory search, we point out here that evidence for serial exhaustive search is not universally found in all search tasks. For example, Egeth, Jonides, and Wall (1972) and Neisser (1963; Neisser, Novick, & Lazar, 1963) found evidence for parallel search through visual displays, Atkinson and Juola (1973) found evidence for serial self-terminating search through long-term memory, and Theios, Smith, Haviland, Traupmann, and Moy (1973) have argued in favor of a serial self-terminating model for memory scanning. Schneider and Shiffrin (1977) and Fisk and Schneider (1983) have shown that extensive practice with memory scanning when the positive and negative items remain constant produces parallel search through both memory and visual display sets. In contrast, they found that changing the assignment of items to positive and negative sets produces serial self-terminating search regardless of practice.

The second puzzle, how the probe is encoded, is also clarified somewhat by the rate of comparison. We are fairly sure the form of encoding is not acoustic or articulatory (e.g., pronouncing each member of the memory set to yourself to see whether it matches the probe) because we know from other studies that it takes much longer than the scan rate of 40 ms to subvocalize well-learned sequences, such as the letters of the alphabet. Landauer (1962) found that subvocalization rates were about 170–200 ms per item for these tasks. Accordingly, the form of encoding must be different from implicit speech, although whether it is a visual image or some more abstract form is not known.

What can we say about the intercept of the RT functions in Figure 5-1? Recall that the intercept of a linear function is that value of *Y* when *X* is zero. Thus, for the RT functions in Figure 5-1, the intercept corresponds to the RT when the set size is zero—that is, when there are *zero* items in memory to be searched. We cannot observe the intercept RT-value empirically—that is, we cannot include a condition in the experiment in which the subject never searches memory. Rather, we infer the value of the zero-intercept statistically. In the memory scanning paradigm, the intercept of the RT function must represent the sum of the times of stage 1, stage 3, and stage 4, since it theoretically represents a case in which there are zero serial comparisons to be made (no stage 2). Now we consider the fact that the intercepts of the positive and negative functions are not the same but differ by 50 ms. (This advantage of positive over negative reaction times when their probabilities are the same is a pervasive finding, although the size of the difference is not as constant as the size of the slope.) This difference between the intercept of positive and negative responses is attributed by Sternberg to the binary decision process of stage 3; it takes longer to decide in favor of a negative than a positive decision.

Factors That Affect Other Stages in Memory Scanning

So far, we have considered the effects of memory set size and type of response (positive versus negative) on two of the four stages. Here we consider the effects of two additional variables—stimulus probe degradation and response probability—on the remaining two stages of stimulus encoding (stage 1), and response organization and execution (stage 4). By *stimulus probe degradation* we simply mean some manipulation that makes the probe more difficult to see.

We might expect that stimulus degradation would affect the stage of stimulus encoding by making it longer. We might also wonder whether it would affect the second stage, stimulus comparison or search as well. Sternberg (1967) compared reaction times for intact visual probes with degraded probes, in which the degradation was accomplished by superimposing a checkerboard pattern on the probe. He found that after some practice, subjects showed a higher intercept for both positive and negative responses for a degraded than for an intact probe (the average difference was about 65 ms), but no change in slope. He interpreted this as meaning that the degradation affected only stage 1 (stimulus encoding) but not stage 2 (comparison). He reasoned that if the comparison process had been slowed by the degradation of the probe, then the slopes of the RT functions would have increased. It is interesting that degrading the visual quality of the probe did not increase the comparison times. This suggests that if comparisons of visual images underlie the serial comparison stage, the encoded version of the probe must be processed to make it equivalent to a nondegraded probe.

We expect response probability to affect the last stage, that of response organization and execution. Many RT experiments show that when response probability in a choice reaction time situation is varied by varying stimulus probability, the more probable response is executed faster and the less probable response is executed more slowly. Sternberg (1969a) manipulated the presentation probability of positive probes (and hence the complementary presentation probability of negative probes) from .25 to .75. He found that presentation probability affected only the intercept of the RT functions, and not their slopes, with the more probable response having a lower intercept (overall faster times regardless of memory set size), and the less probable response having a higher intercept (overall slower RTs regardless of memory set size). This effect is located by Sternberg in stage 4 because response probability does not interact with response type (YES versus NO), and the lack of an interaction between two variables when they are applied together is used as an indication that these two variables do not affect the same stage.

In summary, Sternberg's additive factors method is a type of subtraction method. Here, however, rather than deleting whole stages, variables are manipulated so that differences in RT between different levels of the same independent variable are used as measures of the duration of substages of the major stages. Thus, we use the subtraction method in additive factors to measure substage duration, rather than stage duration.

POSNER'S SAME/DIFFERENT CLASSIFICATION TASK

Michael Posner and his colleagues have used a same/different classification task to isolate and measure components of comparison times. In the Posner paradigm, subjects are asked to classify pairs of stimuli as SAME or DIFFERENT on the basis of some criterion. The classification criteria may vary in abstractness from physical identity, to name identity, to the most abstract level of category or rule identity. As abstractness increases, so do the number of stimuli that are to be considered identical. Posner's method allows us to study the classification problem under experimentally rigorous conditions by using stimuli that are simple and well-learned, yet can be classified by a variety of criteria.

The Letter-Matching Task

The basic paradigm is a letter-matching task, in which the subject is presented with a pair of identical or similar stimuli, such as letters of the alphabet, and is required to judge as quickly as possible whether the pair is the same or different. The basic data are the reaction times required to carry out the task.

In a typical letter-matching task (Posner, 1969; Posner & Keele, 1968), a name-identity criterion is used to classify letters as same. Two letters are shown either simultaneously or successively. The letters may be physically identical (AA, aa), have the same name but different physical forms (Aa, aA), or be different (AB, ab). The subject's task is to classify all the letters with the same name as same and those with different names as different. Thus, both physically identical and name-identical pairs are to be classified as SAME. Figure 5-4 illustrates the name-identical criterion for same judgments under simultaneous and successive presentation conditions.

Well-practiced subjects responding to simultaneously presented letter pairs show a 70- to 100-ms advantage in matching physically identical over name-identical pairs. This result is taken as evidence that subjects match physically identical stimuli on the basis of visual rather than name characteristics even for such familiar stimuli as letters of the alphabet.

Posner (1969) points to other lines of converging evidence for this conclusion. These include the fact that letter-like stimuli without names are matched as fast as physically identical letters and that inverted letters are matched as quickly as upright letters as long as the inverted letters are close to one another in the visual field. The difference in time between physical and name matches also suggests that it takes between 70 and 100 ms to convert a pair of letters into a name code (or alternatively, to convert one of the letters into the opposite case).

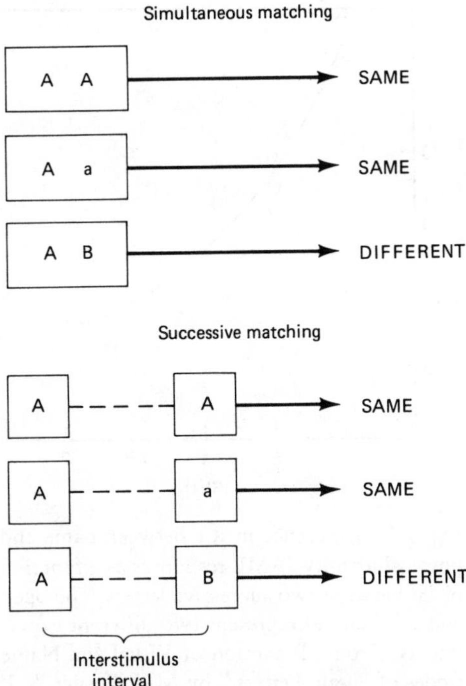

Fig. 5-4 Examples of simultaneous and successive matching in a Posner task with a name-identical criterion.

Another line of converging evidence for the visual basis of physical matches comes from results of experiments studying successive matching (Posner, Boies, Eichelman, & Taylor, 1969). What happens to the advantage of physical matching when there is an interval between the first and second letter in a pair, so that the matching decision must be based on memory for the first letter? Is that memory based on the visual appearance of the first letter or on its name? Figure 5-5 summarizes the results from two experiments in Posner et al. (1969) by plotting differences in matching-time between physically identical and name-identical letter pairs as a function of the interstimulus interval. Time differences rather than absolute times are shown because the absolute times vary widely between the two experiments because of differences in viewing conditions. The zero condition represents the simultaneous presentation condition, and results in about a 90 ms advantage of physically identical over name-identical pairs. However, as the

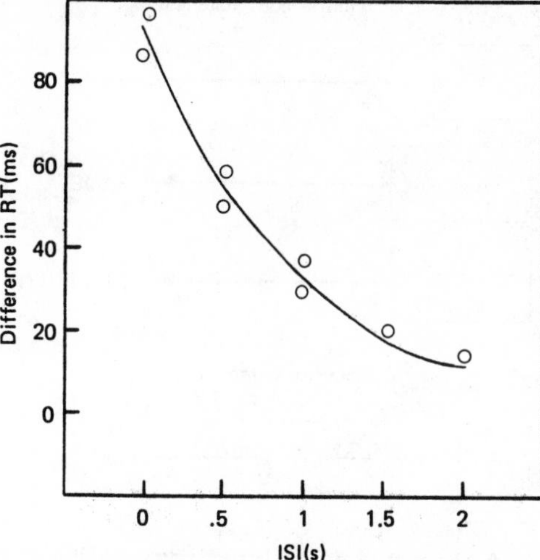

Fig. 5-5 Difference in RT between name and physical identity SAME responses as a function of *ISI* between two successive letters. The open and solid circles represent two different experiments. (From "Retention of Visual and Name Codes of Single Letters," by M. I. Posner, S. J. Boies, W. H. Eichelman, and R. L. Taylor. In *Journal of Experimental Psychology,* 1969, *79* (Monograph Suppl. 1), 1–16. Copyright 1969 by the American Psychological Association. Reprinted by permission.)

interstimulus interval increases, the advantage gradually disappears and is completely absent after an interval of about 2 seconds.

This suggests that subjects after that interval are matching letters on the basis of their names, since a match like AA is made no faster than a match like Aa. Thus, the duration of an efficient visual code for matching appears to be short. Other experiments by Posner and his colleagues have shown that the visual memory code is affected by other attentional demands, since interpolation of a cognitive activity such as addition interferes with the visual matching process but not with the name matching process (Posner, 1969).

Posner and Mitchell (1967) extended the letter-matching paradigm to a matching task involving category (or rule) identity. Subjects were presented with pairs of letters presented simultaneously and asked to classify them as same if they were both vowels or both consonants and as different otherwise. Pairs of same letters could also have the same name or could be physically identical. In this task, letters that were physically identical retained their advantage over those with the same name, but same name pairs were matched faster than those with the same rule of classification (i.e., letters that were both vowels or both consonants).

The times for the four types of same judgments are shown in Figure 5-6, along with the times for different responses. Physical identity matches are about 70 ms faster than name identity matches, which in turn are about 80 ms faster than vowel matches. However, vowel matches are more than 200 ms faster than consonant matches. The difficulty subjects have in deciding whether two letters are both consonants presumably is because there are many more consonants than vowels. In fact, Posner and Mitchell present evidence that the consonant match decisions were

Fig. 5-6 Hypothetical series of stages in Posner and Mitchell's study in which subjects classified letter pairs as same category (both vowels or both consonants) or different category (one of each). Numbers represent time in milliseconds. Node 1 refers to physically identical pairs (AA); node 2 to name identical pairs (Aa), and node 3 to category identical pairs (Ae for vowels and BD for consonants). (From "Chronometric Analysis of Classification," by M. I. Posner and R. F. Mitchell. In *Psychological Review,* 1967, *74,* 393–409. Copyright 1967 by the American Psychological Association. Adapted by permission.)

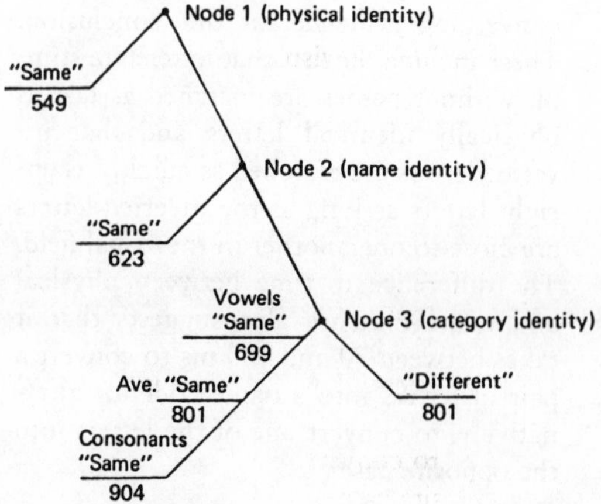

made by exclusion—that is, by checking that neither letter was a vowel.

One way of interpreting the results presented in Figure 5-6 is by assuming that subjects must proceed through all the processing "nodes" in serial order to make the most complex decision. Thus, to decide that B and D are both consonants, a subject checks the physical identity node (node 1), next the name identity node (node 2), next the vowel identity node (node 3), and finally the consonant identity node. If the processing is serial, differences between times for complex decisions and those for simpler decisions reflect times of the interpolated processes. Posner and Mitchell (1967) acknowledge that processes other than serial ones can be invoked to account for their results. Nonetheless, their simple and elegant experiments provide a clear example of another application of the subtraction method in mental chronometry.

Although the use of reaction time to measure the duration of mental events still has a long way to go, the introduction of the additive factors and classification methodologies into the arsenal of the cognitive psychologist has brought the ultimate goal of unraveling mental processes much closer.

METHODOLOGICAL ISSUES IN REACTION TIME

There are a number of methodological issues in the use of reaction time as a dependent variable. Here we survey some of them.

What Is the Minimum Reaction Time?

RT investigators generally assume that there is some minimum RT in simple and choice tasks below which subjects cannot respond. For simple reaction time, this represents the minimum time for stimulus input, decision, and motor response time and has been termed the *irreducible minimum reaction time.* Estimates of this time vary with conditions and subjects, but for auditory stimuli, which produce faster reaction times than visual stimuli, the irreducible minimum is generally estimated to be between 90 and 100 ms. (Snodgrass, 1969; Woodworth, 1938).* Reaction times shorter than the irreducible minimum are called *anticipations.* These may occur if the subject knows with some certainty when the reaction stimulus will occur. Usually, subjects are warned about the presentation of a stimulus by a warning signal that occurs some time before the reaction stimulus.

The first stimulus, the *warning signal,* indicates to the subject that the second stimulus, the *reaction signal,* will occur after some time interval. This time interval is known as the *foreperiod,* and may be fixed in duration or may vary randomly from trial to trial. When the foreperiod is fixed, the subject very quickly comes to know its value. For fixed foreperiods, the optimum duration is between 1 and 2 seconds (Karlin, 1959; Woodrow, 1914). Shorter foreperiods do not permit the subject to prepare sufficiently, and longer ones are too long for subjects to maintain optimum readiness. However, a disadvantage of fixed foreperiods is the large temptation for the subject to anticipate the signal and try to respond just after the signal. Although there are experimental methods for controlling anticipations (Snodgrass, 1969; Snodgrass, Luce, & Galanter, 1967), these are quite time-consuming, so most investigators solve the problem of anticipations by discarding those RTs that are shorter than the irreducible minimum. This minimum is usually taken to be about 100 ms for simple reaction time experiments.

The anticipation problem is less critical for choice reaction time, because subjects cannot respond correctly with more than chance performance until the stimulus has been identified. Thus, investigators who use choice reaction time do not usually need to discard very short RTs.

*In New York City, the irreducible minimum RT to a light stimulus may be defined as the time between a traffic light's turning green and the honk of the taxicab behind you. However, this particular situation has not been investigated in detail.

The Problem of Very Long RTs (Outliers)

The problem of long RTs, or *outliers,* is characteristic of both simple and choice RTs. Very short RTs (or anticipations) are also outliers, but long outliers are more of a problem because they can affect the mean RT more than spuriously short RTs. Furthermore, there are reasons for expecting subjects to produce occasional long RTs. Often subjects report that on that particular trial their attention wandered or they momentarily forgot which key to press for their response. This resulted in a long RT that was outside the normal range.

Accordingly, investigators adopt one of three strategies for dealing with outliers: (a) throw out or (b) replace those that are unreasonably long (we will come back in a moment to the definition of "unreasonable"), or (c) use a measure of central tendency that is less sensitive to outlying observations than the arithmetic mean, such as the median.

When discarding or replacing outliers, investigators may use either a relative criterion, so that an outlier is defined for each subject with respect to the other RT values in that subject's distribution, or an absolute criterion, so that an outlier is defined as any response greater than *k* ms. The value of *k* may be as low as 500 ms for simple reaction time or as high as 3000 ms for choice reaction time.

A commonly used relative criterion is to discard any response that lies more than three standard deviations from that subject's mean for that condition. This criterion is based on a model for RT that assumes RT values are normally distributed. Another widely used criterion is the Dixon test, which is a statistical method for determining the likelihood that a suspected outlier comes from another distribution of RTs. In the Dixon test, we compute the difference between the suspected outlier and the next largest observation, and compare that difference with the entire range of RTs. The Dixon test is described more fully in Chapter 15 on descriptive statistics. Discarding observations from a distribution is known as *trimming*. An alternative to discarding outliers is to replace them with the next largest or smallest value. This procedure is known as *Winsorizing* and it, too, is described in Chapter 15.

The most commonly used alternative measures of central tendency are the median and the geometric mean. The median or 50th percentile is the middle value of a distribution of RTs, and as such is completely insensitive to extreme observations. For example, the median for the set of observations 140, 150, 160, 170, 180 is the same—160—as the median for the set of observations 140, 150, 160, 170, 400. The median is insensitive to the replacement of the value of 180 in the first set by the value of 400 in the second set; in contrast the arithmetic mean is very sensitive to the outlier, being 160 for the first set and 204 for the second.

The geometric mean is the *n*th root of the product of *n* scores. It, like the median, has the property that it is insensitive to extremely long scores. For example, the geometric mean of the series 10, 100, 1000 is 100, while the arithmetic mean is 370. Using the geometric mean as a measure of central tendency is the same as using a logarithmic transformation on the data and then computing the arithmetic mean on the logarithmic transforms. So, for example, the logs to the base 10 of the series 10, 100, 1000 are 1, 2, and 3, and the arithmetic mean of the log transforms, 2, represents the log of the geometric mean. The usual way to calculate a geometric mean is to convert each score into its logarithm, compute the arithmetic mean of the logarithms of the scores, and then find the antilogarithm of that mean.

The use of medians or geometric means is not appropriate when an experimenter is interested in testing an additive type of model, such as Sternberg's, for RT data. The reason these transformations are not appropriate is that the stages that are hypothesized to underly the total RT are additive, and these transformations do not preserve their additivity.

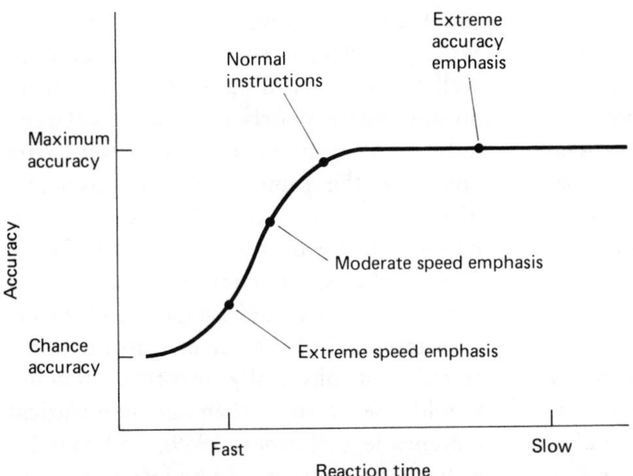

Fig. 5-7 An idealized speed-accuracy trade-off function.

Error Rates and the Speed-Accuracy Trade-Off Function

When RTs are used as the dependent variable, subjects are usually instructed to respond as quickly as possible, consistent with an extremely low (ideally 0%) error rate. Thus, the average RT should represent an ideal performance for that subject for that condition.

However, subjects do make errors. In simple RT experiments, these errors may be anticipations, extremely slow RTs, or omissions. In choice RT experiments, an additional source of error is a response of type B to stimulus A or a response of type A to stimulus B. Regardless of how well practiced subjects are on a choice RT task, there are invariably some small percentage of trials (1 to 2% in the best cases) on which subjects respond to a stimulus with the wrong response. Subjects often explain their errors by saying something like, "I wasn't paying attention on that trial—my mind wandered" or "I forgot momentarily that the right hand response was the correct one." Most investigators merely omit the error RTs from the analysis and report the error rates along with the correct average RTs.

However, it is clear that subjects are capable of manipulating their speed of response by manipulating how many errors they make. For example, if they take a long time to respond, they can approach perfect performance. On the other hand, if they respond too quickly to fully process the stimulus, they can produce very fast RTs but at the cost of lower accuracy. The relationship between RT and accuracy (with increases in RT leading to increases in accuracy) is called the *speed-accuracy trade-off function,* and an idealized one is presented in Figure 5-7.

Here, accuracy of performance is plotted along the ordinate (*y*-axis) against average RT along the abscissa (*x*-axis). If subjects are encouraged to produce very fast RTs (with instructions emphasizing extreme speed), they will also produce low accuracy or a large percentage of errors. If they are given normal instructions, their RTs will increase along with their accuracy. Subjects may differ on where they place themselves along the speed-accuracy operating function, depending on how they interpret the instructions, their own personal biases about which is more important—speed or accuracy—and so on. We might use as an analogy taking a timed achievement test. Some people will race through such tests, preferring to answer all the questions quickly at the expense of some accuracy. Others will take their time and may not answer all questions but will be more accurate on the questions they do answer.

Some investigators (e.g., Pachella, 1974) study the form of the speed-accuracy trade-off function explicitly, by keeping the experimental situation constant and varying payoffs to selectively reward accuracy at the expense of speed (so that subjects adopt a conservative criterion), or to reward speed at the expense of accuracy (so that subjects adopt a liberal criterion). More usually, however, investigators who are interested in the effect of one or more independent variables on RT adopt a standard set of instructions that they hope will produce similar criteria for speed versus accuracy across subjects and conditions.

Thus, most investigators do not worry about the form of the speed-accuracy trade-off function as long as the results from their conditions do not show such a trade-off. When experimenters compare RTs across a number of different conditions, some conditions are usually hypothesized to be more difficult in that they require more processing steps or more complex processing than other conditions. As long as error rates are positively correlated with RT, so that low error rates accompany fast RTs and high error rates accompany slow RTs, the investigator may feel fairly confident that the pattern of RTs cannot be accounted for by a speed-accuracy trade-off. On the other hand, if error rates are negatively correlated with RT, then a speed-accuracy trade-off is a possible alternative explanation to the investigator's preferred hypothesis.

Table 5-2 shows RT and error results from an experiment in which the pattern of RT results *cannot* be explained by speed-accuracy trade-off, and Table 5-3 shows a pattern that *can* be explained by speed-accuracy trade-off.

Both experiments show hypothetical results from a same-different RT experiment in which subjects were presented with letter pairs selected either from a familiar, well-learned class (English letters) or from an unfamiliar, poorly learned class (Greek letters). Within each class, letter pairs could be the same by being physically identical—capital A's (AA) and capital gammas (ΓΓ)—or could be the same by having the same name—a capital and lower-case A (Aa) and a capital and lower-case gamma (Γγ). The investigator hypothesized that physically identical matches would be faster than name-identical matches (e.g., Posner, 1969), and that familiar letter pairs would be faster than unfamiliar letter pairs. (Note that subjects must be familiar enough with the unfamiliar class of Greek letters to know when the letters have the same names.)

Table 5-2 shows just the expected pattern of results: familiar physical matches are faster than unfamiliar physical matches, and unfamiliar name matches are longest of all. The rates of error responses (calling a same pair DIFFERENT) correlate positively with RT in the sense that fast RTs are accompanied by low error rates and slow RTs are accompanied by high error rates, so the RT results cannot be the result of a speed-accuracy trade-off.

Table 5-3 shows the same RT data, but now error rates correlate negatively with RT—fast RTs are accompanied by high error rates and slow RTs are accompanied by low error rates. This pattern of RTs could be explained by a speed-accuracy trade-off. In this particular case, it would be explained by assuming that in the hypothetically "easy" conditions, subjects

Table 5-2 Correct RTs and Error Rates for Familiar and Unfamiliar Letter Pairs in a Same/Different RT Experiment for which no Speed-Accuracy Trade-Off Is Obtained (Only Same RTs Are Shown)

	Mean RT	Error %
Familiar letters (English)		
Physically identical (AA, aa)	400	2
Name identical (Aa, aA)	550	5
Unfamiliar letters (Greek)		
Physically identical (ΓΓ, γγ)	500	3
Name identical (Γγ, γΓ)	700	10

Table 5-3 Correct RTs and Error Rates for Familiar and Unfamiliar Letter Pairs in a Same/Different RT Experiment for which a Speed-Accuracy Trade-Off *Is* Obtained

	Mean RT	Error %
Familiar letters (English)		
Physically identical (AA, aa)	400	10
Name identical (Aa, aA)	550	3
Unfamiliar letters (Greek)		
Physically identical (ΓΓ, γγ)	500	5
Name identical (Γγ, γΓ)	700	2

had a bias toward responding as quickly as possible, thereby producing both fast RTs and high error rates, whereas the opposite occurred for the hypothetically "difficult" conditions. On the basis of Table 5-3, it is impossible to reject the notion that the RTs are really the same across the "easy" and "difficult" conditions, or even that the RTs might run in the opposite direction if error rates were kept constant across the conditions.

SUMMARY

Mental chronometry is the measurement of mental processes by the use of reaction time (RT). Donders pioneered the use of RT to measure mental processes with his subtraction method. However, various problems with Donders' method led to the ultimate rejection of his use of the subtraction method, in part because it involved changing the experimental task so that entire stages were omitted or added. Sternberg's additive factors method revived the subtraction method by manipulating variables that affect various hypothetical stages assumed to underlie the RT, without either adding or omitting stages. We have presented one widely used application of the additive factors method here, namely, its use in short-term memory scanning. By use of this method, Sternberg discovered (a) that scanning through short-term memory was serial and exhaustive, (b) that degradation of the stimulus probe affects the encoding stage but not the search stage of the process, and (c) that factors such as response probability affect only the last stage—response organization and execution—and not the binary decision stage.

Posner's experiments, which apply mental chronometry to classification of letters, showed that physical matching is faster than name matching, which in turn is faster than rule-based matching of vowels and consonants. There is evidence that the extraction of these three levels of information proceeds in a serial fashion, and thus that differences between the RTs for the three matching conditions is a measure of the time for such processing. The advantage of physical matching disappears when the two letters are separated by an interval of two seconds or longer, suggesting that the visual code that is the basis for matching at a physical level is of short duration.

A number of methodological issues in reaction time were discussed to illustrate the correct treatment of RT data. These include the issue of outlying observations, both those that are very short and thus may be produced by anticipating the reaction signal, and those that are very long and thus may be produced by a different process than that under study, such as inattention or response forgetting. Finally, the problem of speed-accuracy trade-offs in RT was discussed.

Reaction time as a method of measuring the speed of mental processes has become increasingly important in recent years and is the dependent variable of choice in many areas. It is important to understand the underlying logic in using reaction time to dissect the workings of the human mind and to be alert to possible confounding variables in reaction time research.

II

Content: Research Areas in Experimental Psychology

This section describes the content areas that have been explored through systematic, well-designed research. First we review how we perceive and attend to our internal and external environments (Chapter 6). The areas of conditioning, learning, and motivation are then reviewed (Chapter 7). In the context of this literature some research on nonhuman (animal) subjects, which provides the experimental roots for these areas, is described. Following this we explore episodic memory—memory for the storage and retrieval of specific autobiographical events (Chapter 8), and semantic memory—memory for the storage and retrieval of information, such as language, common to all members of the same cultural group (Chapter 9). Next, we explore the logical processes used to solve particular problems as well as various types of reasoning (Chapter 10). Finally, we discuss the application of the methodology of experimental psychology to research areas not typically studied by experimental psychologists (Chapter 11). These areas include social psychology, industrial organizations, clinical issues, and parapsychology.

Part II describes the significant research and conclusions that form the substance of human experimental psychology. Obtaining this knowledge of how human beings function is the purpose of our discipline. It must be recognized that the results of these research efforts are intimately tied to the methodology (Parts I and III), which has made all this knowledge possible. Therefore, we emphasize the fact that content and methodology are inextricably interdependent and intertwined.

6
Perception and Attention

It has been said that beauty is in the eye of the beholder. As a hypothesis about localization of function, the statement is not quite right—the brain and not the eye is surely the most important organ involved. Nevertheless it points clearly enough toward the central problem of cognition. Whether beautiful or ugly or just conveniently at hand, the world of experience is produced by the man who experiences it.

This is not the attitude of a skeptic, only of a psychologist. There certainly is a real world of trees and people and cars and even books, and it has a great deal to do with our experiences of these objects. However, we have no direct immediate access to the world, nor to any of its properties. The ancient theory of *eidola,* which supposed that faint copies of objects can enter the mind directly, must be rejected. Whatever we know about reality has been *mediated,* not only by the organs of sense but by complex systems which interpret and reinterpret sensory information. The activity of the cognitive systems results in—and is integrated with—the activity of muscles and glands that we call "behavior." It is also partially—very partially—reflected in those private experiences of seeing, hearing, imagining, and thinking to which verbal descriptions never do full justice.

(Neisser, 1967, p. 3)

Here, Ulrich Neisser, in his 1967 book which marked the beginning of the cognitive revolution in psychology, introduces the problem of perception as one of cognition. As we shall see, perception is an active, constructive process that draws on previous experience and present motivations, not a passive process that necessarily and innately mirrors reality.

This chapter will selectively cover two vast topics in experimental psychology: perception and attention. First, we will explain why the topic of attention is paired with that of perception, and then we will describe the criteria used to select the areas of perception covered in this chapter.

What is attention? We all know intuitively what attention and its opposite, inattention, are. We all know that when we attend to one thing, we find it difficult, if not impossible, to attend to something else. Attention might be described as a searchlight we direct from our conscious mind either outward, toward an event happening in our physical environment, or inward, toward an event happening in our mental environment. The beam of the searchlight might be narrowly focused, so that we are intensely aware of the event we attend to, or more diffuse, so that we can be peripherally aware of other events outside the main focus of attention.

The narrowness of focus of our attentional searchlight depends on both the difficulty of the task and our interest in it. If our attentional beam is focused outward toward a conversation with a colleague who is explaining his new mathematical theory of memory retrieval, our attention will be narrowly focused. This is because we need to concentrate on his every word to understand the theory. If, however, our attentional beam is focused on a conversation with a colleague who is describing his family's vacation in the American southwest, our attention can be more diffuse. During the first conversation, we are likely to be oblivious to the conversation at the next table about the fate of mortgage rates. During the second, we might well follow the neighboring conversation, even though we can maintain those outward manifestations of attentiveness, like orienting the body toward the speaker, maintaining eye contact with him, nodding in appropriate places, and emitting oohs and ahs as the wonders of the Grand Canyon are described.

We can also direct our attentional beam inward, toward out own thoughts and feelings. When we do this we are carrying out that mysterious process called thinking. The stream of thought could be about our own alternative to our friend's mathematical theory of memory retrieval, our new lover, or what we plan to serve at Saturday night's dinner party.

In one sense, the direction of attention can be thought of as voluntary. We can choose to attend to the mortgage rate conversation rather than to our friend's vacation conversation. Or a student in a classroom can choose to attend to the lecture, directing his or her attentional beam outward, or toward memories of last night's party, directing it inward. However, there are certain high-priority environmental events that command attention, which commandeer our attentional beam by their intensity, their unexpectedness, or their symbolic value as danger symbols. It is difficult to be oblivious to the ring of the phone or the doorbell, or to the threat of a mugger.

As we will see, human beings are limited creatures, incapable of being aware simultaneously of everything in their external and internal environment. Attention is the mechanism that lets us selectively sample elements of both. Thus, attention is important in perception, memory, thinking, and problem-solving. It is also important in social relationships, abnormal states of consciousness such as those produced by drugs and alcohol, and psychopathology (see Chapter 11). Despite its wide-ranging applicability to other areas of research, we will consider the topic of attention within the context of perception because the experimental paradigms used to study attention have focused almost exclusively on perceptual tasks—specifically, tasks of selectively attending to subsets of auditory or visual stimuli.

PERCEPTION

We perceive the external and internal environment through our sense modalities—through seeing, hearing, touch, taste, smell, kinesthesis (the awareness of the positions of our body parts)—as well as through sensations arising from within our own bodies. Modern-day sensory physiologists and psychologists have expanded the number of senses from the original five proposed by Aristotle, but there is little agreement on the necessary and sufficient criteria for defining what a separate sense is. Although this is an important and fascinating topic, it lies beyond the scope of this chapter. Here, we consider only visual and auditory perception, and within these two areas, only perception of specific types of materials.

Visual perception permits us to apprehend *objects* in our external environment, and auditory perception permits us to apprehend *events*—primarily those representing movement of objects. Undoubtedly the most important function of auditory perception in today's information society is speech perception, that remarkable ability people have to understand the sounds we call speech produced by air from the lungs rushing over the vocal cords interacting with positions and movements of parts of the mouth and tongue.

There is a large technical literature on speech perception and production (a very readable introduction is provided in Miller, 1981), which we will not cover here. We simply want to point out the importance of speech as a stimulus to the hearing sense. This is not to overlook the importance of hearing for apprehending the approach of another person by their footsteps, the approach of a car by the sound of its motor, or the pleasures of music. Our ancestors undoubtedly survived because of their sensitivity to the rustle of leaves and twigs that signaled the approach of predators. However, anecdotal evidence suggests that the vast majority of people seeking hearing aids do so because they have trouble hearing speech, particularly in a noisy environment, rather than because of a decrease in their enjoyment of music or the loss of variety in the cacophony of city traffic sounds.

Experimental psychologists make a distinction between the areas of sensation and perception. In the field of vision, sensation is concerned with attributes of objects in isolation, such as brightness and color, whereas perception is concerned with the objects themselves. When we look around us, we do not perceive gradations of lightness and darkness, blobs of color, and edges and corners; rather, we perceive an array of objects at particular locations. Yet, if we were to analyze the visual array on which our perceptions are based, we would find that it is composed of these qualities of objects; therefore, it must be from the qualities of the objects that we abstract the object itself.

During the last century, experimental psychologists studying visual perception believed that by studying such attributes of objects as brightness, color, line orientation, depth cues, and so on—in short, by studying the elements of perception—they could come to an understanding of perception itself. Today, we know a great deal about brightness and color discrimination, depth cues, orientation discrimination, and so on. Although these data constitute an important part of the subject matter of classic perception in vision (and corresponding data exist for the other senses), we will have little to say here about these sensory data because they tell us little about perception of the more complex types of verbal and visual stimuli we shall describe in this chapter.

Our treatment here follows the modern approach to perception called *information processing*. The information processing approach is based on the view that the human's primary goal is to process information—that our well-being, indeed our very existence, is based on our capacity to selectively attend to and process various kinds of information and to subsequently incorporate this new information into already existing information structures. Because information is generally delivered through the written and spoken word, and through still and moving pictures, research conducted from the information-processing approach concentrates on perception of written and spoken words and of still and moving pictures.

One issue pervades the discussion of perception: Does the perception of objects such as geometric forms, words, faces, and even scenes and sentences, proceed from parts to wholes or from wholes to parts? Early sensory psychologists believed the appropriate approach to perception was to study human sensitivities to parts or attributes of objects, because they believed that perception must be part-to-whole. How can you perceive a whole *without* first perceiving the parts? Their classic opponents in this view are the *Gestalt* psychologists. The Gestaltists believe that holistic perception precedes part perception, and they proposed laws of perception for figure-ground relationships and rules for how perceptual fields are organized. Current terminology for this issue is the distinction between *bottom-up processing* (part-to-whole) and *top-down processing* (whole-to-part).

Bottom-Up versus Top-Down Processing

The early proponents of the view that perception is part-to-whole (those who attempted to analyze perceptions into their component sensations) were the *structuralists,* and those who believed the whole was greater than its parts were the *Gestaltists. Gestalt* means "form" in German, and the Gestalt psychologists believed that the form is greater than the parts composing it. In fact, they believed that the whole was independent of its parts. They argued that there are intrinsic organizing principles in the perceptual field, in both vision and audition, which transcend the elements that make up the field.

To take a simple example, the form of a triangle may be represented by any of a number of elements, as shown in Figure 6-1. Even though the elements are different in each case—straight lines, dashes, and *a*s in the first three examples—people perceive each figure as a triangle. Example D shows a triangle outlined by *subjective contours.* The sides of the triangle are not outlined by any elements at all, yet we perceive a white triangle. A similar effect occurs in auditory perception. A melody will sound the same when it is transposed into another key, even though the elements that produce the melody have all changed.

The Gestalt psychologists proposed various laws of organization that determine how we perceive coherent form. These laws were considered to be innately determined. Perhaps the most basic organizing principle is that of figure versus ground. In both visual and auditory perception, a segregated segment of the field becomes the figure, and the remainder becomes the ground. It is possible to devise "ambiguous" figures, such as the famous faces–vase or grandmother–daughter-in-law reversi-

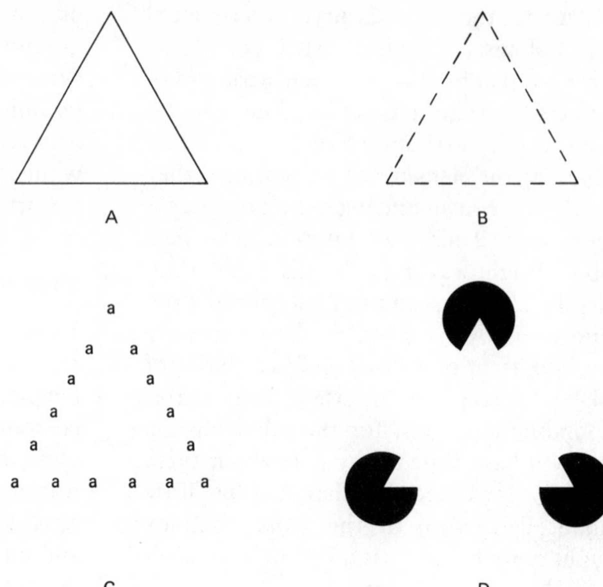

Fig. 6-1 Examples of triangles which are composed of different elements. Example D illustrates subjective contours.

ble figures found in most introductory psychology textbooks. When the observer sees one version of the figure, it is impossible to see the other; the unseen version becomes the ground of the figure.

Figure 6-2 shows two examples of figure-ground reversal from the work of M. C. Escher. In "Fish and Fowl," either the swimming fish or the flying fowls can be seen as figure. In "Sky and Water," the transition from figure to ground for the flying ducks is gradual—the ducks at the top are seen as figure, whereas those on the bottom are seen as ground. M. L. Teuber (1974) has argued that Escher was profoundly influenced by the work of Gestalt psychologists when he investigated figure-ground reversals in his art.

Two other visual organizing principles proposed by the Gestalt psychologists are the principles of *contiguity* and *similarity.* Elements close to one another are organized as segregated forms (contiguity), and elements having similar forms or colors are organized as segregated forms (similarity). Two simple examples of these principles are shown in Figure 6-3. The principle of contiguity causes the collection of small open dots on the left to be seen as three large circles instead of an unorganized group of 17 dots. The principle of similarity of color causes the black and open dots on the right to be seen organized by rows rather than by columns.

This early controversy between the Gestalt psychologists and the structuralists illustrates the difference between top-down and bottom-up processing. We next turn to a more current topic, word perception, in the bottom-up versus top-down processing controversy. The question is whether we read by perceiving whole words rather than their component letters (a top-down strategy) or whether word perception proceeds from the letter to the whole word level (a bottom-up strategy).

VISUAL WORD PERCEPTION

A basic experimental procedure in the study of visual word perception is based on the use of the tachistoscope [or more recently, a cathode ray tube (CRT) connected to an on-line computer], which permits careful control of the duration and intensity of the stimulus being presented. We will begin with a brief history of the use of the tachistoscope to study the issue of whole versus part perception in general, and whole word versus letter-by-letter per-

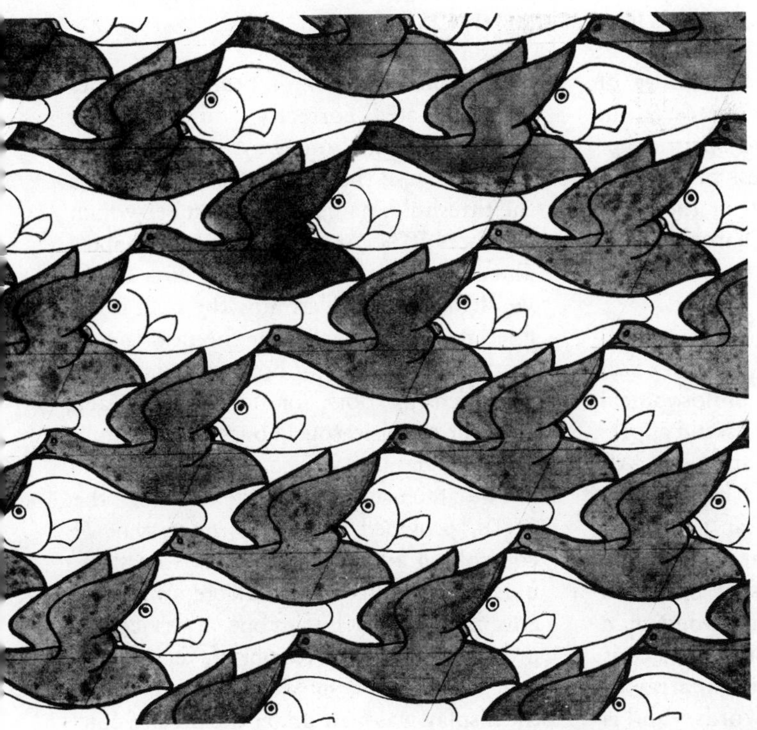

Fig. 6-2 Two woodcuts from the work of M. C. Escher, illustrating ambiguous figure-ground relationships. In the print on the left, "Fish and Fowl," the ambiguity is present throughout, while in the print on the right, "Sky and Water," ambiguity is only present in the center of the print. (© BEELDRECHT, Amsterdam/V.A.G.A., New York, 1984. Collection Haags Gemeentemuseum, The Hague.)

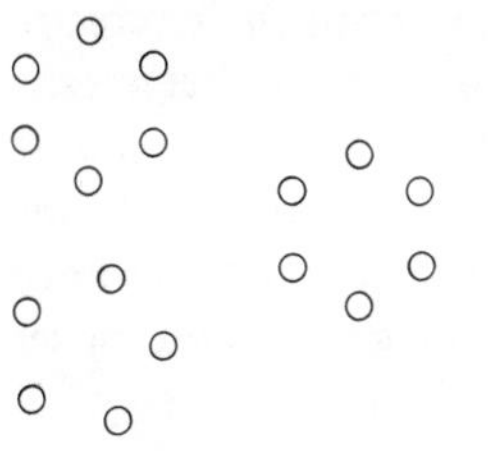

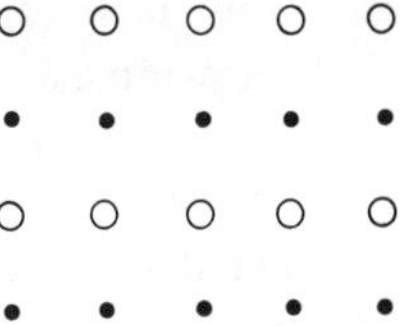

Fig. 6-3 Illustrations of the Gestalt principles of contiguity *(left)* and similarity *(right)* in organizing the perceptual field.

ception in particular. The availability of the tachistoscope produced research in two substantive areas: (1) the span of apprehension and (2) the process of reading. (A more detailed description of the tachistoscope may be found in Chapter 13.)

Span of Apprehension

Experiments on the *span of apprehension* were devised to answer the philosophical question of whether the mind could apprehend more than one object at a time. Although such a "span" could conceivably refer to thought processes (Can you think about more than one thing at a time?), the "span" usually refers to visual processes (Can you see more than one thing at a time?). To measure the span, a subject is presented with a brief view of an array of objects—dots, letter arrays, words—and is asked to report as many objects as possible. When the stimulus objects are all the same, the subject's task is simply to report how many there are. When the stimuli are different (as in letters), the subject must identify each letter.

According to Woodworth (1938), the first systematic experiment that attempted to measure the span of apprehension was carried out by Jevons in 1871, to settle the disagreement among philosophers about whether the span of apprehension could include four, five, or six distinct objects. As was usual in those days, Jevons used himself as the subject.

Jevon's experimental procedure was crude but effective. He began each trial by throwing a handful of black beans toward a cup, into which a variable number would land. He then glanced quickly at the cup and immediately recorded the number he thought was there. Finally, he counted the number actually in the cup and compared it to the number he thought he had seen. Across a large number of trials, he found that he never made an error when three or four beans landed in the cup, but error rates steadily increased as the number of beans increased beyond five. As is customary with psychophysical tasks of this sort, a particular number of beans sometimes was estimated correctly and sometimes not. Accordingly, one way of defining the span is to use the same criterion used for the threshold: namely, that number which produces 50% correct reports (see Chapter 4). For Jevons's data, this number is 10. As we shall see, however, how the span is defined depends on whether the task is estimating the number of homogeneous stimuli, such as dots, or identifying each member of a heterogeneous set of stimuli, such as letters.

The tachistoscope, invented in the 1880s, provided a more elegant way of controlling a subject's exposure to a stimulus than Jevons had available. With the advent of the tachistoscope, a device for presenting stimuli for brief, controlled time periods, the subject's brief glance at the display was now under the precise control of the experimenter. In a typical span experiment for dots arranged randomly, stimuli such as those shown in Figure 6-4 are presented for a brief period in the tachistoscope (100 ms or one tenth of a second is typical). Subjects are asked to report how many dots they see. Figure 6-4 shows random arrays of from 5 to 11 dots. Although people differ in their span, most people report that even as few as 5 dots are not readily apprehended, but rather some cognitive activity that takes place after a brief glance at the array is used to infer the number. Introspective reports of subjects who participated in these experiments were often used to infer such processes. Usually arrays of three or four dots were apprehended directly, those of five and more were often apprehended as several subgroups, and for more numerous groups, subjects often reported counting the dots.

What is of interest in these accounts is that processing larger numbers obviously must have taken longer than the exposure duration. (For example, it has been estimated that subvocal rehearsal, as would be necessary in counting, takes about 170 ms per item.) This suggests that subjects have access to their visual image after the offset of the tachistoscopic exposure.

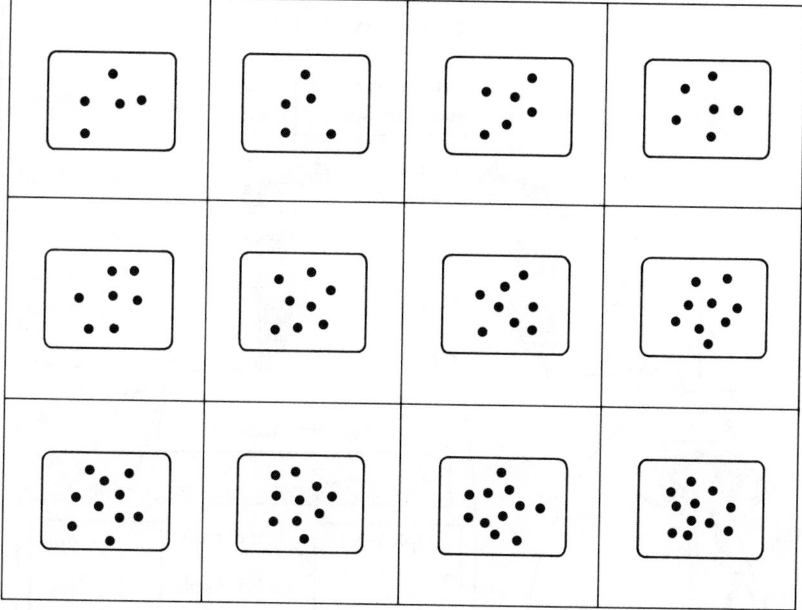

Fig. 6-4 Typical stimuli for a span of apprehension experiment. The number of dots in each display varies from 5 to 11.

Span of Apprehension in Reading. The *word-apprehension effect* refers to the fact that many more letters, when formed into a word, can be apprehended in a single glance than the same letters not forming a word. The word apprehension effect is a special limitation on the span of apprehension—one that illustrates the role of learning in conferring unity on a string of letters previously perceived as individual letters. One process in learning to read is learning to perceive strings of letters that make up words as single perceptual-cognitive units.

To illustrate, a brief exposure of the stimulus *apprehension* can lead to a report of the perception of the entire word, whereas a brief exposure of the stimulus *repenhipnsao* (which contains the same letters as *apprehension* but does not form a word) will result in the report of only a few letters. Before considering this phenomenon in greater detail, it is necessary to consider the chain of events from the brief exposure of a stimulus in a tachistoscopic display to a subject's report of what is seen. As will become clear, the stimulus is available on the subject's internal visual screen far longer than its exposure duration, and there is a complex interaction between the visual image, its prolongation beyond the actual presentation duration, and the memorial processes that intervene between the flash of light marking the visual presentation and the subject's report of what he or she has seen.

Stages in Visual Recognition of Linguistic Material

Figure 6-5 presents stages in the recognition and report of visually presented material such as letters and words. The visual image is prolonged by a very short-term visual memory system, called the *sensory register* or *icon.* The visual image is available for a period equal to the duration of stimulus exposure plus the duration of the icon. During this time period, pattern recognition processes from long-term memory act on the image to extract information. Such information is encoded into a longer-lasting, usually acoustic, store of limited capacity known as the *short-term*

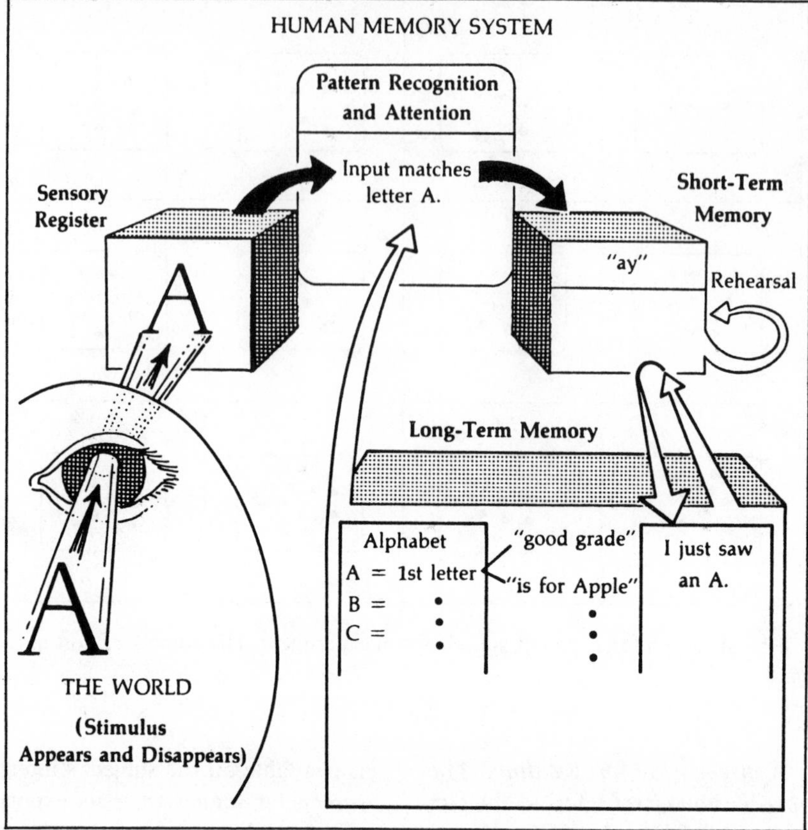

Fig. 6-5 Stages in visual recognition of linguistic material. (From *Human Memory: Structures and Processes* by R. L. Klatzky. Copyright © 1975 by W. H. Freeman and Company. All rights reserved. Reprinted by permission.)

memory system. With continued processing, such as verbal rehearsal, the information may enter an essentially unlimited capacity, long-term system known as *long-term memory.* The subject is usually assumed to report what he or she has seen from short-term memory.

The Sensory Register

During the tachistoscopic exposure, patterned light strikes the retina and produces a visual image somewhere in the visual system (exactly where this image is located anatomically is still a matter of debate). After the stimulus is terminated, the image it produces remains for several seconds in the sensory register. The sensory register facilitates feature extraction and pattern recognition processes of the sensory input and retains an accurate image of sensory events in a raw form that is of large (but not unlimited) capacity. Later stages of analysis such as pattern recognition and feature extraction are of limited capacity and hence operate on only a small amount of what is retained in the sensory register. It is the limitations of these later systems that affect and limit recognition of tachistoscopic images.

The first person to document the existence of the sensory register and to explore its properties was George Sperling, who reported his findings in an influential paper published in 1960 (Sperling, 1960).

The Sperling Experiments. The original purpose of Sperling's research was to investigate how much information can be transmitted by a brief visual exposure. To avoid complications arising from the use of familiar stimuli such as words, Sperling used arrays of consonants or digits.

In one condition of this experiment, subjects were presented with an array of consonants arranged in a 3 × 4 matrix. Each array was presented for 50 ms, preceded and followed by a lighted field. This initial condition was run as a *full report procedure.* Subjects were required to report as many of the 12 letters in the array as they could. They were able to report about 4½ letters from each array, or about 38% of the letters. However, increasing either the duration of the exposure or the number of letters displayed had no effect on the number of letters reported. Sperling speculated that the limit on the number of letters was not due to a limited perceptual system, but rather to a limited memory system. The limit reflected how many of the letters the subject could remember. This was supported by comments from subjects that they could see more than they could report.

To test this hypothesis, Sperling introduced a *partial report procedure* in which subjects had to report only a single row of the display. The particular row was signaled at varying times before and after presentation of a display. The signal for the row to be reported was a tone of high, medium, or low frequency, to indicate report of the top, middle, and bottom row, respectively. Because the selection of each row was determined randomly on each trial, subjects could not anticipate which part of the display they had to report. Therefore, the proportion of the row they were able to report was a valid indicator of the proportion of the entire display they could report if memory factors were not limiting the number of letters they could remember.

Two results from this experiment are of interest: first, when subjects are signaled which row to report at the *offset* of the stimulus, they can report nine of the 12 letters. This suggests that all nine letters were identifiable at that point in time. Second, when the tone is delayed for some period of time after the offest of the stimulus, more than 38% of the letters were reported up to a delay of about 1 second. This suggests that there is some visual trace available to the subject that prolongs the life of the image. Sperling called this visual trace the *sensory information store,* although Neisser in his 1967 book introduced the term *icon* for this brief visual afterimage, and this term is more widely used today. Figure 6-6 shows the data from Sperling's experiment.

The duration of the icon is apparently dependent almost entirely on the physical characteristics of the visual stimulus. This suggests that the icon is a property of the visual system and shares many of the properties of the visual afterimage observed for simpler visual stimuli such as spots of colored light. For example, the duration of the icon is longer when the postexposure field is dark than light, and the icon can be

Fig. 6-6 Sperling's data for number of letters available from a 3 × 4 matrix in a partial report procedure as a function of signal delay. The data shown are the average for four subjects. The bar at right shows whole report performance. (From "The Information Available in Brief Visual Presentations" by G. Sperling. In *Psychological Monographs,* 1960, *74,* No. 11. Copyright 1960 by the American Psychological Association. Reprinted by permission.)

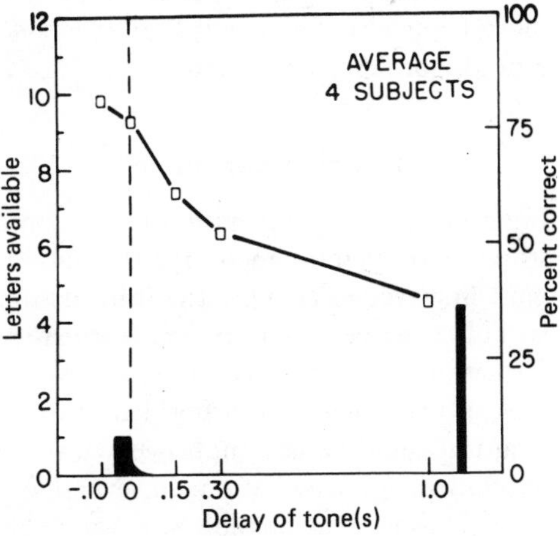

effectively terminated when the stimulus is followed by a visual masking field.

To summarize, the icon is a visual store whose capacity is as large as the capacity of the original image formed during the actual stimulus presentation, but whose clarity fades with time after offset of the stimulus. The rate at which the icon decays is a function of the postexposure field. It is longest lasting (perhaps as long as 4 seconds) for a dark postexposure field, shorter (about 1 second) for a lighted postexposure field, and can effectively be terminated by a *visual noise field.* A *visual noise field* can be constructed by randomly scattering features of letters such as curves and lines over the field, or by rows of Xs or $s covering the area of the letter array. When tachistoscopic exposures are short and there is no postexposure masking field, we can be fairly sure that the subject is actually reading the stimulus from the icon rather than from the visual image itself.

Short-Term Memory

Sperling's subjects who reported they could not remember everything they saw were suffering from limitations on their short-term memory. We shall have more to say about the properties of short-term memory in Chapter 8. We will note here that it has a limited capacity (Sperling estimated it to be between four and five items). Thus, the limit on perception of such unrelated items as consonants and digits from a brief glance is limited by memorial, not perceptual, factors.

Pattern Recognition

In order to enter information from iconic store to short-term memory, the subject must first recognize what the information is. This must be based on well-learned information about the way letters and words look in print or handwriting. Pattern recognition could be accomplished with one of two strategies, and at one of several levels of analysis. One possible way for a pattern recognition system to work is by *feature analysis,* in which the letter "A" is recognized by separate recognition of such visual features as two oblique lines and a cross-bar. Another possibility is *template matching,* in which the pattern recognition system has stored a variety of different templates corresponding to the various ways the letter "A" can look, such as upper versus lower case, its appearance in various type fonts, and even its appearance in different handwritings. In template matching, the degree of match between each of many stored templates and the visual image is used to recognize the pattern. Obviously, there are many difficulties with the template matching scheme, because it requires a different template for each possible appearance of a pattern. For this reason, most researchers in this field favor feature analysis over template matching as the primary process in pattern recognition, although the last word is not in.

Now that the theoretical stages in letter and word recognition have been described, we turn next to the empirical literature to see how an understanding of the stages might help us to understand the empirical data.

The Word Apprehension Effect Revisited

Let us return to the word apprehension effect we mentioned earlier. This effect refers to the fact that words are identified more easily than random letter strings; that a string of letters arranged to make up a word has a unity imposed on it that is not enjoyed by a string of unrelated letters. *Cat* is easier to report than *tca,* and *apprehension* is much easier to report then *repenhipnsao.* The question, then, becomes the point at which the unity is conferred; is it at the level of the construction of the visual image, at the level of the pattern recognition process, at the level of short-term memory, or at the level of decision processes that are invoked to decide what to report?

Actually, the word apprehension effect is just one example of the general rule that familiar stimuli have lower recognition thresholds than unfamiliar stimuli: high-frequency words *(cat)* are easier to see than low-frequency words *(aardvark);* words *(cat)* are easier to see than pronounceable nonwords *(tac);* and pronounceable nonwords are easier to see than nonpronounceable nonwords *(tca).* Thus, as stimuli become less familiar, they become harder to see (or at least to report). However, this is just a description of the phenomenon and does not explain the effect.

EMPIRICAL STUDIES OF THE WORD RECOGNITION PROCESS

In discussing empirical evidence on word recognition processes, we shall concentrate on a single phenomenon, called the *word superiority effect.* The word superiority effect is the effect that words are perceived or reported better than nonwords. We will discuss the word superiority effect within the framework of stages in word recognition, beginning with the last stage in the process, that of converting the stimulus information that has been coded into short-term memory into a vocal or written response.

One theory locates the word superiority effect at this last stage in word recognition—retrieving the information from short-term memory. This theory is called *fragment theory* (Neisser, 1967). *Fragment theory* asserts that when partial information about a stimulus is obtained in a brief tachistoscopic exposure, subjects fill in missing information and attempt to infer what the word must have been on the basis of partial information.

One of the characteristics of all languages (and English is no exception) is the existence of spelling constraints about which letters can follow each other and which letter combinations can occur in which positions of words. These constraints on spelling are known as *orthography.* For example, q is always followed by *u, ck* never begins a word, and *gl* never ends a word. Gibson and her students (Gibson, Pick, Osser, & Hammond, 1962) have shown that nonwords that exhibit English spelling patterns, like *glurck,* have lower tachistoscopic recognition thresholds (i.e., are recognized faster) than nonwords that violate English spelling patterns, like *ckurgl.* Because English spelling is relatively regular, certain constellations of partial fragments often determine what a word can be, and subjects may use their knowledge of English spelling to make an educated guess about what the word is.

Fragment theory implies that the partial information subjects use to construct their guesses is based on letters. However, there are other properties of visual words that can be used to infer which word might have been presented. A very potent property is word shape. One fact about tachistoscopic recognition known since the beginning of its use is that words in lower case type have lower thresholds than those in upper case type. The advantage of lower case words arises from the physical characteristics that distinguish one lower case letter from another and are lost in upper case. These include *ascenders* (the features appearing above the line on the letters *b, d, f, h, k, l, t*) and *descenders* (the features appearing below the line on the letters *g, j, p, q, y*). Ascenders and descenders provide characteristic shapes to lower case words that are lost in the upper case mode. For example, "lint" and "line" have different shapes in lower case, but LINT and LINE have virtually the same shape in upper case.

Experimental evidence for the importance of word shape was provided by Havens and Foote (1963). They compared recognition thresholds for words with many shape-mates (e.g., *lint*) with those having few shape-mates (e.g., *drab*). They found that words having many shape-mates had higher thresholds (were more difficult to perceive) than words having few shape-mates. From this work, they concluded that word shape can contribute to word recognition. This experiment by Havens and Foote shows that word shape is an important variable in word recognition, but it is not the only variable that accounts for the word superiority effect.

Another way in which the role of English orthography in word recognition has been assessed is by using letter strings having various orders of approximation to English. Zero-order approximations are letter strings constructed so that each letter has an equal probability of being selected. First-order approximations choose letters according to their frequency in English (for example, vowels are more common than consonants). Second-order approximations choose pairs of letters according to their frequency in the language (for example, *qe* could never be chosen because *q* must always be followed by *u*). Third-order approximations choose triples of letters according to their frequency. Extending this logic yields the rules for forming fourth-order, fifth-order, and higher-order approximations. *ozhgpmjj* is an example of a zero-order approximation and was constructed by choosing letters randomly from among the 26 letters of the alphabet. For this reason, zero-order approximations do not resemble English words at all. *Therares* is an example of a second-order approximation, and was constructed by choosing pairs of letters according to their frequency in English. *Vernalit* is an example of a fourth-order approximation, and was constructed by choosing quadruples (tetragrams) of letters according to their frequency in English. All of the four-letter strings in *vernalit—vern, erna, rnal, nali,* and *alit*—occur in English and were chosen according to their frequencies in print.

Tables of frequencies of occurrence in English of single letters and digrams by position in words of various lengths may be found in Mayzner and Tresselt (1965), and of trigrams, tetragrams, and pentagrams in Mayzner, Tresselt, and Wolin (1965a, 1965b, 1965c, respectively). Using these stimuli, Miller, Bruner, and Postman (1954) showed that recognition thresholds of letter strings constructed to have different orders of approximation to English decreased as order of approximation increased. Thus, subjects were able to take advantage of the redundancy of the higher-order strings to facilitate perception just as they seem to be able to do with words as opposed to nonwords.

Word Frequency Effects and Strategies of Guessing

Even within the set of English words, there are differences that can produce differences in recognition. Long words are harder to identify than short words, and words that occur more frequently in print have lower thresholds than those that occur rarely. This *word frequency effect* in perception has been a topic of intense interest, with particular emphasis on the question of whether the effect is due to an advantage in "seeing" the word or "saying" (i.e., guessing) the word. The question is whether the effect occurs at an early stage of the recognition process—formation of the icon or pattern recognition—or at a later stage such as recoding into short-term memory, or at the decision stage.

The word frequency effect was first demonstrated by Howes and Solomon (1951), who showed that tachistoscopic recognition thresholds decreased with frequency in print, based on Thorndike and Lorge (1944) word counts (see Chapter 14). The specific function they found was that recognition thresholds decreased linearly with the log of the frequency.

One theory to explain the word frequency effect is known as the *sophisticated guessing model* and is a variant on the fragment theory mentioned earlier. The *sophisticated guessing model* assumes that the subject has some partial information available—a few letters, word shape, or word length. Because instructions in tachistoscopic recognition experiments usually encourage subjects to guess when they are unsure, subjects will tend to guess familiar or common words more often than uncommon words. Experimentally, it has been shown that incorrect guesses tend to be words of higher frequency than the frequency of the words shown (Newbigging, 1961). This evidence tends to support the sophisticated guessing model.

An alternative explanation for the word frequency effect attributes the effect of familiarity to the perceptual process itself. This might occur during the formation of the icon, or perhaps when the pattern recognition system acts on the input to put it into the short-term memory system. Although a number of studies have attempted to examine the perceptual process in the absence of guessing, it was not until 1969 that Gerald Reicher introduced an elegant paradigm for doing this. Because the methodological issues are complex, we shall take some time to discuss these, and their surprising (to sophisticated guessing theorists) findings.

The Reicher/Wheeler Experiments. Prior to 1969, the prevailing opinion about the locus of the word superiority effect was that it was based on constructive and inferential processes carried out by the subject on partial information from the percept. Because the visual image was shown to be available much longer than the stimulus itself (through the iconic storage system), subjects had sufficient time to operate on the image and bring these higher-level cognitive processes to bear on a fragmentary image. As we have noted, this view is known as fragment theory. Fragment theory would hold, then, that letters are not made more visible by their inclusion in a word; rather, knowledge of English words makes the individual letters more guessable.

According to fragment theory, if subjects had to report a single letter from a display containing a word or nonword, the single letter would not be more visible in the word than in the nonword. However, subjects would have a bias toward reporting a letter that makes the stimulus a word rather than a nonword. So, if the stimulus *word* were shown but only *wor* were seen, subjects would tend to guess a *d* or *k* rather than an *f* or c, thereby completing the fragment as *word* or *work* rather than

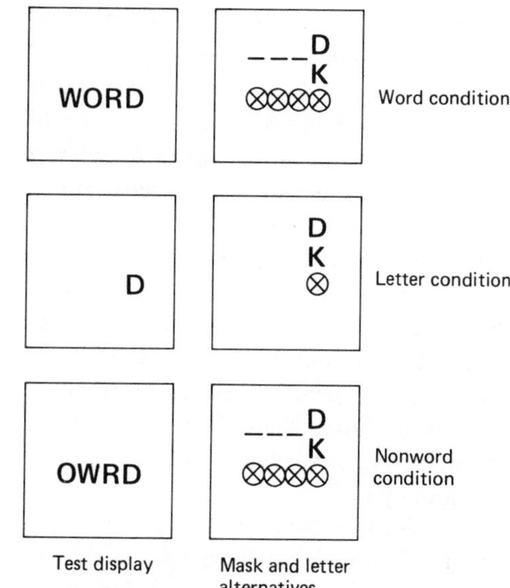

Fig. 6-7 The visual displays used in the Reicher (1959) study.

worf or *worc*. But what if subjects were given a choice between two letters that do make a word on some trials, and two letters that do not make a word on other trials? No response bias toward word guesses could operate, and perceptual processes themselves could be identified.

Just such a procedure was used by Reicher (1969), and later replicated by Wheeler (1970). Subjects were shown a brief flash of a word, nonword, or single letter. Immediately after its presentation, the stimulus was masked and two probe stimuli were presented. These were two letters, one of which was present in the stimulus and the other which was not. The crucial aspect of the experiement is that on the word trials, either letter could make a word, and on nonword trials, neither letter could make a word.

Figure 6-7 shows the sequence of events in the Reicher experiment. On a given trial, subjects are shown a word, a single letter, or a nonword, for some brief period of time (between 35 and 85 ms depending on each subject's threshold). Following the offset of the stimulus, a visual mask was presented (the *X*s enclosed in circles), accompanied by two probe stimuli presented above the spatial position where the crucial to-be-recognized letter appeared in the display. For words and nonwords, these probe stimuli could appear at any one of the four letter positions (only four-letter words and nonwords were used). Single letters had only one position at which the probe stimuli could appear. Subjects were required to choose the letter they thought they had seen, and when in doubt, to guess. (This is known as a two-alternative, forced-choice procedure, as described in Chapter 4). Since there were two choices on each trial, subjects are correct 50% of the time by chance.

The results were clear-cut. Letters were identified much better in the word than in the nonword condition, and letters in words were even more visible than single letters. Thus, words serve to reveal, rather than conceal, their component letters. With respect to the "saying" versus "seeing" question, the Reicher and Wheeler experiments suggest that words are not only "said" more often than nonwords, but they are also "seen" more often than nonwords. In other words, there is a perceptual component to the word superiority effect. Because the letter strings were masked before the alternatives were presented, this effect could not be due to a prolonged icon. Thus, these data suggest that the effect occurs at the pattern recognition stage—that pattern recognition is more rapid and efficient for word strings than for nonword strings (and, by extension, for familiar words than for unfamiliar words).

McClelland and Rumelhart (1981) and Rumelhart and McClelland (1982) have recently proposed an elaborate model to account for the various facts of word perception. In their model, recognition can occur at the level of individual letter features, individual letters, and individual words. Interactions among the various levels account for phenomena such as the word superiority effect. Simulation of their model on a computer has provided impressive confirmation of the model by producing simulated data that are consistent with data produced by subjects in their experiments. Their model proposes specific mechanisms for the perceptual superiority of letters embedded in words, and these mechanisms can be tested by explicitly programming them into a simulation.

In summary, we have reviewed evidence indicating what processes take place during tachistoscopic recognition of verbal material, and we have attempted to relate these processes to various empirical effects in the literature on word recognition. This is a vast literature, and we have only sampled a few crucial experiments from it. However, it should be clear that questions about the locus of effects in perceptual recognition cannot be answered in a simple all-or-none way. The human information processing system is sufficiently complex that a particular effect, such as the word frequency effect, probably occurs at several levels in the process. It will be the task of future researchers to carefully delineate the contribution of each.

SPEECH PERCEPTION

In visual perception of language, we use a tachistoscope, or its modern analog, the computer-driven CRT (a device much like your home TV screen), to present a degraded string of letters. The stimulus can be degraded by presenting it for a very brief duration, at a very low intensity, or accompanied or followed by a visual masking field.

In research on speech perception, the speech signal is passed through a series of electronic devices that degrade the signal in a number of different ways. The speech signal can be degraded by cutting out the high frequencies or the low frequencies, by adding noise, and so on. Subjects in this type of experiment are required to write down or repeat into a microphone the words they think they hear. The percentage correct of the list reported by the subject is the dependent variable.

These tests, called *articulation tests,* were first used by Bell Telephone Laboratories in the 1920s. Telephone engineers had a very practical interest in how degraded a speech signal could be and still be understood. To carry the full range of frequencies present in the human voice across a telephone wire is very expensive. (The range of frequencies carried by a communication system is known as its bandwidth.) The narrower the bandwith required, the cheaper the system can be. The frequencies in the human voice range from 50 to 6500 hertz (Hz or cycles per second), but the modern telephone passes frequencies only between 300 and 3300 Hz. To get an idea of what these ranges mean, the lowest note on the piano has a frequency of about 28 Hz, the highest note of 4180 Hz, and middle C corresponds to a frequency of about 262 Hz. One of the purposes of articulation tests is to determine how wide a band of frequencies needs to be carried and where that band should be centered.

Articulation scores are dependent on many variables. These include the voice frequencies that are filtered out, the type of material used (nonsense syllables are harder to hear than unconnected real words, which in turn are harder to hear than real words that make a sentence), and the amount of background or masking noise. In filtering tests, a high-pass filter passes only high frequencies and cuts off low frequencies, whereas a low-pass filter passes only low frequencies and cuts off high frequencies. Interestingly, it does not matter whether low or high frequencies are cut off—the performance in terms of articulation scores is about the same whether all frequencies above 1900 Hz or below 1900 Hz are removed.

This is quite surprising, because it suggests that no particular part of the frequency spectrum is necessary for speech perception. Although the modern telephone passes a relatively narrow band of frequencies, we have no difficulty understanding what our friend is saying over the telephone. Indeed, we have little trouble identifying his or her voice from a few words.

Later in this chapter, when we consider lateralization of function, we will review evidence that suggests there is a special neurological center which evolved for the specific purpose of producing and understanding speech, localized in the left hemisphere of the brain of most people.

The Role of Context in Speech Perception

We can understand an amazingly degraded speech signal, as long as it is in context, forms grammatical strings, and so on. The complexity of this human performance is truly amazing when we compare it to the performance of computers. The implementation of a device to transcribe speech into written text—the so-called talking typewriter—has so far eluded computer scientists. Transcription of the speech signal into written form, though simple for a stenographer, apparently is so dependent on contextual factors and knowledge that computers cannot yet be programmed to do such a feat. Except when the vocabulary is limited, or there are only a few speakers involved, or both, the talking typewriter is still a device of the future. Although speech synthesizers (machines that talk) have been remarkably successful, speech recognizers (machines that listen and transcribe) have not.

The secret seems to be that the human listener takes advantage of the large redundancy of language, conferred by syntactic constraints and the semantics or meaning of the passage, to decode the speech signal. So much information is needed to use these rules that the computer simply cannot be equipped with all the necessary contextual knowledge.

An experiment by Miller (1962) will illustrate the important role of context in recognizing speech against a background of noise. Miller argues that the reason speech perception is so successful in humans, while machines fail at it, is that humans rely on both top-down and bottom-up processing. In speech perception, top-down processing means that we develop hypotheses about what the next word or words might be and then test them against the incoming input. It also means that our attempts to understand lag behind the speech signal by a few words.

As an example, if you heard the first few words of the sentence "Mary put on her red . . ." you would develop expectations for a class of words that include clothes (such as dress, sweater, scarf, coat), lesser expectations for possible but unlikely words like nose, gun, and telephone, and much lower expectations for "impossible" completions like *gave, the, his,* and *sweeter.* If the next word you heard sounded like *sweeter,* you would probably interpret it as *sweater.*

To demonstrate the role of top-down processing in speech perception, Miller conducted intelligibility tests for different vocabularies of words under six signal-to-noise ratios. Signal-to-noise ratio was varied by recording speech against a background of white noise (sound containing all frequencies) at various intensities. At a signal-to-noise ratio of 0 decibels, the noise has the same amount of energy as the signal, and subjects generally do quite well (virtually 100% articulation scores) regardless of the context. Thus, the noise energy level has to be increased substantially over that of the signal to show differences between types of material.

Miller used four conditions in his experiment, which will be illustrated with the aid of Table 6-1. In one condition, the five-word vocabulary, subjects were presented with permutations (orders) of five words within a single subvocabulary (if subvocabulary 4 were being used, subjects might hear the list: *wet, black, cheap, wrong, good*). Their task was to repeat the words they heard into a microphone after each list. In the sentence condition, five words were selected from each of the five subvocabularies successively, leading to sequences like *Don, loves, some, cheap, shoes.* This selection rule guarantees that grammatical, though not necessarily meaningful, sentences will be generated. In the 25-word vocabulary condition, lists of five words were selected randomly from the entire set of 25 words. Finally, in the most interesting condition, pseudosentences, words were successively selected as in the sentence condition, but in a backwards order, leading to nongrammatical strings like *shoes, cheap, some, loves, Don.*

Table 6-1 Five Subvocabularies Used to Explore the Perceptual Effects of Grammatical Content

1	2	3	4	5
Don	Brought	His	Black	Bread
He	Has	More	Cheap	Sheep
Red	Left	No	Good	Shoes
Slim	Loves	Some	Wet	Socks
Who	Took	The	Wrong	Things

[From "Decision Units in the Perception of Speech," by G. A. Miller. In *IRE Transactions on Information Theory,* 1962, *IT-8,* 81–83. Copyright © 1962 IRE (now IEEE). Reprinted by permission.]

Figure 6-8 shows the articulation scores for this experiment plotted as a function of signal-to-noise ratio. (An articulation score is the percentage of words the subject correctly reported.) As can be seen, differences among the four conditions emerge only when the noise energy is higher than the signal energy (at a signal-to-noise ratio of −12 decibels, the noise contains 16 times the energy of the signal). As can be seen in Figure 6-8, the articulation scores for sentences,which use the 25-word vocabulary with appropriate sequential constraints, were as high as for 5-word vocabularies, whereas pseudosentences, which have the same sequential constraints as sentences, were heard no better than unconstrained lists from the 25-word vocabulary.

Miller argues that sentences are heard better than pseudosentences because subjects can delay their decision about what they have heard, relying on grammatical rules which constrain the grammatical class of successive words to disambiguate the message. Thus, he argues that in speech perception, subjects do a great deal of top-down processing, in addition to bottom-up processing. Further, the strat-

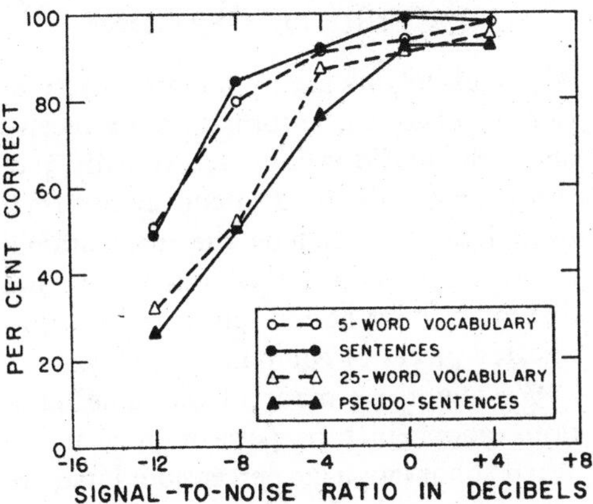

Fig. 6-8 Accuracy as a function of signal-to-noise ratio for different contexts and vocabulary sizes. Grammatical context improves intelligibility, but ungrammatical context does not, even though the number of alternative words that could occur was the same in both cases. (From "Decision Units in the Perception of Speech" by G. A. Miller. In *IRE Transactions on Information Theory,* 1962, *IT-8,* 81–83. Copyright © 1962 IRE (now IEEE). Reprinted by permission.)

egy of delaying the decision about what has been said until several words have occurred is an efficient one.

The Phonemic Restoration Effect

The phonemic restoration effect, first reported by Warren (1970; Warren & Warren, 1970) also shows the strong effect of context in interpreting speech. When a single *phoneme* (the smallest unit of speech, such as the "puh" sound in *peek*) is deleted from a sentence and replaced with a nonspeech sound such as a cough, subjects hear the missing phoneme. They even hear a unit as large as a syllable when it is replaced with the extraneous noise. Even more interesting, they cannot accurately perceive the location of the noise—the extraneous noise appears to lie outside the speech stream and is poorly located within the stream. Thus, if the sentence being read was "The state governors met with their respective legi__latures convening in the capital city" (the cough occurring simultaneously with the missing "s" sound in *legislatures*), subjects trying to guess the location of the cough would locate it anywhere within the preceding and target words—anywhere from a place in *respective* to a place in *legislatures.*

The Warrens also showed that, as Miller had conjectured, subjects delay for several words before making a decision about what they must have heard. This was demonstrated by deleting phonemes from words and then varying the later context to make one completion of the multilated word more semantically congruent than another completion. For example, when the initial phoneme is deleted in the sixth word of the sentence "It was found that the __eel was on the *axle,*" subjects hear the mutilated word as *wheel.* However, if the last word of the sentence is changed to *shoe,* they hear the word as *heel.* Thus a change in a word occurring four words after the ambiguous stimulus is capable of changing the perception of the ambiguous word in conformity with what makes sense in context. Actually, it has been known for some time that skilled transcribers of speech, such as Morse code operators and typists, lag behind a message by as much as six words. A Morse code operator who is transcribing speech from the Morse code waits until a whole phrase or short sentence has been understood before beginning to transcribe it (Bryan & Harter, 1897, 1899).

Speech Segmentation

In written language, words are clearly segregated by the space between adjacent words. In spoken speech, however, no clear physical gap occurs between successive words, even though we perceive the words as separated. When speech is recorded and analyzed by a speech spectogram (a picture of the frequencies in momentary speech sounds as a function of time), no clear-cut silent period, analogous to a space, exists between adjacent words of a sentence. We can observe this informally by listening to someone speak an unknown foreign language. It is often impossible to locate the beginning or end of one word—the speech seems continuous. Yet psychological gaps are heard between adjacent words of speech in a language we know and, as we shall see, even larger gaps are perceived between larger units such as clauses.

To study the reality of such psychological gaps, Fodor, Bever, and Garrett (1974) introduced a task in which subjects had to identify the location of a click which was presented with a spoken sentence. Their research provides a second line of evidence that speech is understood in larger units than at the level of the individual word. In these studies, subjects are presented with two-clause sentences, such as "The boy who bothered Shirley hit the ball." The two clauses in this case are "The boy bothered Shirley," and "The boy hit the ball," and the division between them in the original sentence occurs after *Shirley.*

When clicks are presented within one of the words in either clause, the click appears to migrate to the clause boundary—that is, subjects show a large bias toward locating the click at the clause boundary, after *Shirley.* From these results, the authors conclude that the clause represents a cognitive unit, which resists disruption. Perhaps subjects refrain from encoding the train of speech until they get to a phrase or clause boundary. After encoding the first clause, they turn their attention to the click (which we might conjecture is in a slightly different short-term acoustic store than language), and perceive it as having occurred at the clause boundary.

As we have seen, speech perception is probably the most important use we make of our auditory system. Although this ability might seem like a relatively effortless and automatic activity, the rules by which we decode the speech signal must be very complex indeed—so complex that no computer has yet come close to our ability to do this.

PICTURE PERCEPTION

Although in this highly literate society of ours much of the information we receive about the world is conveyed verbally, pictures can also be used to convey information. Examples include the international traffic signs, maps of various kinds, and diagrams about how to put together complicated pieces of equipment.

We might ask many of the same questions about picture perception that we asked about language perception: First, are pictures perceived whole-to-part or part-to-whole, that is, does picture perception proceed top to bottom or bottom to top? Second, are pictorial symbols, such as line drawings, simply pictorial conventions much as language is a convention, which must be learned in order to be "read," or is there an innate capacity to "read" pictures as symbols of the objects or events in question?

Top-Down versus Bottom-Up Processing in Picture Perception

As we noted in the section on whole-word versus letter-by-letter perception of words, top-down processing implies that the subject has some expectation of what is likely to be seen. Context governs what these expectations are, and these expectations are subjected to continual updating by bottom-up processing.

Research on holistic perception of words has the advantage that words are composed of a well-defined set of elements—the letters of the alphabet. The same question for pictures suffers from the difficulty of defining the elements of which a picture is composed. Because of the problems in defining picture elements, the experimental work we shall describe deals with scene perception, in which a scene is composed of a certain number of objects. The elements of a scene, then, are the objects of which it is composed, and we bypass the problem of defining the elements comprising a picture of a single object. Be-

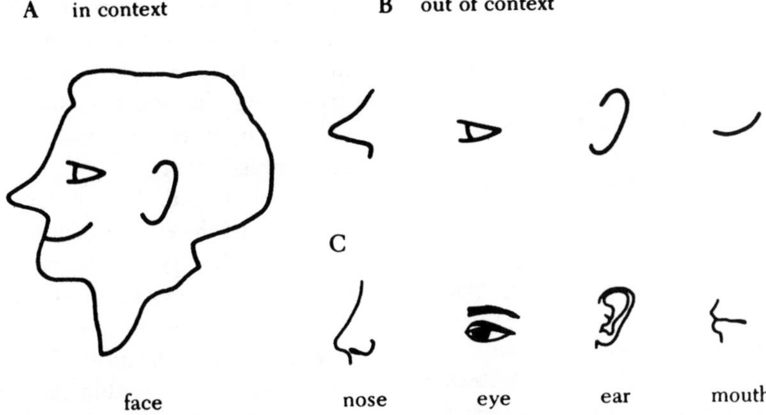

Fig. 6-9 An illustration of part-whole context. Facial features recognizable in the context of a profile (A) are not recognizable out of context (B). It is necessary to make the features more detailed, as in (C), to make them recognizable out of context. (From "Visual Perception and World Knowledge" by S. E. Palmer. In D. A. Norman, D. E. Rumelhart, and the LNR Research Group, *Explorations in Cognition.* Copyright © 1975 by W. H. Freeman and Company. All rights reserved. Reprinted by permission.)

cause scenes generally require more than a single-word description, scene perception is more analogous to sentence or paragraph perception than to word perception.

Before discussing this experimental work, we refer to a demonstration by Palmer (1975b) on how context can work to disambiguate features of pictures that would not be recognized in isolation. Figure 6-9 presents Palmer's demonstration. The features of the face in context, as in A, can be quite sketchy but still recognizable, whereas in isolation, as in B, they are ambiguous. In order to make isolated features recognizable, they must be made more detailed, as in C. Palmer argues from this demonstration that perceptual interpretation cannot be solely bottom-up nor solely top-down, but rather both processes must go on simultaneously.

Strong effects of context in scene perception have been obtained experimentally for both speed and accuracy of locating a cued object. Biederman, Glass, and Stacy (1973) presented subjects with a photograph of an object that subsequently either appeared or did not appear in a photograph of a real-life scene. The task of the subject was to press a YES key if the object appeared in the subsequently presented scene, and a NO key if it did not.

Some objects actually occurred in the scene, and thus a YES response was appropriate. Some objects could have occurred in the scene but did not (e.g., a fire hydrant in a street scene). Here, the correct response is NO, but since the object is possible in the scene, the response is called a POSSIBLE NO. Finally, some objects could not occur in the scene, or were extremely unlikely (e.g., a teacup in a street scene). On these trials, too, the correct response is NO, but since the object is impossible in the scene, the response is called an IMPOSSIBLE NO. The independent variable of object occurrence thus has three levels; Yes, it did; No, it did not but was possible; and No it did not and was impossible, even though the subject's response has only the two levels of YES and NO. Finally, context was varied by presenting either a photograph of the original scene or a jumbled version in which the photograph was cut into six parts and rearranged.

The investigators predicted that a coher-

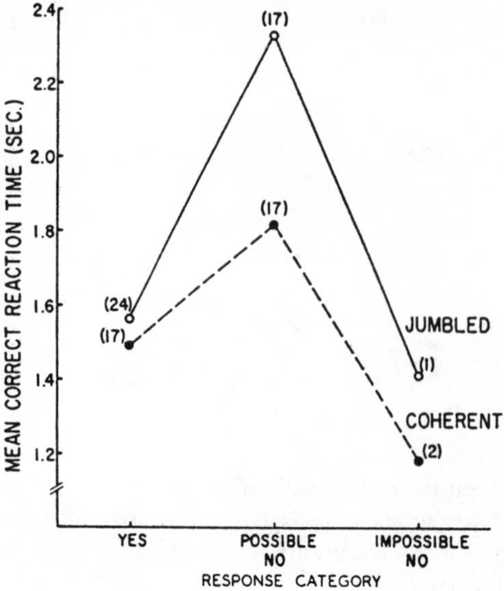

Fig. 6-10 Mean correct reaction times and percent errors (in parentheses) as a function of jumbled versus coherent scenes for the three types of response. (From "On Searching for Objects in Real-World Scenes," by I. Biederman, A. L. Glass, and E. W. Stacy, Jr. In *Journal of Experimental Psychology,* 1973, *97,* 22–27. Copyright 1973 by the American Psychological Association. Reprinted by permission.)

ent context will facilitate performance as measured by time and accuracy for all three types of responses, and that POSSIBLE NOs will be more difficult than IMPOSSIBLE NOs or YES responses. Figure 6-10 presents the results of this study, in which time to make a correct decision is plotted along the *y*-axis for the three types of responses, and the error percentages are shown in parentheses.

Note that jumbled scenes always led to longer times and, usually, higher error rates for all three categories of response, but that the differences between coherent and jumbled scenes are particularly large for POSSIBLE NOs. The authors concluded that subjects process scenes top to bottom. Subjects first access some overall schema which they have for such environments as streets, kitchens, or playgrounds, and then, having accessed that schema, they look for the critical object where it is most likely to be found. Both processes—generating the schema and locating the object—are faster for coherent scenes than for jumbled scenes.

Palmer (1975a), in a similar experiment, investigated the effect of context on the accuracy of identifying objects. In his experiment, subjects were shown a particular context, and then an object was presented briefly for identification. The object was either appropriate within the context (e.g., a loaf of bread in the context of a kitchen table), inappropriate but visually similar to the appropriate object (e.g., a mailbox which is similar in shape to the loaf of bread), or inappropriate and visually dissimilar (e.g., a drum). The point of his experiment was to demonstrate that just as it is easier to hear a word within the context of an appropriate sentence, it will be easier to see an object within the context of its appropriate environment.

He found, as predicted, that accuracy of identification for appropriate objects within contexts was greatest (approximately 85%), and accuracy for inappropriate objects was actually hurt by the context. For inappropriate but dissimilar objects, accuracy was about 45%, whereas for inappropriate but visually similar objects, it was only 35%. Thus, both studies find evidence for strong contextual effects in the speed and accuracy of perception of objects in scenes. This supports the view that scene perception, like sentence or word perception, proceeds both from wholes to parts and parts to wholes.

In short, the human observer walks around with expectations of what things are found where. These expectations, or schemas, have a dramatic effect on performance when unexpected things are observed. We do not expect to find a lion in our office or a desk behind bars in the zoo. These expectations presumably facilitate the ease with which we can perceive our world, and most of the time we are correct in our expectations.

Are Pictures Linguistic Devices, or Are They Innately Perceived?

Do pictures of objects or events have to be learned to be interpreted, or are they innately perceived as veridical (true) representations of the objects they represent? Evidence on this issue is drawn from three areas of research: observations of anthropologists on the reaction of primitive tribes who had never been exposed to photographs or drawings, developmental studies, and studies on the veridicality of depth perception from pictures.

To anticipate somewhat, the available evidence appears to indicate that perception of pictures of objects is direct, inasmuch as no specific training is required to recognize the object depicted. This is true even in impoverished stimuli such as line drawings. However, the depth at which an object appears (and hence its relative size) is imperfectly represented by pictures, even (or especially) those with perfectly rendered perspective.

What this implies is that object perception in the real world is primarily mediated by exterior and interior contours. In contrast, the depth of an object in the real world is dependent on not only static visual cues such as those that can be depicted in pictures, but also on cues available from binocular viewing, in which each eye gets a slightly different view of a scene, and on the movement of the eyes, head, and body, in which cues such as motion parallax and relative size changes provide cues for depth. Although a discussion of the myriad cues to depth perception is beyond the scope of this chapter, useful reviews can be found in Kaufman (1974; 1979), and a fascinating series of demonstrations of the powerful role of retinal disparity may be found in Julesz (1971).

Anthropologists have long been fascinated by the question of the effect of culture on perception. However, as we have seen, perception involves a series of stages, including a memorial one. The effect of culture or learning can intrude in many ways. Segall, Campbell, and Herskovits (1966) and Deregowski (1980) review some of the history of such cross-cultural research, and provide vivid examples of some of the pitfalls of anthropological research.

Two questions have been the focus of anthropological research in this area. First, are the objects in drawings or photographs perceived correctly without any training by people who have not previously been exposed to pictorial representations? Second, are pictorial cues to depth correctly used without training?

Although there are scattered reports of the absence of pictorial perception from photographs or drawings in "primitive" or unacculturated tribes, Kennedy (1974) reviews this literature critically. As he points out, a photograph can be viewed first as an object with a shiny surface, and second as a representation of a real object or scene. When details are pointed out to the respondents, they are usually able to identify the objects, animals, or people. In fact, Deregowski (1972) reports a dramatic example of one group of tribal people who, when shown a projected slide of an elephant, behaved as if they thought it was a real animal by running from the room.

Most evidence suggests that picture perception is immediate, once the unfamiliarity of the material, such as the glossy paper on which a photograph is printed, is discounted. There is, however, a great deal of evidence that certain pictorial cues for depth, such as size, overlap, linear perspective, and position in the field, *are* culturally learned cues for depth. Hudson (1960, 1967) has developed a test of pictorial depth perception that he has used with many different African tribes. This test is a series of line drawings in which size and position in the field are always cues to distance, but in which overlap and linear perspective are sometimes present and sometimes absent. Figure 6-11 presents some examples. P-1 is a picture with neither overlap nor linear perspective cues, P-2 has

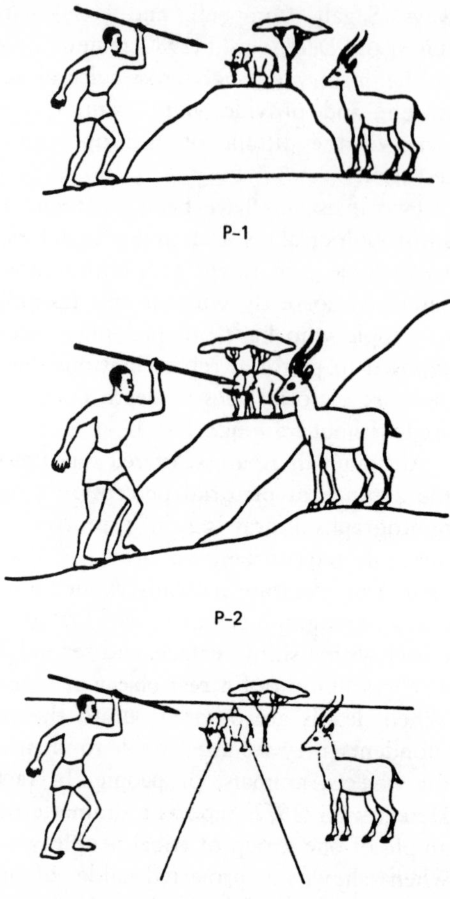

Fig. 6-11 Pictures from Hudson's pictorial depth perception test. P-1 contains only size and position cues; P-2 adds overlap cues; and P-3 adds linear perspective cues. (From "Pictorial Depth Perception in Sub-cultural Groups in Africa" by W. Hudson. In *Journal of Social Psychology*, 1960, *52*, 183–208. Copyright 1960 by the Helen Dwight Reid Educational Foundation. Reprinted by permission.)

overlap cues, and P-3 has linear perspective cues.

In Hudson's study, subjects were first asked to identify the three objects in the pictures—the man, the elephant, and the antelope—and only those who could do so were tested for depth perception. Then they were asked what the man was doing. Finally, they were asked which two of the three objects were closer to one another. Answers that provided evidence for three-dimensional perception from pictorial cues were those that indicated the man was aiming or throwing the spear at the antelope, and that the man and antelope were closer than the man and elephant or the elephant and antelope. Among the 11 samples of subjects tested by Hudson, only those who were attending or had attended school gave evidence of pictorial depth perception.

What this implies is that pictorial cues to depth perception *are* learned. This does not mean, of course, that people unskilled in use of pictorial cues do not see depth in the real world. Depth cues from movement and retinal disparity are very powerful. Indeed, hunters in the jungle would hardly survive if they could not use depth cues to calibrate the force with which to throw a spear or shoot an arrow.

If culture does affect perception, then one should be able to observe parallel results to those in the cross-cultural literature in developmental studies because both reflect learning. In a rather direct test of whether pictures of objects are perceived innately, Hochberg and Brooks (1962) raised a child to the age of 19 months with no exposure to pictures or photographs. The child had learned to name real objects, but was never exposed to pictures of those objects. At 19 months, when first shown a series of both photographs and line drawings of familiar objects, the child had no difficulty naming them. Hochberg and Brooks concluded that a picture directly portrays those features of objects that are important in distinguishing them from one another, and thus that pictures are not linguistic devices but rather accurate depictions of reality. A similar conclusion was reached by O'Connor and Hermelin (1961), who found that adults of below 50 IQ were able to accurately pick out line drawings in response to spoken names of the objects depicted in them.

Pictorial depth cues, on the other hand, show a definite developmental trend. T. G. R. Bower (1971, 1972), in an ingenious series of studies, tested for generalization of an infant's response from a training stimulus to either a pictorial representation or the same stimulus at a different depth. He was interested in the developmental course of shape and size constancy. Shape constancy is the stable perception of the shape of an object regardless of its viewing position (a tilted square still looks square even though its retinal image is trapezoidal). Size constancy is the stable perception of the size of an object regardless of its viewing distance (a distant elephant still looks big even though its retinal image is tiny). The results of Bower's studies show that infants exhibit shape and size constancy when either binocular information (retinal disparity) or head motion (movement parallax) is present.

Bower's infants, however, did not show transfer of their learned responses to a *picture* of the training object. Thus, Bower's infants show the same pattern of development as that inferred from cross-cultural studies—depth cues from movement and binocular vision are primary and seem to be innate, whereas depth cues from pictures must be learned and emerge only with experience.

Finally, we turn to a study showng that even among adults trained in the use of linear perspective, "correct perspective" in pictures appears unnatural. Since the time of Leonardo da Vinci, artists have been using the rules of perspective to convey depth in painting. But since the Renaissance, both painters and, later, photographers have discovered that using true perspective produces pictures or photographs that look unnatural—the convergence of parallel lines appears too abrupt, and the background figures look too small. For example, if you stand at the base of the World Trade Center in New York City and look up, you will see a tall retangular building (i.e., you will see the building as it is). But if you replace your eyes with a camera and look at the resulting photograph, the building will look unnatural—it will look as if it shrinks in width as it gets taller.

Artists have compensated for perceptual distortions arising from true perspective by modifying the rules of perspective, usually intuitively (Pirenne, 1970), while photographers use the zoom lens, so they can move away from too close a vantage point, or the wide angle lens, to make photographs look more realistic.

In a striking demonstration of the failure of true perspective drawings to portray natural-looking objects, Hagen and Elliott (1976) used sets of computer drawings of geometrical objects that were generated to produce perspective views ranging from the traditional linear perspective, in which the convergence of parallel lines is identical to that in a real scene, to parallel perspective, in which there is no convergence of parallel lines.

Figure 6-12 shows two cubes at the extremes of the range of perspective changes, from veridical (conical) on the left, in which the depth information is correctly conveyed by the convergence of the sides of the cube, to nonveridical (axonometric) on the right, in which no convergence of parallel lines occurs. Adult subjects who were instructed to order the pictures from most to least realistic chose the parallel, nonveridical convergence condition on the majority (52%) of the trials. The veridical drawings were chosen only 6% of the time. Thus, even for adult subjects who have presumably been exposed to conventions of perspective drawing, *no* perspective is judged to produce a more realistic image than correct perspective (or anything in between). Hagen and Elliott interpret their results as indicating that subjects prefer to view an object as drawn at least

Fig. 6-12 Examples of two cubes showing the two extremes of perspective changes investigated by Hagen and Elliott (1976).

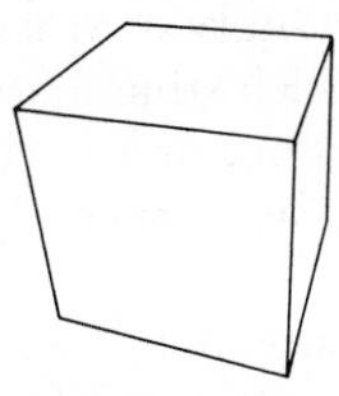

Veridical perspective (conical)

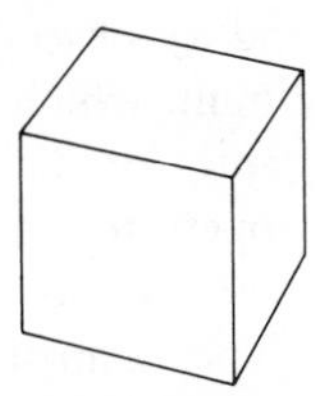

Parallel perspective (axonometric)

ten times the distance of its size (what they term the "Zoom effect") so that perspective changes will be minimal.

In summary, then, what can we conclude about picture perception from this brief review of these three areas of research? First, it seems clear that objects can be recognized from pictorial representations, whether as photographs or simple line drawings, almost as well as the objects themselves are recognized. Little or no training is required to attain this skill.

In contrast, recognition of the distance of objects in pictorial representations is much less direct or innate. Although perception of depth from movement and the two views received by the two eyes seems to be built in, the cues available from pictorial representation seem to require learning.

ATTENTION

There are two questions that have been studied intensively in the area of attention. The first, is, how selective can attention be, and along which dimensions can selectivity operate? This area of research is called *selective attention.* The second question is, to what extent is it possible to divide attention and attend simultaneously to more than one message, channel, or stimulus input? This area of research is called *divided attention.* We first consider experiments in the area of selective attention.

SELECTIVE ATTENTION

This discussion of selective attention will concentrate on experiments that have studied the human ability to selectively attend to subsets of either auditory or visual stimuli, which aspects of such stimuli are usable for directing attention, and what happens to material that is simultaneously presented but unattended.

The control of visual attention seems more straightforward than the control of auditory attention. When we choose a particular part of our visual environment to attend to, we can selectively inspect that part by changing head, eye, and body position. This brings that particular area of the visual field into foveal vision by fixating the field so that the chosen area of the visual field is imaged onto the fovea, the most sensitive part of the retina. While fixating on a particular object, we will be less aware of stimuli in the periphery of our visual field. One reason for this is that our acuity is worse in the periphery. In addition, of course, we will be completely unaware of visual stimuli outside our field of vision. Thus, the question of interest in visual attention is whether we can selectively attend to different visual inputs within the fixated foveal field.

Attention to different aspects of the auditory environment seems less straightforward, although we can certainly direct our ears toward or away from a particular source of sound. Anecdotally, we seem to be able to direct our attention to one or another aspect of our auditory environment, as in attending to a particular conversation at a cocktail party, or listening for the cry of a child in the next room even as the television set blares. However, the way that auditory attention is shifted from one source to another is much less clear than for visual attention. In fact, it was the mysterious nature of auditory attention that prompted an English engineer, Colin Cherry, to study it by means of the *dichotic listening* task.

The Dichotic Listening Task and the "Cocktail Party Phenomenon"

In a typical dichotic listening task, the subject is seated in a quiet room with earphones on. One message is played to one ear, while a second message is played to the other ear. The messages can range from unassociated digits or consonants to connected discourse such as the text of a novel. The subject is instructed to pay attention to one of the two messages. For example, a subject might be instructed to attend to the message coming to the right ear. In order to ensure that full attention is being paid to that ear, the subject is also instructed to repeat each word of the attended message. This repeating task is called *shadowing*.

It is sometimes convenient to think of the two ears in this example as *channels* of communication. Because aspects of the speech signals other than which ear they are delivered to have been used as ways of dividing attention, we shall use the term channel in a more general sense. A *channel* is any dimension in either the auditory or visual realm that can distinguish two classes of stimuli. In the auditory realm, this can be the ear to which the message is delivered, the language in which it is spoken, the speaker (e.g., whether male or female), the intensities of the messages, and their semantic and syntactic continuity if they are prose passages. In the visual realm, a channel can be a spatial location, a color, or a more abstract distinction such as letters versus digits or consonants versus vowels.

The early experiments on dichotic listening were carried out by an English engineer, Colin Cherry (1953). Engineers were interested in the problem of separating one voice from another, as people seem able to do at a cocktail party, because no known electronic device is capable of doing such a thing. That is, it is not possible to program a sophisticated microphone connected to a computer to pick up and record one voice against a babble of voices, yet humans seem to have no difficulty doing so.

Cherry referred to the problem of attending to one conversation among a babble of several conversations as *the cocktail party phenomenon.* He brought this problem into the laboratory by using the dichotic listening task. The reason for transporting the problem from the cocktail party into the laboratory is to exercise more control over the stimuli presented to the subject and to monitor more closely the subject's performance.

The questions that Cherry posed with these early, pioneering experiments are still being asked today. First, what characteristics of a channel will permit us to attend to its message? These characteristics might include the speaker's voice, the direction from which the speech arrives, continuity of the speech in terms of semantic factors, and intensities (as would occur if you were listening to a nearer rather than a more distant conversation). Second, if we are successful at attending to one channel, are we completely unaware of anything being said on the other channel? Do we reject all input from the second channel, or can we monitor it at some low level to see if it contains a high-priority event? Third, if the answer to the second question is positive, what high-priority events will cause us to switch our attention from the attended to the unattended channel? We have probably all had the experience of being deep in conversation with one partner at a cocktail party, yet overhearing our name being mentioned halfway across the room. If this "crosstalk" from another channel can be demonstrated experimentally (and it has), then we must be monitoring other channels at some level.

Cherry's first experiments used binaurally presented speech mixed together. (Binaural presentation means that the same set of stimuli are presented simultaneously to both ears.) In this situation, the same speaker spoke two prose passages and these two messages were tape-recorded over each other and played to both ears. With mixed messages, subjects had no cue as to which message was which, except continuity of meaning and syntax. Despite this, they were able to separate out the two messages, although only with great difficulty and after playing sections over and over again.

When Cherry separated the two messages by presenting them dichotically (one to each ear), subjects had no difficulty whatever attending to one message by shadowing it. However, although they could shadow perfectly, usually with a delay of one or two words between the time they heard a word and the time they repeated it, they retained almost nothing of the meaning of the shadowed message. Furthermore, they were unaware of the message in the other channel except for very obvious physical characteristics such as whether it was speech or pure tones. They were "deaf," on the unattended channel, to changes in language or even to changes from speech played forward to speech played backward.

Let us note here, however, that although Cherry attempted to bring the cocktail party into the laboratory, there are many differences (aside from the absence of cocktails) between the cocktail party and the dichotic listening task with shadowing of one channel. We normally do not shadow when listening to a conversational partner at a party (indeed, shadowing would seem a good way of getting rid of conversational partners). In addition, we usually remember conversations taking place at cocktail parties, while subjects who shadow typically retain little of the meaning of the message they have shadowed.

Despite these differences between real-world and laboratory approaches to selectivity in attention, dichotic listening tasks have provided a new paradigm for psychologists studying attention. The interest of psychologists has shifted to the possible dimensions, or channels, along which subjects can direct attention. What kinds of physical or psychological cues can be used to catch and hold attention?

To anticipate somewhat, most current theories of attention assume that subjects can fully attend to or process only one channel at a time, that switching from one channel to another takes some time and effort, and that such switching is normally done only when something of high priority is happening on the other channel. The issue on which the theories disagree is the degree to which the unattended message is processed: Is it only to such obvious physical characteristics as voice and type of signal (tones versus speech), as Cherry's initial results would suggest? Or does the message get analyzed to the level of meaning, as the ability to hear your own name in the unattended channel would suggest? Is the lack of memory for the unattended channel due to lack of processing to the depth of meaning, or is it simply that information that has been analyzed for meaning does not enter long-term memory after being processed in short-term memory? As we shall see, it depends on the task set to the subject. Subjects appear to be capable of focusing or broadening their attentional field, so that unattended messages can be analyzed to various degrees of depth.

Imagine, as an analogy, a rather noisy radio or television set. You set the dial to a particular channel, but input from other channels or stations come through at an attenuated level. Although the channel to which you are tuned comes in the clearest, it is possible to monitor input from other channels. However, if you try to hear another channel more clearly by turning the dial slightly, you will lose clarity on the channel to which you are tuned. And if the information coming over the other channel seems important enough, you can switch to the other channel, but, as in a radio or television set, switching takes time.

What Are the Characteristics of a Channel?

In one of the first models of selective attention, Broadbent (1958) proposed that a channel of attention is based on the physical characteristics of the incoming signals, such as whether they are auditory or visual, their spatial location, their intensity, and their pitch. In his model, a selective filter was set to admit only stimuli of the attended physical characteristic, and thus input from other physical channels was filtered out. This model, which places the filter of attention right after the sensory stage of perception, is known as *early selection.*

The Split-Span Experiment. Broadbent based his model on results of a series of *split-span experiments.* In a typical split-span experiment, subjects are presented with strings of three digits simultaneously to both ears in a dichotic presentation. Thus, the right ear might be presented *8, 2, 4* while at the same time the left ear is presented with *7, 1, 3.* The subject's task in this experiment is to report the digits in any order, but to report as many as possible.

There are two surprising outcomes of this experiment. First, subjects overwhelmingly preferred to recall the digits by ear, rather than by the order in which they were presented. Thus, they would report *8, 2, 4* followed by *7, 1, 3* rather than *8, 7, 2, 1, 4, 3.* Furthermore, they had difficulty reporting more than 4 or 5 correctly (a number well below the immediate memory span of 7 or 8 for digits presented binaurally). They would, however, normally report all three of the digits from the first-reported ear correctly. The results of this experiment have several implications. First, subjects attend primarily to one channel or ear. Second, switching between channels takes time or effort. Third, the digits presented to the unattended ear are in some sort of short-term acoustic store from which they decay rather rapidly.

The Broadbent model produced a great deal of research, but it seems to be wrong in at least two important aspects: first, the filtering can be done on more than merely physical grounds and, second, the unattended channel does get monitored for meaning—the filtering is not completely all or none.

A split-span experiment by two undergraduates at Oxford, Gray and Wedderburn (1960), will illustrate both these aspects. In their experiment, sometimes known as *the Dear Aunt Jane task* (Massaro, 1975), three digits were alternated between the two ears with either a simple three-word phrase like *dear-aunt-Jane* or three syllables of a word like *ex-tir-pate.* Thus, a subject might get the sequence *dear-2-Jane* in the right ear, and *7-aunt-3* in the left ear. Under these conditions, subjects report the word or phrase together and the digits together. That is, they report *dear aunt Jane* followed by *7-2-3,* thereby grouping by type of material rather than by ear. Although the results of Gray and Wedderburn suggest that meaning is not filtered out, their results have also been attributed to the postperceptual reporting process—the fact that subjects simply found it easier to report the digits together and the word or phrase together, rather than by ear.

Treisman (1964) compared the difficulty of shadowing under a number of different conditions, including physical differences (different ears, or a female versus male voice), phonetic differences (a message in a known language versus another spoken by the same speaker, in a second unknown language), and semantic differences (same condition as before, but with subjects who knew both languages).

Although Treisman found that messages were much easier to shadow when separated by physical factors such as ear and voice, semantic factors also had an effect, in that a known language spoken in the unattended ear caused more errors in shadowing the attended ear than an unknown language. Thus, it would appear that unattended channels are analyzed for meaning to some degree but that it is easier to ignore the unattended channel (for that is the subject's task in the dichotic listening task) when physical parameters can be used. Treisman proposed a new model of attention, in which the unattended channel was not completely blocked, as in the Broadbent model, but rather attenuated. In this model, the meaning of the message in the unattended channel was available and could be used to follow a message that was being switched from one ear to another.

The view that a message on an unattended channel is analyzed for meaning is known as "late" selection, as opposed to the "early" selection model proposed by

Broadbent. It appears that subjects can attend to or analyze meaning on an unattended channel, particularly if it contains a high-priority event. For example, Moray (1959) showed that subjects were usually aware of their own name coming over the unattended ear, even though they were unable to recall a neutral word that had been presented as many as 35 times to that same ear. Thus, subjects are not completely deaf to an unattended channel even if physical parameters of the two are quite different. Unattended messages *are* analyzed for meaning, but the information may never enter long-term memory—it is forgotten once it has been analyzed. This forgetting model of attention was first proposed by Deutsch and Deutsch (1963) and further elaborated by Norman (1968).

One more experiment will demonstrate this point. Subjects in an experiment by MacKay (1973) shadowed sentences containing polysemous words (words with more than one meaning, like *bank,* which can mean a side of a river or a place where you keep money). Simultaneous with the polysemous word, subjects were presented with a word to the unattended ear which biased the subject toward one of the meanings. For example, *bank* might be paired with *river* or *money.* On a subsequent recognition test for the shadowed material, subjects were more likely to select a paraphrase of the sentence that emphasized the biased meaning, even though these same subjects had no memory for the biasing words.

To recapitulate, a channel in an auditory dichotic listening experiment can be either a physical or psychological cue. Subjects seem to process information in unattended channels to the level of meaning, but no residue of memory can be found for that meaning. In effect, this suggests a rather impressive ability on the part of subjects to pay full attention to what they need to attend to and at the same time effectively analyze other unattended sources of information for meaning "just in case." Following this, subjects can reject what they do not need.

Selective Attention in Vision

Obviously, we can selectively attend to different parts of our visual field by moving our bodies, eyes, head, and so forth. But what of our ability to attend to selected channels of a fixated area of the visual field?

Sperling (1960) investigated this question with his partial report procedure. As you may recall, he estimated the number of letters available to the subject at varying intervals of time after the visual display was turned off by instructing them, with tones, to report one of three rows. Subjects giving partial reports by spatial positions (rows) were able to do better than when they had to report the entire set of letters. This indicated that the primary limit on their report of what they could see was their memory, not what they actually saw. It also indicated that because they could selectively attend to a particular spatial location in this experiment, spatial location can serve as a channel of attention.

Sperling found that color was also effective as a channel. Subjects can report as many letters of a particular color in the partial report procedure as they can of a particular row. However, stimuli that differ categorically, such as letters versus digits, cannot be selectively attended to. That is, subjects instructed to report only the digits (or the letters) in a mixed array of letters and digits did no better than subjects instructed to report the whole array. Thus, at least for brief visual presentations, subjects cannot use categorical information as a channel of attention.

In a visual analogue of the dichotic listening paradigm with meaningful messages, Neisser and Becklen (1975) made videotapes of two different games and superimposed them by use of mirrors. The subject's task was to attend to one of the games, and press a key each time a critical event, such as the throw of a ball, occurred. The two games were a *handgame,* in which the critical event was a slap on the hand by the bottom (attacker's) hand, and a *ballgame,* in which the critical event

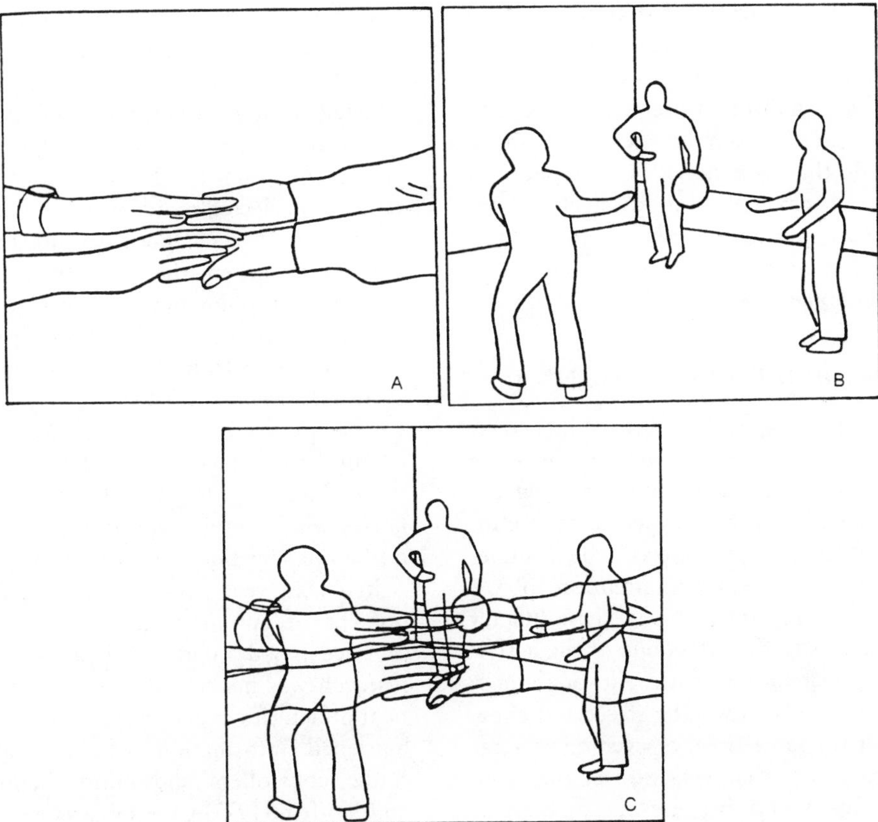

Fig. 6-13 Outline tracings of typical video images. (A) The handgame alone, (B) the ballgame alone, and (C) the handgame and ballgame superimposed. (From "Selective Looking: Attending to Visually-Specified Events," by U. Neisser and R. Becklen. In *Cognitive Psychology,* 1975, 7, 480–494. Copyright 1975 by Academic Press. Reprinted by permission.)

was a throw of the ball from one player to another. Schematic views of how the two games appeared at a particular moment in time are shown in Figure 6-13.

Subjects instructed to attend to one of the two games had no trouble doing so, detecting the critical events on nearly 100% of their occurrences. In addition, they failed to notice "odd" events that occurred during the unattended game, such as replacing the male players with females in the ballgame, or replacing a slap with a handshake in the handgame. Their behavior, then, was very similar to the behavior of subjects shadowing a meaningful passage presented to one ear or spoken by one speaker—they were unaware of what was going on in the other "channel." Thus, subjects can be selective about monitoring a particular visual input when it has a completely different one superimposed.

In contrast, when subjects were asked to monitor both games, by pressing one key for a hand slap and a second for a ball throw, their performance deteriorated markedly, with error rates climbing to about 40%, even though the density of the critical events in each game was cut in half. Thus, subjects were able to *selectively* attend to one game (or channel) but were not able to efficiently *divide* their attention between the two games.

Following the earlier discussion of auditory selection, we would argue that a meaningful stream of action constitutes a "channel." However, this interpretation is different from that which Neisser and Becklen prefer to give to their demonstration. In their words, "It is argued that selective attention does not involve special mechanisms to reject unwanted information, but is a direct consequence of skilled perceiving" (Neisser & Becklen, 1975, p. 480). Be that as it may, the metaphors of "filters," "channels," and "selection" are so deeply ingrained in the attention literature that we find it difficult to talk about the phenomena without them.

DIVIDED ATTENTION

We have been speaking of the ability to attend to one channel and ignore others as a skill well worth having (that is, after all, what subjects in these experiments are instructed to do). In contrast, the complementary ability—paying attention to two sources of information—is very difficult for subjects to do unless one of the activities has become automatic. Although most of us can walk down the street and chew gum at the same time, or even drive a car and carry on a conversation at the same time, this is only because one or both of the activities is highly overlearned. A new driver needs to pay full attention to driving, and even a skilled driver has difficulty carrying on a conversation when traffic conditions become hazardous.

One of the earliest studies on whether as complex a skill as writing words from dictation could become automated was carried out by Leon Solomons and Gertrude Stein (the famous writer and patron of the arts). As undergraduates together at Harvard, Solomons and Stein (1896) practiced writing words from dictation while they progressively carried out more difficult tasks such as reading another passage for meaning. They finally reached the point where they claimed they could read one passage while automatically writing down words from dictation, with no decrement in the speed or comprehension of reading. Evidence that their writing had become automatic was that they did not notice the meaning of the written words.

This study was recently replicated by Spelke, Hirst, and Neisser (1976), whose two undergraduate subjects eventually were able to write from dictation with no loss of speed or accuracy in reading a second text, and apparently no processing of the meaning of the written words. For example, their subjects did not notice when randomly selected words were replaced by words from two categories, although they did notice when the lists rhymed. As Spelke et al. point out, however, just because their subjects did not notice that all the words were from the same category (or even made sentences) does not mean they were not capable of doing so. With some training, their subjects were able to classify the dictated words into one of two categories while simultaneously reading, with no loss of speed or comprehension.

In recent years, research on the development of automatic processes through practice has dramatically increased. This research was inspired in part by the practical difficulties experienced by such overburdened information-processors as air traffic controllers and pilots. Schneider and Shiffrin (1977) gave subjects extensive training in a visual detection task. The subjects were to respond to either a single target letter or to any of four target letters embedded in a background of distractor letters. In one condition, the identity of both the target and distractor letters remained constant across the experiment in what they called a "consistent mappings" condition. In the consistent mappings condition, their subjects could eventually perform the four-target task as well as the one-target task. Schneider and Shiffrin have called this automatic processing, and speculate that no attentional resources need to be allocated to the task; in fact, their subjects reported that after training the targets appeared to "leap out" from the display.

Resource Allocation

A recent approach to divided attention tasks is to assume that humans have limited capacity or resources, that this limit exists somewhere in a "central processor," and that the human is capable of allocating resources between the two tasks. As long as the tasks do not consume more resources than are available, there will be no decrement in either task. However, when the attention demands of the two tasks exceed this capacity, performance on one or both of them suffers. Kahneman, in his 1973 book *Attention and Effort,* suggested that capacity limitations are affected by the degree of arousal of a subject, with the optimum level of arousal occurring at a moderate level for fairly difficult tasks. Highly practiced activities, such as driving for skilled drivers and target search for Shiffrin and Schneider's subjects, can be carried out with little or no resource allocation and are said to be automated.

A paradigm for measuring the capacity demands of a task of interest (the primary task) is to introduce a secondary task and measure how the secondary task suffers when the primary task is varied. Johnston and Heinz (1978) used this technique to measure the differential resource demands of different shadowing tasks. Their secondary task was reaction time to an increase in intensity of a white light. They found that reaction time was longer when subjects had to shadow by meaning than by voice of speaker. Subjects were required to shadow for meaning by repeating words from a single category, when words from two categories (names of cities and names of occupations) were presented to both ears. Johnston and Heinz suggest that a selective filter can be put anywhere in the flow of information. When it can be put earlier, at a physical dimension like voice, as in Broadbent's model, more capacity is left over for the secondary task. When it must be put later, after meaning is extracted, as in the categories condition, less capacity is left over for the secondary task, and so performance on the secondary task suffers.

HEMISPHERIC SPECIALIZATION

Perhaps no other topic in experimental psychology has attracted so much attention from the general public as hemispheric specialization. Hemispheric specialization, also known as lateralization, refers to the hypothesis that in right-handers language functions are primarily carried out in the left hemisphere, while spatial and form functions are primarily carried out in the right hemisphere. Popularized in the 1970s by Robert Ornstein as a way of bridging the gap between "Western rationalism" and "Eastern mysticism," the notion of two sides of the brain, each with its own strengths and weaknesses, goals and wishes, and separate consciousnesses, has captured the imagination of many (Ornstein, 1977).

Experimental psychologists have been understandably uneasy about the public's interest in this topic. This is largely because the claims about the differences between the two hemispheres have been greatly exaggerated. Such claims have led to the proliferation of workshops to train the "neglected" right hemisphere and calls to revamp our educational systems away from left brain skills toward right brain skills. As one experimental psychologist working in this area has written,

> It is becoming a familiar sight. Staring directly at the reader—frequently from a magazine cover—is an artist's rendition of the two halves of the human brain. Surprinted athwart the left cerebral hemisphere (probably in stark blacks and grays) are such words as "logical," "analytical," and "Western rationality." More luridly etched across the right hemisphere (in rich orange or royal purple) are "intuitive," "artistic," or "Eastern consciousness." Regrettably, the picture says more about a current popular-science vogue than it does about the brain.
>
> (Gardner, 1982, p. 278)

Here we will try to give a moderately balanced account of research in hemispheric specialization. We will first describe the experimental paradigms that have been developed to test for hemispheric specialization in normal subjects, and then review briefly some of the experimental differences that have been found.

In order to understand the logic behind experiments with normal subjects in hemispheric specialization (or laterality) studies, it is necessary to review some anatomy. The upper half of the human brain is called the *cerebral cortex.* This is divided into two halves—the left hemisphere and the right hemisphere. These two halves are connected by a massive sheaf of neurons known as the *corpus callosum.* The corpus callosum provides rapid communication between the two hemispheres. (It has been estimated that the time it takes for information from one hemisphere to reach the other is on the order of 3–10 ms).

The two hemispheres need to communicate with each other because each receives different information about the body and the environment. Signals to and from the left half of the body go to the right hemisphere while those to and from the right half of the body go to the left hemisphere. So, for example, the left hemisphere controls the right hand and the right hemisphere controls the left hand. In hearing, input from the right ear goes primarily to the left hemisphere via contralateral, or opposite-sided, fibers, although the right ear is also connected to the right hemisphere by ipsilateral, or same-sided, fibers. Conversely, input from the left ear goes primarily to the right hemisphere, although it, too, is represented in the left hemisphere.

In vision, the division is somewhat different. As shown in Figure 6-14, the split here occurs, not between the two eyes, but between the two hemifields of each eye. Input to the right visual field (RVF) in both eyes goes to the left hemisphere, while input to the left visual field (LVF) in both eyes goes to the right hemisphere. Thus, if you fixate the word RAT · HER between the T and H (indicated by the dot), your right hemisphere receives RAT and your left hemisphere, HER. Of course, your phenomenological impression is that you have seen a whole word synonymous with "somewhat," not two conflicting impressions having to do with a rodent and a female. This example illustrates the very effective communication between the hemispheres in normal people; we do not experience our visual field as split down the middle, but see it as a unified whole.

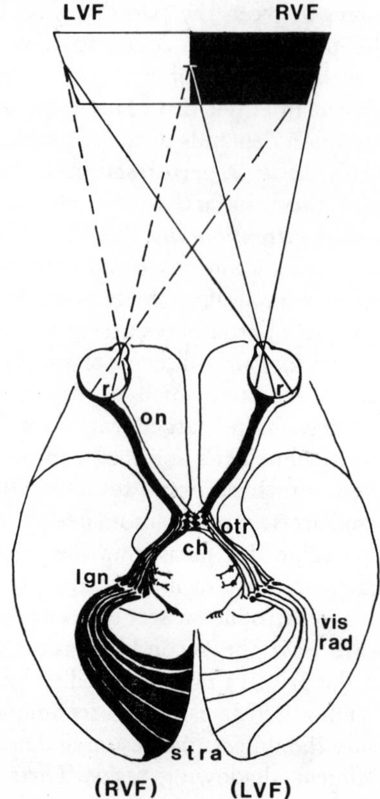

Fig. 6-14 A schematic diagram of the visual pathways of the brain. Stimuli in the right visual field (RVF) are transmitted to the left hemisphere, while those in the left visual field (LVF) are transmitted to the right hemisphere. Abbreviations: r—retina, on—optic nerve, otr—optic tract, ch—chiasma, lgn—lateral geniculate nucleus, vis rad—visual radiations, stra—striate cortex (occipital lobe).

The evidence is compelling that both language production and language reception functions lie in the left hemisphere of the vast majority (95% or so) of right-handers. The picture for left-handers is less clear, although it has been estimated that a major though smaller percentage (70%) also have speech in the left hemisphere (Springer & Deutsch, 1981). The evidence for lateralization of speech initially came from clinical observations of brain-damaged individuals, such as stroke victims. Aphasia, a disturbance in the ability to speak or understand language, was almost invariably accompanied by left-hemisphere damage, and consequent paralysis of the right side. Two general types of language deficits could be identified: difficulty in speech production, associated with lesions of an area in the frontal lobe of the left hemisphere known as Broca's area; and difficulty in spoken and written language reception, associated with lesions of the back part of the temporal lobe of the left hemisphere known as Wernicke's area (Lenneberg, 1967).

Additional evidence came from observations of split-brain patients—those who have had the corpus callosum severed to control severe epileptic seizures (Gazzaniga, 1970; Sperry, 1968). By presenting words visually via tachistoscopic exposures to separate hemifields in such patients, thereby segregating input to one or another of the two hemispheres, it can be shown that language is primarily the function of the left hemisphere.

Until fairly recently, the right hemisphere (sometimes identified as the minor hemisphere, compared to the left or dominant hemisphere), was considered to be less important, or inferior to, the left hemisphere. This inferiority was inferred from clinical observations that left-hemisphere damage led to massive difficulties for the patient in the all-important functions of language, whereas right-hemisphere damage appeared to produce few observable deficits.

More recently, evidence has accumulated that each hemisphere has its own specialties. The picture that emerges is one in which each hemisphere complements the other. What is at issue is exactly how to characterize this complementarity. The dichotomy of left and right hemisphere has variously been described as verbal versus nonverbal, analytic versus holistic, focal versus diffuse, serial versus parallel, rational versus synthetic, categorical versus analogical, and temporal versus spatial (see Bradshaw & Nettleton, 1981, for a recent discussion of the nature of this dichotomy).

Because the field of hemispheric specialization is continuously expanding it is impossible to anticipate what the final resolution of the differences between the two hemispheres will be, other than to note that the picture becomes more complicated with each new experiment. What we shall try to do here is to describe some paradigmatic experiments in both hearing and vision and their implications for hemispheric specialization in people with normal brains.

Experiments in hearing and vision conducted on normal subjects manipulate the hemisphere to which information is *first* delivered, by manipulating which ear gets it, in hearing, or in which hemifield the information is presented, in vision. Unlike the split-brain patient, for whom stimuli can be isolated to one hemisphere, the hemisphere of the normal subject not directly receiving the information receives it very quickly through the corpus callosum.

If the hemisphere specialized for analysis of the material receives it *first,* performance is generally better than if the nonspecialized hemisphere receives its first. Yet, why should this be, since the information is very quickly (within 3 to 10 ms) available to both hemispheres? Various proposals have been made for the advantage a specialized hemisphere obtains by receiving specialized material first. One explanation is that there is a time advantage (albeit a small one). Another explanation is that information transmitted from one hemisphere to another suffers a degradation in either quantity or quality when crossing the corpus callosum. Still a third holds that the hemisphere that initially receives the material will perform the task, and if this is the nonspecialized hemisphere, it will not perform it as efficiently as the specialized hemisphere. These are, at the moment, pure speculations as to why the priority with which the information is received should confer an advantage on the appropriate hemisphere (Springer & Deutsch, 1981).

The Dichotic Listening Task and Hemispheric Specialization

We have previously described the dichotic listening task for attention tasks. It has also been used with normal subjects to study hemispheric specialization. Because the right ear pathways primarily go to the left hemisphere, we expect that verbal material, such as words, will be better reported when delivered to the right than to the left ear. Conversely, if the right hemisphere is specialized for other types of auditory stimuli such as music, the left ear should show an advantage over the right ear in recognition of these types of sounds.

Just such a pattern of results has been reported by Doreen Kimura. In a dichotic listening task, speechlike sounds such as words, nonsense syllables, and even backward speech were recognized more accurately when presented to the right ear than to the left ear. In contrast, both melodic patterns and nonspeech sounds such as coughing, laughing, and crying were recognized more accurately when presented to the left ear (Kimura, 1967).

This suggests that the left hemisphere is not only specialized for understanding language per se, but specifically for recognizing speechlike sounds, regardless of whether they are meaningful or not (as in backward speech). Even more specificity has been provided to this hypothesis by the work of Studdert-Kennedy and Shankweiler (1970), who found a right-ear (hence left hemisphere) advantage for meaningless consonant-vowel syllables such as *ba* and *ga,* but no right-ear advantage for vowels presented in isolation. Thus it appears that the left hemisphere is specialized for processing those elements of speech—the consonants—that make speech most informative.

The right hemisphere advantage for musical stimuli is consistent with the clinical literature. Many patients with left hemisphere damage who cannot speak can nonetheless sing, whereas patients with right hemisphere damage whose speech is intact often lose their ability to sing, as well as their ability to express emotion in their utterances.

However, some evidence suggests that the left-ear advantage for music in dichotic listening tasks only holds true for subjects who are nonexperts in music. Bever and Chiarello (1974) found that although naive subjects recognized melodies better when presented to the left ear, experienced musicians showed the opposite pattern, recognizing melodies better in the right ear (i.e., with the left hemisphere). Bever and Chiarello attribute this difference to a difference in listening strategy. They speculate that naive listeners use a holistic strategy to perceive the melody whereas musicians use an analytic strategy.

As we noted, input from each ear actually goes to both hemispheres, with the contralateral or opposite hemisphere receiving more input than the ipsilateral or same-sided hemisphere. However, this relatively small difference in degree of input to the two hemispheres is not enough to show a laterality difference when linguistic or nonlinguistic stimuli are presented monaurally—usually the asymmetry appears only with dichotic presentation. Kimura has hypothesized that dichotic presentation effectively inhibits the ipsilateral input to the same-sided hemisphere, thereby producing the left- or right-ear advantage, depending on the type of material. Milner, Taylor, and Sperry (1968) showed this hypothesis was correct by comparing monaural and dichotic performance in split-brain patients. The patients had no difficulty understanding such speech sounds as words or nonsense syllables when presented to either ear monaurally, but were effectively "deaf" to speech presented to the left ear when the right ear was listening to different speech, in a dichotic presentation. The patients claimed to hear nothing in the left ear at all, suggesting that the subcortical transmission possible with monaural presentation was inhibited in the dichotic situation.

Tachistoscopic Recognition and Hemispheric Specialization

The technique for demonstrating hemispheric specialization in the visual domain is to present one stimulus tachistoscopically in either the right visual field (so that it goes directly to the left hemisphere) or the left visual field (so that it goes directly to the right hemisphere). Both a brief exposure and steady fixation are important in this procedure to ensure that the stimulus will be transmitted only to one hemisphere. Because the movement reaction time of the eye is on the order of 200 ms or so, the stimulus duration is usually kept below 100 ms.

In this situation, we expect linguistic material to be better perceived when presented to the right of fixation (to the left cerebral cortex), and pictorial or spatial material to be better perceived when presented to the left of fixation. The data from studies using linguistic material quite consistently show a right visual field (left hemisphere) advantage, although the converse—better perception of pictorial or spatial displays in the left visual field—is not quite so clear-cut.

Initially, superior recognition of verbal material presented to the right of fixation was attributed to well-established reading habits, which for English proceed from left to right (Neisser, 1967). As we have seen, a brief tachistoscopic flash produces a long-lasting icon that can be scanned by the subject. In a direct test of the "scanning" hypothesis, Mishkin and Forgays (1952) presented bilingual Hebrew–English subjects with English and Hebrew words presented to the right or left of fixation. Because Hebrew is read right to left and English is read left to right, they predicted that English words would be perceived better in the right field, while Hebrew words would be perceived better in the left visual field. Their hypothesis was confirmed, although the advantage for Hebrew on the left was less than for English on the right. Although scanning strategies undoubtedly enhance the right visual field advantage for words, it has been shown that when English and Hebrew words are printed vertically, thereby destroying any horizontal scanning advantage, *both* are perceived better to the right of fixation by Hebrew–English bilinguals (Barton, Goodglass, & Shai, 1965).

Left visual field (right hemisphere) superiorities have been reported for dot localization (Bryden, 1976), line orientation (Atkinson & Egeth, 1973), depth perception (Kimura & Durnford, 1974), photographs of faces (Rizzolatti, Umilta, & Berlucchi, 1971), and schematic faces (Patterson & Bradshaw, 1975). Thus, the left visual field results are consistent with a view that the right hemisphere is specialized for spatial processing and for processing of complex visual configurations, such as faces, which are indescribable in words. These results are also consistent with clinical findings that patients with right hemisphere damage do poorly on tests of spatial relationships, have difficulty finding their way about, and have difficulty recognizing faces. Unfortunately, for every study showing a left visual field advantage for some stimulus class, there are others showing either no difference or a difference in the opposite direction (Bradshaw & Nettleton, 1981).

What emerges from a review of the experimental literature, then, is a view of the two hemispheres of the normal brain very different from that common in the popular literature. In fact, some of the foremost researchers in the split-brain area have recently argued that the *only* difference between the two hemispheres lies in the fact that because some tissue in the left hemisphere is committed to language, the corresponding tissue in the right hemisphere is free to take over some functions (the manipulospatial ones) not possessed by the left hemisphere (LeDoux, Wilson, & Gazzaniga, 1977). In all other respects, they argue, the two hemispheres duplicate one another in their functions.

A related argument has been proposed by Ross (1982), who suggests that the speech centers in the left hemisphere control *what* we say, while the corresponding areas in the right hemisphere control *how* we say it—the right hemisphere controls the prosodic or emotional aspects of language. Ross has observed patients with lesions in the right hemisphere corresponding to Broca's area in the left (the area controlling speech production) who are unable to express emotion in their speech, although their speech is intact. Others, who have lesions in the right hemisphere corresponding to Wernicke's area in the left (the area controlling language understanding), have no difficulty producing emotion in speech, but cannot understand the emotion conveyed in the speech of others.

In summary, then, although the topic of hemispheric specialization is immensely provocative, leading to speculations ranging from the nature of consciousness to the location of Freud's unconscious in the right hemisphere, the experimental data are extremely complex, contradictory, and, as yet, unresolved.

SUMMARY

We have selectively reviewed two vast areas of research in experimental psychology—perception and attention. We have paired the field of attention with the field of perception because the experimental paradigms developed to study attention and its limits have typically used perceptual tasks.

We use an information-processing approach to perception, in which the act of perception is assumed to consist of several stages that include memorial and judgmental processes as well as sensory and perceptual ones. Within such an information-processing model of the perceptual process, effects of different variables on perceptual performance can affect a perceptual stage, a nonperceptual stage, or both.

A pervasive issue in the perception literature is the distinction between bottom-up (part-to-whole) and top-down (whole-to-part) processing. In the classical perceptual literature, top-down holistic processing characterizes the Gestalt school of perception, whereas bottom-up analytic processing characterizes the structuralist school of perception. In modern information-processing models, top-down processes have been used to characterize everything from whole-word tachistoscopic perception, to ease of identifying objects in scenes, to location of psychological gaps in spoken discourse.

The information-processing approach emphasizes perception of information-rich entities, such as visually and auditorially presented words, and visually presented pictures. Important issues in the area of visual word perception include the questions of whether words are perceived holistically or letter by letter and of whether the locus of the word superiority effect and its related phenomenon, the word frequency effect, occur in a perceptual or nonperceptual stage of perception. Similar issues occur in the area of speech perception, but here an additional puzzle is the mechanism whereby listeners segment the physically continuous speech stream into meaningful units such as words and phrases.

The area of picture perception has been less exhaustively studied than that of word perception, in part because the elements of pictures are less well-defined than the elements of words or phrases. For this reason, the role of context in picture perception has usually been studied by using scenes rather than pictures of single objects. As in visual and auditory word perception, context plays a significant role in facilitating perception of expected objects. A second issue in picture perception is whether pictures, like the words that describe them, act as arbitrary linguistic devices that differ across cultures and must be learned or convey information about their referents more directly. Evidence from cross-cultural and developmental studies suggests that pictures do provide direct, innately determined information about object identity, but not necessarily about relative object location. Pictorial cues to object distance and object location need to be learned to be used as valid cues.

Attention can be divided into two major areas: selective attention and divided attention. Research in selective attention has focused primarily on selecting among auditory inputs, as exemplified by the problem of paying attention to one conversation among a buzz of conversations at a cocktail party. It is clear that humans are usually capable of picking out a particular stream of auditory information from among competing streams, but the question is on what basis this is done. The term *channel* has come to mean a basis on which one stream of information can be segregated and attended to while others can be ignored. An early model of attention by Broadbent suggested that the basis was physical, so that different channels could be defined by separate ears, different voices, or different intensities, but not by different meanings. Modifications of the Broadbent model have included meaning and also have proposed that nonattended channels, once thought to be completely ignored, may be processed to some degree for meaning, even though memory for information coming across them seems to be missing. These modifications provide an explanation for why we can switch attention to a high-priority event like our own name coming over a unattended channel.

The area of divided attention asks the question of whether, and to what extent, two activities or two sources of information can be attended to. In modern information-processing terminology, the question can be phrased as whether the human is a serial processor (can attend to only one thing or channel at a time) or a parallel processor (can attend to multiple sources of information at a time). The answer seems to be that, with sufficient practice under appropriate conditions, processing can become parallel, or automatic, in that two or more sources of information can be attended to with the same efficiency as a single source. An important concept in the area of divided attention is that of resource allocation. As long as multiple tasks do not consume more human resources than are available, two tasks can be carried out in parallel with no decrement in performance on either one.

The area of hemispheric specialization or laterality is of unusual interest to both the lay public and the serious experimental psychologist. In most right-handed subjects, the left cerebral hemisphere appears to be specialized for verbal skills, whereas the right cerebral hemisphere appears to be specialized for visuospatial skills. Hemispheric specialization in normal subjects is studied in audition by use of the dichotic listening task and in vision by use of the split visual field tachistoscopic recognition task. Evidence from normal subjects is generally unanimous in supporting right field–left hemisphere superiority for verbal material, whereas evidence for left field–right hemisphere superiority for visual or spatial material is less compelling.

In this chapter, we have selectively reviewed issues in the vast research areas of perception and attention, with particular attention to ways in which critical questions in both areas have been investigated with experimental paradigms. The area of laterality in human subjects illustrates how experimental methods can be used to investigate neurological organization in the absence of neurological intervention. We hope to give the student in this chapter a glimpse into the complex yet fascinating research topics that comprise the human's first step in gathering information—attending to and perceiving information from the visual and auditory world.

7

Conditioning, Learning, and Motivation

> But yet it is true that at first some lucky hit, which took with somebody and gained him commendation, encouraged him to try again, inclined his thoughts and endeavors that way, till at least he insensibly got a facility in it, without perceiving how . . . which was the effect of use and practice.
>
> (John Locke, "An Essay Concerning Human Understanding," 1690)

In this chapter, we will consider key aspects of three related topics in experimental psychology—conditioning, learning, and motivation. The selection of particular problem areas will be guided by their usefulness to the student in performing experiments on human subjects. However, because many of the principles of learning come from animal research, we will have occasion in this chapter, unlike the other chapters in this book, to describe in detail some experiments that use animals.

The orientation of the theories in this chapter differs from those in the following chapters. Here, psychologists are interested in understanding the *why* of behavior—its motivation. In contrast, research reported in other chapters is concerned with the *how* of behavior. The necessary motivation is assumed and is not usually taken as a variable of interest in studies of perception, memory, concept formation, and problem solving.

Two approaches to behavior's motivation will be examined. The first approach was followed by behavior theorists—psychologists who hoped to explain the gamut of human and animal behavior with a set of simple stimulus-response (S-R) chains. In these early S-R models, motivation is considered an implicit force that impels responsive behaviors through one of several automatic processes, which we will describe.

The second approach follows a cognitive view of learning processes. Cognitive theories differ from strictly S-R theories in that they generally assume a nonautomatic, nonmechanical process in which some degree of thinking and appraisal is involved. We will examine several representative examples of cognitive learning processes in this chapter.

The topics of motivation and conditioning are closely related. This is because the conditioning and learning that occur in both lower animals and humans require some motivating force whose satisfaction acts as a mediator for acquiring or learning the new behavior. Generally, it has been assumed that no learning could take place without motivation, a controversial assumption that was challenged by experiments in latent learning (Tolman, 1951). Given the assumption that all new behavior is motivated, theories of motivation are necessarily closely tied to theories of learning.

THEORIES OF MOTIVATION IN LEARNING

The topic of motivation concerns the purpose of behavior. When we try to explain what causes behavior, we want to know three things: first, what *activates* and *energizes* it, that is, what triggers it and keeps it going? Second, how is it *directed* along one course instead of another? Finally what is it aimed at, or what is the *goal?* However many different ways there are to attain a desired objective, we would expect to find some recognizable consistency in those factors—energy, direction, and goals—with respect to different kinds of behavior. Therefore, they will constitute our working definition of motivation: an activating force that *energizes* the organism and *directs* a specific behavior toward a particular *goal.* The goal provides the reward for the action, and thus the motive for learning.

We mentioned the close relationship between motivation and learning. It is generally assumed that some motivating reward is necessary to make learning appear subsequently in behavior. The converse role of learning in the development of motivation can also be demonstrated. We need only recognize that there must be some memory of previously identified directional cues and goal satisfactions for a particular behavioral response to be repeated. This means there must be learning even in the case of instincts, such as hunger and sex.

Theories of motivation describe the nature of the mental changes that are involved in the learning of new behavior. These theories attempt to provide a single set of principles that will account for all purposive behavior. Early behavior theorists were concerned with those motivating objectives necessary for individual survival, such as food, water, comfort, and avoidance of pain, or for species survival, such as sex, nurturance, and affiliation. Yet humans obviously act from motives other than survival. Many psychologists have proposed additional motives to account for the why of human behavior. These include both cognitive and social motives, such as the reduction of dissonance, as in *cognitive dissonance theory* (Festinger, 1957, 1958), *need for achievement* (McClelland, Atkinson, Clark, & Lowell, 1953; Horner, 1972), *consistency and incongruity theories* (Heider, 1958), *field theory* (Lewin, 1938), and *attribution theory* (Schachter & Singer, 1962; Valins, 1966; Weiner, Russell, & Lerman, 1978). Although these are interesting topics in themselves, they are peripheral to our concern with motivation as a mediator of learned behavior and have been developed within the disciplines of personality and social psychology rather than experimental psychology. We mention them here only to indicate the wider scope of motivation.

In the first part of this chapter, we consider some mechanisms of conditioning and learning, and in the second part, we review how various theories of motivation support these mechanisms.

CONDITIONING AND LEARNING

Associationism

Many attempts to explain the marvelously complex processes of human learning commonly reduce it to the workings of simple, basic principles. One of the oldest and most prominent of these principles is *associationism,* the building of memory, thought, and their related behaviors out of linkages among perceptions and ideas. We are generally aware of our consistent associations between words, images and other sensory stimuli. So it is not surprising that the first theory of associational memory and thinking was propounded by the first philosopher-psychologist, Aristotle. Since the theory readily accounts for so much that we can observe in our thinking, and does so with a few simple concepts, it has dominated psychology, with amendments and amplifications, right up to the present. (An interesting and illuminating history is given by Bolles in Chapter 2 of his book [1975].)

How could associationism's simple connections explain complex learning behavior? This theory states that all that is needed for learning is to link together pairs of contiguous items (words, digits, ideas, etc.). Therefore, the associationist models had only to show how rather simple linkages between perceived stimuli and their associated responses could mediate observed behaviors. Such bondings, or links, became the targets of more experimental manipulations and observations than any other concept in all of psychology. The fact that experimenters find it comparatively easy to manipulate, to control, and to observe S-R behavior sequences has undoubtedly encouraged the endless attention to S-R processes and the abundance of S-R theorizing.

The notion that S-R effects seemed to be automatic supported a mechanistic type of theory and, indeed, provided the foundation for a mechanistic school of motivation—behavioral psychology. The shortcomings of a purely mechanical theory of human behavior were noted early, and it gradually became clear that even animals did more than make simple, automatic connections between stimuli (Tolman, 1948). Nevertheless, the S-R process is still treated as the fundamental principle of behavior in many laboratories and several influential journals today.

Although the stimulus-response concept seems simple enough, a closer look reveals a number of complexities and uncertainties. These include such questions as identification of the controlling stimulus, competing effects of multiple stimuli, the internal means by which the stimulus evokes the overt response, the ability of an organism to perform behaviors that presumably have not been learned, and the behavioral difference between conditioned and unconditioned responses, among other critical issues. We will trace the main line of research that attempts to solve such problems.

In order to understand the questions that are presently holding the interest of theoreticians, we will review some of the landmark developments in S-R behaviorism. Behaviorist theory of motivation and learning is built on two types of conditioning. The first, *classical* or *respondent conditioning*, was introduced by the Russian physiologist Ivan Pavlov (1849–1936). The second, *instrumental conditioning*, was introduced by Edward L. Thorndike (1874–1949) and developed by Burrus F. Skinner (1904–) into a refinement of Thorndike's concepts, known as *operant conditioning*.

The two types of conditioning present many differences, some fundamental and others only apparent. One major difference lies in the methods used in the conditioning procedures. Another difference is whether the conditioned response is involuntary (classical) or voluntary (operant). Yet another important difference is in the explanations for the motivation of the response as offered by the original developers of the two methods. We will shortly see how subsequent research has either supported or contradicted their respective claims.

Classical Conditioning

Pavlov's interest, as a physiologist, was in the digestive reflexes, and accordingly he designed equipment for experiments in eliciting such reflexes. His classical conditioning process was based on the natural, inherent ability of certain stimuli to elicit a particular response, or reflex, without previous training of the subject. That is why the natural, eliciting stimulus is called an *unconditioned stimulus* (US, or sometimes, UCS). A typical US is the aroma of food, which naturally excites salivation, an unconditioned response (UR). Another typical US is a puff of air on the eyeball, which elicits the unconditioned eyeblink response (UR). Note that the UR is a specific, unlearned reflexive response to the US.

In the classical procedure, the US is used as the means of training, or conditioning, a neutral stimulus to evoke a conditioned response (CR) that appears to be identical to the unconditioned response (UR). There are some differences between the CR and UR, which we will discuss later. But first let us see how the CR is conditioned in the Pavlovian procedure (Pavlov, 1927).

Pavlov used a dog as the subject in his original experiments. (Today, rats, rabbits, and humans are conditioned by essentially the same basic procedure.) The dog was held in a harness (see Figure 7-1). Within reach of his mouth was a shelf on which a dish containing meat powder (US) was placed. When the meat powder appeared, it elicited a salivation response (UR). A tube was connected to one of the animal's salivary glands to allow the saliva to drain off and be measured when the flow was stimulated by the US. The experimental sequence was as follows:

Meat powder (US) → Salivation (UR)

Immediately before, during, or after the meat powder was presented, a bell was rung. The bell was the neutral, or conditioned, stimulus (CS) that, by itself, would evoke no specific response, but when bell and meat powder were paired repeatedly, the two would become associated in the dog's perception. Thus,

$$\left.\begin{array}{c}\text{Meat powder (US)}\\ +\\ \text{Bell sound (CS)}\end{array}\right] \rightarrow \text{Salivation (UR)}$$

Fig. 7-1 Pavlov's dog. The dog, held in a harness, is presented with a bell as the CS and meat powder as the US. The conditioned response, salivation, is measured by a tube connected to an opening in the salivary gland. Rate of salivation is measured on the revolving drum. (Reproduced from *Psychology* by Henry Gleitman, by permission of W. W. Norton & Company, Inc. Copyright © 1981 by W. W. Norton & Company, Inc.)

The CS can be presented at various time intervals in relation to the US, either separated or overlapping. (A detailed discussion on comparative conditioning effectiveness of various temporal relations between CS and US appears in Spooner and Kellogg, 1947.)

Finally, after a certain number of paired trials, the bell is sounded but the meat powder is no longer presented. Pavlov observed that the dog salivated at the bell alone as he had when the meat powder had been presented. The bell sound had become conditioned (CS), and was now capable of evoking a conditioned salivation response (CR). The situation is represented thus:

Bell sound (CS) → Salivation (CR)

What this tells us is that the bell sound had become conditioned to the meat powder and, according to Pavlov, substituted for it when the meat (US) was not present. The connection here is between two stimuli, the CS and the US. Notice that throughout the conditioning procedure, the dog initiates no action but merely responds passively to the stimuli.

In this experiment, it would appear that the salivation CR is the same as the salivation UR, but there is evidence that this is not so. For example, the quantity of CR salivation is not the same as that of UR salivation.

An interesting example of the difference between a CR and UR was demonstrated in a conditioned narcotic withdrawal experiment run with eight former drug addicts currently in a methadone maintenance program (O'Brien, Testa, O'Brien, Brady, & Wells, 1977). In the conditioning trials, the subjects were injected with a chemical called naxolone, which produces symptoms usually experienced during heroin withdrawal. Among the withdrawal symptoms are elevated respiration, decreased skin temperature, rubbing of eyes and nose, and sniffing. Eight salient symptoms, including the five just listed, were monitored. These responses were elicited by the naxolone injection, mimicking the effects of heroin withdrawal.

A compound CS was presented with the naxolone (the US) to strengthen the conditioning. The CS, consisting of both a 700-Hz tone and a pronounced odor (oil of peppermint), was presented during the peak of the naxolone-withdrawal effect. Subsequently, after US-CS training trials, only the compound CS was presented in the test trials, without naxolone injection. During the test trials, the conditioned subjects manifested CR symptoms similar to most of the UR symptoms observed during the naxolone-withdrawal peak. However, some of the CR symptoms did not correlate with the UR symptoms, among them pupil size (UR increased, CR no change) and respiration rate (quantitative UR-CR differences for individual subjects).

Some psychologists see such differences as a contradiction of Pavlov's CS-US substitution hypothesis. If the CS were simply substituting for the US, there should be no difference in the effect, that is, there should be no difference between the CR and UR. But because the CR and UR are not identical, the CS must be playing a somewhat different role in relation to the US. They consider that the CS induces an *expectancy* in anticipation of the US. That is, it signals the imminence of the US, which, of course, may not appear. We will look at this possibility more closely later.

Instrumental Conditioning

Having studied examples of the passive responses of animals and humans to classical conditioning, we now consider another type of conditioning that requires an active response in order to gain the reward. Chronologically the two procedures made their experimental appearance at about the same time. The groundwork for *instrumental conditioning,* the active procedure, was developed by Thorndike and first presented in his doctoral dissertation in 1898.

In classical conditioning, the relationships of interest are between the conditioned and unconditioned stimuli and the corresponding conditioned and unconditioned responses. In instrumental conditioning, our interest centers on the relationship between the instrumental response and the reward for its performance. Further, we note that responses that can be classically conditioned are limited to passive reactions of the autonomic nervous system that can be automatically evoked by a natural, unconditioned stimulus. However, with instrumental conditioning, the response can be virtually *any* possible behavior, involving either the voluntary muscles or the autonomic nervous system, that can be evoked by *any* stimulus. During the early days of instrumental conditioning, it was thought that only voluntary muscle actions could be evoked by reward stimuli. More recently, however, it has been demonstrated that autonomic responses, such as blood pressure and heart rate, as well as brain wave patterns, can be conditioned through *biofeedback* methods. In these situations the reward is some indication of success in producing the desired response.

Thorndike's Law of Effect. Pavlov demonstrated a way to link specific acts of behavior to neutral cues. We saw, however, that the CS-CR linkage was a passive reaction, just as the original US-UR linkage had been. The animal's response was a function of the autonomic (involuntary) nervous system, requiring neither initiative nor control on the animal's part.

By the time Pavlov had established the ability of a CS to elicit a counterpart to a US, Thorndike had laid the foundation for a landmark conception in the development of learning theory: the *law of effect* (Thorndike, 1898).

Thorndike sought to prove that there was neither basis nor need for the anthropomorphic notion of animal intellect that became popular after Darwin's theory of animal-human continuity gained acceptance. Impressive examples of animal cleverness were widely acknowledged as indications of sophisticated learning processes. Thorndike undertook to show that it was not necessary to assume a high order of intellect in order to explain such behavior.

Thorndike studied the ability of cats to learn to escape from a puzzle box whose door was pinned by a latch that could be released by pressing on a treadle. The criterion for learning was the time needed (latency) for a successful escape. The cats' learning showed a pattern marked by numerous regressive failures as the correct procedure gradually became "stamped in."

Thorndike's explanation for the learning of the correct response was the formation of an S-R bond, the successful outcome of a series of rewarded trials. Conversely, if trials are unrewarded (i.e., unsuccessful; we now say *extinguished*) the behavior will cease. In short, the animal's learning behavior is governed by its effect, a purely S-R connection. There is no need to ascribe it to some humanlike ingenuity. (The Gestalt psychologists revived the animal ingenuity hypothesis, as we shall see in Chapter 10, with their insight theory of problem solving.) In an interesting inversion, Thorndike supported the animal-human continuity theory by applying the S-R law of effect to human learning as well: Animals and humans were not similarly ingenious, they were similarly mechanistic in their thinking.

The key to instrumental theory is trial-and-error learning, along with the associative stamping-in of successful outcomes and dropping-out of unsuccessful ones. This suggests a process of accidental discoveries that become associated with certain problems or needs and, by their success, develop into habitual responses, stored in memory where they are available for later situations. The entire procedure is quite automatic, or mechanistic, involving nothing more than the S-R linkage formed by successful outcomes. Success makes a habit; failure extinguishes it. That simple doctrine is the basis for S-R discrimination and response selection. It became the keystone of an extensively researched area of S-R theory, *operant conditioning,* a procedure initially developed by B. F. Skinner (1938).

Operant Conditioning: A Type of Instrumental Conditioning

The essential process in operant conditioning consists of a sequence that starts with a behavior emitted by the subject, followed by a reinforcement of that behavior. A positive reinforcement (usually, pleasant or satisfying) increases the likelihood that the particular behavior will be repeated, in accordance with Thorndike's law of effect. These response patterns have been plotted through myriad experiments, which are usually performed in a Skinner box (see Figure 7-2).

A typical Skinner box experiment is performed with an animal (rats and pigeons

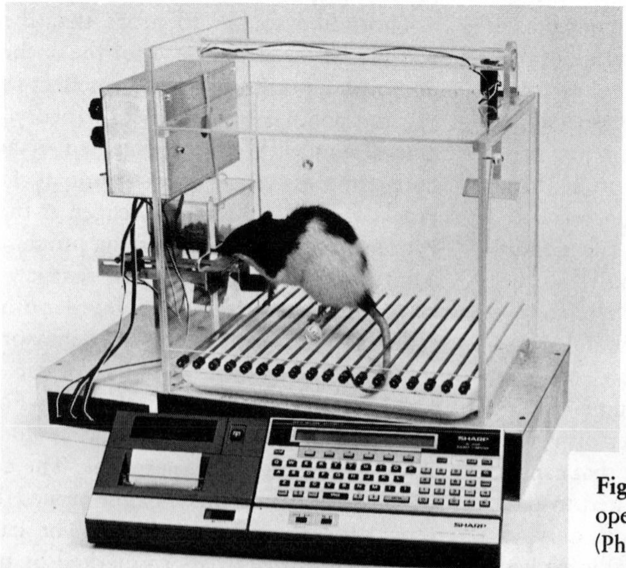

Fig. 7-2 Computer programmed operant chamber (Skinner box). (Photo courtesy of Life Science Associates, Bayport, NY 11705).

are favorite subjects) that has not been fed for a sufficient length of time. This ensures a hunger strong enough to motivate the desired behavior. The rat is placed in a Skinner box, which is equipped with the necessary mechanism to dispense a measured portion of food in response to the rat's bar pressing behavior. The probability of a response depends on a number of factors, the most important of which is the *contingency schedule,* which is the rate and pattern of reinforcements consequent upon the emitted behavior. Various patterns of frequency, timing, and regularity of reinforcement induce corresponding effects in strength and persistence of responding by the subject. The *schedule of reinforcement,* or *contingency schedule,* can be varied. Most experiments consist of mapping the response patterns to various schedules of reinforcement. Schedules refer to the virtually countless variations in the reinforcement rates, their regularity (or intermittency), "tandem" combinations (such as a fixed ratio of reinforcements-to-responses running simultaneously with a variable-time-interval schedule), and deprivation conditions. Figure 7-3 describes the various schedules and shows recordings of typical response patterns to several different rates of reinforcement under the four basic types of schedules. Table 7-1 describes the corresponding response patterns. These schedules are discussed in more detail by Ferster and Skinner (1957).

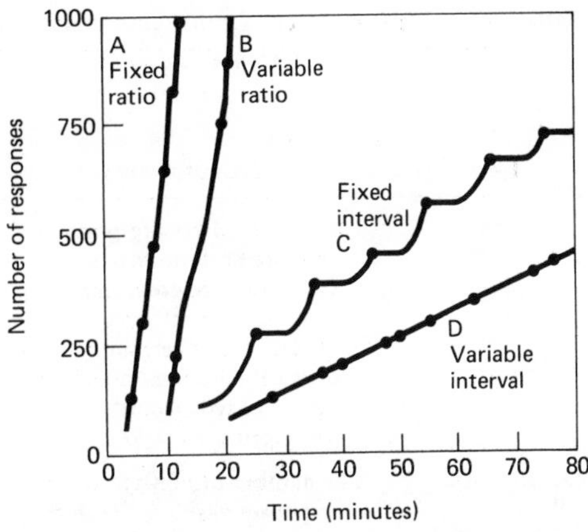

Fig. 7-3 Typical patterns of responding under four schedules of reinforcement. The functions are cumulative response counts, so increasing rates of response produce steeper slopes, and a horizontal line indicates no responding. The solid circles show delivery of a reinforcement. Ratio schedules produce much higher response rates than interval schedules. The scallop shape is typical of a fixed interval schedule, and shows that the pigeon increases its response rate toward the end of a fixed interval, as reinforcement becomes more and more certain. (From "Teaching Machines," by B. F. Skinner. In *Scientific American,* 1961, *205,* 90–102. Copyright© 1961 by W. H. Freeman and Company. All rights reserved. Reprinted by permission.)

Discriminative Stimulus. There is, however, something more in the environment than the appearance of the reinforcement, or reward, that excites the subject's responses. The fact that the animal never fails to contact the same lever, bar, or key, even after interruptions or distractions, suggests a visual cueing function, which provides a means of discriminating the appropriate operating device from alternative objects in view. Accordingly, this device is called a *discriminative stimulus.* As we will see, it plays an important role as a "stand-in" for the forthcoming reinforcer, and, as such, it shares the reinforcer's function of conditioned stimulus in exciting the subject's conditioned responses.

In effect, the discriminative stimulus serves to enable the subject to anticipate the reinforcement. This cueing function can be considered analogous to the fractional anticipatory goal response postulated by Hull as a means of explaining how the subject starts an action sequence leading to a remote goal object (the reward). Hull's concept of goal anticipation will be discussed later in this chapter.

Shaping. In operant conditioning, the subject must emit the desired response before a reinforcement can be given. How, then, does the experiment begin? In some cases, the experimenter simply waits until the animal running about in the box or cage accidentally touches and actuates the

Table 7-1 Reinforcement Contingency Schedules

Type	Contingency	Typical response pattern (see Figure 7-3)	Response characteristics
Fixed ratio (FR)	*Continuous:* Every response is reinforced. *Intermittent:* Occasional reinforcement. A response is reinforced when it occurs after a certain number of unreinforced responses have been emitted, according to a predetermined ratio.	A	Brief pause (horizontal slope) immediately after each reinforcement, followed by a sharp acceleration (vertical slope) to next fixed reinforcement. The faster the required number of responses are made, the sooner the reward is obtained.
Variable ratio (VR)	The number of nonreinforced responses varies between the successive reinforced responses. The sequence of varying ratios is predetermined to center on a specified average ratio.	B	Rapid, stable rate maintained (steep, straight slope) between reinforcements since subject does not know which response will be reinforced but learns that frequent responding brings faster rewards.
Fixed interval (FI)	A response is reinforced only when it is emitted after a preset time interval (e.g., 2 minutes between reinforced responses). Responses emitted during the interval not reinforced.	C	Negligible responding immediately after reinforcement (horizontal slope). Response rate accelerates sharply as subject senses approach of critical time for next reinforcement, producing characteristic FI scallop.
Variable interval (VI)	Reinforcement is given only to the response that is emitted after an unreinforced interval that varies in duration according to a predetermined schedule, ranging from a few seconds to many minutes.	D	As with VR, VI responding is steady and stable, though interval schedules (both FI and VI) tend to induce lower rates of responding generally than ratio schedules, since frequency of response has no effect with temporal contingencies.

trigger mechanism and thereby elicits the reward automatically. Or the experimenter can increase the probability of an "accident" by nudging the animal toward the device. The experimenter may even model the behavior by hitting the bar in view of the animal.

The problem is more difficult in the case of an uncommon response that requires a sequence of steps before it can be performed. For example, changing a light bulb in a ceiling fixture requires getting a ladder from the closet and then finding a good bulb. Yet the reward of a lighted room is not immediately associated with getting a ladder or searching through a cluttered shelf for a bulb. Building an operant response sequence is done by a method of *successive approximations,* often referred to as *shaping.* The shaping process can account for elaborate and complex behaviors, human and animal, and is an essential technique in most animal training. A notable example has been reported by Pierrel and Sherman (1963), demonstrating how an extended series of unnatural behaviors can be operantly conditioned.

They trained a rat to (a) climb a staircase, (b) cross a narrow bridge, (c) climb a ladder, (d) pull a toy auto over the bridge, (e) jump into the auto, (f) pedal it to another ladder, (g) climb the ladder, (h) crawl through a tube, (i) enter a elevator, (j) pull a chain, which raised a flag and lowered him to the starting platform, where he (k) pressed a lever that delivered a food pellet. After eating the food pellet, he started the whole sequence again. As in the training of many complex behaviors, the conditioning process starts with the last action before the reinforcer is presented. Each previous act is then conditioning by *chaining* it to the already conditioned act, until the entire sequence is completed. Thus, the rat was first trained to press the lever for the reward, then to pull the chain, then to enter the elevator, and so on. The new action becomes the discriminative stimulus for the following operant response and a conditioned reinforcer for the preceding one.

Controlling Stimuli

In classical conditioning, the controlling stimulus is the CS, which elicits the CR. Learning in classical conditioning thus consists of associating a new response (CR) with a previously neutral stimulus. The controlling stimulus in classical conditioning thus *precedes* the response. In instrumental conditioning, in contrast, the controlling stimulus is the reinforcer, which occurs *after* the response, and increases the probability that the response will be repeated in the future. Thus, Skinner (1937) argued that the controlling relationship in operant conditioning is between response and reinforcer, as dictated by the law of effect, not an associative S-R bond between discriminative stimulus and response, as in classical conditioning. The operant behavior is influenced solely by its consequences (the reinforcement). Yet, could the operant also be influenced by stimuli presented before the response, as in the classical conditioning case?

Schwartz and Williams (1972) tried to show such discriminative stimulus control in pigeons by pairing the delivery of food with a lighted (pecking) key, requiring no operant response. Yet their pigeons pecked at the lighted key even though the pecking *cancelled* the food that would have been delivered without any response on that trial. Similarly, Gormezano and Hiller (1972) trained a rabbit to perform a jaw movement (CR) to a CS that signalled water even though the CR cancelled the delivery of water on that trial. Of course, we may here be observing a natural behavior (pecking or jawing) that the animal might perform spontaneously in any case. So we now look at an experiment in which control subjects provided a basis for distinguishing conditioned from natural, species-specific behavior. Here, the significant difference in behavior offers more definite evidence of discriminative cueing based on stimulus associations.

Boakes and Ismail (1971) exposed birds to 100% pairings of lighted key and lighted, but *empty*, food magazines. These trained birds, in subsequent instrumental trials, began pecking significantly sooner than other birds that had seen the two stimuli separately. Remember, there had been no food reinforcers during the training trials, so the effect must have come from the pairing of the key and empty magazine stimuli. In short, the birds were responding to the lighted discriminative stimulus.

Our interest in the control of responses goes to the heart of the question of *why* behaviors are performed—the basic issue of motivation that we pointed out at the beginning of this chapter. The question of control thus becomes the critical basis for distinguishing one type of conditioning from another. Pavlov proposed that the formerly neutral CS acquired its power to elicit the CR by *substituting* for the US. Thorndike claimed that the instrumental response became *associated* ("stamped in") with the consequent reward, generating a kind of expectancy effect. Skinner, however, firmly refuses to postulate internal motivational mechanisms, rejecting Thorndike's associationist model. He argues that all we know and all we need to know about the behavioral phenomenon is that the reinforcement stimulus increases the probability of the response being emitted by the subject, and repetition of the reinforcement, contingent upon the performance, ensures repetition of the response.

In order to pursue the question of what governs response behavior, we must probe more deeply into the function of reinforcement. Although reinforcement is identified with operant conditioning, it relates to several functions that are common to both operant and classical processes: *extinction, inhibition,* and *contingency. Extinction* is the elimination of a response by withholding the previous reinforcement of that response. *Inhibition* is the suppression or blocking of a response by following it with negative or aversive reinforcement (punishment, discomfort, etc.). *Contingency* is the direct relationship between the response and the reinforcement, expressed as the probability that the response will be followed by the reinforcement. All of these processes are intimately related to the processes of *generalization* and *discrimination,* to which we turn next.

Generalization and Discrimination

Generalization. Now that we have seen how subjects can use response-contingent reinforcements to discriminate between rewarded and nonrewarded responses, we can understand how that ability enables them to extend a learned S-R behavior to a range of similar stimuli in a process called *stimulus generalization.* A corresponding process permits a single stimulus to elicit a range of related responses in a process called *response generalization.*

Stimulus generalization refers to the fact that stimuli similar to the original CS will elicit similar responding. The strength of responding (measured by rate or latency) follows a curve that declines monotonically with increasing distance from the original stimulus. This falling response curve describes the *generalization gradient* for the particular CS.

To illustrate, Siegel, Hearst, George, and O'Neal (1968) exposed 20 white rabbits to an unconditioned stimulus consisting of a mild shock to a point on the cheek below the left eye. The unconditioned response was an eyeblink. Each rabbit also heard a pure tone of a different frequency (either 500, 1000, 2000, 3000, or 4000 Hz) as a conditioned stimulus, with a CS-US interval of 1 second. During the test trials,

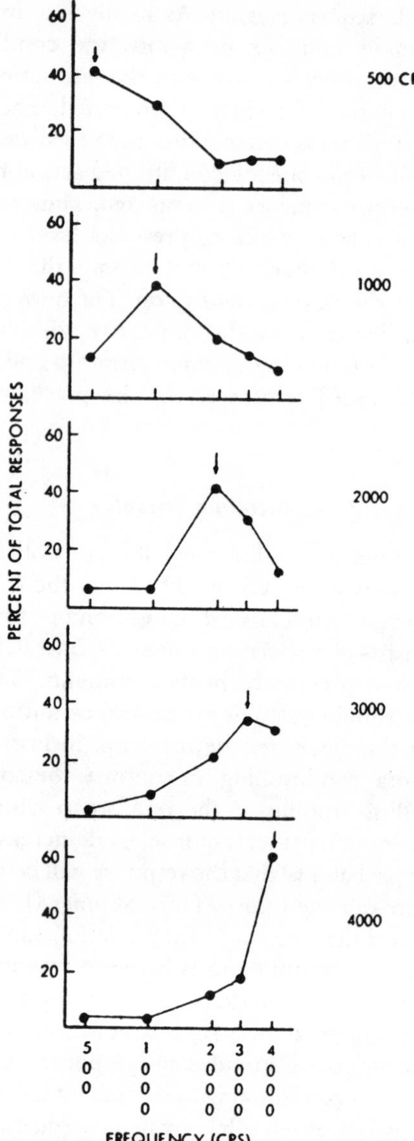

Fig. 7-4 Generalization gradients for five groups of rabbits conditioned to tones at five different frequencies. The tones were paired with a mild shock (US) which elicited an eyeblink (UR). The arrow indicates the conditioning stimulus. As the graphs show, the highest percent of conditioned eyeblink responses were made to the original CS, with monotonic decreases as the test CS departs in frequency from the conditioning CS. (From "Generalization Gradients Obtained from Individual Subjects Following Classical Conditioning," by S. Siegel, E. Hearst, N. George, and E. O'Neal. In *Journal of Experimental Psychology,* 1968, *78,* 171–174. Copyright 1968 by the American Psychological Association. Reprinted by permission.)

tones of all of the frequencies were presented without shock. The graphs in Figure 7-4 show the relative increase of eyeblink CRs as the tone frequencies approached the particular conditioned frequency for each group of subjects. The closer the test stimulus is to the original, conditioned stimulus, the more likely it is to elicit the conditioned eyeblink response. The fact that subjects show weaker responses to stimuli similar to, but not identical to, the original CS, shows not only stimulus generalization, but also stimulus discrimination, a topic that we turn to next.

Discrimination. We owe the classic formulation of *discrimination learning* to Kenneth Spence (1936). The basic idea is a direct offshoot of S-R automaticity: Any creature, however limited in cognitive capacity, will be able to associate a salient cue with a desirable reward, like Pavlov's bell and the aroma of (promise of) meat. If the cue is presented along with other similar cues that are not reinforced with a reward, the subject will eventually recognize and choose the rewarded cue. First, of course, the subject will make a series of trial-and-error choices before it discriminates the rewarded stimulus (S^+) from the unrewarded stimulus (S^-). For example, if you go fishing with several kinds of bait, you will continue using the kind that increases your catch and abandon the kind that brings in no fish. Once the discriminative association has been established, the rewarded stimulus (S^+) acquires an *excitatory* effect while all unrewarded stimuli (S^-) become *inhibitory* cues. The initial trial-and-error responses to the S^- stimuli die out and cease to be made. This process is called *extinction.*

The discrimination can be quite complex. It need not be merely an absolute association between a specific response and its reward, according to Spence (1942). In fact, he showed that performance is a complex function of both generalization and inhibition (discrimination) gradients in the following experiment. He presented chimpanzee subjects with sets of two different-sized squares, one of which had a reward behind it (S^+) and the other, nothing (S^-). The animals learned to choose the positive square over the negative square. Spence's model is shown in Figure 7-5. In this model, the degree of preference for a particular square corresponds to the net *difference* between values of the conditioned generalization (B) and inhibition (A) gradients at the points representing the S^+ and S^- cues (see the A-B difference between the two curve heights in Figure 7-5). When the 160-cm^2 square is conditioned as S^+ against the 100-cm^2 square as S^-, the positive generalization gradient (solid curve) peaks at 160, and the negative inhibition gradient (dashed curve) peaks at 100, predicting a test-preference for the 160

Fig. 7-5 Hypothetical generalization (B) and inhibition (A) gradients hypothesized to develop around the positive (160) and negative (100) squares during training, and used by Spence to account for transfer to new squares. (From "The Basis of Solution by Chimpanzees of the Intermediate Size Problem," K. W. Spence. *Journal of Experimental Psychology,* 1942, *31,* 257–271. Copyright 1942 by the American Psychological Association. Adapted by permission.)

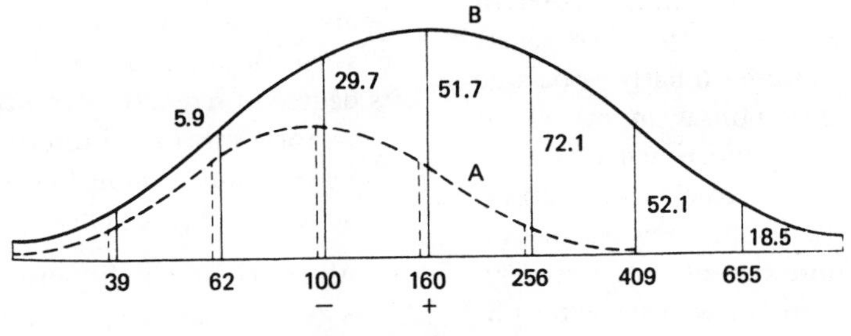

stimulus when the pair is presented, since the difference between habit and inhibition (B-A) is 51.7 at 160 and only 29.7 at 100.

The power of Spence's model is that the relative heights of the habit and inhibition gradients can be used to predict preferences between squares that have never been seen by the chimp. For example, when the test pair of 256 and 160 is presented, the subjects are predicted to choose 256 over 160 (and they do!) because the difference between habit and inhibition is 72.1 for 256 and only 51.7 for 160. The chimps, however, are not simply always choosing the larger square. When the pair 256 and 409 are presented, 256 is chosen. This is because 256 has a net habit strength of 72.1 whereas 409 has a strength of only 52.1. Clearly, these predictions are not in accord with a simple notion of absolute reinforcement discrimination, since the responses are made according to the gradient size relationship rather than the direct size relationship between the stimuli.

The discrimination effect has been elicited with both the discriminative stimulus and the reinforcer in numerous experiments. Using different reinforcers for two responses, Trapold (1970) trained rats to press two different levers to the sound of a click and a tone, each lever-press producing either a food pellet or a sucrose-solution reward:

Lever 1 + Click → Food pellet
Lever 2 + Tone → Sucrose

The differentially trained rats responded more accurately to the lever discrimination task in test trials than the control rats, whose levers had both returned the same reward during the training. Different amounts of the same reward (five pellets versus one pellet) were similarly associated with alternative responses in other discrimination training experiments.

Having seen how subjects can discriminate between successful (rewarded) and unsuccessful (unrewarded) responses in complex combinations, we can better understand the ways in which stimulus and contingency relationships affect the degree, or strength, of the conditioning. In particular, we can distinguish between the effects of *contingency* versus *contiguity* in the conditioning process.

Contingency versus Contiguity

What is the essential requirement for conditioning to occur? It was originally thought that the *contiguous* (adjacent in time) *pairing* of the CS and US was the essential requirement for classical conditioning. Thus, if food was presented within a few seconds of a bell, salivation would be conditioned to the bell. If, however, the food was presented an hour after the bell, no conditioning would take place.

More recently, researchers have begun to question whether contiguity alone can account for conditioning. As we have just seen, studies of discrimination learning show that subjects can distinguish complex relationships between stimuli and reinforcers, so perhaps they can also distinguish between *contingency* (the probability that one event will follow another) and *contiguity* (simple temporal pairing). The research described below shows that contingency, not contiguity, is the essential requirement for conditioning.

The importance of contingency over contiguity was demonstrated in a series of experiments by Rescorla (1966, 1968). He argued that pairing of the CS-US in Pavlovian training was not sufficient to ensure conditioning. Conditioning will occur only if the subject can distinguish between the frequency of the US occurring *with* the CS compared with the frequency of the US occurring *without* the CS. The relative CS-US probabilities (i.e., their contingencies) determine which kind of conditioning (positive, negative, or none) will occur and its degree of strength (Rescorla, 1967).

Rescorla's theory of discriminative contingency can be summed up in these three possible contingency effects:

1. When the probability of CS occurrence is greater than the probability of CS ab-

sence when the US is presented, *positive* (excitatory) conditioning will occur.

2. When the probability of CS occurrence is less than the probability of CS absence when the US is presented, *inhibitory* conditioning will occur.
3. When the probability of CS occurrence equals the probability of CS absence when the US is presented, *no* conditioning will occur.

In one experiment, Rescorla (1966) demonstrated all three types of conditioning—positive, negative, and none. Rescorla trained three groups of dogs to jump over a barrier in a shuttlebox in order to avoid electric shock. Classical fear conditioning was then applied in which tones (CS) were presented during the shock training sessions. Group R (random) received shocks and tones on a random schedule. Group P (predictable positive) received only shocks paired with tones. Group N (predictable negative) received only shocks that were *not* temporally paired with tones, so that tones predicted *absence* of shocks.

During the nonreinforcement (no shock) test, group P, for whom the tone was a positive predictor of shock, responded to the fear-producing tone with a high rate of avoidance jumping compared to baseline. Group N, for whom the *absence* of tone was a predictor of shock, responded to the tone with a low rate of avoidance jumping compared to baseline. Group R (the random pairing group) did not change its response rate, indicating no conditioning effect. The conclusion was that the animals that were contingently conditioned (groups P and N) learned to *predict* the occurrence or nonoccurrence of the shock and to avoid the shock by jumping the barrier (group P) or to use the tone as a "safe signal" meaning they could refrain from jumping (group N).

In subsequent experiments, Rescorla was able to show that neither the absolute number of CS-US pairings nor the absolute number of USs was responsible for the positive conditioning effect; rather, it was the contingency itself. But before turning to Rescorla's next experiment, we first introduce some methodology.

Ordinarily, strength of conditioning is measured by the number of unreinforced trials before the response is extinguished. However, this method is slow and lengthy and, in addition, not precise enough to measure small differences in conditioning strength. Rescorla used another technique that employs *response suppression* as the index of conditioning strength. This technique, which combines classical (Pavlovian) and operant (Skinnerian) procedures, was first described by Estes and Skinner (1941). Because the response suppression method is complex, we take a moment to describe the technique.

Estes and Skinner produced what was called a *conditioned emotional response* (CER) to demonstrate the inhibitory effect of conditioned fear. A group of rats was trained to bar-press for food pellets according to the standard *operant* paradigm. In another location, they were conditioned by a *classical* procedure to associate a tone with shock. The natural response (UR) to the shock is fear. When the CS tone was sounded during the operant trials, the rat's bar-pressing responses were significantly reduced in frequency. Since the two responses (fear and bar-pressing) were conditioned independently, there was no associative response interference. In other words, the fear-associated tone was able to produce the conditioned fear effect so as to inhibit the operant bar-pressing response, even though bar-pressing had not been conditioned to fear. (This experimental technique is referred to as *transfer-of-control*, in which control of an operant response is transferred to another CS, and is useful as a means of determining the relationship between classical and operant processes. In this case, the control of the operant bar-pressing response by the food reinforcer was transferred to the classically fear-conditioned tone.)

In one of Rescorla's (1968) aversive suppression experiments, he first trained three groups of rats to bar-press for food

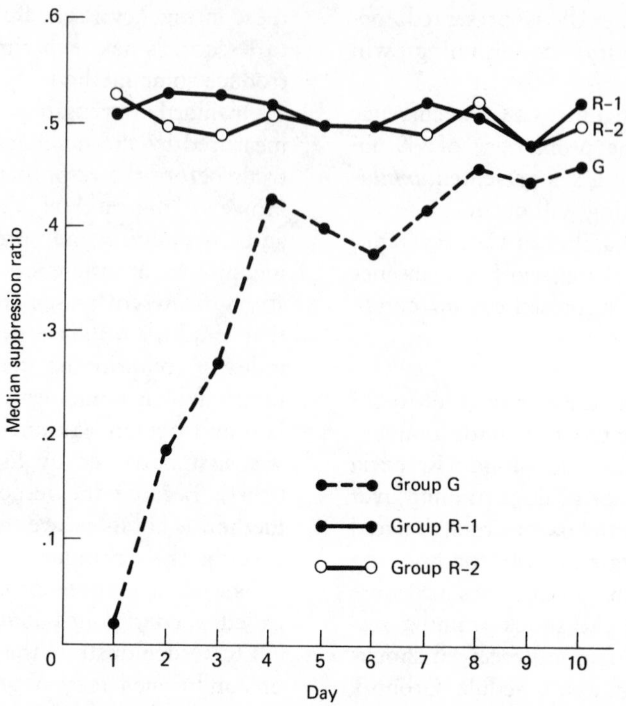

Fig. 7-6 Suppression ratio for each group in Rescorla's experiment. A suppression rate of 0.5 indicates no differential conditioning, while a suppression ratio of 0 indicates maximum conditioning. (From "Probability of Shock in the Presence and Absence of CS in Fear Conditioning," by R. A. Rescorla. In *Journal of Comparative and Physiological Psychology*, 1968, 66, 1–5. Copyright 1968 by *The American Psychological Association.* Adapted by permission.)

pellets on a variable interval reinforcement schedule. Group G, the contingency group, then received shocks in the presence of tones, but never in their absence, although some tones were presented without the shock. Two other groups served as the random control groups. Group R-1 was identical to group G with the exception that some shocks were also presented in the absence of tones. Thus, group R-1 received the same number of CS-US pairings—that is, the same number of tone-shock pairs—as group G, but additional shocks occurred in the absence of tones. Thus, the tone was not a valid predictor of the shock, as it was for group G, but group R-1 received more shocks than group G. The second random control group, group R-2, was also shocked independent of the tone, like R-1, but received the same number of shocks as the G group. Because of the randomness of the tone-shock pairings, however, group R-2 received fewer CS-US pairings than group G. Thus, group R-1 was matched to group G on absolute number of CS-US pairings, and group R-2 was matched to group G on absolute number of shocks.

Subsequently, the three groups were returned to the bar apparatus, where they proceeded to press for food, but also heard four 2-minute tone CSs (without shock). The conditioning effect is measured by the *suppression ratio,* computed from the formula $A/(A + B)$, where A is the rate of responding (bar-press) during CS presentation and B is baseline response rate before CS onset. A suppression ratio of 0 indicates no CS responding, whereas 0.5 indicates equal CS and pre-CS rates. As shown in Figure 7-6, group G clearly shows a suppression effect, but groups R-1 and R-2 do not. We see that group G was strongly conditioned at the outset of the unreinforced test trials, whereas the two noncontingent groups showed no suppression (or conditioning) effect during the unreinforced CS test.

Thus, even though group R-1 got the same number of CS-US pairings as group G, and group R-2 got the same number of shocks (US) as G, neither R-1 nor R-2 were conditioned. Only the higher probability of shock *during* CS than in the *absence* of CS (discriminative contingency) produced conditioning.

Rescorla, in the same series, varied the CS and non-CS contingency probability and showed a nicely graded set of suppression ratios corresponding to the contingency differential between CS and non-CS shocks. The larger the differential, the stronger the conditioning. Thus, Rescorla has made a strong case for the essential function of contingent reinforcement and the ineffectiveness of contiguity alone in the conditioning process.

Avoidance Learning

Avoidance learning combines elements from respondent or classical conditioning with elements from operant or instrumental conditioning. Because the early pioneering work in avoidance conditioning used dogs in shuttle boxes escaping or avoiding shock by jumping over a barrier (Solomon & Wynne, 1954), we use this situation to explain the procedure. In a typical avoidance learning procedure, dogs are given shock from which they can escape by jumping over a barrier from the shocked side to the "safe" side. The onset of shock is signaled by a tone that is presented a short time before the shock is to be turned on. The tone thus acts as a CS to the US of the shock. Dogs initially learn to jump to escape from the shock through a process of trial-and-error. Subsequently, they learn to avoid the shock by jumping when the tone comes on, rather than waiting for the shock to come on.

The theoretical problem in avoidance conditioning is to explain what event reinforces the act of jumping to avoid. When dogs are escaping from shock, it is clear their jumping response is being reinforced by shock termination. But what reinforces the jumping response when the dog fails to experience the shock?

Two-factor theory of avoidance learning, first proposed by Mowrer (Mowrer, 1947; Mowrer & Lamoreaux, 1942, 1946) attempts to answer the question. According to Mowrer, the CS (the tone signaling the shock) evokes a fear-response by mechanisms of classical conditioning, and the avoidance response is reinforced by fear reduction. Thus, the CS (tone) evokes a CR (fear), whose termination by the avoidance response is reinforcing in the same way that the US (shock) evokes a UR (pain) whose termination by the escape response is reinforcing. Thus, the avoidance response is learned by both Pavlovian and instrumental conditioning.

Mowrer and Lamoreaux (1946) developed an ingenious experiment to separate the unconditioned escape response from the conditioned avoidance response, so as to determine how the former affected the latter. In the standard experiment, where tone (CS) and shock (US) were associated, escape and avoidance responses (e.g., jumping) were identical. In their new design, they reinforced an unconditioned *jumping* response (UR) during conditioning trials with shock (US) termination and a *running* response (CR) during test trials with a light (CS) turned on or turned off. They exchanged (i.e., counterbalanced) the response-reinforcer pairings for each half of the subjects, to avoid questions about inherent response-type bias. Thus, half of the subjects were reinforced for jumping in response to the shock US and for running in response to the light CS, while the other half were reinforced for running in response to the shock US and for jumping in response to the light CS. Control group II had the same UR and CR response reinforced (i.e., both reinforced responses were running or both were jumping). Control group III had a shock US of fixed duration regardless of response.

It might have been expected that the UR

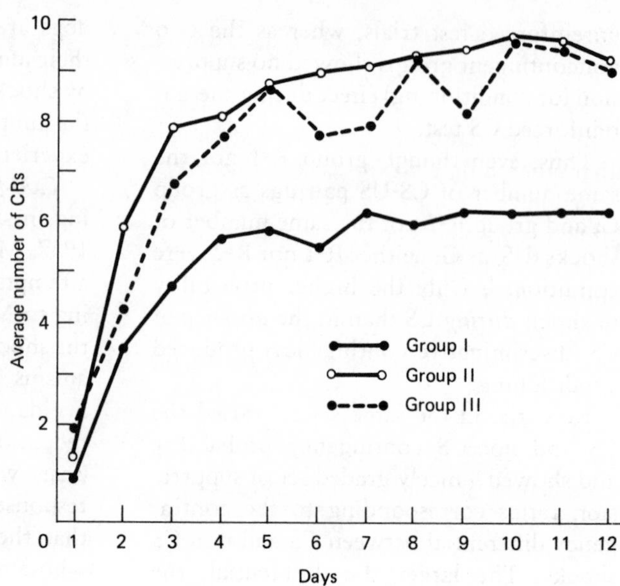

Fig. 7-7 Mean number of conditioned responses made by each group as a function of days. Note the substantial amount of operant (CR) responding by Group I, although this response had not been conditioned to the previous shock US. (From "Fear as an Intervening Variable in Avoidance Conditioning," by O. H. Mowrer and R. R. Lamoreaux. In *Journal of Comparative and Physiological Psychology,* 1946, *39,* 29–50. Copyright 1946 by the American Psychological Association. Reprinted by permission.)

would interfere with acquisition of the different CR for the experimental group I as a result of response confusion or conflict. However, as shown in Figure 7-7, although the response curve for group I (UR different from CR) is significantly lower than the curve for the control groups II (UR same as CR) and III (fixed US), the group I curve shows substantial learning of the previously untrained avoidance response. Thus, we see that the experimental group I made a new response to the avoidance test as a result of the different reinforcement; that is, the new avoidance response had been conditioned to a distinctly different, operant reinforcer (light CS) rather than to the original unconditioned shock (fear). This result strongly contradicts the Pavlovian stimulus substitution thesis by indicating that the avoidance behavior is a learned operant that is reinforced by reduction of fear induced by CS termination. By establishing a second process (avoidance reinforcement) after the initial classical shock conditioning, Mowrer (1947) introduced a *two-process theory* of avoidance conditioning. The two processes are (1) a classically conditioned fear escape response, based on autonomic nervous system function, followed by (2) an operant avoidance response, reinforced by fear (drive) *reduction.* This *two-factor theory* is essentially a motivation theory of avoidance behavior.

Choosing Among Multiple Sources of Reinforcement: The Matching Law

So far we have reviewed effects on behavior of single schedules of reinforcement, the role of generalization and discrimination in extending behavioral repertoires, and the conflicting demands of positive and negative outcomes.

However, human behavior is often the result of choosing among several responses, each with a different schedule of reinforcement. We may have to choose between doing homework and visiting friends, cleaning the supper dishes and watching TV, writing letters and reading a novel, or buying new jeans and buying a new dishwasher. Whichever alternative we as humans choose is affected by the past reinforcement for a particular activity (writing a letter) and the reinforcement histories of alternative activities (reading a novel, doing our homework, etc.). On the other hand, the rat's behavior is usually determined solely by the reinforcement history of the experimental behavior (food for pressing a bar). There is no array of alternative activities for the laboratory rat as there is for the human.

To study the problem of multiple choices, experiments have been designed that study animals exposed to concurrent schedules of reinforcement. In such an experiment a rat may have two levers to press each of which produces food with an independent reinforcement schedule. Through the study of concurrent reinforcement schedules we can begin to investigate choices among alternative behaviors in humans.

As a result of experiments comparing concurrent schedules of reinforcement, Herrnstein (1970) developed a quantitative formula called the *matching law,* which permits the calculation of the relative conditioning effects of conjunctive reinforcement schedules of two or more concurrent CSs. In a typical Herrnstein experiment, pigeons were given a choice of responding to two variable reinforced stimuli. For example, a pigeon might be exposed to one key with a variable interval (VI) 4-minute schedule and a second key with a VI 2-minute schedule. Over time in this situation, the pigeon will respond less to the first key and more to the second.

Data from these experiments show that pigeons respond in a way predicted by the proportion of reinforcements for these responses. The relationship between frequency of pecking responses to the left or right key and frequency of reinforcement on each key is expressed in equation (1) of Table 7.2 (L = left; R = right; R_L = responses on the left; R_R = responses on the right).

In other words, the ratio of one response to all responses is equal to the ratio of reinforcements of that response to all reinforcements. This relationship is called the *matching law,* in which the pigeon matches specific response rates to specific reinforcement rates.

The matching law can be used to successfully predict behavior among alternative choices. It applies not only to reinforcement frequency but also to the magnitude (M) of the reinforcement, as shown in equation (2) of Table 7.2.

Similarly, the matching law can be applied to the delay between the reinforcement of two alternatives. In this application the relative frequency of the response matches the reciprocal of the delay (D) of reinforcement. This is shown in equation (3) of Table 7.2.

Thus, if all factors are constant and the left button has a delay of 8 seconds between response and reinforcement and the right has a delay of 2 seconds, the right response will be chosen four times more often than the left. Combining the independent variables of reinforcement frequency (*r*), reinforcement magnitude (*M*), and delay of reinforcement (*D*), we can state the matching law in its most general form as shown in equation (4) of Table 7.2.

Rachlin and Green (1972) investigated the effect of delay of reinforcement and access time to food (corresponding to magnitude of reinforcement) on choice. Their

Table 7-2 The Matching Law

$$\frac{R_L}{R_L + R_R} = \frac{\text{Reinforcements on L}}{\text{Reinforcements on L} + \text{Reinforcements on R}} \quad (1)$$

$$\frac{R_L}{R_L + R_R} = \frac{M_L}{M_L + M_R} \quad (2)$$

$$\frac{R_L}{R_L + R_R} = \frac{1/D_L}{1/D_L + 1/D_R} \quad (3)$$

$$\frac{R_L}{R_L + R_R} = \frac{r_L + M_L + 1/D_L}{(r_L + M_L + 1/D_L) + (r_R + M_R + 1/D_R)} \quad (4)$$

experiments confirmed the matching law's prediction. Pigeons preferred a smaller immediate reward to a larger, delayed reward. However, if both rewards are delayed past a critical time, then the pigeon will choose the larger, more delayed reinforcement over the less delayed, smaller reinforcement.

As an analogy to humans, we could consider the following example: A person has to choose between organizing his monthly finances (paying bills, balancing his checkbook) and visiting a friend. In this example organizing one's finances represents a greater, though delayed reinforcement whereas visiting friends has a more immediate but small reinforcement. If you asked someone which they would rather do in ten minutes, the individual is likely to choose visiting a friend, which represents the smaller but more immediate reward. But if the choice is required a day before the event is to take place (What will you do tomorrow?) the more delayed, greater magnitude alternative (organizing one's finances) might be chosen. This is exactly what is predicted by the matching law.

In recent years, the matching law has been applied to economics. Here, the available money of the human individual is considered analogous to the response frequency of the experimental animal and the behavior to be predicted is the consumer's choice between commodities. However, in this application to economics, we soon find that there are several additional factors that must be considered. One of these is elastic versus inelastic demand.

Briefly, *demand* is the amount of a particular item that will be purchased at a particular price. For inelastic items, demand is not affected very much by fluctuations in price. Commodities in this category are usually necessities. Thus, if the price of milk or bread doubles, triples, or even quadruples, demand for these inelastic items will probably remain constant. In contrast, demand for elastic items, usually luxury products, fluctuates a great deal with price. Thus, as the price of eating dinner in restaurants increases, the demand for eating out decreases.

How is this relevant to operant conditioning? To answer this question we must reexamine the plight of the rat in the experimental chamber. The rat expresses demand by its bar-pressing behavior (money) and is reinforced with food. In the context of what we have just discussed, this is an inelastic commodity. The rat must obtain food, no matter what the cost.

For example, Hursh and Natelson (1981) gave rats a choice of pressing two levers. Pressing the first lever produced food and pressing the second produced pleasurable brain stimulation. If both are cheap (a small amount of bar pressing produces each reinforcement), the rat will press for stimulation much more frequently than for food. According to the matching law, this implies that pleasure is more valuable. If, however, they are both expensive (many bar presses are required for reinforcement), the animal spends more time bar-pressing for food. Thus, we see that deciding which of two reinforcers is more valuable depends on how inelastic (or necessary) one reinforcer is compared to the other. Further, we learn that the matching law holds only in situations in which the competing reinforcers are equally elastic, since the response rates for food and stimulation are not constant, but change with absolute reinforcement rates.

Other factors also affect the applicability of the matching law. These include whether the amount of resources (money for humans, responses for rats) is limited, what other activities are available in the particular situation, and whether the economic system of interest is open or closed. We will briefly review each of these additional factors.

As the matching law is used in animal studies, resources are rarely limited. Animals are free to make as many responses as physically possible. In the human area, resources are money and money is limited. Furthermore, the determination of which items are luxuries (elastic) and which are necessities (inelastic) depends on availability of resources or income.

The assessment of the available alternative choices is another influence on the matching law's applicability to economics. The relationship between alternatives can be substitutive, complementary, or independent. Only alternatives that can substitute for each other show matching behavior. Thus, the matching law tells us that an 80-second VI schedule with food reinforcement will be maintained when presented alone but will fall off considerably when a 10-second VI schedule with food reinforcement is introduced. However, if one alternative is complementary to another, increasing one may increase rather than decrease the second. For example, an animal might have to choose between two levers, one that gives food and a second that gives water. It turns out that the more attractive one alternative is, the more attractive the second becomes. This is because as the animal's hunger is satisfied, it drinks more, and vice versa (Hursh, 1978). The third possibility is that the two alternatives are independent. Thus manipulating one would have no effect on the second. The matching law applies only in the case in which one reinforcer substitutes for another.

Finally, the matching law is appropriate only for closed systems in which access to items occurs only through expenditure of behavior or income. If items can be obtained in other ways, then the principles of the matching law cannot be applied. Thus, if a person chooses to buy a shirt instead of a sweater because he knows he will receive the sweater as a gift, we cannot apply the matching law to learn about the relative value of these items. Similarly, if the rat knows it will be fed after the experiment, why should it work very hard to receive food as a reinforcer?

Thus, we see that the matching law is really a specific case of many interacting economic principles. These principles include the interrelationship of demand elasticity, income (resource allotment), the substitutability of various alternatives, and whether the system is open or closed. These factors must be considered when applying the matching law to economic systems.

Conditioning and Learning Compared

Generally, the term *conditioning* is used to refer to the two basic types of learning situations studied by behavior theorists: classical or respondent conditioning and instrumental or operant conditioning. Both of these involve learning, of course, but the term *learning* is a broader term used to refer to any change in the behavior of the organism. Experiments on learning with humans have, in many cases, used verbal materials, and have generally been described as verbal learning experiments. Models that have been proposed to account for studies in memorization of verbal materials emphasize both the learning process (the organized storage of information) and the whole process of storage, retrieval, and use. These areas of learning are reviewed in Chapter 8 on *episodic memory,* and in Chapter 9 on *semantic memory.*

MOTIVATION: AROUSAL THEORIES

Arousal and Drive

In our attempt to understand conditioning processes, we are left wanting some explanation of what *makes* the dog (and the human) salivate when it sees and smells meat, and what *impels* the rat to press the food-releasing bar. We look for a prime mover or activating force that *energizes* the behavior, as well as directs it to its selected goal. *Arousal* theories present some testable models of activation mechanisms. Allied with the concept of *homeostasis,* the organism's mechanism for maintaining or restoring a state of equilibrium, these arousal theories account for behaviors induced by biological forces and drives activated by deprivation needs, especially those of instinctual origin, such as hunger and thirst.

The oldest theory of this type is Clark Hull's drive reduction theory. For many years it dominated learning research. More recently Hull's theory has been challenged by theories of optimal arousal and theories of cognition and intrinsic motivation. Let us first consider Hull's extensively developed theory.

Drive Reduction Theory

Hull's (1943) theory is an elaborate S-R model. Its most important aspect is its motivational function. We see in Hull's *drive reduction theory* an integration of motivational and learning theories. One of the more impressive accomplishments in Hull's theoretical conception is that it was built on the rigorous use of empirical data. It is, therefore, subject to experimental testing. Furthermore, it was composed of so many interacting variables that it could be adjusted to accommodate new developments.

Drive reduction theory is based on two principles. The first principle is that the motivating force is a generalized drive, such as hunger, that not only energizes the urge to eat but also energizes *all* potential behaviors. Drives (hunger, thirst, sex, and so on) arise from biological needs. The second principle, which resembles homeostasis, is that the organism seeks to neutralize or satisfy the drive so as to reduce it to a state of no-need. The sensation of reduced drive is a reinforcement.

Hull's essential drive formula is

$$E = D \times H$$

where E is *excitatory* (or *reaction*) *potential*, D is *drive* strength, and H is *habit* strength. (Habit strength is the probability of repeating a learned response.) Hull derived this multiplicative function from studies of the effects of food deprivation on running speeds in animals (Hull, 1943). Since our interest is in experimentation with humans, we will look at another supporting line of research by Janet Taylor (1956) and Kenneth Spence (Spence, Farber, & McFann, 1956; Spence, 1958).

Taylor and Spence decided to test the Hullian model on the Yerkes-Dodson law. The Yerkes-Dodson law (1908) states that there is an inverted U-shaped function relating performance to level of arousal, with the peak of performance occurring at some intermediate level of arousal. Furthermore, this law states the peak of the relationship shifts toward lower levels of arousal when task difficulty is increased. These relationships are shown in Figure 7-8.

Taylor considered anxiety as a suitable, energizing drive and devised a test, the Manifest Anxiety Scale, to classify subjects as *high anxiety* (corresponding to Hull's high drive or high D) or *low anxiety* (low D) types. Groups of high-anxiety and low-anxiety subjects were given word pairs to learn. They were then tested with one of the paired words and asked to recall its mate. Some of the word pairs were close associates (e.g., father-mother), which would be easy to recall because of their high habit strength, and others were unrelated (e.g., quiet-double), which would be difficult to recall because of their low habit strength.

The results supported the Hull and Yerkes-Dodson predictions. High-anxiety subjects did better on the easy recall task, whereas low-anxiety subjects did better on the difficult word-pair task. Hull's equation provides a reasonable explanation.

The E (excitatory) value of the dominant response (the one with highest habit strength H) is strengthened by the high-anxiety subject's high D, increasing in value in relation to the weaker E of competing responses. Since the dominant response is correct on the *easy* task (high-associate pairs), the high-anxiety subjects (those with high drive, D) perform better. Low-anxiety subjects are handicapped here because the inherent excitatory potential (E) of the dominant response does not exceed that of the other responses by enough to induce a correct choice. However, the dominant response is incorrect on the *dif-*

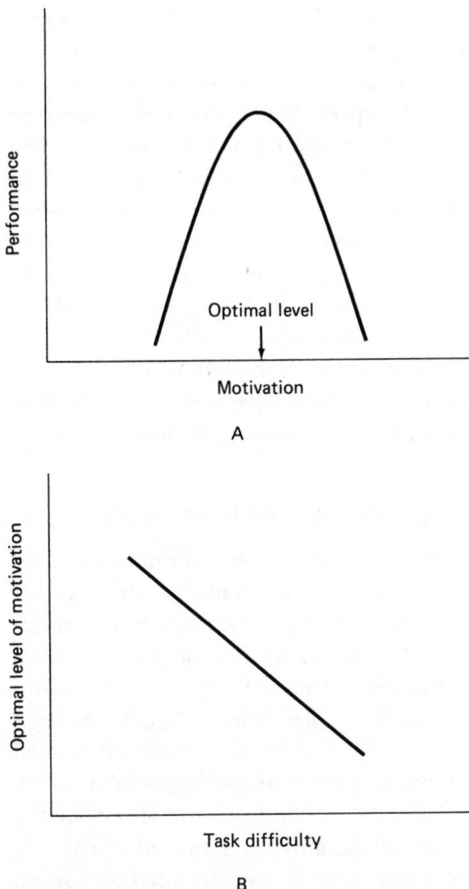

Fig. 7-8 The Yerkes-Dodson law states that (A) there is an optimal degree of motivation for any task, and (B) the more difficult the task, the lower the optimal degree.

ficult task (low-associate pairs). Therefore, increasing *E* with a higher *D* only increases the dominance of the incorrect response, so high-anxiety subjects make more errors.

In a direct comparison of the same groups of high-anxiety and low-anxiety subjects on both simple and complex tasks, Farber and Spence (1953) found similar anxiety-drive effects. On the simple task of eyeblink conditioning, subjects were conditioned to respond with an eyeblink reflex (CR) to a lightflash CS after being trained with a US consisting of a strong puff of air on the cornea. High-anxiety subjects reached criterion performance in fewer trials than low-anxiety subjects. When the same subjects were tested on complex maze solutions, the low-anxiety subjects were superior. Furthermore, low-anxiety subjects showed the largest advantage over high-anxiety subjects at maze choice-points with many possible paths. In other words, more choices increased the low-anxiety advantage. These results are also consistent with Hull's model.

The additive effect of multiple or compound drives (e.g., hunger + fear, hunger + thirst) has been demonstrated in many experiments with animals and in a number of human studies. Epstein and Levitt (1962) found that learning of paired-associate word lists was better before than immediately after the evening meal, presumably because the hunger drive added excitatory potential to the learning drive. In contrast, Taylor (1956) found no difference in recognition memory for food-related or neutral words between deprived and recently fed subjects. In light of Taylor's study, other factors must be taken into account, such as varied emotional responses to different degrees of hunger by different types of people. Then, too, *D* levels above optimum may degrade performance, so deprivation and compound drive experiments should test for effects over a range of intermediate points, not just at one or two extremes (see Chapter 3 on experimental pitfalls).

Drive Selection. One of the major problems with drive theory is the principle of generalized activation of all drives; that is, all drives active at any given time strengthen each other. Such generalized activation could cause many inappropriate responses. Hull solved this problem by postulating a *drive stimulus* (S_D), which is evoked by the drive. The S_D is an internal or external cue that directs the subject to the appropriate goal. (For example, a dry mouth makes you drink to quench your thirst drive.) As we have seen with the operant discriminative stimulus, the S_D could function as a CS. Unlike D, S_D directs the response toward the appropriate goal. It does this by eliciting the *fractional antic-*

ipatory goal response. The connection between the drive stimulus and the fractional anticipatory goal response arises from the fact that the S_D is associated with the goal response itself. Hull's *fractional anticipatory goal response* is the subject's inner reaction to a partial or preliminary drive stimulus cue representing the ultimate goal. The covert response to the stimulus cue then generates an expectation toward the ultimate goal, like the dry mouth that makes you think of the thirst-quenching drink or the aroma of food that elicits a taste response and creates the anticipation of eating.

In Hull's revised model, the reinforcer not only reduces the drive but also serves as incentive manifested by means of the S_D cue and mediated by the fractional goal response en route to the goal. Incentives affect the strength of response performance, not the rate or efficacy of the learning, according to the Hullian model.

Thus, Hull was able to introduce the concept of incentive, *K*, into his theory by the revised formula:

$$E = D \times H \times K$$

Frustration as Drive. Frustration is defined by Amsel (1958, 1962) as the nonreinforcement of a previously reinforced response. Thus, removal or withholding of an expected reward can cause frustration. There is much evidence that the frustration drive leads to increased activity.

Amsel proposed that frustration can assume drive properties under intermittent or variable reinforcement conditions. Under variable contingencies, the subjects learn to respond both to reinforcement anticipations and to nonreinforced frustrations. These hypotheses are based on animal studies. Most experiments on frustration with human subjects deal with aggression in cognitive settings.

For example, Haner and Brown (1955) had children place 36 marbles in a matrix of holes, for which they were to receive a prize. By pushing a hidden button (the "upset" button), the experimenter could cause the marbles to fall out, whereupon the child had to push a reset lever to begin again. Upsetting the marbles presumably frustrated the child, and the degree of frustration should increase with the number of marbles upset. When the child's pressure on the reset lever was recorded, the data showed that the more marbles the child had placed when the experimenter pushed the upset button, the harder the child pushed the reset lever. Thus, increasing the frustration apparently increased the drive. This effect also suggests a basis for the link between frustration and aggression that some researchers have postulated (Dollard, Doob, Miller, Mowrer, & Sears, 1939).

Arousal and Homeostasis

Motivation theories based on arousal and homeostasis are particularly attractive because we can trace the sources of the effects directly to specific organs and areas of the central nervous system. For example, we have determined (largely through animal experimentation) the exciting and inhibiting effects of the hypothalamus on sexual activity, hunger, and thirst; of the effects of the amygdala and other parts of the limbic system on emotional responses, notably fear and aggression; and of the brainstem's reticular activating system effects on general brain arousal and relaxation.

Experimentation on physiological arousal deals with human performance under different types and degrees of arousal, ranging from sleep through wide-awake alertness. Studies of *REM sleep* (named for the rapid eye movements that accompany certain stages of sleep marked by dreaming) are made with electroencephalograph (EEG) instruments that record brainwave patterns characteristic of the different sleep stages. Mapping of the sources of stimulation and suppression of cortical arousal is an important area of motivation research.

Other areas of the study of arousal and its motivational functions center on sexual behavior, emotion, and stress. These excitatory and inhibitory functions are mediated principally by the autonomic nervous system and its chemical transmitting

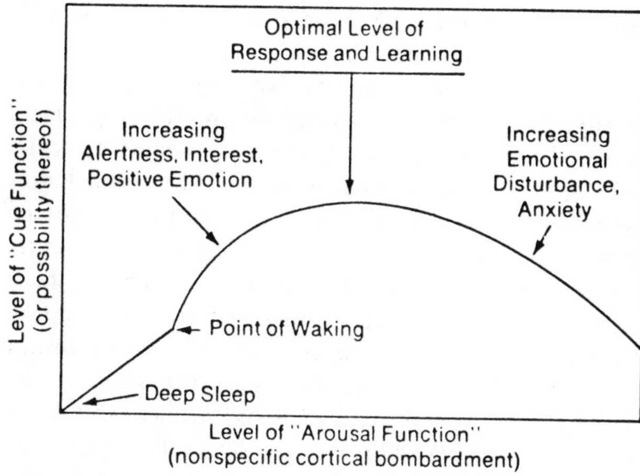

Fig. 7-9 Hebb's inverted-U function relating performance quality to arousal level. Note the continuum from deep sleep to high arousal in the waking state. (From "Drives and the C.N.S. (Conceptual Nervous System)," by D. O. Hebb. In *Psychological Review,* 1955, *62,* 243–254. Copyright 1955 by the American Psychological Association. Reprinted by permission.)

agents. Since a vast literature describes the physiological arousal and regulation of these functions, developed largely through animal studies involving selective stimulation and removal of brain centers, we will confine ourselves to their psychological expression in human studies.

Optimal Arousal Level

Arousal and Performance. Hebb (1955) saw motivation as a diffuse and generalized *energizing* (arousal) system. He expressed the relationship between energy level and performance in an inverted-U function, based on responses to a variety of motor and cognitive tasks (Figure 7-9). The variation in performance effectiveness reaches a peak at some medium arousal level, suggesting an *optimum* level best adapted to task demands, situational conditions, and individual disposition and skill. The Hebb performance function was designated a *stimulus cue function,* relating it to certain "cue" controls in the environment that motivated behavior. These cues would include such aspects as sensory information perceived by the subject.

The *Yerkes-Dodson law,* as we have seen, also postulates an inverted-U function between performance and arousal, with the location of the optimal level of performance at a moderate level of arousal. The law also states that the greater the task difficulty, the lower the optimal level of arousal. In support of the law, Suedfeld and Landon (1970) found that subjects performed best in a simple rote-learning and object naming task when they were given a high money incentive after rather long sensory deprivation (high arousal condition), but no money incentive and no sensory deprivation (low arousal condition) produced best performance on a complex task of naming uses for various pictured objects.

The inverted-U curves, with their mid-range peaks, show the principal characteristic of optimal-level or adaptation-level models, the preference for moderate degrees of arousal in most situations. Various kinds of experiments demonstrate this. Haber (1958) asked subjects to rate the pleasantness of different water temperatures by dipping their hands. Subjects found 68°F was neutral, warmer and cooler temperatures near 68°F were rated pleasant, but temperatures more deviant were rated unpleasant. Figure 7-10 shows how affect (rated pleasantness) is an inverted U-shaped function on either side of a neutral point—small discrepancies from neutrality are pleasant, but large discrepancies are unpleasant.

These connections between arousal and emotion seem to agree with Hebb's (1955) analysis, which links the two functions, and his conclusion that higher levels of arousal produced "extreme loss of adaptation" accompanied by emotional disturbance that degraded performance. "Paralyzing anxiety" causes immobility in response to overwhelming threat, as shown by the upper range of Hebb's arousal function (Figure 7-9).

At the other extreme from the paralyzing anxiety resulting from a flooding of sensation, the absence of stimulation produced in experiments on sensory deprivation also evokes strong reactions. Bexton, Heron, and Scott (1954) paid subjects $20 for each day they stayed in a room devoid of stimulation. The steady hum of an air conditioner masked outside sounds, and subjects were blindfolded and prevented from touching anything. Some subjects experienced hallucinations and no subject was able to remain longer than three days.

In what we have seen of arousal as a motivational force, particularly in the adaptation version of the optimal level model, arousal does more than just energize behavior randomly. There is a direction in the motivated effects we have observed—subjects are motivated to find and stay in a pleasant state, the optimal level. The level may vary in different situations, according to task, duration or repetition of activity, and so on. This stable preference relates to the body's basic *homeostatic,* or equilibrium mechanisms.

This suggests that arousal at a suitable level can indeed be reinforcing. Hebb (1966) argued that play behavior, which raises arousal level, provides needed stimulation for bored (i.e., stimulus-deprived) creatures. We are not speaking here of the effects of deprivation (e.g., hunger, thirst) that experimenters manipulate in conditioning subjects. The reinforcing reward we are speaking of is the sense of the arousal itself. Olds and Milner's (1954) rats worked for nothing but some direct intracranial stimulation. Berlyne (1960) cites numerous experiments of his own and of others demonstrating that infants of three to nine months responded by orienting reflex and continuing attention to novel and more contoured objects in preference to familiar and simpler ones. Presumably, higher arousal was provoked by the more complicated objects. Some theorists consider this response to be the primary motivation for curiosity and exploratory behavior.

The effects of relative complexity of

Fig. 7-10 The effect of discrepancy from adaptation level on affect. As the discrepancy increases in either direction, affect first increases and then decreases. (From "Discrepancy from Adaptation Level as a Source of Affect," by R. N. Haber, *Journal of Experimental Psychology,* 1958, *56,* 370–375. Copyright 1958 by the American Psychological Association. Reprinted by permission.)

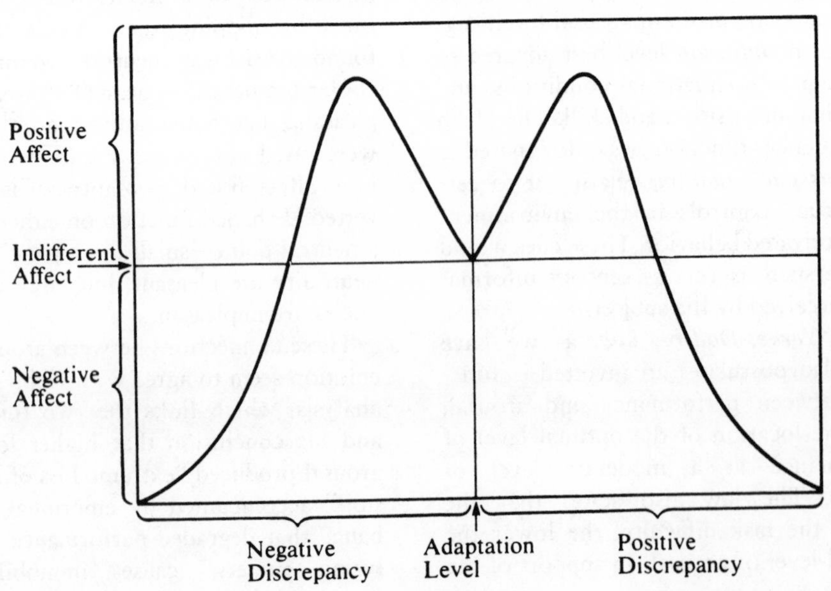

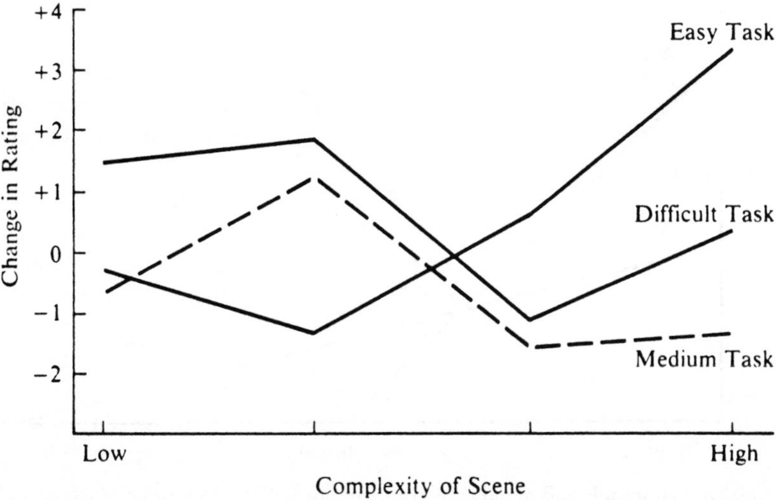

Fig. 7-11 Shifts in preference ratings of environments of differing complexities for three different intervening tasks. The easy task shifts preference toward more complex scenes, while the difficult task shifts preference toward simpler scenes. (Reprinted with permission of authors and publisher from Arkes, Hal R. and Clark, Patricia. "Effects of task difficulty on subsequent preference for visual complexity." *Perceptual and Motor Skills,* 1975, *41,* 395–399, Figure 1.)

stimuli or tasks on subjects' preferences have been studied in a series of interesting experiments by Arkes and Clark (1975). They related the amount of environmental complexity that college students preferred to the complexity of the task performed. The students rated slides showing scenes of varying complexity before and after solving anagrams of varying difficulty. In the posttest rating, students who were required to solve easy anagrams indicated preference for more complex slides, whereas those who had worked on the brainbusters preferred the simpler slides. The before-and-after changes in complexity preference are shown in Figure 7-11. Here we find experimental support for our inclination to relax from easy but fatiguing tasks with puzzles or "heavy" reading and, conversely, to relax from strenuous thinking with entertainment that requires minimal mental exercise, such as television and mystery novels.

Hedonism Theory

The idea that arousal in itself can be pleasurable and, therefore, reinforcing is the centerpiece of *hedonism theory.* Hedonism accounts for the motivation of behavior through the operation of the pleasure-pain principle: we tend to do and want things that give us pleasure, and to avoid things that give us pain.

Approach-Avoidance Conflict. One of the principal applications of hedonism theory is its explanation of *approach-avoidance* behavior. This has to do with the two-way conflict we experience between the desire to do some pleasurable or necessary activity (approach) and the price or discomfort involved in doing it (avoidance).

We previously considered avoidance behavior in terms of the conditioning factors that determined it. Now we examine it in terms of the internal responses that mediate such behavior. Neal Miller and his students have been responsible for both the theoretical development and the experimental testing of approach-avoidance conflict (Dollard & Miller, 1950; Miller, 1951a,1951b). Figure 7-12 illustrates the basic concepts of Miller's approach and avoidance gradients toward a goal that has both positive and negative components.

As shown in Figure 7-12, the gradient of avoidance is steeper than the gradient of

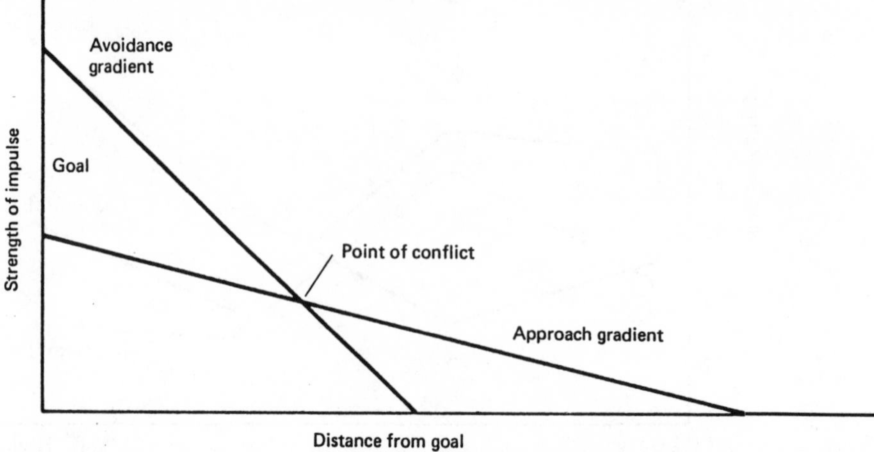

Fig. 7-12 Idealized approach and avoidance gradients, in which the height of each gradient represents the tendency to approach or avoid a goal. When the organism is further from the goal than the point of conflict, the approach gradient dominates, and when it is closer, the avoidance gradient dominates. At the point of conflict, the two tendencies are equal.

approach. This means that as a goal that is both desired and feared is approached, the approach gradient will initially be higher. At the crossover point, the avoidance gradient becomes higher than the approach gradient. The dimension along which the gradients are plotted can be spaces, as when we walk toward a person who we want to meet at a party but are shy about approaching, or time, as when our anticipation of a lecture we are to give is positive further from the target event but becomes aversive as the event looms near.

Approach-avoidance behavior in lower animals can be observed by pairing a positive stimulus such as food with a negative stimulus such as shock. As animals approach a goal box in which they have both been fed and shocked, they reach a point of conflict (the intersection point of the approach-avoidance gradients) at which the behavior of approach is overcome by the behavior of avoidance. The distance from the goal where the animal hesitates can be manipulated by increasing the noxiousness of the shock, (which increases the height of the avoidance gradient) or by increasing the reward value of the food (which increases the height of the approach gradient).

J. S. Brown (1942) designed an ingenious apparatus to measure directly the strength of the approach and avoidance gradients in rats who were either shocked or fed in a goal box. One group of rats was trained to approach a goal box for food, and a second group was trained to leave a goal box they were shocked in. They were then attached to a harness to measure the amount of force they exerted to either avoid the place they had been shocked in, or to approach the place they had been fed in. As predicted by Miller's approach-avoidance gradient theory, the avoidance gradient was found to be steeper than the approach gradient, as measured by the animal's strength of pull, and increasing the drive (fear) to escape by increasing the shock intensity raised the avoidance gradient, while increasing the drive (hunger) to approach raised the approach gradient.

Dollard and Miller (1950) and Miller (1951a, 1951b) suggest how drugs and psychotherapy can adjust approach or aversion responses to reduce conflict and promote movement toward desirable goals. They point out, however, that focusing only on positive motivating factors can actually increase fear, since merely raising the level of the approach gradient without also changing the avoidance (fear) gradient leads to an increase in fear as the subject approaches the goal. You can see this shift of the conflict point toward the goal by increasing the slope or the level of the approach gradient in Figure 7-12. Closeness to the goal, with its associated fear aversion, evokes a more intense fear reaction. For example, when the increasing pain of a toothache finally drives you (raises your approach gradient) to the dentist, you experience renewed fear of dentistry as you enter the office and approach the operating chair. The point of conflict has shifted closer to the feared treatment. To prevent this, it would be necessary to lower the avoidance gradient (by therapeutically reducing fear, e.g., taking a couple of tranquilizers) to eliminate the conflict junction where the gradients now cross.

Conger (in Miller, 1951b), showed that giving alcohol to rats does indeed seem to lower the avoidance gradient rather than raise the approach gradient. Using strength of pull as a measure of gradient strength, Conger trained rats to either approach the end of a runway for food or to avoid the end of a runway in which they had been shocked. After alcohol injections, the rats showed a large decrease in the avoidance response, as measured by their strength of pull against a harness, away from the goal, but actually showed a marginal decrease (rather than increase) in the strength of the approach gradient toward a goal motivated by hunger. This supports the hypothesis that drinking alcohol in a conflict situation is reinforced by its fear-reducing effect rather than its reward-enhancing effect. As we see, most of the investigation of avoidance or conflict theory has been done with animals. In view of the recent advances in instrumental measurement of arousal and other autonomic responses, it is now possible to make meaningful human studies of approach and avoidance in the larger framework of hedonist theory.

The optimal level models of arousal function, with their hedonistic bias, suggest a preference for some "pleasant" level of internal stimulation or excitement based on an interaction between physiological mechanisms and psychological, or behavioral, responses. This preference—a disposition to function more effectively in a particular arousal condition—reflects a basic regulatory process that is observed in many bodily mechanisms. *Homeostasis* (Cannon, 1932) is the process by which the mechanism tends to return to a stable state in which its components and functions are in balance. In motivational terms, the balance point is the optimal arousal level of the organism in a given situation.

Opponent-Process Theory. Another extension of the concept of hedonism under the homeostatic model of emotional balance is *opponent-process theory.* Solomon and Corbit (1974) proposed this theory of hedonic contrast to explain the commonly experienced letdown that follows an exhilarating experience and also the habituating effect of addiction. Figure 7-13 shows the five phases in the opponent-process cycle of an affective reaction. State A is the primary affective reaction and State B is the afterreaction (the opponent process to A). The opposing State B works to reduce state A, resulting in a steady-state level equal to A-minus-B. When State A input ceases, State B reaches its opposite peak (the letdown) and then decays to the homeostatic neutral level, or baseline. On successive experiences with the same stimuli, the intensity of the hedonic A reaction declines and that of the B afterreaction increases, causing a buildup of the opponent effect. This progressive strengthening of the opponent process is what accounts for habituation. The intense pleasure of the stimulation (A reaction) diminishes with repetition, while the opposite, aversive effect (B reaction) increases. In the Solomon and Corbit model, State A can also be unpleasant (extreme terror, for example) and its opponent process, State B, then becomes a pleasant state like relief.

Opponent-process effects were demonstrated for the terror-relief case in a study by Epstein (1967) of parachute jumpers' reactions. In this example, State A is unpleasant and State B is pleasant. State A is terror

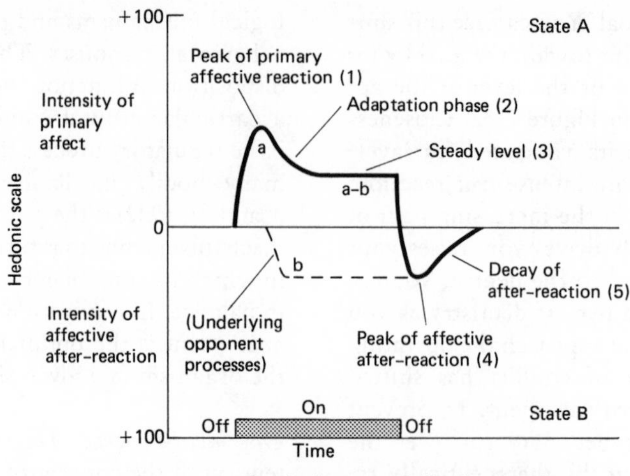

Fig. 7-13 The temporal course of opponent processes in Solomon and Corbit's theory. The primary affective reaction has an initial peak in intensity (1), followed by adaptation (2) to a steady level (3). When the affective stimulus is removed, the after-reaction sets in, with its initial peak (4), followed by return to a neutral resting position (5). (From "An Opponent-Process Theory of Motivation: I. Temporal Dynamics of Affect," by R. L. Solomon and J. D. Corbit. In *Psychological Review,* 1974, *81,* 119–145. Copyright 1974 by the American Psychological Association. Adapted by permission.)

with very high autonomic nervous system arousal as the parachutist contemplates and then launches himself on his first jump. Upon landing, State B, which is relief, reduces the terror to a level of stony-faced, stunned tenseness. With the realization that the jump (and so, the danger) is over, the relief of State B reaches its peak of exuberance and exhilaration, which slowly fades to the parachutist's normal mood. On subsequent jumps, the terror is mitigated to tense expectation (A state) followed, upon landing, by exhilaration (enhanced B state). The changing emotions were detected by telemetered recording of autonomic responses and by automatic photographing of facial expressions in flight.

Solomon and Corbit invoke their theory to explain drug addiction. At first, the use of the drug is repeated for its pleasurable (A phase) sensations. When these sensations lose their impact, the aversive (B phase) opponent reactions gain strength, and now the drug is sought even more compulsively to regain the A effect. But since, through repetition, the A strength wanes in relation to B, larger dosage or higher potency is required to overcome the aversive reaction.

In opponent-process theory, we see another example of a class of motivation models usually referred to as *homeostatic theories.* These include optimal arousal, adaptation level, and hedonic theories. They share a common basis in the inherent tendency of organisms to function best and longest at some suitable average point or level. Presumably, what is most efficient for organic operation also feels best in terms of sensory experience. In the opponent-process model, a sensation of extreme intensity in either direction (pleasant or aversive) is automatically countered by a reactive sensation in the opposite direction, usually balancing the initial sensation in intensity of affect. An interesting and somewhat unique aspect of opponent-process theory is the gradual diminution in the initial A effect and a corresponding increase in the opponent B effect with repetition. This process develops a shift of the homeostatic balance to a new stable point for that particular experience. Since homeostatic motivation theories closely parallel similar processes in human biological systems, it is logical to look for a direct relationship between mental and physical homeostasis. Much experimentation on opponent-process theory is currently directed toward determining underlying physiological mechanisms.

MOTIVATION: COGNITIVE THEORIES

Learned Helplessness

In an effort to account for some of the puzzling inconsistencies in stimulus-response effects, experimentation has been focused more and more on the part played by cognition in motivating behavior. Because other chapters in this book deal extensively with cognitive processes, we will review here just one topic that represents an important line of cognitive motivation research. *Learned helplessness* illustrates the application of basic research to clinical problems. This represents a practical development that is largely confined to behavior modification based on S-R conditioning theory.

The phenomenon of *learned helplessness* was first demonstrated with dogs by Seligman and Maier (1967), who subjected the animals to inescapable, unavoidable shock. When these animals were reexposed to shock from which they could escape merely by pressing their head against the walls, they generally failed to make any attempt to escape. Instead, they hunched down and suffered the repeated shock. Presumably, the S-R escape association had not been formed, and the dogs were unable to experience the reinforced effect of operant behavior.

To show that the failure to escape was not due to the traumatizing effects of shock itself, a second group of dogs also experienced the shock treatment, but they could escape by pressing a panel with their noses. These dogs quickly learned to use the head-pressing escape response. Further, when the animals were trained in the escape response *before* the exposure to inescapable shock, they did not show helpless behavior in the subsequent escape trials. However, without such pretraining, follow-up escape training (being pulled over the barrier) resulted in escape learning, but at a slow rate.

Thus, Seligman and Maier concluded that learned helplessness was manifested in passivity, performance deficits, and learning retardation. On the basis of the similarity of such responses to those of depressed human patients, they proposed a learned helplessness hypothesis (Seligman, Maier, & Solomon, 1971), which explains depression as a conditioned response to the experience of being incapable of avoiding failure or of controlling aversive experiences. This leads to a "demotivation" of behavior, observed as passivity and hopelessness in a person's manner and in his or her responses to new tasks. Experience with helplessness produces not only the emotional disturbances of depression and anxiety, but also undermines the motivation to respond and retards the ability to learn that responding works (Seligman, 1974). Laboratory work with humans has provided support for some of these hypotheses, and has modified others.

For example, Roth and Kubal (1975) showed that the perceived importance of failure affected the magnitude of the helplessness effect, in a complex sequence of two experiments. All subjects signed up for both experiments, which "happened" to be scheduled on the same day in the same building. In Experiment 1 (pretraining), they were given noncontingent (arbitrary, not related to correctness of responses) reinforcement on concept-formation problems. Some of the subjects were told their performance was a good predictor of academic success in college (that is, the results were important), and others were told they were merely solving problems as an experiment in learning (the results were unimportant). In Experiment 2 (test), immediately following, the same subjects were asked to solve a series of five concept-formation problems. Test performance was measured on the basis of ability and persistence (time spent before giving up). The subjects who had done poorly in training in the "important" condition showed greater deficits in ability and persistence in the subsequent test than the ones who believed the first problems were "unimportant." Thus, the importance of the uncontrollable result influenced the helplessness effect on the following task.

Roth and Kubal's finding that helplessness is influenced by task importance added an important concept to the notion of learned helplessness. Seligman's original formulation had not included the variable of task importance in predicting the degree of depression or learned helplessness experienced by subjects in the face of failure. Other challenges and contradictions of the original hypothesis centered on its failure to account for the tendency of depressives to manifest low self-esteem and self-blame for failure. These attitudes would seem to be inconsistent with a sense of personal incapability and helplessness. Seligman and his colleagues (Abramson, Seligman, & Teasdale, 1978) have reformulated the learned helplessness hypothesis to take into account the effect of some of these criticisms.

Seligman et al. reviewed a series of experiments in which attributions were elicited from depressives on failure in problem-solving tasks. The basis of classifying depressive and nondepressive subjects in these experiments was usually their scores on the Beck Depression Inventory (Beck, 1967). They proposed that depressives manifested a strong tendency to attribute internal, stable, and global causes for bad outcomes ("I always fail because I'm not competent") and external, unstable, situational causes for good outcomes ("I succeeded on that occasion because of a lucky break"). In short, this is an expectancy theory of depression in which characteristic patterns of *expectations* determine an attitude of helplessness that motivates depressive responses.

The new notion here is that "mere exposure to objective uncontrollability is not sufficient to render an organism helpless; rather, the organism must form the expectation that future outcomes will be uncontrollable in order to exhibit helplessness" (Alloy & Seligman, 1979, p. 232). In short, it is not just past failures but the prediction of future lack of control that causes helplessness.

In fact, Alloy and Abramson (1979), who tested the ability of depressives compared to nondepressives to detect how much control they had over positive and negative outcomes, found that depressives were actually *more* accurate than nondepressives in their judgment of control. (This somewhat surprising finding is reflected in the title of their paper: "Judgment of Contingency in Depressed and Nondepressed Students: Sadder but Wiser?")

Subjects classified as either depressed or nondepressed by the Beck Inventory were assigned to a pushbutton task that challenged their judgment of contingency (control of outcome). They pressed a button, which was reinforced on 50% of the presses. The reinforcements were contingent on the button-press in the 50% control condition, and were completely random in the noncontingent condition. There were two subconditions that associated reinforcement with either a reward or a loss: the reinforcer (green light) signaled a "win" (with money reward) in one condition and a "lose" (with money deduction) in the other condition. Figure 7-14A shows that in the noncontingent (no control) condition, nondepressed subjects judged they had more control in the "win" condition, whereas the depressives showed no difference in perception of control in either "win" or "lose" conditions. The win-lose judgments showed a similar pattern in the condition in which 50% of responses were contingently reinforced (50% control), except that the nondepressed subjects were less accurate in judging contingency in the "lose" condition (Figure 7-14B). It would seem that depressives are fairly accurate in their contingency judgments, compared to nondepressives, raising a question about the role played by judgment of control in depression. Regardless of contingency, nondepressed subjects attribute wins to control and losses to lack of control. Other factors that have been found influential in depres-

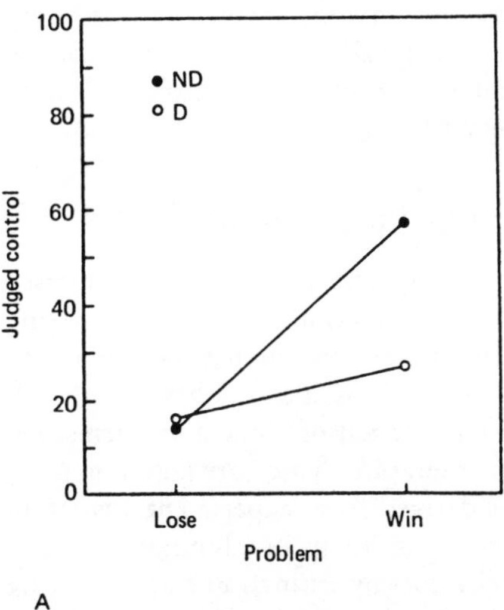

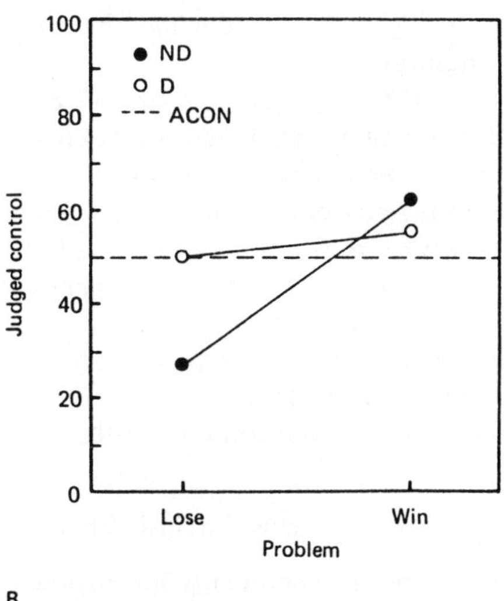

Fig. 7-14 Judged control of depressed and nondepressed subjects for the noncontingent (A) and contingent (B) case. The actual degree of control is shown by the dotted lines. Depressed subjects are actually more accurate than nondepressed subjects in judging degree of control. (From "Judgment of Contingency in Depressed and Nondepressed Students: Sadder but Wiser?" by L. B. Alloy and L. Y. Abramson, *Journal of Experimental Psychology: General,* 1979, *108,* 441–485. Copyright 1979 by the American Psychological Association. Reprinted by permission.)

sives' performance are similarity or difference between uncontrollable training experiences and new tasks and relative importance of task to self-esteem (Seligman, Abramson, Semmel, & von Baeyer, 1979).

INTRINSIC MOTIVATION

The identifying feature of intrinsic motivation is that there must be no external incentive, reinforcement, or reward. In other words, the goal itself must be an internal satisfaction of an internal need. The need, of course, can be developed through external experiences in social learning situations. For example, good school grades and praise for academic achievement can persist in adult life as a need that promotes intrinsic satisfaction in completing intellectual puzzles.

Drive Reduction and Optimal Stimulation

Fowler (1965) proposed that drive reduction could be intrinsically motivated, if we accept the basic need for optimal arousal. This assumption provides a homeostatic basis for the intrinsic drive to attain an optimal level of stimulation, whether it be higher or lower than the prevailing environment provides.

In a test of intrinsically motivated responses to stimulus-rich and stimulus-deprived environments, Smith and Myers (1966) confined 36 volunteer naval men in two conditions: In one condition they spent 24 hours under experimental conditions of solitude, darkness, and sensory deprivation. In the other, control condition, they were exposed to lively recreation (TV, music, magazines), a lighted room, and intercom communication. After spending 24 hours in one condition, the men spent 24 hours in the other. (The sequence of conditions was counterbalanced.) After 9½ hours in each condition, the men were told they could turn on a tape player and listen to boring stock market reports for up to 60 minutes (3600 seconds). Subjects in the sensory deprivation condition listened to an average of 1514 seconds of old market reports compared with 277 seconds during the control condition.

On the other hand, some of Zubek's (1969) subjects in a long-term (14 day) isolation experiment grew accustomed to the peaceful environment and became serenely patient for the duration of the experiment. This recalls the variable, idiosyncratic nature of people's adaptation levels, suggesting the close relationship between optimal arousal and adaptation level theories under the intrinsic motivation umbrella.

Intrinsic versus Extrinsic Effects

A variety of experiments have shown an inhibiting or degrading effect of extrinsic rewards on intrinsic motivation. One example is Deci's (1972) puzzle-solving experiment. He paid experimental subjects for solving each of four puzzles within a time limit. Controls were paid nothing for the same task. When both groups were given free-choice time for preferred activities, the paid subjects spent an average of 109 seconds working on the puzzles, whereas the unpaid controls spent 208 seconds, almost twice as long. This indicates either that the intrinsic interest in puzzle-solving for the unpaid group was not compromised by extrinsic reward payment or that receiving an extrinsic reward for the task diminished its intrinsic reward value for the paid group.

Lepper, Greene, and Nisbett (1973) found a similar effect in children, who were either rewarded or not for drawing with pens. One of the rewarded groups was told about the reward before the activity and the other was given it without a preannouncement. During subsequent free play time, the children were given a choice of the pens or other toys. Both groups of extrinsically rewarded children played with the pens significantly less than the unrewarded group.

Some psychologists see an attribution effect at work in these experiments ("I'm doing this for nothing; therefore I must *like* doing it," or "I used to get paid for this, why should I bother doing it for no money?"). Nonetheless, this research shows the dangers inherent in reducing the reward value of an intrinsically rewarding activity by extrinsic reinforcement.

CLINICAL APPLICATIONS

One of the experimental psychologist's greatest satisfactions comes from seeing principles and techniques developed in basic research used as the basis of the effective treatment of clinical problems. Behavior therapies, which are based on principles derived from experimental work in conditioning, focus on eliminating harmful behaviors by extinction and instituting healthy behaviors by positive reinforcement. Such behavioral extinction procedures, called *counterconditioning,* owe their effect to various processes that have emerged from experimental laboratories. Perhaps the best known and most widely used counterconditioning technique was perfected by Joseph Wolpe (1958), a behaviorally oriented clinician. He based his *systematic desensitization* therapy on a type of counterconditioning called *reciprocal inhibition.* In one version of his reciprocal inhibition process, Wolpe trains the subject to relax in the presence of anxiety-producing stimuli. The positive relaxation response inhibits the anxiety response and supplants the latter as the CR. The desensitization procedure has been used in treating such clinical problems as phobias and stress conditions.

Conditioning is also the essential mechanism in biofeedback training. This is a psychophysiological method used to enable patients to control excessively low or high blood pressure, situational tension, migraine, heart rate, and epilepsy.

McDowell (1981) applied Herrnstein's matching law to clinical behavior problems. An adult male was under treatment for engaging in what was termed "oppositional behavior" (violent outbursts, assaults, threats). Because an attempt at extinction (ignoring the violent behavior) was considered risky, the treatment program was based on the matching law. A token economy was set up to reward unrelated positive behaviors (shaving, reading, performing useful tasks). By increasing the reinforcement rate for the desired behaviors, the *relative rate* of environmental reinforcement of the oppositional behaviors was decreased without changing the *absolute number* of such reinforcements. An 80% decline in frequency of oppositional behavior was observed within the first 8 weeks of treatment, demonstrating the practical validity of the matching law.

It is satisfying to see the successful application of basic psychological research to clinical therapies. We are certainly pleased to see experimental psychology assume the counterpart role for psychotherapy that the biological sciences perform for the practice of medicine.

SUMMARY

Motivation is defined as an activating force that energizes and directs a specific behavior toward a goal, or reward. Mechanistic, stimulus-response (S-R) theories of motivation are based on automatic S-R connections (associationism) in which behavior is governed by its consequences (Thorndike's law of effect). Behaviorism is built on two types of S-R conditioning processes: classical or respondent (Pavlovian) and instrumental or operant (Skinnerian). In classical conditioning, a neutral stimulus is paired with a natural, or unconditioned, stimulus, thereby acquiring the ability to elicit the same, or similar, response. In operant conditioning, a reinforcer (conditioned or natural stimulus) causes a conditioned response to be emitted. A discriminative stimulus (an environmental cue) signals the location or timing of the reinforcement and shares some of the motivating effect of the conditioned stimulus. Discrimination of the conditioned stimulus is the critical factor in effective conditioning. It depends mainly on the latter's contingency of appearance or nonappearance with the unconditioned stimulus. Both positive and aversive classical conditioned stimuli can inhibit, or suppress, operant responding in what is known as counterconditioning. This effect also occurs in avoidance learning, which may invoke a combination of classical fear conditioning and operant avoidance responding (two-process theory). Responses can be generalized to similar or related stimuli, and vice versa, with response strength or probability increasing as the degree of similarity to the conditioned stimulus increases.

Arousal and drive provide biological forces as motivators. Hullian theory postulates drive reduction as the basic reinforcer in S-R motivation processes. Drives energize all potential behaviors, but the drive stimulus, like the operant discriminative stimulus, cues and directs the appropriate response. Arousal and drive motivations are governed by homeostatic mechanisms that tend to return the system to equilibrium or optimal performance levels.

Optimal or adaptation levels of arousal are related to sensory satisfaction and task difficulty. Hedonism associates arousal with the preference for pleasure and aversion to pain and discomfort. This preference accounts for approach-avoidance conflicts, in which the opposing gradients determine behavior toward or away from the target. Opponent-process theory provides another balance model of behavior resulting from opposing emotional sensations. Cognitive theories account for behaviors based on the influence of attitudes and attributions. Uncontrollable experiences (attributed to external forces) can lead to a clinical condition of "learned helplessness," which has been posited as a cause of depression.

Intrinsic motivation theory explains behavior as the result of internal drives and stimulation, involving homeostatic mechanisms. These internal motivations are inhibited by explicit, external rewards.

This chapter reviews theories of conditioning, learning, and motivation. Based primarily on experimentation with animals, models have been formulated, tested, and applied to human behavior. The results have helped us to understand the *why* of behavior.

8

Episodic Memory

> And suddenly the memory returns. The taste was that of the little crumb of madeleine which on Sunday mornings at Combray . . . my aunt Léonie used to give me, dipping it first in her own cup of real or of lime-flower tea. . . . But when from a long-distant past nothing subsists . . . the smell and taste of things remain poised a long time, like souls, ready to remind us, waiting and hoping for their moment, amid the ruins of all the rest; and bear unfaltering, in the tiny and almost impalpable drop of their essence, the vast structure of recollection.
>
> (From *Remembrance of Things Past* by Marcel Proust)

This is how Marcel Proust describes the event—tasting a madeleine (a shell-shaped pastry beloved by the French) dipped in tea—that led him to produce the seven-volume semi-autobiographical novel called *Remembrance of Things Past.* His recollections of his past (even though modified by imagination) are the kind of memories we classify as episodic.

Episodic memory is the repository of personal, unique, concrete experiences that are dated in the rememberer's past. This chapter will selectively review several issues in the episodic memory literature. First, we ask whether memory should be viewed as a structure or a process; second, we review the evidence in favor of the multiple-store view of memory, particularly the distinction between short-term and long-term store; third, we review an alternative to the multiple-store model known as levels-of-processing; fourth, we describe the distinction between recall and recognition at both the empirical and theoretical levels; and fifth, we discuss the role of imagery in memory. Before beginning, however, we take a brief historical detour to review the work of the father of episodic memory reseach, Hermann von Ebbinghaus.

A BRIEF HISTORY OF EPISODIC MEMORY RESEARCH

The study of memory entered the present era of quantitative, empirical research in the late nineteenth century with the pioneering work of the German psychologist Hermann von Ebbinghaus (1850–1909). Ebbinghaus investigated the common, though at that time little studied, human problem of forgetting. He designed ingeniously simple and effective methods and concepts for revealing the course of remembering and the patterns of its failure. His work strongly influenced subsequent memory research and is still referenced in the current verbal learning literature. In fact, his experiments, first published in 1885, have been reprinted by Dover (Ebbinghaus, 1885/1964). Ebbinghaus's experiments marked the first experimental study of memory processes and set the pattern for a century of research. For this reason, it is useful to review his approach and techniques.

Ebbinghaus focused his studies on the learning and forgetting of individual verbal elements. In order to avoid material that his subject (himself) might be able to structure into meaningful combinations (phrases, related concepts, mental pictures), he invented the *nonsense syllable,* a three-letter string consisting of a consonant-vowel-consonant or CVC (for example, BEX), which is pronounceable but does not form a true word.

Another of Ebbinghaus's innovations was a very sensitive measure of learning—the *method of savings.* In this method, a list of nonsense syllables is initially learned; then, after a lapse of time to allow forgetting, relearned. If fewer trials are needed to relearn the list than were required for the initial learning, the difference, or savings, is taken as evidence of retention of the material. The measure of such retention is percent savings, the percentage of relearning trials saved compared to total initial learning trials. Savings is computed as:

$$\text{Savings \%} = \frac{\text{Number of original trials} - \text{Number of relearning trials}}{\text{Number of original trials}} \times 100$$

So, if a particular list of nonsense syllables initially required 40 trials for learning, and only 20 trials for relearning, the amount of savings is 50%: ((40 − 20)/40) × 100. Here, where a recall task, which requires reproducing the list of items, may show little or no retention after an interval of time from presentation of the original list, the method of savings is extremely sensitive to any faint memory traces that would be too weak to emerge under the more stringent requirements of a recall task.

Figure 8-1 shows a typical Ebbinghaus retention curve. The ordinate or *y*-axis shows the percentage of savings. The abscissa or *x*-axis shows the number of days since the original learning. Note that the curve drops to less than 50% savings after one day of forgetting, tapering off to 25% after a week, and to 20% after 3 weeks. In other words, the rate of forgetting is rapid at first and then slows down. Forgetting, measured by the method of savings, is a slow process, and some information seems to be retained almost indefinitely.

Although the nonsense syllable was used extensively by early researchers in verbal learning, recent researchers have used the more meaningful stimuli of words, phrases, sentences, and even whole blocks of text. Materials are no longer exclusively verbal but have been extended to digits, pictures, sounds, odors, and tangible objects. Percentage of savings is now only one of a varied set of measures of retention used as the dependent variable. We next turn to some of the theoretical controversies in the area of episodic memory, and the data on which they are based.

Fig. 8-1 Ebbinghaus' retention curve. The graph plots percentage savings against days since learning. Virtually all forgetting curves show this characteristics shape, with forgetting rapid at first, followed by asymptotic performance. (From *Human Memory: Structures and Processes* by R. L. Klatzky. Copyright © 1975 by W. H. Freeman and Company. All rights reserved. Reprinted by permission.)

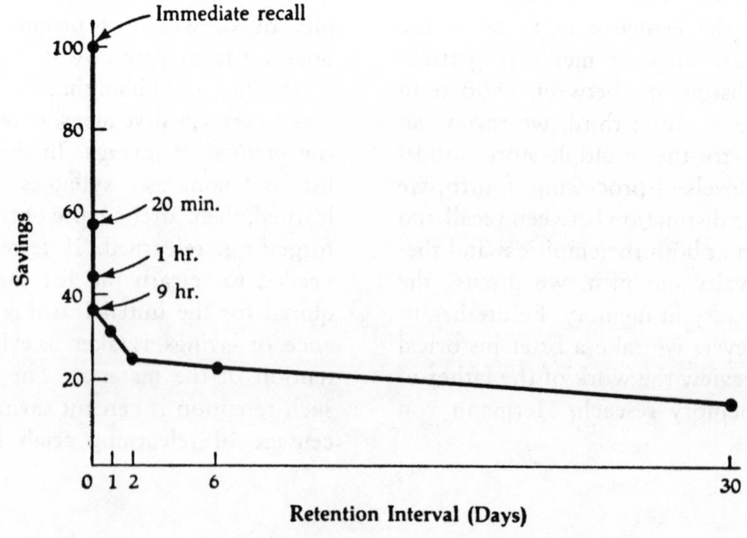

MEMORY AS STRUCTURE OR PROCESS?

There are two major theoretical approaches to episodic memory: structure-oriented and process-oriented. A structural approach to memory views information as passing from one memory system or store to another. As information is passed from one store to another, some may be lost or transformed from one form to another. For example, the visual components of a string of letters making up a word may be encoded into a phonemic (acoustic) form and next the meaning of the word may be retrieved from long-term memory. We describe one such structural model for memory, that of Atkinson and Shiffrin (1968).

In contrast, a processing view of memory sees information as being transformed by the processing that subjects apply to it. This processing can range from the shallowest kind in which only visual (graphemic) characteristics are noted, to a deeper processing in which acoustic (phonemic) characteristics predominate, to the deepest processing in which meaning (semantic) characteristics are paramount. The processing approach is exemplified in the levels-of-processing theory of Craik and Lockhart (1972).

The two approaches, structure and process, are similar in that each assumes some transformation or encoding of information. However, a structural approach emphasizes distinct systems or stores. These are often viewed as storage locations in the brain, each with its own characteristics. A processing approach emphasizes the different processes that subjects use to transform information. These are thought to be easily manipulated by instructions, and sensitive to the different strategies that subjects employ in their efforts to remember.

Atkinson and Shiffrin's Storage Model

A typical storage memory model was proposed by Atkinson and Shiffrin in 1968. Their model is shown in Figure 8-2. (A similar, less elaborate version appears in Chapter 6.) As we indicated in the chapter on perception (Chapter 6), the *sensory register* (or sensory information storage system) is a rapid-transit buffer that holds incoming information briefly in an image-like form for one to four seconds. Subjects can either recode the information from this sensory store to a short-term store by encoding it into a verbal (phonemic or acoustic) form, or they can encode it directly into long-term store. These two possible alternatives are represented in Figure 8-2 by the arrows from the sensory register to short-term store or directly to long-term store. The dotted arrow suggests the uncertainty of direct storage in long-term store. Some information may be lost in transit as a result of interference or other defects in processing.

Short-term storage is longer lasting than sensory storage, but it is of limited capacity (current theory suggests that only three to seven items of information can be stored there). Items can be displaced from short-term memory by new incoming information, can be recycled in short-term memory by rehearsal, and can be transferred to long-term memory either by rote rehearsal or by some more elaborate processing. Whether rote rehearsal is sufficient to transfer information into long-term memory is a much debated issue that we will return to later in this chapter. Items that are displaced from short-term store before they can be transferred to long-term store are considered lost unless reentered into short-term store by re-exposure.

Once information finally enters long-term memory, it may become permanent, or it may be reduced in strength (decay) or become inaccessible. This uncertainty about whether information can ever be lost from long-term memory is represented in the figure by the dotted arrow. (In Freudian analysis, for example, memories repressed in the unconscious are often recalled many years after they have apparently become irretrievable.)

Experimenters who study memory bypass consideration of the sensory register

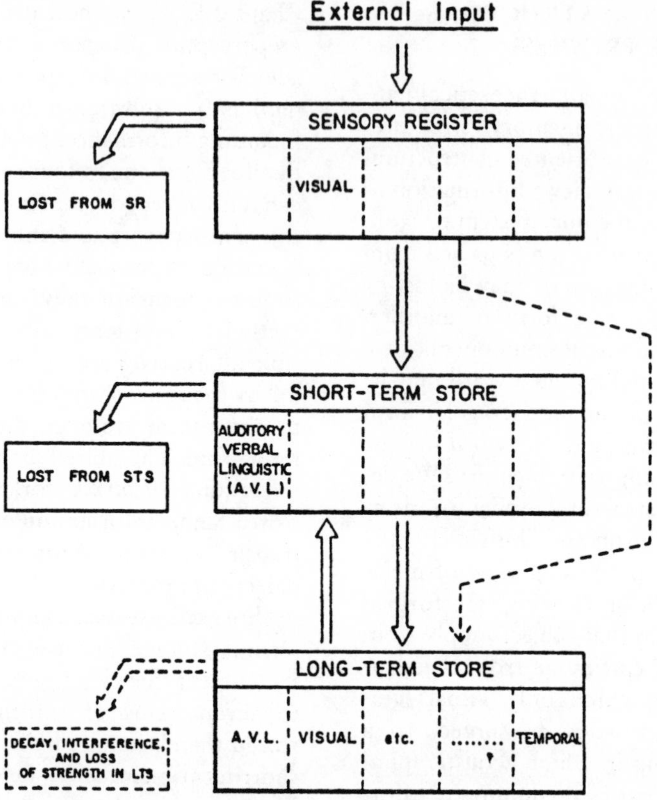

Fig. 8-2 Atkinson and Shiffrin's information-processing model of memory. (From "Human Memory: A Proposed System and its Control Processes," by R. C. Atkinson and R. M. Shiffrin. In K. W. Spence and J. T. Spence (Eds.) *The Psychology of Learning and Motivation* (Vol. 2). Copyright 1968 by Academic Press. Reprinted by permission.)

by presenting stimuli for long enough intervals to ensure perception of each item. Thus, their experimental paradigms have been designed to study the distinction between short-term and long-term storage. The dual, short-term versus long-term store concept has been advanced as an explanation for many results in memory performance. In a moment, we consider one such result—the serial position curve in free recall. First, however, we consider some data and results on short-term memory.

Short-Term Memory

Short-term memory is a working memory that serves as a transfer station between both input from our outside environment and output from our inner environment. We use it to remember the last few words of a phrase we are hearing long enough to understand it, remember a telephone number we have looked up long enough to dial it, and remember what we have seen from a tachistoscopic exposure long enough to say it or write it down. In addition, we use it to remember a conversation we had last night, think about an experiment we are planning, and rehearse an important conversation we are about to have. It has been identified with the primary memory of William James (1890), who defined primary memory as the contents of consciousness and the psychological present (Waugh & Norman, 1965).

Short-term memory differs from long-term memory in three ways. First, items initially stored there are fragile and easily forgotten. Second, relatively few items (from three to seven) can be stored there, so short-term memory is of limited capacity. And third, the coding format of items stored in short-term memory seems to be predominantly acoustic or articulatory in nature. In contrast, long-term memory retention is more permanent, has an apparently unlimited capacity, and stores items in a primarily semantic format.

Fragility of Short-Term Memory traces. How long can items reside in short-term memory without being lost? In order to trace out the time course of forgetting from short-term memory, it is necessary to prevent rehearsal. This is because rehearsal is generally held to be the primary vehicle for maintaining information in short-term memory and of transferring information to long-term memory. Brown (1958) in England and Peterson and Peterson (1959) in the United States almost simultaneously introduced a rehearsal prevention task to observe forgetting from short-term memory. This task is known as the Brown-Peterson paradigm.

In the Brown-Peterson paradigm, a small number of items is presented for the subject to remember, and then memory is tested at various times after presentation (from 0 to 18 seconds in a typical experiment). When this time interval is unfilled, subjects can usually remember the items perfectly, even after an 18-second delay. However, in this paradigm the interval is filled with a task demanding both attention and subvocalization. Subjects are given a task like counting backward by threes from a three-digit number. This task is intended to prevent rehearsal of the to-be-remembered items.

Figure 8-3 presents data from the original Peterson and Peterson paper (1959), which used three unrelated consonants as the material to be remembered. On the same figure, some data collected by Murdock (1961) using a single word, three words, and three consonants are plotted. Although the interfering, rehearsal-prevention task has minimal effects on memory for a single word, memory for three words or three consonants decreases rapidly with time, and the shape of the forgetting function is the same whether the

Fig. 8-3 Percent of correct recall from short-term memory. The graph compares the performance of Peterson and Peterson's (1959) subjects for three consonants with the performance of Murdock's (1961) subjects for three consonants, three words, and one word. (From "Implications of Short-Term Memory for a General Theory of Memory," by A. W. Melton. In *Journal of Verbal Learning and Verbal Behavior,* 1963, *2,* 1–21. Copyright 1963 by Academic Press. Reprinted by permission.)

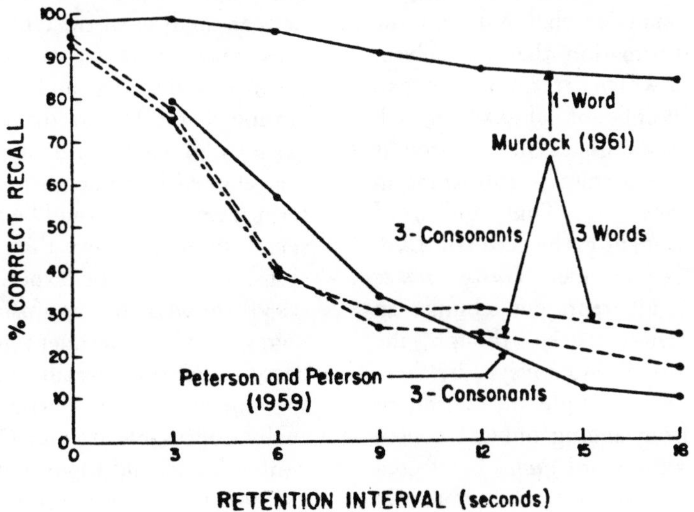

three items are consonants or words. The results of experiments like those illustrated in Figure 8-3 indicate that items residing in short-term memory last for not much longer than 6–9 seconds unless they are maintained by rehearsal.

Limited Capacity of Short-Term Memory. Short-term memory is of limited capacity, and has been variously estimated as seven plus or minus two when its capacity is measured by memory span experiments (Miller, 1956), and as few as four to five items when its capacity is measured by the number of letters we can report from a brief visual exposure (Sperling, 1960).

But how do we count items to measure capacity? Is an item a single letter regardless of whether it is embedded in a list of unrelated letters or in a word? A clue is given by the data shown in Figure 8-3, which indicates that the rate of forgetting from short-term memory is the same whether such forgetting is measured in terms of three unrelated consonants or three three-letter words (which consist of nine letters, related to one another by a well-learned scheme). George Miller, in his justly famous 1956 paper entitled "The Magic Number Seven, Plus or Minus Two: Some Limits on Our Capacity for Processing Information," reviewed a number of studies of short-term memory span (a task that requires subjects to repeat back a string of items in the same order as presented). He concluded that it is not the richness of information that the subject must remember which determines the span but rather the number of "chunks" of such information. A chunk of information is anything that has a unitary representation in long-term memory. Thus, the word *guilty,* the consonant *g*, the acronym *IBM,* and even the platitude *"Haste makes waste"* might all represent chunks in short-term memory even though the amount of information conveyed by them varies widely. (For example, the consonant *g* is selected from among only 21 consonants, whereas the word *guilty* is selected from among thousands of potential words). Miller found that when information in a single item is varied from the smallest possible amount (a binary digit that can take on only the values of 0 or 1), to decimal digits (selected from among the 10 digits 0 through 9), through letters, and through one-syllable words, it was the number of chunks of information rather than the amount of information conveyed that was important.

Coding Format of Items in Short-Term Memory. In addition to the limited capacity of short-term memory and the fragility of items residing there, a third characteristic of short-term memory is its acoustic coding format. Verbal items such as digits, letters, and words appear to be entered into and maintained in short-term memory by translating them from their original form (e.g., visual, auditory, tactual) into an acoustic or articulatory form. This acoustic form is maintained by subvocal rehearsal (repeating the items over and over again). Silent rehearsal, using the mind's tongue to talk to the mind's ear, is apparently a ubiquitous activity of the human adult, which can be used not only to maintain items in short-term memory, as when rehearsing a phone number or the name of a new acquaintance, but also for verbal thinking.

Evidence that information encoded into short-term memory is in an acoustic or phonemic form comes from two sources: first, an analysis of the types of errors subjects make when recalling items from short-term memory, and second, a consideration of the factors that can reduce the capacity of short-term memory. If items are retained in an acoustic form in short-term memory, it should be possible to observe auditory, rather than visual, confusions. In his classic experiment, Conrad (1964) showed that confusion errors in a memory-span experiment are acoustically based rather than visually based. Letters of the alphabet can be classified as being visually confusable (C and O), acoustically confusable (C and B), or neither (C and F). Conrad found that acoustic confusions predominated in short-term recall even when the items are presented visually. In other words, subjects confused the letter C with the letter B (an acoustic confusion) more often than they confused a C with an O (a visual confusion).

Furthermore, the memory span is smaller when items are acoustically confusable than when items are not, for both consonants (Conrad & Hull, 1964; Wickelgren, 1965) and short words (Baddeley, 1966b). Baddeley's experiment is particularly noteworthy because he showed that although fewer words can be recalled when they are acoustically similar, semantic similarity had no effect on the capacity of short-term memory. Thus, a list of words like *bat, hat, cat* are recalled less well than *bat, desk, tiny* (which are unrelated both semantically and acoustically), but a list like *tiny, small, little,* which are semantically related, are recalled as well as an unrelated list. Thus, semantic confusability does not seem to reduce the capacity of short-term memory when short lists of five words are used, which are within the capacity of short-term memory.

In a complementary experiment, using longer lists of ten words, which presumably must be stored in long-term memory, he found just the opposite results: semantically confusable words were now recalled more poorly, while acoustically confusable words were recalled as well as control lists (Baddeley, 1966a).

Having reviewed some of the differences between short-term and long-term memory, we next turn to how the two-store model has been used to account for serial position functions in free recall tasks.

Serial Position Functions in Free Recall. A *free recall* task is the simplest possible memory task in terms of procedure, although the strategies subjects use to succeed in the task are undoubtedly very complex. In a free recall experiment, subjects are presented with a list of 10 to 30 items, usually words, displayed or spoken one at a time, at a predetermined rate and for a fixed duration per item. At the end of the list, subjects are given a recall signal and asked to write down as many of the words from the list as they can remember. Subjects are permitted to recall the words in any order—that is, they need not write down the words in the order they were presented. The procedure is called *free recall* because the task is recall or reproduction of the material presented, and the order of recall is unspecified, or free to vary. This is in contrast to *serial recall,* in which subjects are required to recall the items in the order they were presented.

When recall performance (number or percentage of correct items) is plotted as a function of presentation or input order (not the order in which the subjects actually recalled the words, the output order), the recall performance shows a serial position function of the kind shown in Figure 8-4. Words presented early in the list and those presented late are recalled best, whereas words in the middle of the list are recalled worst. The initial section of the serial position function, which shows good recall of the beginning of the list, is known as the *primacy effect.* The final section of the serial position function, which shows good recall of the end of the list, is known as the *recency effect.*

According to the two-store model of memory, some of the items recalled from a list as long as 10 or 15 items would necessarily be recalled from long-term memory, because the capacity of short-term memory is not sufficient to hold such a long list. Thus, at least some of the items from lists of the length typically used in these free recall experiments must be recalled from the long-term store, and items are assumed to enter long-term store through the mechanism of verbal rehearsal.

On the other hand, some items, particularly the most recent ones, might very well still be in short-term memory and thus be retrieved from short-term rather than long-term store. In fact, one of the interesting aspects about the free recall experiment is the order in which subjects actually write down the words they recall.

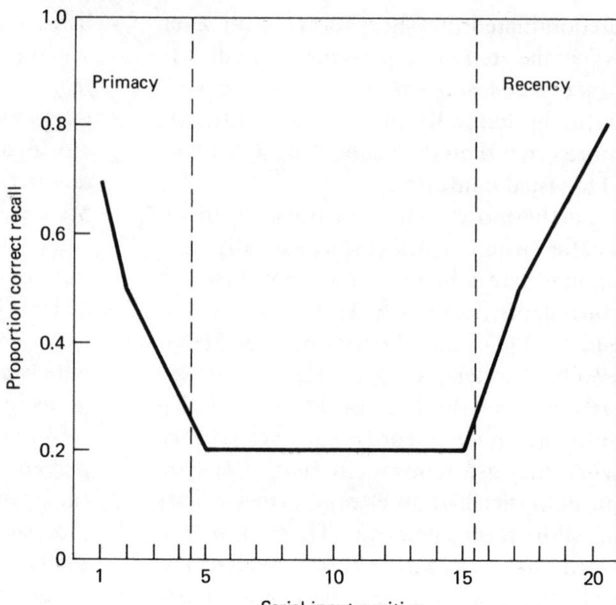

Fig. 8-4 Idealized serial position function for a 20-item free recall task, showing the primacy and recency peaks.

Typically, subjects write down the words from the end of the list first, then words from the beginning of the list, and finally, the words from the middle of the list. In other words, they do not recall the words in the same order they were presented, but "dump out" from memory the most recently presented ones first. Why? We may assume that subjects through long experience know the capacity and time limitations of their short-term memories, and so attend to short-term store first, before the items can be lost or displaced by recall of earlier items. Next, the subject goes into long-term memory to retrieve the earlier items. But why should the words at the beginning of the list be recalled better than those in the middle? Why do we observe both recency effects (presumably due to short-term memory functioning) *and* primacy effects (presumably due to long-term memory functioning)?

In 1966, Murray Glanzer proposed the dual-store hypothesis as an explanation for the shape of the free recall serial position function (Glanzer, 1972; Glanzer & Cunitz, 1966). He suggested that recency effects in free recall were caused by retrieval from short-term store, and primacy effects by retrieval from long-term store. According to the two-store explanation of the serial position function, early items benefit from increased rehearsal opportunities and thus are more likely to be stored in, and retrievable from, long-term memory. Late items, on the other hand, are still in short-term store, in some kind of acoustic or auditory form. When the recall signal is given, they can be "dumped out" even though they have not had sufficient processing to enter long-term store. Items in the middle of the list are also retrieved from long-term store. However, because they have not had as much time to be rehearsed, and also suffer from interference by earlier items *(proactive interference)* as well as by later items *(retroactive interference),* they will not be recalled as well as the first items on the list. In summary, then, the dual-store explanation of the serial position recall function says that the early and middle portion reflects retrieval from long-term store, and the end portion reflects retrieval from short-term store.

If the two serial position peaks are due to two different processes, it should be possible to selectively affect one peak without affecting the other. Glanzer and Cunitz

(1966) reported two experiments, one which affected only the end peak of the serial position function and the other only the beginning peak.

As we have seen, a highly effective method of "clearing out" short-term memory is by use of a rehearsal-prevention task such as counting. When Glanzer and Cunitz had subjects count forward from an arbitrary number for either 10 or 30 seconds (thereby "clearing out" recent words from short-term store), they found that the final peak of the serial position curve was indeed flattened, as shown in Figure 8-5, compared to the control condition (indicated with a 0 in the figure) in which subjects performed no counting and recalled immediately. The 30-second interference condition produced virtual destruction of the end peak. In contrast, the initial peak of the serial position function was unaffected by the counting manipulation. These results were interpreted as evidence that the counting task had cleared out the contents of short-term memory, thereby destroying the recency effect, without having any effect on long-term memory, thus sparing the primacy effect.

In a complementary experiment reported in the same paper, Glanzer and Cunitz sought an experimental manipulation that would affect long-term retention but leave short-term retention unaffected. One such manipulation is study time—the longer each item is presented in a rote learning experiment, the better it is retained. This is understandable within the context of a stores model: the more time an item is available for rehearsal, the more likely it will enter long-term memory. However, retention of items in short-term memory is dependent not on the study

Fig. 8-5 Serial position curves for three delay periods—0, 10, and 30 seconds. (From "Two Storage Mechanisms in Free Recall," by M. Glanzer and A. R. Cunitz. In *Journal of Verbal Learning and Verbal Behavior,* 1966, *5,* 351–360. Copyright 1966 by Academic Press. Reprinted by permission.)

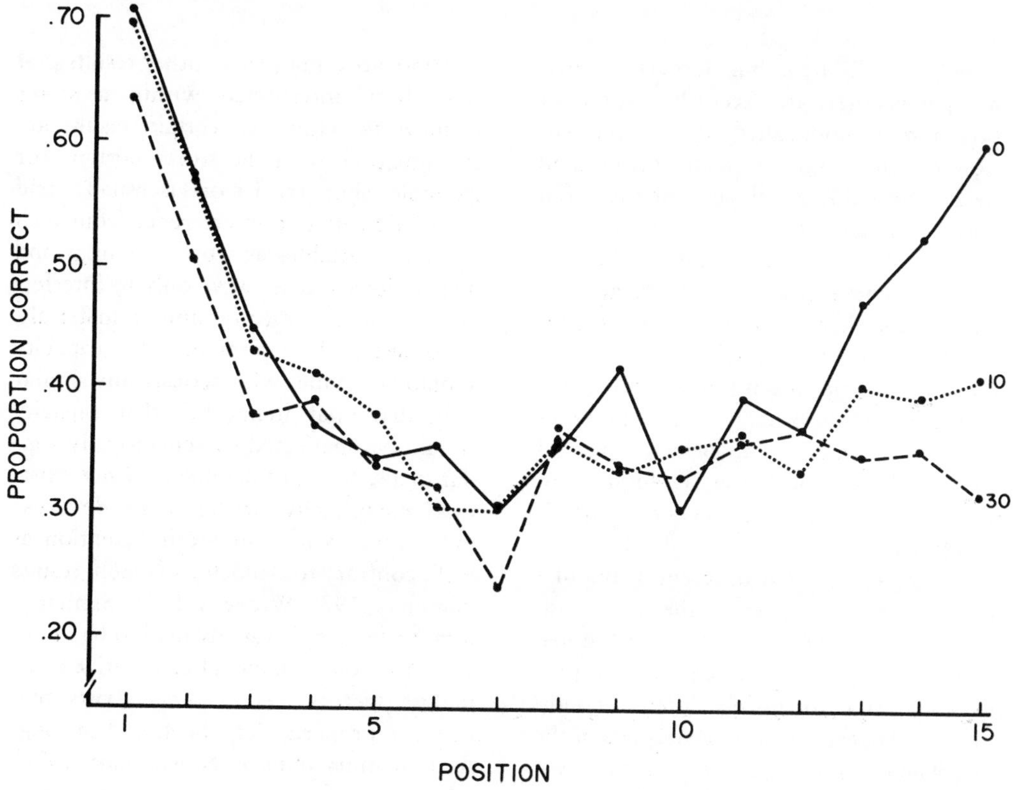

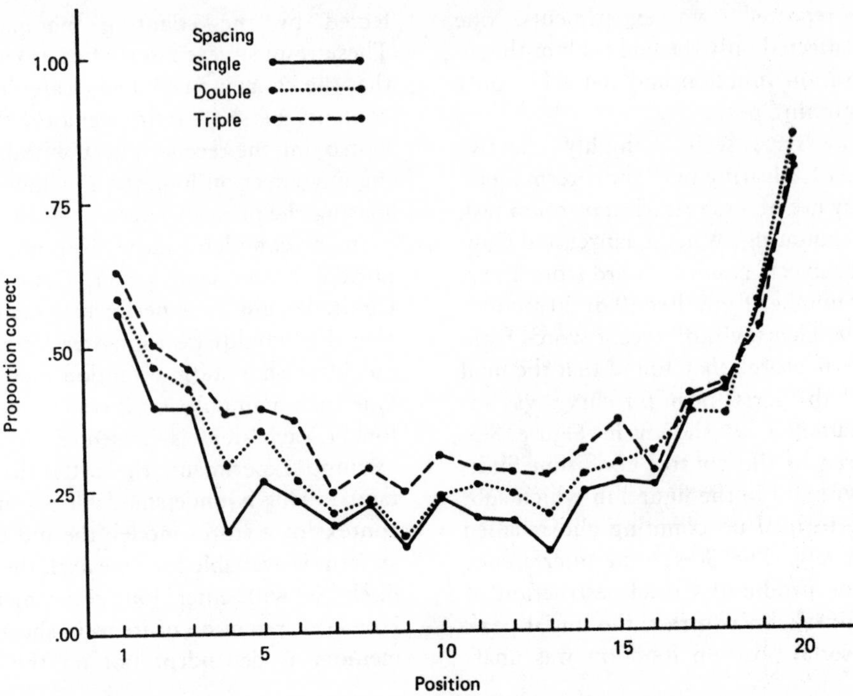

Fig. 8-6 Serial position curves for three different rates of presentation: single (3 seconds); double (6 seconds); triple (9 seconds). (From "Two Storage Mechanisms in Free Recall," by M. Glanzer and A. R. Cunitz. In *Journal of Verbal Learning and Verbal Behavior,* 1966, *5,* 351–360. Copyright 1966 by Academic Press. Reprinted by permission.)

time for each item but rather on how many items there are. Accordingly, rate of presentation should affect long-term retention but not short-term retention, and hence affect the initial peak of the serial position function but not the end peak.

Figure 8-6 shows the results of this second experiment, when rate of presentation was varied. There were three spacing conditions: triple spacing (one item every 9 seconds), double spacing (one every 6 seconds), and single spacing (one every 3 seconds). As predicted, the primacy part of the serial position curve is higher for slower rates, but the recency part is unaffected.

The ability of two different manipulations to affect two parts of the serial position curve independently was interpreted as evidence of two different storage processes sensitive to entirely different conditions, and operating at opposite ends of the list. These results thus support the two-store model.

There are a number of other results that have been interpreted within a stores framework. However, certain results are incompatible with the stores notion. For example, short-term store is usually held to be insensitive to interference from such semantic variables as word meanings and associations and sensitive only to interference from acoustically similar materials. So subjects' short-term memory capacity should be smaller with acoustically similar than dissimilar items, but that capacity should be unaffected by semantically similar items. Yet considerable evidence exists that semantically similar items *do* cause interference with short-term retention as well, contrary to Baddeley's (1966b) results (Shulman, 1971; Wickens, 1973). Similarly, long-term store is usually held to be insensitive to acoustic factors but sensitive to semantic factors, yet evidence exists that acoustic properties can be stored in long-term memory (Nelson & Rothbart, 1972). In the face of evidence that the two stores are not as qualitatively different as was once supposed, Fergus Craik and Robert Lockhart in 1972 proposed an alternative to the stores model of memory, which they called a levels-of-processing model.

Craik and Lockhart's Levels-of-Processing Model

The levels of processing approach proposes that incoming information may go through a variety of encoding operations or processing. The elaborateness of the processing and the type of processing affect how well an item will be remembered. According to this model, information has the potential to be encoded at progressively deeper and more complex levels of meaning. When attention is focused on a word, a memory trace for that word is created. This trace may be very slight and short-lived, or very strong and durable, depending on how the word is being attended to, or, in levels-of-processing terminology, at what depth it is being processed. A word may be encoded at a shallow level according to how it looks, at an intermediate level according to how it sounds, or at a deep level according to what it means. The deeper the level at which a word is processed, the better it will be remembered.

In contrast to the assumption of the stores theory, sheer rehearsal of a word will not help it to be remembered better. Rather, better memory only comes from deeper processing. In the levels-of-processing model, the distinction between short-term and long-term store is not in encoding operations, but rather in attentional characteristics. Craik and Lockhart equate short-term store with primary memory as it was originally used by William James—that is, with the present contents of consciousness, the things that we are attending to at the present moment. In their view, short-term memory is a *process* of attention rather than a *place* to store things. Short-term memory acts as a beacon to illuminate certain characteristics of an item, rather than a box to place things in. For an item to be in primary memory is for an item to be attended to at a certain level. However, Craik and Lockhart assume that simple maintenance of attention on an item at a certain level of processing (maintenance rehearsal) does not act to increase the trace strength of the item. It will merely maintain it in primary memory. The only way to increase an item's strength in long-term memory is to increase the depth of its processing. Thus, items that are stored in long-term memory may have benefited from deeper or shallower processing, and will accordingly be well or poorly remembered.

Some of the characteristics of the levels-of-processing approach may be illustrated with data from experiments reported by Craik and Tulving in 1975. They used an *incidental learning* task to test the levels-of-processing model. The task is called "incidental" because subjects are not intentionally trying to learn the stimulus materials. Rather, during the learning phase subjects are given an *orienting task* in which they are asked to judge whether or not words have some characteristic, and the time required to make the YES or NO decision is measured. The characteristics to be judged are varied to require different *levels of processing,* from a very shallow level in which only the visual or structural characteristics of the word need to be processed, to a deeper level in which the sound or pronunciation of the word must be processed, to the deepest level in which the meaning must be accessed in order to answer the question. Table 8-1 shows examples of each of the three processing tasks.

In the structural coding task, only the visual or orthographic properties of the word are needed, to decide if it is in capital letters; in the phonemic coding task, only the phonological properties of the word need to be accessed to decide if it rhymes with *rain;* and finally, in the semantic coding task, the meaning of the word must be retrieved to decide if it fits into the sentence context. After this incidental task, subjects are given an unexpected memory task—either free recall or, as in this case, recognition.

Table 8-1 Examples of Three Types of Encoding Tasks in an Incidental Learning Task

Coding task	Question	Examples	Answer
Structural (case)	Is the word in capital letters?	CLOUD match	YES NO
Phonemic (rhyme)	Does the word rhyme with "rain"?	TRAIN COUCH	YES NO
Semantic (sentence)	Does the word fit the sentence: "He met a ____ in the street?	FRIEND TABLE	YES NO

There are two dependent variables of interest in this task. The first is the time to answer the initial question, defined as the time between the presentation of the word to which the question refers and the subject's YES or NO response. The second is the recall or recognition scores for the words responded to during the orienting task. Results from one of Craik and Tulving's experiments are shown in Figure 8-7. The right panel of Figure 8-7 presents the results of the memory test, which are of major interest. First, recognition memory performance for words accompanied by sentence (semantic) questions is higher than those with rhyming questions, which in turn is higher than those with case questions. The sentence and rhyme words also show memory results typical of incidental learning tasks: namely, that words eliciting YES responses lead to better memory than those eliciting NO responses.

To use the examples from Table 8-1, *friend* is remembered better than *table* and

Fig. 8-7 Decision latency in the orienting task *(left panel)* and recognition memory performance on the delayed memory task *(right panel)* for three different levels of processing. (From "Depth of Processing and the Retention of Words in Episodic Memory," by F. I. M. Craik, and E. Tulving. In *Journal of Experimental Psychology: General,* 1975, *104,* 268–294. Copyright 1975 by the American Psychological Association. Reprinted by permission.)

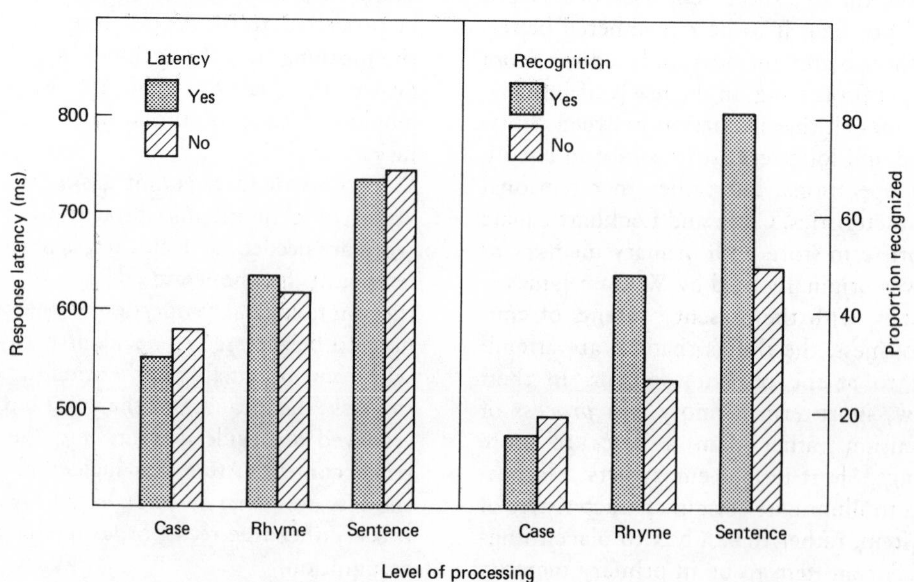

train is remembered better than *couch*, but *cloud* and *match* from the structural task show equivalent, and poorer, memory. The explanation that Craik and his colleagues have given for the advantage of YES words is that for positive questions, both the question and the word are stored as a unit in memory, and hence the word is easier to retrieve because it is part of a more elaborate memory structure.

The latency (reaction time) results, shown in the left panel, exhibit a common pattern of results for such orienting tasks, namely, that questions that require deeper processing also require more time to answer. Sentence questions take longer than rhyme questions, which in turn take longer than case questions.

Although the latency results are intuitively consistent with the notion of the depth of processing required during the orienting task, the fact that items that are remembered better also tend to take longer to process poses the possibility that it is time, rather than depth, which accounts for the memory results. In general, the longer an item is presented for study, the better it is remembered. So it is possible that the depth results are actually an artifact of processing time during learning.

Craik and Tulving (1975) attempted to disentangle the effects of longer encoding time from the effects of depth of processing. They conducted another experiment to compare memory for words requiring a relatively fast but semantic decision (verifying category membership) with memory for words requiring a relatively slow but structural question (deciding whether a word conformed to a particular pattern of consonants and vowels). The encoding times for the structural questions were longer than for the semantic questions. However, words processed semantically were remembered better than words processed structurally. Thus, words accompanied by questions that took longer to answer were less well remembered. They concluded that it was the quality and nature of processing during the orienting task that predicts memory performance, not the time taken for such processing.

Craik and Tulving also showed that the pattern of results from the incidental memory task was not due to the unexpectedness of the test. *Intentional memory* tasks, in which subjects are instructed to remember the words they answer questions about, show the same pattern of results.

Although the influence of the levels-of-processing model has been widespread, the model has its critics. In 1978, Alan Baddeley wrote a critique of the levels-of-processing approach in *Psychological Review*. Baddeley's major criticism concerns the lack of an independent way to assess depth of processing other than by its reflection in memory performance. It seems intuitively plausible that deciding whether a word is in upper or lower case will produce poorer memory than deciding whether the word belongs to the category *animal*. However, no *independent* method of measuring depth appears viable. Thus, the depth notion is circular. Ironically, the very fact that deeper processing does not always require more processing time, and thus that processing time does not always predict processing depth, was used by Baddeley in his criticism of the circularity of the depth approach.

A second criticism made by Baddeley concerns the depth-of-processing assumption that continued processing of, or attention to, a stimulus in short-term memory at the same level does not lead to increased durability of the trace. Baddeley pointed to evidence that simple rote rehearsal (continued attention to the item at the phonological level) *does* produce increased memory for the item. The question whether rehearsal *per se* increases item retention is a thorny one, and there is a great deal of evidence on both sides of the argument. Suffice it to say here that the stores versus levels-of-processing controversy has been productive in generating new paradigms and new data. For this alone, the controversy has been valuable.

Levels-of-processing researchers have used either recall or recognition as measures of the memory strength of an item, with generally consistent results regardless of which measure is used. We next turn to the question of whether recognition and recall are really measuring the same underlying construct—goodness of memory.

RECALL VERSUS RECOGNITION: ARE THEY TWO SIDES OF THE SAME COIN?

There are two basic procedures for testing memory performance: recall and recognition. In recall, subjects are required to reproduce the material they have learned, usually by writing it down. In recognition, subjects are presented with the items they have studied, called target or old items, interspersed with some items they have not studied, called distractor or new items. Subjects must decide which items are old and which are new. Just as there are several different types of recall tasks, there are several different types of recognition tasks.

Methods for Testing Recognition Memory

One way of classifying recognition memory tasks is by the manner of presentation of old and new items. In the *discrete* trials procedure, there are two separate phases to the experiment: the study phase and the test phase. In the study phase, the to-be-remembered items are all presented, usually one at a time. The test phase either follows the study phase immediately or with a delay filled with some distracting task. The test phase consists of the presentation of old, or target, items interspersed with new, or distractor, items.

In the *continuous* trials procedure, the study and test phases are combined. Subjects are presented with a continuous series of items, some of which have been presented earlier. The subject's task on each trial is to say whether the presented item was old or new. (The first few items presented must of necessity be new.)

Shepard and Teghtsoonian introduced the continuous procedure for recognition memory in 1961, in order to more closely mimic the memory requirements of everyday life. There are many real-life situations in which a continuous stream of information is presented and we must continually update our memory of what has happened or what is yet to happen, as in playing out a bridge or poker hand or shopping for a dinner party. Shepard and Teghtsoonian used as their stimulus materials three-digit numbers and carefully constructed their sequence of numbers so as to vary the *lag*, or number of items intervening between the first and second presentations of an item, from its minimum value of zero (i.e., no intervening items between the first and second presentation) to a value as large as 60. The first presentation of each item should be called new, and the second presentation should be called old.

Figure 8-8 presents the recognition memory performance of Shepard and Teghtsoonian's subjects in terms of percentage correct classification of old items as a function of lag. Performance is virtually perfect for a lag of zero, and drops almost to chance after a lag of about 55. In this experiment, chance is 50% because half of the items are old and half are new, and subjects are required to guess on each trial even if they have no idea whether the item is old or new. Thus, their expected score from guessing alone is 50% correct.

A second way of classifying recognition memory tasks is by the nature of the test. There are three types of recognition memory tests: YES/NO, confidence ratings, and forced choice. In some cases, YES/NO tests are combined with confidence ratings.

In the YES/NO test, items are presented to subjects one at a time and the subject must indicate whether the item is OLD, that is, one that has been studied before, or NEW, one that was never studied. This was the procedure used in Shepard and Teghtsoonian's continuous recognition experiment.

The confidence rating procedure obtains more information about the certainty of the subject's judgment than can be obtained from a simple YES or NO. Some theories of the recognition memory process based on signal detection theory (see

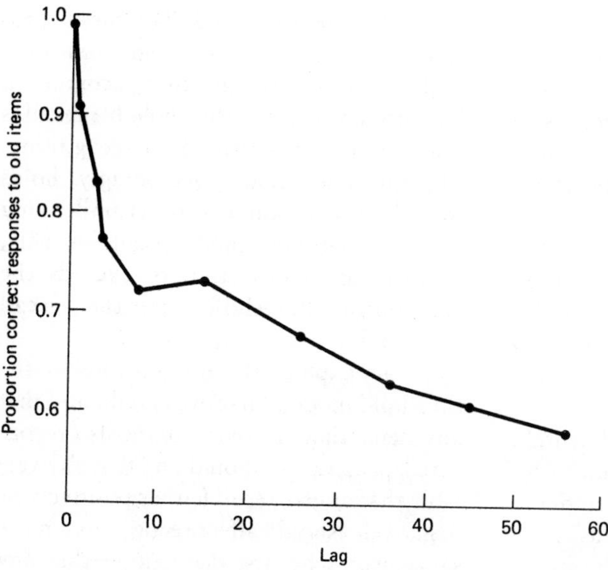

Fig. 8-8 Proportion correct responses to old items (hits) as a function of lag—the number of stimuli intervening between the first and second presentations of the item. (From "Retention of Information under Conditions Approaching a Steady State," by R. N. Shepard and M. Teghtsoonian. In *Journal of Experimental Psychology,* 1961, *62,* 302–309. Copyright 1961 by the American Psychological Association. Reprinted by permission.)

Chapter 4) assume that the decision about whether an item is old or new is made with reference to an underlying continuum of familiarity. Items that appear familiar to the subject are classified as old, and items that appear unfamiliar are classified as new. But if familiarity lies along a continuum, subjects should be able to rate their familiarity experiences into more categories than the extremes of old or new. The confidence rating procedure permits them to do so by dividing the OLD/NEW range into some arbitrary number of rating values or intervals, with one extreme indicating "sure it's new" and the other indicating "sure it's old." Intermediate rating values indicate intermediate degrees of confidence about the old or new judgment.

So, for example, a six-category scale might use the top three numbers (4, 5, 6) to indicate varying degrees of confidence for old judgments, and the bottom three numbers (1, 2, 3) to indicate varying degrees of confidence for new judgments. When a scale with an even number of categories is used, it is also possible to collapse the rating judgments into YES/NO judgments and treat them as simple YES/NO data. This cannot be done for odd-numbered category scales, in which the middle value is used for uncertainty about whether the item is old or new. For this reason, an even number of scales is usually used, permitting all responses to be divided into one of the two YES/NO categories. Appendix B describes models of the recognition process based on signal detection, along with various methods for analyzing YES/NO and confidence rating data using signal detection theory methods.

In the forced-choice procedure, *n* alternatives are presented to the subject simultaneously, among which one is old and the remaining alternatives are new. The simplest version of this procedure is two-alternative forced-choice, in which a pair of stimuli is presented, one of which is old and one new. Subjects must decide which member of the pair is old. The new items are often selected by the experimenter for their distraction effects. For example, including a synonym as a distractor may reveal that the subject had encoded the original word semantically, whereas including a homonym (a word that sounds like the original word but means something different) may reveal that the subject had encoded the original word phonemically.

Having described the two major methods of measuring memory performance—recall and recognition—we next turn to the question of whether they are simply two different ways of assessing memory or two different processes.

Theoretical Differences Between Recall and Recognition

Recognition is usually a much easier task than recall. If you were asked to recall the name of the champion swimmer who won five gold medals in the 1976 Olympics you might have trouble remembering his or her name. However, if you were given the four names Mark Rudd, Tom Jones, Mark Spitz, and Joe Namath, chances are you would recognize Spitz as the almost-forgotten hero.

Although a great deal of experimental evidence indicates that performance in recognition tasks is generally better than performance in comparable recall tasks, it has also been shown that many of the same factors that improve recall also improve recognition. Memory researchers have long been interested in the theoretical question of whether comparable psychological processes underlie the two methods of addressing memory. As we shall see, the question of the relationship between recognition and recall is intimately tied up with the question of the nature of the memory trace, and whether there are separate memory systems for registering occurrence (episodic) information and conceptual (semantic) information.

The earliest theory of how recognition and recall take place, and hence, how they are related, was the *threshold hypothesis* described by McDougall in 1904. The threshold hypothesis says that whether an item is recognized or recalled depends on its strength in memory. All items that you know (for example, all the English words in your vocabulary) have some strength in memory. This means they are all registered with different degrees of memorability in long-term memory. However, when an item is presented for study in a memory experiment, it receives a boost in strength. The amount of that boost will depend on such factors as the duration of the item's presentation, its meaningfulness, the particular encoding strategy a subject uses, and so on. The strength of that item during the test phase of a memory experiment will determine whether it is recognized or recalled. The threshold hypothesis proposes that recall of an item requires a higher memory strength than recognition. Put another way, the threshold for recall is higher than the threshold for recognition. The threshold model, accordingly, holds that there is a single process underlying both recognition and recall—namely, whether an item's strength exceeds the recognition threshold or the recall threshold.

Let us explore the implications of the threshold model. First, we should find that any items that are recalled are also recognized. Second, we should find that any variable that affects recall (either positively or negatively) should affect recognition in the same way. The first deduction—that any item that is recalled should also be recognized—was shown to be false in several studies reported by Endel Tulving and his colleagues (Flexser & Tulving, 1978; Tulving & Thomson, 1973). The phenomenon was termed by him "the recallability of nonrecognized words." This phenomenon was used to support a theory called *encoding specificity,* which we will return to later in this chapter. The second deduction—that any variable that affects recall should affect recognition in the same way—was shown to be incorrect for at least one very important variable in verbal memory—word frequency.

It is a well-documented fact that words of high frequency of occurrence in English, such as dog, are recalled better than those of low frequency, such as aardvark (Hall, 1954; Sumby, 1963). Therefore, word frequency is positively related to recallability. However, just the reverse relationship has been found for recognition; words of low frequency are recognized better than words of high frequency (Allen & Garton, 1968, 1969; McCormack & Swenson, 1972; Schulman, 1967; Shepard, 1967). Therefore, word frequency is negatively related to recognizability. Because the second deduction from a threshold model—that a variable should have the same effects on both recognition and recall—can be shown to be false for the variable of word frequency, we need another model to account for these differences between recall and recognition.

Such a model was proposed by Kintsch in 1970. This model, called a dual-process model, explicitly recognizes the important role of retrieval in recall (as documented by a large body of literature that will not be reviewed here), and its relative lack of importance in recognition. It proposes that recall of an item requires two processes: *retrieval,* that is, a search for a target item through long-term memory, and then a *decision* about whether the item was on the study list by an evaluation of its strength.

To give a concrete example, suppose you have just been presented with a list of words and are now asked to recall them. You remember that some of the words were names of foods, and you dredge up from memory several food words, such as cake. Having retrieved cake, you evaluate its strength to see whether it is high enough to classify it as an old word. If it exceeds your decision threshold, you write it down; if it does not, you do not write it down.

In recognition, however, there is only one process—the decision process. Search and retrieval of the item are not necessary because the item is present at the test. The subject needs only to decide whether it exceeds the recognition threshold (presumably the same threshold used for the recall task). Thus, recall involves the two processes of retrieval and decision, whereas recognition involves the single process of decision. To put it in a simple formula: *recall = retrieval + recognition.*

According to the dual-process model, a variable can have different effects on recall and recognition because it can differentially affect the two stages of retrieval and decision. In the word frequency paradox referred to earlier (that high-frequency words are recalled better but low-frequency words are recognized better), it seems plausible that high-frequency words are more easily retrieved than low-frequency words, thereby giving them a recall advantage. However, low-frequency words might be recognized more easily than high-frequency words because the boost in memory strength produced by the study phase is more detectable. Because retrieval is a more difficult operation, the high-frequency advantage dominates the recall process because the low-frequency words that fail to get retrieved cannot demonstrate the benefit of the greater memory strength boost.

Although the dual-process model can account for the disconfirmation of the second deduction from threshold theory (that variables should affect recall and recognition in the same way) it has trouble with the first (that any words that are recalled should also be recognized). If a word is recalled, it has both been retrieved and passed the decision stage; however, it should then also be recognized because all that is required for recognition is passing the decision stage.

Tulving's Encoding Specificity Model

Contrary to the logic of the dual-process analysis we have just reviewed, Tulving and his colleagues have collected a large amount of data that demonstrate the recallability of nonrecognized words (Flexser & Tulving, 1978; Watkins & Tulving, 1974). Tulving explains his results in the following way. First, he claims that contrary to the dual-process model, recognition does, in fact, require retrieval. Presentation of what he calls a *copy cue* (the item itself on a recognition test) does not automatically guarantee retrieval of the memory trace that was established during the study phase.

The importance of retrieval in recognition may be illustrated by an experiment reported by Tulving and Thomson in 1971. In their experiment, subjects in a recognition memory task were shown pairs of related words during the study phase. During the test phase, the old words were tested either in the same context as studied (with their mates from the study phase), in a changed context (with new related words), or without context (alone). Subjects recognized the same context words better than the no-context words, which turn were recognized better than the changed-context words. These results were interpreted as evidence that retrieval in recognition was important, since the context in which a word appeared affected its recognizability.

The relationship between context and retrieval was even more forcefully demonstrated in another series of experiments by Tulving and Thomson (1973). The subjects were first asked to study a list of word pairs each of which consisted of a target (in capitals) and a cue word weakly associated with its paired target word (e.g., ground–COLD). Then the subjects were presented with the list cues (ground–?) and required to *recall* the corresponding target words, thus ensuring that the targets would be encoded in the cue context. Next they were given a list of new cues that were strong associates of the original target words (hot–?), and told to list all possible associations for each cue word. In this phase, the associations listed by the subjects included about three quarters of the original target words. This, of course, is reasonable since the targets were strong associates of the new cue words, so that *hot* was likely to elicit the associate COLD. Finally, the subjects were asked to look over their responses and circle any word they *recognized* as having occurred on the original paired study list.

Now, consider this carefully: Three quarters of those response words were the actual words that they had *recalled* in the very first test. Yet in the final recognition test they *recognized only 24% of the original target words* they had generated in the free association task immediately before. As an extra check, a posttest was administered in which the original list cues (the context words in the pairings) were presented and the subjects asked to *recall* the corresponding target words. The mean recall score was 63%, far more than the recognition score for the target words on the test just previous to the final recall. Tulving and Thomson counted 69 target words *recalled but not recognized,* indicating that they had been retained in memory and were available. Of course, they were available when retrieval was undertaken with the original context cues but not with the new cues, even though the former were weak associates and the latter, strong associates of the target words.

These remarkable findings led to the development of the *encoding specificity hypothesis.* This hypothesis holds that in episodic memory tasks the occurrence of an item is coded in a specific, cue-dependent way. When the retrieval context does not reinstate those specific cues that were presented during study, memory performance will deteriorate. Thus, recognition may be either easier or more difficult than recall depending on the cues available during the memory test.

In episodic memory tasks, we encode events and objects we observe into a form that can be stored and used in memory. According to Tulving, this encoding records the things on which we focus attention in the setting in which they appear and with a time-tag that reminds us of when we observed or heard them. If you see the instructor write the word *psychology* next to the word *test,* you will remember the two words together and also that they are on the blackboard and that they were written last Tuesday. The two words and their situational context (blackboard, classroom, instructor, Tuesday) are all recorded in some interlinked form in your episodic memory at the time of input.

The idea that the kinds of memories that are studied in the traditional verbal learning and memory tasks are different from memories carrying such conceptual knowledge as word meanings, uses, and relationships led Tulving in 1972 to propose the term *episodic memory* for the first type of memory, as distinct from *semantic memory* for the second. He makes the distinction as follows:

> In this chapter I discuss the possibility that semantic memory, among other things, is not the kind of memory that psychologists have been studying in their laboratories since the time of Ebbinghaus. I will suggest that there are sufficiently fundamental differences between the two forms of memory to recommend that we consider, at least for the time being, the two

categories separately. To facilitate subsequent discussion, I will refer to this other kind of memory, the one that semantic memory is not, as "episodic" memory.

(Tulving, 1972, p. 384)

In the next chapter, on semantic memory, we distinguish the two types of memory systems in greater detail, both theoretically and in terms of the different paradigms that are used to study them. Here, however, we simply point out that the concept of an episodic memory provided the foundation of Tulving's theory of *encoding specificity.* He reasoned that because each observed event is uniquely encoded, a particular word will be encoded in many different ways on different occasions. Each new encoding of the word will incorporate a new and different context. Furthermore, even though the basic meaning of the word in semantic memory might be unchanged, its representations in episodic memory will be different, since each will be modified by the context. Because each encoding of the same word is different, it cannot be found in memory and identified again unless you look for it with an exact copy, or *copy cue,* along with its original context present at study. That is just what Tulving and Thomson's experiment showed. The retrieval context must reinstate the specific cues that established the encoding during study, or recognition is impaired.

Light and Carter-Sobell (1970) demonstrated this phenomenon in an experiment in which they presented target words in one context (e.g., strawberry jam) and tested them in a different context (e.g., traffic jam). Subjects were to remember only the target (the underlined word), but were instructed that the context (the other word) might help them. They found that while the target jam was not likely to be recognized in the context of *traffic,* it was readily recognized in the context of *strawberry* or *raspberry.* Raspberry is not identical with strawberry, but the two have enough orthographic and semantic attributes in common ("berry" + fruit preserves) to establish an adequate copy cue for retrieval.

According to Tulving's theory of encoding specificity, while the episodic representation of the word is affected by the specific context, the semantic representation is not. Tulving proposed that the two memory systems are separate, although clearly interconnected. Semantic memory is protected from loss of information because of its highly organized and meaningful contents. Episodic memory is not protected because it is time and space tagged, and new incoming information will affect the tags and introduce new forms of old items.

Not all theorists have accepted the distinction between episodic and semantic memory (e.g., Anderson & Bower, 1974; Martin, 1975; Reder, Anderson, & Bjork, 1974). According to their views of memory, there is only one long-term memory store—semantic memory. In an episodic memory task, concepts, often viewed as nodes in a richly connected memory system, are *tagged* or incremented in strength. During the test phase of an episodic memory task, a subject addresses the node corresponding to the item in semantic memory to see if it has been tagged, or if it has above-threshold strength. The strong effect of context in recognition is explained by the hypothesis that different concept nodes will be accessed in different contexts. Thus, the word *jam* will have at least two concept nodes—that corresponding to a preserve and that corresponding to a traffic congestion. Only the first concept node will be tagged when the to-be-remembered item is the *jam* in strawberry *jam.*

Here, a node is not a word in its surface form, but rather a concept to which a word can refer. The concept of *jam* in traffic jam is a different concept from that of *jam* in strawberry jam. Accordingly, different nodes in semantic memory are accessed when the context is changed from *traffic* to *strawberry.* In short, words are polysemous (have different meanings), and hence their representations in memory differ with the context. According to this argument, the decrement in recognition memory with changed contexts occurs because a different node in semantic memory is accessed.

According to the semantic theorists, then, there is no necessity to postulate two memory systems, the episodic and the semantic, one is sufficient. Of course, such a model still requires a retrieval function on recognition tasks in order to access one of the semantic representations that corresponds to the context encoding. This model also demands a massive memory store of semantic representations of all the various meanings possible for each word, increasing with each new context encountered. And all of these meanings must reside permanently in a loss-proof memory. The issues cannot be resolved simply on the basis of existing data or hypotheses.

MEMORY AND IMAGERY

So far, we have confined our attention to memory for verbal items. The stores model for memory that we described at the beginning of the chapter proposes that all items must be encoded into a verbal or acoustic short-term memory before they can be stored in long-term memory. This implies that everything we remember, including the appearance of objects, the faces of friends, and the locations of building, must be verbally encoded (i.e., translated into words) in order to be remembered.

The hypothesis that memory for nonverbal objects or events is based on language has a long history. Perhaps its most celebrated advocate was Benjamin Whorf, who proposed that all of perception and memory is influenced by the language into which we must necessarily code these perceptions and memories (Whorf, 1956). In testing the Whorfian hypothesis, several investigators have found that stimuli for which verbal descriptions are short or consistent are remembered better than those requiring longer descriptions, or for which no single term exists (e.g., Brown & Lenneberg, 1954; Glanzer & Clark, 1963a, 1963b).

Yet, as we shall see, impressive evidence exists that pictures of objects are remembered better than their names, that concrete words are remembered better than abstract words, and that instructions to subjects to form mental images of the objects to which words refer have impressive effects in improving memory. One interpretation of these results uses the concept of the visual mental image to account for differences in memory for various kinds of items or for various kinds of strategies subjects use for remembering.

Mental Imagery in Thought and Memory

A mental image is often defined as the experience of a sensation in the absence of the original stimulus. Such an image could thus be visual, auditory, tactual, gustatory, or olfactory, as in remembering how an apple looks, how it sounds when bitten into, how it feels to the hand, how it tastes, or how it smells. For our present purposes, we confine ourselves to visual images and visual imagery.

Imagery is used in psychological research to refer to two kinds of activity: *remembering* the appearance of an experienced event, which results in an image of memory, and *imagining* the appearance of an unexperienced event, which results in an image of imagination. We can remember the appearance of a collie that we saw jumping over a fence yesterday, and we can imagine the appearance of a dog jumping over the moon, even though we have never experienced the latter event. Both kinds of visual images are studied in memory research. Images of memory are based on actual pictorial stimuli presented to subjects. Images of imagination are generated by subjects to verbal stimuli such as the word pair *dog–moon,* to which they might generate an image of a dog jumping over a moon.

Few psychologists today take one of the two extreme positions that either all memories are concretized as mental images or all memories are encoded in verbal terms. Rather, psychologists divide themselves into two main camps: those who believe that there are two memory systems, one for images and one for verbal codes; and those who believe that there is a single amodal system, containing concepts and their relationships, to which both images and verbal codes have access. An amodal system is one that is independent of the form of input of information, in this case, independent of whether concepts are presented as words or as pictures.

The dual-coding hypothesis, first proposed by Paivio (1971), holds that there are two memory systems—the visual-spatial system and the verbal-symbolic system. These two systems are differentiated by neural locus and by specialization for different tasks. However, the two systems are richly interconnected, and many types of material may be encoded into both systems. A subject attempting to remember a concrete word may store both the word itself and its visual image into the two systems, and a subject attempting to remember a picture may store both the memory image of the picture and its description into the two systems. On the other hand, there may be some verbal material that is so abstract it is encoded only into the verbal system, and some visual material, such as faces of strangers and abstract paintings, that is so indescribable that it is encoded only into the visual system.

The amodal hypothesis, sometimes referred to as the conceptual-propositional view, questions the assumption that the visual and verbal memory systems are qualitatively different (Anderson & Bower, 1973; Pylyshyn, 1973). This position has been heavily influenced by computer simulations of human performance that store information about the world in terms of abstract propositions and relationships. The propositionalists argue that humans probably store information in analogous ways, not as mental images and verbal symbols but as a system of abstract propositions and relationships. Before describing how the two hypotheses account for the superiority of imagery in memory, we will first review some of the relevant empirical evidence.

Superiority of Imagery in Memory

Two types of imagery-related variables have been manipulated experimentally: different types of *materials* having different potentials for activating visual memory images and different types of *instructions* to manipulate subjects' encoding strategies.

Stimulus Variables in Imagery Research. Stimulus variables have been manipulated by using pictorial representations of objects, names of those objects (concrete words), and names of abstract concepts (abstract words). When pictures are used as stimuli, the experimenter provides the subject with a prefabricated memory image, and when concrete words are used, the subject may generate his or her own image. In a wide variety of memory tasks, memory performance progressively improves as the concreteness of the stimulus increases: from abstract words, to concrete words, to line drawings of objects, to photographs of objects, to the objects themselves.

To take the single comparison between pictures and concrete words, pictures are superior to words in recognition (Nickerson, 1965; Shepard, 1967; Snodgrass & McClure, 1975; Standing, Conezio, & Haber 1970), as well as in recall (Bousfield, Esterson, & Whitmarsh, 1957; Paivio, Rogers, & Smythe, 1968). Examples of pictures and words used in these sorts of studies are shown in Figure 8-9.

The dual-coding model accounts for the picture superiority effect by two aspects of the visual memory image; first, pictures are more likely to be dually coded than words (i.e., registered in both the image and verbal stores), and second, the image code, which is more likely to be stored to a picture than to a word, is the more effective code for item memory (Paivio, 1971; Paivio & Csapo, 1973).

The conceptual-propositional position has produced a variety of different explanations for the picture superiority effect. One explanation is that pictures produce more spatial predicates than words do,

Fig. 8-9 Examples of pictures and words used in research on memory and imagery. (From "A Standardized Set of 260 Pictures: Norms for Name Agreement, Image Agreement, Familiarity, and Visual Complexity," by J. G. Snodgrass and M. Vanderwart. In *Journal of Experimental Psychology: Human Learning and Memory,* 1980, *6,* 174–215. Copyright 1980 by the American Psychological Association. Reprinted by permission.)

while continuing to contact the same underlying amodal concept (Anderson & Bower, 1973). Another explanation, related to the first, is that pictures produce more elaborate sensory codes than words. Nelson and his co-workers (Nelson, Reed, & McEvoy, 1977; Nelson, Reed, & Walling, 1976) found that increasing the visual similarity of a set of pictures in a paired associate recall task, while keeping conceptual similarity constant, had the effect of destroying, and sometimes even reversing, the superiority of pictures over words. They argue from these results that it is the distinctive surface characteristics of pictures like the intricacy of line and detail that make them more memorable than words, and when such distinctiveness is destroyed by drawing pictures of distinct concepts in visually similar ways, the picture advantage is destroyed.

Yet another hypothesis proposes that

pictures are remembered better than words because of the unique representation of the depicted concept in semantic memory (Durso & Johnson, 1979; Snodgrass, 1980). The argument here is that words, even concrete names, carry more meanings and representations than pictures, and hence a particular semantic representation is less likely to be contacted on a recognition test or retrieved during recall than the word's corresponding picture. For example, the word *saw* has several meanings in addition to its picturable meaning as a tool, and so *saw* may be stored as a verb instead of a noun on a memory test. The argument is similar to arguments made by semantic theorists, referred to earlier, in their criticism of Tulving's encoding specificity hypothesis.

Instructional Variables in Imagery Research. Subjects' encoding strategies have been manipulated by instructing them to form visual images of words or word pairs. When learning pairs of words, subjects do better if they imagine the members of the pair of to-be-remembered items interacting with one another, and the association is usually more effective if the interaction is bizarre. So, to remember the pair *man–hat,* it is better to image the man wearing a hat than to image them side by side (interaction is better), and it is probably better to image the man eating the hat (a bizarre interaction) than wearing it.

The most striking improvement in memory through imagery training occurs in the serial recall task. The Greek orators introduced the *method of loci* as a memory aid, in which prominent locations in the oratory hall were picked as pegs on which to hang key points in the speech. Another well-known peg-word technique is the one-bun method, in which subjects learn concrete words that rhyme with the first 10 digits, and then use imagery to associate items on a to-be-learned list to each of the peg words associated with each digit.

An amusing anecdotal account of teaching the one-bun technique to a recalcitrant subject is given by Miller, Galanter, and Pribram in their book, *Plans and the Structure of Behavior.*

> The antagonistic attitude of experimental psychologists toward mnemonic devices is even more violent than their attitude toward their subject's word associations; mnemonic devices are immoral tricks suitable only for evil gypsies and stage magicians. As a result of this attitude almost nothing is known by psychologists about the remarkable feats of memory that are so easily performed when you have a Plan ready in advance. Anecdotes do not contribute to science, of course, but they sometimes facilitate communication—so we shall lapse momentarily into a thoroughly unscientific vein.
>
> One evening we were entertaining a visiting colleague, a social psychologist of broad interests, and our discussion turned to Plans. "But exactly what is a Plan?" he asked. "How can you say that *memorizing* depends on Plans?"
>
> "We'll show you," we replied. "Here is a Plan that you can use for memorizing. Remember first that:
>
> one is a bun,
> two is a shoe,
> three is a tree,
> four is a door,
> five is a hive,
> six are sticks,
> seven is heaven,
> eight is a gate,
> nine is a line, and
> ten is a hen."
>
> "You know, even though it is only ten-thirty here, my watch says one-thirty. I'm really tired and I'm sure I'll ruin your experiment."
>
> "Don't worry, we have no real stake in it." We tightened our grip on his lapel. "Just relax and remember the rhyme. Now you have part of the Plan. The second part works like this: when we tell you a word, you must form a ludicrous or bizarre association with the first word in your list, and so on with the ten words we recite to you."
>
> "Really, you know, it'll never work. I'm awfully tired," he replied.
>
> "Have no fear," we answered, "just remember the rhyme and then form the association. Here are the words:
>
> 1. ashtray
> 2. firewood
> 3. picture
> 4. cigarette
> 5. table
> 6. matchbook

7. glass
8. lamp
9. shoe
10. phonograph."

The words were read one at a time, and after reading the word, we waited until he announced that he had the association. It took about five seconds on the average to form the connection. After the seventh word he said that he was sure the first six were already forgotten. But we persevered.

After one trial through the list, we waited a minute or two so that he could collect himself and ask any questions that came to mind. Then we said, "What is number eight?"

He stared blankly, and then a smile crossed his face, "I'll be damned," he said, "It's 'lamp.'"

"And what number is cigarette?"

He laughed outright now, and then gave the correct answer.

"And there is no strain," he said, "absolutely no sweat."

We proceeded to demonstrate that he could in fact name every word correctly, and then asked, "Do you think that memorizing consists of piling up increments of response strength that accumulate as the words are repeated?" The question was lost in his amazement.

(From Miller, Galanter, & Pribram, 1960, pp. 132–136)

Results from a myriad of experiments show that visual memory images, whether provided by the experimenter in the form of pictures or generated by the subject to words, provide a powerful alternative to the linguistic associative system of verbal encoding. The question remains, however, whether the effects of mental imagery arise from the operation of two separate memory systems, as dual-coding theory would have it, or both types of encodings access the same amodal system.

There are additional questions that need to be answered by empirical research. What happens to visual mediators when we become familiar with various kinds of knowledge—when we no longer need to visualize a person's face to remember his or her name or when we no longer have to mentally view a map to remember that Lisbon is due west of Madrid? Why can some kinds of images be recalled better than others, and why do certain image details remain in memory indefinitely while others fade rapidly? Why do some of us have better spatial imagery than others have? The list of challenging puzzles that are beyond reach of present theories goes on and on. And the need for further research on these problems is obvious.

SUMMARY

In this chapter, we have reviewed the topic of episodic memory. Episodic memory is concerned with personal, unique, concrete experiences that are dated in the rememberer's past. In contrast, semantic memory refers to a person's abstract, timeless knowledge of the world that he or she shares with others. The topic of semantic memory is reviewed in the next chapter.

The pioneering work of Ebbinghaus set the stage for the experimental study of episodic memory. Ebbinghaus invented both the nonsense syllable and the method of savings as a sensitive measure of memory retention. More recent research in memory has concentrated on theoretical interpretations of the by-now voluminous data on memory. Two recent views of the nature of episodic memory are contrasted—a structural approach and a process approach. Atkinson and Shiffrin's storage model views information as passing through a series of storage locations in the cognitive system. As a function of various processes that the active human rememberer brings to bear on the information, the information may stop at the first stage, the sensory store, may be recoded and stored in a transient short-term memory, or may be transferred to a more permanent long-term memory. The primary process for transferring information to more permanent stores is the mechanism of rehearsal, which means recoding the information into a verbal/phonemic code.

The sensory information store is of little interest to memory researchers, because in memory studies information is presented sufficiently long to be registered there. Short-term memory is of limited capacity (somewhere between two and nine items from a variety of estimates), traces of items are fragile and do not last long in short-term memory unless they are constantly refreshed by rehearsal, and the coding format of items in short-term memory is generally held to be acoustic or articulatory.

Craik and Lockhart's levels-of-processing model proposes a different view of memory. In their model, the durability of memory traces is determined not by how many stores the information passes through but by the depth to which the information is processed. Deeper processing produces more durable memories. The shallowest level of processing is structural processing, which involves attending to only the graphemic properties of visually presented material (usually words). The next deepest processing is phonemic processing, in which words are recoded into their phonemic components. The deepest level of processing is attending to the word's semantic characteristics. The levels-of-processing model has introduced the incidental learning task as its major experimental paradigm.

Another controversy in the area of episodic memory is the distinction between recall and recognition as tests of memory. Do the two methods of testing memory reveal identical aspects of the memory trace? Two empirical facts suggest that the two memory testing procedures reveal different aspects of the memorability of an event. First, some factors that affect recall in one way affect recognition in the opposite way. The most striking example is word frequency: common words are recalled better than rare words, but rare words are recognized better than common words. Second, some items that are recalled under optimum contextual conditions are not recognized when the item itself (a copy cue) is presented. This phenomenon of recognition failure of recallable words has been used by Tulving as evidence for his theory of encoding specificity.

Encoding specificity proposes that items in an episodic memory task are encoded uniquely, depending on the context at the time of study. Such context includes external stimuli manipulated by the experimenter and internal stimuli generated by the subject. The extent to which the same context is reinstated at the time of the test will determine the extent to which the item is retrieved or remembered as having occurred. Thus, it is possible that an item that is not recognized when such context is absent will be recalled when such context is present.

Most models of episodic memory emphasize verbal rehearsal as an important process in establishing and maintaining memories. Thus, the bulk of memory research has used verbal materials as stimuli. However, there is a large literature which suggests that visual memory images and visually rich stimuli, such as pictures and faces, are better remembered than verbal stimuli. Paivio's dual-code hypothesis predicts such pictorial superiority by hypothesizing that there are two memory systems—one that stores visual images and one that stores verbal codes. When a stimulus is encoded into both systems, by being encoded with both a visual and a verbal code, it will be remembered better than one encoded into only a single system. Paivio assumes that symbols that have concrete referents, such as pictures and concrete words, are more likely to be encoded into both systems than abstract symbols, and hence are more memorable. A competing theory, the propositional model, hypothesizes that all information, regardless of its surface form, is encoded into the same amodal system, having the properties of neither visual images nor verbal utterances.

Although the theoretical controversy is far from settled, it is clear that large improvements in memory can be accomplished by using concrete pictorial stimuli rather than abstract verbal stimuli and by instructing subjects to form visual memory images when trying to remember verbal items. The visual imagery mnemonic devices are especially effective for learning lists of serial items, as in the method of loci or the one-bun techniques.

9

Semantic Memory

A single feature—feathers—marks every bird for what it is. Other principle features characteristic of the class are wings and beaks. Together these make birds the most easily classifiable and the most easily identifiable of all animal classes. Even flightless orders like the kiwis and the penguins display structural characteristics so obviously avian that the possibility of alternative classification does not arise. If flight were the only factor distinguishing birds from other vertebrates, then the systematic position of the one mammalian order capable of flight, the bats, would have to be reconsidered. But fur instead of feathers places the bats unquestionably among the mammals. Teeth (not found in living birds) and the absence of a beak simply confirm that they have no place in the avian order.

(Burton, 1980, p. 331)

This is how a biologist describes classification of the category of birds within the animal kingdom. In this chapter, we will consider how information about natural categories such as birds, fish, and mammals is acquired and organized in the minds of our human subjects. Such information is stored in a system of memory called *semantic memory.* Semantic memory, which represents an organized set of knowledge about the world, may be contrasted with episodic memory, described in the last chapter, which is autobiographical and time-tagged.

THE DISTINCTION BETWEEN EPISODIC AND SEMANTIC MEMORY

In 1972, Endel Tulving proposed two distinct memory systems: "episodic" memory and "semantic" memory. According to Tulving, "Episodic memory receives and stores information about temporally dated episodes or events, and temporal-spatial relations among these events" (Tulving, 1972, p. 385). In contrast, "Semantic memory is the memory necessary for the use of language. It is a mental thesaurus, organized knowledge a person possesses about words and other verbal symbols, their meaning and referents, about relations among them, and about rules, formulas, and algorithms for the manipulation of these symbols, concepts, and relations" (Tulving, 1972, p. 386).

Tulving's original definition of semantic memory emphasized the linguistic system as the repository of semantic information. However, semantic memory has also been used to refer to the information available in images, cognitive maps, and spatial representations in general. Thus, semantic memory may include pictorial and spatial information about how things look and where they are found, as well as verbal information about what things are called and how words are defined. That part of semantic memory that stores words and their meanings is often referred to as the *lexicon,* or mental dictionary.

Episodic and semantic memory differ in the ways they are investigated in the laboratory. Episodic memory is studied in the laboratory by the traditional types of verbal learning tasks described in the last chapter. In these tasks, subjects must first learn a set of materials in the laboratory before being tested on them. Thus, episodic memory tasks typically include a learning or study phase before the test phase.

In contrast, subjects in semantic memory tasks are assumed to possess the semantic information being tested when they walk into the laboratory. No new information needs to be learned by the subject; rather the subject's existing knowledge structure is probed. The task may be deciding whether a string of letters like *mant* is a word or a nonword, in a *lexical decision task;* deciding whether a word or picture of a lion is a member of the superordinate category *animal* in a *categorization task;* deciding whether *cat* or *mouse* has more of some attribute such as size in a *symbolic comparison task;* or deciding whether a statement such as a canary can sing, has wings, is a bird, and is not a vehicle is TRUE or FALSE in a *sentence verification task.*

Because the common knowledge structure that is being probed is assumed to be virtually perfect, the dependent variable of choice in semantic memory tasks is the time required by the subject to make a correct decision (reaction time) rather than whether the decision is correct or not. In contrast, an episodic memory task usually overloads the subject's episodic memory capacity. Therefore, the dependent variable in episodic memory experiments is usually proportion correct rather than reaction time.

Tulving has proposed several differences between episodic and semantic memory. He argues that semantic memories are more permanent than episodic memories, are less subject to interference from new learning, and are not changed by retrieval. In contrast, episodic memories are more ephemeral, are prone to interference from new information, and are changed by their retrieval.

In this chapter, we will first consider how concepts might be organized into categories in semantic memory, and how such categorization develops. We will be particularly concerned with classification of objects that occur naturally in the environment, like fruits and animals, as well as those that occur through natural evolution but are man-made, like vehicles and furniture. Next, we will consider some models of the organization and functioning of semantic memory, how these models are tested, and how revisions of semantic memory models have dealt with conflicting data. Finally, we will consider extensions of semantic memory models to more complex human activities such as text comprehension.

CONCEPTS AND CATEGORIES

A concept is a mental category that can be used to refer to a number of different instances of an object, event, person, or entity. Concepts are usually expressed in words, often in only a single word. Thus, *dog, apple, animal,* and *fruit* are all concepts or categories that may be used to refer to a number of past, present, and future instances. Concepts can refer to subsets (subordinates) or supersets (superordinates) of other concepts. Thus *apple* is a subset of *fruit* and *Granny Smith* is a subset of *apple* in the same way as *dog* is a subset of *animal* and *poodle* is a subset of *dog*.

Categorization is a basic human cognitive process that is generally held to be an indispensible tool in structuring both experience and thought. Although some categories are completely arbitrary and must be learned by rote (e.g., letters of the English alphabet), and still others are physiological and appear to be universal across cultures (e.g., color and form), many categories have boundaries that are not well-defined. These include categories of natural objects, emotions, personality types, life-styles, types of music, literary forms, English pronunciation rules, and even psychological theories.

In the following discussion, we will use the terms category and concept interchangeably, as linguistic labels that can be used to classify a number of instances under a single name. Categories permit us to carve up the world of singular and unique instances of entities into a more abstract but simplified world. Before considering how psychologists have dealt with the problem of ill-defined categories, we first review briefly the contributions of philosophers and linguists to the problem of concepts and categories.

A key issue in the learning and use of conceptual categories is the mental bases on which they are differentiated. How does a child learn to distinguish a dog from a cat? And how shall we program our home robot to distinguish a fruit from a vegetable when we send it shopping for groceries?

One approach, known as *semantic feature theory,* is to assume that complex concepts such as dog and bird are made up of bundles of simpler concepts, called features. The conjunction of these simpler features then defines the concept. For a concept like bird, these features might be inclusion in the superordinate *animal,* ability to *fly*, possession of *wings* and *feathers*, and the ability to *lay eggs*. Semantic feature theory attempts to decompose concepts into features so that a set of features can be used to uniquely define a concept. In addition, the hope is that when all such features are listed, the list of all features will be smaller than the list of all concepts.

There are two different approaches to using features to define categories: the classical view and the prototype view. According to the classical view, which goes back to Aristotle, an instance is either a member of a category or not, depending on whether the instance possesses those features that define the category. In the classical view, boundaries between concepts are clearly drawn. The prototype view denies the existence of a set of defining features that will be true of all instances of a category. Instead, it proposes that some members of a category will possess more of the features that are characteristic of a category, and thus instances can belong to categories in a graded fashion, depending on how many and which features they possess. The prototype, or most typical member of a category, belongs maximally to that category because it possesses the maximum number of features that are characteristic of that category. Boundaries between concepts or categories are not clear-cut but fuzzy.

Classical Theory

In classical theory, the features that represent a concept are both singly necessary and jointly sufficient to define the concept. What do we mean by singly necessary? Every instance of the concept must have this feature. What do we mean by jointly sufficient? Every entity having that set of features must be an instance of the concept.

Following Smith and Medin (1981), we use the concept of a square to illustrate the operation of singly necessary and jointly sufficient features. A square might be defined by listing the following four attributes: closed figure, four sides, sides equal in length, and equal angles. Anything that is called a square has these four features (each is singly necessary), and anything that has these four features is called a square (the features are jointly sufficient). Another requirement of the classical theory is that the features of a concept's superordinate must be nested or included within the defining features of the concept. So quadrilaterals, of which squares are subsets, have the defining features of a closed figure and four sides, and these two features are nested within the set of features that define squares.

It was the classical view of concept definition (and hence of concept formation) that led early psychologists, beginning with Clark Hull (1920), to study the processes of concept formation using artificial concepts. These concepts were usually abstract visual patterns, which had the property that a few discrete, easily describable features constituted the definition of the concept the subject was to learn. Research in concept formation, using artificial stimuli of this type, occupied psychologists for decades. Because many of the questions asked in the concept formation literature are peripheral to the concern of how concepts in the real world are defined and used, the research on concept formation is reviewed in Chapter 10 on Thinking and Problem Solving.

The prototype view of concepts was developed to deal with problems in applying the classical definition of concepts to natural categories of real-world objects. Natural categories include biological objects such as animals and fruit as well as human artifacts such as tools and clothing.

Prototype Theory

Prototype theory was developed to deal with the problem that many categories of natural objects have ill-defined or fuzzy boundaries. This is because natural categories appear to lack that set of singly necessary and jointly sufficient features that would let us unequivocally decide whether

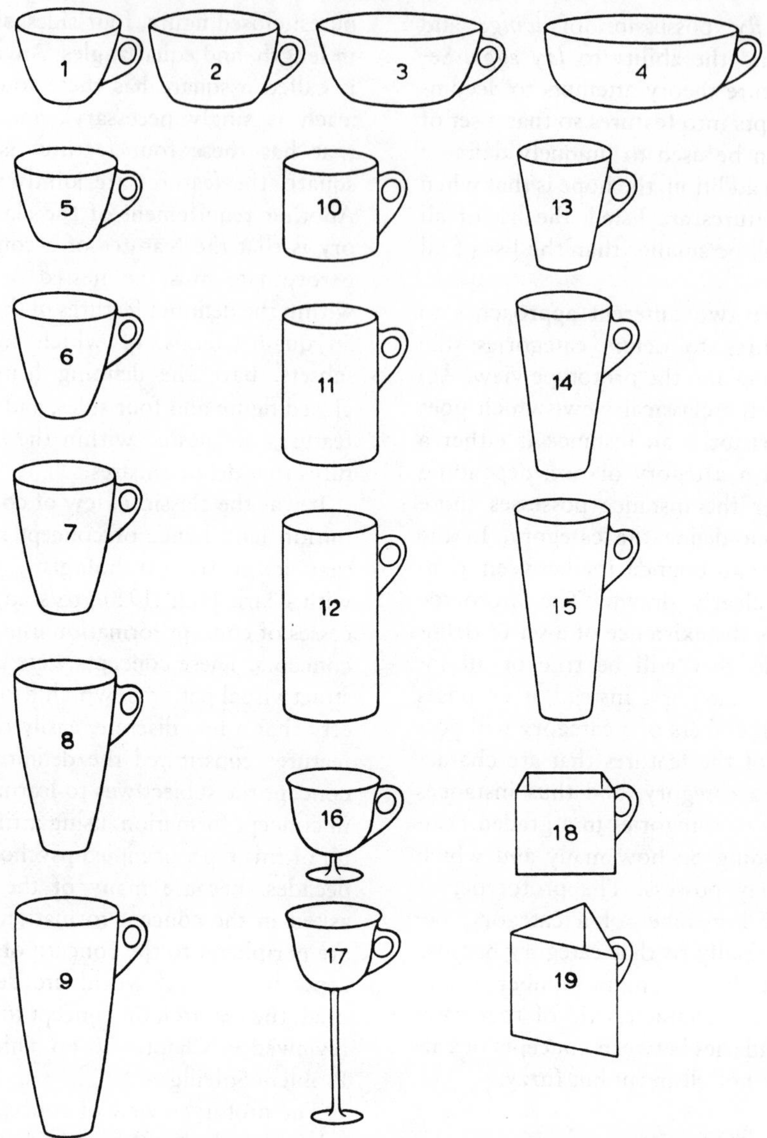

Fig. 9-1 Series of cuplike objects. (From "The Boundaries of Words and Their Meanings," by W. Labov. In C. J. N. Bailey and R. W. Shuy (Eds.), *New Ways of Analyzing Variations in English*. Copyright 1973 by the Georgetown University Press. Reprinted by permission.)

or not a particular object belongs to a particular category.

We will use an example from the research of Labov (1973) to illustrate the fuzziness of boundaries, and the ease with which they can be manipulated. Consider the set of objects illustrated in Figure 9-1. Each of them could be a cup, but some are better cups than others. In fact, some of the wider ones look more like bowls than like cups (number 4, for example). And some of the taller ones look more like vases (number 9, for example).

Labov had subjects name pictures of each of the objects under a variety of different conditions. In the neutral context, subjects were given no instructions but simply asked to describe each object as a picture of it was handed to them. In the food context, subjects were asked to imagine the object sitting on a table filled with mashed potatoes. In the flowers context, subjects were asked to imagine the object sitting on a shelf filled with flowers.

Figure 9-2 shows the percentage of subjects who called each of the objects of four different width-to-height ratios (numbers 1 through 4 in Figure 9-1) either a cup or a bowl. The two solid lines are for subjects in the neutral context, and the two dashed lines are for subjects in the food context. Subjects are more likely to call narrower objects cups than bowls and are more likely to call wider objects bowls than cups. However, objects at the boundaries of the two categories are not always called by one or the other name. Furthermore, context shifts the crossover point, so that all objects are more likely to be called bowls than cups when they are imagined to be filled with food. A similar shift in the crossover point between naming objects as cups or vases occurred in the flower context, when the height-to-width ratio was changed in the opposite direction, from cuplike ratios to vaselike ratios (numbers 5 through 9 in Figure 9-1).

Labov's experiment thus demonstrates that even for such familiar objects as cups, bowls, and vases, both perceptual features such as height-to-width ratio and functional features such as the object's use can determine subjects' categorizations.

EXPERIMENTAL RESEARCH ON PROTOTYPES

We next turn to the contributions of experimental psychologists on the role of prototypes in categorization. We review the research on natural categories first, because this is the research that has supported the prototype view. Next, we discuss some research using artificial categories of experimenter-designed stimuli that mimic prototypicality effects in natural categories. Finally, we review some research that indicates that even when classical definitions for category membership are fulfilled, prototype-like effects are obtained.

Natural Categories

We review three types of evidence that support the prototype theory over the classical theory of categorization. The first

Fig. 9-2 Percent of different names applied to cuplike objects as the width increases and as a function of food versus neutral contexts. The four cups are those labeled 1 through 4 in Figure 9.1. (From "The Boundaries of Words and Their Meanings," by W. Labov. In C. J. N. Bailey and R. W. Shuy (Eds.), *New Ways of Analyzing Variations in English*. Copyright 1973 by the Georgetown University Press. Reprinted by permission.)

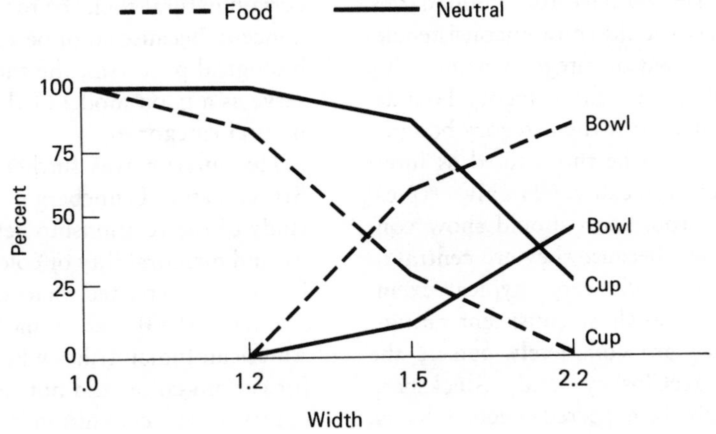

shows that boundaries of natural objects are indeed fuzzy when the frequency of subjects' categorizations are considered. The second shows that exemplars of natural categories are indeed perceived as belonging to the category in a graded fashion and that this perception is mirrored in more objective performance measures. And the third shows that prototypical objects share more features with other members of the category, and this fact provides a mechanism or explanation for why prototypes of categories develop and why category membership is graded rather than all-or-none.

Fuzzy Boundaries in Natural Categories. Interestingly, direct experimental evidence for the fuzziness of category boundaries in natural categories was only recently obtained, even though the research in prototypicality effects that predated it was based on the premise of unclear category boundaries. In 1978, McCloskey and Glucksberg published a paper that provided a direct test of the hypothesis. They selected exemplars from 18 categories selected so that the exemplars would cover a wide range of typicality. Included in the exemplars studied were those that bore no relationship to the category (e.g., *paper* for the category *precious stone*), and thus represented near zero levels of typicality. Subjects were asked to decide on two separate occasions whether or not each exemplar belonged to a particular category.

If categories do have fuzzy boundaries, then subjects should show inconsistencies in their judgment of category membership for exemplars near the category boundaries. Exemplars near the category boundaries are likely to be those rated as intermediate in typicality. Highly typical exemplars (prototypes) should show consistent ratings, because they are central to the category, while very atypical exemplars should also show consistent ratings, because they are completely outside the category. McCloskey and Glucksberg found exactly the expected effects—that is, inconsistent ratings of category membership for such marginally typical objects as pumpkins or tomatoes classified as fruits or vegetables, and consistent ratings for prototypes (apples rated as fruits and carrots rated as vegetables) and noncategory members (apples rated as vegetables and carrots rated as fruits). Consistency was measured in two ways: by agreement across subjects (intersubject consistency) and by agreement within subjects across the two separate sessions (intrasubject consistency). Both measures of consistency showed the predicted effects and thus supported the claim of prototype theorists that natural categories have fuzzy boundaries.

The Role of the Prototype in Categorization. Much of the interest in categorization of natural objects is due to the research of Eleanor Rosch and her students. In this section we trace the development of her research on the role of the prototype in categorization, and in a later section we consider her contribution in discovering the basic level of categorization.

Rosch began her study of prototypicality in the area of color perception with an investigation of what Berlin and Kay (1969) called "focal" color points. She was looking for the core meaning of individual color names. It was Rosch's idea that the core meaning is the heart of the internal structure of all natural categories—that it constitutes the prototype or best example of each category. The prototype centers on certain natural foci, the focal points of the concept. Because color perception involves biological processes, she thought it would serve as a good model of the formation of natural categories.

Her interest was further stimulated by Brown and Lenneberg's (1954) classic study of the relationship between codability and memorability of colors. Brown and Lenneberg reported that Lenneberg and Roberts (1953) had found that certain American Indian tribes who had no names for certain colors did not remember those colors in a recognition test as well as

English-speaking subjects whose language has the necessary names. Furthermore, Brown and Lenneberg found that English speakers remembered best those colors with high codability. Codability was measured in a number of different ways—for example, by the number of different names a color could have—but the best measure appeared to be naming agreement across subjects. Although the Brown and Lenneberg results were intitially interpreted as support for the Whorfian hypothesis of the effect of language on perception (see Chapter 10), another interpretation was suggested by two anthropologists, Berlin and Kay (1969).

Berlin and Kay studied almost 100 languages in an attempt to determine the basic color terms. Their interest was in determining whether different cultural groups carved up their perceptual world of color in different ways, or whether there was communality in how different peoples named colors. Berlin and Kay made two important discoveries. First, they found that all languages draw their basic color terms from a set of 11. In English, these are black, white, red, green, yellow, blue, brown, purple, pink, orange, and gray. Second, they found that regardless of how many or how few of these basic color terms a cultural group possessed, members of a cultural group showed remarkable agreement in picking the best example of the color from among an array of color chips. In fact, this agreement was as high across cultures as within a culture. So, for example, if a culture has a term for red, members of that culture agree with each other and the rest of the world about what a "good red" is. Berlin and Kay called these "best" colors the focal colors.

Another remarkable finding of Berlin and Kay was that the color terms always appeared in a language in the same sequence, as follows (the colors in brackets emerge together): [white, black]—[red]—[green, yellow]—[blue]—[brown]—[purple, pink, orange, gray]. Thus, a people that has only two terms will have terms for white and black (or light and dark), those that have three will have white, black, and red, those that have four will have those three plus green or yellow.

Rosch (publishing under the name of Heider, 1971, 1972) first determined which were the focal colors (i.e., the most favored and most readily named colors) in the spectrum. She found the selection consistent across a wide range of languages and cultures, as well as across all age levels (starting from age three). Then Rosch (1973) tested an Indonesian tribe of stone-age people, the Dani, who have only two color terms in their language (corresponding to light and dark), against a U.S. English-speaking group. The subjects briefly saw a single color chip, which they were asked to find later in a 160-chip array. The Dani did much more poorly than the U.S. subjects but much better on focal than on nonfocal colors. She then taught her Dani subjects to pair-associate the colors with certain clan names. The focal colors were learned with fewer errors than the nonfocals.

Rosch concluded that there are perceptually salient focal colors that serve as natural prototypes for learning color names and that these focal colors tend to be the ones whose names are learned first and best during language acquisition. The focal colors are those colors—white, black, red, green, blue, and yellow—that are thought to be the physiological primaries of the primate visual system. Thus, they presumably serve as built-in prototypes, determined by biology rather than by environment. They are also the very same color terms that Berlin and Kay had found emerged first as color terms in a language. Ratliff (1976) has analyzed in detail the physiological bases for these universal color terms.

Rosch found similar effects of natural, perceptually salient prototypes in geometric figures (e.g., circle, square). Again, the Dani learned the "good" forms faster than the distorted versions (with gaps and curving lines). She notes that this finding accords with the Gestalt principle of "good, ideal forms."

The next question was whether common objects without an obvious physiological basis for categorization fall into natural categories having focal and salient prototypes. That is, are there good examples of birds, fruits, and vehicles in the same way that there are good examples of reds, blues, and greens?

Several lines of evidence have supported the prototype view of natural categories. First, people find it natural to rate degree of typicality of objects within categories, and they agree with one another about what is typical and what is not. Second, the typicality of objects has an effect on objective performance measures—people can categorize an object into a category faster if that object is typical than if it is atypical.

Rosch (1973, 1977) asked subjects to rate the extent to which instances of common superordinate categories represented their "idea or image" of the category name. Not only did subjects show graded responses to the set of objects within categories, rating some of them as highly typical and others as atypical, but there was impressive agreement among subjects. When the mean ratings of a randomly chosen half of the subjects was correlated with the mean ratings of the other half, the split-group correlations were above .97. These impressive measures of agreement have been replicated by other investigators (e.g., Armstrong, Gleitman, & Gleitman, 1983; Mervis, Catlin, & Rosch, 1976; Rips, Shoben, & Smith, 1973).

In addition, typicality affects category verification times. When subjects are given sentences to verify like *a robin is a bird* or *an ostrich is a bird,* both of which are TRUE, they are faster to verify the sentence with *robin* than the one with *ostrich* because robin is rated as a more typical bird than ostrich. (In a sentence verification task of this sort, there must be some false statements. These are usually constructed by re-pairing the TRUE concept-category pairs to make false sentences of the form *a robin is a vehicle* or *a car is a bird.*) The robust effect of typicality in sentence verification tasks has been reported by several investigators (e.g., Rips, Shoben, & Smith, 1973; Rosch, 1973, 1975), and the effect has been shown to be independent of word frequency.

Another indication that prototypes of a category are processed more efficiently than atypical examples comes from the effects of priming on category verification times. Priming is the advance presentation of a stimulus that is related to a following stimulus and speeds its processing; thus, *A* as a primer facilitates *same* judgments of *AA* or *aa.* Rosch (1975) used objects of high, medium, and low prototypicality in nine common categories (furniture, fruit, vehicles, etc.). Then she had subjects perform a same-different matching task with pairs of category members representing these three prototypicality rating levels. The primer was the appropriate category name for the pair of exemplar names. An example of a primer for a good pair is *bird: robin-robin,* and for a poor pair is *bird: chicken-chicken.* The same pairs were presented without a prime to establish baseline levels of response time.

She found that category priming facilitated same-different judgments of good instances of the category compared to baseline conditions, but hindered responses to poor category representatives. These differential results suggest that superordinate semantic categories are represented in memory by something more than a list of critical attributes common to all members of the category, that is, by a set of defining attributes or features. If the primer generated an attribute list, *same* responses to both good and poor examples should be equally facilitated. The fact that priming helped only good-instance pairs suggests that the category name evokes the prototype representation—the best example of the category—rather than the category attributes.

Rosch (1975) noted one important difference between physiologically based categories, like colors, and semantic categories, like furniture. With practice in the primed matching task, the advantage of good over poor examples disappeared when the examples were from semantic categories, but not when they were from color categories. In an earlier test with additional practice on primed color matches, the focal (good example) colors retained their reaction time advantage over the nonfocal colors. The differential advantage, however, was lost in the case of the semantic categories. This apparently indicates that the internal structure of the latter is not immutably fixed, as is that of truly natural categories such as color, but can be altered by training.

The selective priming facilitation of category names was observed identically with both word and picture matches. This suggests that the category representation is neither entirely verbal nor pictorial, but some abstraction that provides necessary information for identification in both modes.

Family Resemblance and Typicality. The concept of family resemblance is a central one in understanding the concept of a prototype. The idea of family resemblance was first introduced by Wittgenstein (1953), the philosopher of language, as an alternative to the classical approach to defining certain concepts. Wittgenstein used as an example the concept of a game, and defied anyone to describe a set of features that would classify all activities we would describe as games into one class and exclude all those we would not describe as games. What attributes do chess, baseball, solitaire, and ring-a-round-the-rosy have in common, which permit us to classify them all as games?

Wittgenstein conjectured that categories such as game were cluster concepts, held together by a cluster of common features, only some of which are possessed by any particular game. For example, many games have the feature that more than one person plays it, yet solitaire is considered a game. Wittgenstein suggested that each type of game bears a family resemblance to all other games, even though none of them need share all the attributes.

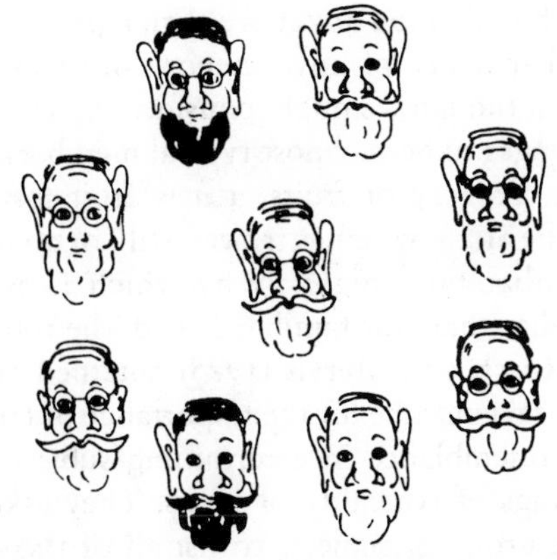

Fig. 9-3 Family resemblance in the Smith brothers. The center brother is the prototype because he exhibits all the model features of the family as a whole—white hair, glasses, mustache, beard, and large ears. (From "What Some Concepts Might Not Be," by S. L. Armstrong, L. R. Gleitman, and H. Gleitman. In *Cognition,* 1983, *13,* 263–308. Copyright 1983 by Elsevier Sequoia. Reprinted by permission.)

Family resemblance means that each member of a family shares some, but not all, of the features of other members of the family. Consider as an example the Smith brothers shown in Figure 9-3. We might consider the following facial features as characteristic of the Smith family: beards, eyeglasses, large ears, white hair, and mustaches. All of the brothers have beards, six of the nine wear eyeglasses, seven of the nine have large ears, five of the nine have mustaches, and seven of the nine have white hair. However, only the brother in the center possesses all of these characteristics, and thus he is the prototypical member of the family. The prototype, then, is the person in the family (corresponding to the exemplar in the category) having the largest number of features in common with all the other members of the category. The prototypical brother, however, need not exist in reality—a prototypical family member need not be instantiated in flesh and blood any more than a prototypical member of any category must exist. Even though we might consider apples and oranges to be the most typical members of the category of fruits, a new fruit might come along which is fruitier still, or an unfamiliar bird might fly by which is even birdier than our familiar friend, the robin.

Rosch and Mervis (1975) obtained empirical evidence for the importance of family resemblance in determining subjective ratings of typicality of items. They asked one group of subjects to list all of the attributes they could think of for each of 20 common objects in the six categories of fruits, vegetables, furniture, vehicles, weapons, and clothing. A separate group of subjects rated the typicality of each object within its category.

An analysis of the attribute listings revealed that few attributes were given to all 20 objects in each category. For example, only four items shared six or more category attributes. It is clear from these data that common defining features do not identify category members. Most important, when ratings of typicality were compared with the number of shared attributes an item possessed (the measure of family resemblance), the correlations within the various categories ranged from .84 to .94. Perception of an item as a good example of its category (its prototypicality) increases with the number of attributes it shares with other category members. This research thus demonstrates two things: first, that members of categories do not all share defining attributes or features, as the classical theory would have it, and second, that the number of attributes shared by an exemplar with other exemplars is an important determinant of its prototypicality.

Rosch and Mervis (1975) have proposed that a prototype provides maximum cue validity. This means that a prototype not only shares a maximum number of features with other members of its category, but also shares a minimum number of features with members of contrast categories. As an example, consider the contrast categories of fruits and vegetables. Is a *tomato* a fruit or a vegetable? People disagree about which category it belongs in, and thus *tomato* is not a prototype for either the fruit or the vegetable category. Fruits tend to be sweet, round, colored red or yellow, grown on trees, and found in fruit bowls. In contrast, vegetables tend to be nonsweet, longish, green, and found in salad bowls. Thus, a tomato fails as a prototypical fruit, first because it does not share many features with other fruits, and second, because it shares some features with exemplars in the contrast category of vegetables.

Criticisms of the Prototype Model of Categorization

As we have seen, supporting lines of evidence for the prototype model consist of graded responses in assigning exemplars to categories. These occur in ratings of typicality, in which subjects rate some exemplars as better examples than others, and in category verification tasks, in which better examples are verified as being members of their categories more quickly than poorer examples.

Recently, Armstrong, Gleitman, and Gleitman (1983) have challenged the view that graded responses support the prototype model. They present evidence that categories that satisfy the classical criteria of class inclusion—that is, categories that are well-defined—also show graded responses. Armstrong et al. compared the well-defined categories of *odd number, even number, female* and *plane geometry figure* with the prototype categories of *sport, vehicle, fruit,* and *vegetable* on the rating and category verification tasks. Well-defined categories are those whose boundaries are clear—there is no question of whether or not an exemplar belongs in the category—whereas prototype categories are those with fuzzy boundaries.

In the typicality rating task, subjects showed graded responses in evaluating the goodness-of-example of well-defined categories in the same way as they did in rating the prototype categories. For example, they rated 2 as a better example of an even number than 806, 7 as a better example of an odd number than 447, mother as a better example of a female than cowgirl, and square as a better example of geometric figure than ellipse. Of course, comparable differences in goodness-of-example ratings occurred for the prototype categories, although the range of the ratings was greater for the latter (specifically, more exemplars were given low ratings in the prototype than in the well-defined categories).

In the category verification task, subjects were given sentences of the form "An *orange* is a *fruit*" or "A 7 is an *odd number,*" and their response times to respond TRUE or FALSE were recorded. The well-defined categories showed the good example superiority in much the same way that the prototype categories did: that is, exemplars rated as more typical in the rating task were verified as being members of their category faster than the less typical ones for both well-defined and prototype categories. Furthermore, the magnitude of the good example advantage was the same for both types of categories—there was no interaction between goodness-of-example and type of category.

Finally, Armstrong et al. verified that their college student subjects did in fact view membership in well-defined categories as all-or-none. They gave a new group of subjects the categories and their exemplars and asked them: "Does it make sense to rate items in this category for *degree of membership* in the category?" For the four well-defined categories studied previously 96% of the responses were NOs (interestingly, the only category in doubt was *female,* and this was doubtful for only 3 of the 21 subjects in the experiment), while for the four prototype categories, only 43% of the responses were NOs. Thus, the well-defined categories studied had nonfuzzy borders, even though they showed the graded response effect.

Armstrong et al. suggest that graded responses to exemplars are not always valid indications of fuzziness of category boundaries and thus do not support a prototype theory of categories over a classical theory. Rather, they suggest that decisions about category membership, which for well-defined categories are all-or-none, concern the concept's core meaning, used in compositional meaning and informal reasoning, whereas goodness-of-example effects are attributable to a concept's identification function, which people may use as an efficient heuristic for picking out likely candidates for a category from obvious and easily processed attributes such as perceptual features.

Armstrong et al. point to the concept of *grandmother* as an example of a well-defined concept with a core meaning, which might be described as "mother of a parent." Yet the identification function for grandmother can function as a useful heuristic to help us pick out the referent of the statement "That's Joey's grandmother over there" from among a host of people over there. This function might include the perceptual features of gray hair, twinkling eyes, and, if over there were to include a stove, the action of stirring chicken soup. None of these perceptual characteristics is part of the core definition, but they provide a thumbnail sketch of a typical grandmother and are useful when more probing questions concerned with the core definition cannot easily be asked.

Basic Level Categories

Rosch and her colleagues have argued that there exists a unique level of abstraction, the *basic level,* which provides an optimum level of specificity so that human information-processing abilities are not overtaxed, yet sufficient specificity so that accurate communication can occur. This optimum level of abstraction is reflected in the names by which subjects choose to call objects. Speakers of a language use words that refer to basic level objects rather than to either superordinates or subordinates.

For example, the categories *furniture, chair,* and *office chair* represent a hierarchy of abstractness. According to Rosch and her colleagues, *chair* is at the basic level, and most conversation is carried on at the basic level. We invite a visiting colleague in our office to "Pull up a chair" rather than to "Pull up the red vinyl office chair" (subordinate to the basic level), or "Pull up a piece of furniture" (superordinate to the basic level).

To illustrate her point, Rosch (1978) quotes the following passage to show the bizarre and humorous effect of communicating in subordinate rather than basic level language: "And so, after putting away my 10-year-old Royal 470 manual and lining up my Mongol number 3 pencils on my Goldsmith Brothers Formica imitation-wood desk, I slide into my oversize squirrel-skin L. L. Bean slippers and shuffle off to the kitchen. There, holding *Decades* in my trembling right hand, I drop it, *plunk,* into my new Sears 20-gallon celadon-green Permanex trash can" (Rosch, 1978, pp. 45–46).

Rosch, Mervis, Gray, Johnson, and Boyes-Braem (1976) used a variety of methods to show that the basic level of categorization is the most useful level. These included determining which features subjects listed for objects at the three levels of abstraction, determining which level produced the most communality of motor movements, and finally, determining the degree to which the visual shape of an object was constant across exemplars at each of the three levels of categorization.

In the attribute listing task, subjects listed attributes for objects in nine categories at the three levels of abstraction—superordinate, basic, and subordinate. For example, subjects would be asked to list all the features they could think of for *furniture* (superordinate category), *chair* (basic level category), and *kitchen chair* (subordinate category). Subjects could think of very few attributes that were true of all furniture (for example, what do things like rug, chair, and desk have in common?), yet they were able to list many more attributes for basic level objects. And although the number of attributes listed for subordinate level objects was somewhat higher than for the basic level objects, the increase was not significant. These results supported their claim that the basic level is the most inclusive level at which useful distinctions can be made.

The same list of objects was presented to another group of subjects who were asked to describe the sequences of muscle movements used when interacting with objects at various levels of abstractness. Movements were broken down into specific body-part movements at each phase of the sequence. There were few common movements involving superordinates. How many common motor programs do we employ with furniture items in general (tables, chairs, lamps)? Very few. However, there were many common movement sequences involved in sitting down on various chairs, whether they be the kitchen or living room variety. Again, commonality of motor movement attributes was found to be concentrated at the basic level with few additional motor movements added by moving down to the subordinate level.

Two further tests were made by Rosch and her associates to provide convergent evidence of the perceptual salience of basic level objects. In one, pictures of objects within selected categories were superimposed on each other. Two objects from the same basic level category (two cars) showed more overlap than two objects from the same superordinate category (a car and a motorcycle). Although there was more overlap for subordinate objects (two sports cars) than for basic level objects (two cars), the differences were small compared to the differences between basic level and superordinate objects.

Figure 9-4 shows some examples. Each of the composite outlines incorporates a pair of tracings of two objects in the same basic level category. Thus, the first outline in the third row is a composite of two automobile tracings. Note that the outline is readily recognizable as a car because of the similarity of shapes of all cars (high over-

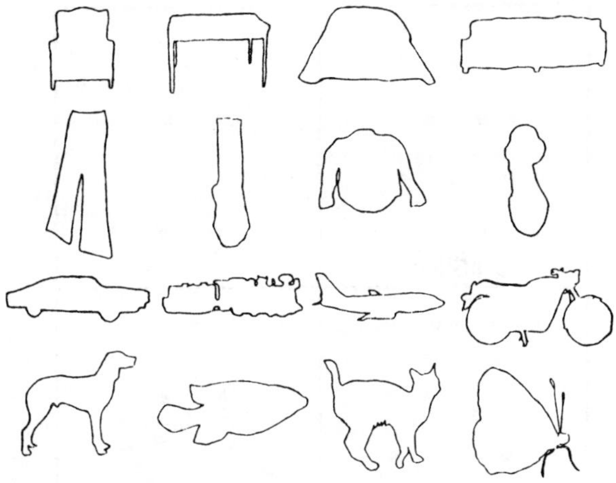

Fig. 9-4 Examples of traced figures from subsets of basic level objects, showing overlap of perceptual characteristics at the basic level. (From "Basic Objects in Natural Categories," by E. H. Rosch, C. B. Mervis, W. D. Gray, D. M. Johnson, and P. Boyes-Braem. In *Cognitive Psychology,* 1976, *8,* 382–439. Copyright 1976 by Academic Press. Reprinted by permission.)

lap). A composite outline of a locomotive and an airplane would not be recognizable as a representative of either basic level category or of their common superordinate, vehicle.

The final test measured the accuracy of identification of outline drawings made from the overlapped shapes at each of the three levels of abstractness. Basic level drawings were most easily identified, superordinate average shapes were more difficult, and subordinate drawings were identified no better than the basic level drawings. This suggests that the basic level provides the mental image that is most useful for distinguishing one object from another, yet is simple enough to be useful.

Experimentation with Artificial Categories

Although natural categories provide a more ecologically valid set of stimuli on which to test various theories about categorization, they suffer from the shortcoming common to any "natural" experiment. Namely, the investigator cannot separately manipulate or control variables that might confound the effects of typicality in natural stimuli. Such variables include familiarity or degree of exposure to both typical and atypical instances. The usual remedy for such lack of control is to use artificial categories whose characteristics may be manipulated directly by the experimenter. Here, we review some of the research on the role of prototypicality in artifical categories. It should be noted that much of this research predates Rosch's important use of natural categories. But as we shall see, many hypotheses about the exact nature of prototypes can be tested directly when artificial categories are used.

Attneave (1957) was one of the first to study the role of the prototype in categorization. He demonstrated that when subjects were pretrained on prototype matrix patterns of letters and polygon shapes, they were more successful in learning to pair associates to a set of variations of the prototypes than were control subjects who had no prototype training. Clearly, the prototype-trained subjects had gained an advantage in recognizing the pattern variations. Some characteristic aspect of the prototype must, therefore, have been evident in the variants. Although Attneave trained his subjects on the exact prototypes, the latter are generally not available in nature, so conventional learning must succeed without them. How do we learn about a category and its boundaries without actual prototypes?

Edmonds, Evans, and Mueller (1966) and Evans (1967) showed that subjects could benefit from training with distortions from the prototype (using as stimuli bar graphs consisting of 12 columns of varying heights). They also found that training with distortions close to the pro-

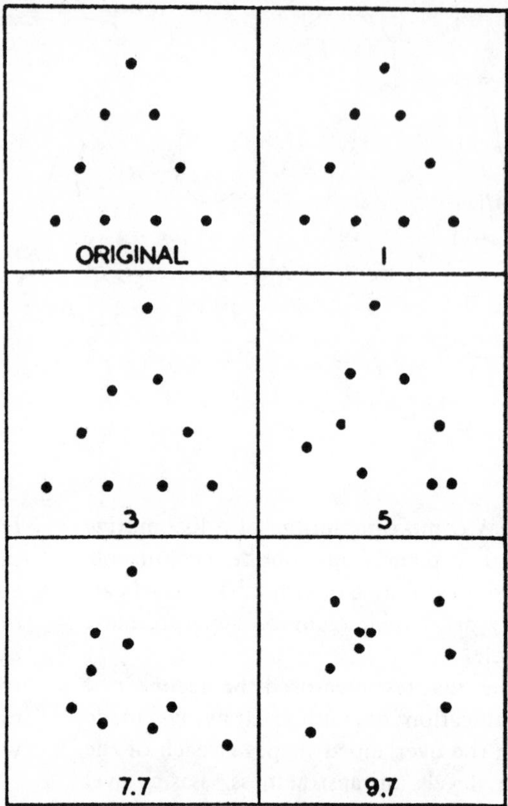

Fig. 9-5 The original and five levels of distortion for the triangle prototype. (From "Perceived Distance and the Classification of Distorted Patterns," by M. I. Posner, R. Goldsmith, and K. E. Welton, Jr. In *Journal of Experimental Psychology,* 1967, *73,* 28–38. Copyright 1967 by the American Psychological Association. Reprinted by permission.)

totype was more beneficial than training with those very different from the prototype.

To investigate the role of distortions from the prototype with more precision, Posner, Goldsmith, and Welton (1967) attempted to establish a psychophysical basis for judging distortions according to degree of deviations from the prototype. Posner et al. used several dot pattern prototypes and generated five degrees of distortions for each by shifting some or all of the dots according to a set of statistical rules, thereby producing patterns that deviated in increasing measure from the prototypes. Figure 9-5 presents the triangular dot pattern prototype along with its five levels of distortion, to illustrate their manipulation.

Subjects were asked to rate each distortion with a number that would indicate its distance from the original in similarity of shape or form. Posner et al. were looking for a scale relating the perceived difference between the prototype and its distortion to the objective difference as determined by the statistical formula for shifting the dots. They found it to be a suitably linear function—that is, the perceived distance between pattern distortions at different levels was a linear function of the objective average distance between corresponding dots at the different levels.

With Posner's psychophysical scale, we can vary the distortion distances and draw conclusions about prototype learning difficulty. Now we want to know how the subject uses the distortions to discover the prototype, that is, what the subject abstracts and stores during the learning phase. To study this, Posner and Keele (1968) presented subjects with three levels of distortions (indexed 1, 5, and 7.7, as shown in Figure 9-5), which were selected to provide stimuli of slight (1), moderate (5), and high (7.7) deviation.

Distortions, *but not prototypes,* were

presented singly to the subjects during learning trials. The subjects practiced classifying the distortions into the four categories and were given feedback. One group of subjects was trained on level 1 distortions and a second group was trained on level 5 distortions. Each group was subsequently tested on levels 5 and 7.7 distortions along with the original prototypes (which had never been seen), and the original training stimuli. Not only were the originally learned distortions more easily and correctly classified than the new ones, but the previously unseen prototypes were classified just as easily as the old, learned patterns. Furthermore, although learning to classify level 5 distortions took longer than level 1 distortions, subjects trained at level 5 showed better class discrimination on the test than those trained at level 1. It would seem that subjects trained on level 5 learned about variability, which was helpful when they attempted to classify level 7.7 distortions.

The research using artificial patterns has thus demonstrated that prototype learning can occur without prototype exposure. However, the research does not permit us to decide how the subject is using the properties of the distortions from the prototype of a category to abstract the prototype. Furthermore, in these experiments, prototypes have been defined as the average, or arithmetic mean, of the distortions. Because the distortion patterns are geometrical, the arithmetic mean is well-defined. However, prototypes in natural categories cannot be defined so easily by the category average—what, for example, is the arithmetic mean of an apple, orange, pomegranate, and grape? As we have seen, models of prototypicality developed from research on natural categories have relied on features, which are qualitative in nature, rather than on quantitative dimensions such as those introduced into these artificial stimuli.

Reed (1972) studied prototype learning with artificial stimuli that were more similar to those in natural categories. Reed used as his stimuli schematic faces, of the sort shown in Figure 9-6, which can be de-

Fig. 9-6 Examples of two categories of faces. The arrows show the prototypes for each category. (From "Pattern Recognition and Categorization," by S. K. Reed. In *Cognitive Psychology*, 1972, *3*, 382–407. Copyright 1972 by Academic Press, Inc. Adapted by permission).

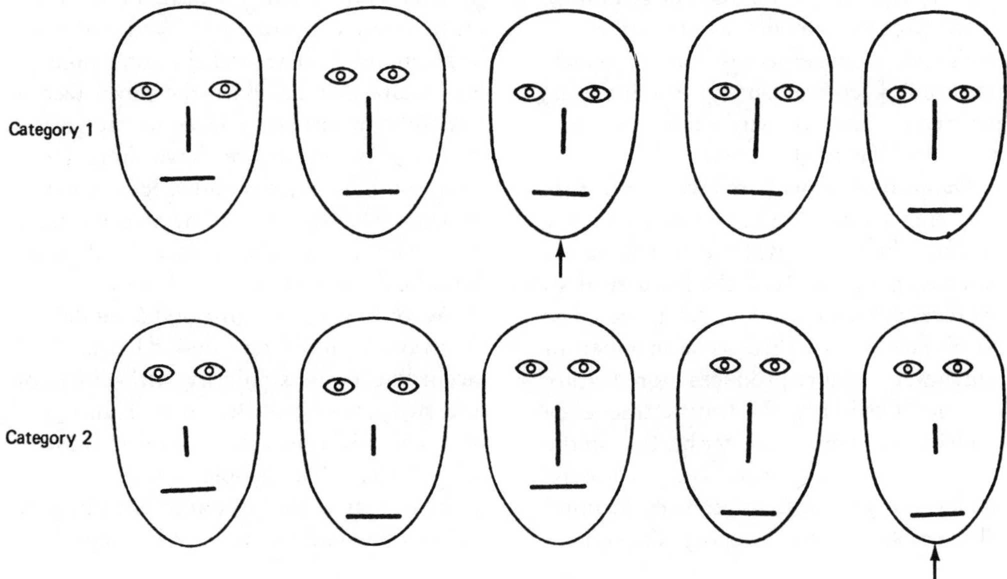

scribed naturally in terms of features. The faces he used vary in four features: forehead, eyes, nose, and mouth. Each feature has three values or variations. So, for example, the face at the top left in Figure 9-6 has a large forehead, wide eyes, medium nose, and high mouth.

Subjects were trained to categorize the top five faces in Figure 9-6 into one category, and the bottom five faces into a second category. The training was accomplished by presenting feedback after every response and having the subjects classify all 10 faces a total of 12 times. The test phase consisted of 24 new faces, which the subjects were to classify into either category 1 or category 2. Performance on the set of new faces was used to determine which of two models of categorization was correct.

The first model, the prototype model, assumes that subjects find the prototype of each category and classify new patterns according to how similar they are to the prototype. The prototype has the average values of the features of the other patterns in the category. In Figure 9-6, the prototype for category 1, shown by the arrow, has large forehead height, average eye separation, average nose length, and average mouth height. The prototype for category 2 has a low forehead, small eye separation, small nose, and low mouth. The advantage of the prototype model, as far as the subject's task is concerned, is that the subject need only keep one pattern in mind—the prototype—and compare each novel pattern with that single pattern.

The second model tested was the feature frequency model. In the feature frequency model, subjects are assumed to compare a new incoming face with the features of all the faces in each of the two categories. The novel face is classified as a member of whichever category produces more feature matches. Obviously, the feature frequency model places a much greater burden on the subject's memory than the prototype model, for the subject must keep in mind all exemplars of the category (or, equivalently, lists of features for all exemplars of the category).

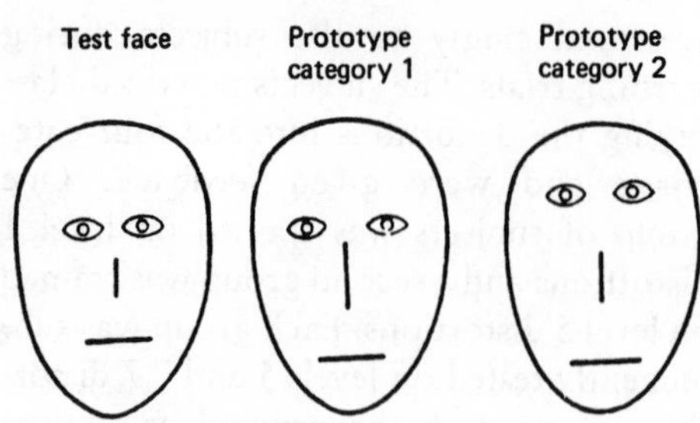

Fig. 9-7 Examples of novel test faces for the two categories shown in Figure 9.6. The face on the left is the novel face used to test various models of categorization. The prototypes of the two categories are shown on the right. (From "Pattern Recognition and Categorization," by S. K. Reed. In *Cognitive Psychology*, 1972, *3*, 382–407. Copyright 1972 by Academic Press, Inc. Adapted by permission).

Reed's test stimuli were designed to distinguish between the prototype model and the feature frequency model. As an example of how he did this, consider the test face, shown with the two prototypes of the two categories, in Figure 9-7. The test face has a large forehead, narrow eyes, a short nose, and a high mouth. An inspection of the two categories in Figure 9-6 show that four faces in category 1 have a large forehead, one has narrow eyes, and one has a high mouth. Therefore, the total number of feature matches with the novel face is six. By contrast, four faces in category 2 have narrow eyes, three have short noses, and two have high mouths, for a total of nine matches. So, according to the feature frequency model, the subject should classify the novel face into category 2.

According to the prototype model, in contrast, the novel face should be classified according to its similarity with either of the two prototypes shown in Figure 9-7. But which is it most similar to? How shall we decide? Most people agree that it is most similar to the prototype for category 1, but we would like to be able to compute similarity directly from the features of the two prototypes.

Reed investigated a number of different similarity measures for the prototype model and found that the best one differentially weighted the different features. For example, forehead (or eye height) was given much greater weighting than the other three dimensions. Thus, according to the weighted features prototype model, the novel pattern would be classified as category 1. The way in which Reed's subjects classified novel patterns supported the weighted features prototype model over the feature frequency model. In addition, subjects' descriptions of their strategies also favor prototype models over feature models.

Subsequent research, however, has produced competing proposals for how subjects learn new categories (see Franks & Bransford, 1971; Neumann, 1974; Hayes-Roth & Hayes-Roth, 1977; Medin & Schaffer, 1978). As Smith and Medin (1981) point out in their excellent review of the categorization literature, despite the volume of research on category learning, there are still many unresolved issues. Nonetheless, it is clear that the use of artificially manipulated stimuli permits the researcher to make more detailed predictions and explore more intricate and complex variations on prototypicality models than use of naturally occurring categories.

Organization of Categories in Semantic Memory

As we have seen, Rosch has proposed a useful way of conceptualizing category structure in terms of both its horizontal and vertical dimensions. The horizontal dimension is affected by the location of the prototype of the category. The vertical dimension is defined by the relation of class inclusion, with the most useful level of abstraction occurring at the basic level.

Figure 9-8 presents such a structure

Fig. 9-8 A proposed category structure based on the work of Rosch. The vertical dimension shows the location of the basic level of categorization, and the horizontal dimension shows the location of the prototype.

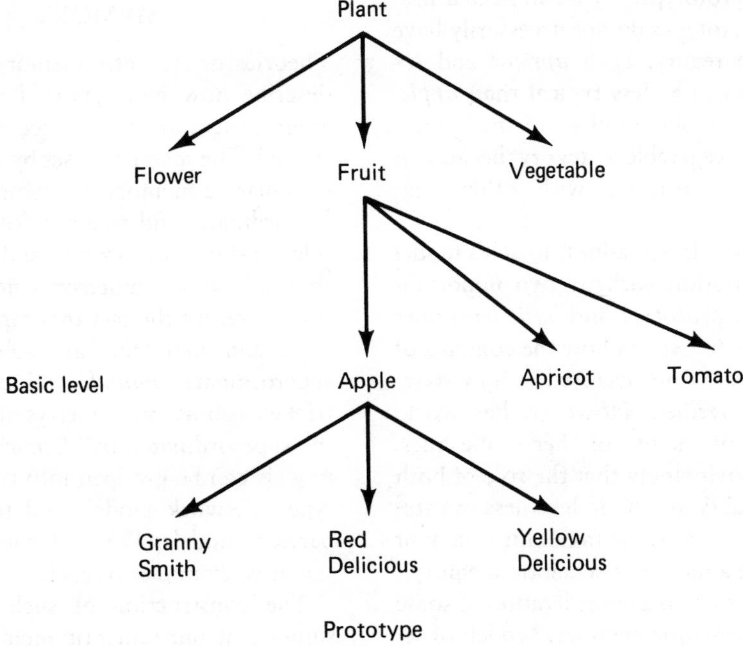

for the super-superordinate category of plant. As we move down in the vertical structure, we come to subordinate levels of plant such as flower, fruit, and vegetable, and as we move down to the subordinates of fruit, we come to the basic level categories such as apple, apricot, and tomato. Finally, the subordinate levels of apple might include Granny Smith, Red Delicious, Yellow Delicious, and so on.

The vertical dimension has as its important focus the basic level of categorization, which provides maximum cue validity because basic level categories have more common attributes shared by the other members of the category than do superordinate categories. That is, apples share more features than do fruits. These common features include perceptual ones such as shape and functional ones such as the motor movements needed to deal with instances within the category.

The horizontal dimension represents the typicality dimension, with the prototype representing the center of the category in that it shares more features with other members of the category (it exhibits maximum family resemblance). A prototype for fruit is *apple,* although it is not necessarily *the* prototype. As we indicated previously, prototypes do not necessarily have to exist in reality. Both *apricot* and *tomato* are rated as less typical than *apple,* and *tomato* is shown close to the boundary of the vegetable category because it shares many features with other vegetables.

As she herself will admit, Rosch's model of categorization with its two important concepts of *prototype* and *basic level* does not attempt to explain how the contents of these categories are accessed or how statements are verified. However, her work, and that of many of her colleagues, showed convincingly that the role of both prototypicality and basic levelness in category structure must be taken into account in building a model of semantic memory.

We next turn to a consideration of some models of semantic memory. Models of semantic memory make two assumptions: the first concerns the way semantic information is represented or structured in memory, and the second concerns the process by which such information is used in order to answer questions and solve problems. In this section, we have considered evidence on how concepts are categorized and some possible organizations of such information. In the next section we consider what semantic memory models assume about the structure of information in long-term memory. We consider three semantic memory models. The first is an early model of Quillian (1968) and Collins and Quillian (1969), which has no provision for the strong effects of prototypicality in semantic memory tasks. The next is a model based on feature comparisons, by Smith and his colleagues, which is designed to reflect the effect of prototypicality (Smith, Shoben, & Rips, 1974). Finally, we discuss a revision of the Quillian model by Collins and Loftus (1975), which is modified to provide both mechanisms for prototypicality and an account of how false sentences are negated in sentence verification tasks.

THEORIES OF SEMANTIC MEMORY

Theories of semantic memory attempt to describe how concepts and relationships among them are stored, accessed, and retrieved. The major task set by most models of semantic memory concerns how subset (subordinate) and superset (superordinate) relationships are stored and accessed—that is, how does a person's memory structure represent the fact that birds, fish, reptiles, and mammals are subsets of the superordinate *animal,* and canaries, ostriches, robins, and bluejays are subsets of the superordinate *bird?* Semantic memory models can be grouped into two principal types: network models and feature comparison models. We will consider representative examples of each.

The construction of such models assumes that our semantic memory is organized according to some sensible, worka-

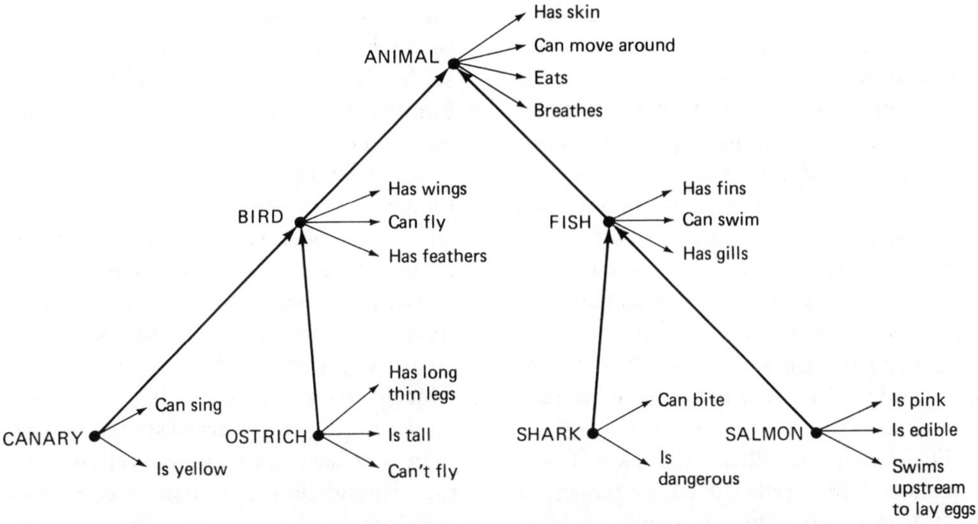

Fig. 9-9. The hierarchical organization of semantic memory proposed by Collins and Quillian (1969) illustrating the principles of cognitive economy—that a property is stored at the highest possible level in the hierarchy. (From "Retrieval Time from Semantic Memory," by A. M. Collins and M. R. Quillian. In *Journal of Verbal Learning and Verbal Behavior,* 1969, *8,* 240–247. Copyright 1969 by Academic Press, Inc. Reprinted by permission.)

ble system. We will see evidence for this reasonable assumption. For example, it has been repeatedly shown that organization of lists into categories facilitates free recall and, under certain conditions, improves recognition memory (Bousfield & Bousfield, 1966; Bower, 1972; Mandler, 1967; Pollio, Kasschau, & DeNise, 1968; Tulving, 1962). The question then becomes how the system is organized so as to provide efficient access to, and retrieval of, stored semantic concepts.

Network Models: The Collins and Quillian Model

Network models have a characteristic structure that resembles an intricate and extensive network consisting of nodes (at which the concepts are stored) joined to each other by links according to some relational scheme.

One of the earliest and best-known of the network structures was proposed by Ross Quillian in his doctoral dissertation (Quillian, 1968), and later tested with human subjects by Collins and Quillian (1969). The original model was implemented as a computer program, called the Teachable Language Comprehender, which was designed to answer real-world questions in as efficient and economical way as possible. A representative part of the model is shown in Figure 9-9. As this figure shows, the principle underlying the organization is logical nesting. The memory structure is a hierarchical network of superordinate-subordinate relations, called superset or S relations, as indicated by pointers between adjacent node levels, and property or P relations, listed by each category or class of objects. The properties belonging to each class of objects are stored with the highest class for which they are appropriate, for purposes of *cognitive economy.* Thus, the properties *has wings, can fly,* and *has feathers* belong to all (or almost all) birds and so are shown as stored at the *bird* node rather than each being stored with its appropriate concept at lower levels. When a subordinate does not possess a feature of the superordinate, that exception is listed explicitly, as in the property *can't fly* stored at the *ostrich* node. In contrast, the properties *can sing* and *is yellow* are specific to canaries but not to all birds, and hence are stored at the *canary* node. Subjects understand and verify sentences by finding a path that connects two concepts. To understand the sentence "A canary is a bird," a path must be found leading from canary to bird, connected by a superset pointer, as shown in Figure 9-9. The sentence, "A canary has skin" requires three steps: tracing the path sequence from *canary* to *bird, bird* to *animal,* and finally to the property of animals *has skin.*

These examples illustrate how subjects understand and verify TRUE sentences, as would be required in a sentence verification experiment. However, sentence verification tasks must include some FALSE sentences, and so the model must describe how subjects can reject as false a sentence like *A canary is a fish.* Finding paths between such remote concepts requires an intersection technique. The subject is assumed to start at both nodes (*canary* and *fish*) and trace pointers to other nodes, leaving tags at each node indicating the starting node, until a common node is found. The path between the two starting nodes is checked for syntactic legality and permissible relationships. "A canary is a fish" could be rejected because of the incompatible properties *has feathers* versus *has fins.*

Collins and Quillian (1969) tested the adequacy of this model as a simulation of human semantic memory by measuring reaction times of subjects in a sentence verification task. Because the model provides predictions for how many levels up or down subjects must move in order to verify true sentences, the model is tested by varying the number of levels across supersets or property lists subjects must move in order to verify the sentence as true. Retrieval time, as measured by reaction time to respond TRUE, should depend on the distance between the reference nodes. In addition, it is assumed that the time to travel successive levels is additive. These two assumptions predict that it should take longer to verify *A canary is an animal,* which requires moving up two superset levels, than to verify *A canary is a bird* (one superset level) or *A canary is a canary* (zero superset levels).

Statements about properties should take longer to verify than statements about relationships because the property list must be searched. Nonetheless, as for superset levels, the number of levels that must be traversed to verify properties should increase with number of levels separating the concept from its property list: Thus, *A canary can sing* (zero levels) should be faster than *A canary can fly* (one level), which in turn should be faster than *A canary has skin* (two levels).

The results from the Collins and Quillian experiment are shown in Figure 9-10. As indicated there, two classes of true sentences were tested—those for supersets and those for properties. As predicted, property sentences take longer than superset sentences. Furthermore, as the number of levels that must be traversed increases, reaction times increase roughly linearly (the exceptions are the S_0 sentences, in which subjects may have used physical matches to verify a sentence like *A canary is a canary.*) The data indicate that the time to travel one level to a superset is 75 ms and recovery of properties at a node take 225 ms.

Criticisms of the Collins and Quillian Model. The hierarchical network model of Collins and Quillian has encountered trouble when others have tried to replicate and confirm their RT results. For example, Conrad (1972) found that, contrary to the hypothesis of *cognitive economy,* which proposes that properties are stored only at the highest superset to which they are appropriate, the same properties were to be found at several node levels and seemed to be available most readily for strong associates. She did not find the expected difference in reaction times to the sentences, *An animal can move, A fish can move, A shark can move,* which should take increasing time to search as we move down

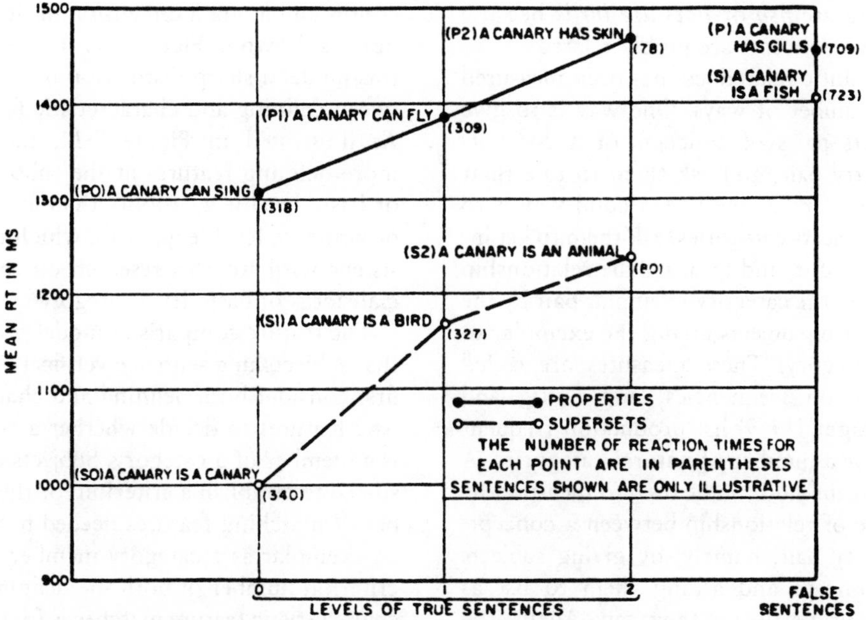

Fig. 9-10 Mean verification times *(RT)* as a function of levels for superset *(S)* sentences compared to property *(P)* sentences. (From "Retrieval Time from Semantic Memory," by A. M. Collins and M. R. Quillian. In *Journal of Verbal Learning and Verbal Behavior,* 1969, *8,* 240–247. Copyright 1969 by Academic Press. Reprinted by permission.)

in the hierarchy from animal to shark if the property *can move* were stored only with the node *animal.* The assumption that *can move* is stored only with animal would require moving up two levels from *shark* to *animal* and one level from *fish* to *animal.* The lack of RT differences among the three sentences indicates that direct access to the property *can move* was available at each of the nodes on all three levels.

Perhaps the most devastating indictment of network models was presented by Smith and his colleagues (Rips, Shoben, & Smith, 1973; Smith, Shoben, & Rips, 1974), who first demonstrated the strong effect of the typicality of an exemplar on verification times for category membership. The Collins and Quillian model predicts that only the internodal distance should affect reaction time. Therefore, it should take no longer to determine that a *chicken* (an atypical bird) is a *bird* than a *robin* (a typical bird) is a *bird* because the subset levels are the same. However, Rips et al (1973) found that typical instances were verified about 50 ms faster than atypical ones. Similarly, Conrad (1972) found a 200-ms RT advantage in verification speed for frequent over infrequent instances of a category.

Semantic Relatedness. The effects of typicality and frequency on categorization latencies are specific examples of the general effect of semantic relatedness on verification times. Many of the failures of the hierarchical network model stem from the fact that there is no explicit provision for the introduction of semantic relatedness among the concepts at the nodes or between the features listed at each node and the concept itself. In verification experiments, subjects are faster in responding TRUE to true statements about supersets and properties when semantic relatedness is high than when it is low. Conversely, subjects take longer to respond FALSE to false statements about supersets and properties when semantic relatedness is high. So it is harder to reject the statement

Whales are fish or *Bats are birds* because the two concepts are highly related.

Semantic relatedness has been measured in a number of ways. One way is to give subjects pairs of concepts or a concept-property pair, and ask them to rate their degree of relatedness. A second way is to give subjects categories, ask them to list instances of it, and measure the relationship between the category-exemplar pair by the number of subjects giving the exemplar to the category. These measures are called production frequencies, and Battig and Montague (1969) list production frequencies for a number of natural categories. A similar method can be used to measure the degree of relationship between a concept-property pair, namely, by giving subjects the concept and asking them to list as many properties as they can. Again, the measure of relatedness is the number of subjects giving that property. It is consistently found that the higher the frequency of production of either exemplars or properties, the faster the verification times for true statements.

Feature Comparison Models

As an alternative to the network models, Smith and his colleagues proposed a model that represents the meaning of a concept in terms of its semantic features (Smith, Shoben, & Rips, 1974). Instead of treating all features as equal in function and importance, as the network models do, they distinguish between two distinct kinds of features: *defining features,* which are essential to the superordinate concept, and *characteristic features,* which often occur in exemplars of the superordinate but are not essential to its meaning. For example, defining features of the concept *bird* include wings and feathers, because all birds possess wings and feathers. In contrast, characteristic features include the ability to fly and the ability to sing, because not all birds can fly or sing but typical birds often do. In line with the consensus that natural categories are not well-defined, the defining and characteristic features form a continuum along a dimension of definingness, as shown in Figure 9-11. However, in this model a sharp distinction is made between defining and characteristic features. As illustrated in Figure 9-11, there are more defining features at the subordinate or basic level (e.g., robin), than at the superordinate level (e.g., bird), which is consistent with Rosch's research on the special status of basic level categories.

The feature comparison model proposes that subjects in a sentence verification task first consider both defining and characteristic features to decide whether a concept is a member of a category. Subjects are assumed to establish a criterion for the number of matching features needed to accept an exemplar as a category member. If the criterion number of both the defining and characteristic feature matches is found, the subject makes an affirmative response. If the criterion number fails to match, the subject proceeds to the more time-consuming step of considering whether the concept matches the category on all the category's defining features. The model correctly predicts that it should take longer to verify the statement *A chicken is a bird* than *A robin is a bird* because robins possess a larger number of characteristic bird features than chickens do.

Smith et al. cite linguistic evidence in support of the distinction between defining and characteristic features. Lakoff (1975) analyzed a class of modifiers he called hedges. They include "a true," "technically speaking," and "loosely speaking." The acceptable use of such hedges depends on the degree to which the subject and predicate nouns in the statement share defining and characteristic features. Thus, *A robin is a true bird* is acceptable to listeners because *robin* shares both defining and characteristic features with *bird. Technically speaking, a chicken is a bird* is acceptable because *chicken* shares only defining features with *bird. Loosely speaking, a bat is a bird* is acceptable because *bat* shares only characteristic features with *bird,* but not its defining features. It is not acceptable to say *Techni-*

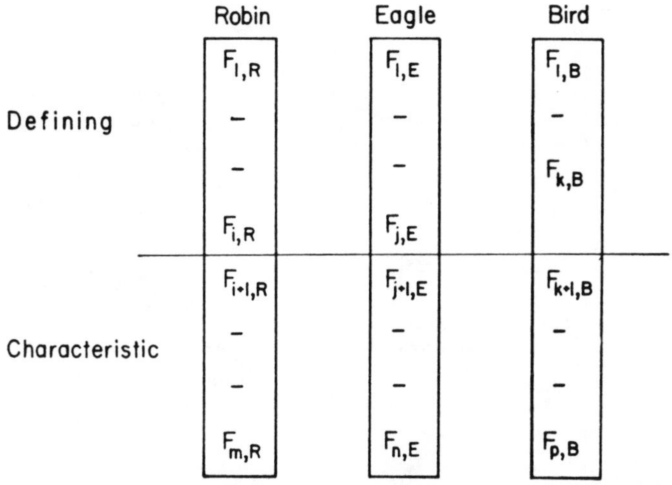

	Robin	Eagle	Bird
Defining	$F_{1,R}$	$F_{1,E}$	$F_{1,B}$
	–	–	–
	–	–	$F_{k,B}$
	$F_{i,R}$	$F_{j,E}$	
Characteristic	$F_{i+1,R}$	$F_{j+1,E}$	$F_{k+1,B}$
	–	–	–
	–	–	–
	$F_{m,R}$	$F_{n,E}$	$F_{p,B}$

Fig. 9-11 The distinction between defining and characteristic features. In general, superordinates like *bird* will have fewer defining features than subordinates like *robin* and *eagle.* (From "Structure and Process in Semantic Memory: A Featural Model for Semantic Decisions," by E. E. Smith, E. J. Shoben, and L. J. Rips. In *Psychological Review,* 1974, *81,* 214–241. Copyright 1974 by the American Psychological Association. Reprinted by permission.)

cally speaking, a robin is a bird because both kinds of features (defining and characteristic) are shared.

Smith and his colleagues used similarity ratings to generate a representation of various categories and their members in a multidimensional space. (For a brief description of multidimensional scaling, see Chapter 4.) Figure 9-12 is a two-dimensional plot of bird and mammal categories based on subjects' ratings of semantic relatedness (or distance) which are presumably based on the degree to which relevant semantic features are the same. In plots such as these, the closer two concepts are to one another, the more similar they are seen to be. There are two interesting characteristics of the plotted data. First, typical birds such as bluejays, cardinals, sparrows, and robins lie closer to the superordinate category *bird* than atypical exemplars such as goose, duck, chicken, hawk, and eagle. (Although a similar pattern can be observed for animals, there are fewer clear-cut differences among the animals with respect to their typicality.) Second, the vertical axis of both graphs appears to measure a dimension such as wildness or predacity, whereas the horizontal dimension appears to measure a dimension such as size.

The feature comparison model of Smith and his colleagues is not without its critics. One criticism is that the model relies on ratings to make predictions about verification times. Although both undoubtedly reflect the degree of semantic similarity between a category and its exemplar, there is no direct test that this similarity is based on the number of defining and characteristic features they share. Indeed, as we have seen, the work of Rosch and others has suggested that many natural categories have *no defining features at all.* Furthermore, the feature comparison model predicts that each category verification decision is made by computing the number of overlapping features. Yet, once a subject has learned that a robin is a bird or a bat is not a bird, why can't subjects simply use those direct relationships in verifying category memberships? These and other criticisms led Collins and Loftus (1975) to propose a revision of the original Quillian model, which they call spreading activation theory.

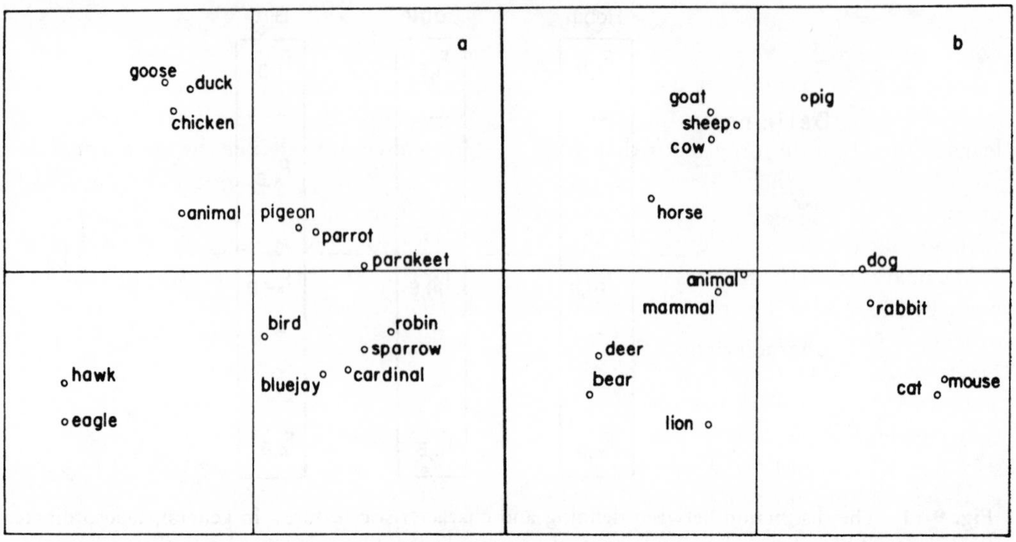

Fig. 9-12 The multidimensional scaling solution for (a) birds and (b) mammals based on subjects' similarity ratings. Distance between points is proportionate to the judged similarity of items. The typicality of an item can be judged by its closeness to the superordinate. (From "Semantic Distance and the Verification of Semantic Relations," by L. J. Rips, E. J. Shoben, and E. E. Smith. In *Journal of Verbal Learning and Verbal Behavior,* 1973, *12,* 1–20. Copyright 1973 by Academic Press, Inc. Reprinted by permission.)

Collins and Quillian Revised—The Spreading Activation Model

Collins and Loftus (1975) proposed a revision of the Collins and Quillian model that maintains a network structure but abandons the notion of hierarchical structure. They assume that concepts are linked to one another with various relational markers. The degree of semantic relatedness—an important variable in accounting for the sentence verification times and rating and production data—is given by the length of the segments joining concept nodes together. Figure 9-13 shows a section of the structure of the model. The important characteristics to note in Figure 9-13 are the nature of the links between concept nodes, and the degree of relatedness of the concept nodes, represented by the length of the links.

Collins and Loftus introduced several unique features to the model in order to account for the large body of findings from semantic memory experiments. To account for the fact that prototypical instances are categorized more easily than nonprototypical instances, the prototypes are located closer to the superordinate than nonprototypes. Thus, in Figure 9-13 *canary* is located closer to the *bird* node than is *ostrich.* Second, some of the relationships between concept nodes and property nodes are specifically labeled with the negative statement ISNOTA; thus, although the node for *bird* and that for *bat* are close together in the network, the fact that the relational marker between them is labeled ISNOTA is a convenient way of permitting the subject to reject as FALSE the statement "A bat is a bird." The ISNOTA link is considered useful for denying particular relationships between two concepts that are highly related. Third, while superset relationships can produce inferred properties and other superset relations, as in the hierarchical model of Collins and Quillian, there can exist redundant links which reflect how closely two concepts are related. Thus, *dog* is linked to both *mammal* and *animal,* even though the fact that a dog is an animal could be inferred from the fact that a dog is a mammal. The organization of semantic memory in such a model can reflect both the order in which information is learned (i.e., that children learn that dogs are animals before they learn that dogs are mammals) as well as the frequency with which that information is encountered.

We next turn to the process assumptions made by the model. The model works by a process called "spreading activation"—hence the name of the model. The model assumes that activation occurs whenever two concepts (e.g., *canary* and *bird*) are stimulated, as would occur when a subject is asked whether a canary is a bird. This activation spreads out across the relational links. If the level of activation linking two concepts rises above some threshold, subjects can verify sentences easily. Because this activation takes some time to reach its maximum, and in the process spreads across the relational links, it will take longer to activate two nodes that are further apart than two nodes that are closer together. Furthermore, the activation decreases in strength as it travels outward from a stimulated node the same way it decreases with time from activation and with intervening activity.

The model is particularly effective in accounting for priming effects in semantic decision. Priming effects occur when presentation of a previous stimulus facilitates a decision on a following stimulus. Priming effects have been studied most extensively in the lexical decision task. In this task, subjects must decide whether or not a string of letters forms a word. Meyer and Schvaneveldt (1971) compared lexical decision latencies for words when preceded by related words (e.g., *butter* preceded by *bread*) with baseline latencies for the same word when preceded by an unrelated word (e.g., *butter* preceded by *doctor*). If the two words are semantically related, sub-

Fig. 9-13 A portion of semantic memory as it might be represented by the theory of spreading activation. Compare this network organization to the hierarchical organization shown in Figure 9-9.

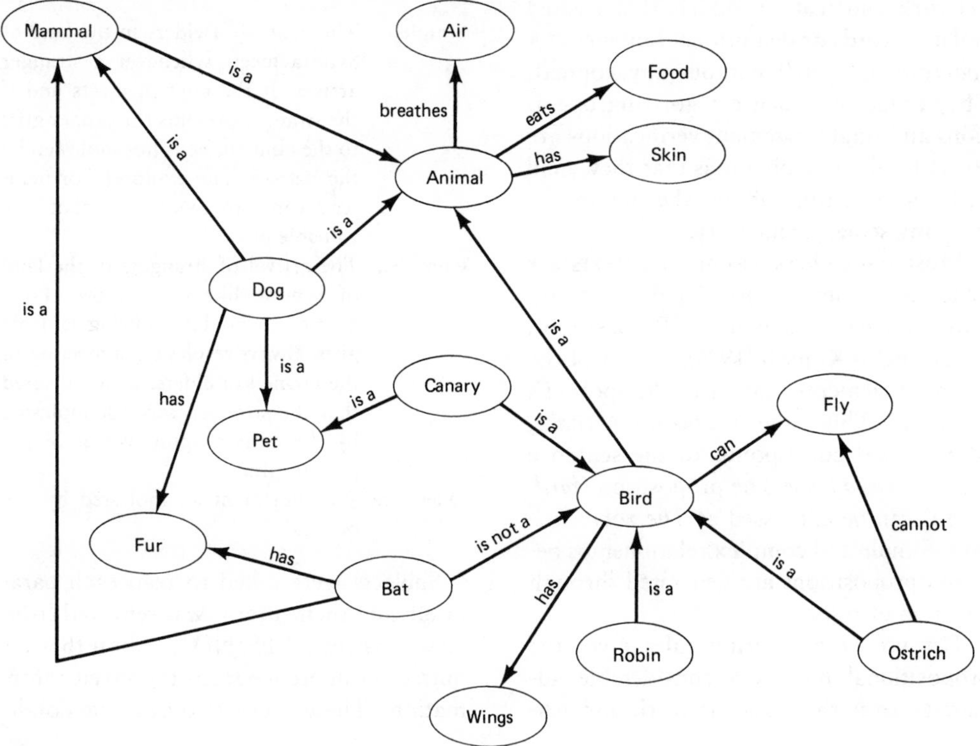

jects are faster in verifying that the second string is a word than if the two words are unrelated.

Although the spreading activation model is quite flexible (e.g., it uses both categories and properties in its representation), its very flexibility means that it is difficult to derive specific predictions from it. In fact, the model was developed to account for existing results that could not be explained by previous models. Its flexibility and complexity have thus been criticized on those very grounds.

Extensions of Semantic Memory Models to Text Comprehension

In the 1970s, after decades of experimental efforts to develop semantic memory models based on list-learning and statement-verification tasks, a growing number of researchers—notably Kintsch, Fredricksen, Winograd, Bransford, and their colleagues—turned their attention to the study of text comprehension as the basis for discovering memory structure. They pointed to the shortcomings of existing network and feature models that treated isolated words or definitional sentences *(A sparrow is a bird)* without any context. They argue that such categorizing operations and single statement verifications are so artificial and ambiguous that they yield little information about the nature of working semantic memory.

Most researchers assume that texts are generated from propositional structures with rule-based dynamics. Propositions, according to Kintsch (1974), consist of the essential elements that carry the speaker's meaning. Thus, the proposition *(bake, Mary, cake)* corresponds to the sentence *Mary bakes a cake.* The proposition *(bird, robin)* can be expressed as *The robin is a bird.* Simple and complex relationships between propositions are generated through a system of rules.

The use of generating rules gives the propositional models a considerable advantage over the static network and feature comparison models. The most important benefit is in providing for *inferred knowledge* in semantic memory, without which it would be impossible to account for the availability of information that had not been explicitly learned. *Semantically acceptable* (i.e., possibly true) sentences are composed of inferred knowledge plus definitional (i.e., stored from previous learning) propositions. Kintsch assumes that well-learned characteristics (e.g., *The shark swims*) would become stored as definitional sentences because of their high frequency of occurrence.

To determine whether semantic information is indeed stored in some abstract logical form, Kintsch and Monk (1972) presented a reading task in which a situation involving four propositions was described in two ways: (a) as a series of simple sentences and (b) as a single, complex sentence composed of various syntactic and semantic transformations. The two versions had the same essential meaning but differed in the complexity of their expression. The two versions are illustrated in the following examples:

Simple: The council of elders in the land of Syndra meets whenever a stranger arrives. If the council meets and if the stranger presents the proper gifts to the council, he is not molested by the natives. The explorer Portmanteau came to Syndra without any valuable gifts.

Complex: The arrival of strangers in the land of Syndra, like the explorer Portmanteau, who did not bring valuable gifts, always resulted in a meeting of the council of elders, which insured that the stranger was not molested by the natives upon receipt of the proper gifts.

Question: Was Portmanteau molested by the natives?

Subjects were asked to read each paragraph and then, after it was removed from view, answer a YES/NO question that required an inference from the given information. There were two reading conditions: self-paced for as long as desired, and restricted to 10 seconds. Subjects responded by pressing an appropriate button.

The results showed significant differences in reading time for complex and simple sentences but inference times for both types were virtually identical. In other words, once comprehension has been achieved, the logical structure for both simple and complex sentences is the same. It is once again important to call attention to the task-oriented nature of the behavior. The subjects were informed that an inference task would be presented after each reading. Therefore, we can speak only of the likelihood that abstract logical (i.e., propositional) storage occurs when someone knows that an inference rather than recall will be required.

To gather more specific evidence of storage of semantic propositions, Kintsch and Keenan (1973) manipulated the number of basic propositions as the principal variable. Subjects read sets of 10 to 20 sentences, in which the number of propositions per sentence varied from 2 to 23. Topics included classical history and psychological terminology. Subjects were asked to recall information (not verbatim) from each paragraph. Timing conditions were either self-paced or restricted. They found a direct relationship between number of propositions per sentence or paragraph and reading time with respect to propositions correctly recalled. There was also a high correlation between number of propositions presented and number recalled (self-paced $r = .91$; restricted reading $r = .74$).

Now that researchers have undertaken the exploration of semantic memory using text blocks and even whole essays as probes, they must cope with complications of a problem that earlier psychologists sought to simplify. The latter concentrated on relatively simple definitional tasks in support of limited models for isolated statement verification. It is vastly more difficult to control variables when the stimuli are complex texts and the task is making inferences or responding selectively to context effects. Kintsch (1980) discusses recent experimental methods and theories in the light of the way they deal with context-free concepts (e.g., categories) and context-bound structures (e.g., texts or discourse). The ultimate objective is the determination of the structures and processes by which meaning is represented in semantic memory. And for a semantic memory model to be a complete description, it must deal with the generation and understanding of sentences. As Armstrong and her colleagues put it, "Since we speak in whole sentences rather than in single words, the chief desideratum of a theory of categories (coded by the words) would seem to be promise of a computable description for the infinite sentence meanings" (Armstrong, Gleitman, & Gleitman, 1983, p. 273).

SUMMARY

In this chapter, we have discussed research in semantic memory. Semantic memory is concerned with the organization and use of conceptual information. Research in this area is thus concerned with the following two issues: how concepts are formed, so that instances of objects, events, or experiences may be generalized and categorized, and how such conceptual knowledge is organized, used, and updated in semantic memory. The first issue is addressed by research in categorization, and the second issue is addressed by the proposals of various theories of semantic memory.

There are two basic theories about conceptual categories—classical theory and prototype theory. Classical theory holds that a concept is defined by a set of singly necessary and jointly sufficient attributes or features. The classical definition of concepts produced research in concept formation that used logical rules for class inclusion and exclusion. The aim of this research was to study how subjects learned such rules; but since the research is more appropriate to the topics of thinking and problem-solving, we review this research elsewhere.

The classical theory of categorization seemed quite inadequate to deal with categories of natural objects, whose boundaries are not well-defined and whose members exhibit different degrees of belongingness to the category. Accordingly, prototype theory was developed to deal with the existence of certain focal or prototypical exemplars that appeared to share features with many other members of the category. The related concept of family resemblance states that different family or category members will possess, to a greater or lesser extent, features they share with other family members. The member who shares the most features with other members is the prototype. A prototype may be an idealized set of features that does not exist in reality.

A great deal of experimental evidence supports prototype theory. Subjects show inconsistencies in classifying exemplars that are of low prototypicality, which would be expected if natural categories have fuzzy boundaries. Subjects can reliably rate the typicality of exemplars within categories, and these prototypicality ratings predict the latencies with which subjects can verify category membership. And finally, the number of attributes that subjects list for exemplars can be used, as a measure of family resemblance, to predict the degree of prototypicality these exemplars will exhibit.

A second aspect of category structure is that of the basic level. Rosch's research reveals that basic level objects show a variety of characteristics that make them ideal for optimally conveying information without burdening the communicator with excess verbal baggage. Experimentally, basic level objects were shown to possess maximum commonality of attributes, motor movements, and perceptual characteristics. Thus, Rosch's work in both prototypicality and basic levels provides a basis for the organization of categories in semantic memory.

Models of semantic memory propose a structure and a representation for semantic information as well as processes that are needed to act on such representations. Most models of semantic memory can be classified into either network models or feature models. An early network model, by Collins and Quillian, proposed a hierarchical organization for concepts and the features that characterize them. The model proposed a principle of cognitive economy, in which features are stored at the highest possible level. Experimental data from sentence verification tasks were used to support the Collins and Quillian model.

However, the early Collins and Quillian model had no provision for prototypicality effects. A feature comparison model, proposed by Smith and his colleagues, attempted to deal with prototypicality effects by proposing two types of features: features that are defining for membership in the category (defining features) and features that are true of many but not all members of a category (characteristic features). An exemplar of a category is prototypical to the extent that it has both types of features. Evidence from both similarity ratings and category verification tasks support the feature comparison model. A major criticism of the model is the lack of any apparent defining features for some categories.

A modification of the original Collins and Quillian model (spreading activation theory) reintroduces the network structure to semantic memory but abandons the original hierarchical structure. The spreading activation theory proposes that semantic information is represented by a set of nodes for both concepts and properties that are connected by relational markers. Prototypicality effects are represented in the model by locating prototypes closer to their superordinates. Semantic distance effects are introduced explicitly by varying the length of the relational markers between properties and categories. Although the spreading activation model accounts for most of the extant data on categorization, it was designed to do just that. One criticism of the model is that so many ad hoc provisions have been built into it that it lacks easily tested predictions.

Most research in semantic memory has been concerned with single concepts or concept-pairs. However, people typically use their semantic memory by processing and generating strings of words that make up sentences, strings of sentences that make up paragraphs, and strings of paragraphs that make up texts. Extensions of semantic memory models to the more complex materials of texts have recently been undertaken.

The research area of semantic memory has a relatively short past but will undoubtedly have a rich and productive future, for it is the acquisition and use of semantic knowledge that is the basis of much of what we call education.

10
Thinking and Problem Solving

Logic, n. The art of thinking and reasoning in strict accordance with the limitations and incapacities of the human misunderstanding. The basic of logic is the syllogism, consisting of a major and a minor premise and a conclusion.

Syllogism, n. A logical formula consisting of a major and a minor assumption and an inconsequent. (See LOGIC.)

(From *The Devil's Dictionary* by Ambrose Bierce)

In this chapter, we consider what is known about thinking and its relation to problem solving. Although thinking is perhaps the most ubiquitous of human activities (thought might be defined as any activity of the human mind), experimental psychologists have primarily confined their research interests to a study of thought processes that are used to solve problems. There are, of course, other varieties of thought. We may remember past events, in the type of thinking called reminiscing. We may imagine future events, as in planning a trip or imagining a reconciliation with a lover. And in that mysterious process known as dreaming, we perform a kind of thinking, even though our thoughts, as represented in dream images, may be obscure to us.

The nature of thought and the mental processes that constitute thinking have engaged the interest of philosophers since Aristotle first pondered the workings of the human mind. We concern ourselves in this chapter with one area of the broad subject of thinking: purposeful thinking, aimed at solving problems or reaching rational conclusions—what we usually call *reasoning*.

In our review of the subject of reasoned, purposeful thinking, we will consider two principal aspects: (1) the forms of logic that underlie reasoning and (2) the various theories of thinking. Our exploration of various types of logic in the first part of the chapter will center on problem solving and its relationship to concept formation. In the second part, we will compare the most prominent theories of the thinking process and evaluate their success in accounting for different kinds of problem-solving behavior. These theories range from the mechanistic associationist models to the insight-motivated Gestalt concepts, and finally to today's information processing models. After considering the role of verbal mediation in problem solving, we will examine the broader issue of the influence of language in directing our thoughts and in forming our view of the world.

In contrast to research on perception, learning, and memory, for which well-defined paradigms exist, research on thinking and problem solving has adopted a variety of paradigms ranging from studies in concept attainment to computer simulations of problem-solving behavior. Because of the diverse approaches to thinking, our commonly used dependent measures of probability correct and reaction time are often inadequate to cope with the complexity of the problem solver's behavior. Thus, other dependent measures such as a subject's protocol—a record of the subject's talking out loud while solving a problem—play an important role in the analysis of the thinking process.

INTRODUCTION TO REASONING

There are two types of reasoning processes: *deductive reasoning,* which proceeds from the general to the specific, and *inductive reasoning,* which proceeds from the specific to the general. In deductive reasoning tasks, subjects are given a set of principles or premises and asked to determine whether a conclusion follows from the premises. *Syllogistic reasoning* and a subset of this type of problem called the *three-term series* problem are the specific types of deductive reasoning most often studied by psychologists. A variant of the deductive reasoning problem is *hypothesis testing.* In a hypothesis testing experiment, subjects are given a premise or hypothesis and asked to test whether or not it is correct by examining selected cases. The measure of interest in hypothesis testing tasks is which cases the subject selects, which in turn determine the conclusion about the hypothesis he or she draws.

In inductive reasoning, subjects are given a set of particular examples and are asked to induce the general principle that characterizes all the examples. The most widely studied area in inductive reasoning is *concept formation,* in which subjects are given sets of examples that comprise positive and negative instances of the to-be-discovered concept and then are invited to state their hypothesis about what the concept is. These are usually fairly artificial concepts, such as *two red squares.* The subject learns the concept by seeing a set of geometric shapes differing in number, shape, and color, and guesses what the concept is after each presentation. These experimental situations are attempts to mimic what happens in more natural settings such as language learning, in which children learn words for concepts such as *chair* in a process of concept-learning or concept-attainment.

As we shall see, whether subjects exhibit correct logical behavior in each of these situations depends on the types of materials used, the types of information given, and the number of items that must be memorized. In hypothesis-testing, a rather pervasive finding is that subjects fail to select cases that could possibly disconfirm the hypothesis; they tend to seek confirmation rather than disconfirmation of the hypothesis they are testing.

Cognitive psychologists have used two basic experimental techniques to investigate reasoning processes: (1) reaction time, which measures the relative difficulty and complexity of various mental operations, and (2) choice of alternative conclusions, which indicate the type of logic being used by the subject. We will examine the theories underlying several systems of logic, to see how they can be used to probe the reasoning processes.

DEDUCTIVE REASONING

Aristotle first presented the syllogism as a most useful tool in deductive reasoning. It has a clear-cut, formal structure and a set of rules that enable the user to determine the proper conclusion in each case directly and without ambiguity. This is the basic structure of deductive reasoning.

The syllogism is composed of two premises and the conclusion deduced from them. For example, the two premises (1) "All cows give milk" and (2) "That animal is a cow" leads to the conclusion "That animal gives milk." *All*-type premises are called *universal affirmatives. No*-type premises ("No bulls give milk") are called *universal negatives. Some*-type premises ("Some cows give milk") are called *particular affirmatives. Some/not*-type premises ("Some cows do not give milk") are called *particular negatives.*

Errors in inferring conclusions arise from misinterpretation of the premises in various combinations of the four types. For example,

> All crows are black.
> That bird is black
> Therefore, that bird is a crow.

The conclusion is invalid, not simply because we know that other kinds of birds are also black, but because the conclusion does not follow logically from the premise. This error is called the *predicate error,* because we invalidly conclude that subjects having identical predicates are themselves identical. If we say: All A are B, All C are B, therefore All A are C, we invalidly equate A with C because they share a common predicate, the attribute B.

Another source of syllogistic error is what Woodworth and Sells (1935) described as the *atmosphere effect*—drawing conclusions on the basis of an overall impression of the premises. Here is an example:

> Some females are women.
> Daisy is a female.
> Therefore, Daisy is a woman.

She may be a woman, or she may be a little girl, or even a family pet. The syllogism leaves room for doubt. Woodworth and Sells found that affirmative premises (both universal and particular) created an affirmative atmosphere, whereas negative premises created a negative atmosphere. That is, the mood of the premises determined the inclination of the subject to come to a corresponding positive or negative conclusion. They successfully predicted the errors that subjects would make for each different combination of premises.

The Chapmans (1959) challenged the atmosphere effect. They tricked their subjects by setting up 42 experimental syllogisms with multiple-choice conclusions, *none* of which was valid. Letters were used instead of real objects to avoid the influence of prior knowledge or opinion (e.g., All Ls are Ks). They found that error results on most premise combinations were consistent with the predictions of the atmosphere theory, but there were significant differences in the particular affirmative–universal negative and particular negative–universal negative combinations. The error predicted by the atmosphere effect on both combinations is the particular negative. Thus, with these premises

Some Ls are Ks (particular affirmative).
No Ks are Ms (universal negative).

the predicted error preference (based on the atmosphere effect) would be

Some Ms are not Ls (particular negative).

Instead, the most commonly made error was the choice of the invalid conclusion

No Ms are Ls (universal negative).

Although the Chapman experiment used undefined letters, it may be helpful for understanding to translate the syllogism into real objects:

Some engineers (Ls) are women (Ks).
No women (Ks) are U.S. presidents (Ms).

The conclusion according to the atmosphere theory would be

Some U.S. presidents are not engineers.

But according to the Chapman results, the error was

No U.S. presidents are engineers.

The Chapmans suggest that this kind of error arises from the general practice of most people to draw inferences on the basis of probabilistic judgment. That is, we regard as proved something that is merely probable. In the preceding example, if we accept the fact that "No Ks are Ms" (and vice versa), then it is unlikely that if Ls and Ks have *something* in common, Ms and Ls would have *anything* in common. Consider the possible real situation:

Most philanthropists are rich men.
No rich men are coalminers.

If we take a commonsense view of likelihood, we might conclude that

No coalminers are philanthropists.

The conclusion may make sense probabilistically, though it would be logically invalid.

Henle (1962) pursued this popular habit of probabilistic inference in an effort to find some relationship between formal logic and ordinary thinking. She took her cue from Aristotle's concept of the *practical syllogism,* a logical structure designed to serve as a guide to action, a tool for rational living. Looked at from that standpoint, errors in formal deduction do not constitute evidence that the laws of logic are irrelevant to actual thinking or that most people are incompetent in logical thinking. Rather, people make errors because they alter the syllogisms to conform to their habit of probabilistic inference.

In a study to determine how educated people dealt with logical deductions, Henle (1962) asked 42 graduate psychology students to evaluate the *logical adequacy* of deductions presented in examples of practical syllogisms. Henle found several logical errors in their reasoning processes:

1. Failure to accept the logical task. Here the students' evaluation of the stated conclusions takes no account of the actual premises but reflects their appraisal of the practical requirements of the situation expressed in the syllogism.
2. Restatement of the premise or conclu-

sion so that the intended meaning is changed. As an example, one syllogism said, "Many youngsters don't get enough vitamins in their daily diet. Some vitamin deficiencies are dangerous to health. Therefore, the health of many of our youngsters is being endangered by inadequate diet." The student response was to agree with the conclusion, although they had changed the particular premises to universals in overstating the health danger of vitamin deficiency.

3. Omission or addition of a premise. In some cases, the response omitted one of the two premises, drawing the inference from just one. In other cases, extraneous premises were added.

What we see in these syllogistic distortions are further examples of the effect of task demands on problem solving. The consequences of logical error may be appropriate to practical reality, though not necessarily so.

The Three-Term Series Problem

A special form of syllogism known as the *three-term series* has received much attention from psychologists because it reveals possible mediation processes in deductive reasoning. Stated as a deductive task, the three-term series problem has this form:

Mary is taller than Jane.
Alice is shorter than Jane.
Who is tallest?

The height relationship among the three girls can be expressed in various ways: by switching the order of one or both premises ("Jane is shorter than Mary"), changing the dimensional pole in the question ("Who is shortest?"), and so on. It is the effect of such alternative arrangements of the conditions that interests experimenters, because the relative difficulty in solving the different arrangements, as measured by reaction time, can indicate the processes that subjects use in working out the relationships in deductive problems. Several models have been proposed for three-term series problems.

The Operational Model. Ian Hunter (1957) proposed an *operational* model, based on the principle that a linear series of relations can be resolved by expunging the intermediate terms. The series $a > b > c > d \ldots > z$ leads directly to the conclusion that $a > z$ by the property of *transitivity.* In the case of the syllogism:

A is larger than B.
B is larger than C.
Which is largest?

we conclude that A is larger than C by dropping the common middle term B.

Some three-term series problems may require restatement or conversion of the terms. For example,

A is larger than B.
C is smaller than B.

requires a *conversion* of the second premise to the necessary form:

A is larger than B.
B is larger than C.

Using reaction times as the index of difficulty, Hunter demonstrated it was faster to solve $A > B$, $B > C$ problems, which are in their "natural" form, than to solve $A > B$, $C < B$ problems, which required a conversion of the second premise. The latter were, in turn, easier to solve than $B < A$, $C < B$, which required a reordering of the second premise ahead of the first. (Hence, conversion is easier than reordering.) Problems that required both conversion and reordering were hardest of all:

C is smaller than B.
A is larger than B.

must first be converted to

B is larger than C.
A is larger than B.

and then the premises must be reordered:

A is larger than B.
B is larger than C.

The Image Model. A second model for the three-term series problem, by DeSoto, London, and Handel (1965), proposed that subjects use spatial imagery as a mediating aid. They maintained that problem solvers formed a mental image of a horizontal or vertical array in which the items are positioned according to the relational terms used in the premises. Some relational terms are more natural in a horizontal array. For example,

A is wider than B, B is wider than C.
Which is widest?

fits most naturally into a horizontal (wide) format. Other relational terms are more natural in a vertical array. For example,

A
is better than
B
B
is better than
C
Which is best?

falls readily into a vertical, *top-down* structure (better is higher). DeSoto and his colleagues found that the format of the problem interacted with the natural horizontal or vertical structure of the relationship, such that solution times were fastest for the pairings in which the spatial format was suited to the comparative relationship.

In addition, the top-down structure, with the best thing at the top, was shown to be easier (shorter RTs) than the bottom-up structure, with the best thing at the bottom, for a "Which is best?" problem. Both these results—differential compatability of type of relationship with either a horizontal or vertical problem format, and *top-down* form preferred to *bottom-up form*—disconfirms the *operational model,* which would seem to predict no effect of format on middle-term cancellation.

Another principle proposed by DeSoto et al. is that of *end-anchoring* as a facilitating form. In the end-anchoring form, the extreme items go at the beginning of both statements, as in

A is better than B.
C is worse than B.

Which is superior to

B is worse than A.
B is better than C.

Huttenlocher (1968) proposed a refinement of the *image* model. She showed that relative difficulty of performance was not associated so much with end-anchor positioning as it was with the *deep structure* of the premise. Deep structure expresses the essential subject-object relationships in a statement, which may be modified for reasons of the speaker's rhetorical style or other communicative purpose. For example, the sentence "The race was won by Tom, who was not as young as the other contestants" is built out of the following deep structure statements: "Tom won the race. Tom was old-more than the other contestants." Passives (the transformation of "Tom won the race" to "The race was won by Tom") and negatives are two of the surface transformations of deep structures.

In a comprehension experiment, Huttenlocher, Eisenberg, and Strauss (1968) found that nursery school and first-grade children could arrange a movable block easier (fewer errors, lower RTs) above or beneath a fixed block when it was the *logical subject* in the instruction. Example: "The green block (movable) is on top of the red block (fixed)" is easier to set up than "The red block (fixed) is under the green block (movable)." This advantage was observed even when the movable block was the grammatical *object* if the sentence was in the passive voice, since it was still the *logical* subject of the sentence. The critical condition is that the perceived actor corresponds to the described actor.

From that discovery, Huttenlocher concluded that the end-anchoring effect was an example of the subject's sensitivity to the deep structure representation of the relation. The leading item in the end-anchored form serves as the grammatical and logical subject of the premise.

The Linguistic Model. In his contribution to the three-term series issue, Clark (1969) constructed a *linguistic* model, in which he went beyond Huttenlocher's use of deep structure, taking a psycholinguistics approach to an explanation of the findings. Clark postulated three principles. The first principle, the *primacy of functional relations,* holds that premises are reduced to their deep structure representation. Thus, "John is worse than Bob" is recoded as "John is bad-more and Bob is bad-less." This form is easier to process than the surface transformation. In general, the premise "A is better than B" is processed as "A is good-more; B is good-less." The comparison premise "C is worse than B" becomes "C is bad-more; B is bad-less." The repeated item B is recoded to "B is middle." The comparatives then are elevated to superlative, and the final form is "A is most good, B is middle, C is most bad." This is the form that all three-term theories agree is easiest to solve.

Clark's second principle is *lexical marking.* This asserts that so-called *unmarked* comparatives are easier to process than *marked* comparatives. Unmarked terms are neutral and do not indicate absolute position on the scale of polar adjectives. Thus, "good" is unmarked and "bad" is marked. We can say "How good is John?" without indicating bias, but "How bad is John?" carries an implication that John is at the "bad" end of the scale. The corresponding unmarked and marked comparatives "better" and "worse" share the lexical qualities of "good" and "bad." Accordingly, "A is more bad and B is less bad" would be harder to process than "A is more good and B is less good."

Finally, Clark's third principle speaks of the value of *congruence.* It is simpler to determine the answer when the question is congruent with the form of the premise. "A is better than B" is coded as "A is more good and B is less good." The question is harder to answer when phrased "Which is worse?" This question can be rephrased "Which is less good?" to yield a form congruent with the premise and so, easier to process.

The linguistic theory seems to do a better job of predicting the effects of the full variety of premise and question forms than the other theories. This is especially true for those involving the *negative equative* construction, "Joe is not as good as Roger," which Clark maintains is converted into "Roger is better than Joe," before proceeding through the deep-structure recoding.

Controversy has swirled about the competing claims of the three major theories—operational, image, and linguistic. All can offer experimental evidence of actual use by subjects, and this fact turns out to be surprisingly noncontradictory, since all are used by different subjects at different phases in the learning-to-solve process. Philip Johnson-Laird (1972), in his comparative analysis of the three theories, describes how the subject, gaining skill rapidly from trial to trial, modifies his or her strategy as the experiment progresses, learning the advantage of reading the question first, eliminating unnecessary analysis of second premises, and ignoring the order of the premises. In short, as Johnson-Laird points out, what we really need to know, as a critical variable, is how many trials the naive or experienced subject has completed when we try to determine his or her strategy on the trial in question.

Hypothesis Testing

Two kinds of hypothesis-testing paradigms have been used in research. In the first, subjects are given a rule or hypothesis and asked to test the validity of the hypothesis in the most efficient way possible by selecting cases to examine. In the second, subjects are given cases and asked to state hypotheses about the general principle that generated the cases. This second paradigm might best be called "hypothesis-guessing," and it rather closely resembles the concept formation procedures. However, because in both paradigms the subject's task is to test, or generate and test, a hypothesis, both types of procedures will be discussed together. Both procedures can be illustrated with experiments devised by Wason (1960, 1968a, 1968b), whose deceptively simple problems have stumped both English undergraduates and an occasional professor of logic!

In an example of the first paradigm, Wason (1968b) presented four specially printed cards to a group of undergraduates. The subjects had been informed that each card had a letter on one side and a number on the other. In the classic version of this experiment, an *A* was printed on the visible side of one card, a *B* on the second, a *2* on the third, and a *3* on the fourth. The subject saw all four cards on the table and was told, "All the cards with a vowel on one side have an even number on the other," and was then asked which cards would have to be turned over to check whether the statement was true. Thus, the hypothesis to be tested is the statement "All the cards with a vowel on one side have an even number on the other," and the task is to test it by turning over as few cards as possible.

Formal logic dictates that two cards must be turned over to test the hypothesis. These are the card with the *A* and the card with the *3*. The first choice gives the hypothesis a chance to be confirmed. (The *A* card must have an even number on the back). The second choice gives the hypothesis a chance to be disconfirmed. (The *3* card cannot have a vowel on the back.) The other two cards are irrelevant—the *B* could have an even number on the back and be compatible with the statement, and the *2* need not have a vowel on the back and be compatible with the statement. These possibilities are illustrated in Figure 10-1. Yet, from 60% to 75% of the adult subjects chose both the *A* and the *2*, or only the *A* card, and ignored the necessity of checking the *3* card. The fact that subjects often choose the 2 card to test is not surprising in light of our previous discussion of syllogistic reasoning. These subjects interpreted the statement "All the cards with a vowel on one side have an even number on the other" to imply the reverse as well, that all cards with an even number on one side must also have a vowel on the other. In short, they assumed that if all As are Bs, then all Bs are As.

We can translate Wason's task into a more concrete example. Instead of "All the cards with a vowel on one side have an even number on the other," we could test the logically similar hypothesis, "All mothers are females." Figure 10-2 shows the possibilities for testing this second hypothesis. To confirm the hypothesis, we would have to make sure that any particular mother was indeed a female. (This is similar to checking that the *A* has an even number on the back.) To check for disconfirmation we would have to make sure that

Hypothesis: "All the cards with a vowel on one side have an even number on the other."

A. Cards presented by the experimenter

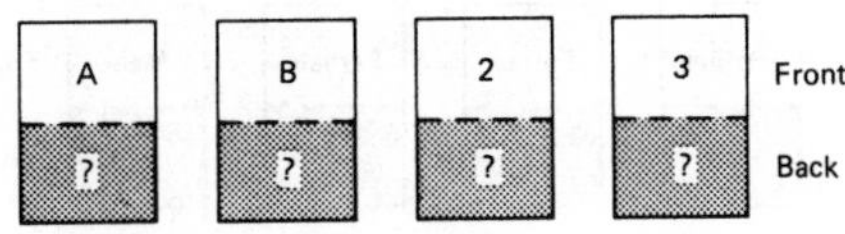

B. Card which can confirm the hypothesis

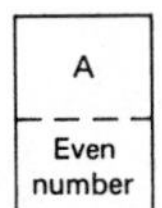

C. Card which can disconfirm the hypothesis

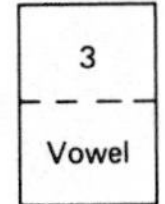

D. Cards which are irrelevant to the hypothesis

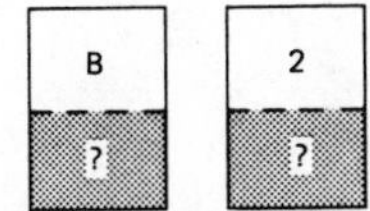

Fig. 10-1 An illustration of Wason's hypothesis testing procedure.

Hypothesis: "All mothers are females."

A. Cards presented by the experimenter

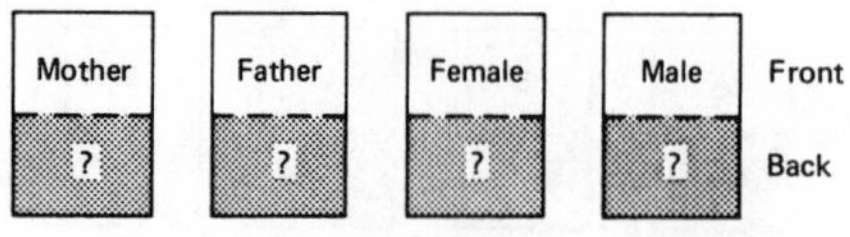

B. Card which can confirm the hypothesis

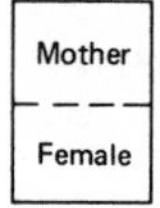

C. Card which can disconfirm the hypothesis

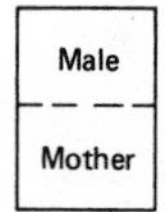

D. Cards which are irrelevant to the hypothesis

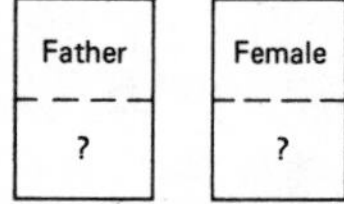

Fig. 10-2 Another illustration of hypothesis testing.

no male was a mother. (This is similar to checking that the *3* does not have a vowel on the reverse side.) The other two situations are irrelevant to this logical problem. Whether a particular father is male (or female) or whether a particular female is a mother (or father) does not bear on the hypothesis being tested.

In a second experiment, Wason (1960, 1968a) presented subjects with a numerical sequence and asked them to generate and test the rule that defined the sequence. Subjects were presented with the initial sequence 2-4-6, and told they could generate as many three-number sequences as they wished before announcing their hypotheses. The subject was told after each sequence whether it was consistent with the rule or not.

The overwhelming majority of subjects adopted the strategy of attempting to confirm, rather than disconfirm, their hypothesis. For example, they might generate a hypothesis such as "sequences of increasing numbers separated by 2," and then *only* generate sequences of numbers that would confirm the hypothesis, such as 10-12-14, 22-24-26, and so on. They rarely generated a sequence of numbers that would permit their "separated by two" hypothesis to be disconfirmed, such as 2-3-4, and thus, many never solved the problem. Subjects who did solve the problem used a high proportion of disconfirmation sequences, and quickly solved the problem. (The rule is: any ascending series of numbers.)

Wason describes the behavior of a subject who failed to solve the problem after fifty minutes of persistent hypothesis-generation. This subject never tried to disconfirm the hypothesis but rather generated increasingly complex hypotheses about the rule, ending with this one before finally giving up: "The rule is that the second number is random, and either the first number equals the second minus two, and the third is random but greater than the second; or the third number equals the second plus two, and the first is random but less than the second" (Wason, 1968a, p. 232). Wason points out many similarities between the thought processes of his subjects, obtained through protocol analysis, and thought disturbances in psychopathology.

INDUCTIVE REASONING: CONCEPT FORMATION

The psychological study of inductive reasoning processes is largely concerned with the formation of concepts. A concept is a set of related attributes that define a class of objects.

Concepts used in everyday life are usually represented by verbal symbols such as "chair," "dog," "my friend Dorothy," or even "cognitive psychology." As we pointed out in Chapter 9, such concepts are hard to define precisely. On the other hand, concepts studied by experimental psychologists in concept formation exper-

Fig. 10-3 Some of the stimulus materials used by Hull (1920). Each of the six different radicals is embedded in a unique character in each list. Each radical is associated with a nonsense name, which is the response to be given to that radical regardless of the character in which it occurs. (From "Quantitative aspects of the evolution of concepts," by C. L. Hull. In *Psychological Monographs,* 1920 (Whole no. 123). Copyright 1920 by the American Psychological Association. Reprinted by permission.)

iments are generally clearly defined with discrete, easily distinguishable, and relatively salient attributes or dimensions. Stimuli in such experiments usually differ on a number of attributes, such as color, shape, size, and quantity, each having at least two different values (e.g., black/white, and circle/square). Only some of these attributes are relevant to the concept, and it is the subject's task to discover which attributes are relevant and which values of the relevant attributes are associated with positive instances of the concept. The subject learns these rules for defining the concept by evaluating positive and negative feedback.

Clark Hull (1920) proposed that concept learning followed the same S-R rules of association that mediated other types of learning. Hull proposed that a concept shared common attributes and that concept learning consisted of the abstraction of the common elements and attachment of a single response to those elements, which he proposed occurred in a gradual, continuous fashion. In addition, new stimuli sharing those elements would elicit the same response, in the process of *stimulus generalization.*

Hull demonstrated the principles of S-R learning in a concept-formation experiment in which subjects learned to associate one of twelve nonsense syllables with one of twelve Chinese characters, each of which contained a different radical. New lists were constructed of different characters in which each character shared one of the twelve radicals with characters from the previous list. Figure 10-3 includes examples of Hull's stimuli. Subjects showed gradual learning across lists by demonstrating gradual increases in their ability to attach the correct response to the correct Chinese character, even though they were unable to verbalize the basis of the common elements among them.

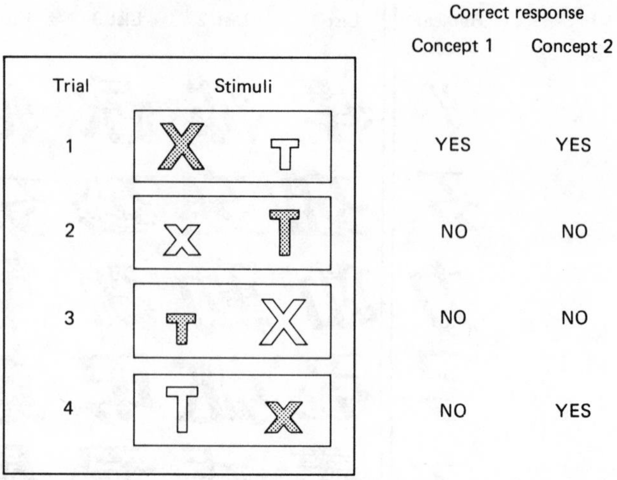

Trial	Stimuli	Correct response: Concept 1	Correct response: Concept 2
1	X T	YES	YES
2	X T	NO	NO
3	T X	NO	NO
4	T X	NO	YES

Fig. 10-4 Four trials of a four-attribute concept formation problem. Concept 1 = shaded large X on left; concept 2 = shaded X.

As can be seen in Figure 10-3, the common radical attribute in Hull's stimuli is very difficult to identify perceptually (i.e., it is not salient). However, in more recent versions of concept learning experiments, easily discriminable and verbally codable attributes such as number, color, and size have been used. Although early theories of the concept formation process continued to invoke associational, S-R principles for acquisition of the concept (e.g., Bourne & Restle, 1959), it soon became clear that concept-attainment was not usually a gradual but rather an all-or-none process, in which subjects developed hypotheses about what the concept was, for example, *two red circles,* and then tested their hypothesis until it was contradicted. Mathematical models for such hypothesis-testing strategies were proposed by several investigators (e.g., Bower & Trabasso, 1964; Restle, 1962) and were generally supported by empirical data. According to most hypothesis-testing models of concept attainment, learning can occur only on an error trial, that is, on a trial when the hypothesis must be rejected. Because the subject's overt response of accepting or rejecting a stimulus as an instance of the concept does not reveal the particular hypothesis held by the subject, subsequent experimenters often asked subjects to state their hypotheses on every trial, or after some number of trials.

As an example, consider the series of trials in a concept formation task shown in Figure 10-4. Stimuli can vary on four attributes: shaded versus unshaded; large versus small; X versus T; and left versus right. Suppose the concept to be learned is shaded large X on left (concept 1). For concept 1, all four attributes are relevant, and only the first trial represents a positive instance of the concept. Next, suppose that the concept to be learned is simply shaded X (concept 2). Now only two attributes are relevant, so both the first and fourth trials are positive instances of the concept. Suppose, in trying to learn concept 2, the subject were to develop the hypothesis that the concept is X on the left. He or she would correctly classify the example on the first trial but for a partially wrong reason. Thus, the hypothesis cannot be disconfirmed on this trial. However, the subject would be incorrect on the second trial, and this would disconfirm the hypothesis.

Experiments on concept formation use either the *reception paradigm* or the *selection paradigm.* In the simplest version of the *reception paradigm,* the experimenter shows the subject a particular stimulus and the subject classifies it as an instance of the concept or not. The subject is told whether he or she is correct and the process is repeated. Thus, each trial consists of stimulus, categorization, and information feedback. This process continues until the subject indicates he or she has learned the concept, either by making a criterion string of correct responses or by stating the correct hypothesis.

In the *selection paradigm,* the subject is presented with the entire population of stimuli at the onset of the experiment. The experimenter then shows the subject one stimulus that is a positive instance of the to-be-discovered concept. The subject uses this information to guess the hypothesis. If he or she is wrong, the subject then chooses another stimulus and the experimenter reports whether this second stimulus is a positive or negative instance of the concept. The subject must then guess the hypothesis. This process—choosing a stimulus, receiving information feedback, and guessing the concept—continues until the subject correctly guesses the concept. From the patterns of stimulus choices coupled with hypothesis guesses, the experimenter can infer the strategy and the process by which the concept is finally attained. The difference between reception and selection, then, is that in reception, the *experimenter* selects the stimuli, whereas in selection, the *subject* selects them.

The selection paradigm was introduced by Bruner, Goodnow, and Austin (1956), who used subjects' selection of the stimuli to infer which strategies they used to discover the concept. They ran a series of tests with children and adults, using cards containing three values on each of four attributes—number, shape, color, and border design—as shown in Figure 10-5. The target concept might be any one of the three values of any one to four of the attributes. The subject's task was to discover the concept by selecting instances and evaluating the feedback from the experimenter about whether the instance was an example of the concept or not. A typical

Fig. 10-5 An array of instances comprising combinations of four attributes, each attribute exhibiting three values. The four attributes with their three values are: (1) Quantity—one, two, three, (2) Shape—cross, circle, square, (3) Color—green, red, black, (4) Border design—single, double, triple. Green figures are shown as plain, red figures as striped, and black figures as solid. (From *A Study of Thinking,* by J. S. Bruner, J. J. Goodnow, and G. A. Austin. Copyright 1956 by John Wiley and Sons. Reprinted by permission.)

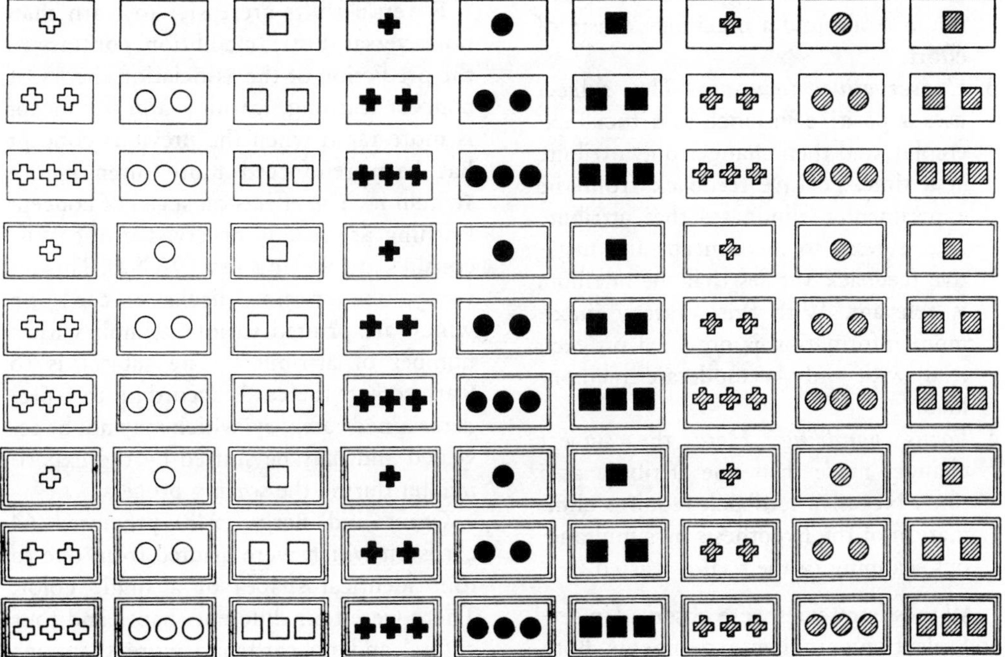

concept might be "all cards with two red circles," in which the three attributes of number (two), shape (circle), and color (red) are relevant and the fourth attribute, border design, is irrelevant.

Bruner and his colleagues centered their interest on the various selection strategies adopted by the subjects. Such strategies are useful for many reasons. First, they increase the likelihood that instances encountered will contain appropriate information. Second, these strategies render less difficult the task of assimilating and keeping track of information. Finally, they regulate the amount of risk one will undergo in attaining a correct solution within a limited number of choices.

The Bruner experiments elicited four different strategies for the selection of hypotheses:

1. *Simultaneous scanning.* This involves checking and remembering all positive and negative feedback instances and making very complicated inferences—an overwhelming cognitive and memory load.
2. *Successive scanning.* With this strategy, the subject tests one hypothesis at a time, covering all instances of a single attribute. This strategy involves a minimum strain and a maximum waste of effort.
3. *Conservative focusing.* The subject uses a positive instance as a focus exemplar, and then changes one attribute at a time. Positive feedback from the experimenter eliminates that attribute as irrelevant to the concept and negative feedback verifies that the attribute is relevant. With this strategy maximum information is obtained on each trial with only a moderate memory load.
4. *Focus gambling.* Here the subject changes more than one attribute at a time. Negative feedback requires elimination of the hypothesis by simultaneous scanning or the trial is wasted.

All these strategies were observed in several selection paradigm experiments. Both focusing and scanning strategies were used, but focusers used fewer choices to discover the concept.

In one experiment, some subjects were given positive feedback only, while others were given negative feedback only. The positive group steadily increased their risk by choosing more and more attributes that differed from the focus card. The negative group tended to choose fewer and fewer different attributes (down to a minimum of 1.08 per trial). Apparently, expectancy of positive or negative feedback either encourages or inhibits risk-taking strategies, depending on favorable or unfavorable results.

Concept researchers are particularly interested in conditions that will improve concept-attainment skills. One procedure that has been used to study the speed of such attainment is *shifting* the target concepts. There are two kinds of shifts: *reversal shifts,* in which the relevant attribute or attributes are kept constant, but the value of the positive attribute is changed (e.g., the concept shifts from all red objects to all green objects), and *nonreversal shifts,* in which the relevant attribute changes (e.g., the concept shifts from all red objects to all square objects).

Reversal shifts are easier to learn than nonreversal shifts. In addition, contrary to the prediction of the association theory of concept learning, learning a new concept is more rapid when the previous concept has been reinforced more often before switching. The effects on speed of concept learning are readily observed in the Wisconsin Card-Sorting Test (WCST). This involves one or more decks of cards on which are printed various stimuli with a number of attributes. The subject is to learn to sort the cards according to a predetermined category, which may not be revealed and may be shifted by the experimenter during the sorting process.

Grant and Berg (1948) presented 64 cards on which were printed from one to four identical shapes of a single color. There were four different shapes and four colors, and no card had more than one type of shape. For example, a card could have one, two, three, or four circles, but it could never have one circle and one square. Sorting was possible according to color, shape, or number of shapes. The sorting category was secretly shifted after from three to ten reinforcing (correct) trials. The results showed that a greater number of reinforcing trials reduced perseveration and led to more rapid attainment of the new concept—the more reinforcements for the old concept, the more flexibility and fewer errors when a new concept was introduced. One interpretation of these results is that after a more extended reinforcement sequence it is easier to tell when a change in contingency has occurred. A subsequent sorting experiment by Grant and Cost (1954) confirmed the salutary effect on learning of longer runs of reinforcing trails (20 and 40 trials) before switching.

Concept formation research is a rather artificial procedure, usually involving sets of arbitrary visual symbols presented in an uncommon, synthetic task. We would like to apply what we have learned from such research to a natural process like language acquisition (even the "simple" process of acquiring a vocabulary). When we do so, however, the principles and methods of concept research seem rather remote from the pragmatic business of learning one's language in a variety of environments and, in particular, in learning how to classify instances of natural categories such as dogs, chairs, and dishes, which cannot be so precisely defined.

Carroll (1964) underscores four differences between concept research and natural language learning. First, although experimental concepts are composed of familiar attributes (the common shapes, colors, etc.), in natural language learning, the child meets mostly new attributes in the early environment. Second, in natural situations, concepts are complexes of previously learned concepts. Sometimes a whole network of prerequisite concepts is necessary to grasp a new one. In contrast, the concepts in concept formation experiments are independent of any content. Third, natural concepts usually exist in relational situations. They less frequently exist in neatly disjunctive or conjunctive classes, as is common with artificial concepts. Fourth, concept learning in school is generally deductive, whereas experimental concept formation is generally inductive. A pattern of positive and negative instances is usually not available for natural concept learning. Instead, verbal descriptions are the common means of teaching these concepts.

Finally, Carroll points to the main difference between experimental and natural concept learning. According to the Piagetian theory, meanings are first learned in the physical world by a process of developing action schemas through sensorimotor experience, whereas in the laboratory situation there is no physical involvement and no experiencing of functional attributes. Of course, the process by which the child learns the meaning of a word through reinforcement and correction parallels the experimental method of concept attainment. In light of these criticisms, Carroll calls for real-life, natural concept learning research.

THEORIES OF THOUGHT PROCESSES

It is somewhat paradoxical that thinking about thinking should be so perplexing and provoke so many different, apparently contradictory theories of how reasoning works. We will look at three models representing three sharply contrasting conceptions of underlying mechanisms of thought: *associationism*, *gestaltism*, and *information processing*.

Associationism

The earliest theory of how we think was inspired by the recognizable connections through which ideas recall related ideas, forming sequences of remembered or imagined events. The way words and ideas are linked in memory often allows a forgotten item to be retraced through a series of related words, each evoking an associate. From this simple observation, it was a straightforward step to explain thinking as a process comprising such verbal connections. In the present century, associationism as a basis for thinking and problem solving was assimilated into the general theory of S-R processes that are identified with the behaviorist school of psychology.

Behavior theorists such as Thorndike, Hull, Spence, and Skinner used the principles of S-R contiguity and contingency coupled with reinforcement to account for learning. Complex chains of behavior that eventually led to a desired goal had to be augmented with unobservable stimuli and responses, called feedback goal stimuli (s_G) and anticipatory goal responses (r_G). These unobservable r_G-s_G anticipatory goal response pairs are assumed capable of migrating backward from the goal in order to provide secondary reinforcement for responses that are not directly followed by the goal. In addition, principles of stimulus and response generalization are invoked to account for identical responses to different stimuli (stimulus generalization) and different responses to identical or similar stimuli (response generalization).

As we shall see, association theory has a heavy burden to bear in accounting for phenomena such as *insight* in problem solving, *hypothesis testing* in concept formation, and various phenomena in deductive reasoning. However, let us illustrate its use in understanding how a child might solve the problem of learning a concept in real life and then describe several experimental tests of association theory.

Imagine that a child is confronted with a red velvet armchair and told its name is "chair." How is he to acquire the concept of chair so that he will apply it appropriately to a kitchen chair, desk chair, or rocking chair? Through stimulus generalization, he might first call everything that is red a chair, or everything that is velvet a chair, or everything with arms a chair. Through negative reinforcement, the links between the irrelevant attributes of the original example and the response *chair* will weaken, and through response generalization, the child may begin to call other nonvelvet nonred armchairs *chair* until finally all chairs will be given their rightful designation.

There may be several alternative chains of S-R connections, elicited by a common stimulus, which lead to a common goal. In the child's case, the goal may be praise from mother or father for acquiring a vocabulary, and the chains could be all the other terms possible to apply to the original red velvet armchair (e.g., *sit, red, comfortable,* etc.). Another example is all the different paths that can intervene between the ringing of your alarm clock (the common stimulus) and arriving at work (the goal). As we saw in Chapter 7, Hull called these paths *habit family hierarchies.* Habit family hierarchies can *converge,* by becoming attached to more than one initiating stimulus, or *diverge,* by becoming attached to more than one goal response.

The mechanisms of convergence and divergence are used by associationists to explain various kinds of generalization. This applies to all kinds of behavior, both verbal and nonverbal. For example, in an experiment by Riess (1940), the stimulus word "urn" was associated by conditioning with a loud buzzer. The buzzer, as we might expect, evoked an elevated galvanic skin response (GSR), indicating a heightened state of nervous excitement. In the test phase, the presentation of the word "urn" evoked a high GSR even when the buzzer was not sounded (remember Pavlov's dog?). "Urn" is also semantically associated with its synonym "vase," thereby forming a divergent response pattern that generalizes the stimulus "urn" to at least those two different responses—i.e., "vase" and the elevated GSR. Since "urn" is a synonym of the word "vase," there is a two-way association—urn-vase and vase-urn. Accordingly, it should come as no surprise that the experiment demonstrated an elevated GSR when the word "vase" was presented without direct conditioning to the buzzer. We have now seen the original divergent pattern lead to a convergent pattern as the GSR is generalized as the single common response to the two stimuli "urn" and "vase".

The companion principles of divergence and convergence are exemplified in certain kinds of errors encountered in the course of learning English. Irregular verbs are a case in point. At an early stage, children generalize the "-ed" as the past tense form for all verbs. This convergence pattern expresses itself in such errors as *goed* and *bringed.* Later, as they hear the correct forms for those words used by adults, children acquire equivalent response chains in a divergent hierarchy. Words like *bring* may acquire additional erroneous associations as a result of class similarities of form: Since *bring* is in the same verb class as *sing* and *ring,* it may produce the erroneous past tense form *brang* (instead of *brought*) by stimulus generalization.

Eventually, if learning is efficient, the similar verb forms acquire equivalent chains in a divergent hierarchy for past tense responses. In the normal course of learning English, the incorrect alternatives will fail to be reinforced in the speech of adults, and so will diminish in probability of occurrence, while the correct forms will increase. The aversive effect of having one's error corrected will further contribute to the extinction of that response.

Associationism, with its modern elaborations, has been more successful in explaining the mechanical modes of learning and thinking, such as rote learning and syllogistic logic, than in explaining the processes of reasoning and creative thinking. It is in dealing with creative thought processes that associationist theory has been hard-pressed to amplify its structures and laws. Because problem solving is common to both learning and thinking, we can evaluate associationism by its ability to explain human performance in finding answers to problems.

Thinking involves the selection of the appropriate habit-family hierarchy and the specific sequences, or chains, within the hierarchy. The anticipatory goal response (r_G-s_G) is the key to learning new ways to use existing knowledge and to develop new information in solving problems. It indicates the association between a stimulus (the problem) and new responses that mark novel, and possibly better, routes to the solution-goal. It does this by focusing on salient stimulus features that are related by semantic or other similarities. These features provide a basis for organizing objects into classes: all members of a class share common reinforcement when one member of that class is reinforced as the correct response to a problem and common inhibition when one member is blocked. Selection of one response causes preference for other responses from that class.

The operation of common reinforcement on all members of a class has mixed effects on success in finding solutions. One effect is called *problem-solving set,* or *einstellung.* This is a preference for repeating a procedure that was successful on a previous problem. It can be useful in working on a series of related problems or on one problem with a series of related answers. An example is the task of solving anagrams. An anagram is a scrambled word, and its solution requires unscrambling the letters to form the word (e.g., unscrambling the anagram *oidgn* to form *doing*). Letter combinations of high frequency can act as aids in rearranging the scrambled letters into words (Mayzner & Tresselt, 1958). Thus, the fact that *ing* is a common word ending aids in determining that *oidgn* is the anagram for *doing.* A second example is memorizing lists of related words, in which categorization of the items aids recall (Mandler, 1967). Here, the fact that the words in a list of, say, twenty can be divided and grouped into four categories of five words each permits the subject to improve memory performance by recalling the category names and using them as cues to recall their associated list words.

Problem-solving set can also hinder problem solving, so that subjects persevere in their responses when alternative strate-

Table 10-1 The Problems Used by Luchins (1942) To Study Problem-Solving Set

Problem	Capacity of jugs a	b	c	To get	Formula	Jug containing the solution
1	29	3	—	20	a − 3b	a
2	21	127	3	100	b − a − 2c	b
3	14	163	25	99	"	b
4	18	43	10	5	"	b
5	9	42	6	21	"	b
6	20	59	4	31	"	b
7	23	49	3	20	a − c	a
8	15	39	3	18	a + c	b
9	28	76	3	25	a − c	a
10	18	48	4	22	a + c	b
11	14	36	8	6	a − c	a

Note. Problem 1 is for illustrative purposes. Problems 2 through 6 are the *einstellung* problems, to establish the problem-solving set. Problems 7 through 8 and 10 through 11 are "catch" problems, which can be solved by two formulas: the direct formula (a − c or a + c) *and* the *einstellung* formula (b − a − 2c). Problem 9 cannot be solved by the *einstellung* formula, and so provides a "recovery" problem.

gies are more advantageous. Luchins (1942) performed an experiment with the classic three-jug problem. In this problem, the subject is presented (on paper) with three jugs of different capacities and a quantity of liquid. One or two of the jugs is to be filled and poured into the others in a sequence that leaves a desired amount of fluid in one of them. Table 10-1 shows the problems and their solutions.

For example, in problem 1 in Table 10-1, the solution is to fill jug *a* to capacity, then pour it into jug *b* three times. What will remain in jug *a* is 20 units of fluid. Problems 2 through 6 all have the same solution—namely, to fill jug *b*, then pour it into jug *a* once and into jug *c* twice. Problems 7, 8, 10, and 11, on the other hand, can be solved either by the same solution as in problems 2 through 6 or by the simpler procedure of filling jug *a* and pouring it into jug *c* ($a - c$), or of filling jug *a* and jug *c* and pouring them both into jug *b* ($a + c$). Problem 9 can only be solved by the solution $a - c$, and so provides a "recovery" problem from the problem-solving set.

When subjects discovered that a certain filling and pouring sequence worked on five variations of the basic problem (problems 2 through 6), they continued to use the same three-jug, four-step formula on the four following "catch" problems. They often failed to observe that the "catch" problems could be solved by a simpler and more efficient procedure.

Associationism runs into its most frustrating challenges when it attempts to explain creative thinking in terms of response hierarchies. Given the well-known disposition of creative people to produce widely deviant associations, the burning question is, how do uncommon responses get reinforced sufficiently to raise their selection probabilities over common ones? Here, associationists have invoked the concept of *self-reinforcement.* According to this principle, responses that occur without either selection or rejection reinforce themselves, and so by being selected less frequently, uncommon responses generate more self-reinforcement than common responses. In addition, all uncommon responses are associated to one another by virtue of their uncommonness rather than only by their semantic relationships. That means, *all* uncommon responses get reinforced when *any one* of them is reinforced, regardless of semantic class! For example, Maltzman, Simon, Raskin, and Licht (1960) showed how instructions and training in "giving uncommon responses" induced subjects to do just that. At this point, however, associationism has introduced so many additional assumptions to the original S-R formulation that its original advantage of simplicity is compromised.

This apparent inadequacy of associationism to provide a satisfactory account of innovative thinking does not disqualify S-R theory altogether. The reason it emerged so early and continued to dominate models of memory and cognition for centuries is that associational mechanisms seem to be necessary for the performance of many acts of memory and, therefore, thinking. We have all, at times, used mnemonic devices of various kinds to help us remember things. The regularity and consistency of word association norms points to a long-term memory structure of S-R connections, and the experimental results we have presented in this section offer strong evidence for such linkages. However, other theories of cognition seem more apt in explaining certain kinds of thinking that strict S-R structures are hard-put to deal with. Gestalt theory is one of these.

Gestalt Theory

Gestalt (literally, "whole shape") is built on a holistic conception of mental processes. Perception of form, in this view, is not merely the summation of components, but rather a comprehension of complete structures that are more than the sum of their parts. We saw the principle at work in perception (Chapter 6). Now we see this fundamental principle applied to the processes of thinking and problem solving.

Gestaltists recognize two kinds of thinking: *reproductive* (recapitulation of old knowledge by rote) and *productive* (bringing imagination and the ingenious use of knowledge to bear on new problems). Wertheimer (1959), one of the seminal Gestalt theorists, wrote the classical exposition of productive thinking. He developed the dynamics of learning and problem solving through detailed examples of the acquisition and use of mathematical and logical concepts. The Gestalt key to Wertheimer's method is in the visualization of the problem. In this view, the solution is almost a by-product of the comprehension of the problem-structure. The way children solve the problem of determining the area of a parallelogram, as shown in Figure 10-6, illustrates this principle. After they learn that the formula for rectangles is area equals base times height ($A = b \times h$), they must see the complementary relationship between the triangle at the left and the triangular space at the right side of the figure. This relationship is the key to the solution. Wertheimer sees the two triangles as points of structural disturbance—focal points whose deviation or eccentricity draws attention to the reorganization necessary to reach the solution.

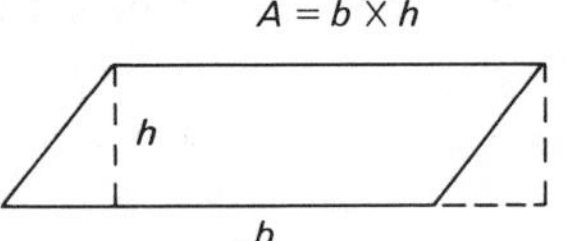

Fig. 10-6 This figure illustrates the Gestalt approach to determining the area of a parallelogram.

The structure of the problem must be understood by the solver, so the trial-and-error experience that associationists use as the source of correct S-R linkages has no place in Gestalt processes. This distinction is demonstrated in Köhler's (1927) classic experiment with the caged ape, who manipulated two sticks ineffectually in efforts to reach and retrieve a banana outside the cage just out of reach of each stick. His failures did not lead to a solution until he had a flash of "insight" resulting from several informative attempts to fit the sticks together. Once the ape recognized the potential function of the sticks when joined, he quickly fitted them together and with the joined sticks poked the banana close enough to grasp. The solution did not emerge as a result of trial-and-error accident, but as a direct consequence of recognition of function. Chance may create useful arrangements, but they are neither necessary nor sufficient for problem solving.

Like the associationists, Gestaltists depend on the goal to motivate and direct the problem-solving process. However, unlike the association chains composed of discrete S-R links, the Gestalt sequence of thoughts or movements is continuous and uniform, sometimes describes as a "melody." Success is the result of insight into the demands of each task. Thus, perception and thought are unified. Correct perception of structure and function are essential to the experience of "seeing the light"—Wertheimer's metaphorical description of insight.

The problem-solving process is largely dependent on the subject's flexibility and skill in perception. If a solution does not emerge from the first view of the situation, the perception must be revised by regrouping or reorganizing parts and relations and by taking a creative, unstereotyped view of object functions related to problem requirements.

Maier (1931) devised an ingenious problem to illustrate the role of changing perceptions. Two cords are hung from the ceiling at a distance apart that makes it impossible to grasp the free ends and bring them together. The problem requires that the ends be tied together. Several objects are also in the room: poles, ringstands, clamps, pliers, extension cords, tables, and chairs. The solution is to use the pliers as a weight, tie them to the end of one of the cords, and then swing the cord like a pendulum so that it can reach and be caught by the subject holding the end of the other cord.

Solving this problem requires a new perception of the function of the pliers, not their standard use as a tool, but the application of an otherwise incidental attribute: weight. It also requires a special perception of the cords, which have a variety of functions, including their use as pendulums. If the subject could not work out the solution in a reasonable time, two hints were given at intervals: (1) the pliers were tied to one cord and twirled, not swung; (2) one of the cords, without pliers attached, was set in motion. The first hint was presented as a "suggestion," while the second was done casually, without calling attention to it.

Some subjects reached the solution as a whole, in one step. They recalled the twirling suggestion, but had no recollection of the swinging cord hint. They credited the twirling action for helping toward the solution. Maier points to this as evidence of unconscious problem solving, because they had not been able to solve the problem after the twirling, but only after the subsequent pendulum hint of which they were apparently unaware. The appropriate organization of the factors is unconscious. Moreover, previous similar problem solutions may either help or hinder, since the subject's thinking converges on a repetition of an unproductive idea with small variations (problem-solving set).

In the Maier experiment, the subjects had to overcome the blinding effect of *functional fixedness,* in which the normal function of an object (the pliers as a tool) prevents them from perceiving other functions (the pliers as a weight). To discover how the function became fixed in the subject's mind, Adamson (1952) presented another problem: Three open cardboard boxes, three candles, some matches, and thumbtacks were displayed. The subject was asked to mount the candles on the wall in some way, and light them. One group of subjects received the boxes containing the matches, candles, and tacks; another group got the empty boxes, along with the other items. Thus, the first group was handicapped (functionally) by seeing the boxes used as containers. The solution required attaching the boxes to the wall with the tacks and then setting the candles in the boxes. The boxes served as shelves instead of containers.

There were twice as many successful solvers in the empty-box group as in the box-as-container group, and the former's solution times were substantially lower. Adamson concludes that "preutilization" (showing the object in a use not suitable for solving the problem) is the critical factor in predisposing subjects to functional fixedness.

The experiments we have reviewed in this section are demonstrations of what the Gestalt experimenters claim is a holistic, or insight, process of problem solving. However, they do not really *explain* what is going on in the process of developing the solution (as the associationists try to do with their hierarchical structures). Gestalt theory failed to integrate its useful laws of perception into a total explanation of cognitive processes and has been overshadowed by later developments in neoassociationism, concept formation, and information processing.

Information Processing

The advent of the computer inspired new ways of thinking about human thought processes. Claude Shannon's original analysis of the nature of information (Shannon & Weaver, 1949) provided the means for dealing with the human mind as an articulated system dedicated to solving problems by logical processes that could be reduced to stepwise procedures. It was inevitable that this would lead to a resurgence of mechanistic S-R models of thinking and problem solving.

The object of the diverse attempts to imitate, or simulate, human thinking processes with computer programs has been to determine the actual minimal processing functions that would be necessary for performing various cognitive tasks. If, for example, the computer could learn (that is, categorize, discriminate, and store in a systematic way) and use a concept appropriately in working out a problem or answering a question, then we would have a clearer understanding of what kind of mental processes are going on or could be going on in our heads when we think through similar tasks. At the very least, the necessarily precise definitions and rules of information theory sharpened experimental methods and theorizing in cognitive research. We will now see the progress and limitations that have developed in the course of investigating information processing by means of computer simulation of thinking.

Information theory opened the way to two parallel lines of research. One was the development of information processing models postulating stages of cognitive behavior of the kind described in Chapters 6, 8, and 9. The second consisted of a succession of attempts to simulate human problem solving with computer programs. Outstanding developers in this work, which John McCarthy dubbed *artificial intelligence,* included Newell, Simon, Reitman, Hunt, Feigenbaum, and McCarthy. We will see how these two approaches have influenced each other.

Getting data into the computer *(input)* is the first step in the data processing sequence. The first step in the human information processing sequence is perception of the object of interest. Because it is not an integral part of the logic apparatus, we note it here in passing merely to acknowledge its place in the total process. Chapter 6 presents a more detailed discussion of perceptual mechanisms.

We assume for our present purpose that the sensory percepts have been processed into usable data that is now "food for thought." At once we face the problem of packaging and transmitting that data as efficiently as possible (i.e., with minimal loss of definition and content). This raises questions about processing capacity, which is analyzed here in terms of information processing concepts.

In his essay on "The Magical Number Seven," Miller (1956) relates what he calls the *span of immediate memory* to an information processing dimension called *channel capacity,* that is, the extent of our capability for making sensible judgments about incoming data. He reviews a number of experiments and concludes that short-term memory capacity has a limit of about seven (plus or minus two) unrelated items. That capacity can be increased, however, by recoding items into *chunks* of information. In order to recode, items must be related to one another by some well-learned system that permits chunking, such as grouping a string of letters into a meaningful word, recoding binary digits into decimal digits, or remembering strings of four digits by historical association to years (e.g., recognizing 1776 as an important date).

Two other information theorists of note, Simon and Feigenbaum (1964; Simon, 1974), extended the chunking process from short-term memory into long-term memory. They showed how it is possible to predict learning times for three-letter nonsense syllables (three chunks) compared to three-letter words (single chunks). To make the prediction, they developed the Elementary Perceiver and Memorizer (EPAM), a computer-programmed memory simulator that breaks down the learning process into discrete steps. These steps include learning to recognize the stimulus, learning to recognize the response for recall, and learning to compound the pair into an associative unit. In learning nonsense syllable pairs, such as *reh-giz,* in which the first trigram, *reh,* is the test-cue for the associated response *giz,* the first step is forming an image of the pair (familiarization). Discrimination learning occurs when a similar trigram cue is met on the list, say, *ruz-fot,* which has an identical initial *r.* Here, the second or third letter must be used for discrimination. The EPAM program then builds a "tree" with separate nodes for each cue as the basis for correct sorting and recognition during subsequent testing.

As Simon and others have pointed out, it is chunking that enables chess experts to reconstruct whole arrangements of pieces in games played or studied long before. Placement of pieces takes longer and is less accurate when the situation on the board is less critical with respect to the outcome. Presumably, when the board situation presents the threat of loss of an important game-piece or of a check-mate, the locations of the individual pieces are remembered better because of their critical relationship to the threat, each relationship between pieces constituting a chunk. The pieces most closely related to the pattern of attack or defense are placed faster than incidental pieces in tests of game recall. The repertory of familiar game-position chunks in a grand master's memory has been estimated at between 25,000 and 100,000—approximately the lexical vocabulary of an educated adult.

Data Versus Resource Limitations. The vital question of processing capacity has been broken down by Norman and Bobrow (1975) into two distinct types of limitations: limitations on *data* and limitations on *resources.* Limitations on data may be produced by presenting stimuli for too short a period, as in tachistoscopic recognition experiments (see Chapter 6), by presenting stimuli against a visual or auditory noise background or preceded or followed by a noise mask, or by testing memory for items after a long delay, when the memory trace is weak. Limitations on resources (lack of processing capacity) may be produced by overloading attention or short-term memory.

An experimental example of resource-limited performance produced by overloading attentional capacity is the dichotic listening task used by Treisman and Geffen (1967). The subject heard two different, simultaneous spoken messages on two earphone channels. He was to repeat aloud *(shadow)* the message heard in one ear (the primary channel) and signal whenever he heard a designated target word that had been inserted into the message presented to the other ear (secondary channel). Performance in shadowing the primary message was usually excellent, indicating ample auditory resources for processing the primary message. However, performance on the secondary message was poor, indicating that the remaining processing resources were inadequate. (There was no deficiency in the clarity of the messages on both channels, hence, no data limitation.)

An example of resource-limited performance by overloading short-term memory capacity can be found in an experiment by Baddeley and Hitch (1974). They taxed what they call "working memory" with a double load. While reciting either a sequence of six random digits, changed on every trial, or the consecutive digits "1-2-3-4-5-6" repeatedly, the subject had to perform a visually presented reasoning task. (Example: "*A* is not preceded by *B—AB*." Answer: TRUE.) The random-digit recitation interfered with the reasoning task and increased the true-false reasoning reaction times above those for consecutive-digits, but the consecutive digits task did not increase reaction times over the reasoning-only (no digits) control condition. This indicates an overload of a resource-limited workspace, which can be allocated either to storage or to processing. The 1-through-6 counting sequence apparently required less memory space (it was probably stored as one chunk rather than the six chunks for the random digits), and so the working memory was adequate for the reasoning task in that case.

Computer Simulations of Human Problem-Solving Models. Many models of human problem-solving have been tested by simulating them on a computer. *A computer simulation* is a program that incorporates the processes thought to be engaged in by a human problem solver. The object is to set up a program that will receive and process the given problem data and compute a correct solution. The types of problems vary, from learning-and-recall tests to drawing conclusions about spatial relations between objects or about logical statements (syllogisms, symbolic logic, and so on). One test of whether the simulation is adequate is to determine whether the computer makes the same types of errors as human subjects do. According to computer simulation developers, the program is the theory, and the simulated performance by the computer validates the theory. But does it? We will consider the question after we have looked at several programs.

One of the earliest attempts to imitate human thinking was Newell, Shaw, and Simon's (1957) Logic Theorist. This information processing program was able to solve logic problems. (It proved theorems in Whitehead & Russell's *Principia Mathematica.*) The Logic Theorist used both logical rules and heuristic methods. The rules were used to generate guesses at likely proofs, and then algorithms (standardized, finite, stepwise procedures, much like cookbook recipes) were applied to work through the proof. This is a heuristic, or selective trial-and-error, approach.

In answer to the challenge to demonstrate more general problem-solving skills, Newell et al. developed the General Problem Solver (GPS) (1959). (A simple description appears in Newell & Simon, 1961.) This is a sophisticated and highly elaborate system that simulates human methods of problem solving. GPS uses a heuristic method called means-ends analysis. As indicated previously, a heuristic is a selective search of certain relations that indicates an approach to the goal. Means-ends analysis compares the present state with the goal and tries to reduce the difference, or distance, between the two by setting up subgoals or subproblems that lead to the main goal. Subproblems are solved by applying certain operations to the objects in the problem. The operators are various arithmetic functions and mathematico-logical transformations. By a means-ends analysis, these are applied to *differences* detected between objects, in order to transform object A into object B or to reduce the difference between A and B.

A simplified example will illustrate how the means-ends analysis works. Imagine you want to change a burnt-out light bulb in a ceiling fixture. There is a ladder in the closet in the same room. Reduced to essentials, these are the conditions you meet en route to the solution of the problem:

1. Distance between floor and ceiling fixture.
2. Distance between ladder (in closet) and point under light fixture.
3. Distance between you and ladder.
4. Closed closet door impeding access to ladder.

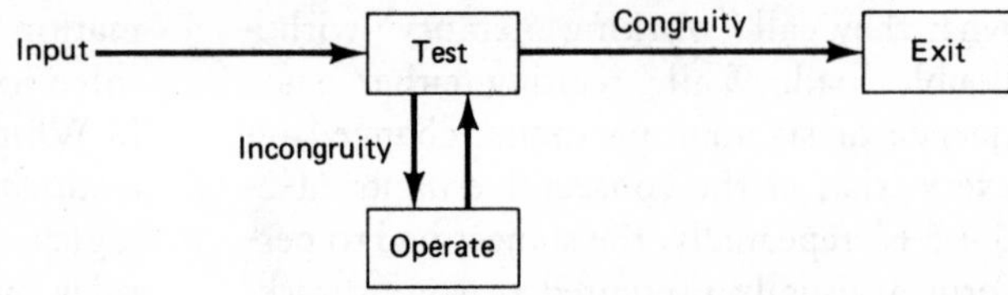

Fig. 10-7 The TOTE loop proposed by Miller, Galanter, and Pribram (1960).

5. Ladder's inanimate state (no locomotive capability).

These differences between existing and necessary conditions can each be eliminated by application of appropriate operators:

1. Get ladder into position under fixture. This breaks down into subgoals:
   a. *Walk* (operator applied to distance/difference between you and closet).
   b. *Open* (operator applied to closed door).
   c. *Remove* (operator applied to difference between ladder in closet and its desired position outside of closet).
   d. *Carry* (operator applied to immobility of ladder).
   e. *Climb* (operator applied to distance/difference between you and ceiling fixture).

In their GPS program, Newell and his colleagues developed an algebraic system for expressing operators and their functions according to mathematical rules. This enabled them to abstract various types of problems in a form that could be solved or proved by the program.

At about the same time Newell, Shaw, and Simon were designing their GPS, Miller, Galanter, and Pribram (1960) were working on a feedback model of behavior, called Test-Operate-Test-Exit (TOTE), that showed how human knowledge is translated into action. Their book, *Plans and the Structure of Behavior,* had a decisive influence on the development of information processing approaches to problem solving. There is a parallel between the way GPS *transformations* operate to reduce differences between objects and the way TOTE *plans* reduce differences between existing and desired states. Miller et al. postulate an *image* representing all of the organized world knowledge accumulated by an individual along with a repertory of *plans* for accomplishing desired objectives.

The *plans* follow a basic operating pattern—a recursive feedback loop, along whose connecting paths energy, information, and control are transmitted. As in the GPS operation, differences are tested and reduced by appropriate operations. Example: A nailhead sticking up is hammered. After each blow, the nail is tested for *incongruity*—is it level with the board? If not, the operation is repeated (another hammer blow). This is the recursive procedure: test-operate-test. When the state of the nailhead is *congruous* (level with the board), the plan switches to *exit.* The TOTE sequence is shown in Figure 10-7.

The goal of every TOTE plan is equilibrium or equalization, which corresponds to the essential principle of homeostasis described in Chapter 7 that governs mind and body functions. If this mechanistic model or any other simulation realistically represents the workings of human intelligence, then we may hope for the eventual development of a computer that will indeed be capable of behaviors that approximate human cognition. However, TOTE is not intended to reproduce all human behavior. For one thing, it does not explain or mimic emotional responses or affects. Most of the information processing models, human and artificial, ignore emotional influences.

Another feature of human cognition that is omitted from most artificial processing models is loss or change of memory items with the passage of time—the general notion of *decay.* One single-purpose simulation, called ARGUS, incorporates a rather limited treatment of such decay effects in memory.

The ARGUS program by Reitman (1965) is dedicated to the solution of analogies of the form A is to B as C is to (select one of four alternatives), symbolically represented as A:B::C: (W, X, Y, or Z). An example is book:page::flower: (leaves, *petals,* stem, roots). An *executive* program generates the analogies according to a set of rules. The words are contained in stored lists of semantic items that include associations and their strength values and relations.

A unique feature of ARGUS that makes its otherwise limited ability of psychological interest is a technique for determining and modifying the current state of the semantic items with respect to *activation.* Activation is represented by a value stored with each item, which is increased each time the item is used in a solution, and which is automatically diminished ("decays") with the passage of time, according to an arbitrary formula. These changing values determine interactive conflicts (e.g., interference between semantically similar or synonymous items), which are resolved by choosing the item with the highest net activation. The use of the semantic units creates "time-line" entries that record the sequence of events, decaying with the passage of time. The net effect is to favor more commonly used words, as is the general case with human memory.

Hunt (1962) designed a concept learning system that stores attributes of each stimulus in memory as they are presented on input. It keeps track of positive ("correct") and negative ("wrong") instances, storing them after each trial. It constructs a decision rule, using a *conditional focusing* routine, as follows:

1. It scans stored instances to determine common attributes that are *exclusive* to *either* positive or negative instances.
2. If exclusive common attributes are found, it uses them to form a decision rule.
3. If not found, it uses common attribute x occurring *most frequently* among positive instances in association with attribute y found exclusively among positive instances.
4. If found, it forms rule based on x and y combination.
5. If not found, it tries again with another high-frequency positive attribute . . .

To demonstrate the procedure in a simplified case, we apply it to the problem of learning to discriminate the concept *cake* from the concept *bread.* There are cakes that resemble bread and breads that are quite cakelike, so we are not able to satisfy the requirements of exclusive attributes in steps 1 and 2. We can find several attributes, such as "sweet" and "soft crust," that are more frequently associated with cake than bread. And we might consider "flavored" (vanilla, chocolate, etc.) as an attribute of cake exclusively associated with the attribute "sweet" to form the required $x + y$ combination in steps 3 and 4, thereby giving us the basis on which the computer could learn the concept for future discrimination problems. Here we have a trial-and-error algorithm that resembles the kind of strategies humans use in concept formation tasks.

As you can see, all computer-based problem-solving programs are of necessity mechanistic—that is, the response decisions are relatively rigid and limited. The computer is a finite machine whose programs are essentially algorithms (i.e., a set of sequential instructions that lead to a result, much like a recipe). Every routine (that term aptly characterizes the process) is constrained by arbitrary limits established by a predetermined method. In contrast to the complexities of human judgment, the decision parameters that determine choice and stopping rules are limited in number and effect on the computer's decision process, even though their values may be varied according to differences in tasks.

In all these instances it is the computer program that attempts to simulate human thought processes (within the limits of the computer). These simulations often have perfect memory, although as we have seen in the ARGUS program described earlier, we can easily simulate the decay or loss of memory for particular items characteristic of human thought by incorporating decay parameters into the computer program. These programs as well as other (noncomputer) models of behavior attempt to simulate human behavior. Their successes and failures help us to understand how the human mind functions, or at least how it might be functioning.

Are Computer Simulations Valid Theories of Human Thinking? You will notice that each of the various simulation programs offers special features designed to mimic certain aspects of human behavior, even to the modest attempt at injecting word frequency and decay variables into the ARGUS program. But yet, the central question remains: If a computer program imitates the results obtained by a human, does that constitute an explanation or theory of human cognitive behavior? The computer's mechanistic functions form an approximation of S-R associations as memory linkages and retrieval devices. How much of human thinking and problem solving does S-R theory explain?

The computer's system stores information items in hierarchical memory structures, called lists. In spite of the hierarchical similarity, the lists do not have the semantic associations that work like the networks in human memory. Finally, it is not possible to verify the human equivalence to the computer's performance by direct comparison with the performance of a human subject on the same task. The computer's architecture and operations do not even approximate the human brain, so whatever the computer does in solving a problem gives us no picture of the relationship between thinking and physiology. At best, it gives us a set of logical operations that can be used to get the answer. All we can do is compare the computer program itself with our subjects' reported protocols. Still, students of human cognition working in the area of artificial intelligence are unanimous in claiming useful insights for developing models of human thought processes and in promising closer approximations as the technology of information processing advances.

LANGUAGE AND THOUGHT

In this section, we will consider two of the functions of language: its constraints on thinking, and its verbal mediation effects in facilitating or inhibiting problem solving. Both functions have been the object of formal study and psychological experimentation for a century or more.

The name most notably associated with the constraints of language on thought is Benjamin Whorf, who developed what is known as the Whorfian hypothesis of *linguistic relativity* (Whorf, 1956). This much-quoted thesis asserts that thought is shaped by the language in which it is couched. In Whorf's own words:

> The background linguistic system (in other words, the grammar) of each language is not merely a reproducing instrument for voicing ideas but rather is itself the shaper of ideas, the program and guide for the individual's mental activity, for his analysis of impressions, for his synthesis of his mental stock in trade. Formulation of ideas is not an independent process, strictly rational in the old sense, but is part of a particular grammar and differs . . . as between different grammars. *We dissect nature along lines laid down by our native language.*
>
> (Whorf, 1956, p. 106. Emphasis added.)

Fishman (1960) analyzed the Whorfian hypothesis into four levels of effects:

Level 1—The effects of *vocabulary* on world view. On this level we find that the Eskimo's score of words for different kinds of snow should make precise communication possible with regard to snow, which is extremely important in their culture. As another example, the Trobriand Islanders have separate names for the maternal and paternal uncle. This is important because in this culture the maternal uncle is responsible for the nephew's discipline (Malinowski, 1927).

Level 2—The effects of *vocabulary* on

nonlinguistic endeavor, specifically memory. Brown and Lenneberg (1954) tested the ability of English speakers to recognize colors that were exposed for a short duration. Recognition was tested by having the subjects pick out the colors they had seen from an array of 120 Munsell color chips. Recognizability was predicted by a variable they call *codability*—the degree to which speakers agree with one another, and with themselves, on the name a color should be called. The importance of codability in recognition increased with the number of to-be-remembered colors (from one to four), and the interval between presentation and test (from 7 seconds to 3 minutes). This study thus showed that speakers remember colors by naming them, and that the more reliable that name is, the better recognition can be. In a parallel study with Zuni Indians, Lenneberg and Roberts (1953) showed that Zuni subjects, who code orange and yellow with a single color name, often confused the two colors in the recognition test, while English speakers virtually never did so.

Similarly, Glanzer and Clark (1963a) found evidence that subjects encoded abstract visual patterns verbally and that the length of such encoding influenced their ability to reconstruct the pattern. They proposed a *verbal loop,* from experience to coding and back to reproduction of the experience. Their subjects produced verbal descriptions that varied in complexity. Further, there was a negative correlation between accuracy of reproduction and length of description. Patterns that required only two-word descriptions were reproduced with 100% accuracy whereas those that required eight-word descriptions were reproduced with only 15% accuracy.

Level 3—The effects of *grammar* on world view. The Navaho language does not make the subject-verb-object distinctions that the English language (among others) does. This is taken as evidence for different points of view regarding activity and control of behavior.

Level 4—The effects of *grammar* on nonlinguistic behavior. Carroll and Casagrande (1958) studied Navaho children, whose language uses different verb forms for objects of different shapes and rigidity. An object (A) was presented which was similar to a second (B) in color and to a third (C) in shape. The question was, would *A* be grouped with *B*, which had a similar color, or with *C*, which had a similar shape? Since shape is distinguished by Navaho verb forms and color is not, we would expect an A-C grouping based on shape. This was the actual result. Shape dominated and dictated Navaho classification.

A more explicit demonstration of verbal mediation in problem solving is provided by an experiment by Glucksberg and Weisberg (1966) designed to eliminate the functional fixedness that prevented subjects from perceiving the use of a box of tacks as a candleholder when tacked to the wall. Labels *(box, tacks, candles)* were attached to the items. Subjects who received the verbal labels were more likely to solve the problem than subjects who did not have the labels. The identification of the box without reference to its contents apparently allowed the subjects to perceive the box separately and recognize its shelf-like attributes, even when filled with tacks.

The strong influence of descriptive coding in object labels, demonstrated in Glanzer and Clark's verbal loop experiment, was first shown in a study by Carmichael, Hogan, and Walter (1932). Each of two groups of subjects saw a series of 12 outline drawings paired with one of two alternative verbal descriptions. Each drawing was ambiguous enough so that either description was appropriate. The 12 drawings, with their two descriptions, are shown in Figure 10-8.

The series of figures was presented one at a time, accompanied by the appropriate description, and then subjects attempted to recall the figures by drawing them from memory. The procedure was repeated until all 12 drawings could be reproduced. The number of trials required for reproduction of the complete set ranged from two to eight. (Note that this procedure is just like free recall of a list of words, except that

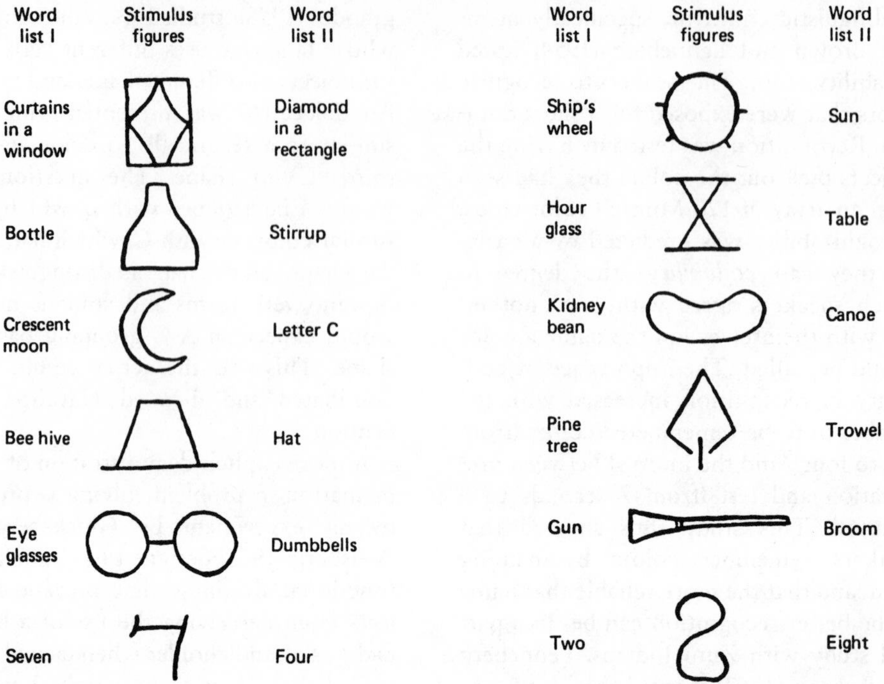

Fig. 10-8 The twelve drawings, with their two alternative descriptions, used by Carmichael, Hogan, and Walter in a study of the effect of language on reproduction of visual form. (From "An Experimental Study of the Effect of Language on the Reproducton of Visually Perceived Form," by L. Carmichael, H. P. Hogan, and A. A. Walter. In *Journal of Experimental Psychology,* 1932, *55,* 73–86. Copyright 1932 by the American Psychological Association. Reprinted by permission.)

here the recall response is drawing the figure rather than writing the word.) Reproduction of objects from memory showed a pronounced influence of the particular name presented with the figure. For example, the drawing of two circles connected by a straight line and labeled *eye glasses* for one group and *dumbbell* for the second group was reproduced by the first group with clear features of eyeglasses and by the second group with clear features of a dumbbell. Based on the ratings of two independent judges, about 75% of the reproduced figures resembled the description read to the subject as opposed to the alternative description.

These studies point to the role of language in constraining and mediating thought. Language is also necessary for reasoning and problem solving, memory mnemonics, and the coding that permits abstracting attributes and identifying objects, to say nothing of its role in making remote reference possible, so that we can make plans and influence the thoughts of others. At the same time, we must acknowledge that some of the theoretical links between verbal and other kinds of encoding are missing. We are not clear on the mechanism of verbal mediation on behavior. As if that were not enough to complicate our study of language and thinking, there is growing recognition of the influence of genetic and physiological factors on language (for a detailed discussion, see the section on hemispheric specialization in Chapter 6). As with the other areas we have reviewed, much more research is needed to answer these questions.

SUMMARY

In this chapter, two kinds of reasoning are considered—deductive and inductive reasoning. In deductive reasoning problems, subjects are given a general rule and asked to apply it to selected cases. In inductive reasoning problems, subjects are presented with specific cases and asked to determine the general rule. Inductive reasoning problems are usually exercises in concept formation.

Psychologists who study deductive reasoning have concentrated their efforts on syllogisms, three-term series problems, and hypothesis testing. A syllogism is a conclusion deduced from two premises. Errors in syllogistic reasoning can be produced by the way in which the premises are stated, as well as by probabilistic inferences or arbitrary changes in the premises made by the subjects.

A three-term series problem is like a syllogism in presenting two premises from which a deduction is required. However it also incorporates relational terms in its expressions. Three principal theories have been proposed to explain the process of reasoning in three-term series problems: (1) an operational model, which is based on the transitivity principle, (2) an image model, which is based on the spatial visualization of the premises, and (3) a linguistic model, which is based on deep-structure and other lexical conditions involved in comparative relations.

Hypothesis testing strategies used in deductive reasoning have been examined to obtain clues about the reasoning process. One major finding is that subjects fail to generate disconfirming cases in testing the hypothesis, even though these are most likely to provide information necessary for solution.

Investigations of inductive reasoning have concentrated on concept formation experiments. A concept is a set of attributes that defines a class. Studies of concept formation follow either reception or selection paradigms. Selection task strategies often involve various scanning and focusing procedures and are influenced by memory load and subjects' skills.

Three representative theories of thought processing are reviewed. The first, associationism, is a stimulus-response model. This model relies on a feedback mechanism that provides for anticipation of the goal stimulus (reinforcement), which in turn directs the intermediate responses toward the goal. These anticipatory responses become chained into habit family hierarchies. In addition, the anticipatory responses are generalized to other response patterns. One result of reinforcement of the response pattern is a form of mental fixedness called problem-solving set.

The second theory of thought processing is the Gestalt theory. This theory explains two kinds of thinking—reproductive (rote) and productive (imaginative and insightful). This view maintains that perception is not merely the sum of components but rather the comprehension of a complete structure, which is more than the sum of its parts. It follows from this that if a solution does not emerge from the first view of the problem, the perception must be revised by reorganizing parts and relationships between the parts. This ultimately yields a creative, unstereotyped view of object functions related to problem-solving requirements.

The third theory of thought processing is the information processing theory. This system compares human thinking to computer data processing. Information processing models take account of input and processing capacity (the latter can be increased by chunking techniques). Computer simulations provide tests of these computer models. Critics have questioned the appropriateness of making analogies between mental and computer processes.

Finally, we discuss the limiting effects of language on thinking. Some have proposed that the available words in a particular language shape thinking, while contributing to the fostering of culturally determined views. This principle of the importance of language in determining a world view, usually attributed to Whorf, is known as linguistic relativity.

This chapter considered the broad areas of thinking, reasoning, and problem solving as they relate to experimental psychology. We considered purposeful thinking as it relates to problem solving. In addition, theories of thought processes—how we think—and the relationship between language and thought were explored.

11

Applying Experimental Methods to Other Areas in Psychology

Throughout this textbook our focus has been on the *pure research* associated with human experimental psychology. The areas of interest we have discussed are concerned primarily with how humans can perceive, store, and use information. The chapters on perception explored how sensory information is analyzed by the mind; the chapters on memory explored some possible ways we store and retrieve information; and the chapters on learning and problem solving explored the ways we acquire knowledge and use it to solve problems. Most of the experiments presented there are pure in the sense that their main purpose is to increase scientific knowledge. Understanding how the human mind works has motivated this research.

In some ways pure or basic research can be considered somewhat contrived. Areas of interest are defined without regard to any specific real-life problems. However, the methods used to successfully answer these questions are often used in more applied areas. All research, to be meaningful, depends on the basic experimental principles we have presented. Good research is the only meaningful way to solve scientific problems. A poorly designed experiment, regardless of the field, tells us nothing.

Applied research, as its name implies, is devoted to finding answers to existing problems. For example, the pure researcher studies the visual system to learn how people recognize letters or words, whereas the applied researcher tries to improve the visual characteristics of letters to help children overcome reading difficulties. Both scientists are interested in the characteristics of the visual system, both have meaningful questions to answer, and both generate and test hypotheses in reasonable and valid ways. Generally, the applied researchers are more restricted in their choice of subjects, stimuli, and experimental design because their goal is to solve existing problems. This can lead to experimental results that are not always generalizable but do resolve specific problems. In contrast, the pure researcher frequently ends up with a generalizable result that has theoretical significance but whose conclusions are not always clearly applicable to specific problems.

This chapter briefly describes four areas of applied research in the specializations of social psychology, industrial organizations, clinical issues, and parapsychology. These topics are selected from the many areas of applied research and will illustrate some of the ways in which the methods of basic research can be applied to more practical applied areas of research.

RESEARCH IN SOCIAL PSYCHOLOGY

Social psychology employs many of the same research techniques as experimental psychology. Social psychology is dedicated to understanding how the individual behaves in particular environments that are social in nature or that include other people. The question asked by the social psychologist is how the particular individual will react to the stimulus of another person or persons in social situations, whereas the question asked by the experimental psychologist is how the individual will react to the stimulus of information that must be perceived, learned, or used to solve problems.

Experimental psychology seeks to establish functional relationships between the properties of the physical world and basic human psychological processes. In social psychology the main focus is the functional relationship between the properties of the social world and basic human psychological processes. Far from being an independent discipline, social psychology is intimately tied to experimental psychology. It seeks to quantify and qualify a science of social behavior based on our growing knowledge of how humans think, perceive, act, and react. In effect, one can consider social psychology the extension of laboratory findings to the real world.

Experiments in social psychology can be done in laboratories where researchers create and manipulate groups or in the field where groups already exist for the social psychologist to study. Laboratory studies usually provide more experimental control; however, it can be difficult to create realistic group situations. On the other hand, field experiments, which are often more realistic, usually provide less experimental control.

One special problem associated with research in social psychology is the need to thoroughly debrief the subject. Often, as we shall illustrate, it is necessary to deceive subjects about the situation they are in. As a result of these experiments, subjects often discover aspects of their own behavior that are not usually obvious and are not always flattering. If these revealed traits are unfavorable or viewed as undesirable by the subjects, then participation in the experiment might make them lose self-esteem, generate self-doubts, and so forth. In these experiments it is incumbent on the researcher to make sure that every subject is completely and carefully debriefed at the end of the session. Reasons for the deception should be thoroughly explained and all questions should be discussed. Participation in an experiment should never have the effect of negatively altering subjects' views about themselves. Failing to properly debrief subjects is unethical and irresponsible.

Regardless of their differences, research in human experimental psychology and social psychology share many properties. In both fields the principles of experimental design are appropriate and important.

First, to illustrate some of these principles we shall review a laboratory and a field experiment on *conformity,* the effect of group behavior on an individual's judgment or behavior. We will review Solomon Asch's (1951, 1955, 1956) classic studies. In his laboratory he created well-controlled experiments that explored the interaction of individuals with their social environments. Although conducted in the laboratory, his work is very relevant to what does happen "in the field." We will then review a field study by Milgram, Bickman, and Berkowitz (1969), which explores the relationship between conformity and group size. This study provides an interesting example of a well-controlled field experiment on conformity.

A second area we will discuss is eyewitness testimony. Research in this aspect of our judicial process provides another application of the methods of experimental psychology to social psychology. Several studies have explored various characteristics of eyewitness testimony. The accuracy of eyewitnesses' perception and reports of events and people is often a main component of jury trials. Research in this area has been divided into two types: system-variable research and estimator-variable research (Wells, 1978). We will discuss two experiments using simulated crimes to explore variables that affect eyewitness accuracy (Loftus & Palmer, 1974; Hosch & Cooper, 1982). As we shall see, the application of experimental methodology to this social institution is appropriate and important.

Conformity

In his classic laboratory experiments, Asch (1951, 1955, 1956) had subjects choose which of three lines matched a stimulus (standard) line. He chose the lines so that the correct choice would be obvious. Each subject had to respond aloud after hearing the responses of the other eight "subjects" in the room. Unknown to the subject, these other subjects were *confederates* given special instructions before taking part in this experiment. The purpose of his experiments was to study group influences on decision making. For most of the judgments, the confederates gave the wrong answer deliberately and usually unanimously. Thus, this experiment was designed to investigate the extent to which a person would answer correctly after hearing the eight preceding subjects make mistakes.

The results showed a strong influence of the majority. One third of the judgments made by the subjects were errors, which were identical to or in the same direction as those of the incorrect majority. The per-

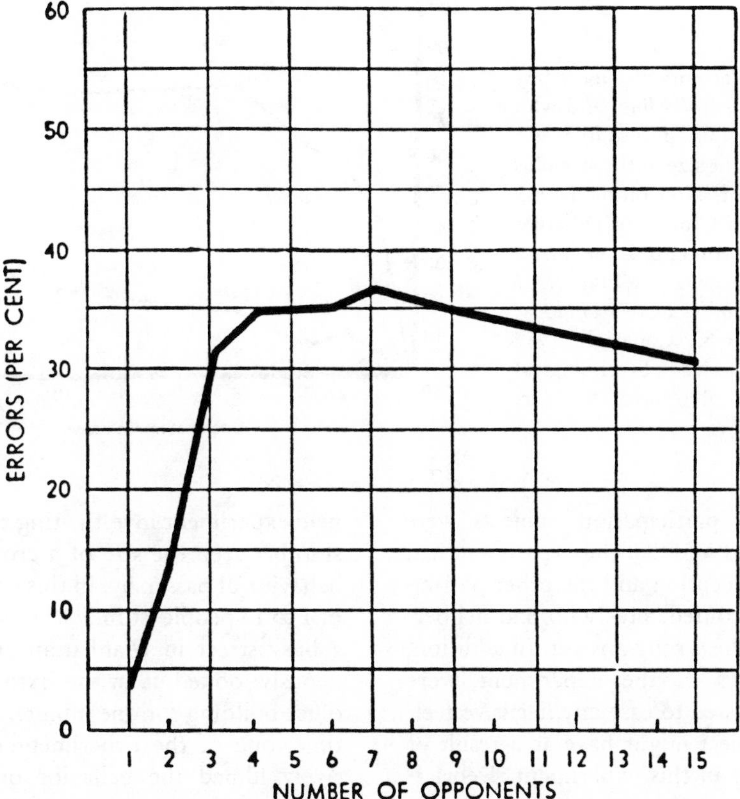

Fig. 11-1 The effect of the size of the majority on the percentage of errors made by subjects in perceptual judgments. With only one opponent, the error percentage is small, but when the number increases beyond two, the error rates increase rapidly to about 30% or more. (From "Size of Majority" by S. E. Asch. In *Scientific American*, November, 1955, *193*, 31–35. Copyright 1955 by W. H. Freeman and Company. Reprinted by permission.)

formance of subjects in a control group, which reported their judgments in writing, was almost error-free. In addition, large individual differences were found. Some subjects always maintained their independence whereas others consistently followed the clearly wrong majority. In follow-up interviews, subjects stated that they knew the majority had been incorrect but followed them anyway.

Figure 11-1 shows the relationship between the number of confederates (opponents) who preceded the subjects' answer with the wrong answer, and the percentage of subjects' errors. When the size of the incorrect majority was manipulated, the influence of group behavior on the individual increased as the group size increased, up to a group size of three. Thus, only one individual had a very small influence on the subject's behavior, a group of two had a substantially greater influence, and a group of three had an even greater influence. As the size of the group continued to increase beyond three, the influence of the group on the individual's behavior remained constant.

These studies show the effect of the size and behavior of the majority on the minority. In summary, even when the majority was clearly wrong and the situation was not of much consequence (i.e., nothing tangible in the person's life depended on "succeeding") subjects preferred to be part of a majority that was wrong to being a minority that was correct.

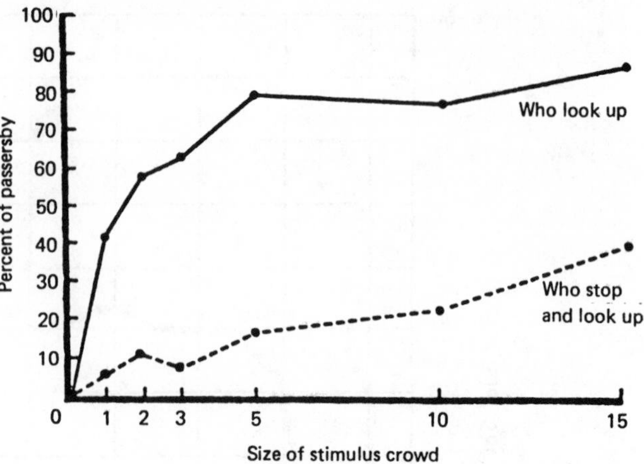

Fig. 11-2 Percentage of passersby who look up *(solid line)* and who stop and look up *(dashed line)* as a function of the size of the stimulus crowd. (From "Note on the Drawing Power of Crowds of Different Size," by S. Milgram, L. Bickman, and L. Berkowitz. In *Journal of Personality and Social Psychology,* 1969, *13,* 79–82. Copyright 1969 by the American Psychological Association. Reprinted by permission.)

Following participation, subjects were debriefed and told that the experiment had employed deception and the other participants were confederates who had deliberately given the wrong answer. In addition, the dynamics of the experiment were openly discussed to ease any negative feelings the subject might have as a result of participating in this experiment. Debriefing is an extremely important component of any experiment, particularly if deception is used.

Although Asch's original experiments were done more than 30 years ago, his findings are still valid and the experimental paradigm he used is still being used today. His classic work provides an excellent example of the importance and power of good experimental techniques.

Even today many published papers addressing the issue of conformity refer to his contribution, both in methodology and findings, to the field of social psychology. Variables including the relationship between sex differences and conformity (Javornisky, 1979) and the influence of television commercials on conformity (Jennings, Geis, & Brown, 1980) have successfully used the Asch paradigm to explore aspects of conformity in the laboratory.

Field studies on conformity must also use the methodology of well-controlled experiments. Milgram, Bickman, and Berkowitz (1969) conducted an interesting field experiment investigating the relationship between the size of a crowd and the behavior of passersby. In this study, groups of 1 to 15 people (stimulus crowd) stood on a busy street in Manhattan and simultaneously looked up at the sixth floor of an office building for one minute. During this time, one of the experimenters unobtrusively filmed the behavior of passersby. This procedure was repeated 30 times with stimulus crowds varying from 1 to 15. The films were later evaluated by two judges who recorded the following behaviors: the total number of passersby, the number of persons who looked up but kept on walking, and the number of persons who looked up and stopped.

The results of this experiment are shown in Figure 11-2. Both the number of passersby who only looked up and the number who looked up and stopped increased as the size of the stimulus crowd increased. The number of persons who looked up but kept on walking was always greater than the number who stopped, probably, the authors posit, because only looking up requires less effort than stopping. Further, the relationship between stoppers and crowd size showed a significant linear trend; every increase in crowd size was associated with an increase in the number of people who stopped.

In contrast, the relationship between those who looked up but kept on walking and crowd size was curvilinear (both linear and quadratic trends were significant). The maximum effect seems to have been attained with a crowd size of five. This suggests that the choice of dependent variable, at least in part, affects the nature of the relationship between stimulus and response. When the dependent variable is how many subjects stop and look up, the relationship between stimulus and response is linear. When, however, the dependent variable is defined as the number of passersby who merely look up, the relationship between stimulus and response is curvilinear. Careful comparison of dependent variables within and across studies is often necessary to reconcile different results.

The preceding study of the relationship between the size of a crowd and its influence on an individual's behavior was done in the field rather than in the laboratory. It is clearly relevant to how pedestrians will behave when in the presence of a crowd. The setting of this experiment did not compromise the need for, or the use of, good methodological techniques. Because the hypotheses were well defined and appropriately tested, the data are meaningful and valuable.

Eyewitness Testimony

One form of evidence that is often used in jury trials is eyewitness testimony. Here, a person's description of a past event or person is retold to a jury. The members of the jury must then evaluate the accuracy and relevance of the witness's testimony and, in conjunction with other information, decide on issues of fact and culpability.

The ability of an eyewitness to accurately remember and relate past events is fundamentally an issue of episodic memory (see Chapter 8). Thus, there is tremendous potential for the application of the research expertise of experimental psychology to this social institution. This section will discuss ways in which research methods borrowed from experimental psychology can illuminate some of the variables that affect eyewitness testimony. (We will not consider deliberate attempts of an eyewitness to distort or misrepresent information. We will assume that the witness wants to communicate what was seen.)

There are many questions of interest that could be pursued. How good is a particular observer? What happens if the observer is also the victim? How does the time elapsed since the event affect the report? Were there other potentially distracting events occurring when the crime occurred? The number of relevant questions is almost endless. Though it is extremely difficult to answer these questions for any particular witness reporting a specific event, research can provide us with some general guidelines and understanding of eyewitnesses' abilities under different circumstances.

Psychological research has the potential to answer these questions. There must, however, be some organization of the variables of interest so that the research in this area will be meaningful and have some value to those involved in the criminal justice system.

Wells (1978) has defined two types of applied eyewitness testimony research. His scheme provides a way of organizing research in this area in terms of variables and goals. One type, system-variable research, pertains to variables that can be manipulated in criminal cases. These variables are considered to be under the direct control of the criminal justice system. The application or goal of this research might be to change (and improve) the justice system.

One example of system-variable research investigates the influence of the time between the crime and the testimony. Evidence in this area (e.g., Lipton, 1977; Shepard, 1967) could be used to schedule police interrogation of witnesses at the most advantageous time. Other examples include research in suggestive interrogation (Loftus & Palmer, 1974; Loftus, Altman, & Geballe, 1975; Loftus, Miller, & Burns, 1978) and question structure (Lipton, 1977; Marquis, Marshall, & Oskamp, 1972; Marshall, 1966). The greatest utility of this type of research is to modify the system with the goal of improving witness accuracy.

A second type of research, estimator-variable research, concerns variables that affect the accuracy of the eyewitness testimony but are not under the direct control of the criminal justice system. Research concerning these variables can serve to estimate the probability of accuracy of a particular witness but cannot affect how accurate a particular witness is. Information gained from these studies can help us to understand how likely it is that the witness is accurate. Since the results of these research efforts are probabilistic, and so many other factors influence the reliability of eyewitness testimony, application of this research in any particular case is quite limited.

Estimator-variable research can be subdivided into three parts: characteristics of the criminal event, characteristics of the defendant, and characteristics of the witness.

One characteristic of the criminal event that has been studied, by Leippe, Wells, and Ostrom (1978), is the seriousness of the crime. They found that witnesses are more accurate for more serious crimes if they are aware of the crime's seriousness at the time of the event. Other important characteristics of the event include increased exposure to the event (Loftus, 1972; Hintzman, 1976), increased complexity of the event (Loftus, 1972; Wells, 1972; Franken & Davis, 1975), and increased familiarity with the event (Grether & Baker, 1972), which are all related to better memory for the event.

Characteristics of the defendant, the witness, and their interaction have been studied. These characteristics include race (Malpass & Kravitz, 1969; Cross, Cross, & Daly, 1971; Elliot, Wills, & Goldstein, 1973; Luce, 1974) and sex (Howells, 1938; Cross, Cross, & Daly, 1971). The general results are that within-race identifications are better than cross-racial identifications, and females can identify other females better than they can identify males.

As we noted before, it is difficult to apply the findings of estimator-variable research to improve the criminal justice system. Knowing, for example, that cross-racial identifications are less accurate than within-racial identifications does not help the jury decide the reliability of a particular black witness identifying a black or white defendant.

It has been suggested that this information could be presented to a jury by expert witnesses. The value of psychologists giving such information in jury trials has been discussed at great length and is quite controversial (McCloskey & Egeth, 1983a, 1983b; Loftus, 1983a, 1983b). After partitioning research in eyewitness testimony into system-variable and estimator-variable research, Wells concludes that the former probably has greater applied utility for the criminal justice system in that it can lead to improvements of the system.

Research in eyewitness testimony relies primarily on simulation of crimes. Here again, the social psychologist is challenged to create a realistic, applicable laboratory experiment. We will discuss two paradigms that have been used, one an example of system-variable research and the other an example of estimator-variable research. In the first, a traffic accident, shown on film, is the criminal event (Loftus & Palmer, 1974). In this paradigm subjects are told from the beginning that they are watching a simulated event. In our second example the subject is the witness and sometimes the victim of crime (Hosch & Cooper, 1982). During the crime, the subject is unaware that it is a fake. Following the staged crime, the subject is told of the deception and thoroughly debriefed.

Loftus and Palmer (1974) were interested in the effect of suggestive interrogation on eyewitness testimony. After showing subjects a film of a multiple-car accident, they asked either "how fast were the cars going when they *hit* each other?" or "how fast were the cars going when they *smashed into* each other?" They wished to test the hypothesis that the choice of the word *hit* or *smashed* would influence the subject's memory of the ac-

Table 11-1 Distribution of "Yes" and "No" Responses to the Question, "Did You See Any Broken Glass?"

Response	Verb condition		
	Smashed	Hit	Control
Yes	16	7	6
No	34	43	44

(From "Reconstruction of Automobile Destruction: An Example of the Interaction between Language and Memory" by E. F. Loftus and J. C. Palmer. In *Journal of Verbal Learning and Verbal Behavior,* 1974, *13,* 585–589. Copyright 1974 by Academic Press. Reprinted by permission.)

cident. A week later, subjects were asked whether they had seen broken glass in the film. (There was, in fact, no broken glass in the original film.) As Table 11-1 shows, subjects who had been questioned with the phrase *smashed into* were more likely to report seeing broken glass. There is a great potential for the application of this system-variable research to requirements of interrogative procedure. In particular, it suggests that eyewitnesses can be led to misremember, or misreport, what they saw by suggestions from the prosecutor or defense attorney.

Hosch and Cooper (1982) used a simulated crime paradigm developed by Wells and his coinvestigators (e.g., Leippe, Wells, & Ostrom, 1978) to investigate whether victims are more likely than nonvictims to give accurate testimony and to explore the relationship between the accuracy of witnesses' reports and how confident the witnesses are about their reports.

Lieppe, Wells and Ostrom (1978) investigated whether different situations affect eyewitnesses' accuracy in identifying a person. In one situation the subject merely had to recognize another person seen before. In a second situation the subject witnessed a theft and had to recognize the thief. In the third situation the subject was the victim of a theft and had to recognize the thief. Subjects participated in pairs in one of the three conditions. In the no-theft control condition, the experimenter gives the subjects forms to fill out and then leaves the room. The confederate enters the room, claims to be a late-arriving subject, fills out the forms and leaves. In the calculator-theft condition, in which subjects merely witness the theft, the experimenter leaves a calculator in the room with the subjects. When the confederate arrives, she speaks to the subjects as in the control condition and then states that she has always wanted a calculator like this. Following this statement, she puts the calculator in her purse and leaves. In the watch-theft condition, in which subjects are the victims of theft, the experimenter takes the two subjects' watches, presumably for later use, and places them on a table. He then leaves the subjects to fill out their forms. The thief-confederate enters, speaks to the subjects as in the control condition, declares that she has always wanted watches like these, puts the subjects' watches in her purse, and then leaves. Approximately a half-minute after the confederate leaves, the experimenter returns, explains the true nature of the experiment and the necessity for deception. Subjects are then asked to identify the thief-confederate from an array of six pictures and to indicate their confidence that the identification was accurate.

Although all the groups were significantly better than chance in identifying the confederate (16.7%), eyewitnesses were more accurate for the theft conditions than the no-theft condition (see Table 11-2). There was, however, no significant difference between the condition in which the subject was the victim (watch-theft) and the condition in which the subject merely witnessed the theft (calculator-theft). These data show that although the presence of a crime increases identification accuracy, it is not necessary for the witness to be the victim. Further analysis showed no relationship between accuracy and confidence ratings. In other words how confident a witness is in the accuracy of his or her report is unrelated to the actual accuracy of the report. This example of estimator-variable research helps us better understand some aspects of eyewitness testimony, but its present applica-

Table 11-2 Frequency of Eyewitness Choice by Condition

	Picture choice						
Condition	1	2[a]	3	4	5	6	None of them
No-theft control	2	7	0	6	1	2	3
Calculator theft	0	16	1	2	0	1	4
Watch theft	0	15	1	1	2	0	2

[a]The actual confederate was picture 2.

(From "Victimization as a determinant of eyewitness accuracy," by H. M. Hosch and D. S. Cooper. In *Journal of Applied Psychology*, 1982, *67*, 649–652. Copyright 1982 by the American Psychological Association. Reprinted by permission of the authors.)

tion to the criminal justice system is unclear. It does, however, suggest that eyewitnesses who merely witness a theft will be as accurate in their identifications as those who are victims. Or, put another way, victims are (at least in some cases) no *more* accurate than other witnesses.

RESEARCH IN INDUSTRIAL ORGANIZATIONS

Industrial psychology provides us with another example of applied psychology. This is the study of the individual's behavior in business and industrial settings. In the past, industrial psychology was primarily concerned with employee behavior, but it now incorporates areas of management and consumer behavior. Among its subdivisions, we can include personnel psychology (job selection and training), human factors psychology (man-machine interface), human relations psychology (interpersonal factors and leadership), organizational psychology (motivation and job satisfaction), engineering psychology (designing equipment that takes the capabilities of potential users into account), and consumer behavior (advertising and public relations). As with research in other applied areas, research in industrial psychology also requires rigid adherence to the principles of experimental methodology.

In this section, we will discuss the Hawthorne studies, which were conducted in the 1920s and 1930s. Although these studies are 50 years old, their results are still widely referred to. These classic studies have been credited with calling attention to the importance of interpersonal factors in the work environment. Recently, these important studies have been reexamined and their methodology criticized. We present some of these issues here to highlight the importance of good methodology and appropriate statistical techniques in research.

From 1924 to 1933 a series of seven studies was carried out by the managers and workers of the Hawthorne Plant of the Western Electric Company in Chicago, who were assisted by consultants from the Massachusetts Institute of Technology and later from Harvard University. The first three of these studies (1924–1927), in collaboration with the National Research Council, were undertaken to explore the relationship between illumination levels and worker production rates. These were followed by four more experiments initiated to study social and physical factors related to work efficiency. One of the most surprising findings to emerge from the initial studies was that worker output and job satisfaction increased regardless of whether the illumination levels were increased or decreased. Puzzled by the illumination studies, the investigators designed the Relay Assembly Test Room experiments. In these, the effect of changes in working conditions (rest pauses and length of working day) was measured. The experimenters felt that these new experiments, which were more carefully designed and controlled, would help clarify the relationship between changes in the workers' environments and productivity. The period from 1927 to 1929 was divided into 13 experimental intervals ranging in length from 2 weeks to 31 weeks. During these periods the number and durations of rest periods were manipulated. In the standard condition (with no rest periods) workers worked for 48 hours per week. In the condition with the most time off, the work week consisted of less than 42 hours. Neither the length of the experimental time periods nor the amount of rest systematically increased or decreased during the course of this experiment.

When the experimental changes decreased the number of hours worked, productivity in terms of number of relays produced per week did not decrease. The experimenters Roethlisberger and Dickson (1939) state, in relation to these data, " . . . it can be seen that all major dips in the output curves correspond to large decreases in time worked which were not due primarily to experimental changes . . . these large decreases in weekly hours of work are primarily due to holidays, absences or hospital visits . . . total weekly output does not decline when rest pauses are introduced, but remains practically the same during all rest period experiments" (pp. 78–79).

Following this series of studies, experiments were designed to investigate the importance of the wage incentive factor (the Second Relay Assembly Group) and to reassess the influence of manipulating rest pauses (the Mica Splitting Test Room). The results of these last two experiments did not alter the conclusions drawn from the earlier studies.

The *Hawthorne effect* is the name given to the observation that increased worker output results from the workers' transformed interpersonal relationship with management rather than from any specific variations of the workers' environment. Put more generally, the Hawthorne effect asserts that workers will produce more if they perceive that they are receiving special treatment or attention.

The Hawthorne effect is well known and widely referred to in industrial, experimental, and social psychology. For almost 50 years it has been accepted as a scientific fact, proven by research. Recently, the research on which this phenomenon is based and the conclusions originally drawn from these studies (Roethlisberger & Dickson, 1939) have been questioned (Bramel & Friend, 1981; Carey, 1967; Franke, 1979; Franke & Kaul, 1978). We will discuss the major criticisms leveled against these studies—methodological flaws.

There are several alleged methodological flaws in the research. First, there were no statistical analyses of the data. Argyle (1953) points out that there is no quantitative evidence supporting the conclusion that the changed relationship with supervision caused an increase in worker output. Correctly quantifying and analyzing experimental data allows us to accept or reject the null hypothesis and draw conclusions from experimental manipulations. Without quantification and statistical analysis of data, one cannot know or discuss the results of an experiment. This is because statistical analyses are needed to learn whether the obtained results can be reasonably attributed to the experimental manipulation or to chance factors.

A second methodological problem stems from the fact that two of the five workers in the experiment (workers 1A and 2A) were replaced 8 months after the experiment had begun. Franke (1979) quotes the original log notes (Roethlisberger & Dickson, 1939) on some circumstances surrounding the change in subjects: "Log notes from the observer record that in the second of these experiments the foreman told the workers that they 'would be taken back to the regular department and in the most offending cases laid-off (dismissed from the company), if improvement was not made'" (Franke, 1979, p.863). "Two of these workers in particular (operators 1A and 2A) failed to display 'that wholehearted cooperation' desired by the investigators" (Roethlisberger & Dickson, 1939, p. 53).

Mayo, one of the Harvard consultants for this project, refers to the change in subjects in much more neutral terms. He states (1933) that they were "permitted to withdraw" (p. 110) and "At no time . . . did the girls feel they were working under pressure" (p. 69). Years later, Wardwell (1979) defends the dismissal of these two workers by stating that two of the remaining three workers asked that these two be dismissed and that one of the dismissed workers was later found to be anemic while the other had family problems. Bramel and Friend (1981) criticize the workers' dismissal. "Six months into the experiment, with productivity thought to be static or falling, these two women were being continually reprimanded and threatened with disciplinary action. Finally, after 8 months, operators 1A and 2A were dismissed from the experiment for 'gross insubordination' and low output" (p. 871). These two workers were replaced by pro-establishment workers, which Bramel and Friend speculate may have affected the results of the experiment.

A third methodological flaw was the failure of the experimenters to consider ongoing historical events that occurred during the course of the study. Probably the most obvious and important event was the Great Depression, which began when the experiment was about half over. One can reasonably speculate that during such a time of national economic hardship, workers would fear losing their jobs and consequently try to please management. This factor was not considered when the original experimental results were evaluated.

Franke and Kaul (1978) took the quantitative data from the original reports (Roethlisberger & Dickson, 1939) combined with certain categoric changes that occurred during the course of the experiment, and performed time-series regression analyses. The variables originally recorded included the independent variables of rest pauses, hours of work per day, and hours of work per week. The dependent variables were measures of the quantity and quality of output. The two categoric changes that were considered were the replacement of two of the workers (supposedly for their unsatisfactory attitudes) and the beginning of the Great Depression halfway through the experiment.

The results of these analyses show that three factors can account for most of the variance in the quantity of group and individual output (Franke & Kaul, 1978). These factors are managerial discipline (this refers to the replacement of the two independent workers for more agreeable workers), the Depression, and the time set aside for rest periods (worker fatigue).

The weight of the last 10 years of reinterpretation and reanalysis and the lack of specific replication of the Hawthorne effect in 50 years makes the experimental validity of this effect seriously questionable. This is not to say that the phenomenon does not exist, but rather that the research so long credited with validating this phenomenon is not adequate proof. It is important to keep in mind that the Hawthorne effect can be related to other well-established psychological phenomena such as the placebo effect (i.e., the positive effect of expectation of treatment results regardless of any direct beneficial effect of the particular treatment).

Carey (1967) asks a most relevant question: How is it possible for "conclusions so little supported by evidence to gain so influential and respected a place within scientific disciplines and to hold this place for so long" (p. 403)? One possibility is that the findings agreed with the prejudices of the times. This, however, is a matter of speculation. Regardless of the reasons for these severe methodological problems with the Hawthorne studies, they illustrate the importance of rigorous scientific methodology and the necessity for appropriate quantification and analysis of data.

RESEARCH IN CLINICAL ISSUES

The nature and treatment of psychological and psychiatric disorders have been extensively investigated. There are certain special problems associated with research on clinical issues using patient populations. First, defining the severity and characteristic symptoms of psychiatric disorders is no simple matter. Unclear, jargon-filled labels such as "personality dysfunction with borderline paranoid tendencies of moderate severity" are often used to describe patients. Labels of this sort make definitions of particular disorders difficult and comparison of research results between research groups nearly impossible.

In 1980, the American Psychiatric Association published the third edition of its *Diagnostic and Statistical Manual (DSM-III)*. This volume tries to establish specific criteria for different psychiatric disorders. Though it is sometimes criticized by the psychological community for being too medically oriented, it is widely used in research. It represents one attempt to define standardized homogeneous patient populations. This facilitates relevant comparison of the results obtained from different researchers in different facilities.

A second difficulty, once the class of patients has been defined, is locating and recruiting a sufficient number of subjects. Patients differ in the severity of their illness and their willingness to participate in research.

In addition, many patients are already receiving psychological or drug therapies, or both, for their psychiatric or psychological conditions and frequently for other related and unrelated physical disorders. Once recruited, many subjects drop out for one reason or another. This is a particular problem because research that examines the response of illness to particular treatments often lasts a long time (6 to 12 months is not unusual). Others who do remain subjects do not always follow the experimenter's instructions. All these factors make it difficult to know how representative the patient sample is.

When designing an experiment that uses a group of patients as subjects, it is difficult to select a group of experimental controls sufficiently similar to the patient group. It is important to have a control group that is matched to the patient group on a number of characteristics so that the effectiveness of a particular therapy can be tested. Without a control group, it is difficult to assess the separate influences of time alone and of the experimental manipulation. (See Chapter 2 on experimental design.) An additional difficulty is assembling a control group that is equated to the patient group for diagnosis, severity of disease, and history of treatment.

An alternative research strategy (when selection of control groups is not possible) is to test each person before and after a particular treatment or experimental manipulation. This can be done when testing the efficacy of a particular treatment for a particular disorder. In this way the patient acts as his or her own control. But this, too, has problems. It is important to control for the effects of time—would the patient have improved spontaneously during this length of time regardless of treatment? Also, this method does not reveal anything specific about the therapy or manipulation. It is possible that the nonspecific effects of the treatment, including the attention of an interested party (i.e., the therapist), or the environment that was conducive to discussion of the patient's problems, or even the a priori belief that the therapy would be effective, could account for positive results.

These control problems are not always insurmountable. Patients can sometimes be matched on relevant attributes, divided into groups, and given either a placebo (inactive substance) or medicine. In addition, periodic evaluations can be made to monitor the time course of the effect of the treatment. Alternatively, subjects could be given a placebo at the start of the study to see if the nonspecific effects of the treatment will be effective. Then only those who fail to improve on the placebo would be tested on the medication or treatment of interest.

Finally, there are serious ethical considerations. For example, if you want to test the effectiveness of a particular therapy, can the group of patients be randomly divided so that half receive treatment and half do not? This could mean that treatment is being withheld from certain patients. Or is it justified to give a drug therapy of unknown action to a person who is ill? Generally, the answer to this depends on the condition of the patients, the available treatments, and how much is known about the drug being tested. Still another ethical problem is that of informed consent. Who is competent to judge whether a person with a psychological or psychiatric disorder can participate in a research project and how much information must be given? (See Chapter 12 for a discussion on subjects' rights.)

These factors contribute to making applied research of clinical populations quite difficult. Even though not all of these problems can be surmounted, it is possible to design meaningful research in this area.

In this section we will briefly discuss two types of research. In the first, treatment of anxiety disorders is investigated. This research extends a clinical observation that a particular drug therapy helps people who suffer from frequent and spontaneous panic attacks. The second area of research explores the association between attention deficits and schizophrenia. Here an attempt is made to understand the nature of a particular disorder by the demonstration of attentional deficits in schizophrenic patients.

The Treatment of Anxiety Disorders

Many psychiatrists and psychologists agree that it is necessary to establish the efficacy of available treatment for different disorders. We will discuss research that shows the efficacy of a particular medication for patients who suffer from panic attacks. Panic attacks are the major symptom of an anxiety disorder, which typically develops in the following way: For no apparent reason, the person will experience intense feelings of anxiety. The symptoms include a racing heart, sweating, and an overpowering fear of impending death or losing rational control. After a short time these feelings subside, leaving the individual quite shaken and wondering what has happened. Usually medical attention is sought. Often the individual goes to a cardiologist who finds nothing wrong and tries to reassure the patient. Several days or a week pass and the individual again has an intense and unexplainable anxiety attack. Again there is no apparent cause; again medical attention is sought; again nothing physical is found. After one or more repetitions, the person finally seeks psychological or psychiatric help.

In addition to the panic attacks themselves, other phobias or irrational fears usually develop. This is thought to be a consequence of the fact that the individual cannot predict where or when the next attack will occur. Often the person will become agoraphobic, refusing to go out in crowds. Some people only travel in the company of people they know, only sit in the aisle seats at movies, only travel using routes that pass hospitals, and so forth. In extreme cases, individuals have to give up their jobs and can travel only within a short distance of their homes.

Early clinical observations by Klein and Fink (1962) showed that the drug imipramine (a tricyclic antidepressant) was associated with the cessation of panic attacks, although it had little effect on the phobic reactions of these patients. (Phenothiazines and sedatives that do have a positive effect on other types of anxiety are ineffective in treating panic anxiety.) In order to experimentally verify the observations that imipramine selectively affects panic attacks but not other types of anxiety, controlled studies were done by Klein, Zitrin, and Woerner (1978). Three groups of subjects were tested. The first group was composed of agoraphobic patients who have panic attacks and are afraid to go out. (These are the patients previously described who, on the basis of clinical observation, seemed to be responsive to imipramine.) The second group was composed of simple phobics, patients who have narrowly defined fears, such as a fear of heights or needles. They rarely have generalized phobias and they do not have spontaneous panic attacks. The third group was composed of mixed phobics. They share some of the characteristics of both the other two groups; they have well-defined specific phobias and also have panic attacks. It was predicted that the two groups with panic attacks would improve on imipramine while simple phobics would show no change.

Patients were admitted to the study and given either a placebo (an inactive substance) or imipramine in increasing amounts until an appropriate therapeutic dose was reached. Because all the patients needed treatment, everyone in the study received either behavior therapy or supportive therapy. The study lasted for 26 weeks. The patients' improvement during the 26 weeks of treatment was rated by an evaluator who was unaware of which group had received medicine and which had received a placebo. (This is technically known as a double-blind experiment, in which both the patient and the experimenter evaluating the degree of improvement are blind to, or unaware of, the experimental condition. It is interesting to note that many researchers in double-blind studies use side effects to correctly guess which group is receiving the active medication.)

In support of the hypotheses, both the agoraphobic group and the mixed phobic group improved with the imipramine therapy. There was no improvement with imipramine for the simple phobic group. Thus, this experiment established that for patients with spontaneous panic attacks, the drug imipramine can be effective therapy and that this treatment is not uniformly good for all anxiety disorders. This experiment does not show, however, whether other drugs or psychological therapies (e.g., desensitization) would also be appropriate or even superior for the treatment of patients who suffer from spontaneous panic attacks. Further research is needed to answer these questions as well as to investigate the mechanisms involved in panic attacks and how this disorder differs from other anxiety disorders. This extension of clinical observations to research helps the clinician deal more effectively with patients and increases our knowledge about mental disorders.

Attention and Schizophrenia

The tools of experimental psychology have been effectively used to explore the underlying cognitive deficits of psychiatric and psychological disorders. One such research interest is the relationship between attention and schizophrenia. Attention has long been the object of experimental study, and schizophrenia has long been associated with attentional deficits.

Tasks with attentional demands seem particularly sensitive to schizophrenic pathology. As early as 1919, Kraepelin referred to attention deficits as a major symptom of schizophrenia (what he called dementia praecox). He wrote about both active attention deficit—the inability of patients to voluntarily concentrate on external events—and passive attention deficit—an undue susceptibility to distraction by irrelevant features of the environment. Since then others have referred to deficits in selective attention (McGhie & Chapman, 1961; Reed, 1972), segmentalized set (Shakow, 1977), the inability to deal appropriately with incoming stimuli (Silverman, 1967), and overinclusive thinking—the breakdown of an appropriate filter mechanism (Payne & Caird, 1967).

As previously discussed, it is necessary to carefully define the disorder of interest, in this case schizophrenia. For our purposes we can use the definition of schizophrenia in *Stedman's Medical Dictionary* (1982):

> . . . the most common type of psychosis, characterized by disorder in thinking processes, such as delusions and hallucinations, and extensive withdrawal of the individual's interest from other people and the outside world, and the investment of it in his own.

We must also define what we mean by attention. (See Chapter 6 for discussions of attention relevant to experimental psychology.) For our discussion of possible attention deficits related to schizophrenia, we will use the following definition. Attention is the ability to focus in a sustained manner on one task, activity, or stimulus. Disturbances in attention may be manifested by easy distractibility or the inability to concentrate. Now that we have definitions of both schizophrenia and attention, we can begin to explore the relationship between attentional deficits and schizophrenia.

In order to effectively study this complex and hard-to-define relationship, it is necessary to address a specific question with a well-defined experimental paradigm. In other words, the researcher must choose an operational definition of attention that defines it by the subject's performance in a specific task. One experimental paradigm that has been useful in exploring this complex area involves measuring the smooth pursuit eye movements of a subject required to visually follow a moving target such as a pendulum. Thus, in this task, good attention is operationally defined as the ability to visually follow a moving target. Conversely, an attention deficit is the inability to visually follow a moving target.

A brief review of the work done by Holzman, Levy, and Proctor (1976) will illustrate this experimental paradigm. They instructed subjects to visually follow a pendulum swinging within 20° of visual arc at a frequency of 0.4 Hz (2 cycles every 5 seconds or 24 cycles per minute). During this procedure, electrodes which record the electrical activity of the muscles that surround and control voluntary eye movements are attached near the subjects' eyes. This gives a record (EOG) of the subject's eye movements.

Figure 11-3 shows four eye-tracking patterns in response to a moving pendulum. When normal controls are tested in this manner, their eye movements closely parallel the sinusoidal movement of the pendulum (tracings a and b). In contrast to this, deviant eye-tracking patterns (tracings c and d) are typical of the eye movements of schizophrenic patients. Instead of continuously following the moving target, patients' eyes often cease to follow the target. These failures to track the target are called velocity arrests. In addition, even when they do visually follow the target, the pattern of their eye movements does not mimic the sinusoidal movement of the target as well as those of normal subjects.

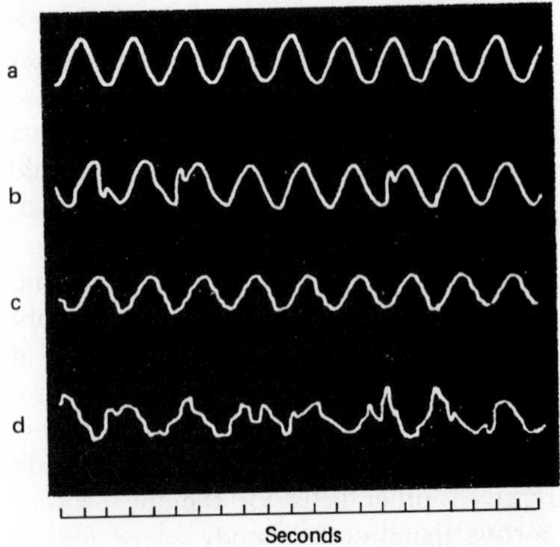

Fig. 11-3 Four eye-tracking patterns in response to a moving pendulum: (a) smooth pursuit, (b) smooth pursuit with occasional brief interruptions and resumption of accurate tracking, (c) deviant tracking pattern in which rapid saccadic movements are superimposed on the slow pursuit, and (d) deviant tracking with alternations in amplitude, frequency, and symmetry. (From "Eye-Tracking and Optokinetic Tests: Diagnostic Significance in Peripheral and Central Vestibular Disorders," by J. T. Benitez. In *Laryngoscope,* 1970, *80,* 834–848. Copyright 1970 by The Laryngoscope Co. Reprinted by permission.)

Holzman et al. (1976) suggest that this demonstrated deficit in schizophrenics reflects their inability to focus and concentrate in a consistent and uninterrupted manner. These data are consistent with the hypothesis that schizophrenia is, at least in part, an attention disorder.

The work of Shagass, Roemer, and Amadeo (1976) provides additional support for the relationship between attention and the eye tracking deficit in schizophrenic patients. Schizophrenic and normal subjects were compared in four experimental conditions that followed one another. The first and fourth conditions were identical and closely duplicated the experimental conditions of Holzman and his colleagues cited previously. That is, subjects were required to visually follow a moving target (pendulum). Repetition of this task (condition 4) investigated whether learning or practice affected the ability to track a moving target. During the second and third conditions, numbers were randomly displayed one at a time superimposed on the moving target. Subjects were required to visually track the moving stimulus and, at the same time, to read the numbers either silently (condition 2) or aloud (condition 3). Table 11-3 shows these four conditions.

The eye trackings of schizophrenic patients were examined in all four conditions. The data are shown in Figure 11-4. When compared with the standard tracking conditions (1 and 4), the silent reading condition (2) showed fewer velocity arrests, and the accuracy of the waveform increased. When the reading-aloud condition (3) was compared to the standard tracking conditions, the accuracy of the waveform increased, though the number of velocity arrests remained the same. Thus, it was shown that forcing schizophrenic patients to increase their attention by reading numbers on the tracking stimulus improved performance, even though patients in this condition still did not do as well as normal controls. The patients and controls showed a similar pattern of results, but the performance of the patients was always worse.

Table 11-3 Four Conditions Comparing the Eye Movements of Normal and Schizophrenic Subjects

Condition	Description
1	Track pendulum—no numbers
2	Track pendulum—with numbers, silent reading
3	Track pendulum—with numbers, reading aloud
4	Track pendulum—no numbers

In addition, the patients' improvement during the reading conditions did not have any positive effect on the final pendulum tracking condition. Patients' performances were just as bad during the final standard tracking condition as they were during the

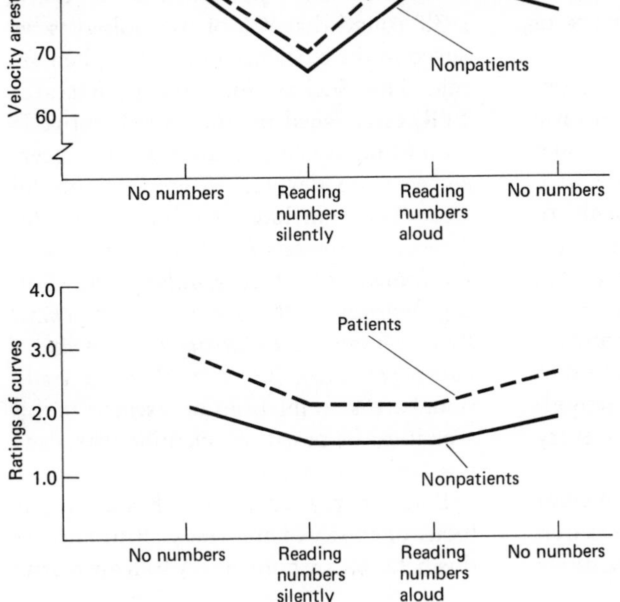

Fig. 11-4 Data from an eye-tracking experiment plotting the velocity arrests *(top)* and ratings of the normality of curves *(bottom)* for patients compared to nonpatients as a function of the different number conditions. (From "Eye Tracking Performance and Engagement of Attention," by C. Shagass, R. A. Roemer, and M. Amadeo. In *Archives of General Psychiatry,* 1976, *33,* 121–125. Copyright 1976 by the American Psychological Association. Reprinted by permission.)

first tracking condition. Thus, improvement during the second and third conditions was due to having the patients read the numbers on the pendulum and not to repetition of the task.

A related study (Holzman, Proctor, Levy, Yasillo, Meltzer, & Hurt, 1974) tested the eye tracking abilities of the first-degree relatives (parents, siblings, or offspring) of schizophrenic patients. They found that a significant number of nonschizophrenic, normal relatives demonstrated aberrant eye tracking under these visual eye tracking conditions. This evidence suggests a heritable component of the attention deficit in schizophrenic disorders.

This experimental paradigm has many advantages when investigating the deficits associated with schizophrenic disorders. First, it provides a way of measuring a component of attention that can be objectively defined. Second, because of the short duration of the procedure, the attention effects studied here are less likely to be confounded by boredom, fatigue, or some type of "attention wandering" not related to the particular type of attention being measured. Third, because of the familial findings, this measure seems to be a quite sensitive and selective measure of at least one component of attention that might be used to identify genetic components of schizophrenia.

As mentioned, there are special problems associated with doing research on a clinical population. All the critical issues discussed in the chapter on subjects (Chapter 12) become particularly difficult to manage with schizophrenic subjects. Do the patients understand the directions, and are they willing and able to cooperate? Are they capable of giving informed consent? Is the sample group generalizable to other patient groups? These and other methodological issues must be resolved for every experimental situation.

To increase our knowledge of mental illness and to improve treatment, research is essential. It is critical that investigations of these and other issues be well-designed if the resulting data are to be meaningful.

RESEARCH IN NONTRADITIONAL AREAS—EXTRASENSORY PERCEPTION

Research in extrasensory perception (ESP) provides an example of scientific research principles applied to parapsychology, a nontraditional area. Beginning in the late 1800s, researchers in this field began to introduce scientific methodology to the study of psychic phenomena. Charles Richet introduced the use of statistical methodology with data from ESP card experiments in 1884. Sometime later, in 1917, John Cooper at Stanford University used scientific methodology to demonstrate the presence of ESP. Probably the best-known personality in ESP research was Joseph Rhine. Beginning in the 1930s he studied ESP using Zener cards. (Zener cards form a deck consisting of 25 cards each showing one of five symbols. In ESP experiments the subject usually tries to guess the sequence of cards.) Rhine continued his work in this field until his death in 1980.

Although never in the forefront of psychological research, parapsychology did enjoy some popularity in the 1930s and 1940s. In 1938 a poll (Warner & Clark, 1938) found that 9% of psychologists believed in the existence of psychic phenomena. The Society for Psychic Research (SPR) established in 1882 is still active in promoting psychic research. Many current journals are devoted to research in this area. These include the *Journal of the American Society for Psychic Research*, the *Journal of Parapsychology*, the (British) *Journal of the Society for Psychical Research* and the *European Journal of Parapsychology*. Just as with more traditional areas, evaluations of research in this area must be based on scientific merit and not prejudice or belief.

Extrasensory perception has been the focus of much of the research interest in this field. Its proponents try to legitimatize it, while its opponents claim and often prove that demonstrations of psychic phenomena are really trickery. Regardless of the fact that these phenomena are not the traditional subject matter of scientific investigation, the principles of research that have been covered in this book can be applied to these areas as well.

Extrasensory perception is the apparent access to external information without the use of either direct sensory information or rational inference. Traditionally, four areas of ESP have been investigated: telepathy, clairvoyance, precognition, and retrocognition.

The studies discussed here provide an example of the application of scientific research principles to a nontraditional area of research. The subject of this research is the ability to influence dreams telepathically. *Telepathy* (literally, "distant feeling") is the apparent, direct mental communication between two organisms. In telepathic communication, one organism appears to have access to the thoughts or experiences of another organism. An examination of research in this nontraditional area is independent of any belief in the phenomenon itself. Good research, in any field, can withstand critical evaluation.

An attempt was made by Krippner and Ullman (1970), working at the Maimonides Medical Center in New York, to experimentally induce telepathic dreams. The experiment was conducted using a single subject who had successfully participated in a similar experiment several years earlier (Ullman, Krippner, & Feldstein, 1966). The aim of this experiment was to see if the content of pictures viewed by an agent could influence the subject's dreams.

The subject slept in an acoustically isolated room on eight consecutive nights. A member of the staff who was not present at any of the experimental sessions chose eight different art prints for each night of the research project. Each print was then sealed in separate opaque envelopes and randomly assigned numbers. The content of these target pictures was unknown to the experimenters, the agent who later tried to transmit the pictures, or the subject himself.

On each of the eight experimental nights the subject was allowed to select any member of the staff as an agent. (An agent is the sender in tests for telepathy. This is the person whose mental images are to be sent to the subject.) Electrodes to record brainwave patterns (EEG) during sleep were attached to the subject and he was sent to bed. A random digit was then chosen and the agent picked out the corresponding envelope containing the stimulus print for that night. The agent then went to his room (96 feet from the subject's room) and opened the envelope. The agent was instructed to write down associations, visualize the picture, and attempt to do anything possible to make its contents a more active part of his thought processes.

Whenever the electrodes attached to the subject detected that he was dreaming (i.e., in the rapid eye movement or REM phase of sleep) the agent was awakened by a buzzer and told to concentrate on the picture. At the end of the REM period, the experimenter woke the subject and received a verbal dream report via a two-way intercom system. The subject was completely alone from the time he was sent to bed until his report to the experimenter the next morning. Through the entire procedure, the agent and subject were not together and were not observed to communicate with each other.

The data were evaluated in the following manner. In the morning the subject was given a set of eight pictures, one of which was the target picture. The subject ranked, according to a rather elaborate system, how the pictures were related to his dream. The most similar received a rank of 1 and the most dissimilar received a rank of 8. These eight rankings, the eight pictures and the transcripts of the dream interviews were given to an outside judge who tried to determine the target picture.

If the target picture was perceived by the

subject as similar to the dream (by receiving a rank of 1, 2, 3, or 4) it was considered a *hit*. If the target picture was perceived by the subject as dissimilar to the dream (by receiving a rank of 5, 6, 7, or 8) it was considered a *miss*. According to the subject's rating, all eight were hits. In other words, on all eight nights the subject dreamed about the picture that was shown to the agent. (This outcome is significantly different from chance when evaluated with a binomial test.)

The evaluation of the outside judge yielded similar results. The authors concluded that these results strongly suggest the operation of telepathy.

Figure 11-5 shows the target for the eighth night of Krippner and Ullman's (1970) experiment. Upon waking the subject gave the following report of his dream:

> There were three men. . . . This word "gunslinger" came through and it could have fitted in with these three men, and it also could have fitted in with the Western theme. . . . A rope theme seemed to come through. . . . My guess would be that it was a scene of Western life involved. People with guns. . . . Somewhere in the picture rope imagery appears in a very prominent or conspicuous way. . . . That would be my surmise as to what the target picture would be like.
>
> (Krippner & Ullman, 1970, pp. 402–403)

This dream received a rank of 1. In other words, the judges found a very high correspondence between the target picture and the dream imagery.

Belvedere and Foulkes (1971) tried and failed to replicate Krippner and Ullman's 1970 findings. Using the same subject in a similar setting at the University of Wyoming, another series of eight nights were investigated. Again, a pool of stimulus pictures was chosen and placed individually in sealed opaque envelopes. (This time magazine illustrations were used instead of art prints.) As in the previously described study, there were several agents from whom the subject could choose to receive telepathic pictures. Again, as before, electrodes were attached to the subject and he was sent to bed. The agent then went to a different room and opened the randomly chosen envelope containing the stimulus pictures for that particular night. At the beginning of each dreaming (REM) period, the agent was awakened with instructions to concentrate on the stimulus picture. On the average, the subject was awakened between 7.5 and 20 minutes after the beginning of the dreaming (REM) period. Upon awakening, he gave a description of his dream. After each description the subject was allowed to guess what the stimulus picture looked like.

In the morning the subject was given the tapes of the preceding night's interviews and the set of eight pictures, which included the target picture. He was asked to rank the pictures in relation to their correspondence to his dreams. Two outside judges who did not know the target stimulus also ranked the pictures based on the recorded dream descriptions.

The subject and one of the judges had three hits and five misses over the eight nights and the second judge had only two hits and six misses. These results can readily be predicted by chance (indeed, they are below chance because the expected number of hits, if no telepathy exists, is four). Thus, this experiment represents a failure to replicate the earlier findings.

What does this tell us about the existence of telepathy in dreams? If ESP *does not* exist, how did the first experiment achieve its results? If ESP *does* exist, why did the second experiment fail to show evidence of its existence?

There are only a few methodological differences between the two experiments. One experiment used prints of paintings whereas the other used magazine pictures. The agents were different in each of these experiments, although all the agents did try to transmit the images. Perhaps these phenomena strongly rely on the relationship between the agent (sender) and the subject (recipient).

Other differences include the fact that extra precautions were taken in the second experiment to keep the identity of the tar-

Fig. 11-5 "Man with Arrows and Companions" by Bichitr. This was the target picture for the eighth night of Krippner and Ullman's (1970) telepathy experiment. (Reprinted with permission from Tudor Publishing.)

get known only to the agent, and there was a different investigator in each experiment. In addition, the subject felt that in the first experiment the researchers believed in the phenomenon being tested, whereas in the second the researchers were quite skeptical. These differences do not appear to be of much experimental significance, and yet the fact that these two experiments produced opposite results must be accounted for.

It is also possible that the significant

findings in the first experiment were the result of chance effects (Type I error). This is unlikely, however, since their various statistical procedures yielded data significant at the .003 level or better. This means that a result as extreme as this would occur by chance only three times out of a thousand.

Based on these two experiments we are unable to conclude whether or not telepathy in dreams does, in fact, exist. The first experiment provides support for the notion that telepathy is possible, but the second seems to refute the existence of this phenomenon. Neither experiment can cancel the results of the other, nor can we choose which experimental results we wish to believe. Only demonstrated flaws in the experiments themselves can invalidate them.

Perhaps telepathy exists but cannot be demonstrated at will. The existence of phenomena such as insight and creativity are accepted even though they cannot be demonstrated at will. Other phenomena such as communication by telephone could not be demonstrated 200 years ago, but was possible then and is commonplace now. However, the fact that 100 years of research have not been able to satisfactorily demonstrate the existence of ESP casts serious doubt on whether it exists at all, though it does not disprove its existence. It remains for further research to show whether and under what circumstances these and other extrasensory phenomena exist.

SUMMARY

This chapter has explored the application of the methodology of experimental psychology to the areas of social psychology, industrial organizations, clinical issues, and parapsychology. Experiments were presented to illustrate the ways in which the methodology of pure research can be best used to solve problems in these applied areas. This coverage is not intended to be comprehensive. Rather, certain subtopics were used to illustrate the kinds of questions that might be asked, the experimental paradigms that are appropriate, and some of the special methodological considerations in each area. For a more complete review of the research in these areas, the student should seek a text specializing in applied research in the particular area of interest.

In the first section we discussed applications of experimental method to social psychology. Social psychology is dedicated to understanding how the individual behaves in particular environments that are social in nature or that include other people. We first contrasted laboratory and field experiments that investigate issues of conformity (the majority's influence on the minority). Asch's laboratory experiments on conformity showed that subjects who are in a minority will change their opinions to conform to those of the majority, even when they believe the majority is incorrect. A field experiment by Milgram and his co-workers showed some of the ways people are affected by a crowd's behavior. Special research problems of deception and debriefing were discussed. In addition the influence of task definition on the data was considered.

Next, we looked at research in eyewitness testimony. The parameters that influence the accurate report of past events are fundamentally a problem of episodic memory. A scheme for dividing the potential variables of interest and examples of two simulated crime experiments were discussed. The implications of findings in this area for modifying the criminal justice system, a social institution, were reviewed.

Industrial organizations provide another arena in which experimental techniques have been applied. Here we reviewed the studies on which the Hawthorne effect is based. (The Hawthorne effect is the name given to the observation that increased worker output results from the workers' transformed interpersonal relationship with management rather than from any specific variations in the workers' environment.) Data from these studies have been credited with calling attention to the importance of interpersonal factors in the workplace. Some methodological flaws in this research were discussed. One major problem was that the original studies did not have the appropriate statistical analyses, a second was that two recalcitrant workers were dismissed during the experiment, and the third was the uncontrolled onset of the Great Depression in the middle of the study. Recently, Franke and Kaul have analyzed these data and come to very different conclusions about the nature of changes in worker output. The necessity for appropriate statistical analyses in research was emphasized.

The next applied area discussed was clinical issues. Here we highlighted two areas of research application: the treatment of anxiety disorders and attention deficits in schizophrenics. Special research problems in research on clinical issues were reviewed. These include the definition of both the disorders and the behaviors of interest, as well as ethical issues involved when doing research on clinical populations.

Finally, we reviewed parapsychology, a nontraditional research area. Two experiments in telepathy, a facet of extrasensory perception, were presented. Using similar experimental paradigms, one team of researchers found evidence supporting the existence of telepathy whereas the second group failed to find such evidence. The point was made that regardless of the nontraditional nature of this research area, the research itself must be judged solely on its scientific merit.

This chapter has reviewed some of the ways in which research tools can be applied to areas other than experimental psychology. Increasing knowledge requires experimentation. Experimentation has certain requirements for validity, which are independent of the particular hypothesis being tested. The methodological tools of valid research in experimental psychology are also the methodological tools of valid research in many different fields.

III

Procedural Methodology: The Nuts and Bolts of Experimentation

This section provides the detailed instruction necessary for executing an experiment. First, we explore how to choose representative subjects (Chapter 12). Next we discuss the properties of apparatus (Chapter 13) and stimulus materials (Chapter 14) that are used in experimentation, and some of their limitations. Once the particulars of the experiment have been worked out and the data have been collected, it is necessary to analyze the experimental results.

Data must first be organized and summarized. Chapter 15 covers the fundamentals of descriptive statistics, which are methods for summarizing and describing data—for transforming a virtually uninterpretable mass of numerical information into an organized systematic presentation that can be described with a few numbers (perhaps only one or two), and presented in tabular or graphical form. Inferential statistics (Chapter 16) are methods with which we can generalize data from our sample. Using the data that has been collected, inferences, or predictions, can be made about what will most likely be true about an entire population. Inferential statistics permits you to infer from your data that your experimental manipulation "really did" make a difference—that there was a significant difference between two conditions or groups or among three or more conditions or groups. Finally, it becomes important to develop the skills necessary to communicate clearly and effectively the experimental processes: hypothesis, design, analysis, and conclusions. The appropriate form for this communication is the written research report (Chapter 17).

Part III is essential for properly executing the experimental process and for evaluating the experimentation of others. It is intended that the student will use these chapters not only to understand and design good research (thus supplementing Part I) but also as a framework for understanding and evaluating research in the content areas of experimental psychology (Part II).

12

Human Subjects

While the individual man is an insoluble puzzle, in the aggregate he becomes a mathematical certainty. You can never fortell what any one man will do, but you can say with precision what an average number will be up to. Individuals vary but averages remain constant.

(Arthur Conan Doyle)

When we wish to measure a characteristic of an entire population of subjects, it is impractical, if not impossible, to test every individual in that population. Instead we choose sample subjects, measure their performances or characteristics of interest, and apply this information to the population. This chapter reviews the following issues that arise when conducting an experiment involving human subjects: selecting the appropriate sample subjects, obtaining the desired performance from subjects, excluding irrelevant data, and preserving the rights of subjects.

First we discuss the problem of selecting sample subjects whose data will be scientifically meaningful. This includes determining which of an individual's many characteristics are relevant, how many subjects are necessary for the particular study, and how the subjects will be recruited. Second, we consider ways to ensure that the performance the subject gives is the same performance that the experiment requires. How can subjects be instructed so that they know what to do and, equally important, how can subjects be motivated so that they do their best? Third, we discuss the important issue of deciding when, if ever, a subject's data should be excluded from the data analysis. Finally, we discuss the all-important issue of subjects' rights. Once subjects are chosen, how is their informed consent obtained? How much should subjects be told about the experiment they are about to participate in without jeopardizing the study itself, and how much must subjects know in order to fairly judge their willingness to participate? In addition, we discuss the procedure of debriefing subjects after their participation in a study and safeguarding their psychological and physical health.

SELECTION OF SUBJECTS

Subject Characteristics

When choosing a sample subject group, the characteristics of the population that are being studied must be enumerated. In some cases these characteristics are obvious, but in others they are more subtle. For example, if you are designing a study to test the extent to which six- and eight-year-olds use verbal coding strategies to remember pictorial material, the age of the subject is one of the relevant characteristics that will determine the choice of the sample group. Similarly, if you wish to determine whether left-handed individuals are more creative than right-handed individuals, the handedness of the subjects must be considered. In both these cases, decisions must still be made concerning the range of relevant characteristics which define each experimental group. In the first example, the experimenter must decide what is the acceptable range of ages that define six- or eight-year-olds. Perhaps any child between the ages of five-and-a-half and six-and-a-half will be considered six for the purpose of the study and any child between the ages of seven-and-a-half and eight-and-a-half will be considered eight.

In the second example, right- and left-handedness must be defined. Some people do virtually everything with their left hand except write, possibly the result of school training. The criteria for defining right- and left-handedness must be decided on when choosing relevant subject groups. (Some tests for "handedness" include testing the individual's dominant hand, eye, and foot.)

The relevance of other independent variables such as sex, IQ, and grade in school must also be determined, and the criteria used for inclusion in a particular subject group must be clearly stated. (For example, if IQ is the basis of group definition, the particular method of assessing IQ must be selected.)

Choosing other relevant characteristics of a subject population is often quite difficult. Because it is necessary to choose a sample of subjects from whom it is reasonable to infer behaviors of the population of interest, one must first clearly define the group of people about whom information is sought. What characteristics of the population are relevant to this particular behavior and therefore essential to consider when choosing a sample of subjects? What qualities are irrelevant and therefore unnecessary to consider when choosing the sample subjects? In a study to determine how individuals solve verbal problems, the amount of formal education of the individual would probably be considered a relevant attribute and would therefore have to be considered when choosing a sample. The individual's height, on the other hand, is an irrelevant attribute when the ability to solve verbal problems is of interest and would not be considered when choosing a sample.

Sometimes it is obvious which attributes should be considered and which should be eliminated. When choosing a sample for the investigation of visual eye tracking behavior in normal human subjects, it is obvious that one wants to use only subjects with adequate binocular coordination and either normal or corrected vision, whereas it is probably not necessary to consider whether a subject is color blind. It might not be obvious, however, that individuals whose first-degree relatives are schizophrenic should not be included in the sample because they may show deviant eye tracking behavior even though they themselves are not schizophrenic (Holzman et al., 1974).

Other characteristics of subjects that are only temporary must also be taken into account. When experiments use college students, it is usually not advisable to test any subject who stayed up the preceding night studying for an exam, a subject who is weary from partying the previous night, or a subject who is taking antihistamines because the experiment happens to coincide with the hay fever season. Such considerations are often hard to anticipate but can nonetheless contaminate data so carefully and painstakingly gathered. One partial safeguard, in addition to careful planning, is to interview the subject after the experimental session (usually while debriefing) and ask for opinions about the task, the behaviors required during the experimental situation, and if there was anything about the abilities needed for the experiment that were affected by something the experimenter did not know about.

Asking the subject to volunteer anything about his or her personal history or temporary state of being often reveals interesting and important information about the subject. Subjects commonly volunteer information like, "I probably would have done better but I am taking medication for a cough right now," or "I just took a course in speed reading in which I used the technique illustrated in this experiment five times in the past week," or "I just couldn't pay attention to the task because I have family problems." Such information is usually given voluntarily by the subject. Although it is sometimes difficult to interpret, this information can lead to *post hoc* explanations of the data of a particular subject whose behavior does not look at all like that of other subjects. Although this practice may not save you from running subjects who are unusable for your research, it can sometimes save you from obscuring a meaningful result with data from subjects who are not true members of the sample you have chosen. (The issue of excluding subjects' data will be discussed later in this chapter.)

Another valuable safeguard in subject selection (as well as many other facets of experimental design) is to solicit advice from other researchers in the same experimental field. Find out if the effect you are looking for is influenced by sex, age, or any other subject characteristics. In a university, there are often many experienced researchers willing, able, and even flattered to answer questions concerning experimental design and subject selection. If you are interested in conducting an experiment on the development of reading ability, you might not be familiar with all the relevant characteristics. Consulting a researcher whose area of expertise is reading development might be enormously helpful. From this person you might learn, for example, whether children with working mothers learn to read earlier or later and therefore whether the employment status of the child's mother should be considered when choosing children as subjects.

Looking up the description of subjects in journal articles reporting related research also may help, although these descriptions tend to be rather brief and may eliminate information that is unimportant to the author but important to you. For example, a particular finding may result from a study done at an American medical school twenty years ago. The description of the subjects may not include the sex or race of the subjects, although probably most of the subjects were white males. If the phenomenon being investigated is influenced by sex or socioeconomic status (which is often correlated with race), then this subject information is quite relevant even though these characteristics were not described explicitly.

Another determinant of the relevant characteristics of the subject population depends on whether the experimenter is interested in what a subject *can* do or what a subject *does* do. Psychologists who investigate questions of the limits of human performance, such as the minimum duration of a tone needed to distinguish it from another tone, are interested in what subjects *can* do. Here, the psychologist would want to use well-practiced, highly motivated subjects, perhaps even subjects with perfect pitch and advanced musical training.

Other experimenters are more interested in what people habitually do so they can learn about typical (rather than possible) human behavior. Thus, if experimenters were interested in tone durations that people find pleasant, they might use naive, unpracticed subjects. (For a more complete discussion of this topic, see Chapter 2.)

Number of Subjects

Once the characteristics of potential subjects are specified, the next step is to determine how many subjects to include in the experiment. With the exception of single-subject experiments (discussed later), determining the number of subjects to use in an experiment can be quite difficult. The larger the sample, the more likely it is that the behavior of the sample will closely approximate the behavior of the population. In the extreme, if the population consists of 10,000 individuals, one could choose 9999 members for the sample and its behavior will practically duplicate that of the population. Conversely, the behavior of only a few of the members of the population will be less likely to duplicate the behavior of the population. More, however, is not invariably better. The enormous resources necessary to measure the behavior of the entire population is the reason a sample group is desired in the first place.

When choosing the sample size, one should consider the *power* of the statistical test that will be used to evaluate the significance of the data. The probability of a Type II error—accepting a false null hypothesis— is β. Its complement, $1 - \beta$, is known as *power*. The greater the power, the more likely we are to correctly reject a false null hypothesis. Put more simply, as the power of the test increases, the likelihood that even a small difference between experimental groups will be significant increases.

One way to increase power is to increase the number of subjects in the sample. This is especially important when there is variability in the subject group or when the phenomenon being investigated is weak or elusive. This does not mean, however, that by adding enough subjects any experimental hypothesis can be supported. It only means that weak effects are more likely to be detected as the number of subjects increases.

Failure to detect large differences between experimental groups could result from variability among subjects. If the group of subjects is homogeneous, it is likely that a small experimental effect will be observable, even with a small number of subjects. With a diverse group, more subjects will be needed to distinguish differences resulting from the experimental manipulation from those resulting from inherent differences among the subjects themselves. If there is a great deal of variability within the group being tested, then increasing the power of the test by increasing the number of subjects is advantageous.

Some phenomena do not produce striking differences between experimental groups. The relationship between handedness and certain brain functions provides an example. The two halves of the human brain have been shown to be specialized for different types of functions (Sperry, 1968); the left cerebral hemisphere is specialized for verbal information and the right for spatial/pictorial information. Although this differential specialization is fairly clear from data on subjects with various types of brain damage, it is difficult to observe these hemisphere differences in normal subjects with intact brains. Therefore, experiments on these laterality effects in normals benefit from techniques that increase power. This includes reducing subject variability (e.g., carefully choosing subjects who have strong differences between the functions of the two hemispheres) and increasing the number of subjects.

In addition to the factors discussed so far, there are several practical guidelines one can follow when choosing the number of subjects necessary for an experiment. Researchers often consult the literature to determine how many subjects are usually used for each condition in a particular experimental paradigm and a particular area of research. Thus, if 12 subjects per condition is common, an experimenter will probably design the experiment with 12 subjects in each experimental condition. When this is the method used, the experimental design will determine the number of subjects necessary for the experiment. If the experimental design has three conditions with different subjects participating in each condition (between-subjects design), then the experiment will require 36 subjects. If the experimental design calls for three conditions with the same subjects participating in each condition (within-subjects design), then the experiment will require only 12 subjects. This method works particularly well when the effect being studied is expected to be fairly strong. If the experimental manipulation is expected to have only a small effect on behavior, then a larger sample should be chosen because increasing the number of subjects increases the probability of detecting even small differences between groups (i.e., increases power).

Although precedent often determines the number of subjects, there are other methods available. Some attempts have been made to develop more objective criteria to determine how many subjects to use in a particular study. These methods take into account the probabilities of achieving particular levels of accuracy given certain information about the sample.

Cohen (1977) provides numerical procedures for choosing the desired number of subjects for different types of experimental paradigms. These formulas will not be discussed here, and the interested reader is referred to this source.

"$N = 1$" Experiments

Although most experiments examine the behavior of a group of representative sample subjects, some human performances, particularly sensory performances, are assumed to be produced in exactly the same way from subject to subject (for subjects without deficiencies in that sensory modality). For these simple sensory tasks, in theory a single subject or a few well-practiced subjects should be sufficient to reliably reveal the phenomenon in question. (Although some single-subject studies reported in the literature are merely case histories, the majority of single-subject reports are experimental in nature.) In these experiments, a large amount of data is recorded and analyzed for a few subjects, whereas experiments with many subjects compare a relatively small amount of data from a large number of subjects.

The landmark studies of Ebbinghaus (1885/1964) on memory belong to this category. Interested in memory, he acted as his own subject and studied many lists of nonsense syllables. He then tried to recall the syllables he had studied and examined the characteristics of the serial learning of these stimuli. Because of his tremendous tenacity, he was able to discover certain principles of memory that probably would have remained undetected if he had used many subjects in his experiments. Of major importance is his discovery of *savings* in memory. He discovered that when he tried to learn a list that he had learned once but forgotten, this relearning could be accomplished more quickly than learning a new list. Apparently, even though he had no recollection of the items previously learned, some features of the old list had remained in his memory, and this information could be utilized when the same stimuli appeared again. This discovery was made possible because one subject, Ebbinghaus, studied memory for lists of nonsense syllables over a period of many years.

In many sensory experiments in which it is advantageous to compare different experimental conditions, it is common practice to use only a small number of long-term subjects. (The classic studies of Hecht, Shlaer, and Pirenne in 1942 provide a superb example.) In experiments of this nature, an experimenter might be interested in detection thresholds to a visual stimulus as a function of certain characteristics of the stimulus. Here the experimenter might train only a few subjects in a detection task and after many trials of training begin to test each subject on various stimulus intensities. The data from each subject would then be analyzed and reported separately. In such an experiment, it is necessary to establish that the subjects whose data are so critical for the study are normal with respect to the ability being investigated—in this case visual detection.

In this type of study, a few subjects are tested over a long period of time. Each subject is usually tested for thousands of trials and each subject's data are analyzed separately. Ideally, all of the subjects will show a similar pattern of results, which provide important parameter estimates of the phenomenon under investigation. Experiments in which a few long-term subjects are investigated are considered single-subject experiments because subjects are regarded as though they participated in separate experiments. Comparisons between subjects are made in the same manner as one would compare replications of the same experiment. In their classic study, Hecht, Shlaer, and Pirenne (1942) investigated the minimum energy required for threshold vision under optimal physiological conditions. In their experiments, they studied the thresholds of between three and seven subjects (including the authors). They analyzed and reported these data individually for each subject in order to explore the parameters of human visual thresholds.

Recruitment

Once the relevant characteristics of the subject population and the desired number of subjects have been determined, a method must be found to recruit these individuals. The goal when choosing a sample is that it be as representative of the population as possible. *Random sampling* is one method of choosing a representative sample from the population. This means that every member of the population has an equal chance of being included in the sample. Theoretically, one could achieve this by using a lottery. The names of every possible subject would be placed in a basket and then the names pulled out until the required number of subjects had been selected. Because subjects are chosen without any bias whatsoever with this method, a randomly chosen sample is assumed to be truly representative of the population.

Unfortunately, this method is usually impossible for several reasons. First, it is not always possible to enumerate every member of the population of interest. If you are interested in studying human visual thresholds, the population of interest is every human being with a normal visual system who ever lived or who ever will live. To enumerate this group is an impossibility. Second, not every member of the population could possibly have an equal chance of being chosen for the sample. In the present example, a researcher obviously cannot have equal access to every person who ever lived or ever will live. He only has access to a small group of people who are willing and available to be subjects in the specified time and place.

This does not mean that one has to abandon the notion of random selection altogether. Often experimenters choose subjects from a much more limited group, such as a university subject pool or those who answer advertisements in a local newspaper or on bulletin boards, rather than randomly choosing subjects from the entire population. When doing this, one assumes that either inclusion in this restricted group is itself random with respect to the phenomenon being tested or some aspect of the experimental design such as random assignment of subjects to groups will eliminate potential biases. (Experimental design controls are discussed in Chapter 2.)

Most psychological experiments (70%–80% of those published in psychological journals) use college students, often students enrolled in introductory psychology classes who are fulfilling a course requirement. How representative of the population at large are college students? One could muse over the possibility that we are developing a literature on the behavior of the college sophomore and not of humans in general. The validity of this concern depends on the relationship between what is being tested and those characteristics peculiar to a college population such as high IQ or, depending on the school, a particular socioeconomic level or a particular level of motivation. The validity of this concern depends on what is being manipulated by the experimenter and which behavior of the subject is being measured.

For example, volunteer subjects are more highly motivated and have a higher need for approval than nonvolunteers. If need for approval interacts with the phenomenon being studied, then it would be unwise to use volunteer subjects exclusively. If, however, the experiment were designed to investigate factors that increase motivation, one might use the volunteer status of the subject as an independent variable.

For some human characteristics it may not be important that the subjects are college students. Practice has been shown to improve performance of many skills. The possibility that college students are better than noncollege students in their ability to solve problems does not mean that either group would make better subjects in a study of the effect of practice on problem solving. Here the relative differences in performance, rather than their absolute values, are of interest.

In some cases it is false to assume that the group from which the subjects are chosen is free from bias, and consequently the experimental results will be quite misleading. Subjects solicited from a roster of the conservative party for a study concerning the welfare system may not fairly represent the population at large. Results from such a survey could only be generalized to conservative citizens and not to all citizens.

In some cases *stratified samples* are more appropriate than random samples. Stratified samples are chosen by recruiting relevant subsections of the population in proportion to their presence in the general population. It is crucial that only relevant factors are taken into consideration when choosing these subgroups. This method is usually used in public opinion polls and election predictions.

Another method commonly used when choosing samples for public opinion polls is *cluster sampling*. This technique takes advantage of naturally occurring groups or clusters such as apartment buildings or city blocks. Here one might randomly select ten city blocks and then randomly choose a sample from the households in each of these blocks.

There are other sampling techniques that can be used. Common to all these methods is the desire to choose a sample whose behavior will be representative of the population while striking a balance between precision and cost as measured in time and money.

SUBJECTS' PERFORMANCES

Instructions to Subjects

Once the experimental design is established and the subjects have been chosen, care must be given to instruct a subject so that the task is executed in exactly the way it was designed. If the subject does not faithfully perform the task as intended, the validity of the entire experiment (i.e., whether the experiment does in fact test the hypotheses) is in jeopardy.

There are a few guiding principles that should be followed when preparing instructions. First, make the instructions as clear and simple as possible. Tell the subject exactly what is required. It is often good to tell the subject the topic being studied in order to help the subject know what is expected. In an experiment on human attention one might tell the subjects, "The tests you are about to participate in are designed to isolate and study ways in which people pay attention to different things. For this reason it is extremely important that you pay as close attention to what you see as possible" or, "In this experiment we are measuring how fast you can make the decision that two items are the same, so please try to answer as quickly as possible without making mistakes."

While giving this information to the subject, guard against using jargon or giving the subject more information than is needed. Instead of saying, "We are measuring latency of responses and in view of the speed-accuracy trade-off, please respond so as to minimize latencies and errors," say "Please respond as fast as you can without making any mistakes." Keep instructions accurate, simple, and clear.

Do not under any circumstances discuss the specific predictions or hypotheses with the subjects prior to their participation in the experiment. This is especially important with experiments that involve some amount of deception. The famous Milgram studies (1963, 1973), which found that subjects would administer pain to others on the orders of an authority figure, could never have been done if the subjects knew beforehand that the hypothesis was that people would obey an authority figure even when they disagreed with him. Even in experiments in which no deception is practiced, it is poor experimental procedure to explain the predictions and hypotheses before the subject participates in the experiment. If the subject knows the experimental hypothesis before participating in the study, it can never be clear whether this knowledge influenced the behavior. Subjects might try to be "helpful" by behaving in a way they think will yield "good" results. If the subject knows the particular differences that are expected, then the data can easily be contaminated by contrived responses. If the subject begins to ask questions about the point of the experiment, tell the subject you will be happy to explain everything at the experiment's conclusion.

Even when the experiment is not intended to investigate the experimenter's influence on the subject, Rosenthal (1976) has demonstrated that the experimenter's expectations about the subject's behavior can affect the subject's performance. For example, an experimenter who believes that college men will be better at mathematical problems than college women might transmit these expectations to the subjects and affect their performances; the women might sense that they are not supposed to do well, while the men sense that they are supposed to do well.

Many subjects apparently wish to behave in "the right way" and pick up behavioral cues from the experimenter, which often conform to the experimenter's hypotheses. Orne (1962) has termed these tacit wishes of the experimenter that are conveyed to the subject *demand characteristics.* These *demand characteristics* can lead to experimental findings that are biased and falsely support the hypotheses being tested. Although it is hard to know exactly how to eliminate this danger, one can avoid this problem by designing experiments in which the experimenter does not know which condition the subject is currently participating in.

In *double-blind experiments,* neither the subject nor the experimenter knows the experimental condition the subject is participating in. Drug studies demonstrate the usefulness of this procedure. If an experimenter is testing the tranquilizing properties of a new drug, it is useful for both the subject and the experimenter to be blind (i.e., unaware) as to whether a particular subject is receiving a placebo (inactive substance) or the drug itself. In this way, knowledge of the expected effect of the drug cannot influence the subject's or the doctor's report of its effect. Though this is not always possible, awareness of this problem can lead to more careful procedures, which will reduce the probability that the subject is aware of and influenced by the experimental hypothesis.

After explaining the instructions to the subject, it is usually helpful to provide the subject with an example of what has to be done. After the example is completed, ask the subject if there are any questions, and reiterate the instructions if the performance on the example indicates that he or she does not really understand what the task involves.

Two methods of presenting the instructions to the subject are commonly used. One is to give the subject written instructions, have the subject read them, and then answer any questions the subject might have. In the second method, the experimenter reads the instructions to the subject and then solicits questions.

The use of either of these methods does not preclude the use of the other. Often a combination of both is used. For example, a subject might be given written directions, which the experimenter reads aloud while the subject follows along. What is important is that the instructions are clear and that every subject in a particular experimental condition receives the same in-

Table 12-1a Sample Instructions for an Experiment on Tachistoscopic Recognition

In the first half of this experiment, you will be given a list of 10 one-syllable words and 10 nonwords. We will ask you to memorize this list by presenting it over and over again. After each presentation, you will be asked to write down all the words and nonwords you can recall. This process will continue until you are able to recall all 20 items. It is to your advantage to memorize this list because these words and nonwords will appear in the second half of this experiment.

In the second half of this experiment, 20 words and 20 nonwords (including the 10 words and 10 nonwords you have just memorized) will be flashed on a screen for a short time interval. Each stimulus will be presented one at a time in this machine you see in front of you, called a tachistoscope. Preceding the presentation of each stimulus, brackets will appear indicating the position of the word or nonword on the screen. The time interval will be increased until you are able to recognize the letter-string. You must spell out each word or nonword. Make an attempt to spell out each stimulus at each time interval.

Are there any questions?

Table 12-1b Sample Instructions for an Experiment Comparing Memory for Pictures and Words under Two Interference Conditions

In this experiment you will be shown 14 lists of either 12 pictures or 12 words. After each list, you will perform a task for a period of 18 seconds and then write down as many items as you recall, in any order. There will be three types of tasks to perform within the 18-second interval between presentation and recall.

1. If a three-digit *number* appears on the screen, you are to *count* backwards by threes until the 18-second interval is up. So, if the number 197 appears, you will count silently to yourself 194, 191, 188, and so on. Count once every 2 seconds as indicated by the experimenter, who will snap his fingers every 2 seconds.
2. If a *tic-tac-toe board* appears, you are to *rotate* it mentally by 90 degrees (one quarter of a circle). Two Xs will appear in two squares on the board, and they are to be rotated with the board. The figure is to be rotated every 2 seconds as indicated by finger snapping.
3. If a *large* X appears following the last item on the list, the experimenter will still snap his fingers every 2 seconds, but you are to just *wait* without performing a task.

Once the task has been performed for 18 seconds, you are to write down either (1) the final 3-digit number obtained or (2) the final position of the figure after rotations or (3) a large X if no task was performed, in the appropriate blank space on the data sheet (see example). When this is done, you are to write down as many items as you remembered from the 12-item list and for this you will be given 90 seconds. The above procedure will continue until all 14 lists have been shown.

If there are any questions about the instructions, please feel free to ask, as the instructions are a crucial part of this experiment.

Table 12-1c Sample Instructions for an Experiment on Levels-of-Processing

This is an experiment involving questions about words. You will be presented with a series of stimuli, each of which has a question concerning either the meaning of a word or the letter configuration of a word. The stimuli will be presented in the tachistoscope. All the questions can be answered with either a yes or a no. If you wish to answer "NO," you are to hit the button on your left marked "NO." If you wish to answer "YES," you are to hit the button on your right marked "YES." When you are not responding to the stimuli, you are to keep your dominant hand in the middle of the box, between the two buttons. The meaning questions are self-explanatory. An example would be:

Is This a Fruit?
POTATO

You would then hit the button on your left marked "NO."

The letter configuration questions are in the form of a sequence of Vs and Cs, where V represents the vowels a, e, i, o, u, and y, and C represents the consonants, that is, any letter that is not a vowel. If the pattern of Vs and Cs exactly matches the word, it should be considered a "YES"; if it does not, consider it a "NO." An example would be

VCVCCV
ORANGE

You would then hit the button on your right marked "YES." Because your responses are being timed, please respond as quickly as possible, but without making errors. Are there any questions?

(After the incidental learning phase of the experiment, give the following instruction.)

Now we would like you to recall as many of the words you answered questions about as you can. Write the words you remember on the data sheet in front of you. Write them in any order they come to mind. You will be given 2 minutes to recall the words.

structions. If the instructions are clear, simple, and accurate, then the subject will do the task that was designed.

Table 12-1(a–c) presents sample instructions for three typical experiments in human experimental psychology. The first is for a tachistoscopic recognition experiment in which recognition thresholds for words and nonwords are compared when they have been memorized before the experiment (the preexposed condition) compared to when they have not (the control condition) (see Chapter 6). The second is for a free recall experiment comparing pictures and words under two interference conditions—backward counting and mental rotation (see Chapter 8). The third is for an experiment using an incidental learning paradigm in a test of the levels-of-processing theory of memory (see Chapter 8), in which subjects first make timed judgments about words based on meaning or structure and then are given an unexpected memory test for the words.

Motivating Subjects to Perform Well

Subjects who participate in experiments are usually volunteers who may receive money for their participation or, in the case of the often-used college sophomore, fulfill a class requirement. Whether or not the subject is compensated (with money or credit), it is necessary to motivate the subject to perform the task as well as possible. Just as subjects must understand what behavior is desired from them, they must also be motivated to do what is required as best as they can. If, for example, you are testing to see if a subject can learn to recall high-frequency words (e.g., *dog*) more easily than low-frequency words (e.g., *aardvark*), it is imperative that subjects try to learn the words they are given. If the subject is not motivated to perform the task well, then it is likely that recall performance of test words will be equally poor regardless of word frequency. Thus, the effect of the experimental manipulation (word frequency) will not emerge even when a true difference between conditons does exist.

One way of encouraging the subject to do well is to use verbal encouragement when giving instructions. A subject who is given a feeling of the importance of the pursuit of knowledge and the experimenter's appreciation of his or her participation will be a well-motivated subject who performs well. In fact, since subjects' participation is essential for research, the experimenter's appreciation of the subject is appropriate and should be communicated.

Two methods generally employed to motivate subjects are feedback and payoffs. We have learned from a vast literature on reinforcement theory on human (as well as nonhuman) subjects that reinforcement manipulates performance: positive reinforcement increases the frequency of the reinforced behavior (see Chapter 7). This knowledge has led to two ways of increasing subjects' motivation—information feedback and payoffs.

For many subjects, the knowledge of being correct (which can be provided by feedback) is enough of a reward and will improve the subject's motivation and, consequently, performance. This is particularly true of college students, who have been extensively trained to strive for the maximum number correct (i.e., "A" performance).

Information feedback is often provided to the subject after each trial or after each group of trials. The most common feedback is indicating whether a performance is good or bad according to some preset criterion. Frequently in choice tasks, the subject is told on every trial whether the response was correct or incorrect. (This can be done by indicating only whether the subject was wrong with the understanding by the subject that if nothing was indicated, the response was correct.) Sometimes the feedback includes more information than just correct or incorrect. In reaction time tasks the subject can be given the response time for each trial and encouraged to minimize the time that responses take. A person may be told at the end of a trial that the response was correct but slow. The underlying theory is that when information is given to a subject about performance, he or she becomes interested in being "correct" as much as possible. Thus, feedback can motivate a subject to improve performance. Humans generally strive for positive reinforcement (being told they are correct or "good"), and research subjects are no exception.

Another method that has its roots in reinforcement theory is the use of payoffs. Instead of assuming that knowledge of being correct will motivate the subjects, they are told that they will be rewarded for good performances. Schemes usually involve a monetary reward for each correct response coupled with a monetary penalty for errors. Other systems involve a bonus system in which the subject is told that at the end of the study the five best subjects will receive, say, \$10. The specifics of the system are explained to the subject prior to the experimental session in the belief that subjects will behave in a way that will maximize their earnings.

Often payoff schemes are used to let the subject know the relative importance of correct and incorrect performance. For example, an experimenter might want subjects to behave in a conservative manner. In this case subjects might be informed that they will receive one penny every time they correctly answer a question, be penalized 25¢ every time they give an incorrect answer, and if they refuse to answer they will neither receive nor lose any money. With such a payoff system, one could expect subjects to respond only when they are very sure of an answer. Conversely, if subjects know they will never be penalized for a wrong answer and will receive \$1.00 for every correct answer, their behavior will be much less conservative. In fact, subjects will probably try to answer every question regardless of how little confidence they actually have in their answer. It is easy to see that subjects' response criteria can be greatly influenced by payoff schemes.

EXCLUDING SUBJECTS' DATA

Under certain circumstances, a subject's data may be excluded from analysis. If legitimate reasons are discovered for believing that the subject or the subject's performance is not representative of the population, the subject's data should be discarded from the sample. Legitimate reasons can include subject variables such as neurological damage, experimental variables such as equipment failure at the time the subject is being tested, or design variables such as a preset performance criterion that must be met before the subject's data can be included. It is not legitimate, however, to look at a subject's data, observe that it does not conform to theoretical expectations or to the data from other subjects, and then discard it as unrepresentative. Eliminating subjects' data from analysis is a procedure to be done only under circumstances like those described previously or based on an objective statistical criterion. Without this precaution, the validity and integrity of an experimental study is in jeopardy.

There are statistical techniques for eliminating extreme scores from analyses. These include Winsorizing (Dixon & Tukey, 1968) and trimming means (Yuen, 1974; Yuen & Dixon, 1973). These techniques are discussed in more detail in Chapter 15.

SUBJECTS' RIGHTS

Protecting the Subject's Physical and Psychological Health

It must be kept in mind when conducting experiments on humans that the subjects have several legal and moral rights that must be carefully guarded. First, the subject's physical well-being must be protected at all costs. No equipment or procedure should be used that might harm the subject. If drugs must be used, the health of the subject should be ascertained before experimentation and a licensed physician should be present. (An example of an experiment using drugs is presented in Chapter 11.)

Of equal importance is the psychological well-being of the subjects. At the end of each experiment, all subjects should be debriefed. During this time, care should be taken to assure subjects that their performance will be kept confidential. It is extremely important to alleviate any feelings of inadequacy that a subject who did not perform well might have. Subjects should not be made to feel inferior or embarrassed as a result of their performance. Experiments that influence subjects to go against the community's moral code can cause subjects to feel guilty about the way they behaved. For example, a subject influenced to help plan a robbery may still feel guilty about having been willing to cooperate in an illegal action even after being debriefed. It is the responsibility of the researcher to ensure that the subject does not feel guilty and, if necessary, to recontact the subjects to guard against any postexperimental psychological discomfort. At the time subjects are debriefed, they should be allowed to ask questions about the experimental procedure and hypotheses. These questions should be answered to the best of the researcher's ability. The experimenter can, of course, stress to the subjects that they should not discuss the experiment with potential subjects and can offer to forward information when the study is completely finished. (Examples of experiments in which subjects are debriefed can be found in Chapter 11.)

Informed Consent

Subjects' participation must never be the result of coercion or intimidation. No subject should participate in an experiment without his or her informed consent obtained in writing prior to the experimental session. The subject should be told that participation can be discontinued at any time for any reason, stated or unstated, without penalty. In addition, information about the subject should be kept in the strictest of confidence and if some dysfunction in the subject's behavior is discovered, the subject should be told confidentially in order that he or she might seek professional help.

The American Psychological Association has established and published guidelines to protect subjects' rights. Most universities, hospitals, and government agencies that sponsor research have very strict guidelines about obtaining the informed consent of subjects. New York University's guidelines are typical of these:

"Informed consent" means the knowing agreement of an individual or his or her legally authorized representative without undue inducement or any element of force, fraud, deceit, duress, or other form of constraint or coercion.

The basic elements of *informed consent* are:

1. A fair explanation of the procedures to be followed, including an identification of those which are experimental;
2. A description of possible discomforts and risks;
3. A description of possible benefits to be derived;
4. A disclosure of appropriate alternative procedures, if any, that would be advantageous for the subjects;
5. An offer to answer any inquiries concerning the procedure to be followed;
6. A statement that the subject is free to withdraw and to discontinue participation in the program or activity at any time without prejudice.

A sample consent form is shown in Table 12-2.

The Debriefing

Subjects should be debriefed at the conclusion of the experiment. The purpose of the debriefing statement is to inform the subject about the purpose of the experiment so that the subject is aware of how essential his or her participation was. In addition, the debriefing serves to assuage any doubts the subject may have had about his or her performance and to explain any deception that may have been used in the interests of the experiment's validity.

Generally, the experiments in the areas of research covered in human experimental psychology entail neither physical discomfort, mental discomfort, nor deception. The typical debriefing statement in these areas serves merely to inform the subjects of the purpose of the experiment, and thereby to enhance their knowledge of the subject matter of human experimental psychology. When subjects are recruited through an introductory psychology subject pool, participation in experiments is intended to improve subjects' knowledge of experimental method and content. As

Table 12-2 A Sample Consent Form

CONSENT FORM

PLEASE READ CAREFULLY BEFORE SIGNING

I have agreed to participate in the experiment (name of your experiment) and hereby give my consent to be a subject. (Include a description of the procedures used in your experiment here.) I understand that my responses will be kept in the strictest of confidence and anonymity. I have the option to withdraw from this experiment at any time without penalty and I also have the right to request that my responses not be used.

Subject's Signature	Experimenter's Signature
Date	Date

such, it is important that the debriefing statement carefully explain the purpose of the experiment to the subject and improve his or her understanding of certain areas of research.

Table 12-3(a–c) presents three debriefing statements that might accompany the three experiments described earlier, for which sample instructions were provided. The first is a debriefing statement for the experiment comparing recognition thresholds for words and nonwords that were either memorized or not before the experiment. The second is a debriefing statement for the experiment comparing memory for pictures and words after an interference task designed to selectively interfere with rehearsal of visual memory images and verbal codes, in a test of dual-coding theory. The third is a debriefing statement for the experiment testing certain assumptions of the levels-of-processing model of memory.

The issues of protecting subjects' rights by obtaining informed consent and debriefing them appropriately are extremely important and should never be taken lightly. It is only with the cooperation of subject volunteers that so much information has been gathered about human subjects. As researchers, we must continue to ensure their well-being to the limit of our ability.

Table 12-3a Sample Debriefing Statement for an Experiment on Tachistoscopic Recognition

This experiment was designed to compare two theories that attempt to explain the word frequency effect. The word frequency effect is the tendency to recognize familiar stimuli, such as words, more easily than unfamiliar stimuli. One theory, the perceptual theory, says that exposure to stimuli facilitates our perception of them. The second theory, the response-bias theory, says that familiar stimuli are guessed more frequently than unfamiliar stimuli.

This experiment compared very familiar stimuli, high-frequency words, with very unfamiliar stimuli, nonwords. Half of each type of stimulus were memorized before the experiment to see if memorizing nonwords would make them as easy to see as words. If we get this last result, this is support for the response bias theory. If words are still easier to see, this is support for the perceptual theory.

Are there any questions?

Table 12-3b Sample Debriefing Statement for an Experiment Comparing Memory for Pictures and Words under Two Interference Conditions

---

Rehearsal is a process by which items are retained in short-term memory. Some researchers have proposed that there are two memory systems—one that stores visual images (pictures) and another that stores verbal codes (words). This theory is known as the dual coding model, and has been proposed by Paivio (1971). The dual-coding model predicts that if an interference task that is specific for one of these modalities is presented between memorization and a free recall task, then that type of storage will be degraded and the other type of storage will be much less affected. Spatial rotation of a tic-tac-toe board is a visual interference task and counting backward is a verbal interference task. So we expect that picture memory would be degraded most by rotation and word memory degraded most by counting, if the dual-coding model is correct.

Are there any questions?

Table 12-3c Sample Debriefing Statement for an Experiment on Levels-of-Processing

---

The purpose of this experiment is to compare memory for words that were given semantic encoding (meaning questions) to those given structural encoding (letter configuration questions). This experiment is based on an experiment performed by Craik and Tulving (1975), who found that semantically processed words were better remembered than structurally processed words. It is our hypothesis that the semantic stimuli will be remembered better than the structural stimuli, even though the meaning questions were answered more quickly than the structural questions.

Are there any questions?

SUMMARY

In this chapter we discussed the object of our research effort—the human subject. First we described how to choose the sample subjects from the population of interest. Important characteristics of the population must be clearly defined and methods of measuring them consistently applied. Next, the number of subjects necessary for the sample was discussed. Generally, the larger the sample, the more closely it will approximate the behavior of the population. Elusive or weak phenomena benefit from large samples. However, very large samples are neither feasible nor practical. Practically speaking, one can usually use the size of samples reported in published research articles as a guide.

Some experiments use only a small number of highly practiced subjects. This is particularly true when investigating the function of behaviors assumed to be the same for all normal subjects. In these experiments, each subject participates in thousands of trials and data are analyzed and reported separately for each subject. Technically, each subject participates in a separate experiment and data from different subjects are considered experimental replications.

Once the characteristics and number of subjects have been determined, a method of recruitment has to be devised and implemented. Among the most commonly used sampling techniques are random sampling, in which each member of the population has an independent and equal chance of selection; stratified sampling, in which the sample includes the same distributions of relevant characteristics as the population; and cluster sampling, in which natural groupings of potential subjects (e.g., apartment buildings) are chosen and then sampled. Whichever method is used, care must be taken to choose a sample that will represent the population in an unbiased way.

Next, we turned to ways of instructing and motivating subjects so that their performances match the requirements of the experimental design. Instructions should be clear, precise, and consistent without revealing the specific hypotheses or predictions. Experimenters should be aware that even subtle behaviors can give the subject information about the hypotheses and thereby cause contamination of the data. In double-blind studies neither the subject nor the experimenter knows which condition a particular subject is participating in.

Subjects must be motivated to give their best performances. Investigators can encourage subjects to do well by giving them appropriate feedback as well as explicit payoffs for good performances. Payoff schedules can also be used to indicate to the subject the relative importance of correct responses and errors.

Finally, the important topic of subjects' rights was discussed. Researchers are morally and legally bound to preserve subjects' physical and psychological well-being and to obtain written, informed consent from all subjects.

Because the central focus of research is the behavior of the subject, learning to choose, instruct, motivate, and protect the subjects are all of vital concern. Without the proper consideration of these issues, experimental research runs the risk of being both meaningless and unethical.

13

Apparatus

Virtually all experiments can be divided into two parts—stimulus presentation and response recording. The experimenter is always interested in a subject's behavior (response) as a consequence of a particular set of circumstances (stimuli). For a better understanding of the functional relationships, we will discuss stimulus-presenting devices and response-recording devices separately. We will limit ourselves to equipment that presents visual and auditory information because stimuli are usually directed to these two senses. Research involving the senses of taste, smell, and touch will not be discussed.

Apparatus for experiments varies in variety and complexity, ranging from index cards and stop watches to computers with custom-built peripheral devices. Some experimenters manage with homemade devices while others can afford complicated and quite sophisticated equipment. The most sophisticated or the most expensive equipment is not always necessary or desirable. More complicated items are more likely to break down and are more expensive (in both time and money) to maintain.

The choice of equipment is limited by availability, the training of the researcher, the budget for the research project, and the type of experiment being conducted. Ideally, whatever piece of apparatus the experimenter wishes to use exists and is available for his or her use. In the real world, however, researchers must often make do with what their budget and institution will allow. Consequently, the available equipment is considered when designing an experiment.

In this chapter we shall discuss the use of equipment in relation to the areas of research for which they are most commonly used. As you begin to explore the literature in experimental psychology, two facts will emerge. First, different content areas traditionally use certain types of equipment and, second, certain types of equipment dominate the literature. It is important to keep in mind that equipment is only a means to an end. It is one of the tools that helps to uncover knowledge. Try not to let the traditional uses of equipment or the traditional equipment used in an area confine or inhibit your experimental ideas. For example, a deck of cards could be used in a memory experiment instead of the more traditional memory drum or slide projector. What is important is to test your hypothesis as meaningfully as possible.

STIMULUS-PRESENTING APPARATUS

The Tachistoscope

One frequently used apparatus for visual experiments is the tachistoscope (sometimes called T-scope or Tach). Although there are many different varieties and manufacturers (e.g., Scientific Prototype and Iconix), all tachistoscopes share two characteristics. They precisely control both the duration and the intensity of visual stimuli.

The simplest, one-channel tachistoscope is a lightproof rectangular tube with a viewing aperture for the subject at one end and a lighted object (stimulus) at the other end (see Figure 13-1). When the subject

Fig. 13-1 Basic design of a one-channel tachistoscope.

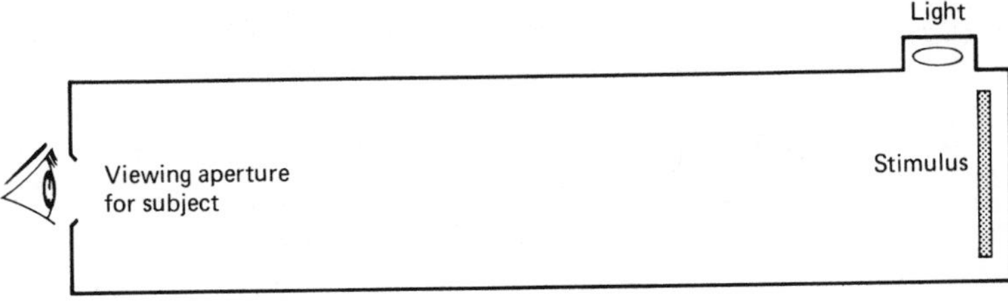

first looks into the tube, the stimulus is not visible. Then the light inside the tube is turned on by the experimenter and the subject is able to see the stimulus. When the light is turned off, the stimulus once again is out of view. By using specially designed timers, the experimenter is able to control the exact stimulus duration. The characteristics of the light enable the experimenter to adjust the intensity of the stimulus.

It is usually desirable for the experimenter to present a sequence of stimuli rather than only one stimulus. Special mirrors and additional lightproof boxes, which present sequences of stimuli for exact durations and at precise intensities, can be added to the basic tachistoscope. The mirrors are half-silvered, enabling the viewer to see whichever stimulus field is lit. Figures 13-2 and 13-3 show the arrangements needed to allow the subject to view two and three different stimuli, respectively. As can be seen in these diagrams, each stimulus can be illuminated by its associated light. Thus, the experimenter uses the lights to control which of the stimuli will be seen at any particular time. All stimuli appear to the subject as though they are in the same location. Coordination of these channels, as each of these stimulus pathways is called, allows the experimenter to design experiments that will present different sequences of stimuli in a predetermined manner.

The tachistoscope can be used to investigate the recognition thresholds or detection characteristics of visual stimuli, since the perception of a visual stimulus is affected by its intensity (energy) and duration. We might wish to test the hypothesis that three-letter words (e.g., *tap*) are recognized more easily (faster) than nonmeaningful three-letter nonwords (e.g., *tlp*) by comparing their tachistoscopic recognition thresholds (TRTs). In such an experiment (see Figure 13-4), a subject looking into the tachistoscope sees a fixation point indicating the stimulus location followed by a brief presentation of a word or nonword (stimulus). Usually the first presentation of the stimulus is subthreshold. This means that it is presented too quickly for correct detection. The same stimulus is presented again and again for increasingly longer periods of time until the TRT, the minimum time needed to correctly report the stimulus, is achieved. Comparison of the average TRTs for words and nonwords can provide the data necessary to test the hypothesis that three-letter words are recognized more easily than three-let-

Fig. 13-2 Basic design of a two-channel tachistoscope.

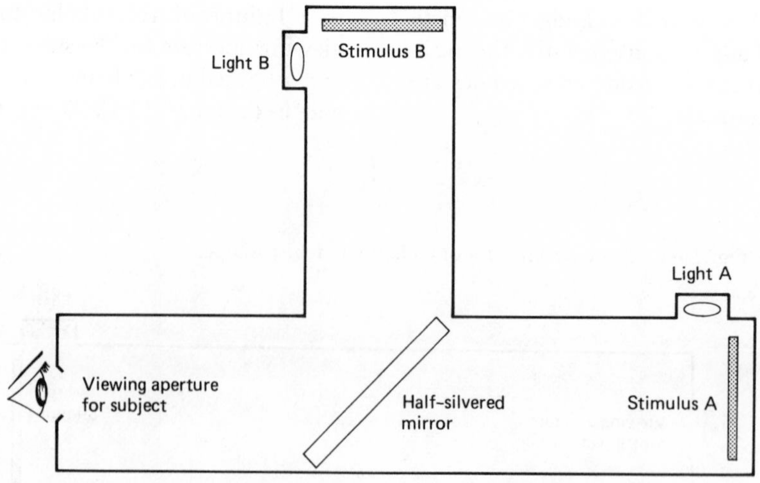

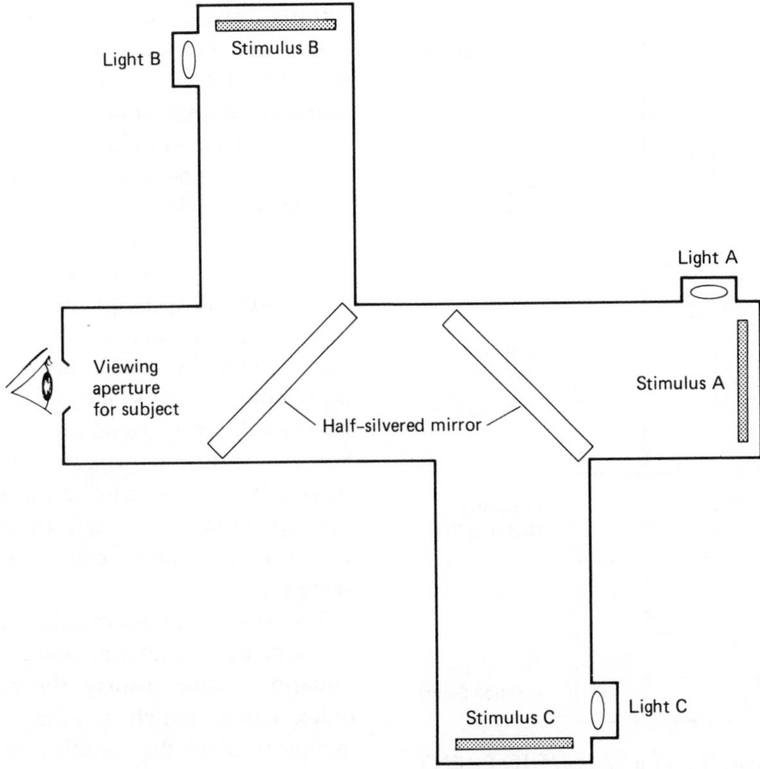

Fig. 13-3 Basic design of a three-channel tachistoscope.

ter nonwords. (For a more complete discussion of recognition thresholds see Chapter 6.)

A two-channel tachistoscope is used in the preceding experiment. The first channel presents the fixation point and the second channel presents the stimulus. If it were sufficient for the subject to see only a dark, blank field before and after the stimulus, a one-channel tachistoscope could have been used. A more complicated experiment investigating the types of trigrams more easily judged the same as, or different from, other stimuli would probably require a three-channel tachistoscope (see Figure 13-5). In one possible experimental design, the subject first sees the fixation point (channel 1), then is shown the first trigram (channel 2), then the fixation point (channel 1) again, and finally the second trigram (channel 3). The subject in this experiment would be required to judge whether the second trigram was the same as the first and indicate the decision by pressing one of two buttons that would record response time. (Devices used to re-

Fig. 13-4 Diagram of a tachistoscopic recognition threshold (TRT) experiment with trigrams.

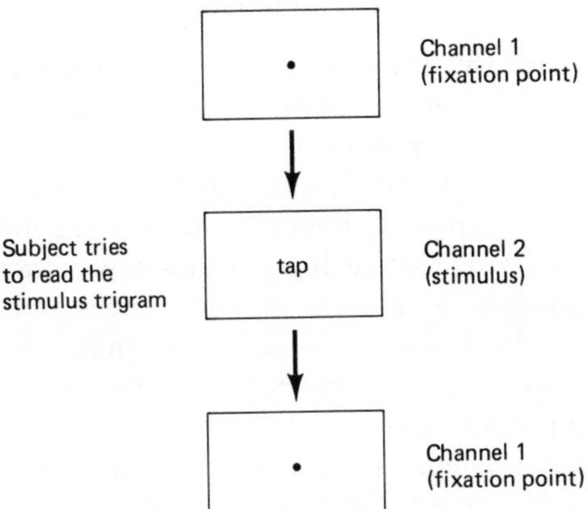

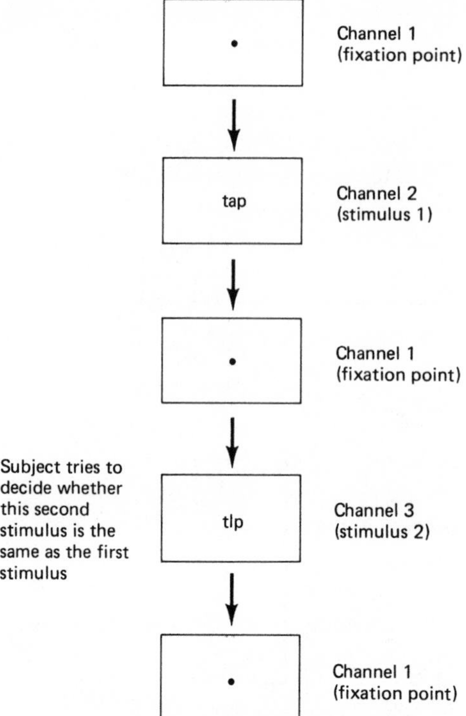

Fig. 13-5 Diagram of a SAME/DIFFERENT experiment.

cord reaction time data are discussed later in this chapter.)

Figure 13-6 shows several time arrangements of channels. In all cases, the blank field is visible whenever the timing apparatus of the tachistoscope is not actuated. The arrangement in part A is the simplest possible, in which the blank field follows the first stimulus field. In part B, the second stimulus field follows the first stimulus field, in part C it precedes it, and in part D it both precedes and follows it. Finally, in part E it follows with a delay during which the blank field is on. In all of these illustrations, we assume that the blank field is dark, the stimulus 1 field contains the stimulus to be reported, and the stimulus 2 field contains a visual masking pattern, as illustrated. Visual noise, composed of a field of Xs, is used to prevent the visual image from persisting after the stimulus is turned off. Using a visual mask of this type (or, alternatively, a field composed of $s or fragments of letter segments such as straight lines and curves) gives the researcher precise control over the actual and perceived stimulus duration.

Tachistoscopes come in a variety of sizes and with a variety of modifications. Some models have two, three, or four channels, which permit more complicated patterns of stimuli and consequently more complicated experimental designs. Each additional channel of the tachistoscope allows more complicated strings of presentations for the subject to attend to and respond to. Some models can project stimuli onto a screen. Instead of just one subject looking through a tube to see each stimulus presentation, many subjects can be tested at the same time.

Tachistoscopes also differ with respect to their ease of operation and degree of automation. Some display the contents of index cards, which require the experimenter to place the stimulus for each trial in the tachistoscope one at a time, whereas others allow the use of slide trays, which automatically feed the next stimulus into the tachistoscope. Regardless of their differences, all tachistoscopes present visual stimuli at specified intensities for precise durations. This makes them especially well adapted for exploring the characteristics of the visual system and certain types of cognitive processing.

The Computer

Since the 1960s, two types of computers have become increasingly important tools for the psychologist. Larger computers (e.g., IBM and CDC computers) have become extremely important for storing and analyzing vast qualities of data in ways not possible with data sheets, pencils, and hand calculators. As is true for many disciplines, psychology benefits from the tremendous speed and efficiency of these large computers. The second type, which is the subject of this section, is the smaller, on-line, interactive minicomputer (e.g., DEC PDP-11).

Small on-line computers have become a vital part of the psychology laboratory in the past decades. Although you may not have access to an on-line computer at this stage of your education, if you attend a fairly large university you can probably go to such a laboratory and ask to be shown around. Perhaps you have participated in an experiment that uses a small on-line computer. In many cases, the on-line computer is used as a tachistoscope with a very large number of channels. On-line computers can be programmed to operate cathode ray tubes (CRTs, which are like a television set or oscilloscope) or other graphics devices to present pictures, words, or other visual information. The program designed by the experimenter to run these experiments has two major characteristics that make the function of a computer similar to that of the tachistoscope. The program controls the exact duration of the stimulus and can often regulate the intensity of the stimulus, depending on the mechanical characteristics of the graphics display device and the graphics language that is being used. In addition, the small on-line computer permits the experimenter to control the timing of every aspect of the experimental trial, including the time between stimuli and the time between trials. The on-line computer combined with a peripheral CRT can be considered a tachistoscope with virtually unlimited channels.

The computer has many advantages over the tachistoscope. First, there is much more flexibility. The experimenter is no longer confined to two, three, or four discrete channels, but now is free to have any number of different events in a particular trial. Second, the computer allows uniform

Fig. 13-6 Some possible stimulus sequences for a three-channel tachistoscope.

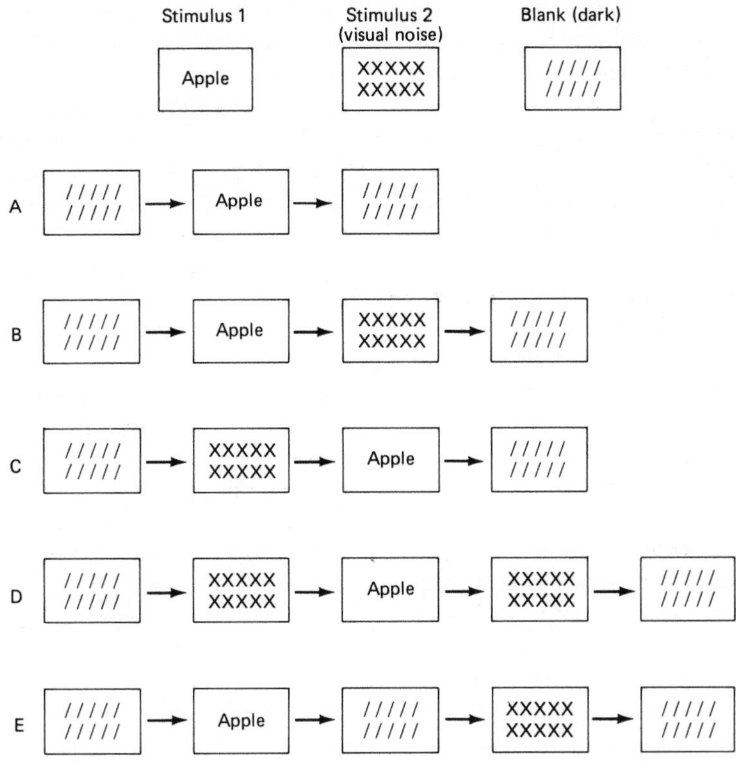

automated running of all subjects. Each subject is given the same items in the same or an experimentally controlled order. Third, the computer allows randomization of stimuli and automatic gathering of data on related response selection or reaction time devices. Finally, data can be stored automatically in a form usually convenient for later automated analyses.

The computer is an efficient and helpful tool. We can compare the activity of the experimenter when using computers and tachistoscopes. In a typical experimental session in a computerized experiment, the experimenter has to set up the experiment (usually by loading disks or other storage media onto the computer), instruct the subject, and begin the session, usually with a code indicating the particular condition and relevant subject information. At the end of the experiment, the experimenter needs to make certain that all the data have been properly stored for later analysis. The computer programs will present the stimulus trials (in a random order if necessary) and collect the data automatically. Contrast this with the role of the experimenter in an experiment using a tachistoscope. Here the experimenter has to set up the machine, instruct the subject, organize and present each stimulus appropriate for different conditions, and record the data. As this comparison shows, once the computer is properly programmed, the experimenter is freed from many of the activities required when using the tachistoscope. This allows the experimenter to pay closer attention to the subject's behavior and reduces the amount of human error introduced into the experimental procedure and data collection.

The small on-line computer has several disadvantages. First, it is relatively costly, although advances in microchip technology are steadily decreasing the cost. Second, because it is such a complicated piece of apparatus and because the computer industry is developing seemingly daily advances and improvements, this equipment requires specialized maintenance and updating. Third, it requires some degree of training before use. Whereas students can be taught to run a tachistoscope in less than an hour, they require much more time to learn how to program an on-line computer. Even for very simple computerized experiments, the prospective experimenter cannot begin implementing experiments for several weeks and often months.

Recently, microcomputers (e.g., TRS-80, IBM-PC, Apple) have been introduced into the psychology laboratory. Although these do not have the power of minicomputers, they provide many of the same on-line and off-line functions at a fraction of the cost. (A practical laboratory can be set up with a microcomputer for a few thousand dollars.) The microcomputer requires less sophistication to use than the minicomputer and also less maintenance.

In addition to experiments that explore properties of visual stimuli, the small on-line computer can also be used effectively in experiments dealing with properties of the auditory system and in those investigating how auditory information is utilized by the brain. It can be used to investigate various aspects of subjects' sensing and perceiving abilities. Many computer installations have a capability for closing switches and generating specific voltages. These capabilities can be used to turn on peripheral equipment including noise generators, tone generators, or tape recorders. As described earlier, the computer can precisely regulate the time that one or several of these devices goes on and off. The computer (depending on its programming and sophistication) is generally capable of automatically recording the subject's particular responses and the reaction time of the response. The data are then stored automatically and can be retrieved at a later time for computer analysis.

The Memory Drum

Many traditional experiments in the research area of learning and memory have used a memory drum to present stimuli.

Essentially, a memory drum consists of a roll of paper containing printed stimuli housed inside a container. This container has a window that allows only a small area of the roll of paper to be seen at any one time. The roll of paper moves at a speed set by the experimenter, and each stimulus is displayed through the window one at a time at some predetermined rate.

List learning by the anticipation method has traditionally used the memory drum. These experiments, which are designed to determine the number of list presentations needed to recall perfectly all of the items on that list in their correct order, use this apparatus in the following typical manner. The roll of paper may have ten words printed on it. The memory drum is set so that every four seconds (the duration can be varied) the roll of paper advances and the next word appears. The subjects are instructed to read each word aloud on the first cycle of the list. In the next and subsequent cycles of the list, the subject will be told to anticipate the following word, saying it before it actually appears. The experimenter will then repeat this procedure until the subject's anticipations are correct for every item on the list. In this experiment the variable of interest is the number of cycles or repetitions of the list needed for a particular subject to learn a particular list presented in a particular order.

The Index Card

Index cards are frequently used to present stimulus materials in learning experiments. They are particularly useful when the exact timing of the presentation of each stimulus is not critical. Index cards have several advantages. First, they are inexpensive to use. Second, experiments that use index cards to present stimuli can be set up very quickly and by persons without any specific training. (This does not refer to the designing of the stimuli or of the experiment, but rather, to the stimulus presentation itself.) Third, if the experimental design requires the randomization of stimuli for each subject or between conditions for a given subject, the cards can be easily shuffled to provide this randomization. (This may be contrasted to the randomization of a list presented on a memory drum, which requires the experimenter to physically make a new list for each order of stimuli even when the individual items remain the same.)

Recognition memory experiments often use index cards to present stimuli. In a typical experiment of this kind, subjects might be shown 30 cards, one at a time, each with one word printed on it. During this presentation, they would be instructed to read each word carefully and try to remember it in any way possible. Cards would be shown to subjects at approximately the rate of one card every five seconds. This series of to-be-remembered words is known as the *study sequence.* (A wristwatch or a metronome is often used to help the experimenter regulate the time.) After the cards are presented once, the experimenter takes these 30 "old" cards and mixes them with 30 previously unseen ("new") cards. The experimenter then shows these 60 cards to the subject and asks him or her to identify the words that have been seen previously (old words) and the words that have not been seen previously (new words). This sequence of old and new words is known as the *test sequence.*

In such an experiment, performance would be measured by determining the number or frequency of words that were correctly identified as old (these responses are called *hits*) and the number or frequency of words that the subject identified as old but were, in fact, new words (these responses are called *false alarms*). (Chapter 4 and Appendix B discuss this terminology and the appropriate analyses for such an experiment.)

The Slide Projector

Another apparatus often used in learning and memory experiments is the slide projector. An experiment similar to the one described previously with index cards might be performed with pictures. Here pictures could be drawn and presented with index cards. If, however, the pictures are too complicated to be drawn on index cards or if they are real scenes, slides could be procured. The study sequence would then consist of a slide tray with the to-be-remembered items, and the test sequence would be loaded into a slide tray containing these to-be-remembered (old) items mixed with the new (distractor) items.

Specially modified slide projectors exist for experimental use. Random access slide projectors provide a way of presenting stimuli in a randomly chosen sequence. Here slides are randomly chosen for presentation from the pool of possible slides.

One advantage in using a slide projector is that many people can be tested at the same time. Slides can be made with words on them instead of pictures, and the index card experiment, which must be individually administered, could be performed on a fairly large group of people at once when the words are transferred to slides. The efficient collection of data is always a big advantage and is worth considering when designing an experiment.

Other Devices that Present Stimuli

There are many devices that can be used to create stimuli for perceptual experiments (e.g., experiments that determine recognition thresholds for particular stimuli) and psychophysical experiments (experiments that relate psychological scales, such as loudness, to physical scales, such as intensity). These devices generate specific types of stimuli whose characteristics can be precisely controlled. One example of this class of devices is a white noise generator. This is a device that produces noise containing tonal components of all frequencies at a particular, adjustable intensity. It sounds to the listener like static on an electrical device. (Because every audible frequency is represented with equal intensity, white noise can be used in auditory experiments in which it is important to avoid spurious findings that might otherwise result from the interaction of a particular frequency with the phenomenon being tested.) For example, it can be useful for experiments in loudness detection, because perceived loudness is affected by both stimulus intensity and stimulus frequency.

Another device often used in auditory experiments is a tone generator. This device allows the experimenter to present a particular tone or sound frequency at a particular intensity. An experiment investigating the function that relates the physical property of intensity to the psychological sensation of loudness might attempt to do this for different frequencies or tones. In such an experiment it would be imperative for the experimenter to have precise knowledge and control over the intensity and frequency of an auditory stimulus. A tone generator is an ideal stimulus-presenting apparatus for an experiment of this type.

The speech synthesizer is another device used in auditory perception experiments. This device can duplicate the sound of words by imitating the sound characteristics of human speech production (the words produced, however, usually sound artificial). This apparatus can be used to study the essential characteristics of speech sound necessary for word perception.

When visual stimuli are desired for an experiment, an oscilloscope is sometimes used to create a visual stimulus of a certain intensity and frequency. This device can be used to determine the properties of the visual thresholds of particular, well-defined stimuli (e.g., spatial frequencies).

In experiments using auditory stimuli, tape recorders and headphones (monaural or stereo) are often used to present stimuli. Information can be presented in a consistent and controlled way to all subjects with the aid of these devices. Similarly, slide projectors are frequently used to present visual stimuli, as previously described.

RESPONSE-MEASURING DEVICES FOR REACTION TIME AND PERCENT CORRECT DATA

A subject's performance on the types of tasks mentioned here is usually measured in either the time it takes to correctly perform a certain task (reaction time) or the accuracy with which a task is performed (percent correct). These measures of performance are used to indicate the complexity of the process being studied. (A more complete discussion of these measures can be found in Chapters 4 and 5.) As an analogy, let us assume you wished to know which of two homework assignments is harder. You might decide that one homework assignment is harder than another because this second, harder, assignment took three hours whereas the first, easier one, took only 15 minutes. Or you might decide that one is harder than the other because the first had 80% errors and the second had only 5% errors, even though they were each completed in 1 hour. Similarly, reaction time and percent correct data can be used as important behavioral measures in an experiment.

If an experimenter wishes to know which of two classes of decisions requires more mental processing, he or she can compare the time needed to make each type of decision and (if the error rates are equally low for both situations) assume that the decision that takes more time requires more mental processing. Reaction time data have been used in this way to explore the characteristics of many types of information processing from the storage of word information in memory (e.g., Meyer & Schvaneveldt, 1971) to cerebral hemispheric organization (Patterson & Bradshaw, 1975). (These dependent measures of behavior are discussed in more detail in the section on reaction time in Chapter 5.)

Reaction time devices are also used to investigate the properties of learning and memory. Often an experimenter is interested not only in whether subjects can recognize or recall a particular stimulus, but also in the amount of time needed to make some judgment about a particular word, to explore how memory is organized. For example, an experimenter might be interested in the ability of a subject to decide whether a written stimulus is a word or a nonword, in order to evaluate which is harder and, in turn, make some assumptions as to how words are stored in the human lexicon (mental dictionary). Such a semantic memory experiment might present strings of letters (either words or nonwords) and require subjects to press one button if the stimulus is a word and a different button if it is not a word. Collecting data about accuracy and reaction time in this *lexical decision* task will provide valuable clues about the organization of the human lexicon.

Once the experimenter has decided to collect reaction time data, certain characteristics of the experimental paradigm will help to determine the appropriate reaction time measurement device. The appropriateness of a reaction time device depends on the scale of time that is relevant to the experiment and the phenomenon being explored. These factors will determine the most appropriate device for the type of activity being measured, the magnitude of the times being measured, and the nature of the expected differences between times. When studying reading rates for paragraphs that differ in their vocabulary level, for example, reading times might be expected to be on the order of minutes, and consequently a stop watch with a minute sweep would be adequate. If seconds are of interest, as with certain stimulus interference tasks (e.g., Stroop, 1935) then a special stop watch or timepiece capable of measuring seconds and tenths of seconds is appropriate. For several types of experiments (many of which are found in both the literatures on sensory thresholds and word memory) a device that measures reaction time in milliseconds (thousandths of a second) becomes necessary.

Another essential characteristic of a reaction time device is that it starts to measure time at the appropriate moment and correctly records the elapsed time from the beginning of the important event to the subject's response. Suppose that an experimenter is interested in comparing the time it took people to read aloud a paragraph of familiar material and the time needed to read a paragraph of complicated, unfamiliar technical material. The appropriate measure would be time, probably in minutes, and a stop watch that records minutes would be used. It is extremely important for the experimenter to start the clock when the subject begins reading the particular paragraph of interest and stop it when the subject finishes that paragraph. If the experimenter fails to carefully start and stop the clock at the proper times, then the measure of reading time will be distorted and the results of the experiment inaccurate, meaningless, or uninterpretable.

The classic Stroop (1935) experiments provide another example of the importance of both choosing the appropriate measuring device and accurately starting and stopping it. In one form of this experiment, subjects are required to report the various colors that words and patterns are printed in on two different sheets of paper. On one, the words "blue," "green," "yellow," and "red" are printed in different colors in sentence-like rows, covering the entire page (about 100 words). Each name of a color is written in the other three colors. The word *red,* for example, appears in blue, green, or yellow ink, but never in red. On a second sheet, nonword stimuli consisting of groups of asterisks (e.g., ***) are arranged on the page in a pattern that resembles the names of the colors on the previously described sheet. Each group of asterisks (the pattern stimulus) is printed in red, blue, green, or yellow ink.

Subjects are given the sheets, one at a time, and required to say aloud the name of the color in which each word (sheet 1) or pattern (sheet 2) appears. This is easy to do for patterns, but it is quite difficult when the stimuli themselves are incompatible color names. In other words, subjects have no trouble saying a pattern of asterisks (***) is blue but do have difficulty saying that the word *red* written in blue ink is "blue." This incompatibility between the correct response (the ink color) and the irrelevant stimulus information (the printed color names) hinders subjects' performance.

To assess this interference effect experimentally, the total time taken to report all of the colors on the sheet containing patterns is compared with the total time required to report all of the ink colors on the sheet with words that themselves are noncorresponding color names. (Recall that for this sheet, if the word *red* appears in green ink, the correct response is "green.") In this experiment the time required to read each sheet is measured in seconds with either a stop watch or other clock capable of recording time in seconds and tenths of seconds. Because the magnitude of the effect is in seconds, a clock whose smallest units are minutes would be inappropriate. Also, because the error in time introduced by the experimenter having to start and stop the clock adds errors of only fractions of a second, which are too small to obscure the effect, a hand-operated clock is appropriate. The subject must read the sheet aloud not only to let the experimenter know if the subject is performing the task correctly but also to signal the experimenter when to turn the clock on and off. For each sheet, the subject is timed from the instant he or she begins reading the sheet to the time he or she finishes it. Finally, the reading time for sheets 1 and 2 can be compared to determine which sheet is easier. These reaction time data reveal that incompatibility between the word's meaning and physical color significantly impairs the subject's ability to report the ink color of the stimulus, even though the subject is never required to read the words that are printed on the page. In other words, the subject is unable to completely ignore the meaning of the word whose ink color he or she is naming.

When time is measured in smaller units,

such as milliseconds, a similar consideration holds. There must be both an appropriate timing device and a way of accurately turning it on and off, so that the interval between the beginning of the stimulus presentation and the response can be recorded to determine how long it took the subject to respond. In this case, no experimenter is fast enough or coordinated enough to turn a clock on and off when the unit of response is in milliseconds. For this purpose there exists a whole line of reaction time devices. Some are custom made, whereas others are constructed according to general standards, and still others are standard models that are modified to work in conjunction with other equipment (e.g., tachistoscopes or computers). These devices are usually clocks that are automatically started by the mechanism that presents the stimulus and stopped by the response mechanism such as the push-button with which the subject responds.

Suppose, for example, an experimenter wants to know if it is harder to detect the letter B when it is presented with a group of other letters (S, G, *B*, M, R, L) than when it is presented with a group of numbers (2, 3, *B*, 7, 9, 4). The purpose of such a study might be to explore the characteristics of detection as a function of category membership. In this experiment, the subject would see displays of six stimuli (letters or numbers) on each trial. Half of the trials would contain the letter *B* and half would not. Here, the experimenter will manipulate the presentations to determine under which condition it is easier to detect the letter *B*. This will enable him or her to make some assumptions about how people analyze visual stimuli.

A reaction time device that measures time in milliseconds would be used in this situation because the data are expected to be on the order of fractions of a second. The subject could have two buttons and be instructed to press one button if the *B* is present and the other button if the *B* is absent. The experimenter could then calculate which was easier—to detect a *B* presented in an array of letters or a *B* presented in an array of numbers. Also interesting for the experimenter would be the difference, if any, between the time needed to decide that the *B* was present versus the time needed to decide that the *B* was absent.

In such an experiment, the stimulus would probably be presented on a tachistoscope or a computer-operated graphics display. With either apparatus, the same device that presents the stimulus would start a timer. When the subject presses a response button, the timer stops and records the time. These data might be recorded on a computer storage device (e.g., magnetic disc or tape), printed on a paper tape, or visually displayed so that an experimenter could copy the response time on paper for later analysis.

For some experiments, it is desirable to measure the reaction time for a subject's spoken response. In these cases, it is not acceptable to have someone, either the subject or the experimenter, push a button as soon as a response is uttered because of the unknown added time required to hear a response, process it, and push a button. In these experiments, a voice key (sound detector and relay) can be used to help collect reaction time data. This is a device that can be set to respond to sounds by either starting or stopping a clock. Thus the subject's oral response can stop the timer.

A variation of the Stroop test described here provides an example of when such a device may be used. An experimenter might wish to record the time needed to read each color stimulus instead of the time needed to read all the stimuli on each page. In this case, each stimulus could be presented individually and a voice key could be used to measure the reaction time for each oral response. In this application, the voice key is essentially a push button that is activated by sound instead of by tactile pressure.

In this section we have presented some of the devices used to record reaction time and percent correct data. More discussion of experimental designs that make use of these various types of apparatus can be found in Chapter 5.

SUMMARY

This chapter described the most commonly used pieces of apparatus in experimental psychology laboratory courses. For the purpose of our discussion, we have divided equipment into two groups based on their functions—stimulus-presenting apparatus and response-measuring apparatus.

The tachistoscope is one of the most frequently used pieces of equipment in perceptual and memory experiments. Although tachistoscopes are available in a variety of models, they all provide precise control of both the duration and intensity of visual stimuli. Tachistoscopes range from simple one-channel models to rather complex multichannel models with custom-built peripheral devices. Tachistoscopes are frequently used to investigate recognition thresholds or detection characteristics of visual stimuli.

Since the 1960s, computers have become increasingly important in the psychology laboratory. Small, on-line computers are used to present stimuli and often to automatically record the subjects' responses. Like a tachistoscope, computers can be programmed to control the exact duration and intensity of the stimuli. Compared to the tachistoscope, a computer's main advantage is its capacity for automation. This not only provides more flexibility in the experimental design but also makes experiments more uniform and better controlled. Unfortunately, computers are quite expensive and require more sophisticated knowledge to operate them. Recently, microcomputers have been developed which provide many of the automated capabilities of the minicomputer at a fraction of the cost, requiring considerably less human expertise.

Though not used frequently today, the memory drum was the traditional apparatus for learning and memory experiments. It allows a list of stimuli to be presented to a subject at a predetermined rate. Many list learning experiments (especially those that used the anticipation method) have successfully used this apparatus.

Index cards can be used as stimulus-presenting devices when precise timing of the presentation is not necessary. They have the advantage of being inexpensive and easy to use. Recognition memory experiments (see Chapter 8) often use index cards to present both the to-be-remembered words and the test sequence.

Slide projectors are also used in learning and memory experiments. Slide projectors allow many subjects to be tested simultaneously. They are relatively inexpensive and easy to use. In addition, slides are well-adapted to experimental designs that require pictorial stimuli.

Devices that are used in experiments of the auditory system include white noise generators (all frequencies present at the same intensity), tone generators, speech synthesizers, and tape recorders.

Response-measuring devices are used to measure and sometimes record subjects' data. We focused here on two types of measures—reaction time and percent correct data. These measures have been used to infer the complexity of mental processing and to explore the properties of learning and memory. The particular reaction time device that is used depends on the scale of time that is relevant to the experiment and the phenomenon being explored. Appropriate measuring devices range from simple stop watches capable of accurately measuring minutes or seconds to elaborate clocks capable of measuring milliseconds (thousandths of a second).

In addition to measuring time in the appropriate scale, a reaction time device must be capable of being started when the stimulus is presented and stopped when the response is initiated. When time is measured in minutes, a hand-held clock can be used. When responses are expected to be in the order of milliseconds, an automatic timer that is started by the stimulus presentation and stopped by the subject's response (e.g., push button or voice key) can be used.

It is important to accurately assess the equipment needs of a particular experimental design. The apparatus chosen to present stimuli and record data must be available, practical, and appropriate. As with most tasks, using the correct tools is essential.

14
Stimulus Materials

Choosing the most appropriate stimuli for an experiment requires knowledge about the characteristics of stimuli that may affect your experimental task and about sources of stimulus materials. Investigators who study aspects of verbal processes have long had access to extensive normative data on various objective and subjective dimensions of their verbal materials. In contrast, normative data on characteristics of pictorial representations are not as readily available.

In this chapter, we will restrict ourselves to the types of stimuli that are most commonly encountered in experimental psychology laboratories that investigate human memory and perceptual processes. Stimulus materials will be classified with respect to two dimensions: verbal (e.g., letters) versus pictorial (e.g., geometric shapes) and meaningful (e.g., words) versus nonmeaningful (e.g., nonsense syllables). Figure 14-1 presents examples of this classification scheme. These two dimensions are independent; that is, knowing whether a particular stimulus is meaningful does not tell you if it is verbal or pictorial. Both these factors have been shown to influence the way people perceive and remember information. Because it is vital for the experimenter to have as much control of the experimental situation as possible, careful selection of the stimuli is necessary. We will present the important characteristics of stimuli in the context of research in learning, memory, and perception.

Experiments in the research area of learning and memory are designed to determine how people learn new information, the characteristics of the storage of this information, and how this information is retrieved (i.e., remembered). Experiments in this area generally use either verbal or pictorial materials. Verbal materials may be letters, nonword strings of letters, words, sentences, or paragraphs. Pictorial materials might be nonsense figures and pictures or drawings of objects, faces, or scenes. In these experiments the materials chosen are crucial to both the outcome and relevance of the experiment itself. Because the experimenter is interested in testing learning and memory, it is important to control for the subject's learning history up to the time he or she enters the laboratory.

For example, an experimenter may wish to investigate the characteristics of memorizing a group of words for later recall. The characteristics of this learning process depend in part on the particular words chosen. If they are extremely familiar to the subject or can generate very strong images, it might be much easier to recall them than if they are not familiar or cannot very easily be associated with an image. Similarly, if subjects are required to decide if a string of letters is a nonword, it will be much easier if the string does not resemble English at all (e.g., *btxrq*) than if it looks and sounds like an English word (e.g., *nerse*). Although it is not always possible to assess the learning history of individual subjects, it is possible to apply what is known generally about the characteristics of stimuli in order to approximate what most people's previous experiences with these stimuli have been.

VERBAL STIMULI

Knowledge of the characteristics of verbal stimuli that have been extensively studied is useful when designing experiments. [Brown (1976) has catalogued 172 of these studies.] Many of the characteristics of meaningful words, nonwords, and letters will be discussed separately in the following sections.

Words—Meaningful Verbal Stimuli

Words are a complex and meaningful group of verbal stimuli. When a subject sees or hears a word in an experiment, it is not usually the first exposure to the word or its root. (If it were, the experimenter's definition of the stimulus as a word would be in error, because for this subject it would be a "nonword.") Words as stimuli have many characteristics that can strongly influence the subject's ability to

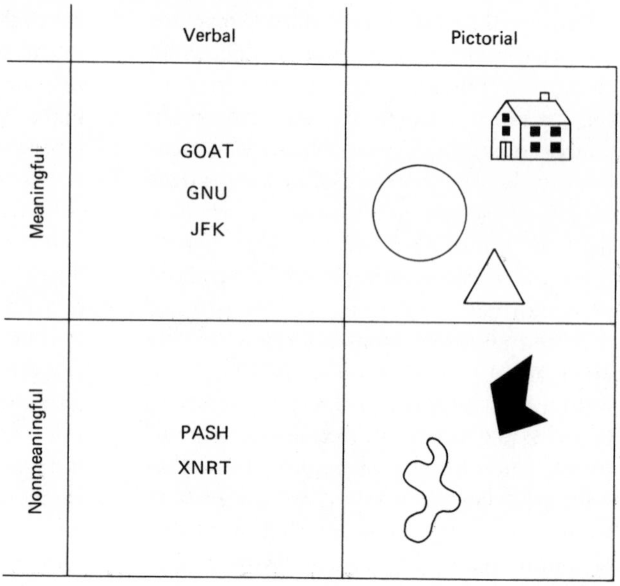

	Verbal	Pictorial
Meaningful	GOAT GNU JFK	
Nonmeaningful	PASH XNRT	

Fig. 14-1 Examples of stimuli classified along two dimensions—verbal versus pictorial, and meaningful versus nonmeaningful.

perceive, learn, and remember that particular word.

Imagine that you were conducting an experiment to assess how easily subjects could remember a list of words arranged in pairs. The type of words chosen as stimuli would make a great deal of difference to the outcome of the experiment. Do you think a subject could as easily memorize familiar words as nonfamiliar words? Would longer words be harder or easier than shorter words? Would words learned as a child be easier than those learned at a later age? How would the relationship between the members of each pair affect learning? Because words have been so widely used as stimuli in experiments on human perception and memory, we know a great deal about the effect of these characteristics of words. This section will discuss some of the more commonly controlled attributes of words.

Frequency. The *frequency* with which words occur in print in the English language has been measured, and frequency counts can be used as an index of how familiar the average person is with certain words. Thorndike and Lorge (1944) reported the frequency of words in such materials as textbooks, the Bible, and popular magazines, as an aid to teachers. More recently, Kučera and Francis (1967) compiled the frequencies they felt were "reasonably representative of current printed American English." They divided their count into categories, including press, reportage, skills and hobbies, learned and scientific writings, and fiction. These two frequency counts were made 23 years apart and are based on different materials. It is therefore not surprising that there are some differences. For example, *radar* was counted at a higher frequency by Kučera and Francis than by Thorndike and Lorge. Despite the difference in date of these two counts, the two sets of ratings are generally quite compatible and both are widely used. As we will see, frequency is an extremely important property of stimulus words.

Word frequency has large and somewhat paradoxical effects on memory performance. Memory for words is usually studied in two ways: by recall and by recognition. In recall tasks subjects are first given words to learn and then are required to produce them without the help of any stimuli or "cues." Recognition tasks first expose subjects to OLD words and then later present these words mixed with another group of NEW words that were not part of the previous set. The subject must recognize the OLD words embedded in this new list. Words of high frequency (high familiarity) are easier to *recall* than those of low frequency. Conversely, words of low frequency are easier to *recognize* than those of high frequency (see Chapter 8 for a discussion of this word frequency paradox).

Word frequency has also been shown to affect word recognition thresholds, or the minimum exposure necessary to correctly perceive a visual stimulus. Howes and Solomon (1951) found that visually presented words can be perceived more easily if they have a high-frequency count (i.e., are more familiar) than if they have a low-frequency count. Although there are several explanations of these effects (some of the hypotheses are discussed in Chapter 6), it is clear that word frequency must be controlled in any experiment on memory or perception. Failure to control this variable could spuriously affect the phenomena being investigated.

For example, suppose a researcher decided to test the hypothesis that older children have a better recognition memory than younger children. To do this the same children were tested twice, once in the third grade and once in the sixth grade. If the children were tested on high-frequency words in the third grade and low-frequency words in the sixth grade, results favoring the older children would not reveal true differences between the two ages. The fact that low-frequency words are recognized more easily would confound the experimental results. In less extreme cases, researchers may fail to control for the effects of word frequency and unknowingly give the two groups different types of stimuli. In these cases, the hypothesis of interest—differences between groups of subjects—will not be fairly tested. Instead, differences between groups of stimuli will be tested.

Age of Acquisition. It is possible that the influence of word frequency on learning, memory, and perception depends on other, more fundamental attributes of words, such as the age at which the particular word was first learned. In many cases, the words that were learned at an early age are the same words that have high-frequency counts. Some investigators (Carroll & White, 1973a) suggest that the variable of *age of acquisition* is a more important determinant of various memory and perception tasks than frequency in print.

Carroll and White found that when subjects are required to name pictures, they can name pictures of words that are learned early in life faster than pictures of words learned later. This effect still holds when word frequency is controlled. Though one cannot automatically generalize this picture-naming result to all verbal behaviors, it does suggest that the age of acquisition of a word, which measures the length of time a word has resided in memory, might account for some of the data previously attributed to word frequency. Norms for the age of acquisition of 220 picturable nouns can be obtained from the work of Carroll and White (1973b).

Word Length. The *length of a word,* measured either by the number of letters or the number of phonemic (sound) units, is another factor that can affect performance. Generally, shorter words are easier to learn and have lower recognition thresholds. This, too, has been shown to interact with word frequency. It has been established (Landauer & Streeter, 1973) that low-frequency words have more phonemic units than high-frequency words with the same number of letters. Thus, we see that both the phonemic length and the frequency of a word should be considered when choosing stimuli.

Concreteness, Imagery, and Meaningfulness. Three additional attributes of words that should be considered in designing a stimulus list are *concreteness, imagery,* and *meaningfulness.* Subjects required to rate words for their concreteness (Paivio,

Yuille, & Madigan, 1968) were told, "Any word that refers to objects, materials, or persons should receive a high concreteness rating; any word that refers to an abstract concept that cannot be experienced by the senses should receive a high abstractness rating . . . " (i.e., low concreteness). Paivio and his colleagues, among others, have shown that this property correlates with performance in experiments on free recall, recognition memory, short-term memory, paired-associate learning, association speed, recognition speed, and physiological indices of arousal. (Ratings of the concreteness, imagery, and meaningfulness of 925 nouns can be found in Paivio, Yuille, and Madigan, 1968.)

The imagery ratings of a word (the extent to which a word evokes a mental image—Gorman, 1961) is highly correlated with its concreteness (Paivio & Simpson, 1966) and has a similar influence on performance. A word such as *dog,* for example, is both concrete and imageable. Most people can, when given the word *dog,* think of exactly what it is and form a mental image, which can function as a memory aid. Some nouns that are associated with sensory experiences but not specific things, including affective attitudes such as "affection" and fictitious creatures such as the "devil," were judged to be high in imagery but low in concreteness. A few words, mostly of low frequency, have higher ratings for concreteness than for imagery. The words *bivouac* and *gadfly* fall into this category. Perhaps the fact that they have few associations but are, nevertheless, recognized as concrete accounts for this finding. These nouns can rely only on one type of memory aid—concreteness or imagery—to help the memory process. Words that are neither concrete nor easily imageable, such as *chance* or *concept,* are usually even harder to remember because they can provide no extra cues for memory such as concreteness or the ability to evoke a mental image.

The meaningfulness of a word is defined as the mean number of written associations that can be made within 30 seconds. Meaningfulness has been found to correlate with performance in most verbal learning situations. In paired-associate learning, in which subjects are required to learn to produce the second member of a pair of words (response) when given the first member of the pair (stimulus), the effect of meaningfulness is greater when applied to the response member of the pair, and the attributes of concreteness and imageability are more effective when applied to the stimulus member of the pair (Goss & Nodine, 1965; Noble, 1963). Although the exact functions and differences among these three variables are still the subject of much research, these characteristics of words must be considered when designing learning experiments.

Category Membership. Another important property of words is their *category membership.* Battig and Montague (1969) have provided lists of words generated by subjects as associates to category names for 56 categories, such as birds, vegetables, and four-legged animals. The frequency with which their respondents wrote down each of the possible exemplars is also reported, and permits investigators to choose exemplars of categories that are most typical of that category. The opportunity to categorize words has been shown to be particularly important in recall memory studies, for which lists of words from a few selected categories can be recalled much better than lists of unrelated words. Subjects are apparently able to use the semantic information about category membership to retrieve items they have learned, as discussed in Chapter 8.

Social Acceptability. The social and sexual implications of words can also affect performance. A classic experiment of McGinnies (1949) showed that recognition thresholds were higher for taboo words than for neutral words (a phenomenon known as *perceptual defense*) and furthermore that the galvanic skin response (GSR) was higher prior to verbal recognition of the taboo word, thereby showing some sort of unconscious recognition of the taboo word prior to the conscious verbalized response. This phenomenon has been termed *subception.* Since McGinnies's experiment, a great deal of research has been directed toward elucidating the nature of these phenomena. (For a review of these phenomena, see Erdelyi, 1974.)

The perceptual defense phenomenon has been challenged on various grounds. First, the taboo and neutral words were not equated for frequency in print, which has been shown to affect recognition thresholds (Howes & Solomon, 1951). Second, response suppression—the failure to say a taboo word until the subject is absolutely sure of its identity—could account for most if not all of the perceptual defense effect. Response suppression could also account for the GSR results, because if the subject recognized a taboo word before reporting it, his or her GSR might be elevated before the response. Other researchers have manipulated this effect while controlling for frequency (Postman, Bronson & Gropper, 1953) and requiring subjects to report words in ways other than by saying them (Zajonc, 1962). Thus, the *social acceptability* of words must also be considered when designing an experiment. Unfortunately, this variable does not have easily accessible norms. However, awareness of these phenomena when designing experiments, and even having a separate group of subjects rate words before an experiment, can be very helpful.

It must seem by now that the list of word attributes that should be controlled in an experiment is endless. In practice, the careful consideration of which words to use as stimuli in relation to their frequency, age of acquisition, length, concreteness, imageability, meaningfulness, category inclusion, and more subjective attributes such as tabooness is often quite tedious, but nevertheless essential. An experiment that does not control the relevant attributes of words used as stimuli can lead to erroneous or unexplainable results. The word characteristics mentioned here can act as confounding variables (see Chapter 3) in experiments in which they are not controlled.

Nonwords—Meaningful and Nonmeaningful Verbal Stimuli

There are several properties of nonword letter combinations to consider when choosing nonwords as stimuli. These properties include their *similarity to English graphemic and phonemic rules,* their *pronounceability,* and their *meaningfulness.*

Similarity to English. Nonwords can be constructed to conform to the structure of English words (e.g., PLUT). There are several systematic ways to construct nonwords that are "legal" (i.e., that conform to the spelling patterns of English). One way is to change one or two letters of existing English words, by replacing a consonant with another consonant or a vowel with another vowel, so that the resulting nonword is pronounceable but not a member of the English language. Another way is to take advantage of published tables giving the frequency of occurrence of single letters or combinations of letters in various positions in English words. Tables of frequencies of occurrence in English of single letters and digrams by position in words of various lengths may be found in Mayzner and Tresselt (1965), and of trigrams, tetragrams, and pentagrams in Mayzner, Tresselt, and Wolin (1965a, 1965b, 1965c, respectively). Alternatively, nonwords may be constructed that are "illegal" (e.g., *qxtl*). This nonword could never be an English word for at least two reasons. First, the graphemic and phonemic rules of English do not permit the letter *q* to be followed by any letter but *u.* Second, every word in English must contain a vowel.

In an experiment designed to study how words are stored, subjects might be required to determine whether a particular group of letters is a word. (Tasks of this type are called lexical decision tasks. The time needed to make this decision is used to infer certain schemes of word storage.) To ensure that decisions are based on the meaning of the word, it would be desirable for the nonwords to resemble real words. If the stimulus does not resemble the structure of a word or is not pronounceable, then subjects can use this information about these characteristics of words to complete the task instead of exploring his or her "internal dictionary" (lexicon) to see if the particular stimulus exists as a meaningful word. In other words, a subject can determine *plut* is not a word only by failing to find its internal representation, whereas subjects can determine *qxtl* is not a word because it does not look like an English word (*q* is not followed by *u*) or because it is not pronounceable (it contains no vowels). Thus, using legal nonwords like *plut* would be better for this experiment. It has been demonstrated experimentally that it is easier to reject an impossible string of letters as being a word than to reject a possible nonword (Snodgrass & Jarvella, 1972).

Conversely, nonwords that are not similar to English words may be desirable stimuli in some experiments. For example, an experiment that explores memory and learning might want to study aids to memory using stimuli that are unfamiliar to all subjects. In such a case, the stimuli chosen for this experiment might not resemble the graphemic or phonemic structure of words at all.

Meaningfulness. It is possible for a nonword to be meaningful, and this, too, can influence how it is perceived and encoded by a human observer. For example, nonwords that are acronyms, such as *JFK* or *IBM*, are meaningful and familiar to most people. Thus, they will not be perceived in the same way as nonmeaningful nonwords such as *JGV* or *FRD*. Acronyms are not the only nonwords that are meaningful. *Nerse* is a nonword that is similar to the real word NURSE and is more meaningful than SENER, for example. *Nerse* will be learned and remembered in a different way from *sener*, which has no meaning or association for most people.

The effects of pronounceability and meaningfulness of nonword trigrams (groups of three letters) have been studied experimentally. Gibson, Bishop, Schiff, and Smith (1964) have shown that recognition thresholds (the minimum time necessary to correctly detect a visually presented stimulus) for pronounceable trigrams (e.g., *kor*) are lower than for either meaningful trigrams (e.g., *rko*) or control trigrams (e.g., *okr*) composed of rearrangements of the same three letters. In contrast, they found that memory as measured by both recognition and recall tests is better for meaningful trigrams than for either pronounceable or control trigrams. The explanation posited for the superiority of pronounceable trigrams in perceptual tests is the fact that pronounceability confers unity by permitting the subject to encode the trigram with a single unit (or chunk) whereas nonpronounceable trigrams must be encoded with three separate units. Regardless of whether this explanation is correct, these data should be taken into account when experiments are designed with nonword stimuli (Badia, Rosenberg, & Langer, 1965; Hayden & Loud, 1969; Nobel, 1967; Smith, Badia, & Rosenberg, 1968, 1969; Underwood & Schulz, 1960).

The aspects of nonword stimuli discussed here—their similarity to English words, their pronounceability, and their meaningfulness—must be considered with care. An experiment testing the characteristics of learning and memory must consider the similarity of nonwords to English and the meaningfulness of nonword stimuli, whereas experiments of perceptual detection must consider the pronounceability of the stimuli. These stimulus characteristics must be considered as they relate to the variables the experimenter wishes to manipulate and test. As previously discussed (Gibson et al., 1964), the effect of a particular stimulus characteristic interacts with the experimental paradigm.

Letters—Nonmeaningful Verbal Stimuli

Verbal and Visual Similarity. Letters are often used as stimuli in experiments. Memory for letters has been investigated to determine which characteristics of letters—their sound or their shape—will cause two letters to be confused with each other. This issue of *verbal* versus *visual similarity* has been important to research. Conrad (1964) has shown that the letters that are most confused in an auditory task (e.g., *c* and *t*) will also be more confusable in a visual task. In Conrad's experiments, there were two sets of stimulus letters. One set consisted of the letters *b, c, p, t,* and *v* and the second set consisted of the letters *f, m, n, s,* and *x.* Each of these two sets of letters was constructed so that all the letters within a set contained the same vowel sound and were shown to be highly confusable when presented acoustically. Subjects were shown six letters, one at a time, for 750 ms each (three quarters of a second). Following this, subjects were required to write down all six letters. The errors that subjects made in this visual task were the same type of errors made by subjects in auditory tasks. Thus, letters that sounded alike were confused with each other more than letters that did not sound alike. In this and other studies (Conrad & Hull, 1964), recall errors varied inversely with acoustic similarity even in nonauditory visual tasks. [However, the work of Gibson et al (1964) reveals that when perceptual similarity is the salient dimension, in a same-different reaction time paradigm, visual similarity is important.]

Although these studies were carried out to answer some questions concerning the characteristics of short-term memory (e.g., whether there are auditory components of this memory), they provide valuable help for choosing stimuli. If a study is undertaken to determine how many letters a person can remember after a brief presentation, it is desirable to choose letters that will not be confused in short-term memory. This way, memory characteristics can be investigated without interference from another phenomenon, namely, acoustic similarity. The data reported above would warn an experimenter to avoid acoustically similar pairs, such as *E* and *D*.

Other experiments (e.g., Gibson et al., 1964) demonstrate that the visual properties of stimuli are critical. In a recognition threshold experiment using letters, one would expect the visually confusable pair *E* and *F* to introduce problems, whereas the acoustically similar pair *E* and *D* might be harmless. As can be seen, it is important to consider the acoustic and visual properties of letters in relation to the experimental paradigm.

PICTORIAL STIMULI

Like verbal materials, pictorial stimuli also have characteristics that must be controlled in an experimental design. These characteristics are, however, more difficult to enumerate and less well understood. We will divide pictorial stimuli into four categories—random shapes, matrix patterns, pictures of objects (line drawings), and photographs of objects—and discuss each separately. As with the verbal stimuli, these stimuli can be described with respect to meaningfulness. The first two categories include nonmeaningful stimuli and the second two include meaningful stimuli. As with any other class of stimuli, the more the experimenter knows about its attributes, the more likely he or she is to design an experiment that is not confounded by stimulus properties.

One important characteristic of a pictorial stimulis is its degree of visual complexity. Early research using pictorial stimuli has established that when complexity is manipulated, more complex stimuli are more difficult to reproduce from memory (Attneave, 1955; Fehrer, 1935) and more difficult to learn by name (Attneave, 1955; French, 1954) than simple stimuli. These findings point to the fact that simple stimuli are easier to process than complex stimuli.

The effects of language on memory of pictorial stimuli have been studied. Glanzer and Clark (1963a) found evidence that subjects verbally encode visual patterns. They found that the ability to reconstruct patterns was influenced by the length of the verbal description. Visual patterns that required descriptions of eight words were reproduced with 15% accuracy, whereas visual patterns that required descriptions of only two words were reproduced with 100% accuracy.

Random Shapes—Nonmeaningful Stimuli

Random shapes such as the one in Figure 14-2 have been generated according to a method described by Attneave and Arnoult (1956) in which certain physical characteristics are systematically varied while the remaining characteristics are randomly determined. Vanderplas, Sanderson, and Vanderplas (1965) conducted experiments that required subjects to scale 1100 figures for their association value and information content. The use of these figures with established association value and information norms allows different research groups to use the same stimuli and yields results that are comparable across studies.

Matrix Patterns—Nonmeaningful Stimuli

Matrix patterns like the ones in Figure 14-3 have been used as stimuli in visual perception and learning experiments. Attneave (1955) used matrices that varied in both complexity and symmetry to investigate performance in three experiments, including reproduction of a matrix from memory, use of a matrix as the response member in a paired associate task (matrices were paired with letters of the alphabet), and identification of a matrix. His results consistently showed that symmetry aids performance and complexity hinders it.

Fig. 14-2 An example of a random figure.

Fig. 14-3 Two matrices with the same amount of white and black spaces. The figure on the left is less complex and more symmetrical than the righthand figure.

Snodgrass (1971) generated matrix patterns and developed three sets of objective complexity measures for them (the first two within the framework of information theory and the third based on symmetry and grouping of identical elements). This study presents a method of producing visual patterns for research and explores a number of methods of analyzing the characteristics of unique patterns that can be applied to other visual patterns. When employed, this method of creating and evaluating matrix patterns allows objective comparisons and evaluations of experiments that use visual patterns for stimuli.

Pictures of Objects (Line Drawings)—Meaningful Stimuli

In recent years experiments employing the pictorial form of concepts have proliferated (Paivio, 1971). Unlike verbal stimuli, which have been extensively standardized (see previous section), little standardization of line drawings exists. In general, the stimuli used in these experiments have been simple drawings of familiar objects. There are, however, many ways to draw even the simplest concept. To date, each investigator has been forced to develop his or her own set of pictures, which are necessarily highly idiosyncratic. One cannot assume that the results of studies employing such different representations of the same concept are comparable.

Snodgrass and Vanderwart (1980) have recently provided a set of 260 pictures (black and white line drawings) that have been standardized on four variables of relevance to experimentation in visual perception and memory. The four variables collected are name agreement (the degree to which subjects agree on the name of a picture), image agreement (the degree to which images generated by subjects to a picture's name agree with the picture's appearance), familiarity (the familiarity of the pictured form of the concept), and visual complexity (the amount of detail in the drawing). Familiarity of pictures should act in much the same way that frequency of words does, affecting both perception and memory. Name agreement is important in determining how easily subjects are able to identify stimuli in tachistoscopic recognition experiments and how easily they can recall stimuli in memory experiments. Visual complexity is also likely to affect perceptual recognition thresholds and to act similarly to the variable of complexity in less meaningful visual stimuli, such as the matrix patterns discussed previously.

Photographs of Objects—Meaningful Stimuli

Of all the types of pictorial stimuli discussed here, the least is known about photographs of real objects, scenes, faces, and so forth. Here the potential variety of color, complexity, ambiguity, and asymmetry is virtually infinite. Although no norms exist for photographs, prudent review of pictures prior to experimentation can lead to some kind of informal control. In addition, independent raters can be asked to judge potential stimuli on variables that may be relevant to the particular study.

For example, an investigator wishing to use photographs of faces in a recognition memory test might first select a group of portraits and then have subjects rate these potential stimuli on their distinctiveness, similarity, or any other relevant attribute. Based on these data, a final group of photographs could then be chosen for use in the experiment with another group of subjects not involved in the rating. This would help ensure that no characteristic of the photographs themselves would be likely to confound the independent variables manipulated by the experimenter.

The careful selection of stimuli is a critical factor of experimental design. Table 14-1 provides a summary of the different types of verbal and pictorial, meaningful, and nonmeaningful stimuli we have discussed. The characteristics of these stimuli must be carefully considered in order to design a reliable and valid experiment.

PERCEPTIBILITY OF STIMULUS MATERIALS

Up to this point, we have been concerned primarily with the properties of stimuli that can be presented either visually or auditorily. Whenever we present material to these two senses, we must consider the perceptual properties of vision and audition. In this section we will very briefly review some properties of visual and auditory perception. (For a complete review, the reader should consult a textbook on perception.)

Visual Perception

For a stimulus to be perceived visually, radiant electromagnetic energy must activate light-sensitive receptors (photoreceptors) in the eye. Visible light can be described by two characteristics—wavelength and intensity.

We are visually sensitive to only a narrow range of wavelengths. Light that we can see ranges from 400 nanometers (1 nm = one billionth of a meter) to 760 nm. This corresponds to our perception of

Table 14-1 Types of Stimuli and Some of Their Characteristics

	Verbal		Pictorial	
	Stimulus type	Characteristics	Stimulus type	Characteristics
MEANINGFUL	Words	Frequency Age of acquisition Length Concreteness Imagery Meaningfulness Category membership Social acceptability	Photographs Line drawings	Complexity Name agreement Image agreement Familiarity Visual complexity
NONMEANINGFUL	Nonwords	Meaningfulness Graphemic properties Phonemic properties Pronounceability	Matrices	Complexity Symmetry
	Letters	Acoustic properties Visual properties	Random shapes	Complexity Randomness

colors ranging from violet, the shortest visible wavelength, to red, the longest visible wavelength.

Intensity is the second important characteristic of visible light. Two aspects of intensity that are measured are illuminance and luminance. Illuminance, or incident light, is the amount of light *falling on* a surface. This property of light is measured in footcandles (the amount of illumination received on a surface with an area of one square foot located one foot from a standard candle). Luminance, the amount of light *reflected from* a surface to the eye, is measured in footlamberts (the amount of light emitted in all directions one foot away from a perfectly reflecting surface receiving one footcandle of illumination).

Our sensitivity to visual stimuli, or the threshold for a particular stimulus, is affected by the part of the retina that is stimulated. When we are in a well-lit area and our visual system is light-adapted, photoreceptors called *cones* are maximally stimulated. This results in a shift in visual sensitivity to the longer wavelengths, good visual acuity, and good color detection. When we are dark-adapted to a poorly lit area, photoreceptors called *rods* are maximally stimulated. This results in a shift in sensitivity to the shorter wavelengths and improved motion detection.

Because of the effect of retinal sensitivity (cone or rod vision) on visual perception, the researcher needs to be aware of the lighting properties of the room where the experiment will be conducted. In addition, it should be noted that it takes about 35 minutes to become fully dark-adapted when entering a darkened room, whereas becoming light-adapted takes only a few minutes. The careful researcher must take this temporal factor into account. A subject being tested in a darkened room must be given sufficient time for his or her visual system to adjust before the experiment begins.

There is a variety of spatiotemporal factors that affect visual sensitivity. There are known relationships between stimulus intensity and duration when determining visual thresholds. For stimuli shorter than 100 ms, stimulus intensity (I) and stimulus duration (T) bear a reciprocal relationship for the amount of stimulus energy necessary for a constant threshold (k) (Bloch's law).

$$k = I \times T$$

The relationship between intensity and retinal area (A) for small retinal areas is reciprocal (Ricco's law).

$$k = I \times A$$

Piper's law for larger retinal areas states that intensity is reciprocal to the square root of the retinal area that is stimulated.

$$k = I \times \sqrt{A}$$

Critical flicker fusion, the rate at which a flashing light is perceived as continuous, is a temporal phenomenon that affects visual perception. Motion pictures, which consist of a series of rapidly presented still pictures, take advantage of this phenomenon.

Other factors that can affect visual perception include contrast effects (e.g., simultaneous brightness contrast, mach bands, and lateral inhibition). Contrast effects are caused by the light that falls on adjacent areas of the retina that are involved in the perception of stimuli. Still other factors that could be considered when designing a visual experiment are binocular vision, depth perception, visual illusions, and constancy.

Auditory Perception

The physical basis for hearing sounds is vibration. There are three properties of sound waves that are frequently measured—*amplitude, frequency,* and *phase.* The *amplitude* of a sound wave is a measure of its pressure. The psychological experience that corresponds to this pressure is *loudness.* (Loudness also depends on the wave's frequency, since our ears are not equally sensitive at all frequencies.) Pressure changes caused by sound waves are measured in decibels (dB). An audible whisper is about 20 dB; a conversation is about 60 dB; a subway is about 100 dB; and a jet at takeoff is about 140 dB. It is estimated that an amplitude of 130 dB is sufficient to cause hearing loss.

The second physical property of sound waves is *frequency,* measured in Hertz (Hz), or cycles per second. This corresponds to the psychological experience of *pitch.* The human ear is most sensitive to stimuli ranging from 1000 to 4000 Hz, although our entire range is much wider (from 20 to 20,000 Hz).

The third physical property of sound waves is *phase.* Phase is the part of the cycle that a wave is in at a specific point of time. Usually we are interested in the phase relationship between two waves. Analyzing the phase relationship between sound waves from a single source as they are perceived by the two ears helps us localize sounds in space. The ear nearer the sound source will receive the sound wave slightly sooner, which provides an important cue for localizing the sound source. If a sound source is directly in front or in back of us, the waves perceived by both ears will be in phase. This is why it is difficult to determine whether a sound is coming from a source directly in front or directly behind us. There is, however, no direct psychological experience always associated with phase.

Another psychological characteristic of sound not directly related to any of its physical properties is *timbre,* the purity of sound. A tuning fork, which produces a single frequency, has a very pure sound whereas instruments with a mixture of frequencies produce relatively impure sounds.

These properties of perceived sounds

have an influence in experiments with auditorily presented stimuli. Paying careful attention to the properties of auditory stimuli will prevent confounding of experimental effects.

SUMMARY

This chapter reviewed some of the characteristics of stimulus materials commonly used in experimental psychology laboratory courses. Stimuli are categorized as either verbal or pictorial and as meaningful or nonmeaningful. According to this scheme, we first discuss properties of words (verbal and meaningful), nonwords (verbal and meaningful or nonmeaningful), and single letters (verbal and nonmeaningful).

Attributes of words that need to be considered when choosing experimental stimuli include frequency, age of acquisition (length of time a word has resided in long-term memory), word length (number of letters and phonemes), concreteness, imagery, meaningfulness, category membership, and social acceptability. High-frequency words (i.e., commonly used words such as *dog*) are recalled better than low-frequency words (i.e., uncommon words such as *aardvark*). Conversely, low-frequency words are recognized better. Naming objects is faster for words learned at an earlier age. Generally, shorter words are easier to learn and have lower recognition thresholds. Usually, the more concrete, imageable, and meaningful a stimulus is, the better the performance of subjects in memory and perception experiments. Category membership is particularly helpful in recalling a list of words. Social acceptability is an important variable. Subjects may fail to perceive words that are considered socially unacceptable. There is a great deal of interaction among these stimulus attributes. Careful consideration of these characteristics can prevent confounded experimental variables.

Nonwords are frequently used as stimuli in memory and perception experiments. These stimuli, composed of two or more letters, can be either meaningful (e.g., *IBM*) or nonmeaningful (e.g., *XBT*). Meaningful nonwords are not perceived in the same way as nonmeaningful nonwords. Recognition thresholds are lower for pronounceable nonwords regardless of their meaningfulness. Memory (recall and recognition) has been shown to be better for trigrams that are meaningful. Combinations of letters can also vary in the degree to which they resemble English words. It is harder to reject a nonword that conforms to graphemic and phonemic rules of English (i.e., looks and sounds like an English word, e.g., *plut*) than one that does not resemble a word (e.g., *pszt*).

Single letters are nonmeaningful verbal stimuli. The similarity among letters—either visual (*E, F*) or verbal (*E, D*)—must be considered when choosing letters. Research has shown that even for visually presented stimuli, confusions occur between letters that are acoustically rather than visually similar.

Pictorial stimuli are the second group of stimuli discussed here. These stimuli can be meaningful (pictures of objects and photographs of objects) or nonmeaningful (random shapes and matrix patterns). Generally, the more visually complex a pictorial stimulus is, the more difficult it is to reproduce from memory and correctly name. Simple stimuli seem to be easier to process mentally than complex stimuli.

There is little specific knowledge about the relevant attributes of the pictorial stimuli, though some data have been collected. Standards have been established for random shapes. For experiments that use matrix patterns, it has been shown that symmetry aids performance whereas complexity impairs performance. Line drawings of objects have been rated on name agreement, image agreement, familiarity, and visual complexity. Little is known about the experimental characteristics of photographs.

We have concluded this chapter with a brief review of visual and auditory perception, because stimuli are most often presented to these two sense modalities. This information is presented to remind the student of certain aspects of stimulus presentation that must be considered.

We have described some of the fundamental characteristics of stimuli. When choosing stimulus materials, it is extremely important to understand and account for the characteristics of the stimuli themselves and to understand how these characteristics interact with experimental paradigms. Appropriate stimuli are an essential part of well-designed and meaningful experiments.

15

Descriptive Statistics: Describing and Displaying Data

Everywhere Nature works true to scale, and everything has its proper size accordingly. Men and trees, birds and fishes, stars and star-systems, have their appropriate dimensions. . . . The scale of human observation and experience lies within the narrow bounds of inches, feet or miles, all measured in terms drawn from our own selves or our own doings.

(D'Arcy Thompson,
"On Growth and Form," 1915)

What would you think if you settled down to watch the weather report on the 6 o'clock evening news and heard, "Today's temperature was measured to be 23°F, 24°F, 21°F, 20°F, 26°F, 27°F, 22°F, 28°F, 29°F, 30°F, 36°F, and 38°F between 7 A.M. and 6 P.M."? You would probably change the channel seeking a report in which the data collected every hour were condensed or summarized in a more manageable way. Hearing instead that "the average temperature today was 27°F with a high of 38°F and a low of 20°F" would provide a much clearer and more meaningful temperature report.

The experimenter faces much the same problem when analyzing data from an experiment. Once the data have been collected, a way must be found to organize and describe it. Usually the data from an experiment are at first a series of numbers. Just as it is nonsense for the weather reporter to present all of the recorded temperatures for a particular day, so, too, experimental data are not meaningful if they are reported in a raw, disorganized manner. The function of descriptive statistics is to organize and describe the data in a relevant and meaningful way.

Examples of the necessity for describing data are abundant. Imagine, for example, the predicament of a high school principal who wants to show that his school contains smarter students than a rival school. To support this hypothesis, he may wish to show that his students received higher SAT scores. He cannot, however, merely list all of the scores for his 400 students and all of the scores for the rival school's 500 students and expect these lists to be useful. He must instead apply descriptive statistical techniques to these data. He might calculate the arithmetic mean of each group of scores so that the information contained in the data (the performance of the students in each school) can be assessed.

Similarly, if a psychologist wanted to evaluate the effectiveness of three different therapies, she would first have to collect measurements from clients in each of the three groups and then organize and describe these data in a meaningful way. In fact, almost anytime measurements (data) are collected, descriptive statistics must be used as a first step in understanding the data.

The problem of organizing and describing data is the subject of this chapter. We will first discuss scales of measurement of the dependent variable, that is, the characteristics of data that are collected and that determine the types of statistical procedures appropriate and mathematically justified. Next, descriptive statistics will be discussed. These are procedures that, as the name implies, allow the useful description and summary of large amounts of information.

SCALES OF MEASUREMENT OF THE DEPENDENT VARIABLE

As was discussed in Chapter 2 (Designing the Experiment), a dependent variable is a characteristic of a subject's performance that is observed and measured by the experimenter. The results of an experiment always consist of an analysis of the dependent variable. The particular descriptive and inferential statistics that are appropriate depend in part on the scale of measurement of that dependent variable.

A famous psychologist once defined measurement as "the business of pinning numbers on things." The way in which the number is pinned onto a particular thing defines the scale of measurement on which that thing is measured. In turn, the scale of measurement determines which statistical techniques are mathematically appropriate for a particular set of numbers assigned to a particular set of things. In psychology, the things that we assign numbers to are usually properties of individuals. These properties may be inherent characteristics of individuals, such as eye color or height, or they may be properties of responses that individuals make to environmental manipulations, including answers to personality questionnaires or reaction times to various sorts of stimuli. In both cases, the thing that we measure is never the individual subject, but rather some property (e.g., behavior) of the individual.

There are four scales of measurement: nominal, ordinal, interval, and ratio. These are presented in order of their relative power, beginning with the least powerful. The number of statistical techniques that are appropriate to use with a scale increases with the power of that scale, and all the techniques that are appropriate for lower scales are also appropriate for higher scales.

Nominal Scale

The nominal scale is the weakest scale of the four—in fact, most people would not consider nominal scale data as information that is measured. Nominal scale data are qualitative data and reflect the fact that the dependent variable differs only in quality, not in order or quantity. Although numbers can be assigned to qualitative data, the numbers act only to distinguish the various data points or individuals, and do not give information about order or differences between categories.

We shall use attributes of individual subjects as examples of all the scales. Suppose we have a group of 50 subjects, and we wish to determine their eye color. We might come up with the following classifications of eye color: blue, green, brown, hazel, and gray. Each subject could then be assigned a number from one to five based on eye color. Thus, in our example if blue-eyed people were assigned the number 2, we would know that all "2s" have the same eye color, blue. However, the fact that we have used numbers for eye color does not permit us to order people with regard to eye color—if green eyes are 3, that does not mean green-eyed subjects have more of some property than blue-eyed subjects, but simply that they are qualitatively different. Eye color is a qualitative rather than a quantitative variable.

Two examples of nominal scale measurement in psychology are classification of mental patients into various psychiatric categories such as paranoid schizophrenic or manic-depressive, and classification of qualitatively different behaviors of nursery school children into such categories as playing alone, playing together, crying, eating, or sleeping.

Ordinal Scale

In ordinal scale measurement, the order of the assigned numbers reflects the order of the variables, but the differences between them or ratios among them are meaningless. As an example, suppose we obtained birth order data from our group of 50 subjects. We could assign numbers to the variable of birth order by assigning a 1 to all firstborn subjects, a 2 to all second-born, and so on. The numbers would tell us how many siblings were already present in the family when each subject was born, but would not tell us anything about the intervals of time separating successive births. A particular second-born subject may have been born one year later than his older sibling whereas another may have been born five years later. In addition, a particular second-born subject from one family may be older than the firstborn subject from another family. The numbers tell us only about order of births. It gives no information concerning the time intervals between them.

As a second example, we might be interested in measuring leadership ability in a group of five subjects. To do this, we could observe interactions among the subjects as they solved problems together and rank-order them in leadership ability by assigning a 1 to the subject who appeared to be most influential in leading the group to a solution and a 5 to the subject who appeared least influential. From the numbers assigned to the subjects on this variable of judged leadership, we can decide that the first-ranked subject has more leadership ability than the second-ranked, and in turn that the second-ranked has more than the third-ranked; however, we cannot decide that the difference in leadership between the first- and second-ranked subjects is equal to the difference between the second- and third-ranked subjects. Ordinal scale measurements tell us about ordering of individuals on a dependent variable, but not about the differences between or the ratios among them.

Examples of ordinal scale measurement in psychology are any data in which rankings of a set of subjects or stimuli are obtained from one or more observers. This includes rankings of the judged beauty of paintings, rankings of the complexity of geometric forms, rankings of aggressiveness in children, and rankings of sociability in adults.

Interval Scale

In interval scale measurement, both the order of numbers and the differences between them are significant, but the ratios between numbers are not meaningful. As an example, IQ test scores are usually assumed to be on an interval scale of measurement. Although the rationale for this is too long and complicated to go into here (and is also somewhat controversial), what this means is that the difference in intelligence between an IQ of 110 and 100 is the same as the difference in intelligence between an IQ of 100 and 90. Thus, if we had IQ scores for 50 subjects, we could both order them in terms of intelligence and talk about meaningful differences between them in intelligence. A subject whose IQ is 120 is as different in intelligence from a subject with an IQ of 100 as she is different from a subject with an IQ of 140.

In interval scale measurement, it is not possible to talk about ratios between numbers on the scale, because there is no absolute zero. In intelligence testing, there is no meaningful concept of zero intelligence; thus, it is not possible to claim that a subject with an IQ of 140 has twice the intelligence of a subject with an IQ of 70.

Another psychological variable that is often assumed to be an interval scale is reaction time (RT), the time between the presentation of some stimulus and a subject's observable response. It is possible to lengthen the RT by introducing additional operations the subject must perform. However, it is impossible to reduce the RT to zero because, even for the simplest tasks, there is some irreducible minimum time required to merely perceive the stimulus and perform a motor response. Thus, psychologists talk about differences between RT but not about ratios among them.

Ratio Scale

In ratio scale measurement, both the differences and the ratios between numbers are meaningful because a ratio scale has an absolute zero. Examples in the realm of physical measurement are height and weight. An individual who is 6 feet tall is twice as tall as one who is 3 feet tall, and a person who weighs 200 pounds weighs twice as much as a person who weighs 100 pounds. Ratio scale measurement has all of the properties of the lower scales as well as the property of an absolute zero. A child who is 60 inches tall is different from one who is 40 inches tall (nominal), is taller (ordinal), is taller by 20 inches (interval), and is 1.5 times as tall (ratio).

An example of ratio scale measurement in psychology is something called ratio scaling. In ratio scaling, subjects are asked to give numbers to stimuli that are proportional to the magnitude of their sensation. A stimulus that sounds twice as loud as another must be given a number twice as large as the first, and so on. For example, the subject might assign the number 10 to a particular sound. If he or she then perceives that another sound is twice as loud,

Table 15-1 Data on Eye Color, Birth Order, IQ, and Height for a Group of 50 Subjects

Subject number	Eye[a] color	Birth order	IQ	Height (inches)	Subject number	Eye color	Birth order	IQ	Height (inches)
Nominal scale	Nominal scale	Ordinal scale	Interval scale	Ratio scale	Nominal scale	Nominal scale	Ordinal scale	Interval scale	Ratio scale
1	2	1	105	65	26	3	1	140	67
2	4	1	132	64	27	1	1	139	63
3	2	2	144	63	28	2	2	103	67
4	1	4	121	66	29	1	1	123	65
5	3	2	116	64	30	1	2	109	58
6	2	1	99	64	31	5	4	123	71
7	1	1	118	61	32	3	1	116	63
8	5	2	124	59	33	1	1	125	70
9	1	1	123	66	34	4	3	113	66
10	4	5	111	64	35	1	1	131	69
11	1	3	107	61	36	2	6	118	64
12	3	1	135	59	37	5	1	126	64
13	2	2	140	65	38	1	4	98	63
14	1	1	136	72	39	1	1	132	62
15	1	2	100	76	40	4	2	127	68
16	4	1	95	62	41	4	1	114	65
17	1	1	122	60	42	1	2	115	68
18	3	3	126	74	43	2	1	109	75
19	1	3	124	64	44	4	3	107	64
20	5	1	117	62	45	1	4	122	60
21	2	2	112	64	46	1	1	129	72
22	5	1	113	73	47	2	2	119	73
23	1	1	130	63	48	2	2	136	59
24	1	2	125	62	49	4	2	137	61
25	1	2	98	64	50	1	1	121	65

[a] 1 = brown, 2 = blue, 3 = hazel, 4 = green, 5 = gray.

the number 20 should be assigned to it. The subject's response numbers are treated as if they were on a ratio scale of measurement in the data analysis.

The various scales of measurement are important in determining which of a number of descriptive and inferential statistics may be used to analyze the results. However, there are other factors besides scale of measurement of the dependent variable that determine which particular statistical test is most appropriate when analyzing data. These other factors include the number of independent variables that have been manipulated, the number of levels of each independent variable that have been studied, and whether subjects participated in only a single condition, were matched on certain variables to other subjects, or served as their own controls in several conditions. The properties of the distribution underlying the data also help determine the appropriate statistical test. These factors are considered in the next chapter on inferential statistics.

FREQUENCY DISTRIBUTIONS

A frequency distribution is a tabulation of the frequency with which each of the possible values of the dependent variable appears in the sample. We will illustrate the construction and graphing of frequency distributions with measurements made on a group of 50 subjects for the dependent variables of eye color, birth order, IQ, and height.

Table 15-1 shows the raw data for each of these variables collected for the 50 subjects. The subjects have been numbered in a completely arbitrary manner, and this numbering itself constitutes measurement on a nominal scale. We have numbered subjects to keep them distinct from one another, and subject number tells nothing about each subject except that he or she is different from a subject with another number. We could as easily have used subject names, subject initials, or any other identification scheme that uniquely identifies each subject.

The second column shows eye color, which is also on a nominal scale of measurement. We have assigned numbers to color in a completely arbitrary manner, and neither the order of the numbers, their differences, nor their ratios have any meaning with respect to the variable of eye color.

Table 15-2 shows the frequency distribution of eye color for the subjects. The number of subjects who have a particular eye color has been recorded in the frequency column. We have also shown the percentage of subjects with each color in the next column. The percentage is calculated by dividing each frequency by N (the total number of subjects) and multiplying by 100. The sum of the percentages must equal 100.

The frequency distribution in Table 15-2 has been plotted as a *bar graph* in Figure 15-1. The various values of the dependent variable, determined by the experimenter's categorization, eye color, are shown along the horizontal or x-axis, and the frequency with which each occurs is shown along the vertical or y-axis of the graph.

Note that the bars erected above each eye color in Figure 15-1 are not adjacent. Bar graphs are appropriate for nominal scale measurement because the order in which the variables are plotted is not related to the differences among the variables. They are qualitatively different, and we could have plotted them in a different order—say, gray, hazel, blue, green, brown— and have gotten a differently shaped distribution. Because there is no continuity between adjacent values of the variables of eye color, the bars representing their frequencies are plotted separately.

The order of the bars is completely arbitrary for a frequency distribution based on a nominal scale, but the height of the bars is not because the heights represent frequencies. There are exactly twice as many blue-eyed as gray-eyed subjects in our sample, and the height of the bar for blue eyes is twice that of the bar for gray eyes. Because the width of the bars is constant for each eye color, this also means that the *area* of each bar is proportional to its frequency. This will be true for each of the graphed frequency distributions we consider.

Table 15-3 shows the frequency distribution for birth order, based on the data in Table 15-1. For ordered data (i.e., data on an ordinal, interval, or ratio scale), the convention used is to order the dependent variable from the highest rank at the top to the lowest rank at the bottom, as shown in Table 15-3.

Birth order is ordinal scale data, and ordinal scale data are also plotted as bar graphs because differences between adjacent values of the dependent variable are not necessarily equal. However, unlike

Table 15-2 Frequency Distribution of Eye Color Based on Data in Table 15-1

Eye Color	Frequency (f)	Percentage (%) = (f/N) × 100
Brown (1)	22	44
Blue (2)	10	20
Hazel (3)	5	10
Green (4)	8	16
Gray (5)	5	10
	$\Sigma = N = 50$	$\Sigma = 100$

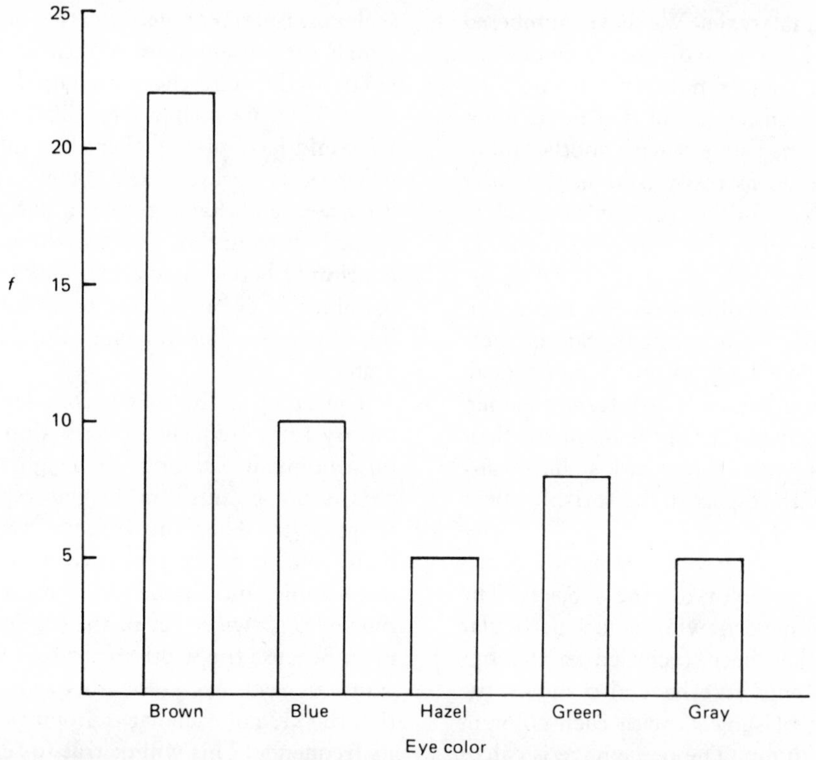

Fig. 15-1 Bar graph for the eye color frequency distribution presented in Table 15-2. (From *The Numbers Game: Statistics for Psychology* by J. G. Snodgrass. Copyright 1977 by Oxford University Press. Reprinted by permission.)

Table 15-3 Frequency Distribution of Birth Order Based on Data in Table 15-1

Order of Birth	*f*	%
6	1	2
5	1	2
4	4	8
3	5	10
2	15	30
1	24	48
	$\Sigma = 50$	$\Sigma = 100$

nominal scale data, the *order* in which the bars are plotted is fixed and proceeds from lowest rank at the left to highest rank at the right along the abscissa.

Figure 15-2 shows the bar graph for the frequency distribution of birth orders. As was true for the nominal scale data, the heights of the bars and their areas are proportional to the frequencies they represent. For example, birth order 2 is three times as frequent as birth order 3, and the bar erected above 2 is three times the height of the bar erected above 3.

The frequency distribution of IQ scores is shown in Table 15-4. In contrast to eye color and birth order, there is a quantitative relationship between adjacent values of IQ scores, because IQ is measured on an

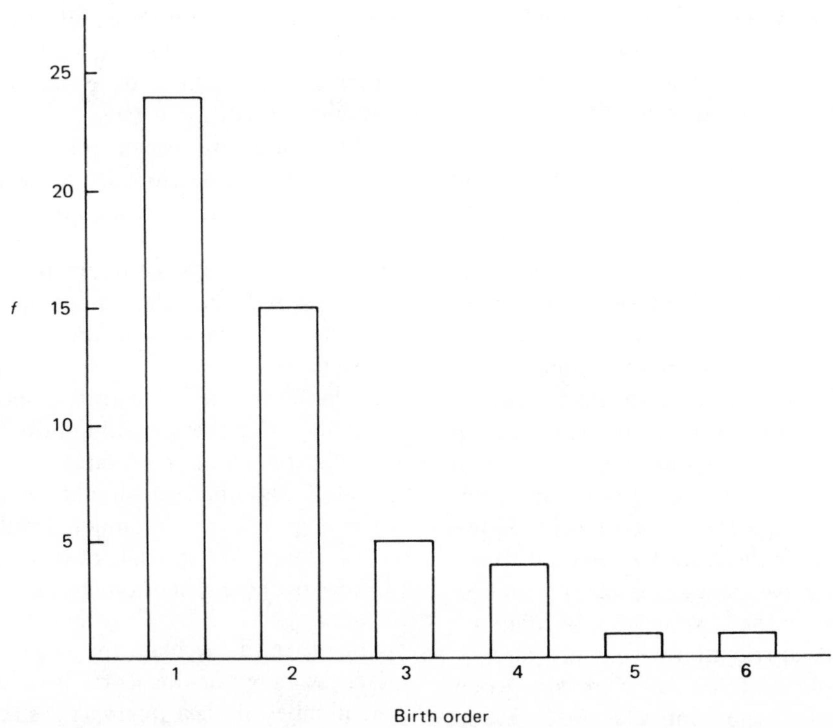

Fig. 15-2 Bar graph for the birth order frequency distribution presented in Table 15-3. (From *The Numbers Game: Statistics for Psychology* by J. G. Snodgrass. Copyright 1977 by Oxford University Press. Reprinted by permission.)

Table 15-4 Ungrouped Frequency Distribution of IQ's Based on Data in Table 15-1

IQ	f	IQ	f	IQ	f
144	1	127	1	110	
143		126	2	109	2
142		125	2	108	
141		124	2	107	2
140	2	123	3	106	
139	1	122	2	105	1
138		121	2	104	
137	1	120		103	1
136	2	119	1	102	
135	1	118	2	101	
134		117	1	100	1
133		116	2	99	1
132	2	115	1	98	2
131	1	114	1	97	
130	1	113	2	96	
129	1	112	1	95	1
128		111	1		$\Sigma = 50$

interval scale. Thus, the order of IQ scores represents order among subjects on intelligence, and quantitative differences between them represent meaningful differences in intelligence.

Although Table 15-4 is a better organization of the IQ data than the listing shown in Table 15-1, it still leaves much to be desired. Because of the wide range of IQ scores and the relatively small number of subjects in our sample, there are many gaps in the frequency distribution, and therefore certain IQ scores have zero frequency. Table 15-4 is an example of an *ungrouped* frequency distribution. We have listed each possible value of IQ score and indicated its frequency of occurrence. However, because there are 50 potential values in our sample, ranging from the highest IQ of 144 to the lowest of 95, we obtain a frequency distribution with many gaps.

The solution to this problem is to group individual IQ scores into *class intervals,* so that the separate frequencies for each of the individual scores may be pooled. The width of the class interval will determine the number of class intervals used. For example, we could group according to a class interval of 10 by listing frequencies for the IQ score intervals 90–99, 100–109, 110–119, and so on, or we could group according to a class interval of 2 by setting up our intervals as 95–96, 97–98, 99–100, and so on. For this set of data, neither solution would be ideal. A class interval of 10 would lose too much detail and would produce only five intervals, whereas a class interval of 2 would produce twenty-five intervals and still show gaps.

The following rough rules of thumb will provide some guidance for setting up grouped frequency distributions:

1. The number of class intervals should be between 5 and 20, depending on the range of scores and the number of subjects.
2. The class interval width, i, should be odd, so that the midpoint of the interval falls at a whole score value.
3. The class interval should be narrow enough that not too much detail is lost but large enough that the overall picture of the distribution emerges.

In order to calculate the class interval size, the range of the scores is divided by the number of class intervals desired. The range of the scores equals the highest score minus the lowest score plus 1, and for the IQ data is $144 - 95 + 1 = 50$. For these data, 10 class intervals might be appropriate, so the class interval size, i, is found by

$$i = 50/10 = 5$$

Table 15-5 shows a *grouped frequency distribution* for the IQ scores for an interval width of 5. We have listed the boundaries of the class intervals and the midpoint of each interval, which may be

Table 15-5 Grouped Frequency Distribution of IQ's Based on Interval Width, i, of 5

Interval	Midpoint	f
140–144	142	3
135–139	137	5
130–134	132	4
125–129	127	6
120–124	122	9
115–119	117	7
110–114	112	5
105–109	107	5
100–104	102	2
95–99	97	4
		$\Sigma = 50$

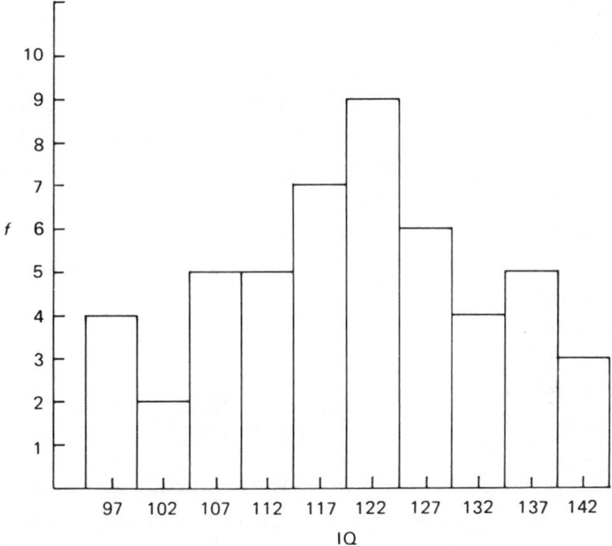

Fig. 15-3 Histogram for the grouped IQ frequency distribution presented in Table 15-5.

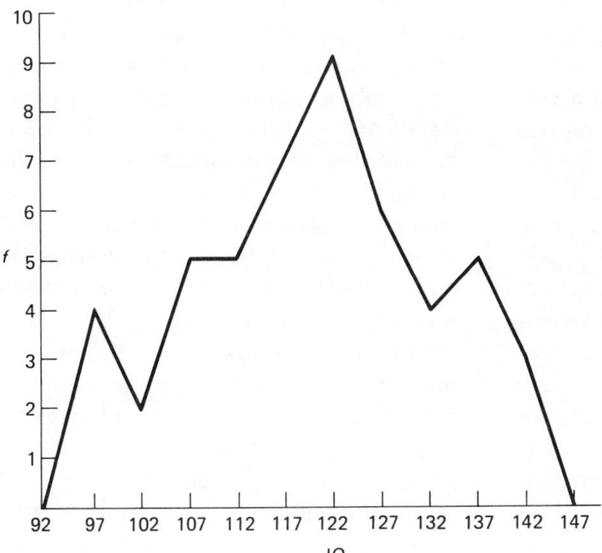

Fig. 15-4 Frequency polygon for the grouped IQ frequency distribution presented in Table 15-5.

calculated by adding $(i - 1)/2$, or 2, to the lower limit of each interval.

Figure 15-3 shows the frequency of each interval plotted against the midpoint of that interval. This plot is known as a *histogram,* as distinguished from a bar graph, because the bars are adjacent to one another. A histogram is used for interval and ratio scale variables for which there is continuity between adjacent class intervals. The histogram of the IQ scores gives us a clearer picture of the distribution of IQ scores in our sample. We see that the highest frequency of subjects scored in the interval 120–124 and that there is generally a decrease in frequency as IQ scores deviate from that interval.

Another type of graphed frequency distribution, shown in Figure 15-4, is known as a *frequency polygon.* Instead of representing frequency by the height of a bar above each class interval, we use single points above the midpoint of each interval and connect them. Note that the frequency polygon is closed at each end by plotting zero frequency for the midpoints of the intervals below the lowest and above the highest intervals in the frequency distribution. The data shown are the IQ data from Table 15-5. Frequency polygons are particularly useful when the number of class intervals is very large, say 20 or more.

In summary, then, *bar graphs* are used to plot frequency distributions for nominal and ordinal data, and *histograms* and *frequency polygons* are used to plot frequency distributions for interval and ratio data.

PERCENTILES AND PERCENTILE RANKS

As many students soon come to realize, a raw test score on an examination is relatively meaningless. To be told that a particular student received a 38 gives no real indication as to how well he or she actually did. A 38 might be the highest score, the lowest score, or any score in between. This same principle can be applied to psychological testing. Knowing that a subject scored 82 on an anxiety inventory or needed seven repetitions to learn a list of nonsense syllables does not tell us how well he or she did in relation to other people who are tested in a similar way. The ability to place a test score in an appropriate context or distribution of scores is essential for the understanding of behavioral and psychological data.

One way of evaluating the individual's performance is by the use of *percentile ranks.* The percentile rank of a person's score is the percentage of scores below his or hers in the comparison group (usually others who have taken the same or a similar test). Put another way, the individual's percentile rank is the percentage of subjects in the comparison group he or she surpassed on the test. For example, if a score of seven repetitions in a list learning experiment places a subject in the 67th percentile, then we know that he or she outperformed 67% of the people who were tested in this way.

Note that the percentile rank is a *percentage,* and as such lies between the limits of 0% and 100%. A test score, on the other hand, can take on a range of values dictated by the test itself. The results of many standardized examinations are reported both as score values and as percentile ranks.

MEASURES OF CENTRAL TENDENCY

Measures of central tendency are used to summarize a large group of data with a single number. This number provides us with the most representative or typical type of behavior, subject, score on a test, income, color of eyes, and so forth. For example, when a researcher measures the behavior of a group of schizophrenic patients on a behavioral test, or the intelligence of college students on an IQ test, he or she would be unlikely to attempt to report the data simply as lists of tens or hundreds of individual scores. Such a report would be quite difficult to interpret and virtually meaningless, particularly with a large number of individual scores. Instead it is much more desirable to condense the information by reporting the typical or average or most usual score for a particular group of patients or students.

The three measures of central tendency most often used are the *mode, median,* and *arithmetic mean.* Which statistic of central tendency is used depends on both the scale of measurement and the purpose of the statistic.

The Mode

The mode is the most frequent score or value in a distribution of scores. It is the only measure of central tendency that is appropriate for nominal (qualitative) data. For example, we could describe the modal handedness of a group of subjects as right-handed, the modal favorite ice cream flavor of a group of children as chocolate, or the modal choice of president in 1960 as John Kennedy. These are all examples of using the mode to describe the most typical measure on a nominal scale.

The major disadvantages of the mode is that it does not take into account each datum in the distribution. Instead the typical, most representative score is defined as the single most frequent value. However, this value could by chance occur at the extreme end of the distribution, in which case it would not represent a typical score in the distribution. For this reason the mode is considered unstable. When the scale of measurement permits the use of another measure of central tendency, the mode is rarely used.

The Median

A second measure of central tendency is the median. The median is that value which lies directly in the middle of the distribution—that is, the score that has 50% of the distribution below it and 50% above it. In terms of percentiles, it is the score that corresponds to the 50th percentile.

Finding the median score is quite simple. First the data are placed in order from smallest to largest. If the number of scores, N, is odd, then the median is the value of the $[(N + 1)/2]$th observation. For example, if the data are the five scores 50, 20, 60, 80, and 10, you would first place the scores in order (10, 20, 50, 60, 80) and then pick the third score $[(5 + 1)/2 = 3]$, 50, as the median. When N, the number of observations, is even, the median is the mean (average) of the $N/2$ and $N/2 + 1$ observations. Thus, to find the median for the group of six scores 90, 60, 20, 40, 30 and 70 one would first arrange the scores in order (20, 30, 40, 60, 70, 90). Following this, the third $(6/2 = 3)$ and fourth $(6/2 + 1 = 4)$ scores would be identified as 40 and 60. Finally, the two scores 40 and 60 would be averaged to yield 50 as the median score.

Typically, the median is used under two conditions. The first condition is when the data have been measured on an ordinal scale of measurement. For example, if we asked subjects to rank the ten most popular movies released in a particular year, then an appropriate measure for the popularity of each movie would be the median rank assigned by the subjects. The second condition under which the median is used is when data have been measured on a higher scale (interval or ratio), but the distribution of scores is either highly skewed or artificially bounded at one end.

One example of a skewed distribution is annual income. Although yearly income is measured on a ratio scale of measurement, because money is on a ratio scale, the typical income is usually reported as the median rather than the arithmetic mean. This is because a small percentage of individuals who have very large incomes would artificially inflate the mean income but not affect the median income. The great advantage of the median is that it is not affected by extreme scores. Thus, the two sets of numbers (10, 30, 40, 50, 70) and (10, 30, 40, 50, 2000) have the same median (40), though their means are very different (40 and 426, respectively).

The median is also used when scores are artificially bounded. An example of scores that are artificially bounded from above are the times required by rats to escape from shock. Usually, the experimenter imposes some sort of time deadline, so that if a rat does not escape by a certain time (e.g., 3 minutes) the trial is ended and a score of 3 minutes is recorded. This score, however, is artificial because the real time it took the rat to escape is unknown and could be anytime between 3 minutes and infinity. For such situations, the median is the preferred measure of central tendency.

The Arithmetic Mean

The arithmetic mean will be familiar to most of you. It is commonly referred to as the average. This is the most widely used of all the measures of central tendency and has the advantage of taking all the data into account.

The sample mean is denoted by the symbol $\overline{X}$ (*X*-bar), and the population mean is denoted by the symbol μ (Greek *mu*). Usually only the sample mean is computed, since all the values in the population are usually unknown. For ungrouped data, the sample mean is computed by summing (Σ) all of the scores (*X*) in the sample and dividing by the total number of scores (*N*), expressed by the equation:

$$\overline{X} = \frac{\Sigma X}{N}$$

For example, the mean of the seven values 1, 1, 4, 8, 9, 12, and 77 is computed in the following way:

$$\overline{X} = \frac{(1 + 1 + 4 + 8 + 9 + 12 + 77)}{7}$$

$$= \frac{112}{7} = 16$$

The mean for this set of numbers, 16, is larger than the median of 8 because the score values are not symmetric around 8. If the largest value of 77 were replaced by the value 21 then the mean would be

$$\overline{X} = \frac{(1 + 1 + 4 + 8 + 9 + 12 + 21)}{7}$$

$$= \frac{56}{7} = 8$$

The new mean is 8, which is the same as the median (which remains unaffected). The mean now equals the median because changing the score of 77 to 21 makes the distribution more symmetric around the value 8. In both cases, the mode is 1, which in this example is not a good indicator of the most typical score.

As can be seen in these examples, the mean, unlike the median, is affected by extreme scores. This property sometimes makes the mean a less than desirable measure of central tendency. In general, however, whenever the data are on an interval or ratio scale and are fairly symmetric, the mean is the most representative and meaningful measure of central tendency.

To compute the mean for a frequency distribution, we multiply each score by its frequency of occurrence, sum, and divide by *N*, as expressed in the following equation:

$$\overline{X} = \frac{\Sigma fX}{N}$$

Note that multiplying each score by its frequency, *f*, is a shorthand way of summing the *f* scores together. If we have some number, *f*, of scores, all of which are the same value, then the sum of the scores can be obtained by multiplying the number, *f*, by the score value, X.

For example, instead of computing the mean of the seven values 7, 7, 7, 3, 3, 4, 4 in the first manner described:

$$\overline{X} = \frac{7 + 7 + 7 + 3 + 3 + 4 + 4}{7}$$

$$= \frac{35}{7} = 5$$

one can make use of the repetition of values and calculate the mean in the following way:

$$\overline{X} = \frac{3(7) + 2(3) + 2(4)}{7}$$

$$= \frac{21 + 6 + 8}{7} = \frac{35}{7} = 5$$

On some occasions, the data are first grouped into intervals of a convenient size, forming a grouped frequency distribution. A researcher collecting IQ scores from 1000 high school seniors might, for convenience, group the raw data into intervals of width 5 and then calculate the mean. Thus, he or she would record the number of students who achieved a score between 80 and 84 in a single group, those who achieved between 85 and 89 in a single group, those who achieved between 90 and 94 in a single group, and so forth. (Grouping data in this manner was quite common when data were hand-collected and analyzed. Now with the growing use of calculators and computers to collect and analyze data, these grouping techniques are used much less frequently.)

To compute the mean for a grouped frequency distribution, we multiply the midpoint of each interval, denoted by X_m, by its frequency of occurrence. This proce-

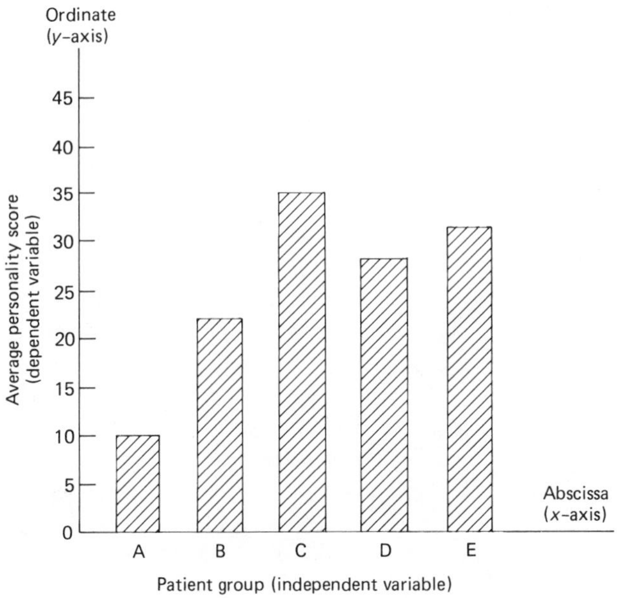

Fig. 15-5 Sample bar graph. The independent variable (patient group) is graphed on the abscissa (*x*-axis); the dependent variable (personality score) is graphed on the ordinate (*y*-axis). Note that the length of the ordinate is approximately three-quarters of the width of the abscissa.

dure makes the assumption that the scores are equally distributed throughout each interval. The products for all intervals are summed and divided by *N*, the number of scores. This is shown in the following equation:

$$\overline{X} = \frac{\Sigma fXm}{N}$$

The grouped formula for the mean yields a value that is close, though rarely equal, to the mean computed from the raw scores themselves.

GRAPHING SUMMARY STATISTICS

One of the clearest ways to display data is with a graph. For the knowledgeable researcher, a graph can often reveal relationships between different groups of data more effectively and more simply than several pages of text. Like most tools, graphs can provide clear presentations of data only when certain rules and conventions are followed. If these rules are ignored, the results can be disastrous—ranging from mildly confusing to meaningless or misleading. Learning to draw careful and accurate graphs is an important skill well worth developing.

Certain rules apply to all graphs regardless of their particular type. We shall illustrate them using graphs of means, although other summary statistics such a medians or standard deviations can be graphed in this way. The horizontal axis, known as the *x*-axis or abscissa, contains the values of the independent variable. The vertical axis, known as the *y*-axis or ordinate, contains the values of the dependent variable on the scale of measurement of the data.

To standardize the method of graphing, there exists a convention known as the "three-quarter rule." This rule advises that the ordinate should be three quarters of the width of the abscissa. Following this rule usually provides a clear and pleasing graph. This is only a suggestion, however, and if it is inconvenient for your particular set of data it can be ignored.

The independent variable (experimenter's manipulation) generally determines the correct type of graph for a particular data set. If the independent variable is qualitative, a bar graph is used. For example, if a researcher collected data on the mean personality scores of five groups of mental patients, the graph might look like the one in Figure 15-5. As this bar graph

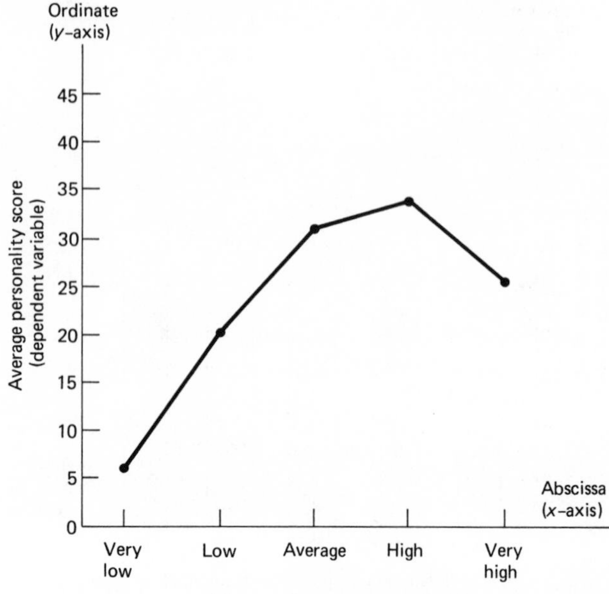

Fig. 15-6 This is a sample line graph using hypothetical data. The independent variable is quantitative and lies along a continuum.

shows, the ordinate (y-axis) contains the dependent variable (personality scores) and the abscissa (x-axis) contains the independent variable (patient groups). Because the independent variable is a qualitative designation of patient group, a bar graph is used.

If the independent variable is quantitative, as when subjects are categorized by range of intelligence, then a line graph is appropriate. Here the categories along the x-axis form a continuum and therefore the points of the graph are connected by a line. Figure 15-6 shows the results of a hypothetical study that examined the personality scores of individuals with different levels of intelligence. Here, the mean personality scores of the different groups are connected by a line because the categories of intelligence along the abscissa form a continuum.

MEASURES OF VARIABILITY

Measures of variability describe the degree to which individuals vary from one another on some attribute or the degree to which an individual's behavior varies from trial to trial in an experiment. We shall describe three widely used measures of variability: (1) the range, (2) the interquartile range, and (3) the variance and its square root, the standard deviation. These three measures of variability are usually associated with the three measures of central tendency discussed earlier; modes and medians are often associated with either the range or the interquartile range, and the mean is usually associated with the variance and the standard deviation.

The Range

As its name indicates, the range is the distance between the largest and the smallest values in a distribution. It is calculated by subtracting the smallest value from the largest value and adding one unit of measurement. The range is a very unstable measure of variability. First, it is based on only two values from the entire distribution—the largest and the smallest scores. Second, the range can be affected by extreme values. For these reasons it is not often used as the only measure of variability.

The Interquartile Range

The interquartile range is the difference between the 75th percentile and the 25th percentile in a distribution. Like the range, it is the difference between two scores in a distribution, but it is more stable than the range because these scores are selected from the middle of each of the two halves of the distribution. For this reason it is completely unaffected by any values that lie in the lower or upper 25% of the distribution, and so it is usually unaffected by extremely high or extremely low scores in the distribution. It is often used as a measure of variability when the median is used as a measure of central tendency.

The Variance and Standard Deviation

The variance and the standard deviation are appropriate only for interval and ratio data. They are the most extensively used measures of variability in psychology. They are really only one measure, since the standard deviation is the square root of the variance. Like the mean, the variance and standard deviation are based on every value in the distribution. Thus, all the information in the distribution of scores is utilized.

The variance is the average squared deviation from the mean, and the standard deviation is the square root of that value. The symbols for the sample variance and standard deviation are s^2 and s, respectively. The symbols for the population variance and standard deviation are σ^2 and σ (Greek sigma). As with the mean, the sample statistics rather than the population parameters are usually computed because all the population scores are usually unknown. The sample variance is described by the following equation:

$$s^2 = \frac{\Sigma(X - \overline{X})^2}{N}$$

This equation instructs us to compute the mean ($\overline{X}$) of the sample, subtract the mean score from each score (X) in the distribution to find the deviation score, square (^{2}) each deviation score, sum (Σ) them, and divide by the total number of scores (N) in the sample.

For example, this is how you would calculate the variance and standard deviation of the values 1, 2, 3, 4, and 5. The mean of this set of values is 3, so the variance is calculated as follows:

$$\begin{aligned} s^2 &= \frac{(1-3)^2 + (2-3)^2 + (3-3)^2 + (4-3)^2 + (5-3)^2}{5} \\ &= \frac{(-2)^2 + (-1)^2 + (0)^2 + (1)^2 + (2)^2}{5} \\ &= \frac{4+1+0+1+4}{5} \\ &= \frac{10}{5} = 2 \end{aligned}$$

and the standard deviation is calculated as follows:

$$s = \sqrt{s^2} = \sqrt{2} = 1.414$$

Because the variance is the average squared deviation from the mean, the variance is reported in squared units. However, since the standard deviation is the square root of the variance, it is reported in the same units as the original scores. For instance, the variance of a set of heights measured in inches is expressed as inches squared, whereas the standard deviation is expressed in inches.

STANDARD (z) SCORES

A z or standard score provides one way of relating a single score to its distribution. Instead of reporting the subject's actual score on a particular test, his or her z score can be reported. This is the score in standard deviation units with respect to the mean of the distribution. The formula for a z score is as follows:

$$z = \frac{X - \overline{X}}{s}$$

To illustrate the computation of z scores, let us assume that IQ scores are distributed with a mean of 100 and a standard deviation of 15. Then Nancy, who scored 115 on an IQ test, has a z score of $+1.00$ ($z = (115 - 100)/15 = 1$), or she scored one standard deviation above the mean, whereas Arnold, who scored 90, has a z score of -0.67 ($z = (90 - 100)/15 = -0.67$), or two thirds of a standard deviation below the mean.

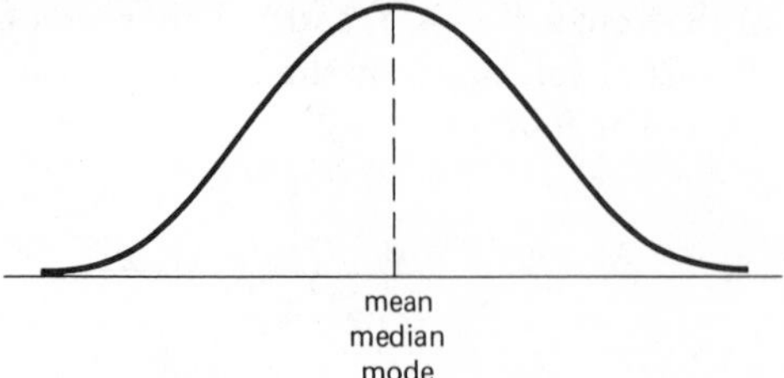

Fig. 15-7 The standard normal distribution. Note that the mean, median, and mode coincide.

Knowing a *z* score can be extremely valuable when the distribution is normal. The normal distribution is the familiar bell shaped curve shown in Figure 15-7. We can observe several properties of this distribution from this figure. First, the normal distribution is symmetric and unimodal, and consequently the mean, median, and mode all coincide. Second, its tails extend infinitely in both directions. This allows for the possibility of any score occurring, no matter how large or small.

A valuable property of the normal distribution is that we know the proportion of scores that lies between any two *z* scores in the normal distribution. Many of the traits we study in psychology are assumed or observed to be normally distributed. Knowing the *z* score that corresponds to a particular raw score enables us to state the percentage of the distribution that lies above or below that score.

We will use the IQ example mentioned previously to illustrate this point, since IQ scores are constructed to conform to a normal distribution. The distribution of IQ scores has a mean of 100 and a standard deviation of 15. Nancy obtained an IQ score of 115, which corresponds to a *z* score of +1.00. It has been calculated that the proportion of scores between the mean and a *z* score of +1.00 is .3414. (This value can be obtained from prepared tables of the normal distribution. See Table A-4 in the Appendix.) Since we know that 50% of the distribution lies below the mean (remember the mean and median coincide) we know that Nancy has an IQ score that lies above approximately 84% of the population (.5000 + .3413 = .8413). Similarly, it can be ascertained from Table A-4 that the proportion of scores between the mean and a *z* score of −0.67 is .2486. Thus, Arnold's score corresponds to approximately the 25th percentile (.5000 − .2486 = .2514). The *z* score, which allows us to relate individual scores to their appropriate distributions in a meaningful way, is an extremely important statistical tool.

CORRELATION COEFFICIENTS

In the preceding sections we have introduced descriptive statistics for a *single* variable measured on a sample of subjects. However, there are many situations in which we have measures on *two* variables for a sample of subjects and we wish to describe the degree of relationship between them. For example, we may wish to describe the relationship between students' scores on a midterm and a final examination in a statistics course, the relationship between Scholastic Aptitude Test scores and grade point averages for a set of graduating high school seniors, or the relationship between subjects' recall of a set of pictures and their recall of a set of words in a memory experiment in which both types of materials are used.

The statistic that we calculate to describe this relationship is known as the *correlation coefficient.* In order to calculate a correlation coefficient, we must have two samples of scores, denoted *X* and *Y*, which are paired on some basis. In psychology, the pairing of scores is usually based on individual subjects, so that a particular subject's score on the first variable is paired with his or her score on the second variable. However, the pairing could be based on any unit of analysis for which we have pairs of values. In addition, there must be more than a single pair of measurements on which to compute a correlation coefficient. If we had only a single pair of scores for a single subject, there would be no basis on which to calculate a correlation coefficient.

There are a number of correlational methods; which method is used depends on the scales of measurement on which the two variables are measured. We will discuss two of these measures—Pearson *r* and Spearman *rho.*

Pearson *r*

The most widely used correlation coefficient is the *Pearson product moment correlation coefficient,* or Pearson *r.* The Pearson *r* is appropriate when both variables are measured on an interval ratio or scale, as in test scores, proportion correctly recalled, height, weight, and reaction time. The Pearson *r* is a measure of the degree of *linear* relationship between two variables, X and Y. A linear relationship is one in which equal relative increments in one variable are accompanied by equal relative increments in the other.

The Pearson *r* is a standardized measure, with a maximum positive value of +1.0 and a maximum negative value of −1.0. Complete lack of correlation would lead to an *r* of 0. An *r* of +1.0 or −1.0 indicates a perfect relationship between two variables. Although such a perfect relationship is never observed between two psychological variables, they are the rule in the realm of physical measurement.

For example, suppose we measure the heights of a group of students in both inches and centimeters. The heights in inches would constitute the X measurements, the heights in centimeters would constitute the Y measurements, and these two sets of heights are paired according to the individuals they are measured on. We naturally expect the two sets of heights to be perfectly correlated, or to yield a Pearson *r* of +1.0.

But now consider an analogous situation in psychological measurement. Suppose we wish to measure knowledge of statistics in a group of college students on two occasions, separated by a week. We carefully construct two parallel tests designed to tap the same range of knowledge, but each test contains somewhat different problems. Again, the test scores for one measuring device are the X measurements and the test scores for the second measuring device are the Y measurements, and the pairing of the scores is by the individuals they are measured on. In this situation, it is very unlikely that there will be a perfect relationship between the two sets of test scores, although we would expect a high positive correlation if the two tests do in fact measure the same knowledge.

One clear way to show the qualitative relationship between two variables is by using a scatter graph. In a scatter graph, each value of Y is plotted against its paired X value in a two-dimensional graph. Thus, a pair of X, Y values is represented as a single point in two-dimensional space. Several scatter graphs, showing various degrees of correlation, are shown in Figure 15-8. Note that for either a perfect positive ($r = +1.0$) relationship or a perfect negative ($r = -1.0$) relationship, the data points lie on a straight line, whereas for nonperfect relationships they form ellipses or circles of various proportions. Figure 15-8F illustrates what appears to be a perfect but nonlinear relationship between the two variables, in that the Y values increase regularly with increases in the X values until a certain value of X, after which Y values decrease regularly with further increases in X. This is known as a curvilinear relationship between X and Y, because one variable neither regularly increases nor regularly decreases with increases in the other variable. Because Pearson *r* is a measure of *linear* relationship, the value of Pearson *r* in this instance is only +.29.

Although a scatter graph can provide

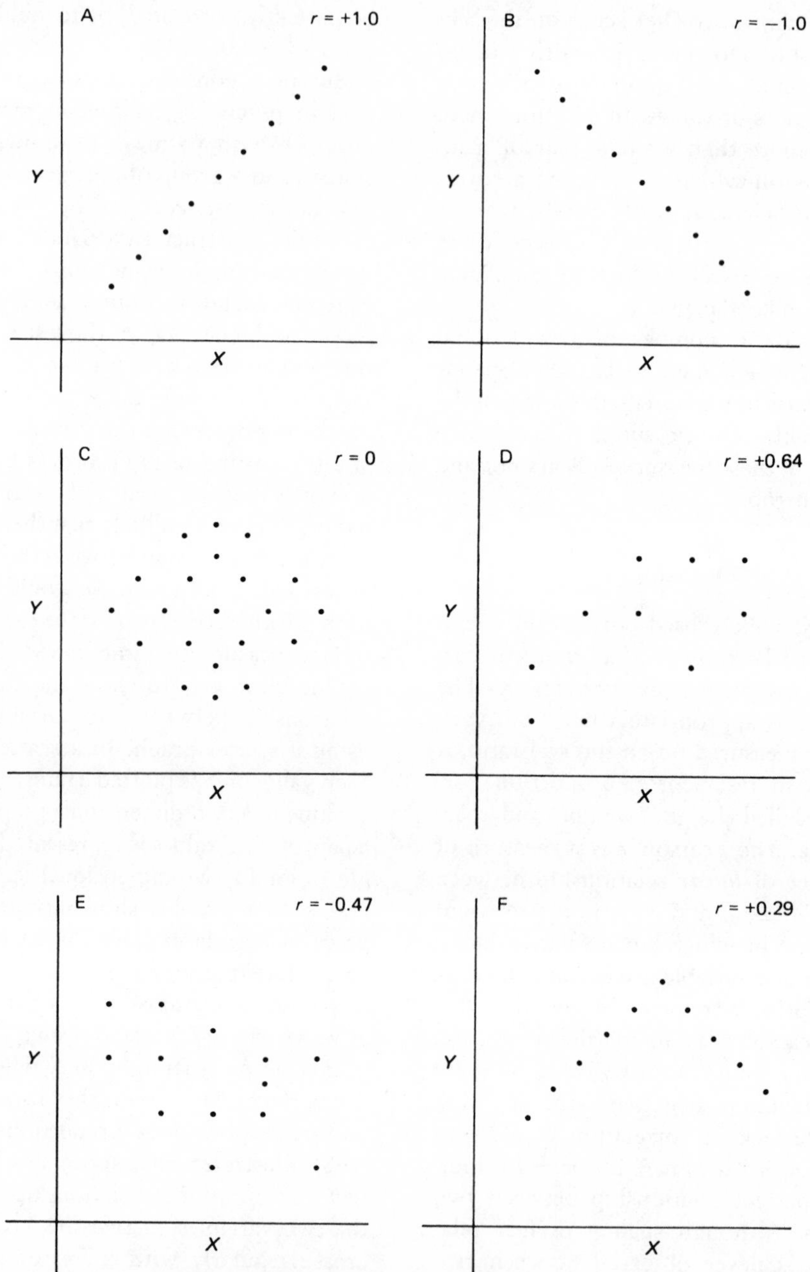

Fig. 15-8 Scatter graphs illustrating various kinds and degrees of correlation. (From *The Numbers Game: Statistics for Psychology* by J. G. Snodgrass. Copyright 1977 by Oxford University Press. Reprinted by permission.)

some qualitative indication of whether a correlation is positive or negative and whether the degree of relationship is high or low, we must actually compute the correlation coefficient from the set of paired data points to measure the relationship quantitatively.

The Pearson r is a standardized measure, and its computation takes into account differences in means and standard deviations between two sets of scores. We can, therefore, compute the correlation of two sets of scores recorded in incommensurate units. For example, it is no problem to relate such diverse measures as feet to pounds or IQ to artistic ability.

The definitional formula for Pearson r (as opposed to the computational formula) is expressed in terms of standard or z scores, as follows:

$$r = \frac{\Sigma z_x z_y}{N}$$

where z_x is the z score on variable X and z_y is the z score on variable Y.

The definitional formula is not usually convenient for actual calculations. Instead, we usually compute it using the raw scores, X and Y. The raw score formula is expressed entirely in terms of the sums of the raw scores, ΣX and ΣY, the sums of the squared raw scores, ΣX^2 and ΣY^2, and the sum of the cross-products, ΣXY, in which each X score is multiplied by its corresponding Y score and the products are summed. Two versions of the raw score formulas are as follows:

$$r = \frac{\Sigma XY - \dfrac{(\Sigma X)(\Sigma Y)}{N}}{\sqrt{\left[\Sigma X^2 - \dfrac{(\Sigma X)^2}{N}\right]\left[\Sigma Y^2 - \dfrac{(\Sigma Y)^2}{N}\right]}} \tag{1}$$

$$r = \frac{\dfrac{\Sigma XY}{N} - \overline{X}\overline{Y}}{\sqrt{\left(\dfrac{\Sigma X^2}{N} - \overline{X}^2\right)\left(\dfrac{\Sigma Y^2}{N} - \overline{Y}^2\right)}} \tag{2}$$

Table 15-6 Raw Scores, Deviation Scores, and z Scores for Two Sets of Paired Scores, X and Y

Subject	X	Y	XY	x	y	xy	z_x	z_y	$z_x z_y$
A	3	22	66	−2	+2	−4	−1.0	+0.5	−0.5
B	4	16	64	−1	−4	+4	−0.5	−1.0	+0.5
C	5	22	110	0	+2	0	0	+0.5	0
D	5	18	90	0	−2	0	0	−0.5	0
E	6	20	120	+1	0	0	+0.5	0	0
F	8	24	192	+3	+4	+12	+1.5	+1.0	+1.5
G	4	20	80	−1	0	0	−0.5	0	0
H	2	12	24	−3	−8	+24	−1.5	−2.0	+3.0
I	1	14	14	−4	−6	+24	−2.0	−1.5	+3.0
J	3	16	48	−2	−4	+8	−1.0	−1.0	+1.0
K	7	24	168	+2	+4	+8	+1.0	+1.0	+1.0
L	3	22	66	−2	+2	−4	−1.0	+0.5	−0.5
M	7	18	126	+2	−2	−4	+1.0	−0.5	−0.5
N	5	16	80	0	−4	0	0	−1.0	0
O	9	28	252	+4	+8	+32	+2.0	+2.0	+4.0
P	6	26	156	+1	+6	+6	+0.5	+1.5	+0.75
Q	5	20	100	0	0	0	0	0	0
R	7	18	126	+2	−2	−4	+1.0	−0.5	−0.5
S	4	24	96	−1	+4	−4	−0.5	+1.0	−0.5
T	6	20	120	+1	0	0	+0.5	0	0

$\Sigma X = 100$ $\Sigma Y = 400$ $\Sigma XY = 2098$ $\Sigma x = 0$ $\Sigma y = 0$ $\Sigma z_x = 0$ $\Sigma z_y = 0$

$\Sigma X^2 = 580$ $\Sigma Y^2 = 8320$ $\Sigma xy = 98$ $\Sigma x^2 = 80$ $\Sigma z_x z_y = 12.25$ $\Sigma z_x^2 = 20$

$\bar{X} = 5$ $\bar{Y} = 20$ $N = 20$ $\Sigma y^2 = 320$ $s_x^2 = 4$ $\Sigma z_y^2 = 20$ $s_x = 2$ $s_y = 4$

$s_y^2 = 16$

Table 15-6 provides an example of some data that might have been collected on 20 subjects. We use these data to illustrate the application of the three formulas for r just presented—the definitional formula, and the two raw score formulas.

By the definitional or z score formula:

$$r = \frac{\Sigma z_x z_y}{N} = \frac{12.25}{20} = +0.612$$

By the raw score formula:

$$r = \frac{\Sigma XY - \dfrac{(\Sigma X)(\Sigma Y)}{N}}{\sqrt{\left[\Sigma X^2 - \dfrac{(\Sigma X)^2}{N}\right]\left[\Sigma Y^2 - \dfrac{(\Sigma Y)^2}{N}\right]}}$$

$$= \frac{2098 - \dfrac{(100)(400)}{20}}{\sqrt{\left[580 - \dfrac{(100)^2}{20}\right]\left[8320 - \dfrac{(400)^2}{20}\right]}}$$

$$= \frac{2098 - 2000}{\sqrt{(580 - 500)(8320 - 8000)}} = \frac{98}{160} = +0.612$$

or alternatively,

$$r = \frac{\dfrac{\Sigma XY}{N} - \overline{XY}}{\sqrt{\left(\dfrac{\Sigma X^2}{N} - \overline{X}^2\right)\left(\dfrac{\Sigma Y^2}{N} - \overline{Y}^2\right)}}$$

$$= \frac{\dfrac{2098}{20} - (5)(20)}{\sqrt{\left[\dfrac{580}{20} - (5)^2\right]\left[\dfrac{8320}{20} - (20)^2\right]}}$$

$$= \frac{104.90 - 100}{\sqrt{(29 - 25)(416 - 400)}} = \frac{4.90}{8.0} = +0.612$$

Spearman *rho*

One way to measure the correlation between rank or ordinal data is by the *Spearman rank order correlation coefficient,* or Spearman *rho.* Spearman *rho* is appropriate to use whenever we have rankings of subjects on one or both variables. If the ranking is only on one variable and the other variable has been measured on an interval or higher scale, the interval data must be transformed to ranks and the correlation computed on the two sets of ranks.

As an example, suppose an art teacher has a class of ten students, each of whom has produced a work of art as part of the course requirement. The teacher feels competent to rank order the works of art in terms of creativity, but does not feel able to give them a more quantitative rating. The students have also taken a standardized test that purports to measure creative ability, and the test scores are assumed to be on an interval scale of measurement. The teacher wishes to determine the degree of relationship between the ranking on creativity measured by actual productions and the ranking on creativity measured by the standardized test.

Table 15-7 Data on Students' Creativity as Measured by Teacher's Ranking and Standardized Test

Student Number	Rank on Art Work (X)	Score on Test	Rank on Test (Y)	$D = X - Y$	D^2
1	5	82	4	+1	1
2	2	80	5	−3	9
3	7	75	6	+1	1
4	10	40	10	0	0
5	1	92	1	0	0
6	4	85	3	+1	1
7	3	86	2	+1	1
8	6	70	7	−1	1
9	8	42	9	−1	1
10	9	63	8	+1	1
				$\Sigma D = 0$	$\Sigma D^2 = 16$

$$r_{\text{rho}} = 1.0 - \frac{6\Sigma D^2}{N(N^2 - 1)} = 1.0 - \frac{6(16)}{10(99)} = 1.0 - 0.097 = +0.903$$

Table 15-7 presents the two sets of measures of creativity for a sample of ten art students. The X variable is the rank on creativity given by the teacher to the art works. The highest ranking individual is given the rank of 1, and the lowest ranking individual is given the rank of 10. The next column shows the score on the standardized test of creativity. The highest score indicates the most creative individual and the lowest score the least creative. Thus, in order to transform these scores to ranks, we give the highest score a rank of 1 and the lowest a rank of 10.

The formula for the Spearman *rho* is based on differences in ranks between the two sets of measurements and is given by the following formula:

$$r_{\text{rho}} = 1.0 - \frac{6\Sigma D^2}{N(N^2 - 1)}$$

where D is the difference between the rank on X and the rank on Y for each individual.

The column marked D in Table 15-7 shows the difference in ranks (with regard to sign) between the rank given by the teacher and the rank on the test, and the next column shows the rank difference squared, or D^2. Note that the sum of the differences, ΣD, must equal 0. To apply the formula for r_{rho}, we need to know only ΣD^2 and N, so

$$r_{\text{rho}} = 1.0 - \frac{6(16)}{10(99)}$$
$$= 1.0 - .097 = +.903$$

Thus, there is very good agreement between the ranking in creativity based on the students' productions and their ranking based on a standardized test of creativity.

Correlation Is Not Causation

It is important to be aware of the fact that a relationship between two variables says nothing about causation between them. For example, a correlation between memory for pictures and memory for words says nothing about the degree to which one causes the other. In fact, we would probably regard such a relationship as springing from a general memory factor that accounted for similar performance on both tasks. However, there are many cases in which investigators attempt to use a correlation between two variables to suggest a causal or directional influence. A recent relevant example is the relationship between cigarette smoking and lung cancer. Data revealed a high correlation between cigarette smoking and cancer. On logical grounds, investigators concluded that smoking caused lung cancer rather than that the onset of lung cancer caused an increase in smoking. However, it is possible that some other factor, such as genetic predisposition, caused both smoking and lung cancer. To properly assign cause and effect, investigators found it necessary to actually produce lung cancer in the laboratory. Thus, the demonstration that lung cancer could be produced in the laboratory with animal subjects was convincing evidence to many skeptics that the correlation observed between smoking and lung cancer in the human population was actually a causal relationship.

LINEAR REGRESSION

Unlike correlation, regression is concerned with the problem of actually predicting one variable from another. The variable that is predicted is known as the dependent variable, and the variable that is used as the predictor is known as the independent variable. As with correlation, causation need not be assumed to use these methods of prediction. One might use high school averages to predict performance in college without assuming that one causes the other. In other situations causation is assumed. An investigator might seek to predict reading time from word familiarity. Here the investigator does believe that word familiarity (the independent variable) causes the reading time (the dependent variable) to be shorter or longer. Independent of this issue of causation, predictions can be made using methods of linear regression that are closely connected with the methods of linear correlation.

A linear equation is an equation that describes a straight line:

$$Y = bX + a$$

This linear equation describes a functional relationship between X and Y such that for every value of X there is a unique value of Y that can be calculated. If there is a perfect functional relationship between X and Y, this equation will always yield a perfect prediction. If we wish to predict ounces (Y) from pounds (X), for example, we would use the following equation:

$$Y = 16X + 0$$

Because these two measures of weight are perfectly correlated ($r = +1.00$) the prediction will always be perfect. In other words, if we know the weight of an object in pounds we can always predict its exact weight in ounces.

Usually when we wish to predict one value from another the correlation between the two scores is not perfect. (Indeed, when it is perfect we really have two ways of measuring the same thing.) In these cases we would like to generate a set of predictions that will minimize our errors of prediction.

The statistician's criterion for minimizing error is known as the least-squares criterion. This is because it minimizes the sum of squared deviations of the data points from the prediction line. The linear regression line that we will use is often referred to as the best fitting least-squares line.

The simplest form of the regression line occurs when both sets of scores are expressed as z scores. In this case, the regression line is written as

$$\hat{z}_y = r\, z_x$$

The "hat" over $\hat{z}_y$ indicates that it is a predicted rather than an observed score, and r is the Pearson r. This definitional formula for the regression line also provides us with another definition of Pearson r—it is the slope of the regression line when both sets of scores are expressed as z scores. The intercept of the regression line is zero, indicating that $\hat{z}_y$ is zero when z_x is zero. This means that the regression line always passes through the points $\overline{X}$, $\overline{Y}$ or that Y is always predicted to be $\overline{Y}$ when X is $\overline{X}$.

The regression line in z scores can be al-

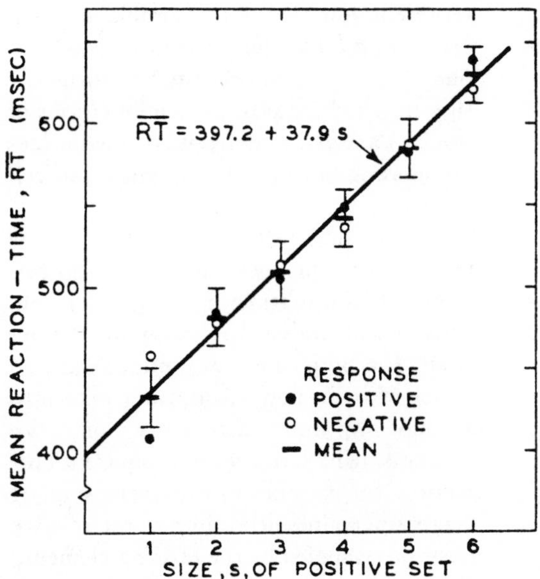

Fig. 15-9 These are the results of Sternberg's classical finding that reaction time increases linearly with the number of items in the memory set. (From "Memory-Scanning: Mental Processes Revealed in Reaction Time Experiments," by S. Sternberg. In *American Scientist,* 1969, *57,* 421–457. Copyright 1969 by Sigma XI. Reprinted by permission.)

gebraically converted to a regression line in raw scores:

$$\hat{Y} = r\left(\frac{s_y}{s_x}\right)X - r\left(\frac{s_y}{s_x}\right)\overline{X} + \overline{Y}$$

When the regression line is expressed as a linear equation of the form

$$\hat{Y} = b_yX + a_y$$

$$b_y = r\left(\frac{s_y}{s_x}\right)$$

and

$$a_y = \overline{Y} - b_y\overline{X}$$

Usually, the direction of prediction is obvious. Returning to our earlier example, it is clear that one would attempt to predict college scores from high school scores and not vice versa. In theory, however, it is possible to predict scores in either direction. Keep in mind that the regression line for predicting X from Y is different from the regression line that predicts Y from X (except when the correlation between X and Y is perfect). The regression lines differ because the squared deviations that are minimized are vertical with respect to the x-axis in the first and vertical with respect to the y-axis in the second.

An important application of linear regression in psychology is provided by the classic work of Saul Sternberg (1969a, 1969b). He used reaction time data to study stages of information processing. With his experiments he explored the time needed for memory search by accounting for the times needed for the underlying component processes by the use of an *additive factors method.* For illustration we will discuss his work investigating the effect of memory set size using an item recognition task.

On each trial, subjects were given from one to six digits to memorize (positive set). Following this they were presented with a single target digit. Their task was to indicate whether this target item was a member of the memory set. The reaction time (time required for responding) was measured.

For example, a subject would be given the items 3, 6, 2, 5, 1 for memorization. If this were followed by 5, the correct response would be "yes." If, however, a 4 were presented, the correct answer would be "no." The time between the presentation of the target item (5 or 4 in this example) and the response (yes or no) is recorded as the reaction time.

As can be seen in Figure 15-9 a straight

line can be reasonably fitted to these data. This illustrates Sternberg's classic finding that reaction time (RT) increases linearly with the number of items in the memory set. The slope of the function that relates RT to the number of items in the memory set provides an index of memory search and comparison time. Here the equation derived from the data allows the prediction of RT (*y*-axis) from memory set size (*x*-axis).

MISSING DATA

There are times when an experimenter is faced with an incomplete set of data. This might occur if a subject fails to complete a questionnaire or if there is an equipment malfunction. Often it is not practical or desirable to discard the rest of that subject's data and find a replacement subject. In other situations, there might be an entire cell missing in a factorial experiment because a particular level of one independent variable was not run with a particular level of a second independent variable for that subject. In situations such as these there are statistical methods that can be used to make unbiased estimates of the missing data.

We will illustrate Winer's (1971) method for the second situation (missing cells in a factorial experiment) when there are no interactions present in the data. We show how this method works by applying it to the 4 × 5 data matrix shown in Table 15-8.

The rows ($a_1 \ldots a_5$) represent five levels of variable *A* and the columns ($b_1 \ldots b_4$) represent four levels of variable *B*. Each cell (e.g., a_1b_1) contains the mean score for one of the 20 conditions in a factorial design in which all possible combinations of levels *A* and *B* are represented. Two values are missing (u_{21} in cell a_2b_1 and u_{34} in cell a_3b_4).

The missing values are constructed by taking the simple mean of the row and column cells and subtracting the grand mean. This yields a value that maintains the average for both the row and column in which it is located. It does not take into account any trends across rows or down columns. (The latter would require a correction for monotonically increasing or decreasing values according to the relative position occupied by the missing element.)

In general, the formula is

$$u_{ij} = \overline{A}_i + \overline{B}_j - \overline{T}$$

where

$\overline{A}_i$ = the mean of the known row values at level *i*

$\overline{B}_j$ = the mean of the known column values at level *j*

$\overline{T}$ = the mean of all known cell values for the whole matrix

u_{ij} = the missing value of row *i* and column *j*

The computation for the two missing values is

$$u_{21} = \frac{39}{3} + \frac{51}{4} - \frac{225}{18} = 13.25$$

$$u_{34} = \frac{41}{3} + \frac{41}{4} - \frac{225}{18} = 11.42$$

Thus by using this method, we can estimate the two values that were lost. Fol-

Table 15-8 A 4 × 5 Matrix of Condition Means in which Two Cells Are Missing, Illustrating the Calculation of Missing Cell Means

	b_1	b_2	b_3	b_4	Total
a_1	10	12	20	9	51
a_2	u_{21}	16	12	11	$39 + u_{21}$
a_3	15	13	13	u_{34}	$41 + u_{34}$
a_4	12	11	15	11	49
a_5	14	12	9	10	45
	$51 + u_{21}$	64	69	$41 + u_{34}$	$225 + u_{21} + u_{34}$ (*T*)

lowing this, data analytic methods can be applied to the data.

EXTREME SCORES

Sometimes a researcher observes one or more extreme scores in the data. Extreme scores can distort many of the test statistics we might want to calculate. Obviously, we cannot arbitrarily eliminate any score that looks deviant. Several methods can be used to eliminate these seemingly extreme scores. Some researchers, for example, merely discard any score above or below three standard deviations from the mean. If the distribution is normally distributed, they reason, this method will eliminate only the extreme scores. Another technique, Winsorizing, changes the values of the most extreme scores in the distribution to be equal to the next most extreme values.

Dixon (1953) has provided one statistical method to determine if a particular score can be considered an outlier. The test is simple to apply. First, you order and number the set of sample data from largest to smallest, if the suspected outlier is the largest value (as would typically be the case for data such as reaction times). Alternatively, you order and number the data from smallest to largest if the suspected outlier is the smallest value.

We illustrate the Dixon method for the first case, so the largest value is designated X_1 and the smallest X_k, where k is the number of sample values. The Dixon test consists of finding the ratio of two ranges. The range in the numerator is the difference between the second largest and largest value, $X_2 - X_1$. The range in the denominator is the total range of scores, the difference between the smallest value of the series and the largest value (the suspected outlier), denoted $X_k - X_1$. As the number of scores increases, the two ranges that are compared are modified slightly. For example, for 14 to 25 scores, the ratio is $(X_3 - X_1)/(X_{k-2} - X_1)$. Again, X_1 is the suspected outlier, X_3 is the third largest, and X_{k-2} is the third smallest. If the ratio

Table 15-9 Dixon Test for Extreme Scores as a Function of k, the Number of Scores in the Sample, for $\alpha = .05$ and $\alpha = .01$

Statistic	Number of scores, k	$\alpha = .05$	$\alpha = .01$
$R = \dfrac{X_2 - X_1}{X_k - X_1}$	3	.941	.988
	4	.765	.889
	5	.642	.780
	6	.560	.698
	7	.507	.637
$R = \dfrac{X_2 - X_1}{X_{k-1} - X_1}$	8	.554	.683
	9	.512	.635
	10	.477	.597
$R = \dfrac{X_3 - X_1}{X_{k-1} - X_1}$	11	.576	.679
	12	.546	.642
	13	.521	.615
$R = \dfrac{X_3 - X_1}{X_{k-2} - X_1}$	14	.546	.641
	15	.525	.616
	16	.507	.595
	17	.490	.577
	18	.475	.561
	19	.462	.547
	20	.450	.535
	21	.440	.524
	22	.430	.514
	23	.421	.505
	24	.413	.497
	25	.406	.489

(From *Introduction to Statistical Analysis* by W. J. Dixon and F. J. Massey, Jr. Copyright 1969 by McGraw-Hill Book Company. Reprinted by permission.)

of ranges is larger than the critical value of ranges at the .05 or .01 level, we reject the outlier as being from a different population and recalculate the data with the outlier removed. Table 15-9 shows the rules for which ranges to calculate and their critical values for various sample sizes.

For example, suppose we have the four observations (326, 177, 176, 157), and want to know if 326 is an outlier. We compute the ratio

$$R = \frac{X_2 - X_1}{X_4 - X_1} = \frac{177 - 326}{157 - 326}$$

$$= \frac{-149}{-169} = .882$$

This is greater than the critical value of .765 for $k = 4$ at $\alpha = .05$, so we reject the largest value at $p < .05$ (but not at $p <$ .01).

To illustrate the calculation for a sample size of 14, suppose we have the following 14 observations, ordered from largest to smallest: 402, 242, 216, 214, 210, 192, 185, 183, 181, 180, 177, 175, 163, 152.

We need to compute the range

$$R = \frac{X_3 - X_1}{X_{k-2} - X_1},$$

where X_1, the largest score, is 402; X_3, the third largest is 216; and X_{k-2}, the twelfth largest, is 175, so

$$R = \frac{216 - 402}{175 - 402} = \frac{-186}{-227} = .819$$

This is greater than the critical value of .641 for $k = 14$ for $\alpha = .01$, so we reject the outlier at $p < .01$.

It should be noted that once one outlier has been identified and discarded, it is possible to test the next largest or smallest value as a potential outlier using the reduced set of data. For the preceding data and $k = 13$, the next outlier is 242. We compute the ratio

$$R = \frac{X_3 - X_1}{X_{k-1} - X_1} = \frac{214 - 242}{163 - 242}$$

$$= \frac{-28}{-90} = .354$$

and 242 is *not* an outlier according the critical values for $k = 13$ in Table 15-9. Thus, we would not reject this score and we would conclude that the data are free from outliers and ready for further analyses.

SUMMARY

In this chapter we discussed statistical techniques for organizing and describing data. The scale of measurement of the dependent variable partially determines the appropriate statistical technique. There are four scales of measurement—*nominal, ordinal, interval,* and *ratio.* Nominal scale data are qualitative data. The dependent variable differs only in quality, not in order or quantity. In ordinal scale measurement, the order of the assigned numbers reflects the order of the variables, but differences and ratios between them are meaningless. In interval scale measurement, both the order of the numbers and the differences between the numbers are significant, but ratios between numbers are not. In ratio scale measurement, both the differences and the ratios between numbers are meaningful.

Next we discussed techniques for graphing data. Graphic displays of data often provide clear pictures of the important variables and their relationships. When graphing data, the independent variable is plotted along the abscissa (x-axis) and the dependent variable along the ordinate (y-axis). The independent variable determines the correct type of graph. If the independent variable is qualitative, a bar graph is appropriate, whereas if the independent variable is quantitative, a line graph is appropriate. Histograms or frequency polygons are used when plotting frequency distributions for interval and ratio data. *Percentiles* and *percentile ranks* are used to relate a particular score to the distribution. The percentile rank tells the percentage of scores that fall below the particular score.

There are three common measures of central tendency that are used to describe the typical observation in a group of observations. The *mode* is the most frequent observation in a distribution. It is the only permissible statistic of central tendency for observations on a nominal scale. The *median* is the observation that divides the distribution of observations in half, so that half of the remaining observations in the sample lie above it and half below it. It is the measure of central tendency of choice for ordinally scaled variables and is also used when the distribution of observations measured on a higher power scale includes extremes or when scores are bounded artificially from above or below. Another name for the median is the *50th percentile.* The *mean,* the most useful measure of central tendency, is commonly known as the average. The mean can be used only for interval and ratio scale measurements. The mean is generally used when the distribution of sample values is relatively symmetric because it takes into account each and every observation in the sample and can therefore be distorted by extreme scores.

Measures of variability are used to describe the degree of dispersion of a group of observations, or how different one observation is from another. There are three commonly used measures of variability, and which is used depends both on the scale of measurement of the observations and on which measure of central tendency has been calculated.

The *range* is the simplest measure of variability to calculate and it is also the least useful. The range is simply the difference between the highest and lowest score in a distribution and as such is completely dependent on those two extreme values. The *interquartile* range is more useful and is often used in conjunction with the median. The interquartile range is the difference between scores at the 75th and 25th percentiles and as such is completely insensitive to the extremes of the distribution in the upper and lower 25% of the distribution. The *variance* and its square root, the *standard deviation,* are the most useful measures of variability. They are often associated with the mean and are appropriate only when the dependent variables are measured on interval or ratio scales. The variance is the average squared deviation from the mean, and the standard deviation is the square root of this quantity.

The z or standard score provides a way of relating a single score to its distribution. Here the score is represented by the number of standard deviation units it deviates from the mean of the distribution. The z score is most useful when the distribution is normal. A normal distribution forms a symmetric and unimodal bell-shaped curve. In normal distributions the mean, median, and mode all coincide. Many of the traits we study in psychology are known or assumed to be normally distributed. With normal distributions, we can relate z scores to percentile ranks.

Correlation coefficients measure the degree of relationship between two variables. They range in value from +1.0 (a perfect positive correlation) to −1.0 (a perfect negative correlation). The Pearson product moment correlation coefficient or Pearson r is appropriate when both variables are measured on an interval or ratio scale. The graphic representation of this relationship is called a scatter graph. Spearman *rho* is the correlation coefficient for variables measured on an ordinal scale. If one of the variables is on a higher scale, it must be converted to ranked data when Spearman *rho* is calculated.

The relationship between two variables, whether measured by the Pearson r or the Spearman *rho*, tells only the statistical relationship between the two variables and nothing about whether one of the variables caused the other. Linear regression is concerned with the problem of predicting one variable from another. Here a functional linear relationship between two variables is defined. Then knowledge of the first variable can be used to predict behavior on the second.

Statistical procedures exist to correct data sets that are either incomplete or include extreme values. Missing data can be calculated in an unbiased way using Winer's method. The deviance of seemingly extreme scores can be determined using Dixon's outlier method. This technique provides one way of objectively eliminating extreme scores.

Collected data must be organized and described in an appropriate way. Knowledge of these techniques is extremely important. Without these techniques we would be incapable of understanding or interpreting the data we have so carefully collected.

16

Inferential Statistics: Drawing Conclusions from Data

> It doesn't help to run the data from a bad experiment through a computer—it's not a washing machine.
>
> (Wike, 1971, p. 6)

In this chapter, we present techniques for drawing conclusions from data by the use of statistical tests. In the first section of the chapter, we present two parametric statistical tests—the *t* test and the analysis of variance—which are used to determine whether two or more sample means are significantly different from one another. These tests are called parametric because they require that the dependent variable in question be quantitative in nature (i.e., be on an interval or ratio scale of measurement) and that several other assumptions, described in detail later, be fulfilled.

Later in the chapter, we consider nonparametric statistical tests. Nonparametric tests are appropriate for either ordinal data (rank order data) or nominal data (data based on frequencies categorized according to some criterion). Both parametric and nonparametric tests ask the question whether or not a set of scores (quantitative values, ranks, or categorized frequencies) differ from one another beyond what might be expected on the basis of chance—that is, whether or not the results of our experiment are statistically significant.

THE MEANING OF STATISTICAL SIGNIFICANCE

When we perform an experiment, we obtain two or more samples of observations on two or more groups of people, or on two or more occasions for the same people. These observations may be qualitative, such as classifications of people or responses into categories, or quantitative, such as proportions of correct responses, reaction times, heights, weights, and scores on a personality inventory.

For simplicity, let us assume that we have measured two groups of subjects on a quantitative variable such as their scores on a midterm examination. These scores will be assumed to be on an interval scale of measurement. We wish to ask the question whether the mean (average) scores of the two groups of subjects are really different.

Suppose an instructor in an introductory psychology course wants to find out if people with last names that begin with letters early in the alphabet do better in the course than people with last names beginning with letters late in the alphabet. (Since a rational hypothesis that might predict such a difference is unlikely, the origin of the hypothesis for this experiment might best be classified among the "What would happen if ..." sources of hypotheses described in Chapter 1.)

After giving the midterm exam, the instructor records the scores in his grade book by alphabetic order of students' last names. He divides the 100 students in the class into two groups, according to whether they are in the first or second half of the alphabet. He then computes the mean score for the first 50 names in the roll book, and finds it to be 76.8, and computes the mean score for the last 50, and finds it to be 74.2. He now must determine if these two means are "really" different.

It should be obvious that the means for any two sets of scores, however arbitrarily divided, will rarely be numerically equal. The reason for this is that any measurement procedure is subject to some chance error. When we attempt to measure a characteristic such as knowledge in a course, our measurement of a particular individual is likely to contain some error. Our questions may not all be equally good, the student may have a cold, there may be distractions in the room, and so on. For example, we know that if we construct two equivalent examinations, we are unlikely to obtain exactly the same scores for the same individual on the two equivalent tests.

In statistical inference, we evaluate the probability that an obtained difference between means could have arisen by chance. If that probability is low enough, we reject the chance explanation in favor of a nonchance, or systematic explanation. Usually, the probability that is low enough is .05 (i.e., one chance out of twenty).

To return to our example, if the instructor discovers that the difference between 76.8 and 74.2 could arise by chance with a probability less than .05, he will conclude that students with last names early in the alphabet do, indeed, learn more than students with last names late in the alphabet. He does so with some risk, however. He will be wrong 5 times out of 100. Nonetheless, according to his criterion, he has obtained a significant difference from his experiment. He now may wish to act on it, for example by instructing the college admissions committee to apply more stringent criteria to aspiring students whose last names begin with letters at the end of the alphabet.

The preceding example is both fanciful and loosely stated. We next provide a more rigorous statement of the formal application of statistical inference, or hypothesis testing.

HYPOTHESIS TESTING

In hypothesis testing, we divide all the possible states of the world into two competing hypotheses, such that if one is true the other is not, and vice versa. One of these hypotheses is called the *null hypothesis*, and the other is called the *alternative hypothesis*. The only hypothesis that is tested directly is the null hypothesis. The investigator either rejects, or fails to reject, the null hypothesis. The alternative hypothesis is tested indirectly. If the null hypothesis is rejected, then the alternative hypothesis is accepted. If the null hypothesis is not rejected, then the alternative hypothesis is not accepted.

The null hypothesis, as its name implies, is virtually always a hypothesis that states there is a null or zero true difference between conditions of an experiment. The alternative hypothesis, which is usually the one the experimenter *wishes* to accept, either states there is a difference, or there is a difference in a particular direction.

Whether the alternative hypothesis is directional or not determines whether the statistical test that is performed is *one-tailed* or *two-tailed*. A nondirectional alternative hypothesis states there is a difference but does not predict the direction of the difference. Examples are this roulette wheel is biased (either toward or away from red); students whose last names begin with letters early in the alphabet differ in performance from those whose names begin with letters late in the alphabet; males and females differ in reaction times. A directional alternative hypothesis states the direction of the predicted difference. Examples are this roulette wheel is biased toward red; students whose last names begin with letters early in the alphabet will perform better than those whose names begin with letters late in the alphabet; females have faster reaction times than males.

The null hypothesis is tested by the following steps. A *test statistic* is computed that has a known distribution under the null hypothesis. This distribution is known as a *sampling distribution*. The position of the test statistic in this sampling distribution is determined, usually by looking up its value in a statistical table. (Statistical tables for significant values of various test statistics are given in Appendix A.) If the test statistic is unlikely in the null hypothesis sampling distribution, the experimenter rejects the null hypothesis. The test statistic is unlikely if it falls into one or another tail of the test statistic distribution. These tails of the sampling distribution are known as the *rejection regions*.

Here is where the distinction between one-tailed and two-tailed tests, corresponding to the distinction between directional and nondirectional hypotheses, is important. If the alternative hypothesis is directional, only one tail of the test statistic distribution is used, whereas if the alternative hypothesis is nondirectional,

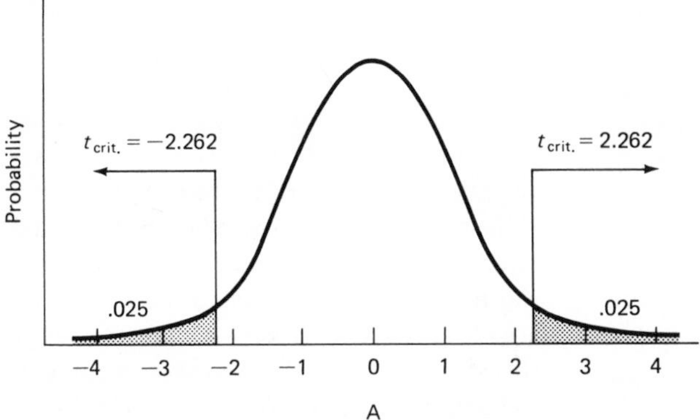

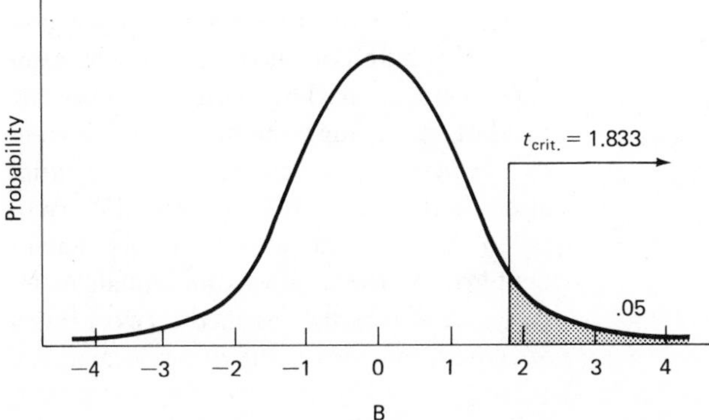

Fig. 16-1 Two-tailed (A) and one-tailed (B) rejection regions for a t distribution with 9 degrees of freedom, where the level of significance (α) equals .05.

both tails are used. What this means in practice is the following. If a directional hypothesis is formulated, the only way a result can be significant is by finding a difference in the expected direction. However, the size of this difference can be smaller in absolute value than the size of a difference whose direction was not predicted.

Figure 16-1 shows the rejection regions of a sampling distribution for a particular test statistic (the t test) used in two-tailed (A) and one-tailed (B) tests. The t test is used to decide whether two sample means are significantly different. In two-tailed tests, we divide the probability equally between the two tails of the distribution, so that a difference in either direction could be in the rejection region, whereas in a one-tailed test, all the probability is located in one tail of the distribution. This means that when results of a one-tailed test are in the predicted direction, we do not need as large a value of the test statistic to reject the null hypothesis at a given level of significance. In other words, we need a smaller difference between means to obtain significance with a one-tailed test than with a two-tailed test.

In the example in Figure 16-1, the t distribution with 9 degrees of freedom (df) is the sampling distribution, and the critical values of the t statistic for a two-tailed test are $t > 2.262$ or $t < -2.262$. In contrast, the critical value of the t statistic for a one-tailed test is only $t > 1.833$. Because the critical value of t for a one-tailed test is less than that for a two-tailed test (1.833 versus 2.262), the difference between the two means needed for significance is less, as long as the difference is in the expected direction. This is because the t statistic has as its numerator the difference between the two means being compared.

The directional/nondirectional distinction in statistical inference is only practicable for comparisons between two groups or conditions. Accordingly, we demonstrate the general principles of hypothesis testing, and the specific principle of two-tailed as opposed to one-tailed tests, for the two-sample case.

In our first example, we test a nondirectional alternative hypothesis. Let us return to our instructor who wishes to compare scores between students with names early and late in the alphabet. Suppose the instructor merely wondered whether the alphabetic order of the last names of his students (the independent variable) made any difference to the scores (the dependent variable) in either direction. In order to test this hypothesis, he needs to calculate the means and variances of the two groups of scores. These data are shown below:

First half

$$\overline{X}_1 = 76.8$$
$$s_1^2 = 27.4$$
$$N_1 = 50$$

Second half

$$\overline{X}_2 = 74.2$$
$$s_2^2 = 25.9$$
$$N_2 = 50$$

The appropriate statistical test to compare these two means is a t test for independent groups. The t test statistic is the ratio of the difference between the two sample means to the standard error of the difference. The notation and formulas are shown below:

$$t = \frac{\overline{X}_1 - \overline{X}_2}{s_{\overline{X}_1 - \overline{X}_2}}$$

where

$$s_{\overline{X}_1 - \overline{X}_2} = \sqrt{\frac{s_1^2 + s_2^2}{N - 1}}$$

or

$$\sqrt{\frac{\hat{s}_1^2 + \hat{s}_2^2}{N}}$$

In this formula, N refers to the number of subjects in either group when both Ns are equal.

The significance of the t ratio is evaluated by referring to the list of critical t ratios shown in Table A-5 of Appendix A. If the obtained t ratio exceeds one of the critical values at an acceptable level of significance, we reject the null hypothesis and conclude that the two groups of subjects are really different on the dependent measure in question. The critical t values depend on two things: the number of *degrees of freedom (df)* associated with the t ratio, and whether the test is one-tailed or two-tailed. For a t test between two independent groups, the number of df equals $N_1 + N_2 - 2$. When the Ns in the two groups are equal, this means the df also equals $2N - 2$.

To illustrate, we compute the t ratio for our two examination groups as follows:

$$s_1^2 = 27.4, \qquad s_2^2 = 25.9, \qquad N = 50$$

$$s_{\overline{X}_1 - \overline{X}_2} = \sqrt{\frac{27.4 + 25.9}{49}} = 1.043$$

$$t = \frac{76.8 - 74.2}{1.043} = 2.49, \qquad df = 98$$

To see whether this t ratio is significant, we consult Table A-5 in Appendix A. Our df is 98, which is not listed in the table, so to be conservative, we use the next lower value of 60 rather than the closer but higher value of 120. For 60 df and a two-tailed test, we need a t value greater than 2.000 to be significant at the .05 level, and greater than 2.666 to be significant at the .01 level. Our obtained t of 2.49 lies between these two critical values, so it is significant at the .05 level but not at the .01 level. We therefore reject the null hypothesis at the .05 level in favor of the alternative hypothesis that the two groups are really different.

Had our initial hypothesis been directional, so that we predicted that students in the first half of the alphabet would be better than those in the second half, we would have rejected the null hypothesis at the .025 level. That is, the probability of having obtained this result by chance under a one-tailed hypothesis is half that for the two-tailed hypothesis, so the result of this experiment is *more* significant under a one-tailed than under a two-tailed hypothesis. (Remember, a result becomes *more* significant as the probability of obtaining it by chance becomes *less*.)

On the other hand, had the result turned out in the opposite direction, so that the last half of the alphabet did better than the first half, we could never reject the null hypothesis regardless of how large the difference was because the result came out opposite from that predicted.

Because effects in the opposite direction from those predicted can never be significant under a directional hypothesis, investigators use one-tailed tests sparingly. They are typically used when a hypothesis about a directional effect is based on a well-developed theory or when the predicted effect has been obtained in previous experiments and there is no conceivable explanation for an effect in the opposite direction. In short, the investigator of a one-tailed hypothesis should be willing to discount any effect in the opposite direction, no matter how large, as simply due to chance.

Many psychologists have argued persuasively against one-tailed tests because they preclude possibly important discoveries. As Sidman (1960) has expressed it, "Those who have no hypotheses or who hold their hypotheses lightly are likely to be alert to the accidental discovery of new phenomena" (p. 10).

Two Types of Errors in Hypothesis Testing

Regardless of whether we reject or fail to reject the null hypothesis, we always run the risk of error. We have already referred to one type of error—that occurring when we reject the null hypothesis when it is true. The probability of this occurring is known as the significance level. When we reject the null hypothesis at the .05 level, this means that we could have obtained a result equal to or more extreme than the one we observed with a probability of .05 solely as the result of chance. This type of error—rejecting the null hypothesis when it is true—is called a *Type I error.* The other type of error we can make is to accept a false null hypothesis. This means we fail to find a significant result when the alternative hypothesis is, in fact, true. This kind of error is called a *Type II error.* The probability of a Type I error can be controlled by judiciously selecting a significance level. However, the probability of a Type II error depends on a number of factors, some of which are under the control of the experimenter and some of which are not.

One very important factor is how large an effect the independent variable really has on the dependent variable. When the effect is large, the experimenter is likely to observe it statistically. Another factor is sample size—the larger the sample size, the more likely we are to correctly reject the null hypothesis. Another factor is whether we use a parametric or nonparametric statistical test. Generally, parametric tests are more powerful—that is, they are more likely to permit us to reject a false null hypothesis. Power is a statistical term that refers to the likelihood that a statistical test can correctly reject a false null hypothesis, so powerful experimental designs and statistical tests are to be desired in experimentation.

STATISTICAL TESTS FOR QUANTITATIVE DATA: PARAMETRIC TESTS

In the previous section, we illustrated the principles of hypothesis testing with a comparison between two groups in which we used a *t* test. In this section we formally introduce those parametric tests—*t* test and analysis of variance—appropriate for comparing two or more than two groups of subjects or sets of observations. The parametric tests are appropriate for quantitative dependent variables, such as reaction time, proportion or number correct, mean GSR, and so on. These tests compare sample means from two or more conditions or groups to see if they are significantly different from one another.

The tests are called parametric because their derivation is based on assumptions about certain *parameters* of population values from which sample measures are drawn. Specifically, the parent populations are assumed to be normally distributed, and the variances of the two or more populations are assumed to be equal. This second assumption is known as *homogeneity of variance.*

In fact, however, the two parametric tests we introduce in this section (the *t* test and analysis of variance) are *robust statistical tests.* This means that modest deviations from normality or homogeneity of variance in the population distributions will not affect the probability values of the test statistic (*t* or *F* ratio) very much, and thus that the probability values reported for the test statistic will be quite accurate even when the parametric assumptions are violated.

Both the *t* test and the analysis of variance are computed by dividing some measure of the difference between or among the various means in the conditions by some measure of the difference among the scores within each condition. This last measure is also known as *error variance.* Error variance is that constellation of factors in an experiment that account for noisy or variable data. These include such factors as individual differences among subjects in the performance being measured, changes in attention and motivation of a single subject over the course of the experiment, errors in experimental procedure, and generally any factors over which we have not established control in the experiment.

The error variance is measured statistically by the error term, or denominator of the *t* ratio and *F* ratio. (The *F* ratio is the test statistic computed in the analysis of variance.) If the error variance is large, it will reduce the size of the *t* or *F* ratio, and we will have difficulty demonstrating effects of our experimental manipulation. If it is small, we will have an easier time demonstrating such effects. Thus, it is to our advantage to reduce error variance as much as possible. In fact, all of the design and control features of an experiment are selected for their effects in reducing error variance.

In presenting the tests and their computational procedures, we will follow the same classification of experiments that was introduced in Chapter 2. Which test is used will depend on three aspects of the experimental design: whether one or two independent variables have been manipulated, whether there are two or more than two levels of the independent variable, and whether the design is within or between subjects.

Table 16-1 presents the parametric statistical tests covered in this chapter as a function of this classification.

A TEST FOR TWO GROUPS: THE *t* TEST

A *t* test is appropriate for testing whether the means of two sets of scores are significantly different or not. There are two types of *t* tests, one for when the two sets of scores are based on independent groups of subjects and one for when the two sets of scores are paired on some basis. The pairing or matching may be based on equating pairs of subjects on some criterion variable or may be based on having the same subject generate two scores under the two conditions of an experiment. The first type of *t* test is called an *independent* t *test,* and the second type is called a *matched* (or *matched pairs*) t *test.* We

Table 16-1 Classification of Parametric Tests Based on Three Aspects of Experimental Design: (1) the Number of Independent Variables, (2) the Number of Levels of Each Independent Variable, (3) Whether the Design Is Within Subjects (Repeated Measures) or Between Subjects (Random)

	One independent variable		Two independent variables
	Two samples	More than two samples	
Independent groups (between)	*t* test (independent)	One-way ANOVA (randomized)	Two-way ANOVA (randomized) Two-way ANOVA (mixed)
Matched groups (within)	*t* test (matched)	One-way ANOVA (repeated measures)	Two-way ANOVA (repeated measures)

present formulas and sample calculations for an independent *t* test for both equal and unequal *N*s in the two groups, and for a dependent *t* test for which there must be equal numbers of scores in the two groups because the scores have been paired on some basis.

Independent *t* Test

An independent *t* test is used when there are two groups of independent subjects, each participating in a different condition or treatment. The *t* statistic is the ratio of the difference between the two sample means to the standard error of the difference between the two sample means. The formulas, which were presented earlier in the example on exam scores, are repeated here for completeness.

When the number of subjects in group 1 equals the number of subjects in group 2 ($N_1 = N_2 = N$):

$$t = \frac{\overline{X}_1 - \overline{X}_2}{s_{\overline{X}_1 - \overline{X}_2}}$$

where

$$s_{\overline{X}_1 - \overline{X}_2} = \sqrt{\frac{s_1^2 + s_2^2}{N - 1}}$$

where

$$df = 2N - 2$$

Table 16-2 presents the application of the formula for an independent *t* test for equal *N*s to some sample data.

When the number of subjects in group 1 does not equal the number of subjects in group 2 ($N_1 \neq N_2$):

$$t = \frac{\overline{X}_1 - \overline{X}_2}{s_{\overline{X}_1 - \overline{X}_2}}$$

where $s_{\overline{X}_1 - \overline{X}_2}$

$$= \sqrt{\left(\frac{N_1 s_1^2 + N_2 s_2^2}{N_1 + N_2 - 2}\right)\left(\frac{1}{N_1} + \frac{1}{N_2}\right)}$$

where

$$df = N_1 + N_2 - 2$$

Table 16-3 presents the applications of the formula for an independent *t* test for unequal *N*s to some sample data.

Matched Pairs *t* Test

A matched pairs *t* test is used when there are two groups of subjects who are matched on some basis or two groups of scores matched by having the same subject produce them. The matched pairs might be first- and second-born siblings in the same family, or pairs of children matched on IQ. An important way of matching subjects is by having the same subject participate in two different conditions of an experiment so that the matched pairs consist of two scores from each subject. For example, children might be tested before and after a special teaching program.

Whether the matching is between two separate subjects, or occurs because the same subject is tested under two different

Table 16-2 Number of Problems Correctly Solved in an Experiment in which Feedback Was Given for Correct Performance to Group 1 and No Feedback Was Given to Group 2 (Independent *t* Test; Equal *N*'s)

Subject Number	Group 1 Number Solved (X_1)	X_1^2	Subject Number	Group 2 Number Solved (X_2)	X_2^2
1	11	121	1	10	100
2	17	289	2	15	225
3	14	196	3	14	196
4	10	100	4	8	64
5	11	121	5	9	81
6	15	225	6	14	196
7	10	100	7	6	36
8	8	64	8	7	49
9	12	144	9	11	121
10	15	225	10	13	169
	$\Sigma X_1 = 123$	$\Sigma X_1^2 = 1585$		$\Sigma X_2 = 107$	$\Sigma X_2^2 = 1237$

$$\bar{X}_1 = \frac{\Sigma X_1}{N_1} = 12.3 \qquad \bar{X}_2 = \frac{\Sigma X_2}{N_2} = 10.7$$

$$s_1 = \sqrt{\frac{\Sigma X_1^2}{N_1} - \bar{X}_1^2} \qquad s_2 = \sqrt{\frac{\Sigma X_2^2}{N_2} - \bar{X}_2^2}$$

$$= \sqrt{\frac{1585}{10} - (12.3)^2} \qquad = \sqrt{\frac{1237}{10} - (10.7)^2}$$

$$= \sqrt{158.5 - 151.29} = \sqrt{7.21} = 2.685 \qquad = \sqrt{123.7 - 114.49} = \sqrt{9.21} = 3.035$$

$$s_{\bar{X}_1 - \bar{X}_2} = \sqrt{\frac{7.21 + 9.21}{9}} = 1.351, \quad t = \frac{12.3 - 10.7}{1.351} = 1.18, \quad df = 18, \text{n.s.}$$

Table 16-3 Comparison of Left and Right Handers on Reaction Time to Tones Delivered to the Right Ear (Independent *t* Test, Unequal *n*'s)

Group 1 (left-handers)	Group 2 (right-handers)
$\bar{X}_1 = 240$ ms	$\bar{X}_2 = 210$ ms
$s_1 = 32$ ms	$s_2 = 40$ ms
$N_1 = 6$	$N_2 = 14$

$$s_{\bar{X}_1 - \bar{X}_2} = \sqrt{\frac{6 \times (32)^2 + 14 \times (40)^2}{(6 + 14 - 2)}\left(\frac{1}{6} + \frac{1}{14}\right)}$$

$$= \sqrt{\frac{6144 + 22{,}400}{18}(0.238)}$$

$$= \sqrt{377.42} = 19.427$$

$$t = \frac{240 - 210}{19.427} = 1.54, \quad df = 18, \text{n.s.}$$

conditions, the number of scores (or subjects) in each group must be equal. The number of paired scores will be denoted as *N*, so the total number of different scores in the analysis equals 2*N*.

There are two alternative formulas for a matched pairs *t* test. The first uses the correlation coefficient (Pearson *r*) between the scores, and the second uses the difference between the paired scores.

Table 16-4 Number of Problems Correctly Solved by Two Groups of Subjects Matched on Verbal SAT Scores, in which Feedback Was Given to Group 1 and No Feedback Was Given to Group 2

Subject Number	Group 1 (feedback) Number correct (X_1)	Group 2 (no feedback) Number correct (X_2)	$D = X_1 - X_2$	D^2
1	11	10	1	1
2	17	15	2	4
3	14	14	0	0
4	10	8	2	4
5	11	9	2	4
6	15	14	1	1
7	10	6	4	16
8	8	7	1	1
9	12	11	1	1
10	15	13	2	4
Σ	123	107	16	36

$$\overline{X}_1 = \frac{123}{10} = 12.3,\ \overline{X}_2 = \frac{107}{10} = 10.7,\ \overline{D} = \frac{16}{10} = 1.6$$

$$s_D^2 = \frac{\Sigma D^2}{N} - \overline{D}^2 = \frac{36}{10} - (1.6)^2 = 1.04 \qquad s_{\overline{D}} = \sqrt{\frac{s_D^2}{N-1}} = \sqrt{\frac{1.04}{9}} = 0.340$$

$r = +.944,$

$$s_{\overline{X}_1} = \frac{s_1}{\sqrt{N-1}} = \frac{2.685}{\sqrt{9}} = 0.8950$$

$$s_{\overline{X}_2} = \frac{s_2}{\sqrt{N-1}} = \frac{3.035}{\sqrt{9}} = 1.0117$$

$$s_{\overline{X}_1-\overline{X}_2} = \sqrt{(0.8950)^2 + (1.0117)^2 - 2(+0.944)(0.8950)(1.0117)} = 0.339$$

(a) t (Direct-Difference Method)

$$t = \frac{\overline{D}}{s_{\overline{D}}} = \frac{1.6}{0.340} = 4.71, \quad df = 9, \quad p < .01$$

(b) t (Correlation Method)

$$t = \frac{\overline{X}_1 - \overline{X}_2}{s_{\overline{X}_1-\overline{X}_2}} = \frac{12.3 - 10.7}{0.339} = 4.72, \quad df = 9, \quad p < .01$$

Correlation formula:

$$t = \frac{\overline{X}_1 - \overline{X}_2}{s_{\overline{X}_1-\overline{X}_2}}$$

where

$$s_{\overline{X}_1-\overline{X}_2} = \sqrt{s_{\overline{X}_1}2 + s_{\overline{X}_2}2 - 2rs_{\overline{X}_1}s_{\overline{X}_2}}$$

and

$$s_{\overline{X}_1}{}^2 = \frac{s_1^2}{N-1},\ df = N - 1$$

Difference formula:

$$t = \frac{\overline{D}}{s_{\overline{D}}},\ \overline{D} = \overline{X}_1 - \overline{X}_2$$

where

$$s_{\overline{D}} = \frac{s_D}{\sqrt{N-1}} = \sqrt{\frac{s_D^2}{N-1}}$$

and

$$s_D^2 = \frac{\Sigma D^2}{N} - (\overline{D})^2,\ df = N - 1$$

Table 16-4 presents computational examples for both the correlation formula and the difference formula. As shown there, both formulas produce identical answers (within rounding error). The correlation formula is computationally more complex, so the difference formula is usually preferred unless the correlations have already been calculated for other purposes.

Degrees of Freedom

In evaluating the significance of statistical tests, we need to know how many degrees of freedom we have. This is because sampling distributions such as the *t* and *F* distribution are really families of distributions that differ depending on the *df* associated with them. As the *df* increases, the difference between means needed for significance decreases. The *t* distribution has a single *df* and the *F* distribution has a pair of *df*. Degrees of freedom are related to sample size, with the number of *df* increasing with the sample size. Roughly speaking, degrees of freedom refers to the number of values in our sample that are free to vary once we have computed certain sample statistics. For example, given that you know the mean of a set of *N* scores, the number of scores that are free to vary is one less than *N*, or $N - 1$.

In an independent *t* test, there are $N_1 + N_2$ different scores, a mean is known for each set of scores, so the number of *df* associated with an independent *t* test is two less than the total number of scores, or $N_1 + N_2 - 2$. In a matched-pairs *t* test, in contrast, there are *N* paired scores. Because these scores are paired on some basis, the two scores are not independent, but dependent. The number of *df* associated with a dependent *t* test is one less than the number of pairs, rather than two less than the number of scores, so the *df* for a matched-pairs *t* test is half the number for an independent *t* test. This means that the *t* ratio for a matched groups design must be larger than that for an independent groups design to lead to the same level of significance.

On the other hand, to the degree that pairs of scores are correlated because of the matching, the error term (denominator) of the *t* ratio will be smaller in matched than independent *t* ratios, so we expect the calculated *t* ratio to be larger.

In all of the examples shown, we have indicated the significance level for a two-tailed test by referring to Table A-5 in Appendix A. Students should make sure they understand how these significance levels were obtained by checking the critical values of *t* shown in the table.

A TEST FOR MORE THAN TWO GROUPS: THE ANALYSIS OF VARIANCE

Whenever more than two means are to be compared, we use an analysis of variance (ANOVA). The analysis of variance compares two variance estimates. One is based on differences between means and is called the *between-groups variance estimate.* The second is based on differences between individual scores within groups and is called the *within-groups variance estimate.* If the variance between groups is large in comparison with the variance within groups, we conclude that our experimental manipulations had a real effect, and we reject the null hypothesis. If the two variance estimates are nearly equal, we conclude that our experimental manipulations did not have a real effect, and we fail to reject the null hypothesis.

The test statistic that we use to compare two variances is the *F* ratio. The *F* ratio is computed by dividing the between-groups variance estimate by the within-groups variance estimate. If the *F* ratio is large enough, we reject the null hypothesis. If it is too small, we accept it.

Table A-6 in Appendix A gives critical values for *F* ratios. Evaluating *F* ratios is somewhat more complicated than evaluating *t* ratios because we need two values of *df* to determine the value of critical *F*s. The first *df* is that associated with the numerator of the *F* ratio, and the second is that associated with the denominator.

In the next sections, we present the five types of ANOVAs shown in Table 16-1: one-way randomized, one-way repeated measures, two-way randomized, two-way repeated measures, and two-way mixed. For each type of ANOVA, we first show

Table 16-5 Glossary of Notational Terms for a One-Way Randomized ANOVA

s	=	number of subjects in each group.
a	=	number of groups, or number of levels of the independent variable.
N	=	total number of observations, given by $a \times s$.
A	=	general designation for the single independent variable or single factor being manipulated.
A_1	=	sum of subject scores run under the first level of factor A.
A_2	=	sum of subject scores run under the second level of factor A.
A_3	=	sum of subject scores run under the third level of factor A.
T	=	total sum of all scores.
C	=	"correction factor" = T^2/N
TS	=	total sum of all squared scores (i.e., each score is first squared, then summed with all others).
SS_{tot}	=	total sums of squares, which in turn can be divided into SS_A and SS_{err}.
SS_A	=	sums of squares due to differences among means on factor A.
SS_{err}	=	sums of squares due to differences among scores within each group. (Note that $SS_{tot} = SS_A + SS_{err}$, so $SS_{err} = SS_{tot} - SS_A$.)
X_{ij}	=	score for *i*th subject under the *j*th level of factor A. So, for example, X_{62} is the score for the sixth subject run under the second level of factor A.
MS_A	=	mean square between groups of subjects on factor A, computed by dividing the sums of squares for A by the number of *df*, or $a - 1$.
MS_{err}	=	mean square within subjects, computed by dividing the sums of squares within subjects by the number of *df*, or $N - a$.

Table 16-6 Computations for a One-Way Completely Randomized ANOVA (Equal *N*'s)

Subject Number	Factor A		
	Level 1	Level 2	Level 3
1	X_{11}	X_{12}	X_{13}
2	X_{21}	X_{22}	X_{23}
3	X_{31}	X_{32}	X_{33}
4	X_{41}	X_{42}	X_{43}
5	X_{51}	X_{52}	X_{53}
6	X_{61}	X_{62}	X_{63}
7	X_{71}	X_{72}	X_{73}

$$A_1 = \sum_{i=1}^{7} X_{i1} \qquad A_2 = \sum_{i=1}^{7} X_{i2} \qquad A_3 = \sum_{i=1}^{7} X_{i3}$$

$$s = 7; \qquad a = 3; \qquad N = s \times a = 21$$

$$T = \sum_{i=1}^{7} \sum_{j=1}^{3} X_{ij} = A_1 + A_2 + A_3$$

$$TS = \sum_{i=1}^{7} \sum_{j=1}^{3} X_{ij}^2$$

$$C = \frac{T^2}{N}$$

$$SS_{tot} = TS - C$$

$$SS_A = \sum_{i=1}^{3} \frac{A_i^2}{s} - C = \frac{A_1^2 + A_2^2 + A_3^2}{7} - C$$

$$SS_{err} = SS_{tot} - SS_A$$

$$F = \frac{SS_A/(a-1)}{SS_{err}/(N-a)} = \frac{MS_A}{MS_{err}}$$

$$df = (a - 1), \qquad (N - a)$$

Table 16-7 Numerical Example of Computations for a One-Way Completely Randomized ANOVA (Equal N's)

Subject Number	Factor A		
	Level 1	Level 2	Level 3
1	10	17	20
2	12	13	25
3	15	16	14
4	11	12	17
5	5	7	12
6	7	8	18
7	2	3	7
Means	8.86	10.86	16.14

$A_1 = 62 \quad A_2 = 76 \quad A_3 = 113$

$s = 7; \quad a = 3; \quad N = 21$

$T = 251$

$TS = 3675$

$$C = \frac{(251)^2}{21} = 3000.05$$

$$SS_{tot} = 3675 - 3000.05 = 674.95$$

$$SS_A = \frac{(62)^2 + (76)^2 + (113)^2}{7} - 3000.05$$

$$= 3198.43 - 3000.05 = 198.38$$

$$SS_{err} = 674.95 - 198.38 = 476.57$$

$$F = \frac{198.38/2}{476.57/18} = \frac{99.19}{26.48} = 3.75; \quad \text{df} = 2, 18; \quad p < 0.05$$

Table 16-8 Computations for a One-Way Completely Randomized ANOVA (Unequal N's)

Subject Number	Factor A		
	Level 1	Level 2	Level 3
1	X_{11}	X_{12}	X_{13}
2	X_{21}	X_{22}	X_{23}
3	X_{31}	X_{32}	X_{33}
4	X_{41}	X_{42}	X_{43}
5	X_{51}	X_{52}	X_{53}
6	X_{61}		X_{63}
7	X_{71}		

$$A_1 = \sum_{i=1}^{7} X_{i1} \quad A_2 = \sum_{i=1}^{5} X_{i2} \quad A_3 = \sum_{i=1}^{6} X_{i3}$$

$s_1 = 7, \quad s_2 = 5, \quad s_3 = 6; \quad a = 3; \quad N = s_1 + s_2 + s_3 = 18$

$T = A_1 + A_2 + A_3$

$$TS = \sum_{i=1}^{7} X_{i1}^2 + \sum_{i=1}^{5} X_{i2}^2 + \sum_{i=1}^{6} X_{i3}^2$$

$$C = \frac{T^2}{N}$$

$$SS_{tot} = TS - C$$

$$SS_A = \frac{A_1^2}{7} + \frac{A_2^2}{5} + \frac{A_3^2}{6} - C$$

$$SS_{err} = SS_{tot} - SS_A$$

$$F = \frac{SS_A/(a-1)}{SS_{err}/(N-a)} = \frac{MS_A}{MS_{err}}$$

$$\text{df} = (a-1), \quad (N-a)$$

Table 16-9 Numerical Example of Computations for a One-Way Completely Randomized ANOVA (Unequal *N*'s)

Subject Number	Factor *A*		
	Level 1	Level 2	Level 3
1	100	86	75
2	120	22	42
3	118	47	35
4	42	51	56
5	63	63	70
6	72		46
7	110		
Means	89.29	53.80	54.00

$A_1 = 625 \quad A_2 = 269 \quad A_3 = 324$

$s_1 = 7, \quad s_2 = 5, \quad s_3 = 6; \quad a = 3; \quad N = 18$

$T = 1{,}218$

$\text{TS} = 96{,}766$

$$C = \frac{(1{,}218)^2}{18} = 82{,}418$$

$$\text{SS}_{tot} = 96{,}766 - 82{,}418 = 14{,}348$$

$$\text{SS}_A = \frac{(625)^2}{7} + \frac{(269)^2}{5} + \frac{(324)^2}{6} - 82{,}418 = 87{,}771.77 - 82{,}418 = 5{,}353.77$$

$$\text{SS}_{err} = 14{,}348 - 5{,}353.77 = 8{,}994.23$$

$$F = \frac{5353.77/2}{8994.23/15} = \frac{2676.88}{599.62} = 4.46; \quad \text{df} = 2, 15; \quad p < 0.05$$

the procedures and formulas in notation, and then present a numerical example. Table 16-5 presents a glossary of notational terms we shall use for a one-way randomized ANOVA.

ONE-WAY ANALYSIS OF VARIANCE

A one-way ANOVA is appropriate whenever we have a single independent variable and we have used three or more levels of the independent variable. If separate groups of subjects have participated in each condition, in a between-subjects design, a randomized ANOVA is the appropriate test. If the same subjects have participated in each condition, in a within-subjects design, a repeated measures ANOVA is the appropriate test. In this section, we give formulas and numerical examples for randomized ANOVAs with equal and unequal *N*s, and formulas and a numerical example for a repeated measures ANOVA. Repeated measures ANOVAs, by the nature of the design, require that there be equal *N*s in each condition.

One-Way ANOVA, Randomized

A randomized one-way ANOVA is used whenever three or more groups of independent subjects are given three or more conditions or levels of a single independent variable. The ANOVA answers the question of whether there are any significant differences among or between means of the conditions. A significant *F* ratio indicates that two or more of the means are significantly different, although additional tests are needed to determine which of the possible differences are significant. There are a number of different tests to make these specific comparisons between means, and we will return to a brief discussion of these multiple comparison tests at the end of this section.

Table 16-6 presents computational procedures for a completely randomized ANOVA with equal *N*s in all groups, and Table 16-7 presents a numerical example.

A single *F* ratio is computed in a one-way ANOVA by dividing the between-groups variance estimate by the within-groups variance estimate. We denote the between-groups variance estimate by MS_A, where *MS* refers to mean square (and is identical to the term variance) and *A* refers to the single independent variable that has been manipulated. The error variance is denoted MS_{err} for the same reasons.

The *df* associated with the numerator is $a - 1$, or one less than the number of groups. The *df* associated with the denominator is $N - a$, or the total number of subjects or scores being analyzed minus the number of conditions.

Tables 16-8 and 16-9 present the computational procedures and a numerical example for a completely randomized ANOVA with unequal *N*s in the various groups. The only computational difference between ANOVAs with unequal *N*s and ANOVAs with equal *N*s is in computing SS_A.

Table 16-10 Computations for a One-Way Repeated Measures ANOVA, Denoted $(A \times S)$

Subject Number	Factor *A*			
	Level 1	Level 2	Level 3	
1	X_{11}	X_{12}	X_{13}	$S_1 = \sum_{j=1}^{3} X_{1j}$
2	X_{21}	X_{22}	X_{23}	$S_2 = \sum_{j=1}^{3} X_{2j}$
3	X_{31}	X_{32}	X_{33}	$S_3 = \sum_{j=1}^{3} X_{3j}$
4	X_{41}	X_{42}	X_{43}	$S_4 = \sum_{j=1}^{3} X_{4j}$
5	X_{51}	X_{52}	X_{53}	$S_5 = \sum_{j=1}^{3} X_{5j}$
6	X_{61}	X_{62}	X_{63}	$S_6 = \sum_{j=1}^{3} X_{6j}$
7	X_{71}	X_{72}	X_{73}	$S_7 = \sum_{j=1}^{3} X_{7j}$
	$A_1 = \sum_{i=1}^{7} X_{i1}$	$A_2 = \sum_{i=1}^{7} X_{i2}$	$A_3 = \sum_{i=1}^{7} X_{i3}$	

$$s = 7; \quad a = 3; \quad N = s \times a = 21$$

$$T = A_1 + A_2 + A_3$$

$$TS = \sum_{i=1}^{7} \sum_{j=1}^{3} X_{ij}^2$$

$$C = \frac{T^2}{N}$$

$$SS_{tot} = TS - C$$

$$SS_A = \sum_{i=1}^{3} \frac{A_i^2}{s} - C$$

$$SS_S = \sum_{j=1}^{7} \frac{S_j^2}{a} - C$$

$$SS_{A \times S} = SS_{tot} - SS_A - SS_S$$

$$F_A = \frac{SS_A/(a-1)}{SS_{A \times S}/(a-1)(s-1)} = \frac{MS_A}{MS_{A \times S}}$$

$$df = (a-1), \quad (a-1)(s-1)$$

Table 16-11 Numerical Example of Computations for a One-Way Repeated Measures ANOVA

Subject Number	Factor A Level 1	Level 2	Level 3	
1	10	17	20	$S_1 = 47$
2	12	13	25	$S_2 = 50$
3	15	16	14	$S_3 = 45$
4	11	12	17	$S_4 = 40$
5	5	7	12	$S_5 = 24$
6	7	8	18	$S_6 = 33$
7	2	3	7	$S_7 = 12$

$A_1 = 62 \quad A_2 = 76 \quad A_3 = 113$

$s = 7; \quad a = 3; \quad N = 21$

$T = 251$

$TS = 3675$

$C = 3000.05$

$SS_{tot} = 3675 - 3000.05 = 674.95$

$$SS_A = \frac{(62)^2 + (76)^2 + (113)^2}{7} - 3000.05 = 3198.43 - 3000.05 = 198.38$$

$$SS_S = \frac{(47)^2 + (50)^2 + (45)^2 + (40)^2 + (24)^2 + (33)^2 + (12)^2}{3} - 3000.05 =$$

$$3381 - 3000.05 = 380.95$$

$SS_{A \times S} = 674.95 - 198.38 - 380.95 = 95.62$

$$F_A = \frac{198.38/2}{95.62/12} = \frac{99.19}{7.97} = 12.45; \quad df = 2, 12; \quad p < 0.01$$

One-Way ANOVA for Repeated Measures

A repeated measures one-way ANOVA is appropriate when subjects serve in all conditions of a one independent variable experiment that has more than two levels. Repeated measures designs are very sensitive because they permit the experimenter to decrease the error variance by subtracting from it the variability attributable to individual differences. We will point out how this is done in a moment.

Tables 16-10 and 16-11 present the computational procedures and a numerical example for a one-way repeated measures ANOVA. Note that the error term is now denoted $MS_{A\times S}$. $MS_{A\times S}$ stands for the mean square or variance attributable to the interaction of subjects with the various levels of the independent variable. Note how it is computed—by subtracting from the total sums of squares (SS_{tot}) both the sums of squares due to the independent variable (SS_A) and the sums of squares due to subjects (SS_S). SS_S is a measure of how much subjects differ from one another, and that component of the total error variance can be subtracted from the error term of the F ratio because each subject participated in all conditions of the experiment.

TWO-WAY ANALYSIS OF VARIANCE

A two-way analysis of variance is used whenever two independent variables are manipulated and all combinations of levels of each of the two variables are used. So, we would use a two-way ANOVA for an experiment in which we manipulated both the sex of subject and type of instructions, for a 2 × 2 design, or when we gave three types of reward under four learning conditions, for a 3 × 4 design.

The advantage of combining two or more independent variables in an experimental design is that the effects of one variable may be changed when combined with a second, and vice versa. For example, praise may be an effective reward for people who are sensitive to the opinions of others but ineffective for people who are self-motivated. Thus, the presence or absence of praise may interact with personality type. Or certain combinations of drugs such as alcohol and tranquilizers may be lethal, even though separately they may be harmless.

In a one-way ANOVA, we obtain a single F ratio, F_A, which tells us whether any of the differences among the mean scores obtained under each of the levels of A is significant. When we carry out a two-way ANOVA, we obtain three F ratios. The first is F_A, which tells us whether the differences among the various levels of factor A, collapsed or summed over the levels of factor B, are significant. The second is F_B, which tells us whether the differences among the levels of factor B, collapsed over factor A, are significant. The third is $F_{A \times B}$, which tells us whether the *interaction* between factor A and factor B is significant.

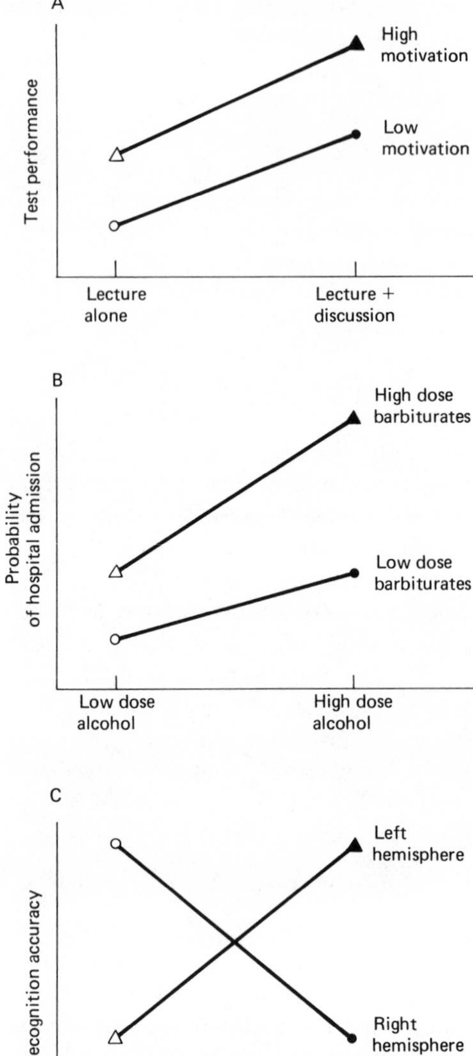

Fig. 16-2 Some examples of outcomes of 2 × 2 designs. (A) Significant main effects but no interaction. (B) Significant main effects and an interaction. (C) No significant main effects but a significant interaction. This is called a crossover interaction.

The Concept of Interaction

The concept of interaction between variables is a very important one when more than one variable is manipulated. An interaction occurs whenever the effect of one variable depends on the level of a second variable with which it is combined. Another way of describing interaction is to say that the effects of the two variables are not additive.

It will simplify our discussion of interaction to consider the simplest two-factor design, one in which each of the two independent variables has only two levels. We refer to this as a 2 × 2 experimental design (see Chapter 2).

Figure 16-2 presents several graphs of data from a 2 × 2 design. First, let us take a moment to explain how to read such graphs. The ordinate (vertical or y-axis) represents values of the dependent variable. The two levels of independent variable A are represented along the abscissa (horizontal or x-axis). The two levels of independent variable B are represented by the two separate lines in the graph. Each figure displays the values of four means, represented by unfilled and filled symbols, and corresponding to each possible combination of the two levels of *A* and the two levels of *B*.

Panel A in Figure 16-2 shows the results of a hypothetical experiment in which we evaluated the effects of both teaching method and level of motivation on test performance. Independent variable *A* is the teaching method, with level 1 defined as traditional lecture method and level 2 defined as lecture plus group discussion. Independent variable *B* is level of motivation, with subjects under level 1 (the low motivation group) instructed that performance on the test is not important, and subjects under level 2 (the high motivation group) instructed that performance is very important. The dependent variable is test performance. The results show that adding group discussion to lectures improves performance and that increasing motivation improves performance, but there is no interaction between the two variables. That is, the two variables add together in their effects on test performance. This can be observed graphically by the fact that the two functions in panel A are parallel.

Panels B and C both illustrate interaction effects, shown graphically by the fact that the lines are not parallel. Panel B illustrates the interactive effects of drugs on probability of hospital admission. If *A* is alcohol and *B* is barbituates, and level 1 is a low dosage of the drug and level 2 a high dosage, panel B in Figure 16-2 shows that a high dose of either drug coupled with a low dose of the second will increase the likelihood of hospital admission, but high doses of both drugs together will more than additively increase risk. The drugs interact because, when taken together, the effects are larger than would be predicted by a consideration of either of them alone. (In pharmacology, this kind of interaction between drugs is known as potentiation).

Panel C shows the most dramatic form of interaction, the *crossover interaction*. A crossover interaction is predicted by the hemispheric lateralization hypothesis, which proposes that the two cerebral hemispheres in humans are specialized for different functions (see Chapter 6). For virtually all right-handers and some left-handers, language processing is localized in the left hemisphere and spatiopictorial processing in the right hemisphere. In order to test the hemispheric lateralization hypothesis, an investigator presents either pictures or words (independent variable *A*) initially to either the right or left hemisphere (independent variable *B*) by exposing the material briefly to the left or right of fixation. The dependent variable is accuracy of recognition. Subjects do well for pictures presented to the right hemisphere and words presented to the left hemisphere, and do poorly for pictures presented to the left hemisphere and words presented to the right hemisphere, producing the crossover interaction shown in panel C of Figure 16-2.

In the next sections, we present computational and numerical examples for three kinds of two-way ANOVAs: randomized, repeated measures, and mixed.

Two-Way ANOVA, Completely Randomized

A completely randomized two-way ANOVA is used when separate groups of subjects are assigned to each of the conditions formed by pairing each level of *A* with each level of *B*. We show an example of a 2 × 2 completely randomized ANOVA with equal numbers of subjects in each of the four groups. Computational procedures for ANOVAs for unequal *N*s are more complicated, and examples can be found in Keppel (1973) and Winer (1971).

A 2 × 2 Completely Randomized ANOVA with Equal Ns. A 2 × 2 ANOVA with equal *N*s is used when there are two levels of *A* and two levels of *B* and different groups of subjects have been assigned to each combination. Thus, there are four separate groups of subjects.

Table 16-12 presents the computational procedures for a 2 × 2 completely randomized ANOVA. The two levels of factor

Table 16-12 Computational Procedures for a 2 × 2 Completely Randomized ANOVA (Five Subjects in Each Group)

	Factor A		
	a_1	a_2	
Factor B			
b_1	X_{111} X_{211} X_{311} X_{411} X_{511}	X_{121} X_{221} X_{321} X_{421} X_{521}	
	A_1B_1	A_2B_1	B_1
b_2	X_{112} X_{212} X_{312} X_{412} X_{512}	X_{122} X_{222} X_{322} X_{422} X_{522}	
	A_1B_2	A_2B_2	B_2
	A_1	A_2	$T = \Sigma\Sigma X$ $TS = \Sigma\Sigma X^2$

$a = 2;\quad b = 2;\quad s = 5;\quad N = abs = 20$

$C = T^2/N$

$SS_{tot} = TS - C$

$$SS_A = \sum \frac{A^2}{bs} - C$$

$$SS_B = \sum \frac{B^2}{as} - C$$

$$SS_{A\times B} = \sum \frac{AB^2}{s} - C - SS_A - SS_B$$

$SS_{err} = SS_{tot} - SS_A - SS_B - SS_{A\times B}$

$$F_A = \frac{SS_A/(a-1)}{SS_{err}/ab(s-1)} = \frac{MS_A}{MS_{err}};\quad df = (a-1),\quad ab(s-1)$$

$$F_B = \frac{SS_B/(b-1)}{SS_{err}/ab(s-1)} = \frac{MS_B}{MS_{err}};\quad df = (b-1),\quad ab(s-1)$$

$$F_{A\times B} = \frac{SS_{A\times B}/(a-1)(b-1)}{SS_{err}/ab(s-1)} = \frac{MS_{A\times B}}{MS_{err}};\quad df = (a-1)(b-1),\quad ab(s-1)$$

A are called a_1 and a_2, and the two levels of factor *B* are called b_1 and b_2. Capital letters, as before, refer to sums. So, for example, the sum of all the scores under the first level of *A* and the second level of *B* is denoted A_1B_2, and the sum of all the scores under the first level of *A* for both levels of *B* is denoted A_1. For clarity in presenting these more complicated ANOVAs, we shall omit the equations for the terms that contribute to a sum. However, by referring to the computational examples, the student should be able to figure out which terms have been added together.

For a particular score, X_{ijk}, *i* indexes subject number, *j* indexes the level of factor *A*, and *k* indexes the level of factor *B*. Because this is a 2 × 2 analysis, the number of *df* associated with each of the three numerators in the three *F* ratios is always 1. That is, the *df* is $a - 1$ for factor *A*, $b - 1$ for factor *B*, and $(a - 1)(b - 1)$ for the *A* × *B* interaction.

Table 16-13 presents a numerical example of a 2 × 2 completely randomized ANOVA. The means are shown at the right of the table and Figure 16-3 presents the graphed means. Calculating the means and graphing them first, before carrying out the ANOVA, can often help the student know what to expect from the results of the ANOVA. From the graph of our results, we see that there is no apparent overall effect of variable *A*, because the means for level a_1 and level a_2 when taken over the two levels of factor *B* (by averaging the two factor *B* functions) are the same. However, there appears to be an overall effect of factor *B*, since the average b_1 function is lower than the average b_2 function (obtained by averaging across the two factor *A* points). In addition, because the two functions are not parallel, we might suspect that there is an interaction between the two factors. That is, moving from level a_1 to level a_2 at level b_1 increases performance, whereas moving from level a_1 to a_2 at level b_2 decreases performance.

Table 16-13 Numerical Example for a 2 × 2 Completely Randomized ANOVA (Equal *n*'s)

	Factor *A*		
	a_1	a_2	
Factor *B*			*Means*
	5	8	$\overline{A_1B_1} = 4.60$
	2	6	$\overline{A_2B_1} = 7.80$
b_1	3	5	$\overline{A_1B_2} = 16.20$
	7	11	$\overline{A_2B_2} = 13.00$
	6	9	
	$A_1B_1 = 23$	$A_2B_1 = 39$	$B_1 = 62$
	15	13	
	14	12	
b_2	17	9	
	19	16	
	16	15	
	$A_1B_2 = 81$	$A_2B_2 = 65$	$B_2 = 146$
	$A_1 = 104$	$A_2 = 104$	$T = 208$
			$TS = 2652$

$a = 2; \quad b = 2; \quad s = 5; \quad N = 20$

$$C = \frac{(208)^2}{20} = 2163.20$$

$$SS_{tot} = 2652 - 2163.20 = 488.80$$

$$SS_A = \frac{(104)^2 + (104)^2}{10} - 2163.20 = 0$$

$$SS_B = \frac{(62)^2 + (146)^2}{10} - 2163.20 = 352.80$$

$$SS_{A \times B} = \frac{(23)^2 + (39)^2 + (81)^2 + (65)^2}{5} - 2163.20 - 0 - 352.80 = 51.20$$

$$SS_{err} = 488.80 - 0 - 352.80 - 51.20 = 84.80$$

$$F_A = \frac{0/1}{84.80/16} = \frac{0}{5.30} = 0; \quad df = 1, 16; \quad \text{n.s.}$$

$$F_B = \frac{352.80/1}{5.30} = 66.57; \quad df = 1, 16; \quad p < 0.001$$

$$F_{A \times B} = \frac{51.20/1}{5.30} = 9.66; \quad df = 1, 16; \quad p < 0.01$$

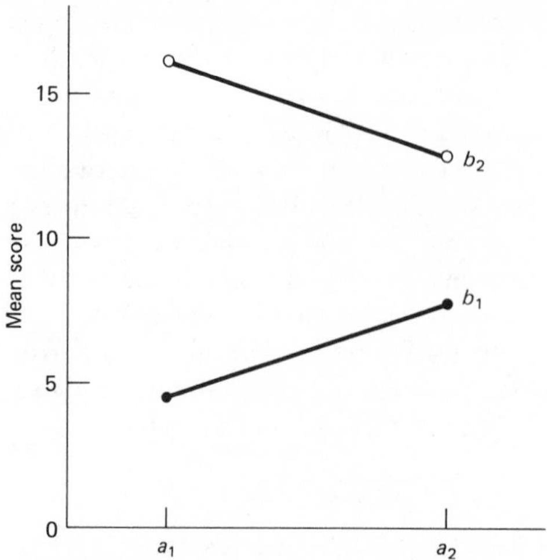

Fig. 16-3 Graphic presentation of the means presented in Table 16-13. (From *The Numbers Game: Statistics for Psychology* by J. G. Snodgrass. Copyright 1977 by Oxford University Press. Reprinted by permission.)

The results of the ANOVA are consistent with our intuitions from the graphed results. There is no overall effect of variable A, because F_A is zero, but there is a significant overall effect of variable B, and a significant $A \times B$ interaction.

Two-Way ANOVA with Repeated Measures on Both Factors

In a repeated measures design, all subjects participate in all conditions of the experiment. Repeated measures ANOVAs differ from completely randomized ANOVAs in two ways. First, the variance resulting from individual differences in subjects is subtracted from the error term. Second, there is a different error term for each of the three F ratios, F_A, F_B, and $F_{A\times B}$. Because the error term is different for each F ratio, a different notation will be used for each error term to distinguish them.

Table 16-14 Computational Procedures for a 2 × 2 Repeated Measures ANOVA, Denoted ($A \times B \times S$)

	Factor A			
	a_1	a_2	BS matrix	
Factor B				
	X_{111}	X_{121}	B_1S_1	
	X_{211}	X_{221}	B_1S_2	
	X_{311}	X_{321}	B_1S_3	
b_1	X_{411}	X_{421}	B_1S_4	
	X_{511}	X_{521}	B_1S_5	
	X_{611}	X_{621}	B_1S_6	
	A_1B_1	A_2B_1		B_1
	X_{112}	X_{122}	B_2S_1	
	X_{212}	X_{222}	B_2S_2	
	X_{312}	X_{322}	B_2S_3	
b_2	X_{412}	X_{422}	B_2S_4	
	X_{512}	X_{522}	B_2S_5	
	X_{612}	X_{622}	B_2S_6	
	A_1B_2	A_2B_2		B_2
	A_1	A_2		

Table 16-14 (*Continued*)

AS matrix		S matrix
A_1S_1	A_2S_1	S_1
A_1S_2	A_2S_2	S_2
A_1S_3	A_2S_3	S_3
A_1S_4	A_2S_4	S_4
A_1S_5	A_2S_5	S_5
A_1S_6	A_2S_6	S_6

$T = \Sigma\Sigma X$

$TS = \Sigma\Sigma X^2$

$a = 2; \quad b = 2; \quad s = 6; \quad N = abs = 24$

$C = T^2/N$

$\text{SS}_{\text{tot}} = \text{TS} - C$

$$\text{SS}_A = \sum \frac{A^2}{bs} - C$$

$$\text{SS}_B = \sum \frac{B^2}{as} - C$$

$$\text{SS}_S = \sum \frac{S^2}{ab} - C$$

$$\text{SS}_{A\times B} = \sum \frac{AB^2}{s} - \text{SS}_A - \text{SS}_B - C$$

$$\text{SS}_{A\times S} = \sum \frac{AS^2}{b} - \text{SS}_A - \text{SS}_S - C$$

$$\text{SS}_{B\times S} = \sum \frac{BS^2}{a} - \text{SS}_B - \text{SS}_S - C$$

$$\text{SS}_{A\times B\times S} = \text{SS}_{\text{tot}} - \text{SS}_A - \text{SS}_B - \text{SS}_S - \text{SS}_{A\times B} - \text{SS}_{A\times S} - \text{SS}_{B\times S}$$

$$F_A = \frac{\text{SS}_A/(a-1)}{\text{SS}_{A\times S}/(a-1)(s-1)} = \frac{\text{MS}_A}{\text{MS}_{A\times S}}; \quad \text{df} = a-1, \quad (a-1)(s-1)$$

$$F_B = \frac{\text{SS}_B/(b-1)}{\text{SS}_{B\times S}/(b-1)(s-1)} = \frac{\text{MS}_B}{\text{MS}_{B\times S}}; \quad \text{df} = b-1, \quad (b-1)(s-1)$$

$$F_{A\times B} = \frac{\text{SS}_{A\times B}/(a-1)(b-1)}{\text{SS}_{A\times B\times S}/(a-1)(b-1)(s-1)} = \frac{\text{MS}_{A\times B}}{\text{MS}_{A\times B\times S}}; \quad \text{df} = (a-1)(b-1), \quad (a-1)(b-1)(s-1)$$

This type of design is denoted ($A \times B \times S$), indicating that a third factor, subjects, enters into the computation. The parentheses enclosing *A*, *B*, and *S* reflect the fact that *A* and *B* are both repeated measures variables.

A 2 × 2 ANOVA with Repeated Measures. Table 16-14 presents the computational procedures, and Table 16-15 presents a numerical example for a 2 × 2 ANOVA with repeated measures on both factors.

The *AS* matrix is obtained by summing across the two levels of factor *B* for each level of factor *A* for each subject, and the *BS* matrix is obtained by summing across the two levels of factor *A* for each level of factor *B* for each subject. The *S* matrix is obtained by summing the scores for each subject across both levels of *A* and *B*. This can be accomplished for the *i*th subject by either adding A_1S_i to A_2S_i or by adding B_1S_i to B_2S_i.

Two-Way ANOVA with a Mixed Design

In a mixed design, factor *A* is a completely randomized or between-subjects variable and factor *B* is a repeated measures or

Table 16-15 Numerical Example for a 2 × 2 Repeated Measures ANOVA ($A \times B \times S$)

	Factor A: a_1	a_2	BS matrix	
Factor B				
b_1	2	4	$B_1S_1 = 6$	
	4	5	$B_1S_2 = 9$	
	7	10	$B_1S_3 = 17$	
	6	8	$B_1S_4 = 14$	
	5	6	$B_1S_5 = 11$	
	3	7	$B_1S_6 = 10$	
	$A_1B_1 = 27$	$A_2B_1 = 40$		$B_1 = 67$
b_2	12	16	$B_2S_1 = 28$	
	10	14	$B_2S_2 = 24$	
	19	19	$B_2S_3 = 38$	
	15	18	$B_2S_4 = 33$	
	15	15	$B_2S_5 = 30$	
	10	17	$B_2S_6 = 27$	
	$A_1B_2 = 81$	$A_2B_2 = 99$		$B_2 = 180$
	$A_1 = 108$	$A_2 = 139$		

AS matrix		S matrix
$A_1S_1 = 14$	$A_2S_1 = 20$	$S_1 = 34$
$A_1S_2 = 14$	$A_2S_2 = 19$	$S_2 = 33$
$A_1S_3 = 26$	$A_2S_3 = 29$	$S_3 = 55$
$A_1S_4 = 21$	$A_2S_4 = 26$	$S_4 = 47$
$A_1S_5 = 20$	$A_2S_5 = 21$	$S_5 = 41$
$A_1S_6 = 13$	$A_2S_6 = 24$	$S_6 = 37$

Means

$\overline{A_1B_1} = 4.50$

$\overline{A_2B_1} = 6.67$

$\overline{A_1B_2} = 13.50$

$\overline{A_2B_2} = 16.50$

$T = 247$

$TS = 3235$

$a = 2; \quad b = 2; \quad s = 6; \quad N = 24$

$$C = \frac{(247)^2}{24} = 2542.04$$

$$SS_{tot} = 3235 - 2542.04 = 692.96$$

$$SS_A = \frac{(108)^2 + (139)^2}{12} - 2542.04 = 40.04$$

$$SS_B = \frac{(67)^2 + (180)^2}{12} - 2542.04 = 532.04$$

$$SS_S = \frac{(34)^2 + (33)^2 + \cdots + (37)^2}{4} - 2542.04 = 90.21$$

$$SS_{A\times B} = \frac{(27)^2 + (40)^2 + (81)^2 + (99)^2}{6} - 2542.04 - 40.04 - 532.04 = 1.05$$

$$SS_{A\times S} = \frac{(14)^2 + (14)^2 + \cdots + (24)^2}{2} - 2542.04 - 40.04 - 90.21 = 14.21$$

Table 16-15 (*Continued*)

$$SS_{B\times S} = \frac{(6)^2 + (9)^2 + \cdots + (27)^2}{2} - 2542.04 - 532.04 - 90.21 = 8.21$$

$$SS_{A\times B\times S} = 692.96 - 40.04 - 532.04 - 90.21 - 1.05 - 14.21 - 8.21 = 7.20$$

$$F_A = \frac{40.04/1}{14.21/5} = \frac{40.04}{2.84} = 14.09; \quad df = 1, 5; \quad p < 0.05$$

$$F_B = \frac{532.04/1}{8.21/5} = \frac{532.04}{1.64} = 324.41; \quad df = 1, 5; \quad p < 0.001$$

$$F_{A\times B} = \frac{1.05/1}{7.20/5} = \frac{1.05}{1.44} = 0.73; \quad df = 1, 5; \quad \text{n.s.}$$

within-subjects variable. This means that each subject is run on only one level of factor *A* but on all levels of factor *B*. This design is designated $A \times (B \times S)$, and the parentheses enclosing *B* and *S* indicate that only factor *B* is a repeated measures variable.

A 2 × 2 Mixed ANOVA. Table 16-16 presents the computational procedure, and Table 16-17 presents a numerical example for a 2 × 2 mixed ANOVA.

Computationally, the mixed ANOVA is more complicated than either the completely randomized or the completely repeated measures ANOVA. The reason is that the error terms used in the denominators of the *F* ratios are more complex. The error term for evaluating the significance of factor *A* is based on the variability of subjects within groups, called $SS_{\text{subjects within groups}}$ or $SS_{S/A}$. Since the same subject participates in only one level of factor *A*, *A* is tested by comparing its variability (i.e., the variability among the means of the levels of factor *A*) with the variability of the subjects within the groups.

The error term for evaluating the significance of both factor *B* and the $A \times B$ interaction is the interaction of *B* with subjects within groups, called $SS_{B\times\text{subjects within groups}}$ or $SS_{B\times S/A}$. This is the error term used because each subject has participated in each level of *B*, and so an interaction term that measures the degree to which the same subjects were affected equivalently by various levels of *B* is appropriate.

Degrees of Freedom for the Three Types of Two-Way ANOVAs

The three ANOVAs differ in the number of *df* associated with the error term, or denominator, of the *F* ratios. The repeated measures design has the fewest *df* and the randomized has the most. Table 16-18 summarizes the *df* associated with the three types of two-way ANOVAs.

The *df* associated with the numerator is the same for all three types of ANOVA. However, the *df* associated with the denominator, MS_{err}, differs depending on the design. The *df* for the completely randomized ANOVA is the largest of the three types and is the same for all three *F* ratios. The *df* for the completely repeated measures ANOVA is the smallest of the three types and is different for each *F* ratio, because the error terms are different for each *F* ratio. The *df* for the mixed design is intermediate in value and is the same for F_B and $F_{A\times B}$.

MULTIPLE COMPARISON TESTS BETWEEN MEANS

After we have carried out an ANOVA for an experiment with more than two conditions and find that our *F* ratio is significant, what do we do? We now know that somewhere among that set of means there is one or more significant differences. But

Table 16-16 Computational Procedures for a 2 × 2 Mixed ANOVA, Denoted $A \times (B \times S)$

	Factor A		
	a_1	a_2	
Factor B			
b_1	X_{111} X_{211} X_{311} X_{411}	X_{121} X_{221} X_{321} X_{421}	
	A_1B_1	A_2B_1	B_1
b_2	X_{112} X_{212} X_{312} X_{412}	X_{122} X_{222} X_{322} X_{422}	
	A_1B_2	A_2B_2	B_2
	A_1	A_2	$T = \Sigma\Sigma X$ $TS = \Sigma\Sigma X^2$

	AS matrix	
	A_1S_1 A_1S_2 A_1S_3 A_1S_4	A_2S_1 A_2S_2 A_2S_3 A_2S_4

$a = 2;\quad b = 2;\quad s = 4;\quad N = abs = 16$

$C = T^2/N$

$SS_{tot} = TS - C$

$$SS_A = \sum \frac{A^2}{bs} - C$$

$$SS_B = \sum \frac{B^2}{as} - C$$

$$SS_{A\times B} = \sum \frac{AB^2}{s} - SS_A - SS_B - C$$

$$SS_{Ss\text{ within groups}} = SS_{S/A} = \sum \frac{AS^2}{b} - SS_A - C$$

$$SS_{B\times Ss\text{ within groups}} = SS_{B\times S/A} = SS_{tot} - SS_A - SS_B - SS_{A\times B} - SS_{S/A}$$

$$F_A = \frac{SS_A/(a-1)}{SS_{S/A}/a(s-1)} = \frac{MS_A}{MS_{S/A}};\quad df = (a-1),\quad a(s-1)$$

$$F_B = \frac{SS_B/(b-1)}{SS_{B\times S/A}/a(b-1)(s-1)} = \frac{MS_B}{MS_{B\times S/A}};\quad df = (b-1),\quad a(b-1)(s-1)$$

$$F_{A\times B} = \frac{SS_{A\times B}/((a-1)(b-1))}{SS_{B\times S/A}/a(b-1)(s-1)} = \frac{MS_{A\times B}}{MS_{B\times S/A}};\quad df = (a-1)(b-1),\quad a(b-1)(s-1)$$

Table 16-17 Numerical Example for a 2 × 2 Mixed ANOVA, $A \times (B \times S)$

	Factor A: a_1	Factor A: a_2	Means
Factor B			
b_1	10	26	$\overline{A_1B_1} = 11.75$
	13	19	$\overline{A_1B_2} = 14.00$
	8	27	$\overline{A_2B_1} = 23.00$
	16	20	$\overline{A_2B_2} = 17.25$
	$A_1B_1 = 47$	$A_2B_1 = 92$	$B_1 = 139$
b_2	12	20	
	16	14	
	11	20	
	17	15	
	$A_1B_2 = 56$	$A_2B_2 = 69$	$B_2 = 125$
	$A_1 = 103$	$A_2 = 161$	$T = 264$
			$TS = 4786$

AS matrix

$A_1S_1 = 22$	$A_2S_1 = 46$
$A_1S_2 = 29$	$A_2S_2 = 33$
$A_1S_3 = 19$	$A_2S_3 = 47$
$A_1S_4 = 33$	$A_2S_4 = 35$

$a = 2;\quad b = 2;\quad s = 4;\quad N = 16$

$$C = \frac{(264)^2}{16} = 4356.00$$

$$SS_{tot} = 4786 - 4356 = 430$$

$$SS_A = \frac{(103)^2 + (161)^2}{8} - 4356 = 210.25$$

$$SS_B = \frac{(139)^2 + (125)^2}{8} - 4356 = 12.25$$

$$SS_{A\times B} = \frac{(47)^2 + (92)^2 + (56)^2 + (69)^2}{4} - 210.25 - 12.25 - 4356 = 64.00$$

$$SS_{S/A} = \frac{(22)^2 + (29)^2 + (19)^2 + (33)^2 + (46)^2 + (33)^2 + (47)^2 + (35)^2}{2}$$

$$- 210.25 - 4356 = 140.75$$

$$SS_{B\times S/A} = 430 - 210.25 - 12.25 - 64.00 - 140.75 = 2.75$$

$$F_A = \frac{210.25/1}{140.75/6} = \frac{210.25}{23.46} = 8.96;\quad df = 1, 6;\quad p < 0.05$$

$$F_B = \frac{12.25/1}{2.75/6} = \frac{12.25}{0.46} = 26.63;\quad df = 1, 6;\quad p < 0.01$$

$$F_{A\times B} = \frac{64.00/1}{2.75/6} = \frac{64.00}{0.46} = 139.13;\quad df = 1, 6;\quad p < 0.001$$

the ANOVA itself does not tell us the source of the differences. Thus, after computation of the analysis of variance, it is often desirable to carry out various comparisons on pairs of means, or pairs of combinations of means, in order to determine the locus of the significance.

The correct method for comparing individual means is somewhat controversial, and for this reason there are many differ-

Table 16-18 Comparison of the *df* Associated with the Numerator and Denominator of Each *F* Ratio for the Three Types of Two-Way ANOVAs

		Randomized $A \times B$	Repeated Measures $(A \times B \times S)$	Mixed $A \times (B \times S)$
F_A	MS_A	$a - 1$	$a - 1$	$a - 1$
	MS_{err}	$ab(s - 1)$	$(a - 1)(s - 1)$	$a(s - 1)$
F_B	MS_B	$b - 1$	$b - 1$	$b - 1$
	MS_{err}	$ab(s - 1)$	$(b - 1)(s - 1)$	$a(b - 1)(s - 1)$
$F_{A\times B}$	$MS_{A\times B}$	$(a - 1)(b - 1)$	$(a - 1)(b - 1)$	$(a - 1)(b - 1)$
	MS_{err}	$ab(s - 1)$	$(a - 1)(b - 1)(s - 1)$	$a(b - 1)(s - 1)$

a = number of levels of factor A
b = number of levels of factor B
s = number of subjects in each group

ent tests available to compare means. Each test reflects a different position on how conservative or liberal the tests should be. We will describe briefly most of the available tests and refer the interested student to appropriate sources for the computational procedures.

Planned Versus Post Hoc Comparisons

A major distinction between the various tests is whether the comparisons are planned or post hoc. Planned comparisons are those based on predictions derived from an experimenter's hypothesis. For planned comparisons, it is not necessary for the overall ANOVA to be significant in order to carry them out. That is, it is possible that a particular planned comparison will be significant in the absence of an overall significant *F* from the ANOVA.

Planned comparisons use the same error term as the ANOVA in evaluating the significance of differences between any pair of means or combinations of pairs of means. Thus, the computational labor for planned comparisons is relatively small, once the overall ANOVA has been carried out. Specific computational procedures may be found in Keppel (1973), Snodgrass (1977), and Winer (1971).

Post hoc comparisons, on the other hand, may not be carried out unless the overall ANOVA is significant. The purpose of post hoc comparisons is to determine exactly where among the set of conditions of an experiment the significant differences lie. The experimenter who carries out post hoc comparisons often has a rather diffuse hypothesis about what the effects of the manipulation should be, and thus is simply interested in where the significant effects occur. Post hoc tests typically test all possible difference among all possible pairs of means. The number of such comparisons, for k conditions of an experiment, equals $[k(k - 1)]/2$. So, for four conditions, there are six possible comparisons, and for 10 conditions, there are 45. Clearly, as the number of conditions being compared increases, so does the probability that a statistically significant difference will be found by chance. The post hoc tests for such multiple comparisons all adjust, to one degree or another, for the increase in the probability of a Type I error as the number of comparisons is increased. They differ in the degree to which the probability of a Type I error is reduced. The following list of post hoc tests is ordered according to the severity with which a Type I error is controlled. As we go down the list from top to bottom, the probability of a Type I error decreases, and thus the magnitude of the difference between any pair of means needed for significance increases.

The list of post hoc tests is as follows:

1. Duncan test.
2. Newman-Keuls test.
3. Tukey B test.
4. Tukey A test (HSD, or honestly significant difference).
5. Scheffé test.

Thus, the Duncan test is the most liberal in the sense that the investigator is most likely to make a Type I error, and the Scheffé test is the most conservative, in that the investigator is least likely to make a Type I error. On the other hand, use of a conservative test will increase the probability of a Type II error—that is, it will increase the chance of accepting the null hypothesis when the alternative hypothesis is correct. More details on post hoc tests may be found in Kirk (1968) and Winer (1971).

COMPARISONS BETWEEN PARAMETRIC AND NONPARAMETRIC TESTS

In the preceding section, we have discussed at length the application of the parametric tests of *t* test and analysis of variance. These tests are appropriate for quantitative dependent variables measured on an interval or ratio scale. Because most experimental techniques applied to the content areas covered in this text yield quantitative data, such as reaction times and proportion correct, and because most introductory statistics tests do not cover the more complex two-way ANOVAs we have covered here, we have presented these in some detail.

For dependent variables measured on an ordinal scale of measurement (i.e., for dependent variables that consist of ranked data), nonparametric tests are appropriate. Nonparametric tests do not make the assumptions about population parameters, such as normal population distributions and equal population variances, made by parametric tests. Nonparametric tests for ordinal data use only the ranks of scores, rather than their actual values. For this reason, these tests are essentially tests of medians rather than means. They answer the question whether the medians of two or more populations from which samples are obtained are equal. In addition, they are considerably easier to calculate than the parametric tests.

Table 16-19 presents a classification of parametric and nonparametric tests according to the classification scheme we employed earlier for tests on means. This classification is based on whether there are two or more than two samples, whether the groups are independent or matched, and whether one or two independent variables have been manipulated. As shown in Table 16-19, there is no nonparametric test on medians corresponding to a two-way ANOVA. This means that there is no nonparametric way to test for an interaction between two independent variables when the dependent variable consists of ranks.

NONPARAMETRIC TESTS: TESTS ON RANKS

The nonparametric tests we introduce here are used for rank-ordered data. If they are to be used for interval-scale data, the scores must be ranked first before the test is applied. We show both types of data in our numerical examples.

Because only the ordinal ranks, rather than the absolute values, of scores are used in nonparametric tests, these tests can be considered tests on medians rather than means. They ask the question whether or not the medians of the samples of scores come from populations whose medians (rather than means) are the same. The tests are called nonparametric, or distribution free, because they make no assumptions about the parameters of the distributions of population values—specifically, they do not assume that the populations are normal or that they have equal variances.

Table 16-19 Classification of Parametric and Nonparametric Statistical Tests Based on Three Aspects of Experimental Design: (1) the Number of Independent Variables, (2) the Number of Levels of Each Independent Variable, (3) Whether the Design is Within Subjects (Repeated Measures) or Between Subjects (Random)

	One independent variable				Two independent variables	
	Two samples		More than two samples		More than two samples	
	Independent	Matched	Independent	Matched	Independent	Matched
Means (parametric)	*t* test (independent)	*t* test (matched)	One-way ANOVA (randomized)	One-way ANOVA (repeated measures)	Two-way ANOVA (randomized)	Two-way ANOVA (repeated measures)
					Two-way ANOVA (mixed)	
Medians (nonparametric)	Median test Mann-Whitney *U* test	Sign test Wilcoxon signed ranks test	Median test Kruskal-Wallis test	Friedman test		

Table 16-20 Scores on a Test of Prejudice for Two Groups

Experimental	Control
5	10
7	12
10	13
6	6
11	5
4	11
8	12
5	9
6	14
2	15
	4

Ranking of Scores
E: 2 4 5 5 6 6 7 8 10 11
C: 4 5 6 9 10 11 12 12 13 14 15

Median = 8

Median Test

The median test is appropriate for two or more independent groups. The test uses the median score across the groups to split the total frequencies of scores into two halves—those above the median and those below the median. The median test then determines whether the *frequencies* of scores within each group are approximately evenly split (which they would be if there were no differences in medians across groups) against the alternative hypothesis that there is a greater imbalance in frequencies than would be found by chance (as there would be if the medians of the two or more groups were really different).

The median test uses the frequencies above or below the median rather than the ranked scores themselves. Because the tests are based on comparing observed with expected frequencies, the median test uses the chi-square test statistic.

The chi-square test compares a set of observed frequencies with a set of expected frequencies to determine whether the two sets differ more than would be expected by chance. A chi-square analysis is performed on a table of observed frequencies with r rows and k columns, and the df for the test equals $(r - 1) \times (k - 1)$. When the $df = 1$ (which would be true for a 2×2 table), a correction for continuity is used in which .5 is subtracted from the absolute difference between the expected and observed frequencies.

The general formula for the chi-square statistic is as follows:

$$\chi^2 = \Sigma \frac{(f_o - f_e)^2}{f_e}$$

and the χ^2 is evaluated for significance by using the critical χ^2 values listed in Table A-7 of Appendix A, for the appropriate df.

Median Test for Two Independent Samples. The data shown in Table 16-20 will be used to illustrate the median test for two independent samples. In this example, the experimenter was interested in determining if showing a film designed to reduce prejudice against minorities would produce a reduction in prejudice, as evaluated by subjects' test scores. The experimental group was shown the film before being tested, and the control group was shown nothing. The experimenter's hypothesis is that the film will reduce prejudice, so he predicts that the experimental group will score lower on the test of prejudice. He decides to use a median test, rather than the appropriate parametric method—an independent t test—because

Table 16-21 Median Test for the Prejudice Scores of Table 16-20

		Group Experimental	Control	
Above median	f_o	2.5	8	10.5
	f_e	5	5.5	
Below median	f_o	7.5	3	10.5
	f_e	5	5.5	
		10	11	

$$\chi^2 = \frac{(|2.5 - 5| - 0.5)^2}{5} + \frac{(|8 - 5.5| - 0.5)^2}{5.5} + \frac{(|7.5 - 5| - 0.5)^2}{5} + \frac{(|3 - 5.5| - 0.5)^2}{5.5}$$

$$= 3.05; \quad df = 1; \quad p < 0.05$$

he is not sure that scores on the test, which was designed specifically for the purposes of the experiment, fulfill the assumptions of the *t* test.

The first step in using the median test is to determine the median of the combined sample, which in this example is 8. Next, the number of subjects scoring above and below the median is determined for each group and constitutes the observed frequencies. The expected frequencies are simply one half the number in each group (10 for the experimental group and 11 for the control group), because if the two groups do not really differ in their population medians, we expect half the subjects in each sample to fall above the median of the combined sample. This results in the 2 × 2 table of expected and observed frequencies shown in Table 16-21. Because one of the subjects in the experimental group scored exactly at the median, this subject is halved (statistically, of course) and half of his score frequency of 1 is assigned to the cell above the median and half to the cell below the median, resulting in observed frequencies of 2.5 and 7.5 for the experimental group. Because this is a $df = 1$ problem, the correction for continuity is used, as shown in Table 16-21. The computed χ^2 value is 3.05, which is significant at the .05 level for a one-tailed test (see Table A-7 in the Appendix).

Median Test for More than Two Independent Samples. The median test for more than two independent samples is conducted in exactly the same way as that for two independent samples, except that no correction for continuity is made. The *df* for a median test for *k* groups has $k - 1$ *df*.

Table 16-22 shows the results of an experiment that is an extension of the two-group experiment described above. Five groups of subjects were given five different treatments to determine whether there would be differences among the treatments in reducing prejudice. Group I was the control group and was given no treatment. Group II was shown a movie, group III was given a lecture, group IV was given a pamphlet to read at home, and group V engaged in a discussion with members of minority groups. The numbers of subjects scoring above and below the grand median across the five groups are shown in Table 16-22. As can be seen there, some of the treatments appeared to be more effective than others, with group discussion (group V) and movie (group II) showing particularly large effects.

To determine whether there was a statistically significant difference among the median prejudice scores of the five groups, a χ^2 was calculated as shown in Table 16-22. The obtained χ^2 of 43.02 for 4 *df* is highly significant, at the .001 level for a two-tailed test (see Table A-7 in the Appendix). Thus, we conclude that the treatments differ from one another in differentially affecting prejudice.

Mann-Whitney *U* Test

When there is one independent variable with two independent groups, the appropriate test is the Mann-Whitney *U* test. The Mann-Whitney *U* test answers the question whether the median scores of populations from which two independent samples of subjects were drawn are the same or not. The data used by the *U* test are the rank orders of some aspect of behavior, regardless of whether those data have been obtained as rankings in their original form (e.g., from a single judge ranking the leadership abilities of two groups of subjects) or by converting quantitative scores to rank orders.

The *U* statistic is a transformation of the sum of ranks of one of the two groups (whichever transformation yields the smaller value), and it is evaluated by looking up tabled values of critical values of *U* in Table A-8 in the Appendix. If the obtained value is smaller than the relevant critical value, the investigator rejects the null hypothesis and concludes that the medians of the two populations are different.

Only the lower tail of the *U* distribution is tabled (in much the same way that only the upper tails of the *F* distributions are tabled), which is why the lower of the two possible *U* values is used to evaluate significance and why the result is significant only if the obtained value is smaller than the tabled value.

We illustrate the computation of the *U* test with some quantitative data, which first must be ranked, in order to illustrate some points about ranking. Table 16-23 presents data on the number of cooperative behaviors observed in a group of six girls and nine boys in a nursery school over a one-week period. We want to know whether girls are more cooperative than boys (or vice versa). First, we rank order the entire set of 15 children in cooperativeness by assigning a 1 to the least cooperative and a 15 to the most cooperative. This way of assigning ranks may be confusing at first, because ranking as used in sports, beauty contests, and academic standing usually goes in the opposite direction—that is, the person with the most of something is assigned the lowest numerical rank. In all of the examples shown, we will assign the lowest rank to the lowest numerical score and the highest rank to the highest numerical score. In ranking scores, tied scores are given the average rank they would have if they were not tied. In the example in Table 16-23, a boy and a girl both obtained a score of 12, so each is given the average rank of 10.5, because

Table 16-22 Median Test for Prejudice Scores of Five Groups of Subjects

		Group I	Group II	Group III	Group IV	Group V	
Above median	f_o	17	5	10	16	2	50
	f_e	10	12.5	8.5	9	10	
Below median	f_o	3	20	7	2	18	50
	f_e	10	12.5	8.5	9	10	
		20	25	17	18	20	100

$$\chi^2 = \sum_{i=1}^{10} \frac{(f_o - f_e)^2}{f_e} = \frac{(17-10)^2}{10} + \frac{(3-10)^2}{10} + \ldots + \frac{(18-10)^2}{10}$$

$\chi^2 = 43.02$; $df = k - 1 = 4$; $p < 0.001$

Table 16-23 Mann-Whitney *U* Test on Number of Cooperative Behaviors of 15 Nursery School Children

Boys		Girls	
No.	(Rank)	No.	(Rank)
8	(6)	12	(10.5)
15	(13)	16	(14)
12	(10.5)	17	(15)
9	(7)	10	(8)
6	(4)	11	(9)
4	(2)	5	(3)
0	(1)		
13	(12)	$T_2 = 59.5$	
7	(5)	$N_2 = 6$	
$T_1 = 60.5$			
$N_1 = 9$			

$$\text{Check: } T_1 + T_2 = \frac{N(N+1)}{2} = \frac{15(16)}{2} = 120$$

$$U_1 = N_1N_2 + \frac{N_1(N_1+1)}{2} - T_1$$

$$= 9(6) + \frac{9(10)}{2} - 60.5$$

$$U_1 = 38.5$$

$$U_2 = N_1N_2 + \frac{N_2(N_2+1)}{2} - T_2$$

$$= 9(6) + \frac{6(7)}{2} - 59.5$$

$$U_2 = 15.5$$

$$\text{Check: } U_1 + U_2 = N_1N_2 = 54$$

in the absence of a tie they would receive ranks of 10 and 11.

The ranks of the two groups are summed, and the sums denoted T_1 and T_2. Each sum is transformed to a *U* score by the formulas

$$U_1 = N_1N_2 + [N_1(N_1 + 1)]^2 - T_1$$

and

$$U_2 = N_1N_2 + [N_2(N_2 + 1)]^2 - T_2$$

As checks on the ranking, summing, and transformation to *U* scores, the following equalities must hold:

$$T_1 + T_2 = \frac{[N(N+1)]}{2}$$

where

$$N = N_1 + N_2$$

and

$$U_1 + U_2 = N_1N_2$$

The smaller of U_1 and U_2 is defined as *U*, and its value is referred to Table A-8 in the Appendix. If the obtained value of *U* is equal to or smaller than one of the two critical values for the two values of sample size N_1 and N_2, the null hypothesis is rejected.

For our example, $U = 15.5$, $N_1 = 9$, and $N_2 = 6$. We find from Table A-8 that we need a *U* of 10 *or smaller* to reject the null hypothesis at the .05 level of significance. Our test statistic is not small enough, so we fail to reject the null hypothesis that there is no difference in cooperativeness between girls and boys. A difference as large as the one we observed could easily have arisen by chance.

Sign Test and Wilcoxon Signed Ranks Test

When we have a single independent variable with two levels, and the subjects are matched between the two conditions, there are two possible nonparametric tests—the *sign test,* and the *Wilcoxon signed ranks test.* For both tests, subjects must be paired on some basis and their performance compared. The tests differ in how much information they use from the data. In the sign test, the only information used is the number of pairs of subjects showing better performance under one condition than the other. In the Wilcoxon test, both the direction of the difference and the rank order of the difference are used. To facilitate comparison between the two tests, we apply them to the same set of data.

As an example, suppose an investigator hypothesized that subjects will show more emotion when viewing a "taboo" movie than a "neutral" movie. Thirteen subjects were shown a taboo movie (showing scenes of nude members of the opposite sex) and a neutral movie (showing scenes of the same actors clothed) in a counterbalanced order. The average GSR during each movie was used as a measure of emotion. Table 16-24 presents these GSRs for each condition and subject. This is a matched subjects design with two conditions, because each subject participated in each of the two conditions of the experiment. We will analyze the data shown in Table 16-24 with both the sign test and the Wilcoxon test.

Sign Test. Both tests begin by subtracting the subject's score in one condition of the experiment from his or her score in the second condition. The sign test considers only the number of signs in one direction (positive or negative) out of the total number of pairs. The sign test uses the test statistic *r*, the smaller of the number of signs in one direction out of *N*. The logic of the sign test is as follows. If the two groups are identical with respect to their medians, then we would expect the number of pairs having signs in one direction to approximately equal those with signs in the other direction. For a small *N*, we can calculate the probability that as small a number of

Table 16-24 Wilcoxon Signed Ranks Test for Median GSR Scores to Taboo and Neutral Pictures of 13 Subjects

Subject No.	Taboo	Neutral	Difference	Rank	Postive Signed Rank	Negative Signed Rank
1	56	25	+31	12	+12	
2	40	36	+4	5	+5	
3	30	32	−2	2		−2
4	47	40	+7	8	+8	
5	63	40	+23	11	+11	
6	60	61	−1	1		−1
7	54	32	+22	10	+10	
8	55	50	+5	6	+6	
9	61	67	−6	7		−7
10	75	40	+35	13	+13	
11	67	57	+10	9	+9	
12	42	39	+3	3.5	+3.5	
13	58	61	−3	3.5		−3.5
					$T_+ = 77.5$	$T_- = 13.5$

Check: $T_+ + T_- = \dfrac{N(N+1)}{2} = 91$

$T = T_- = 13.5; \quad p < 0.025$

signs in one direction as r would occur by chance by using the binomial distribution with $p = .5$. Table A-9 in the Appendix lists critical numbers for the smaller value of r for various values of N. If our obtained r is smaller than or equal to one of the critical values, we reject the null hypothesis that the medians of the two groups are equal at the given level of significance. In the example provided, r (the number of negative signs) is 4 out of 13. However, Table A-9 reveals that we need an r at least as small as 3 for the result to be significant with a one-tailed test at $p < .05$, so we cannot reject the null hypothesis.

Table A-9 is based on the binomial distribution for $p = .5$ and N ranging from 5 to 35. For N larger than 35, we can use the normal approximation to the binomial, compute a z score, and use the tables of the normal distribution to see whether the result is significant. The expected mean of the normal distribution under the null hypothesis of no difference is $N/2$, the standard deviation is $\sqrt{N/4}$, and z is computed by

$$z = \frac{|r - N/2| - 0.5}{\sqrt{N/4}}$$

where r is the obtained number of signs in one direction, N is the sample size, and .5 is subtracted from the absolute difference as a correction for continuity. Tables of the normal distribution (Table A-4 in the Appendix) may be used to determine whether the z score is sufficiently large to reject the null hypothesis that the two medians are really the same.

The Wilcoxon Signed Ranks Test. The Wilcoxon signed ranks test takes into account both the sign of the difference between pairs of scores and the rank of their difference. It uses the test statistic T, the smaller of the two sums of ranks of the differences associated with each of the two signs. Table 16-24 also shows the application of the Wilcoxon test to the data on emotionality.

The first step in the data analysis is to compute the set of signed differences between the two sets of scores. This is done by subtracting each neutral score from each taboo score. Next, the differences are ranked from lowest to highest by absolute value. If the difference between any pair of scores is zero, there can be no sign attached to this difference and so the pair is omitted from the Wilcoxon test and N is reduced accordingly. Finally, the sign of each difference is assigned to the ranks, and the sum of the positive and negative signed ranks are separately summed. The Wilcoxon test uses as the test statistic the sum of ranks associated with either the positive or negative sign, whichever is smaller. For this example, the sum of negative differences is smaller than the sum of positive differences so the negative sum is used.

The smaller sum of ranks is called T, and the significance of T is evaluated by looking up its critical value in Table A-10 in the Appendix. If the obtained value of T is equal to or smaller than the critical value of T listed in the table, the null hypothesis is rejected at the given level of significance. For this example, our obtained T of 13.5 is smaller than the critical T of 17 needed for significance at the .025 level (one-tailed test), so the null hypothesis is rejected at the .025 level of significance. We use a one-tailed test because the original hypothesis of the investigator was that the GSR to taboo stimuli would be higher than to neutral stimuli (a directional alternative hypothesis).

With the Wilcoxon test, we conclude there is a significant difference between emotional reactions to taboo and to neutral movies whereas with the sign test the differences were not significant. The Wilcoxon test is more powerful than the sign test in that if the two populations really have different medians, the Wilcoxon test will be more likely to detect this difference than the sign test will. The reason that the Wilcoxon test succeeded where the sign test failed can be seen in Table 16-24. Not only are there more positive than negative

Table 16-25 Kruskal-Wallis Test for Data from Table 16-9

Condition 1		Condition 2		Condition 3	
Score	(Rank)	Score	(Rank)	Score	(Rank)
100	(15)	86	(14)	75	(13)
120	(18)	22	(1)	42	(3.5)
118	(17)	47	(6)	35	(2)
42	(3.5)	51	(7)	56	(8)
63	(9.5)	63	(9.5)	70	(11)
72	(12)			46	(5)
110	(16)				
$T_1 = 91$		$T_2 = 37.5$		$T_3 = 42.5$	
$n_1 = 7$		$n_2 = 5$		$n_3 = 6$	$N = 18$

Check: $\Sigma T_i = \dfrac{N(N+1)}{2} = 171$

$$H = \frac{12}{N(N+1)} \sum^{3} \frac{T_i^2}{n_i} - 3(N+1)$$

$$= \frac{12}{(18)(19)} \left[\frac{(91)^2}{7} + \frac{(37.5)^2}{5} + \frac{(42.5)^2}{6} \right] - 3(19)$$

$= 4.94; \quad \text{df} = 3 - 1 = 2; \quad \text{n.s.}$

signs, in that 9 of the 13 subjects show larger GSRs to the taboo than to the neutral pictures, but the magnitude of these differences, and hence the ranks of the differences, are larger for the subjects showing positive differences than for subjects showing negative differences. The sign test ignores the magnitude of the differences and considers only their signs, but the Wilcoxon test takes into account both the number of differences and their magnitude, by considering the ranks of the differences.

The corresponding parametric test for this experiment is the matched-groups *t* test, which uses the actual values of the differences, whereas the Wilcoxon test uses only the ranks of these values.

Kruskal-Wallis Test

When there is one independent variable with more than two levels, and independent groups of subjects are assigned to each level, the appropriate nonparametric test is the Kruskal-Wallis test. The parametric equivalent to the Kruskal-Wallis test is the one-way completely randomized analysis of variance.

The Kruskal-Wallis test can be considered an extension of the Mann-Whitney *U* test. As in the Mann-Whitney test, scores of all subjects across the three or more conditions are ranked, and the sum of ranks are obtained for each group. The test statistic used to evaluate whether or not the medians of the populations from which the *k* samples were drawn are the same is a transformation of the sums of ranks called *H*. *H* is defined as

$$H = \frac{12}{N(N+1)} \sum^{k} \frac{T_i^2}{n_i} - 3(N+1)$$

where n_i stands for the number of subjects in each group, N stands for the total number of subjects in the experiment, and T_i is the sum of ranks of each group.

In Table 16-25 is an application of the Kruskal-Wallis test to scores of 18 subjects run in three conditions. (These data are the same as those in Table 16-9 used to illustrate a one-way ANOVA for unequal *N*s.) The entire set of scores is ranked, and then the ranks for each group are summed. We follow the same procedures here as for the Mann-Whitney test in computing ranks of tied scores.

The test statistic *H* has a chi-square distribution with *df* equal to one less than the number of groups, or $k - 1$. Accordingly, to evaluate whether *H* is large enough to permit us to reject the null hypothesis that the three groups come from populations with the same medians, we consult the table of critical chi-square values in Table A-7 with $k - 1$ *df* and two-tailed *p* values. Our observed *H* value of 4.94 with 2 *df* does not exceed the critical χ^2 value of 5.99 for a two-tailed test at $p < .05$, so we fail to reject the null hypothesis.

We might contrast this result with the result obtained using a one-way ANOVA for this problem. As shown in Table 16-9, for the same data, our *F* ratio was significant at the .05 level of significance. However, when we used ranks, and tested with Kruskal-Wallis's *H*, we failed to attain significance. This illustrates the fact that the nonparametric methods usually require larger differences among the groups to produce a significant result. Put another way, they are less powerful than the parametric methods.

Friedman Test

When there is one independent variable with more than two levels, and subjects are run repeatedly in each of the conditions, the appropriate nonparametric method is the Friedman test. The Friedman test is the nonparametric equivalent to the one-way repeated measures ANOVA. In the Friedman test, as in the Kruskal-Wallis test, the score values are converted to ranks. However, instead of ranking the scores across the conditions, as a group, the scores are ranked within each row or individual. Then the sum of the ranks for each of the *k* conditions in the experiment are found.

The Friedman test uses as a test statistic χ_r^2, defined as

$$\chi_r^2 = \frac{12}{Nk(k+1)} \sum^{k} T_i^2 - 3N(k+1)$$

where *N* is the number of subjects, *k* is the number of conditions, and T_i is the sum of ranks for the *i*th condition. The obtained χ_r^2 is evaluated by referring to Table A-11, which presents critical values for $k = 3$ or 4 (i.e., for three or four levels of the independent variable) and for *N* ranging from 3 to 9 for $k = 3$ and from 2 to 4 for $k = 4$.

Table 16-26 presents some data that were previously analyzed by a one-way repeated measures ANOVA (see Table 16-11). The scores across the three groups are ranked for each subject. Note that the ranking of subjects' scores across the three conditions is identical (with the exception of subject 3) in that condition 1 produces the lowest rank, condition 2 the next lowest, and condition 3 the highest rank. The Friedman test determines whether or not the variation in the sum of ranks among the various conditions is large enough to permit us to reject the null hypothesis that the ranking of scores across the three conditions is really random (or that the three groups of scores were drawn from populations with the same medians).

The value of χ_r^2 computed for the data in Table 16-26 is 8.86, as shown at the bottom of the table. By referring to Table A-11 in the Appendix, for $N = 7$ and $k = 3$, we see that the obtained value of χ_r^2 is significant at the .01 level because it exceeds the critical value of 8.856, and so we reject the null hypothesis at the .01 level of significance. In this case, the Friedman test gives the same results for these data as were obtained with the one-way repeated measures ANOVA. In both cases, we conclude that the three groups are significantly different from one another.

When *N* and/or *k* exceed the values in Table A-11, the significance of χ_r^2 can be evaluated by looking up its value in the chi-square table (Table A-7) with $df = k - 1$ and two-tailed *p* values.

Table 16-26 Friedman Test for Data from Table 16-11

S No.	Condition 1		Condition 2		Condition 3		
	Score	(Rank)	Score	(Rank)	Score	(Rank)	
1	10	(1)	17	(2)	20	(3)	
2	12	(1)	13	(2)	25	(3)	
3	15	(2)	16	(3)	14	(1)	
4	11	(1)	12	(2)	17	(3)	
5	5	(1)	7	(2)	12	(3)	
6	7	(1)	8	(2)	18	(3)	
7	2	(1)	3	(2)	7	(3)	
	$T_1 = 8$		$T_2 = 15$		$T_3 = 19$		$N = 7$ $k = 3$

$$\text{Check: } \Sigma\, T_i = \frac{Nk(k+1)}{2} = 42$$

$$\chi_r^2 = \frac{12}{Nk(k+1)} \sum T_i^2 - 3N(k+1)$$

$$= \frac{12}{(7)(3)(4)} [(8)^2 + (15)^2 + (19)^2] - 3(7)(4)$$

$$= 8.86; \quad k = 3; \quad N = 7; \quad p < 0.01$$

TESTS ON FREQUENCIES AND PROPORTIONS: THE CHI-SQUARE TEST

We obtain frequency data whenever we classify subjects into one of several mutually exclusive and exhaustive categories on the basis of some characteristic. Often such a categorization is used because the categories in question differ qualitatively, such as sex and birth order. In other cases, categorization is imposed on a quantitative dependent variable by the nature of the measurement process, as happens when subjects check age categories on a questionnaire.

All of the tests used for frequencies or proportions use the chi-square test, or some variant of it, as the test statistic. Use of the chi-square test involves comparing a set of observed frequencies or proportions with a set of expected frequencies or proportions based on a null hypothesis. The chi-square distribution is a continuous approximation to the probabilities associated with discrete distributions, and a number of constraints are imposed by the use of such a continuous approximation that must be followed when using the chi-square test.

There are four rules for using chi-square tests. First, the expected frequency in any category should not be less than 5; second, a correction for continuity should be applied for chi-square tests with 1 *df*; third, the sum of expected frequencies must equal the sum of observed frequencies; and fourth, each observed frequency in a chi-square table should be independent of every other observed frequency. What the independence rule means in practice is that a single subject should be represented in only a single cell of the chi-square table, and the groups of subjects being compared should be independent of one another. We warn here that there are many pitfalls to using the chi-square test. Although it is a very simple test to apply, it is probably the most misused statistical test that we cover here. More than a quarter of a recent book of readings in statistics (Steger, 1971) is devoted to criticisms and rebuttals to criticisms of psychologists' use of the chi-square test.

Chi-Square Test for One-Way Classification

We illustrate the chi-square test for one-way classification with some data on subjects' preferences for faces that either follow the normal growth function (normal), or show one of two abnormalities—a jutting jaw (prognathic) and a receding jaw (retrognathic). Table 16-27 shows the observed frequencies of choices (f_o) of 36 subjects for the three types of faces. The expected frequencies of choices (f_e) based on the null hypothesis of no preference for the normal over the abnormal growth patterns is equal to one third of the total sample, or 12 in each cell. The χ^2 of 13.17, with 2 *df*, is significant at $p < .005$ with a one-tailed test. A one-tailed test is used because the investigator's hypothesis is that normal faces will be seen as more attractive than faces following an abnormal growth pattern.

Table 16-27 χ^2 Test for Preferences among Three Facial Types

	Facial type			
	Normal	Retrognathic	Prognathic	N
f_0	22	5	9	36
f_e	12	12	12	36

$$\chi^2 = \Sigma\frac{(f_0 - f_e)^2}{f_e} = \frac{(22-12)^2}{12} + \frac{(5-12)^2}{12} + \frac{(9-12)^2}{12}$$

$$= \frac{100 + 49 + 9}{12} = 13.17$$

$$df = 2, \qquad p < .005$$

Chi-square Test for Two-Way Classification (Chi-square Test for Association)

We illustrate a two-way classification chi-square, sometimes called the chi-square test for association, with an expanded example from the previous study. Suppose that the experimenter is interested in the effect of exposure on preference choices for faces. She studies this by exposing one group of subjects to a growth sequence of an adult with a prognathic face, and asks the 36 subjects given this exposure to express their preferences for the three types of faces. She obtains the data shown in Table 16-28, which also shows the preferences of the previous group of unexposed subjects (control subjects). The experimenter now wants to know whether there is any difference between the two groups in their pattern of preferences.

Note that this is a different question

Table 16-28 χ^2 Test of Association Between Exposure Condition and Preference (Expected Frequencies Are in Parentheses)

	Facial type			
	Normal	Retrognathic	Prognathic	N
Control subjects	22 (17)	5 (5.5)	9 (13.5)	36
Exposed subjects	12 (17)	6 (5.5)	18 (13.5)	36
	34	11	27	72

$$\chi^2 = \Sigma\frac{(f_0 - f_e)^2}{f_e} = \frac{(5)^2 + (5)^2}{17} + \frac{(0.5)^2 + (0.5)^2}{5.5} + \frac{(4.5)^2 + (4.5)^2}{13.5}$$

$$\chi^2 = 5.99,\ df = 2$$

$$p < .025$$

from that asked in the previous example. There, we asked whether there was an uneven distribution of preferences across the three types of faces. Here, the experimenter accepts as given the fact that subjects will prefer normal faces to abnormal ones, but asks whether there is an association, or interaction, between the training that subjects have had and their subsequent preferences. To test for association, the expected frequencies are computed based on the row and column totals, under the null hypothesis of no association between exposure condition and preference.

This procedure is illustrated in Table 16-28. The expected frequency for each cell of the table, shown in parentheses, is calculated by multiplying its row frequency (r) by its column frequency (c) and dividing by N, or

$$f_e = \frac{r \times c}{N}$$

The computed χ^2 of 5.99 with 2 df is just significant at $p < .025$ with a one-tailed test.

In this two-way classification chi-square, when expected frequencies are computed on the basis of the row and column sums, the null hypothesis being tested is *not* that the observed frequencies are distributed equally across the three facial categories, but rather that there is no differential effect on the choices of the subjects by the exposure conditions, or no association between choices and experimental manipulation. In terms of analysis of variance, this would be stated as a *no interaction* hypothesis. The fact that this χ^2 is significant tells us there is an effect of exposure condition on facial preference. It does not tell us that there are significant overall differences between the different facial types (i.e., in ANOVA terms, it does not test for a main effect). In chi-square tests, the null hypothesis determines the basis for calculating expected frequencies. In association chi-square tests, the null hypothesis is one of no association between rows and columns.

Chi-Square Tests for Correlated Frequencies

All of the χ^2 applications we have discussed are for independent groups of subjects. The parametric test equivalents are the independent t test and the randomized one-way ANOVA. If we want to test significance of differences between correlated frequencies, in which the frequency in one cell of a table *is not* independent of the other frequencies, it is necessary to modify χ^2 tests to take into account this lack of independence. These tests, which include the McNemar test and the Cochran test, are discussed more fully in Wike (1971) and will not be covered here.

SUMMARY

In this chapter, we have reviewed some principles of inferential statistics, and then presented computational formulas and examples of two major parametric tests—the t test and the analysis of variance (ANOVA).

The t test is appropriate when two groups of subjects or two conditions have been run in an experiment and the investigator wishes to determine whether the two groups are significantly different. If the two sets of scores are independent of one another, an independent t test is used. If the two sets of scores have been matched, either on the basis of some other criterion variable or by virtue of having the same subject participate in both conditions of the experiment, a matched-pairs t test is used. In general, within-subjects or repeated-measures (matched) designs are more sensitive than between-subjects or randomized designs, although the former, because of the lack of independence of scores, have fewer degress of freedom (df) than the latter.

Whenever more than two conditions or groups of subjects are being compared, the appropriate test is an ANOVA. When only a single independent variable has been manipulated, we use a one-way ANOVA to analyze the data. For a between-groups design, a randomized ANOVA is used. Computational procedures differ somewhat depending on whether there are equal or unequal *N*s in the various groups. For a repeated measures design, a repeated measures ANOVA is the appropriate test.

The *F* ratio that is computed in an ANOVA has two *df* associated with it, one for the numerator of the *F* ratio, which measures how different the means of the various groups or conditions are, and one for the denominator of the *F* ratio, which measures how different subjects within groups or conditions are. The numerator of the *F* ratio is known as the between-groups mean square (MS_{bet}) and the denominator is known as the within-groups mean square (MS_{with}) or error mean square (MS_{err}). For conformity of notation with more complex ANOVAs, we refer to the between-groups mean square as MS_A, where *A* refers to the factor that has been manipulated.

When two independent variables have been manipulated, in a factorial design, we use a two-way ANOVA to analyze the data. In these analyses, three *F* ratios are computed—one that evaluates the significance of the first factor, *A,* one that evaluates the significance of the second factor, *B,* and one that evaluates the significance of their interaction, $A \times B$. An interaction between two variables means that the effects of the two are not additive, but instead, the effect of one variable depends on which value of the other variable it has been paired with.

We presented three types of two-way ANOVAS—(1) completely randomized, used when separate groups of subjects have been run in each condition, (2) completely repeated measures, used when the same subjects have been run in each condition, and (3) mixed, used when different subjects have participated in the various conditions of one factor (called factor *A* by convention) but the same subjects have participated in the various conditions of the second factor (factor *B*).

Multiple comparison tests are used to determine which differences among a set of means are significant and which are not. They can be divided into planned comparison tests and post hoc tests. Planned comparison tests are used whenever an investigator's hypothesis predicts that certain differences will be significant and others will not. Post hoc tests are used whenever no specific prediction has been made about which conditions will differ.

Nonparametric tests, which are appropriate for dependent variables measured on an ordinal (ranked) scale, make fewer assumptions than parametric tests do. On the other hand, they are also less powerful than parametric tests in that they are less able to reject a false null hypothesis. Accordingly, the vast majority of researchers in experimental psychology employ parametric statistical tests whenever their use seems justified.

Nonparametric tests are all tests on medians rather than means. They ask the question whether or not the medians of the populations from which the two or more groups of subjects have been selected are different. The median test is appropriate for two or more than two independent groups of subjects and uses the chi-square test to determine whether the observed frequencies of scores above and below the grand median are significantly different from chance. The Mann-Whitney *U* test compares the ranks of two groups of independent scores, and is the nonparametric equivalent to the independent *t* test. The sign test and Wilcoxon signed ranks test are both appropriate for testing whether the ranks of two matched groups of subjects differ. The sign test uses only the frequency of signs in one or the other direction, whereas the Wilcoxon text uses the sum of signed ranks, and thus is more powerful than the sign test. The parametric equivalent is the matched *t* test.

For more than two groups of subjects, the two nonparametric tests reviewed here are the Kruskal-Wallis test, for more than two independent groups of subjects, and the Friedman test, for more than two matched groups of subjects (or for the same subject run repeatedly across the various conditions). Their parametric equivalents are the randomized groups ANOVA and the matched groups or repeated measures ANOVA, respectively. No nonparametric tests are appropriate for two or more independent variables, and so there is no nonparametric way to test for interactions among conditions of a two-factor experiment.

Tests for frequencies or proportions can all be accomplished with the use of the chi-square test. The chi-square test is appropriate for independent groups of subjects, in which a single subject contributes only a single frequency to a chi-square table. We reviewed chi-square tests for one-way classification and two-way classifications in which the test for association between two variables is made (chi-square test for association).

The methods of inferential statistics permit us to go beyond the results from our samples of subjects to predict what is likely to be true of the population at large. For that reason, the principles of inferential statistics are indispensible in all empirical science, and experimental psychology is no exception.

17

The Research Report

> Research is complete only when the results are shared with the scientific community. Although such sharing is accomplished in a variety of formal and informal ways, the traditional medium for communicating research results is the scientific journal.
>
> (*Publication Manual of the American Psychological Association,* 1983, p. 17)

We carry out research in psychology to increase our knowledge of human behavior. We communicate the knowledge obtained from research through published research reports. To make this communication as efficient as possible, the American Psychological Association (APA) has established a set of guidelines for the organization of the research report. Having a standard organization helps readers to find out what they want to know about a study as quickly and easily as possible. Students writing a research report in a laboratory in experimental psychology should also learn APA style, for it will help them to better organize and communicate information, and also help them to read journal articles more efficiently.

The APA guidelines are followed for all APA journals, and also for many journals not published by the APA. This chapter follows the most recent APA guidelines to describe both the sections of a research report and the form in which they are presented. More detailed descriptions of these guidelines may be found in the latest edition of the APA Publication Manual (1983).

SECTIONS OF THE RESEARCH REPORT

The research report should contain the following major sections in the order shown. The italicized sections also appear as section headings in the report. Each section is described in detail below.

Title
Author's name and affiliation
Abstract
Introduction
Method
Subjects
Apparatus and materials
Procedure
Results
Discussion
References

A good research report will communicate clearly and unambiguously the following points about the experiment: (1) what you did, (2) why you did it, (3) what you found, and (4) how you interpret your findings. The "why" of the research is presented in the introduction, the "what" in the section on method, the outcome in the results section, and the interpretation in the discussion section.

The research report has been described as a double funnel (Anderson, 1971), as shown in Figure 17-1. The *introduction* begins broadly by introducing the historical and conceptual background of the experiment, narrows as it focuses on specific issues within the general area, and finally reaches its narrowest, most focused point as it introduces the rationale for the experiment. Both the *method* and *results* sections are shown as occupying the narrow tube of the funnel. These sections are precise and narrowly confined to a description of this specific experiment. The research report expands at the other end of the funnel in the *discussion.* First, the results of the present experiment are discussed, and then their implications for the hypothesis being tested, their relevance for previous research and competing theories, and their suggestions for future lines of research are explored.

Title

"A title should summarize the main idea of the paper simply, and, if possible, with style" (American Psychological Association, 1983, p. 22). It may either describe what was done *(Testing the role of vertical symmetry in letter matching),* the nature of the question being asked *(Is no-stimulus a stimulus?),* or the interpretation

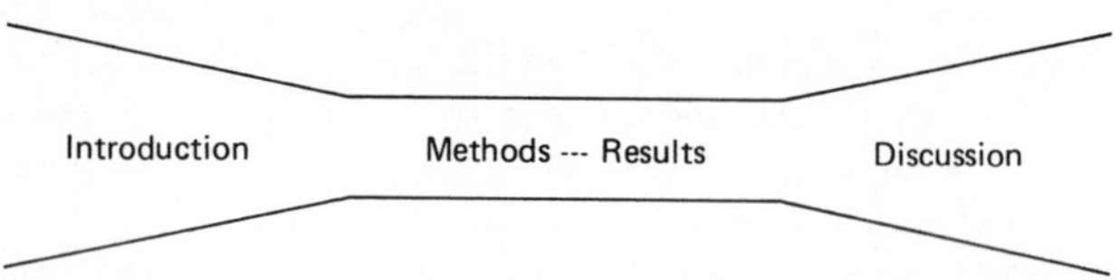

Fig. 17-1 The research paper as a double funnel.

of results *(Stimulus information as a determinant of reaction time).*

Avoid redundant words. It is not necessary to preface a title with "An experimental study of . . . ," since a paper published in an experimental journal is, by definition, an experimental study of something.

Author's Name and Institutional Affiliation

The author or authors are listed by full names without title (e.g., Dr., Professor). The affiliation is the institution at which the research was done. A footnote is used to indicate a new affiliation for one or more of the authors. People who have assisted in the research in one way or another (a principal from a school providing children as subjects, a research assistant, a computer programmer, or a person reading and criticizing the manuscript) are thanked in a footnote. Funding or supporting sources are also acknowledged here.

Abstract

The *abstract* is a brief summary of the experiment. It should permit potential readers to determine whether it is worth their time to read the entire article. Thus, it should communicate what the experiment was all about, what was done, what was found, and what it means.

The abstract should be no longer than 150 words and is often considerably shorter. It should contain only the essential aspects of the experiment—its purpose, the dependent variable used (i.e., tachistoscopic recognition thresholds, recall performance, recognition memory performance), the major results, and conclusions. Procedural details such as numbers of subjects, number of trials, and type of counterbalancing should be omitted unless one or another of these aspects is particularly important. If an unusually large sample of subjects has been used, their number might be reported, or if the subjects are an unusual group, such as split-brain patients, their number is often very small and is often reported. (For an example, see the abstract of *Metacontrol of hemispheric function in human split-brain patients* at the end of the chapter.) Statistical details of the results should be omitted. A result is reported in the abstract *only* if it is statistically significant. The statement in an abstract, "Subjects recalled more high-frequency than low-frequency words" means that in the statistical analysis of your results, high-frequency words were *significantly* better than low-frequency words. References are usually not cited in an abstract unless the work of a particular investigator was central to the aim of the experiment.

Many students have a great deal of difficulty writing an acceptable abstract. Their main fault is including too many details of procedure and results and omitting the main focus and implications of the study. Generally, their abstracts are too long, even though they may omit the most crucial findings of the experiment. Producing a good abstract almost always requires painstaking rewriting, to delete unnecessary material and to express concisely and clearly why a reader should pursue your article.

Some examples of good abstracts taken from published journal articles are presented at the end of this chapter. The student is urged to study these abstracts before attempting to write one.

Introduction

The introduction is of central importance in giving the reader a clear rationale for the experiment and its objective. After reading the introduction, the reader should know the general background of the problem, what the experiment will contribute to its investigation, the expected results, and why these particular results are expected.

The first part of the introduction usually consists of a review of related research literature. It summarizes what other investigators have done in the problem area, with what results, and how these results are relevant to the purposes of the present experiment. In summarizing previous work, major conclusions should be emphasized and unnecessary detail should be avoided. When several investigators have obtained similar results, the results should be summarized in a general statement, followed by citations to the relevant research. The correct form of citation is described more fully under the section on *References.*

Previous research should be summarized in your own words, not quoted from published reports. Seldom should reports be quoted verbatim. Be selective in choosing citations. Most citations should be directly related to the specific problem being investigated, although references to a general article reviewing the background literature may be given.

After introducing the problem and its background, you are now in a position to develop the rationale for your experiment. If the experiment tests a hypothesis, or compares differing predictions from two conflicting hypotheses, you should state the hypothesis or hypotheses at the beginning and then show how the experiment tests it (or them).

The final paragraph or paragraphs of the introduction should introduce the experiment by describing its general plan. Then the implications of various results of the experiment for the hypotheses being tested should be described. Here is an example:

> If the dual-encoding hypothesis is correct, and if visual codes are superior for spatial memory and verbal codes are superior for temporal memory, we would expect that subjects would perform better on spatial memory for pictures than for words, but that they would perform equally well (or perhaps only slightly better) on temporal memory for pictures and for words." (Snodgrass & Antone, 1974, p. 140.)

The Literature Search

Before beginning an introduction (and usually before beginning an experiment), the researcher engages in the literature search. The purpose of this search is to discover the most recent and relevant research papers in the particular area of interest. If the literature search is done before the experiment is performed, the purpose is also to discover the most promising direction for the new experiment being planned as well as to avoid foredoomed repetition of a line of research that has already been tested and rejected. If the literature search is done after the experiment has been performed, its purpose is to provide post hoc reasons for having done the experiment. Although in theory each experiment planned should be preceded by a literature search, in practice many experiments are planned without a complete literature search.

Let us assume that you have done an experiment, and you now want to identify the appropriate research papers to cite in the introduction. In most cases, your research problem will have a history in that there will be one or more classic research papers that are central to the problem. Every paper reporting a new study of the problem will refer to those seminal papers in its introduction. Your task is to trace the web of research from the classic papers up to the present.

There are at least three ways to do this. In the first, you look through the most recent issues of the journals covering the general area of the research topic (e.g., memory, thinking, perception, social psy-

Table 17-1 Some Selected Journals Classified by the Types of Articles They Publish (the Publisher is Given in Parentheses)

Experimental reports of human experimental research
- Journal of Experimental Psychology: General (APA)
- Journal of Experimental Psychology: Learning, Memory, and Cognition (APA) (formerly Journal of Experimental Psychology: Human Learning and Memory)
- Journal of Experimental Psychology: Human Perception and Performance (APA)
- Cognitive Psychology (Academic Press)
- Journal of Language and Memory (Academic Press) (formerly Journal of Verbal Learning and Verbal Behavior)
- Memory & Cognition (Psychonomic Society)
- Perception & Psychophysics (Psychonomic Society)
- Bulletin of the Psychonomic Society (Psychonomic Society [short reports])
- Developmental Psychology (APA)
- Journal of Abnormal Psychology (APA)
- Journal of Applied Psychology (APA)
- Journal of Consulting and Clinical Psychology (APA)
- Journal of Counseling Psychology (APA)
- Journal of Educational Psychology (APA)
- Journal of Personality and Social Psychology (APA)

Experimental reports of animal experimental research
- Journal of Experimental Psychology: Animal Behavior Processes (APA)
- Journal of Comparative Psychology (APA) (formerly contained within Journal of Comparative and Physiological Psychology)
- Behavioral Neuroscience (formerly contained within Journal of Comparative and Physiological Psychology)
- Animal Learning and Behavior (Psychonomic Society)

General review papers
- American Psychologist (APA)
- Psychological Bulletin (APA)
- Psychological Review (APA)

chology) to find articles specifically related to your research area. These papers will cite earlier related literature (including the classic papers), so their citations can be used as a guide back to the more remote research past. By continuing to look up articles cited by more recent articles, you are able to unravel the web of research linking the most recent research to the earliest research. (A list of journals with the topics they cover is given in Table 17-1.)

A more efficient way to discover the most recent publications in various journals is by the use of *Current Contents for the Social and Behavioral Sciences. Current Contents* is a weekly announcement journal that reproduces contents pages of journals in the area of interest. A quick perusal of the titles of journal articles, along with attention to which journals are relevant to your research interest, will often lead you to relevant research papers.

The second method is more systematic than the first in that it uses a formal tool, citations, to discover related research papers. The idea behind use of citations is simplicity itself: If someone is working on a topic related to the area of research of the classic papers, that researcher will very likely cite those seminal papers. Thus, recent papers in a topic of interest may be found by determining those that cite the authors of those seminal papers. Use of citations, rather than key words or topic headings, is often more exact because scientific nomenclature and terminology change rapidly, whereas the names of the authors of classic papers remain constant.

A *Citation Index* for a particular period of time (they are usually published every three months) is an ordered list of references (cited works) followed by sources (citing works). The list of references is alphabetized by senior author, followed by a list of his or her articles or books cited by the articles in the surveyed journals. Each article or book is followed by a list of all the articles or sources that cited this particular article or book. Thus, if Jane Doe had two of her journal articles cited by the journals surveyed for the period in question, the two articles would be listed separately, followed by a list of citors, also listed in alphabetical order, with the source of the citors' articles.

There are two citation indices that are relevant to psychological research: *Science Citation Index* and *Social Science Citation Index.* Both cover the major psychological journals, but *Science Citation Index* also samples from the physical sciences and *Social Science Citation Index* from the social sciences.

A subsidiary index to the *Citation Index* itself is the *Source Index,* which lists the citors by name, then by journal and date, and finally by the title of the article. The *Source Index* may permit you to determine, from the title of the article alone, whether the citing article is actually relevant. A third index is the *Permuterm Subject Index,* which consists of title words in permuted pairs followed by those articles that contain that pair of permuted terms in their title. If the topic can be easily identified by a single term or pair of terms (e.g., *iconic storage* or *signal detection*), then the *Permuterm Subject Index* may be helpful. On the other hand, if the term describing the area of research interest is ambiguous, or used in several contexts in psychological research, then the *Permuterm Subject Index* will produce many sources that are of no interest. A good example is the term *recognition,* which has many meanings in psychological research. It refers to identification of briefly presented items in tachistoscopic exposures, memory for previously presented items in a recognition memory test, and the degree to which a product's name is easily identified with the product's purpose, as in "recognition factor."

Table 17-2 presents two extracts from the *Citation Index* of 1980. The first shows citations for George Sperling, whose seminal paper in *Psychological Monographs* of 1960 demonstrated the existence of a poststimulus perceptual store. (See Chapter 6 for a description of Sperling's results.) Because this paper is of historic importance in the area of short-term visual memory, experimenters working in similar areas will almost invariably cite this paper. Those papers citing Sperling's publications are identified by author, journal, volume number, page number, and year. The second excerpt shows citations for Endel Tulving, whose chapter in a book published in 1972 first introduced the distinction between episodic and semantic memory (see Chapters 8 and 9). An experimenter who studies, supports, or challenges this distinction will almost invariably cite this chapter by Tulving.

A third method of locating relevant literature uses *Psychological Abstracts.* The *Abstracts* list journal articles by content area and by year of publication. Thus, articles are listed by the content of the research rather than by the articles they reference. Although this method might seem to be the most direct of the three, it has one main disadvantage. Content areas of psychological research have not been well-defined or, more accurately, content areas may be defined in a variety of ways. The particular content areas or categories that are used depend heavily on the abstracter's expertise and skill. In many cases, a particular research paper's content could be listed under a number of categories. It was for this reason that *Citation Index* was developed, since a behavioral measure of whether the content of one article is similar to that of another is whether the first paper cites the second paper. However, if your area of research has no seminal, historically important antecedents, or little research work has been done on the problem recently, then *Psychological Abstracts* may be the only source available.

Table 17-3 includes an excerpt from the subject index of the 1976 *Psychological Abstracts,* listing all of the references for that year concerned with lateral dominance (see Chapter 6).

A computer search can combine these various methods of searching the literature. You can indicate key references (as in

Table 17-2 Excerpts from the May–August *Citation Index* for 1980, Showing (A) Citations to the Sperling 1960 *Psychological Monographs* Article [Sperling, G. (1960). The Information available in brief visual presentations. *Psychological Monographs, 74,* No. 11] and (B) Citations to the Tulving 1972 Chapter in an Edited Book [Tulving, E. (1972). Episodic and semantic memory. In E. Tulving & W. Donaldson (Eds.), *Organization of Memory.* (pp. 381–403). New York: Academic Press]

			Vol.	Pg.	Yr.
(A) SPERLING, G.					
60 Psychological Monogr 11					
MEWHO DJK	Mem Cognit		8	15	80
60 Psychological Monogr 74					
AARONSON D	Bk# 12877		1979	65	79
ADELSON EH	J Exp Psy P		6	486	80
APPELMAN IB	Am J Psycho		93	79	80
DUNCAN J	Psychol Rev		87	272	80
HUBA ME	J Exp C Psy		30	88	80
KLIMESCH W	Exp. A Psy		27	245	80
LONG GM	QJ Exp Psy		32	269	80
MADDEN DJ	BK #14120	R	1980	141	80
OHMAN A	BK #12666		1979	443	79
PLACE EJS	J Abn Psych		89	409	80
SANDERS AF	BK #13080	R	1979	409	79
SCHEERER E	Psychol Res.		42	135	80
SIMON HA	Science		209	72	80
URQUHART C	J Inf Sci		1	333	80
60 Psychological Monogr 74 1					
BOWLING A	Perc Psych		27	574	80
COLTHAER M	Perc Psych	R	27	183	80
"	Phi T Roy B		290	57	80
JONIDES J	Can J Psych		34	103	80
MATSUKAW J	JPN J Psych		51	37	80
OSTROM TM	BK # 12667		1980	55	80
THOMASSE AJ	BK # 13080	R	1979	75	79
WYER RS	BK # 12667	R	1980	227	80
60 Psychological Monogr 74 11					
GRAHAM NC	BK # 12556		1980	69	80
JUTTNER C	Psychl BE		22	70	80
PENCHEV A	Behav Brain		2	276	79
(B) TULVING E					
72 Org Memory					
CARLSTON DE	BK # 12667		1980	89	80
CARLSTON DE	J EXP S PS1		16	202	80
COLTHEAR M	Perc Psych	R	27	183	80
DAMBROT F	Teach Psych	N	7	94	80
EBBESEN EB	BK # 12667		1980	179	80
GREENWAL AG	Am Psychl		35	603	80
HANNIGAN ML	Mem Cognit		8	278	80
HASTIE R	BK # 12667	R	1980	1	80
HOFFMAN ML	BK # 12324		1980	295	80
KESNER RP	Behav Brain		2	509	79
KINSBOUR M	BK # 14120		1980	325	80
LARSEN SF	Nord PSYKOL		32	55	80
LEVELT WJM	BK # 13080	R	1979	347	79
UNDERWOO G	BK # 11541 (?)		1979	51	79
WYER RS	BK # 11647	R	1980	227	80
72 Org Memory 381					
AUSUBEL DP	BK # 12563 (?)		79	227	80
COLTHAER M	Phi T Roy				

Note. The Sperling Monograph appears to be listed as several articles because of inconsistency of citation of volume numbers.

Table 17-3 Excerpt from the Subject Index of the 1976 *Psychological Abstracts* Showing Topics of Selected Papers in the Area of Lateral Dominance

Lateral Dominance
acoustic structure variations of dichotic CV syllables, identification responses, college students, implications for prototype model assuming dichotic integration of information between stages of auditory & phonetic processing, 2651.
age & sex & spatial ability, development of lateralization in somesthetic functioning, 5–11 year olds, 3102.
body sidedness, Jungian psychological type & value & behavioral preferences, hospital employees, 7553.
cerebral lateralization/manual-praxis measures, left hemispheric perceptual asymmetry for nonverbal rhythms, right handed college students, 4734.
characteristics of left vs. mixed handedness, 4–9 year olds with myelomeningocele & hydrocephalus, 5695.
consistent & mixed & inconsistent lateral preference patterns, IQ & reading & arithmetic & spelling achievement, 5–12 year old elementary school students, 12632.
coordination of hand preference & manual skill, college students, replication of previous study using 12 year olds & college students, 225.
development of ear asymmetry, speech sound discrimation, 7–8 versus 9–10 versus 11–12 year olds, 9297.
development of left side preference for holding a carrying doll representing newbon, 1.5–16.5 year olds, 5086.
door position & interviewer's & subject's sex & hemispheric dominance & self esteem, eye contact & direction of gaze aversion & smiling & other nonverbal behaviors during embarrassing situation resembling clinical interview, 3299.
ear & hand dominance, 8–9 versus 10–11 year old normal versus retarded readers, 3566.
errors in halving a horizontal line binocularly, right versus left hemisphere damaged patients with cerebral focal lesions with versus without visual field defects versus right versus left handed normals, 5658.
ESP scores, left versus right handed Ss, 6551.
family history of handedness, language lateralization measured by recognition of meaningful versus meaningless trigrams & vowel versus consonant strings presented to right versus left visual field, college students, 2585.
genetic & learning & pathological antecedents of human handedness, literature review, 234.
hand preference & thumb-to-finger opposition performance, female manic depressives & schizophrenics versus nonpsychotic patients with CNS diseases versus normal subjects, 11785.
handedness & eyedness, intellectual & cognitive performance, 6th graders, comparison with prior studies & implications for concept of cognitive deficits associated with left handedness, 4773.
handedness, lateral distribution of conversion reactions, adults diagnosed as having conversion type of hysterical neurosis, 5542.
handedness, lateral eye movement, male versus female college students, 4714.
lateral eye movements & field dependence & hypnotic susceptibility, female right handed college students, 3365.
lateral preference & unimanual motor speed & RT to lateralized stimuli & dichotic ear advantage, minimal brain damaged children, 5650.
mothers holding infants on left side, origin of right handedness as predominant chirality in humans, 5098.
performance on dichotic ear preference & laterality measures & fine motor skills tasks, 5–7 year olds with articulation disorders & with minimal brain dysfunction, 9636.
presentation rates & number of pairs of spoken digits & attention restriction to right versus left ear, dichotic listening, college students, 6812.
presentation to left versus right visual field & backward visual masking, iconic musical symbol recognition thresholds & critical interstimulus intervals, college students with formal music training, 4707.
reading & writing habits, asymmetry of visual perception, right versus left handed German & Israeli students, 6782.
removal of left hemisphere arteriovenous congenital malformation, maintenance of right hemisphere language dominance, 31 year old left handed male, 5728.
sex & eye dominance, color discrimination, right handed college students, 10904.
signal detection analysis & right hand effects & right ear advantage, development of hemispheric specialization for speech perception, right handed 5 versus 7 year olds, 5139.
tests of lateral asymmetry & determination of constitutional predisposition to CNS disease, right handed college students, 11940.
unilateral ECS therapy with varying electrode positions, changes in immediate & delayed memory & forgetting, depressed patients, 5738.
visual similarity judgments among rectangles varying in form & area, right handed controls & right versus left brain damaged patients, 5657.

the use of citations) as well as key words. A computer search can automatically use all of the sources we described previously to produce a listing of references and, where desired, abstracts, of articles that may be relevant to your research interest.

If all else fails, a final approach is to ask your instructor or another faculty member whose interests are related to the problem area. He or she will often be able to suggest specific papers or the names of authors who have done work on that problem.

Method

The method section should provide sufficient detail so that (1) the experiment can be replicated by another investigator, and (2) the methodological soundness of the procedure can be evaluated. In particular, enough detail should be given so that any discrepancies between your results and the results of another investigator who has conducted a similar experiment can be evaluated. Because it is sometimes not clear which particular procedural differences might be important in obtaining a particular result, it is wise to err on the side of too much detail than too little.

The method section is usually divided into three subsections, although which sections are included will depend on what the experiment is and how it was executed. These subsections are subjects, apparatus or materials (or both), and procedure. If an experiment is complex in its design, sometimes a subsection entitled *Design* is included.

Subjects. The number of subjects and the population from which they were selected should be given. The population could be "undergraduates at ______ University," "children enrolled in the public schools in ______ City," "construction workers," and so on. Any other characteristics of the subjects that might be relevant to the experiment should be listed. The numbers of male and female subjects might be included for a study of perception of sexually arousing words, but they may not be included for a study of memory for high- and low-frequency words. (However, as noted in Chapters 2 and 3, the trend toward ignoring the sex of the subject has reversed somewhat. Because it is impossible to predict what perceptual and cognitive abilities might be dependent on sex, and because data on sex of subjects are easy to collect, it is probably wise to err on the conservative side and report numbers of males and females in each condition regardless of the experiment.) The numbers of right- and left-handed subjects would be included for a study of laterality effects, but not for one studying tachistoscopic recognition thresholds for centrally presented words. Whether or not subjects are volunteers might be important for a compliance study but not for a study on visual perception. The number of subjects wearing glasses or contact lenses might be important for an experiment on visual perception but not one on memory.

Most experiments in human experimental psychology do not randomly sample from the population in question, for both practical and theoretical reasons (see Chapter 2). However, when two or more groups of subjects are given different conditions or treatments, it is important to either randomly or systematically divide the subjects into groups to avoid differences between groups that might bias the results. Accordingly, any characteristics that are reported for the group of subjects as a whole should also be reported for each subgroup.

Apparatus. If a standard piece of apparatus is used, such as a tachistoscope, reaction time device, slide projector, or on-line computer with attached peripheral devices, simply identify it by the firm's name and model number. Examples are: "A Scientific-Prototype two-channel tachistoscope, Model 800F, was used to present the stimuli," or "Slides were projected on a screen in front of the room by a Kodak carousel projector." Specially designed equipment not commercially available is described briefly. If no special piece of apparatus has been used, other than 3 × 5 cards or data sheets, omit the *Apparatus* heading from the research report.

Materials. Both the characteristics of stimulus materials and the manner in which they were presented to subjects are given here. If words are used, the sample of words should be described, and the source from which they were drawn cited. These sources might include the Kučera–Francis (1967) or Thorndike–Lorge (1944) word counts and the norms for imagery, concreteness, and meaningfulness published by Paivio, Yuille, and Madigan (1968). Any characteristics of the words that are relevant to the experimental task should be included, such as their frequency counts, their lengths, their imagery and concreteness values, the number of syllables, and so on. (More information about sources for words and other stimuli may be found in Chapter 14 on materials.)

If materials, such as nonsense syllables, were constructed, give the manner in which they were constructed and the characteristics of the sample. For example, "Eighty CVC nonsense syllables were constructed with the restriction that no repeated consonants occurred in any syllable, and all five vowels were used equally often."

If visual patterns or pictorial materials were used that are not available from a published source, describe how the materials were generated. For example, "The line drawings were obtained by first having a pilot group of 35 subjects draw the simplest possible picture for each of 100 concepts, and then choosing representative examples of each."

Describe the manner in which the stimuli were presented to subjects. When perceptual acuity is a factor, as in measuring tachistoscopic recognition thresholds, describe the typeface in which the words were typed or printed, and the size of the stimulus in degrees of visual angle.

When both apparatus and materials sections are included, they may be described under the single heading *Apparatus and Materials.*

Procedure. The procedure section describes in detail, and usually in chronological order, how the experiment was carried out. The typical order is first to describe instructions to subjects, usually by paraphrasing them, then describe any pretest procedure that was used, and finally outline the experimental procedure itself. If instructions were a major independent variable, they should be quoted verbatim. Any randomization or counterbalancing procedures in the ordering and presentation of the stimuli are given here. For example, if two types of stimulus faces were presented in a random order, you might say, "The two types of faces were presented in a random order to the subject, subject to the constraint that no more than three faces of the same type were presented sequentially."

Results

The results are first presented and described qualitatively, and then details of the statistical tests are given. Usually only summary descriptive statistics, such as averages, proportions, and variances, are presented, rather than data from individual subjects. If the number of conditions is small, these statistics may be presented in the text. If the number of conditions is large, statistics should be presented in tables or figures (but usually not both). The important qualitative features of these results should be pointed out to the reader first, as in "It is apparent from Table 1 that female subjects performed better on the verbal task, and male subjects performed better on the spatial task."

Only after the summary statistics are presented and the pattern of results is described should the results of statistical tests be presented. The most common error made by students writing their first research report is to reverse the order, presenting the statistical test results first and then the summary data (or even omitting the summary data if they showed no significant effects). Beginning the results section with a statement like "The results of a two-way mixed analysis of variance revealed that neither of the two independent variables was significant" omits two items of essential information: first, it neglects to remind the reader which dependent variable you have measured and, second, it fails to restate the nature of the two independent variables you have manipulated.

Even if none of the results is significant, you should present the summary statistics because the actual values obtained may be of interest to some readers. There are many reasons for failing to obtain significant results when, under other circumstances, the same manipulations may have an effect. These include ceiling effects (performance was too high across all conditions to show an effect), floor effects (performance was too low), faulty design, or confounding (see Chapter 3). At the very least, some indication should be given to the reader of the absolute values of the dependent variables that might be obtained for these conditions. In short, it is important to make the results available to readers whether or not they are significant.

Tables and Figures

Summary data are usually presented in either a table or a figure, but not both. For clarity of presentation, figures are usually preferred. In particular, if the purpose of your experiment is to test whether a certain relationshiop (e.g., linear, logarithmic, etc.) exists between the independent and dependent variable, a figure can show that graphic relationship better than any table.

To illustrate, in the Sternberg paradigm (see Chapter 5), one result of interest is whether or not the relationship between set size (the independent variable) and reaction time (the dependent variable) is linear, and a figure is indispensible to portraying this relationship. On the other hand, it is hard to present a large amount of data clearly in a figure, so if the number of conditions is large, a table may be preferable.

Tables and figures are both numbered with Arabic numerals. Do not use the term *graph* for a figure. As a matter of style, figures and tables should be presented on separate pages. Titles and captions should be reasonably self-explanatory so that your reader does not have to go back to the text to see what the table or figure is about.

Some Points about Tables. Table numbers and titles go at the top of the page above the table. The title should be a single phrase, such as "Mean correct RTs (ms) and mean error rates (%) in Experiment 1." Additional explanatory notes should be listed as footnotes, rather than appearing as part of the title.

In two-independent-variable experiments, the levels of one variable appear as column headings, and the levels of the second variable appear as row headings. When more than one dependent variable is presented (as in the preceding example, in which both RT and error rates are given) the two values for a given condition are presented adjacent to one another.

Some Points about Figures. Figure numbers and captions go at the bottom of the page, below the figure. Data from different conditions should be distinguished in some way. For example, open and closed circles, solid and dotted lines, or both may be used to distinguish conditions. Different colors are never used, because psychological journals are published in black and white. The dependent variable is plotted along the ordinate (y-axis) against the independent variable along the abscissa (x-axis). Both ordinate and abscissa are labeled and must include the units of measurement. For example, if reaction time is plotted as the dependent variable, you must indicate whether the time is measured in seconds, hundredths of seconds, or thousandths of seconds (milliseconds). Pips along both the ordinate and abscissa indicate units and should be labeled at intervals with numerical values. However, it is not necessary to use a large number of values; between four and ten values should be sufficient. When one of the two axes is not measured continuously from zero, a break in the scale is indicated with slash marks.

Statistical Tests. The statistical tests that are widely used, such as t test, analysis of variance, χ^2 (chi-square), and Pearson r, are reported without citing the formulas used or references. Present the numerical value of the statistic, its degrees of freedom (*df*), and the probability level if it is significant. If a statistical test was not significant, either report its value with the notation *n.s.*, or state that it was not significant. The number of degrees of freedom is given in parentheses before the value of the test statistic. Usually, the highest level of significance a test statistic reaches is reported. Test statistics (e.g., *t*, *F*, etc.) are underlined, so that they will appear italicized in print. Some examples are shown below:

The difference in reaction time between auditory and visual stimuli was highly significant, $\underline{t}(22) = 3.21$, $\underline{p} < .005$, one-tailed test.

A 2 × 2 analysis of variance was performed to determine whether recognition thresholds for taboo and neutral words were differentially affected by the alcohol and placebo conditions. Both main effects and their interaction were significant. For type of word, $\underline{F}(1,20) = 5.30$, $\underline{p} < .05$; for alcohol versus placebo condition, $\underline{F}(1,20) = 4.67$, $\underline{p} < .05$; and for their interaction, $\underline{F}(1,20) = 9.61$, $\underline{p} < .01$.

The results of a two-way repeated analysis of variance revealed that the difference between pictures and words was highly significant, $\underline{F}(1,38) = 23.08$, $\underline{p} < .001$, but that neither the difference between high and low salience items nor the interaction between item form and salience was significant; $\underline{F} < 1$ and $\underline{F}(1,38) = 2.31$, respectively.

Note that the number of *df* for the test statistic is given in parentheses but that no *df* is shown if the *t* or *F* ratio is less than 1 (since regardless of the number of *df*, no *t* or *F* ratio less than 1 can be significant).

An alternative way of presenting the results of statistical tests is to state ahead of time the level of significance that will be used (the usual level is $p < .05$), and then merely report the values of the test statistics and their *df*s without repeating the level of significance.

Discussion

The discussion is the other end of the funnel. The discussion begins with a brief statement of the significance of the results in light of the hypotheses that were advanced in the introduction. When results of the study are perfectly consistent with predictions made on the basis of the hypothesis, the discussion is relatively straightforward and may conclude with suggestions for further research. On the other hand, some of the results may be consistent with the hypothesis being tested, and others may not. In still other cases, results may be inconsistent with any hypothesis proposed, or internally inconsistent. Although it is often not possible to resolve inconsistencies or come to definite conclusions, it is important to attempt to explain your results, however tentatively. In addition, you should attempt to relate your results to others in the literature and to resolve inconsistencies among empirical findings of various investigators or among their interpretations.

References

Every research paper ends with a list of all the references cited in the text. Note that every reference cited should be included but no references should be listed that are not cited in the text.

Form of Citation. References are cited in the body of the paper (usually in the introduction and discussion sections) by listing the author's (or authors') last name (or names) and presenting the date of publication in parentheses. When the author or authors are referred to in the text, only the date appears in parentheses and the authors' names are joined by "and." When the authors are referred to parenthetically, both the names and dates are enclosed in parentheses, and authors' names are joined by "&." For papers authored by more than two people, all authors are listed the first time the paper is cited and subsequent citations use only the first author's name followed by "et al." Examples are shown below.

Averbach and Coriell (1961) and Sperling (1960) were among the first to introduce partial report procedures in tachistoscopic recognition experiments.

Partial report techniques in tachistoscopic recognition were introduced by several investigators (Averbach & Coriell, 1961; Sperling, 1960). The concept of converging operations was introduced by Garner, Hake, and Eriksen (1956). Garner et al. (1956) suggested . . .

Form of the Reference List. References are listed at the end, arranged alphabetically by the senior author's last name. References are not numbered, the journal title is written out, only the first word and proper nouns are capitalized, and journal names, volume numbers, and book titles are underlined.

The 1983 edition of the *APA Publication Manual* recommends placing the year of publication in parentheses immediately after the author's name. This has been done in the references listed here. This date placement is a change from the former editorial style, which placed the year of publication at the end of the reference. Journal articles published before the implementation of this style change will show the former date placement.

Reference lists cite material that has been published and is available to the public, as well as material published that is not generally available (previously listed under a separate section entitled *Reference Notes*). Published material includes journal articles, chapters in books, books, published symposia, doctoral dissertations available on University Microfilm, and monographs. Citation forms for material previously listed under *Reference Notes* may be found in the *APA Publication Manual.* Representative forms of citation are shown below:

Journal Article—Single Author:

Dyer, F. N. (1973). The Stroop phenomenon and its use in the study of perceptual, cognitive, and response processes. Memory & Cognition, 1, 106–120.

Journal Article—Two or More Authors:

Eimas, P. D., Cooper, W. E., & Corbit, J. D. (1973). Some properties of linguistic feature detectors. Perception & Psychophysics, 13, 247–252.

Only the initials of the author's first name(s) are given, only the first word of the title is capitalized, the title of the journal is written out instead of being abbreviated, and the journal title and volume number are underlined (which means they will appear italicized in the published form). The first line, with the senior author's last name, is flush with the left margin, and following lines are indented.

Chapter in Book

Atkinson, R. C., & Shiffrin, R. M. (1968). Human memory: A proposed system and its control processes. In K. W. Spence & J. T. Spence (Eds.), The psychology of learning and motivation: Advances in research and theory (Vol. 2, pp. 84–115). New York: Academic Press.

The book title is underlined, the editors' surnames and initials are not inverted, the editors' names are not separated by a comma, page numbers are given, and no state is given for a well-known city name.

Book

Chomsky, C. S. (1969). The acquisition of syntax in children from 5 to 10. Cambridge, MA: MIT Press.

Book titles are not capitalized, except for the first letter of the first word or, when parts are separated by a colon, the first letter of the first word after the colon. When state names are given, use the official two-letter U.S. Postal Service abbreviations for the names of states.

More detailed descriptions of forms of references may be found in the APA Manual.

Appendices

The typical research report does not need appendices. However, an appendix is appropriate for such materials as a complicated mathematical proof or a list of stimulus materials used in the experiment. Many instructors in an experimental laboratory course may require more detailed appendices for student laboratory reports than are appropriate for a published report, such as instructions to subjects or details of the particular data analysis used. The student should be aware that these are usually superfluous in published research.

WRITING STYLE

The most difficult task faced by students of experimental psychology (and all too often professors of experimental psychology) is that of putting their thoughts, deeds, and interpretations into clear language. Although much has been made recently of "Why Johnny can't write," even students whose spelling and grammar are beyond reproach have difficulty writing with clarity and conciseness.

We believe that writing effectively is a skill everyone should possess. Even those who never have occasion to publish in the *Journal of Experimental Psychology* may very well want to compose a clear, concise memorandum, a convincing and literate letter to a newspaper, or a warm and interesting letter to a friend. And many job advertisements specify "good oral and written communication skills" as a requirement.

Principles of effective communication are the same for memoranda, letters, and research reports. Even though the research report is a structured document, as discussed in the previous sections, the style in which the various sections is written should conform to certain standard principles of writing style. There are a number of discussions of technical writing (American Psychological Association, 1983; Bernstein, 1971; Boring, 1957; Harlow, 1962, Strunk & White, 1979; Woodford, 1967). The following discussion is based on the rules presented by Strunk and White in *Elements of Style* (1979). To illustrate our points, we will present examples of poor writing style taken from students' laboratory reports, with corrections.

Seven principles of clear and concise writing are given below. If they are followed conscientiously, they will lead to clear communication, described by the *APA Publication Manual* as follows:

> Clear communication, which is the prime objective of scientific reporting, may be achieved by presenting ideas in an orderly manner and by expressing oneself smoothly and precisely. By developing ideas clearly and logically, you invite readers to read, encourage them to continue, and make their task agreeable by leading them smoothly from thought to thought.
>
> (American Psychological Association, 1983, p. 31)

Principle 1: Use Definite, Specific, Concrete Language

Writing should be vigorous, colorful, and streamlined, not pedantic, dull, and verbose. This is probably the most difficult principle to apply. There is a widely accepted feeling that scientific communication requires jargon language, that the only way to express complicated ideas is by complicated language. Although we want to express ideas precisely, precision need not imply incomprehensibility. We know of no better example of vigorous writing than the opening and closing paragraphs of George Miller's (1956) influential paper, "The Magical Number Seven, Plus or Minus Two: Some Limits on Our Capacity for Processing Information."

He begins his review paper as follows:

> My problem is that I have been persecuted by an integer. For seven years, this number has followed me around, has intruded in my most private data, and has assaulted me from the pages of our most public journals. This number assumes a variety of disguises, being sometimes a little larger and sometimes a little smaller than usual, but never changing so much as to be unrecognizable. The persistence with which this number plagues me is far more than a random accident. There is, to quote a famous senator, a design behind it, some pattern governing its appearances. Either there really is something unusual about the number or else I am suffering from delusions of persecution.
>
> (Miller, 1956, p. 81)

Miller then goes on to review data on absolute judgments of unidimensional stimuli that show we can identify only about seven plus or minus two stimuli in an absolute judgment task and the data on memory span experiments that show we can remember only about seven plus or minus two stimuli in an immediate memory task, and concludes that the processes limited by the magic number seven are not the same in the two cases. He concludes as follows:

> And finally, what about the magical number seven? What about the seven wonders of the world, the seven seas, the seven deadly sins, the seven daughters of Atlas in the Pleiades, the seven ages of man, the seven levels of hell, the seven primary colors, the seven notes of the musical scale, and the seven days of the week? What about the seven-point rating scale, the seven categories for absolute judgment, the seven objects in the span of attention, and the seven digits in the span of immediate memory? For the present I propose to withhold judgment. Perhaps there is something deep and profound behind all these sevens, something just calling out for us to discover it. But I suspect that it is only a pernicious, Pythagorean coincidence.
>
> (Miller, 1956, p. 96)

These two paragraphs illustrate the maxims of Strunk and White to use definite, specific, and concrete (albeit metaphorical) language. Although most of us do not have the opportunity to speculate as colorfully as Miller did in his article, description of the most pedestrian of experiments can be improved by rewriting in concrete and specific words. In the following examples, we quote excerpts from student papers that illustrate confusion and verbosity rather than clarity and conciseness in expression, and provide the appropriate corrections to make the examples clearer and more concise.

Poor: Using a relatively uncomplicated task in which performance before and after positive and negative feedbacks are compared, the present experiment is carried out with the expectation that results will follow a trend such that conclusions similar to those of the above mentioned experimenters can be made.

Better: This experiment attempts to replicate previous results of the effect of positive and negative feedback on task performance by presenting the feedback after a first trial of a simple arithmetic task.

Poor: This research looked at the English language and how the reader conceptualizes letters or groups of letters that may or may not form a word.

This sentence could refer to a large number of experimental paradigms. It is so vague it is meaningless.

Better: Tachistoscopic recognition thresholds for words, pronounceable nonwords, and nonpronounceable nonwords were compared for lower- and upper-case letters.

This revision specifies what was done and is appropriate as the first sentence of the abstract. The abstract should then go on to say why the manipulations in question should yield interesting information about how human subjects process visual information.

Principle 2: Use the Active Rather than the Passive Voice

This will add vigor to the writing and usually shorten the text. Compare "Sperling showed that one limitation on perception is memory" with "That one limitation on perception is memory was shown by Sperling." The first sentence is simpler and therefore preferred to the second.

Use of principle 2 can be particularly effective when an experiment is being interpreted. It is perfectly legitimate to use *I* (or when the paper is coauthored, *We*) as the subject of a sentence. It is much better to write "I conclude that memory is context-specific" than to write "The results of this experiment lead one to the conclusion that memory is context-specific."

The exception to this rule occurs when the experimenter is the actor. In describing the procedure of an experiment, the experimenter is almost always the actor, but here it is preferable to use the passive rather than active voice. Contrast "The experimenter showed the slides to the subjects at a 5-second-per-stimulus rate" with

"The subjects were shown the slides at a 5-second-per-stimulus rate." The latter, passive, sentence is actually shorter than the former, active sentence and is preferable because the reader will know that the experimenter was the person showing the pictures. In a similar spirit, "The cards were shuffled before each subject was run" is preferable to "The experimenter shuffled the cards before each subject was run."

In short, use the active voice except when the actor, or subject of the sentence, is the experimenter. For these cases, omit the actor and use the passive voice.

Principle 3: Omit Needless Words

Omitting needless words will lead to a clear and concise report. As Strunk and White put it, "Every word should tell."

Clarity and conciseness are difficult to achieve and require thought, patience, and rewriting. When we try to describe a complicated thought, procedure, result, or interpretation, we are tempted to ramble on and on in the hope that some random combination of our words will trap the fugitive idea. To be concise, we must first sharpen our understanding of the idea we want to present, and then search for the words that precisely express that idea. It takes longer to "write short" than to "write long." In a letter to a friend written in 1656, Blaise Pascal apologized, "I have made this letter rather long only because I have not had time to make it shorter."

Student research reports tend to be too verbose in the introduction and discussion sections. The following is the first paragraph in the introduction to a paper on perceptual defense and could be eliminated entirely:

> The effect of an emotional stimulus upon biological processes has often been a perplexing problem to the human animal. We are nervous that everything does not always obey our conscious control. In stressful mental situations the body also reacts: intensive pumping of the heart, perspiration, etc. We struggle for rational, intellectual control and feel weakened when we are unable to do this.

This paragraph represents the student's own, unformed ideas on the perceptual defense issue and adds nothing to the background of the problem. Students have difficulty plunging into a discussion of the problem at the beginning of an introduction, and often avoid the problem by digression, using paragraphs like the one above.

At a more microscopic level, many sentences can be rewritten to be shorter and less redundant. Instead of "It is clear that the results show that . . ." write "The results show that . . ." Instead of "It is undoubtedly true that the most difficult task faced by students of experimental psychology . . ." write "The most difficult task faced by students of experimental psychology . . ." If something is clear or true, simply state the fact without a preamble.

Lest we emphasize conciseness at the expense of completeness, we have also observed that students omit important information in the procedure and results section of the report. The reader must be told everything that was done in running the experiment and everything that was found.

Incomprehensible telegraphic style is particularly common in the results sections. Students are often so dazzled by the fact that they have performed a number of statistical tests that they report the tests without reminding the reader what the dependent variable is, and which way the results came out. The following two paragraphs constitute the entire results section of a laboratory report of an experiment in which tachistoscopic recognition thresholds for words printed in different colors were measured, when the words corresponded to the color name (congruous condition, e.g., the word "red" printed in the color red), the name of a different color (incongruous condition), or a neutral or unrelated name (neutral condition). Try to tell what happened in the experiment by reading this results section!

> Three by three factorial with repeated measures on both factors, color (red, green, blue) and type of word (congruous, incongruous, neutral) was

means of analysis. The color factor was found to be significant ($F(2,32) = 4.16, p < .05$), as was the type of word ($F(2,32) = 4.39, p < .05$). The interaction between these factors was not significant.

A one-way ANOVA with repeated measures was used to determine the effect of words, which was found significant ($F(7,112) = 4.81, p < .001$). This method was also used to determine the effect of practice, significant too ($F(8,128) = 7.41, p < .001$).

The following points have been omitted: (1) the dependent variable that was analyzed by the analysis of variance, and (2) the direction of the results—for example, which color was better, which type of word was better, what was the effect of practice? These omissions could be corrected by first presenting the results qualitatively and then presenting their statistical analysis.

Principle 4: Use Simple Sentences

Use two short sentences instead of one long one whenever possible. This principle should be applied only if the short sentences are intelligible, not telegraphic. Sentences should be simple, rather than complex. They should contain a minimum number of subordinate clauses, particularly if the clauses are themselves complex. The following student example illustrates the violation of principle 4, and its correction follows.

Poor: The six practice trials were used to determine roughly where to start the use of the ascending method of limits for the six types of stimuli.

Actually, this sentence contains two ideas—that the method of ascending limits was used to obtain thresholds and that the practice trials were used to set the starting durations and increments. Accordingly, we could write:

Better: The method of ascending limits was used to obtain recognition thresholds. The six practice trials were used to determine the starting durations and increments for the six types of stimuli.

Principle 5: Use Parallel Construction

When compound sentences *are* used, use parallel construction: Do not change the subject halfway through the sentence. As the *APA Publication Manual* puts it, "When involved concepts do require long sentences, the components should march along like people in a parade, not dodge about like broken-field runners" (p. 34).

Poor: The experimenter first gave the subject a color blindness test, and then subjects participated in the experiment.

Better: Subjects first took a color-blindness test and then participated in the experiment.

Principle 6: Keep Related Words Together

Separation of subject and object can lead to ambiguity, particularly in long sentences. "Throw mother from the train a kiss" is a dramatic example, but some more mundane examples are shown below:

New York's first commercial human-sperm bank opened Friday with semen samples from 18 men frozen in a stainless steel tank.

He noticed a large stain in the rug that was right in the center.

You can call your mother in London and tell her all about George's taking you out to dinner for just sixty cents.

Even though no ambiguity results from separating related ideas, the following sentence is difficult to understand:

Poor: In order to control for practice effects, which in previous studies have been found to be severe (see, e.g., Chase & Smith, 1970; Smith & Chase, 1976), the three types of trials were randomized across the session.

Better: Previous research has shown strong practice effects (Chase & Smith, 1970; Smith & Chase, 1976). Accordingly, presentation of the three types of trials was randomized across the session to control for such effects.

Principle 7: Use Abbreviations Sparingly

Although this principle violates the principle of conciseness, it serves the interest of clarity. Abbreviations (except those of the most commonly accepted kind, as given in the *APA Publication Manual*) save little space and make unwarranted demands on the reader's memory. Contrast the comprehensibility of the first paragraph with that of the second:

Poor: For S pairs it was hypothesized that RTs would be shorter for PI pairs than for NI pairs. Also, RTs would be shorter for NI pairs presented to the RVF and shorter for PI pairs presented to the LVF for RH Ss, and the converse for LH Ss.

Better: For same pairs it was hypothesized that reaction times would be shorter for physical-identical pairs than for name-identical pairs. Also, reaction times would be shorter for name-identical pairs presented to the right visual field and shorter for physical-identical pairs presented to the left visual field for right-handed subjects, while the converse was expected to hold for left-handed subjects.

Many abbreviations previously used in APA journals are no longer acceptable: S (subject) and E (experimenter) should both be written out, as should journal titles (as illustrated in the section on references). The only accepted abbreviations are those that appear as word entries in *Webster's New Collegiate Dictionary* (1981), such as IQ, LSD, REM, ESP; commonly used abbreviations, which should first be written out in full (these include MMPI, CS, ITI, CVC, STM, RT); and abbreviations for various units of measurement, such as Hz for hertz, s for second, ms for millisecond, and cd for candela.

SUMMARY

In this chapter, we have reviewed two aspects of the research report: its formal structure, in terms of its various sections and subsections, and its preferred writing style, in terms of rules for communicating clearly and effectively.

The research report should convey why an experiment was carried out, how it was carried out, what was found, and how the results are interpreted. The *why* of an experiment is conveyed by the *introduction.* The introduction describes the background of the problem being studied, various interpretations or theories that have been proposed to explain the problem, and how the present experiment will advance our knowledge in the problem area.

The *method* section describes how the experiment was conducted. It is typically divided into three sections: subjects, apparatus and materials, and procedure, although a design subsection is also often included. The *subjects* subsection describes the number, characteristics, and population of the subjects. The *apparatus and materials* subsection describes the characteristics of the apparatus and materials used. The *procedures* section is the centerpiece of the method section. It describes, usually step-by-step, the way in which the experiment was carried out. Here, instructions to subjects, counterbalancing or randomization of materials or trials, and the sequence of steps through which the subject passed are described in complete detail. It is important to describe the procedure completely, so that other investigators can attempt to replicate the experiment or to explain why their results from a similar experiment might be different from yours.

The *results* section presents the data collected in the experiment in two ways. First, we describe the results by presenting summary statistics, such as means, in tabular or graphic form. Then, we present our statistical inferences from the results, by presenting the results of statistical tests that reveal which of the observed effects of the manipulations are significant.

The purpose of the results section is not to discuss the implications of the findings but to state them as clearly as possible. Here, it is important to remind your reader of the independent variables that were manipulated, the dependent variables that were measured, and the direction of the significant effects. This can be done by reiterating in the text the nature of the independent variables and clearly labeling the tables and figures.

The purpose of the *discussion* section is

to bring together the problem and expected results, as developed in the introduction, with the obtained results, as described in the results section. It is important to point out any discrepancies between what was expected and what was found and to account for unexpected results or results at variance with previous research. The discussion section is a place where the researcher can speculate about possible reasons for present and past results and possible directions for future research.

The summary of the experiment is presented in the *abstract,* which appears at the beginning of the research report. The purpose of the abstract is to summarize in a clear and succinct way the major purpose and findings of the experiment and their implications. It is an invitation to the reader to peruse the entire paper and for that reason serves an important function in conveying accurately and clearly what was done, why, and what was found. Although an abstract is short (100–150 words is recommended), writing it requires the most care.

There is more to a good research report than simple adherence to the rules of form that are outlined here and in the *APA Publication Manual.* The clarity and vigor of the writing style determines how well your ideas are communicated. No matter how good your idea is, it will have little or no effect on your audience if it is not expressed clearly.

Good writing is an art and a craft. It is difficult to teach, and even more difficult to learn. In this chapter, we try to facilitate the process of learning to write by discussing seven principles of good writing drawn from Strunk and White. We have illustrated violations of these principles with poor examples of writing from student reports and the application of these principles by rewriting the student examples. Some of the principles are concerned with the vigor and clarity of language, such as the use of concrete language, the active rather than the passive voice, simple sentences and parallel construction, and avoidance of abbreviations. We have advocated conciseness and simplicity of expression by encouraging the omission of needless words. Clarity suffers from verboseness, the use of longer and rarer synonyms for shorter and more common words, and the use of technical jargon. We have tried to convince you that complex and profound ideas can be expressed in simple and straightforward language.

Finally, clear writing can come only from clear thinking. If your understanding of a problem or issue is not clear, your writing about it will reflect your confusion. In a complementary fashion, trying to write clearly about an issue may help to clarify your own thoughts about it. So here, in the last chapter of our book, we encourage students to persevere and triumph in this, the most difficult step of doing research—putting ideas into words.

SAMPLE ABSTRACTS

Abstract 1

Metacontrol of Hemispheric Function in Human Split-Brain Patients

Jerre Levy
University of Pennsylvania

Colwyn Trevarthen
University of Edinburgh, Scotland

Four commissurotomy patients were tested for ability to match tachistoscopically presented stimuli with pictures in free vision, according to either structural appearance or functional/conceptual category. Patients were given ambiguous, structural, or functional instructions on any given run of trials with simultaneous double stimulus input to the two cerebral hemispheres. With ambiguous instructions, appearance and function matches were performed by the right and left hemispheres, respectively. When instructions were specific, appearance instructions tended to elicit appearance matches and right-hemisphere control. When function instructions were given, left-hemisphere control and function matches tended to be elicited. In three of the four patients, however, there was a significant number of dissociations between controlling hemisphere and strategy of matching.

From *Journal of Experimental Psychology: Human Perception and Performance,* 1976, Vol. 2, No. 3, 299–312.

Abstract 2

Perceived Informativeness of Facts

Baruch Fischhoff
Decision Research, Eugene, Oregon

There are many tasks in which people are called on to disregard information that they have already processed. Dealing with inadmissible evidence in a courtroom setting, second-guessing the past, and responding to experimental psychologists' debriefing instructions are three tasks of this type; in all these cases, people have been found to experience considerable difficulty. The present experiment investigates these difficulties in a general form, using almanac-type questions. Subjects told the correct answers to such questions were found to overestimate both how much they would have known about the answer had they not been told and how much they actually did know about the answer before being told. Attempts to undo this *knew-it-all-along* effect by exhorting subjects to work harder or telling them about the bias failed. These results were discussed in terms of how the structure of one's knowledge is altered to accommodate new information.

From *Journal of Experimental Psychology: Human Perception and Performance,* 1977, Vol. 3, No. 2, 349–358.

Abstract 3

Use of Orthographic and Word-Specific Knowledge in Reading Words Aloud

Jonathan Baron and Carol Strawson
University of Pennsylvania

Words that conform to spelling-sound correspondence rules (e.g., SWEET) are read aloud more quickly than words that do not conform (e.g., SWORD). This suggests that the rules are used in reading a word, in spite of past learning of the association between the word and its entire pronunciation. This effect is larger in subjects who rely heavily on the rules, as determined by independent tests. In addition, mixing case affects reading of nonconforming words more than of conforming ones, suggesting that word-specific associations use units larger than single letters.

From *Journal of Experimental Psychology: Human Perception and Performance,* 1976, Vol. 2, No. 3, 386–393.

Abstract 4
Differential Interpolation Effects in Free Recall

William M. Petrusic
Carleton University,
Ottawa, Canada

Donald G. Jamieson
University of Calgary
Calgary, Canada

A very demanding task, shadowing digits, is shown to produce substantial amounts of forgetting at all serial input positions when interpolated between the presentation and free recall of lists of 10 or 16 unrelated words. Similar but smaller recall decrements relative to an unfilled delay separating presentation and recall were produced by merely listening to vocal or instrumental music. These differential interpolation effects support views that serial position effects reflect a single process. With respect to dual process theory, recency as a pure "primary memory" phenomenon and the use of interpolated tasks to study properties of pure "secondary memory" are questioned by these data.

From *Journal of Experimental Psychology: Human Learning and Memory,* 1978, Vol. 4, No. 1, 101–109.

Abstract 5
Speech Recoding in Reading Chinese Characters

Ovid J. L. Tzeng and Daisy L. Hung
University of California, Riverside

William S. Y. Wang
University of California, Berkeley

Two experiments were conducted with Chinese subjects to investigate whether phonemic similarity affected the visual information processing of Chinese characters. The first experiment used a short-term retention paradigm and the second, a sentence judgment task. In both experiments the subject's performance was found to be impaired by the introduction of phonemic similarity into the test materials. The results were discussed with respect to the issues of orthographical differences and of speech recoding in reading.

From *Journal of Experimental Psychology: Human Learning and Memory,* 1977, Vol. 3, No. 6, 621–630.

Abstract 6
Semantic and Perceptual Processes in Symbolic Comparisons

William P. Banks and Julianne Flora
Pomona College

This article studies the processing of pictures and words as symbols. Pictures lead to faster and more accurate responses than words when the task is to decide which member of a pair of pictures or words denotes the larger or smaller object. The present experiments show that the superiority of pictures results from the fact that pictures are interpreted more quickly than words, but that after the interpretation is made, processing is the same. These experiments also give evidence that pictures and words are both processed in terms of linguistic codes rather than mental images. The results are well accounted for by an information-processing model that is based on two general assumptions: (a) The stimuli and the instructions are represented as discrete codes, and (b) processing proceeds until one and only one of the stimulus codes is the same as the code for the instructions.

From *Journal of Experimental Psychology: Human Perception and Performance,* 1977, Vol. 3, No. 2, 278–290.

Abstract 7

Testing the Role of Vertical Symmetry in Letter Matching

Howard E. Egeth, Hiram H. Brownell, and Leo D. Geoffrion
Johns Hopkins University

A series of experiments tested a recent suggestion that vertical symmetry of a stimulus display can serve as a visual diagnostic for responding "same" in a letter-matching task. The data of chief interest were *same* reaction times to vertically symmetric (e.g., AA) and asymmetric (e.g., LL) displays, each composed of two side-by-side uppercase letters. Overall, the data argue against subjects' use of vertical symmetry as a diagnostic in dealing with letter pairs. The results were interpreted within the context of recent work on symmetry. In particular, it was suggested that the importance of structural diagnostics in a matching task may be inversely related to the codability of the stimulus elements being compared.

From *Journal of Experimental Psychology: Human Perception and Performance,* 1976, Vol. 2, No. 3, 429–434.

Appendix A
Statistical Tables

The authors wish to thank the following authors and publishers for their kind permission to adapt from the following tables:

Table A-1. Table XXXIII of R. A. Fisher and F. Yates. *Statistical tables for biological, agricultural, and medical research,* 6th edition. London: Longman Group, 1974.

Table A-2 and A-3. Table XXXIII_1 and XXXIII_2 of R. A. Fisher and F. Yates. *Statistical tables for biological, agricultural, and medical research,* 6th edition. London: Longman Group, 1974.

Table A-4. Table III of A. L. Edwards. *Experimental design in psychological research,* 3rd edition. New York: Holt, Rinehart and Winston, 1968.

Table A-5. Table 12 of E. S. Pearson and H. O. Hartley (Eds.). *Biometrika tables for statisticians,* vol. I, 2nd edition. London: Cambridge University Press, 1958.

Table A-6. Table 5 of E. S. Pearson and H. O. Hartley (Eds.). *Biometrika tables for statisticians,* vol. II, 3rd edition. London: Cambridge University Press, 1972.

Table A-7. Table IV of R. A. Fisher and F. Yates. *Statistical tables for biological, agricultural, and medical research,* 6th edition. London: Longman Group, 1974.

Table A-8. Table 11.4 in D. B. Owen. *Handbook of statistical tables.* Reading, MA: Addison-Wesley, 1962. D. Auble, Extended tables for the Mann-Whitney statistic. *Bulletin of the institute of educational research at Indiana University 1,* No. 2, 1953.

Table A-10. Table J of R. P. Runyon and A. Haber. *Fundamentals of behavioral statistics.* Reading, MA: Addison-Wesley, 1968. Based on values in F. Wilcoxon, S. Katti, and R. A. Wilcox. *Critical values and probability levels for the Wilcoxon rank sum test and Wilcoxon signed rank test.* New York: American Cyanamid Co., 1963; and F. Wilcoxon and R. A. Wilcox. *Some rapid approximate statistical procedures.* New York: Lederle Laboratories, 1964.

Table A-11. M. Friedman. The use of ranks to avoid the assumption of normality implicit in the analysis of variance. *Journal of the American Statistical Association,* 1937, *32,* 688–689.

Table A-1 Random Digits

03 47 43 73 86	36 96 47 36 61	46 98 63 71 62	33 26 16 80 45	60 11 14 10 95
97 74 24 67 62	42 81 14 57 20	42 53 32 37 32	27 07 36 07 51	24 51 79 89 73
16 76 62 27 66	56 50 26 71 07	32 90 79 78 53	13 55 38 58 59	88 97 54 14 10
12 56 85 99 26	96 96 68 27 31	05 03 72 93 15	57 12 10 14 21	88 26 49 81 76
55 59 56 35 64	38 54 82 46 22	31 62 43 09 90	06 18 44 32 53	23 83 01 30 30
16 22 77 94 39	49 54 43 54 82	17 37 93 23 78	87 35 20 96 43	84 26 34 91 64
84 42 17 53 31	57 24 55 06 88	77 04 74 47 67	21 76 33 50 25	83 92 12 06 76
63 01 63 78 59	16 95 55 67 19	98 10 50 71 75	12 86 73 58 07	44 39 52 38 79
33 21 12 34 29	78 64 56 07 82	52 42 07 44 38	15 51 00 13 42	99 66 02 79 54
57 60 86 32 44	09 47 27 96 54	49 17 46 09 62	90 52 84 77 27	08 02 73 43 28
18 18 07 92 46	44 17 16 58 09	79 83 86 19 62	06 76 50 03 10	55 23 64 05 05
26 62 38 97 75	84 16 07 44 99	83 11 46 32 24	20 14 85 88 45	10 93 72 88 71
23 42 40 64 74	82 97 77 77 81	07 45 32 14 08	32 98 94 07 72	93 85 79 10 75
12 36 28 19 95	50 92 26 11 97	00 56 76 31 38	80 22 02 53 53	86 60 42 04 53
37 85 94 35 12	83 39 50 08 30	42 34 07 96 88	54 42 06 87 98	35 85 29 48 39
70 29 17 12 13	40 33 20 38 26	13 89 51 03 74	17 76 37 13 04	07 74 21 19 30
56 62 18 37 35	96 83 50 87 75	97 12 25 93 47	70 33 24 03 54	97 77 46 44 80
99 49 57 22 77	88 42 95 45 72	16 64 36 16 00	04 43 18 66 79	94 77 24 21 90
16 08 15 04 72	33 27 14 34 09	45 59 34 68 49	12 72 07 34 45	99 27 72 95 14
31 16 93 32 43	50 27 89 87 19	20 15 37 00 49	52 85 66 60 44	38 68 88 11 80
68 34 30 13 70	55 74 30 77 40	44 22 78 84 26	04 33 46 09 52	68 07 97 06 57
74 57 25 65 76	59 29 97 68 60	71 91 38 67 54	13 58 18 24 76	15 54 55 95 52
27 42 37 86 53	48 55 90 65 72	96 57 69 36 10	96 46 92 42 45	97 60 49 04 91
00 39 68 29 61	66 37 32 20 30	77 84 57 03 29	10 45 65 04 26	11 04 06 67 24
29 94 98 94 24	68 49 69 10 82	53 75 91 93 30	34 25 20 57 27	40 48 73 51 92
16 90 82 66 59	83 62 64 11 12	67 19 00 71 74	60 47 21 29 68	02 02 37 03 31
11 27 94 75 06	06 09 19 74 66	02 94 37 34 02	76 70 90 30 86	38 45 94 30 38
35 24 10 16 20	33 32 51 26 38	79 78 45 04 91	16 92 53 56 16	02 75 50 95 98
38 23 16 86 38	42 38 97 01 50	87 75 66 81 41	40 01 74 91 62	48 51 84 08 32
31 96 25 91 47	96 44 33 49 13	34 86 82 53 91	00 52 43 48 85	27 55 26 89 62
66 67 40 67 14	64 05 71 95 86	11 05 65 09 68	76 83 20 37 90	57 16 00 11 66
14 90 84 45 11	75 73 88 05 90	52 27 41 14 86	22 98 12 22 08	07 52 74 95 80
68 05 51 18 00	33 96 02 75 19	07 60 62 93 55	59 33 82 43 90	49 37 38 44 59
20 46 78 73 90	97 51 40 14 02	04 02 33 31 08	39 54 16 49 36	47 95 93 13 30
64 19 58 97 79	15 06 15 93 20	01 90 10 75 06	40 78 78 89 62	02 67 74 17 33
05 26 93 70 60	22 35 85 15 13	92 03 51 59 77	59 56 78 06 83	52 91 05 70 74
07 97 10 88 23	09 98 42 99 64	61 71 62 99 15	06 51 29 16 93	58 05 77 09 51
68 71 86 85 85	54 87 66 47 54	73 32 08 11 12	44 95 92 63 16	29 56 24 29 48
26 99 61 65 53	58 37 78 80 70	42 10 50 67 42	32 17 55 85 74	94 44 67 16 94
14 65 52 68 75	87 59 36 22 41	26 78 63 06 55	13 08 27 01 50	15 29 39 39 43
17 53 77 58 71	71 41 61 50 72	12 41 94 96 26	44 95 27 36 99	02 96 74 30 83
90 26 59 21 19	23 52 23 33 12	96 93 02 18 39	07 02 18 36 07	25 99 32 70 23
41 23 52 55 99	31 04 49 69 96	10 47 48 45 88	13 41 43 89 20	97 17 14 49 17
60 20 50 81 69	31 99 73 68 68	35 81 33 03 76	24 30 12 48 60	18 99 10 72 34
91 25 38 05 90	94 58 28 41 36	45 37 59 03 09	90 35 57 29 12	82 62 54 65 60

Table A-1 *Continued*

34 50 57 74 37	98 80 33 00 91	09 77 93 19 82	74 94 80 04 04	45 07 31 66 49
85 22 04 39 43	73 81 53 94 79	33 62 46 86 28	08 31 54 46 31	53 94 13 38 47
09 79 13 77 48	73 82 97 22 21	05 03 27 24 83	72 89 44 05 60	35 80 39 94 88
88 75 80 18 14	22 95 75 42 49	39 32 82 22 49	02 48 07 70 37	16 04 61 67 87
90 96 23 70 00	39 00 03 06 90	55 85 78 38 36	94 37 30 69 32	90 89 00 76 33
53 74 23 99 67	61 32 28 69 84	94 62 67 86 24	98 33 41 19 95	47 53 53 38 09
63 38 06 86 54	99 00 65 26 94	02 82 90 23 07	79 62 67 80 60	75 91 12 81 19
35 30 58 21 46	06 72 17 10 94	25 21 31 75 96	49 28 24 00 49	55 65 79 78 07
63 43 36 82 69	65 51 18 37 88	61 38 44 12 45	32 92 85 88 65	54 34 81 85 35
98 25 37 55 26	01 91 82 81 46	74 71 12 94 97	24 02 71 37 07	03 92 18 66 75
02 63 21 17 69	71 50 80 89 56	38 15 70 11 48	43 40 45 86 98	00 83 26 91 03
64 55 22 21 82	48 22 28 06 00	61 54 13 43 91	82 78 12 23 29	06 66 24 12 27
85 07 26 13 89	01 10 07 82 04	59 63 69 36 03	69 11 15 83 80	13 29 54 19 28
58 54 16 24 15	51 54 44 82 00	62 61 65 04 69	38 18 65 18 97	85 72 13 49 21
34 85 27 84 87	61 48 64 56 26	90 18 48 13 26	37 70 15 42 57	65 65 80 39 07
03 92 18 27 46	57 99 16 96 56	30 33 72 85 22	84 64 38 56 98	99 01 30 98 64
62 95 30 27 59	37 75 41 66 48	86 97 80 61 45	23 53 04 01 63	45 76 08 64 27
08 45 93 15 22	60 21 75 46 91	98 77 27 85 42	28 88 61 08 84	69 62 03 42 73
07 08 55 18 40	45 44 75 13 90	24 94 96 61 02	57 55 66 83 15	73 42 37 11 61
01 85 89 95 66	51 10 19 34 88	15 84 97 19 75	12 76 39 43 78	64 63 91 08 25
72 84 71 14 35	19 11 58 49 26	50 11 17 17 76	86 31 57 20 18	95 60 78 46 75
88 78 28 16 84	13 52 53 94 53	75 45 69 30 96	73 89 65 70 31	99 17 43 48 76
45 17 75 65 57	28 40 19 72 12	25 12 74 75 67	60 40 60 81 19	24 62 01 61 16
96 76 28 12 54	22 01 11 94 25	71 96 16 16 88	68 64 36 74 45	19 59 50 88 92
43 31 67 72 30	24 02 94 08 63	38 32 36 66 02	69 36 38 25 39	48 03 45 15 22
50 44 66 44 21	66 06 58 05 62	68 15 54 35 02	42 35 48 96 32	14 52 41 52 48
22 66 22 15 86	26 63 75 41 99	58 42 36 72 24	58 37 52 18 51	03 37 18 39 11
96 24 40 14 51	23 22 30 88 57	95 67 47 29 83	94 69 40 06 07	18 16 36 78 86
31 73 91 61 19	60 20 72 93 48	98 57 07 23 69	65 95 39 69 58	56 80 30 19 44
78 60 73 99 84	43 89 94 36 45	56 69 47 07 41	90 22 91 07 12	78 35 34 08 72
84 37 90 61 56	70 10 23 98 05	85 11 34 76 60	76 48 45 34 60	01 64 18 39 96
36 67 10 08 23	98 93 35 08 86	99 29 76 29 81	33 34 91 58 93	63 14 52 32 52
07 28 59 07 48	89 64 58 89 75	83 85 62 27 89	30 14 78 56 27	86 63 59 80 02
10 15 83 87 60	79 24 31 66 56	21 48 24 06 93	91 98 94 05 49	01 47 59 38 00
55 19 68 97 65	03 73 52 16 56	00 53 55 90 27	33 42 29 38 87	22 13 88 83 34
53 81 29 13 39	35 01 20 71 34	62 33 74 82 14	53 73 19 09 03	56 54 29 56 93
51 86 32 68 92	33 98 74 66 99	40 14 71 94 58	45 94 19 38 81	14 44 99 81 07
35 91 70 29 13	80 03 54 07 27	96 94 78 32 66	50 95 52 74 33	13 80 55 62 54
37 71 67 95 13	20 02 44 95 94	64 85 04 05 72	01 32 90 76 14	53 89 74 60 41
93 66 13 83 27	92 79 64 64 72	28 54 96 53 84	48 14 52 98 94	56 07 93 89 30
02 96 08 45 65	13 05 00 41 84	93 07 54 72 59	21 45 57 09 77	19 48 56 27 44
49 83 43 48 35	82 88 33 69 96	72 36 04 19 76	47 45 15 18 60	82 11 08 95 97
84 60 71 62 46	40 80 81 30 37	34 39 23 05 38	25 15 35 71 30	88 12 57 21 77
18 17 30 88 71	44 91 14 88 47	89 23 30 63 15	56 34 20 47 89	99 82 93 24 98
79 69 10 61 78	71 32 76 95 62	87 00 22 58 40	92 54 01 75 25	43 11 71 99 31

Table A-2 Permutations for $N = 10$

03528	28071	97041	45167	35421	71345	47286	83567	94170	46789	56471	65132	18294	73618	89714
49761	39465	52683	82093	09867	06982	10359	49102	65328	02531	93208	74809	50376	04952	02365
80219	29485	85093	45687	32579	52867	70851	03621	51490	53180	76283	90287	34605	67295	82906
43657	70361	24176	30129	48016	03194	29463	94587	32768	76924	90451	56314	12879	10834	45137
36524	07561	67820	20739	68045	54978	90317	64529	57319	74861	94816	10798	06431	53984	07196
97801	98234	13459	58146	13782	36102	48562	78301	64802	39502	05723	32546	29857	16072	32584
56913	06289	64527	30265	43209	84152	69183	01278	41973	03471	85014	01628	42016	90164	90418
84027	51734	80193	49718	81675	69307	47250	39546	25068	56829	27639	73954	58379	53827	73625
70523	83297	81239	05913	75206	18350	81623	59327	08317	39581	45736	12987	40568	20915	40819
68194	60541	06745	68742	38491	67924	07549	64081	56492	60247	19802	54360	23917	48367	32367
59208	56078	74268	54981	12573	51246	43985	04628	54670	93108	86341	10678	70468	53920	91478
13674	31492	09351	27630	68490	38097	27160	97531	32918	67542	95207	42593	51239	74618	32650
40329	15237	65897	18693	43709	10783	41237	72168	87194	80472	38125	23945	73981	31749	52831
71568	98604	13402	20547	58612	95426	89605	35904	23506	69351	46970	10687	06254	26580	49760
78136	62531	92143	28935	98410	78059	76901	24618	85102	30642	10378	61739	41980	59761	65943
09452	84097	05876	46107	75236	61432	35482	57093	93647	15987	24956	08245	25763	42803	80172
58236	29871	53107	50762	47103	81973	35716	83924	21593	98432	95260	83496	27810	82193	24851
10974	64350	89264	41839	69852	65042	42089	67501	40678	57601	84371	17250	95634	67450	90367

83417	26179	19562	71358	78542	72896	74312	57346	16248	68102	76581	73294	02698	72850	35710
29065	45038	38704	90246	13069	43105	85960	82019	97305	53794	24309	86015	43517	94316	98624
48210	25789	52193	36489	82167	01325	52839	25301	24150	71306	06417	23057	80129	82439	34620
79365	31460	04687	17502	49053	74896	70614	78649	63987	94258	58329	94168	65374	16075	87915
67439	45961	21035	64530	84067	32516	57819	23461	15894	20935	37198	67983	94786	96408	58037
10285	80723	64789	81972	51923	07498	04623	80957	06723	78641	65240	02514	02315	57123	92164
25481	69345	02391	32647	27845	92017	82401	95342	02538	15230	60125	97813	57493	27386	13450
70963	17820	68574	85091	16093	64538	93756	01786	67419	84679	84937	04625	20681	90514	97286
59816	13897	31250	32940	28754	48721	31748	43960	93028	93802	26039	47605	84961	39274	13064
47023	45260	47896	68751	61039	63905	96250	78521	54176	47651	78145	81239	75203	86105	58927
03957	87529	60895	27615	21875	74590	90758	29064	57408	28947	69210	89710	53076	10578	36809
84612	61403	23714	40839	69403	31286	34621	87513	63219	16053	37485	54236	92184	34269	14275
69012	15203	94652	47395	93605	43895	60274	40519	06384	27149	58302	76523	89631	18594	41059
74385	47689	18073	01628	72148	20167	18359	28736	95721	30586	41679	91408	07524	07236	62738
57693	32816	87162	61348	15237	17620	17096	50139	56192	31970	32781	79358	23695	13864	24538
48012	50749	45930	72509	86094	98543	34258	74286	73048	28564	50469	42061	04817	07529	60917
69407	45982	71896	32891	67984	93618	54867	28730	12674	84715	74269	28940	50628	92810	49168
52138	70316	20453	64057	01325	25470	30912	51946	03895	23069	03851	65317	39417	34576	53270
20531	59762	71692	25684	39425	90132	14379	16720	16732	07423	71893	48307	64192	76915	79431
98746	81340	84305	17309	86107	68547	56802	45983	84590	89165	02546	15269	85307	84023	05628

Table A-3 Permutations for $N = 20$

1	15	6	8	5	2	13	7	4	10	11	9	10	1	6	10	2	12	13	9	7	6	10	0	1	16	19	14	8	18	1	15	3	10	17	3	16	0	15	9	14	19	12	17	10	13	17	11	12	14
10	17	12	11	9	18	19	9	3	15	8	5	14	2	16	0	14	7	4	8	19	8	11	17	5	0	12	13	3	4	18	7	2	8	16	17	8	6	14	7	11	13	7	5	3	10	4	8	6	9
2	16	18	0	3	11	1	6	12	0	0	7	15	4	17	5	15	6	3	19	12	16	9	2	4	6	10	2	5	7	0	11	5	12	9	5	12	1	10	13	0	2	6	8	18	1	0	3	18	16
14	7	4	13	19	17	5	14	8	16	3	18	13	19	12	16	1	17	11	18	13	15	18	3	14	1	17	9	15	11	14	19	13	6	4	11	4	19	18	2	1	16	9	4	15	2	7	19	5	15
11	19	2	15	1	3	16	13	7	12	3	15	5	0	11	12	9	16	10	1	2	16	6	18	19	11	14	10	13	5	4	14	3	10	1	6	4	19	14	17	18	17	9	19	6	0	13	18	16	2
7	14	5	4	3	6	18	8	2	19	7	12	13	18	4	6	13	2	19	5	0	7	10	15	3	0	17	4	9	7	8	11	18	9	6	16	7	3	11	2	5	14	13	1	4	11	6	12	14	17
16	9	18	0	12	9	1	11	10	5	8	10	17	6	16	18	4	0	8	7	8	14	5	9	13	8	12	16	6	15	16	2	15	12	13	10	8	0	9	5	7	15	12	3	2	8	15	1	19	10
8	13	10	17	6	0	17	14	15	14	9	1	14	19	2	11	17	14	15	3	1	11	4	12	17	3	18	19	2	1	19	7	17	5	0	1	18	15	12	13	0	10	8	11	16	7	5	4	9	3
18	8	11	9	15	19	13	4	1	11	18	6	3	17	11	3	1	14	12	0	2	17	0	7	19	1	2	10	9	12	17	7	4	3	19	13	0	9	5	17	1	12	9	3	16	0	11	8	4	12
4	5	14	3	0	2	0	7	16	18	4	14	9	10	16	8	2	10	13	18	14	9	12	11	8	6	11	15	0	17	10	0	13	11	14	15	11	1	12	7	5	17	0	7	13	7	2	15	3	18
7	10	16	12	6	5	17	6	8	14	1	12	2	8	19	17	7	11	16	4	6	3	16	13	5	16	8	4	18	5	8	9	5	2	18	10	14	4	18	16	18	4	19	11	15	10	13	6	16	5
19	2	1	13	17	9	10	12	15	3	15	5	0	13	7	5	15	9	19	6	15	10	1	4	18	13	3	14	19	7	16	12	6	15	1	3	2	19	6	8	8	6	2	10	14	9	17	19	1	14
4	0	1	12	7	12	9	0	5	19	15	16	2	5	19	5	14	16	11	6	11	7	5	12	2	15	11	8	5	3	18	14	8	19	15	8	16	19	0	4	13	8	5	1	14	1	11	3	17	7
3	14	5	15	6	7	3	4	6	1	7	8	3	4	12	15	13	3	1	17	13	19	15	14	3	1	9	18	0	14	6	4	3	7	1	13	5	11	14	6	18	11	2	4	12	9	16	0	6	5
8	17	11	19	10	8	13	2	18	16	6	1	0	17	10	19	2	7	8	18	9	10	8	6	1	4	12	16	6	17	0	13	12	2	10	1	18	17	7	12	10	9	3	15	6	4	18	8	15	2
9	18	16	13	2	11	17	14	10	15	9	13	18	11	14	12	9	0	10	4	16	0	4	18	17	19	10	2	7	13	17	9	16	5	11	15	10	3	2	9	17	16	0	7	19	13	14	12	19	10
0	2	5	1	18	14	16	19	7	8	14	6	8	1	19	5	2	3	14	13	18	9	2	12	16	0	1	18	4	15	13	14	0	2	11	0	14	5	12	13	0	6	18	7	16	7	9	19	11	5
15	6	14	12	8	1	11	9	3	4	10	7	12	13	5	18	9	0	12	16	3	10	7	8	13	17	8	13	6	16	3	19	18	1	6	9	16	7	6	4	8	11	1	10	15	18	16	2	12	9
13	16	17	3	19	10	6	5	17	13	17	0	15	18	4	10	6	15	17	7	15	14	17	0	6	14	9	12	19	3	12	10	4	15	17	3	19	18	10	1	3	17	5	2	13	14	13	1	17	0
10	9	7	4	11	12	15	2	18	0	3	9	11	16	2	8	19	1	11	4	11	19	4	1	5	11	5	2	10	7	5	9	16	7	8	2	17	15	11	8	14	4	9	12	19	3	15	4	10	8
6	2	8	4	14	7	16	6	2	1	18	8	3	19	4	7	16	11	19	17	2	11	0	1	7	10	4	12	5	19	4	13	11	9	2	1	6	19	16	11	5	3	11	9	0	3	6	7	9	1
8	1	10	16	9	5	8	17	0	12	9	15	0	11	5	5	14	18	9	3	19	13	18	8	6	8	7	14	2	18	10	15	16	17	6	17	5	14	9	13	2	7	12	15	10	11	16	4	12	10
17	15	5	3	12	9	18	10	3	11	1	6	2	18	7	0	10	4	8	12	9	15	3	17	16	0	3	9	15	13	19	8	14	3	7	10	18	8	2	15	8	6	19	1	14	17	8	2	13	19
13	0	11	19	17	15	19	4	14	13	13	16	17	10	12	15	13	1	6	2	4	12	5	10	14	6	17	1	16	11	18	0	1	12	5	3	0	7	12	4	16	17	13	4	18	0	5	14	18	15

19	13	17	0	9	8	7	10	5	4	12	15	5	17	9	17	19	0	14	11	4	10	7	19	2	17	10	3	0	14	19	9	4	17	1	11	7	17	3	10	5	18	1	13	8	13	10	18	16	19
3	5	1	7	14	9	1	15	6	12	6	1	18	14	4	3	2	18	8	16	0	16	3	8	6	2	9	18	19	1	10	14	15	18	3	14	1	2	19	6	11	0	6	3	19	1	11	18	8	4
8	6	15	10	4	13	18	19	2	11	2	16	19	7	11	4	10	6	12	1	14	11	17	18	15	8	15	6	11	12	6	16	5	13	7	15	0	5	9	8	17	9	16	10	15	0	6	5	9	17
2	11	12	18	16	14	17	16	0	3	0	8	13	3	10	7	15	5	9	13	12	9	13	5	1	4	5	13	16	7	0	8	11	12	2	12	16	13	4	18	4	14	12	2	7	15	2	12	3	7
3	1	17	13	19	14	1	12	6	8	16	12	6	7	1	2	18	3	8	6	11	1	6	8	9	6	1	10	11	15	2	11	10	9	8	17	7	6	15	19	10	0	14	3	19	1	3	13	9	14
5	18	12	15	2	18	17	2	3	5	15	5	18	0	17	4	7	14	0	10	18	12	15	0	19	8	7	2	14	4	1	13	18	3	16	18	0	16	4	3	13	18	1	8	2	6	12	4	18	11
0	9	16	4	10	15	19	13	16	4	8	10	19	3	11	19	1	9	11	13	13	2	10	14	5	13	17	0	9	19	12	14	17	6	19	10	2	9	5	12	12	11	15	9	7	16	8	2	17	7
11	8	14	7	6	0	7	10	9	11	2	4	9	13	14	15	12	16	5	17	4	3	7	16	17	16	3	12	18	5	5	15	7	4	0	14	8	1	11	13	4	5	16	6	17	0	19	15	5	10
19	16	6	8	15	10	11	9	3	12	13	6	4	8	5	13	7	6	1	2	12	15	13	5	3	10	15	0	11	9	19	18	7	11	17	13	14	10	6	18	18	10	17	7	1	8	10	6	18	11
2	10	4	14	18	14	2	4	17	0	1	2	9	14	11	8	9	0	12	11	4	9	18	16	7	3	16	13	5	2	4	5	0	16	2	2	12	4	1	3	12	13	4	8	9	9	17	13	19	1
9	0	12	5	13	15	5	16	18	6	3	12	0	15	7	19	14	5	4	3	2	10	0	17	1	18	19	14	4	12	12	1	6	10	3	17	19	9	16	15	14	16	3	15	5	15	14	4	16	3
11	1	7	3	17	19	7	13	8	1	16	10	17	18	19	15	17	10	18	16	6	11	19	8	14	17	6	1	7	8	13	14	15	9	8	11	8	7	0	5	2	0	19	11	6	2	5	12	0	7
2	7	18	0	17	5	6	13	15	16	4	15	9	3	10	13	18	19	4	3	9	17	15	11	10	13	10	11	3	14	6	13	1	19	12	9	16	2	8	6	13	2	1	9	5	3	15	10	5	1
3	11	1	16	15	7	9	19	10	4	13	8	6	14	12	9	16	14	5	0	6	1	4	16	7	7	9	0	12	5	4	7	15	8	3	19	14	5	15	10	8	6	14	4	16	16	8	12	13	0
13	19	12	6	8	3	1	12	18	8	0	16	7	5	2	17	1	11	15	10	19	5	14	3	0	18	19	17	8	6	2	18	14	16	5	1	4	13	18	11	0	18	11	17	12	7	9	4	2	11
9	4	10	14	5	17	11	2	0	14	18	17	11	1	19	2	6	8	12	7	12	2	8	13	18	2	16	15	4	1	9	0	17	11	10	3	17	12	7	0	19	15	10	3	7	18	6	17	14	19

Table A-4 Areas and Ordinates of the Normal Distribution

z	(1) $A(0, z)$ or $A(-z, 0)$	(2) $A(-\infty, z)$ or $A(-z, +\infty)$	(3) $A(z, +\infty)$ or $A(-\infty, -z)$	(4) $f(z)$ or $f(-z)$
0.00	0.0000	0.5000	0.5000	0.3989
0.01	0.0040	0.5040	0.4960	0.3989
0.02	0.0080	0.5080	0.4920	0.3989
0.03	0.0120	0.5120	0.4880	0.3988
0.04	0.0160	0.5160	0.4840	0.3986
0.05	0.0199	0.5199	0.4801	0.3984
0.06	0.0239	0.5239	0.4761	0.3982
0.07	0.0279	0.5279	0.4721	0.3980
0.08	0.0319	0.5319	0.4681	0.3977
0.09	0.0359	0.5359	0.4641	0.3973
0.10	0.0398	0.5398	0.4602	0.3970
0.11	0.0438	0.5438	0.4562	0.3965
0.12	0.0478	0.5478	0.4522	0.3961
0.13	0.0517	0.5517	0.4483	0.3956
0.14	0.0557	0.5557	0.4443	0.3951
0.15	0.0596	0.5596	0.4404	0.3945
0.16	0.0636	0.5636	0.4364	0.3939
0.17	0.0675	0.5675	0.4325	0.3932
0.18	0.0714	0.5714	0.4286	0.3925
0.19	0.0753	0.5753	0.4247	0.3918
0.20	0.0793	0.5793	0.4207	0.3910
0.21	0.0832	0.5832	0.4168	0.3902
0.22	0.0871	0.5871	0.4129	0.3894
0.23	0.0910	0.5910	0.4090	0.3885
0.24	0.0948	0.5948	0.4052	0.3876
0.25	0.0987	0.5987	0.4013	0.3867
0.26	0.1026	0.6026	0.3974	0.3857
0.27	0.1064	0.6064	0.3936	0.3847
0.28	0.1103	0.6103	0.3897	0.3836
0.29	0.1141	0.6141	0.3859	0.3825
0.30	0.1179	0.6179	0.3821	0.3814
0.31	0.1217	0.6217	0.3783	0.3802
0.32	0.1255	0.6255	0.3745	0.3790
0.33	0.1293	0.6293	0.3707	0.3778
0.34	0.1331	0.6331	0.3669	0.3765
0.35	0.1368	0.6368	0.3632	0.3752
0.36	0.1406	0.6406	0.3594	0.3739
0.37	0.1443	0.6443	0.3557	0.3725
0.38	0.1480	0.6480	0.3520	0.3712
0.39	0.1517	0.6517	0.3483	0.3697

Table A-4 *Continued*

z	(1) $A(0, z)$ or $A(-z, 0)$	(2) $A(-\infty, z)$ or $A(-z, +\infty)$	(3) $A(z, +\infty)$ or $A(-\infty, -z)$	(4) $f(z)$ or $f(-z)$
0.40	0.1554	0.6554	0.3446	0.3683
0.41	0.1591	0.6591	0.3409	0.3668
0.42	0.1628	0.6628	0.3372	0.3653
0.43	0.1664	0.6664	0.3336	0.3637
0.44	0.1700	0.6700	0.3300	0.3621
0.45	0.1736	0.6736	0.3264	0.3605
0.46	0.1772	0.6772	0.3228	0.3589
0.47	0.1808	0.6808	0.3192	0.3572
0.48	0.1844	0.6844	0.3156	0.3555
0.49	0.1879	0.6879	0.3121	0.3538
0.50	0.1915	0.6915	0.3085	0.3521
0.51	0.1950	0.6950	0.3050	0.3503
0.52	0.1985	0.6985	0.3015	0.3485
0.53	0.2019	0.7019	0.2981	0.3467
0.54	0.2054	0.7054	0.2946	0.3448
0.55	0.2088	0.7088	0.2912	0.3429
0.56	0.2123	0.7123	0.2877	0.3410
0.57	0.2157	0.7157	0.2843	0.3391
0.58	0.2190	0.7190	0.2810	0.3372
0.59	0.2224	0.7224	0.2776	0.3352
0.60	0.2257	0.7257	0.2743	0.3332
0.61	0.2291	0.7291	0.2709	0.3312
0.62	0.2324	0.7324	0.2676	0.3292
0.63	0.2357	0.7357	0.2643	0.3271
0.64	0.2389	0.7389	0.2611	0.3251
0.65	0.2422	0.7422	0.2578	0.3230
0.66	0.2454	0.7454	0.2546	0.3209
0.67	0.2486	0.7486	0.2514	0.3187
0.68	0.2517	0.7517	0.2483	0.3166
0.69	0.2549	0.7549	0.2451	0.3144
0.70	0.2580	0.7580	0.2420	0.3123
0.71	0.2611	0.7611	0.2389	0.3101
0.72	0.2642	0.7642	0.2358	0.3079
0.73	0.2673	0.7673	0.2327	0.3056
0.74	0.2704	0.7704	0.2296	0.3034
0.75	0.2734	0.7734	0.2266	0.3011
0.76	0.2764	0.7764	0.2236	0.2989
0.77	0.2794	0.7794	0.2206	0.2966
0.78	0.2823	0.7823	0.2177	0.2943
0.79	0.2852	0.7852	0.2148	0.2920

Table A-4 *Continued*

z	(1) $A(0, z)$ or $A(-z, 0)$	(2) $A(-\infty, z)$ or $A(-z, +\infty)$	(3) $A(z, +\infty)$ or $A(-\infty, -z)$	(4) $f(z)$ or $f(-z)$
0.80	0.2881	0.7881	0.2119	0.2897
0.81	0.2910	0.7910	0.2090	0.2874
0.82	0.2939	0.7939	0.2061	0.2850
0.83	0.2967	0.7967	0.2033	0.2827
0.84	0.2995	0.7995	0.2005	0.2803
0.85	0.3023	0.8023	0.1977	0.2780
0.86	0.3051	0.8051	0.1949	0.2756
0.87	0.3078	0.8078	0.1922	0.2732
0.88	0.3106	0.8106	0.1894	0.2709
0.89	0.3133	0.8133	0.1867	0.2685
0.90	0.3159	0.8159	0.1841	0.2661
0.91	0.3186	0.8186	0.1814	0.2637
0.92	0.3212	0.8212	0.1788	0.2613
0.93	0.3238	0.8238	0.1762	0.2589
0.94	0.3264	0.8264	0.1736	0.2565
0.95	0.3289	0.8289	0.1711	0.2541
0.96	0.3315	0.8315	0.1685	0.2516
0.97	0.3340	0.8340	0.1660	0.2492
0.98	0.3365	0.8365	0.1635	0.2468
0.99	0.3389	0.8389	0.1611	0.2444
1.00	0.3413	0.8413	0.1587	0.2420
1.01	0.3438	0.8438	0.1562	0.2396
1.02	0.3461	0.8461	0.1539	0.2371
1.03	0.3485	0.8485	0.1515	0.2347
1.04	0.3508	0.8508	0.1492	0.2323
1.05	0.3531	0.8531	0.1469	0.2299
1.06	0.3554	0.8554	0.1446	0.2275
1.07	0.3577	0.8577	0.1423	0.2251
1.08	0.3599	0.8599	0.1401	0.2227
1.09	0.3621	0.8621	0.1379	0.2203
1.10	0.3643	0.8643	0.1357	0.2179
1.11	0.3665	0.8665	0.1335	0.2155
1.12	0.3686	0.8686	0.1314	0.2131
1.13	0.3708	0.8708	0.1292	0.2107
1.14	0.3729	0.8729	0.1271	0.2083
1.15	0.3749	0.8749	0.1251	0.2059
1.16	0.3770	0.8770	0.1230	0.2036
1.17	0.3790	0.8790	0.1210	0.2012
1.18	0.3810	0.8810	0.1190	0.1989
1.19	0.3830	0.8830	0.1170	0.1965

Table A-4 *Continued*

z	(1) $A(0, z)$ or $A(-z, 0)$	(2) $A(-\infty, z)$ or $A(-z, +\infty)$	(3) $A(z, +\infty)$ or $A(-\infty, -z)$	(4) $f(z)$ or $f(-z)$
1.20	0.3849	0.8849	0.1151	0.1942
1.21	0.3869	0.8869	0.1131	0.1919
1.22	0.3888	0.8888	0.1112	0.1895
1.23	0.3907	0.8907	0.1093	0.1872
1.24	0.3925	0.8925	0.1075	0.1849
1.25	0.3944	0.8944	0.1056	0.1826
1.26	0.3962	0.8962	0.1038	0.1804
1.27	0.3980	0.8980	0.1020	0.1781
1.28	0.3997	0.8997	0.1003	0.1758
1.29	0.4015	0.9015	0.0985	0.1736
1.30	0.4032	0.9032	0.0968	0.1714
1.31	0.4049	0.9049	0.0951	0.1691
1.32	0.4066	0.9066	0.0934	0.1669
1.33	0.4082	0.9082	0.0918	0.1647
1.34	0.4099	0.9099	0.0901	0.1626
1.35	0.4115	0.9115	0.0885	0.1604
1.36	0.4131	0.9131	0.0869	0.1582
1.37	0.4147	0.9147	0.0853	0.1561
1.38	0.4162	0.9162	0.0838	0.1539
1.39	0.4177	0.9177	0.0823	0.1518
1.40	0.4192	0.9192	0.0808	0.1497
1.41	0.4207	0.9207	0.0793	0.1476
1.42	0.4222	0.9222	0.0778	0.1456
1.43	0.4236	0.9236	0.0764	0.1435
1.44	0.4251	0.9251	0.0749	0.1415
1.45	0.4265	0.9265	0.0735	0.1394
1.46	0.4279	0.9279	0.0721	0.1374
1.47	0.4292	0.9292	0.0708	0.1354
1.48	0.4306	0.9306	0.0694	0.1334
1.49	0.4319	0.9319	0.0681	0.1315
1.50	0.4332	0.9332	0.0668	0.1295
1.51	0.4345	0.9345	0.0655	0.1276
1.52	0.4357	0.9357	0.0643	0.1257
1.53	0.4370	0.9370	0.0630	0.1238
1.54	0.4382	0.9382	0.0618	0.1219
1.55	0.4394	0.9394	0.0606	0.1200
1.56	0.4406	0.9406	0.0594	0.1182
1.57	0.4418	0.9418	0.0582	0.1163
1.58	0.4429	0.9429	0.0571	0.1145
1.59	0.4441	0.9441	0.0559	0.1127

Table A-4 *Continued*

z	(1) $A(0, z)$ or $A(-z, 0)$	(2) $A(-\infty, z)$ or $A(-z, +\infty)$	(3) $A(z, +\infty)$ or $A(-\infty, -z)$	(4) $f(z)$ or $f(-z)$
1.60	0.4452	0.9452	0.0548	0.1109
1.61	0.4463	0.9463	0.0537	0.1092
1.62	0.4474	0.9474	0.0526	0.1074
1.63	0.4484	0.9484	0.0516	0.1057
1.64	0.4495	0.9495	0.0505	0.1040
1.65	0.4505	0.9505	0.0495	0.1023
1.66	0.4515	0.9515	0.0485	0.1006
1.67	0.4525	0.9525	0.0475	0.0989
1.68	0.4535	0.9535	0.0465	0.0973
1.69	0.4545	0.9545	0.0455	0.0957
1.70	0.4554	0.9554	0.0446	0.0940
1.71	0.4564	0.9564	0.0436	0.0925
1.72	0.4573	0.9573	0.0427	0.0909
1.73	0.4582	0.9582	0.0418	0.0893
1.74	0.4591	0.9591	0.0409	0.0878
1.75	0.4599	0.9599	0.0401	0.0863
1.76	0.4608	0.9608	0.0392	0.0848
1.77	0.4616	0.9616	0.0384	0.0833
1.78	0.4625	0.9625	0.0375	0.0818
1.79	0.4633	0.9633	0.0367	0.0804
1.80	0.4641	0.9641	0.0359	0.0790
1.81	0.4649	0.9649	0.0351	0.0775
1.82	0.4656	0.9656	0.0344	0.0761
1.83	0.4664	0.9664	0.0336	0.0748
1.84	0.4671	0.9671	0.0329	0.0734
1.85	0.4678	0.9678	0.0322	0.0721
1.86	0.4686	0.9686	0.0314	0.0707
1.87	0.4693	0.9693	0.0307	0.0694
1.88	0.4699	0.9699	0.0301	0.0681
1.89	0.4706	0.9706	0.0294	0.0669
1.90	0.4713	0.9713	0.0287	0.0656
1.91	0.4719	0.9719	0.0281	0.0644
1.92	0.4726	0.9726	0.0274	0.0632
1.93	0.4732	0.9732	0.0268	0.0620
1.94	0.4738	0.9738	0.0262	0.0608
1.95	0.4744	0.9744	0.0256	0.0596
1.96	0.4750	0.9750	0.0250	0.0584
1.97	0.4756	0.9756	0.0244	0.0573
1.98	0.4761	0.9761	0.0239	0.0562
1.99	0.4767	0.9767	0.0233	0.0551

Table A-4 *Continued*

z	(1) $A(0, z)$ or $A(-z, 0)$	(2) $A(-\infty, z)$ or $A(-z, +\infty)$	(3) $A(z, +\infty)$ or $A(-\infty, -z)$	(4) $f(z)$ or $f(-z)$
2.00	0.4772	0.9772	0.0228	0.0540
2.01	0.4778	0.9778	0.0222	0.0529
2.02	0.4783	0.9783	0.0217	0.0519
2.03	0.4788	0.9788	0.0212	0.0508
2.04	0.4793	0.9793	0.0207	0.0498
2.05	0.4798	0.9798	0.0202	0.0488
2.06	0.4803	0.9803	0.0197	0.0478
2.07	0.4808	0.9808	0.0192	0.0468
2.08	0.4812	0.9812	0.0188	0.0459
2.09	0.4817	0.9817	0.0183	0.0449
2.10	0.4821	0.9821	0.0179	0.0440
2.11	0.4826	0.9826	0.0174	0.0431
2.12	0.4830	0.9830	0.0170	0.0422
2.13	0.4834	0.9834	0.0166	0.0413
2.14	0.4838	0.9838	0.0162	0.0404
2.15	0.4842	0.9842	0.0158	0.0396
2.16	0.4846	0.9846	0.0154	0.0387
2.17	0.4850	0.9850	0.0150	0.0379
2.18	0.4854	0.9854	0.0146	0.0371
2.19	0.4857	0.9857	0.0143	0.0363
2.20	0.4861	0.9861	0.0139	0.0355
2.21	0.4864	0.9864	0.0136	0.0347
2.22	0.4868	0.9868	0.0132	0.0339
2.23	0.4871	0.9871	0.0129	0.0332
2.24	0.4875	0.9875	0.0125	0.0325
2.25	0.4878	0.9878	0.0122	0.0317
2.26	0.4881	0.9881	0.0119	0.0310
2.27	0.4884	0.9884	0.0116	0.0303
2.28	0.4887	0.9887	0.0113	0.0297
2.29	0.4890	0.9890	0.0110	0.0290
2.30	0.4893	0.9893	0.0107	0.0283
2.31	0.4896	0.9896	0.0104	0.0277
2.32	0.4898	0.9898	0.0102	0.0270
2.33	0.4901	0.9901	0.0099	0.0264
2.34	0.4904	0.9904	0.0096	0.0258
2.35	0.4906	0.9906	0.0094	0.0252
2.36	0.4909	0.9909	0.0091	0.0246
2.37	0.4911	0.9911	0.0089	0.0241
2.38	0.4913	0.9913	0.0087	0.0235
2.39	0.4916	0.9916	0.0084	0.0229

Table A-4 *Continued*

z	(1) $A(0, z)$ or $A(-z, 0)$	(2) $A(-\infty, z)$ or $A(-z, +\infty)$	(3) $A(z, +\infty)$ or $A(-\infty, -z)$	(4) $f(z)$ or $f(-z)$
2.40	0.4918	0.9918	0.0082	0.0224
2.41	0.4920	0.9920	0.0080	0.0219
2.42	0.4922	0.9922	0.0078	0.0213
2.43	0.4925	0.9925	0.0075	0.0208
2.44	0.4927	0.9927	0.0073	0.0203
2.45	0.4929	0.9929	0.0071	0.0198
2.46	0.4931	0.9931	0.0069	0.0194
2.47	0.4932	0.9932	0.0068	0.0189
2.48	0.4934	0.9934	0.0066	0.0184
2.49	0.4936	0.9936	0.0064	0.0180
2.50	0.4938	0.9938	0.0062	0.0175
2.51	0.4940	0.9940	0.0060	0.0171
2.52	0.4941	0.9941	0.0059	0.0167
2.53	0.4943	0.9943	0.0057	0.0163
2.54	0.4945	0.9945	0.0055	0.0158
2.55	0.4946	0.9946	0.0054	0.0154
2.56	0.4948	0.9948	0.0052	0.0151
2.57	0.4949	0.9949	0.0051	0.0147
2.58	0.4951	0.9951	0.0049	0.0143
2.59	0.4952	0.9952	0.0048	0.0139
2.60	0.4953	0.9953	0.0047	0.0136
2.61	0.4955	0.9955	0.0045	0.0132
2.62	0.4956	0.9956	0.0044	0.0129
2.63	0.4957	0.9957	0.0043	0.0126
2.64	0.4959	0.9959	0.0041	0.0122
2.65	0.4960	0.9960	0.0040	0.0119
2.66	0.4961	0.9961	0.0039	0.0116
2.67	0.4962	0.9962	0.0038	0.0113
2.68	0.4963	0.9963	0.0037	0.0110
2.69	0.4964	0.9964	0.0036	0.0107
2.70	0.4965	0.9965	0.0035	0.0104
2.71	0.4966	0.9966	0.0034	0.0101
2.72	0.4967	0.9967	0.0033	0.0099
2.73	0.4968	0.9968	0.0032	0.0096
2.74	0.4969	0.9969	0.0031	0.0093
2.75	0.4970	0.9970	0.0030	0.0091
2.76	0.4971	0.9971	0.0029	0.0088
2.77	0.4972	0.9972	0.0028	0.0086
2.78	0.4973	0.9973	0.0027	0.0084
2.79	0.4974	0.9974	0.0026	0.0081

Table A-4 *Continued*

z	(1) $A(0, z)$ or $A(-z, 0)$	(2) $A(-\infty, z)$ or $A(-z, +\infty)$	(3) $A(z, +\infty)$ or $A(-\infty, -z)$	(4) $f(z)$ or $f(-z)$
2.80	0.4974	0.9974	0.0026	0.0079
2.81	0.4975	0.9975	0.0025	0.0077
2.82	0.4976	0.9976	0.0024	0.0075
2.83	0.4977	0.9977	0.0023	0.0073
2.84	0.4977	0.9977	0.0023	0.0071
2.85	0.4978	0.9978	0.0022	0.0069
2.86	0.4979	0.9979	0.0021	0.0067
2.87	0.4979	0.9979	0.0021	0.0065
2.88	0.4980	0.9980	0.0020	0.0063
2.89	0.4981	0.9981	0.0019	0.0061
2.90	0.4981	0.9981	0.0019	0.0060
2.91	0.4982	0.9982	0.0018	0.0058
2.92	0.4982	0.9982	0.0018	0.0056
2.93	0.4983	0.9983	0.0017	0.0055
2.94	0.4984	0.9984	0.0016	0.0053
2.95	0.4984	0.9984	0.0016	0.0051
2.96	0.4985	0.9985	0.0015	0.0050
2.97	0.4985	0.9985	0.0015	0.0048
2.98	0.4986	0.9986	0.0014	0.0047
2.99	0.4986	0.9986	0.0014	0.0046
3.00	0.4987	0.9987	0.0013	0.0044
3.01	0.4987	0.9987	0.0013	0.0043
3.02	0.4987	0.9987	0.0013	0.0042
3.03	0.4988	0.9988	0.0012	0.0040
3.04	0.4988	0.9988	0.0012	0.0039
3.05	0.4989	0.9989	0.0011	0.0038
3.06	0.4989	0.9989	0.0011	0.0037
3.07	0.4989	0.9989	0.0011	0.0036
3.08	0.4990	0.9990	0.0010	0.0035
3.09	0.4990	0.9990	0.0010	0.0034
3.10	0.4990	0.9990	0.0010	0.0033
3.11	0.4991	0.9991	0.0009	0.0032
3.12	0.4991	0.9991	0.0009	0.0031
3.13	0.4991	0.9991	0.0009	0.0030
3.14	0.4992	0.9992	0.0008	0.0029

Table A-5 Critical Values of t

	Level of Significance for One-Tailed Test						
	0.10	0.05	0.025	0.01	0.005	0.001	0.0005
	Level of Significance for Two-Tailed Test						
df	0.20	0.10	0.05	0.02	0.01	0.002	0.001
1	3.078	6.314	12.706	31.821	63.657	318.31	636.62
2	1.886	2.920	4.303	6.965	9.925	22.326	31.598
3	1.638	2.353	3.182	4.541	5.841	10.213	12.924
4	1.533	2.132	2.776	3.747	4.604	7.173	8.610
5	1.476	2.015	2.571	3.365	4.032	5.893	6.869
6	1.440	1.943	2.447	3.143	3.707	5.208	5.959
7	1.415	1.895	2.365	2.998	3.499	4.785	5.408
8	1.397	1.860	2.306	2.896	3.355	4.501	5.041
9	1.383	1.833	2.262	2.821	3.250	4.297	4.781
10	1.372	1.812	2.228	2.764	3.169	4.144	4.587
11	1.363	1.796	2.201	2.718	3.106	4.025	4.437
12	1.356	1.782	2.179	2.681	3.055	3.930	4.318
13	1.350	1.771	2.160	2.650	3.012	3.852	4.221
14	1.345	1.761	2.145	2.624	2.977	3.787	4.140
15	1.341	1.753	2.131	2.602	2.947	3.733	4.073
16	1.337	1.746	2.120	2.583	2.921	3.686	4.015
17	1.333	1.740	2.110	2.567	2.898	3.646	3.965
18	1.330	1.734	2.101	2.552	2.878	3.610	3.922
19	1.328	1.729	2.093	2.539	2.861	3.579	3.883
20	1.325	1.725	2.086	2.528	2.845	3.552	3.850
21	1.323	1.721	2.080	2.518	2.831	3.527	3.819
22	1.321	1.717	2.074	2.508	2.819	3.505	3.792
23	1.319	1.714	2.069	2.500	2.807	3.485	3.767
24	1.318	1.711	2.064	2.492	2.797	3.467	3.745
25	1.316	1.708	2.060	2.485	2.787	3.450	3.725
26	1.315	1.706	2.056	2.479	2.779	3.435	3.707
27	1.314	1.703	2.052	2.473	2.771	3.421	3.690
28	1.313	1.701	2.048	2.467	2.763	3.408	3.674
29	1.311	1.699	2.045	2.462	2.756	3.396	3.659
30	1.310	1.697	2.042	2.457	2.750	3.385	3.646
40	1.303	1.684	2.021	2.423	2.704	3.307	3.551
60	1.296	1.671	2.000	2.390	2.660	3.232	3.460
120	1.289	1.658	1.980	2.358	2.617	3.160	3.373
∞	1.282	1.645	1.960	2.326	2.576	3.090	3.291

Table A-6 Critical Values of F

df for denominator	α	1	2	3	4	5	6	7	8	9	10	12	15	20	24	30	40	60	∞	df for denominator
3	.05	10.1	9.55	9.28	9.12	9.01	8.94	8.89	8.85	8.81	8.79	8.74	8.70	8.66	8.64	8.62	8.59	8.57	8.53	3
	.01	34.1	30.8	29.5	28.7	28.2	27.9	27.7	27.5	27.3	27.2	27.1	26.9	26.7	26.6	26.5	26.4	26.3	26.1	
	.001	167	148	141	137	135	133	132	131	130	129	128	127	126	126	125	125	124	123	
4	.05	7.71	6.94	6.59	6.39	6.26	6.16	6.09	6.04	6.00	5.96	5.91	5.86	5.80	5.77	5.75	5.72	5.69	5.63	4
	.01	21.2	18.0	16.7	16.0	15.5	15.2	15.0	14.8	14.7	14.5	14.4	14.2	14.0	13.9	13.8	13.7	13.7	13.5	
	.001	74.1	61.2	56.2	53.4	51.7	50.5	49.7	49.0	48.5	48.1	47.4	46.8	46.1	45.8	45.4	45.1	44.7	44.1	
5	.05	6.61	5.79	5.41	5.19	5.05	4.95	4.88	4.82	4.77	4.74	4.68	4.62	4.56	4.53	4.50	4.46	4.43	4.36	5
	.01	16.3	13.3	12.1	11.4	11.0	10.7	10.5	10.3	10.2	10.1	9.89	9.72	9.55	9.47	9.38	9.29	9.20	9.02	
	.001	47.2	37.1	33.2	31.1	29.8	28.8	28.2	27.6	27.2	26.9	26.4	25.9	25.4	25.1	24.9	24.6	24.3	23.8	
6	.05	5.99	5.14	4.76	4.53	4.39	4.28	4.21	4.15	4.10	4.06	4.00	3.94	3.87	3.84	3.81	3.77	3.74	3.67	6
	.01	13.7	10.9	9.78	9.15	8.75	8.47	8.26	8.10	7.98	7.87	7.72	7.56	7.40	7.31	7.23	7.14	7.06	6.88	
	.001	35.5	27.0	23.7	21.9	20.8	20.0	19.5	19.0	18.7	18.4	18.0	17.6	17.1	16.9	16.7	16.4	16.2	15.7	
7	.05	5.59	4.74	4.35	4.12	3.97	3.87	3.79	3.73	3.68	3.64	3.57	3.51	3.44	3.41	3.38	3.34	3.30	3.23	7
	.01	12.2	9.55	8.45	7.85	7.46	7.19	6.99	6.84	6.72	6.62	6.47	6.31	6.16	6.07	5.99	5.91	5.82	5.65	
	.001	29.2	21.7	18.8	17.2	16.2	15.5	15.0	14.6	14.3	14.1	13.7	13.3	12.9	12.7	12.5	12.3	12.1	11.7	
8	.05	5.32	4.46	4.07	3.84	3.69	3.58	3.50	3.44	3.39	3.35	3.28	3.22	3.15	3.12	3.08	3.04	3.01	2.93	8
	.01	11.3	8.65	7.59	7.01	6.63	6.37	6.18	6.03	5.91	5.81	5.67	5.52	5.36	5.28	5.20	5.12	5.03	4.86	
	.001	25.4	18.5	15.8	14.4	13.5	12.9	12.4	12.0	11.8	11.5	11.2	10.8	10.5	10.3	10.1	9.92	9.73	9.33	
9	.05	5.12	4.26	3.86	3.63	3.48	3.37	3.29	3.23	3.18	3.14	3.07	3.01	2.94	2.90	2.86	2.83	2.79	2.71	9
	.01	10.6	8.02	6.99	6.42	6.06	5.80	5.61	5.47	5.35	5.26	5.11	4.96	4.81	4.73	4.65	4.57	4.48	4.31	
	.001	22.9	16.4	13.9	12.6	11.7	11.1	10.7	10.4	10.1	9.89	9.57	9.24	8.90	8.72	8.55	8.37	8.19	7.81	

The first F ratio is the critical value for $\alpha = .05$, the second for $\alpha = .01$, the third for $\alpha = .001$.

Table A-6 *Continued*

df for denominator	α	1	2	3	4	5	6	7	8	9	10	12	15	20	24	30	40	60	∞	df for denominator
10	.05	4.96	4.10	3.71	3.48	3.33	3.22	3.14	3.07	3.02	2.98	2.91	2.85	2.77	2.74	2.70	2.66	2.62	2.54	10
	.01	10.0	7.56	6.55	5.99	5.64	5.39	5.20	5.06	4.94	4.85	4.71	4.56	4.41	4.33	4.25	4.17	4.08	3.91	
	.001	21.0	14.9	12.6	11.3	10.5	9.93	9.52	9.20	8.96	8.75	8.45	8.13	7.80	7.64	7.47	7.30	7.12	6.76	
11	.05	4.84	3.98	3.59	3.36	3.20	3.09	3.01	2.95	2.90	2.85	2.79	2.72	2.65	2.61	2.57	2.53	2.49	2.40	11
	.01	9.65	7.21	6.22	5.67	5.32	5.07	4.89	4.74	4.63	4.54	4.40	4.25	4.10	4.02	3.94	3.86	3.78	3.60	
	.001	19.7	13.8	11.6	10.3	9.58	9.05	8.66	8.35	8.12	7.92	7.63	7.32	7.01	6.85	6.68	6.52	6.35	6.00	
12	.05	4.75	3.89	3.49	3.26	3.11	3.00	2.91	2.85	2.80	2.75	2.69	2.62	2.54	2.51	2.47	2.43	2.38	2.30	12
	.01	9.33	6.93	5.95	5.41	5.06	4.82	4.64	4.50	4.39	4.30	4.16	4.01	3.86	3.78	3.70	3.62	3.54	3.36	
	.001	18.6	13.0	10.8	9.63	8.89	8.38	8.00	7.71	7.48	7.29	7.00	6.71	6.40	6.25	6.09	5.93	5.76	5.42	
13	.05	4.67	3.81	3.41	3.18	3.03	2.92	2.83	2.77	2.71	2.67	2.60	2.53	2.46	2.42	2.38	2.34	2.30	2.21	13
	.01	9.07	6.70	5.74	5.21	4.86	4.62	4.44	4.30	4.19	4.10	3.96	3.82	3.66	3.59	3.51	3.43	3.34	3.17	
	.001	17.8	12.3	10.2	9.07	8.35	7.86	7.49	7.21	6.98	6.80	6.52	6.23	5.93	5.78	5.63	5.47	5.30	4.97	
14	.05	4.60	3.74	3.34	3.11	2.96	2.85	2.76	2.70	2.65	2.60	2.53	2.46	2.39	2.35	2.31	2.27	2.22	2.13	14
	.01	8.86	6.51	5.56	5.04	4.70	4.46	4.28	4.14	4.03	3.94	3.80	3.66	3.51	3.43	3.35	3.27	3.18	3.00	
	.001	17.1	11.8	9.73	8.62	7.92	7.44	7.08	6.80	6.58	6.40	6.13	5.85	5.56	5.41	5.25	5.10	4.94	4.60	
15	.05	4.54	3.68	3.29	3.06	2.90	2.79	2.71	2.64	2.59	2.54	2.48	2.40	2.33	2.29	2.25	2.20	2.16	2.07	15
	.01	8.68	6.36	5.42	4.89	4.56	4.32	4.14	4.00	3.89	3.80	3.67	3.52	3.37	3.29	3.21	3.13	3.05	2.87	
	.001	16.6	11.3	9.34	8.25	7.57	7.09	6.74	6.47	6.26	6.08	5.81	5.54	5.25	5.10	4.95	4.80	4.64	4.31	
16	.05	4.49	3.63	3.24	3.01	2.85	2.74	2.66	2.59	2.54	2.49	2.42	2.35	2.28	2.24	2.19	2.15	2.11	2.01	16
	.01	8.53	6.23	5.29	4.77	4.44	4.20	4.03	3.89	3.78	3.69	3.55	3.41	3.26	3.18	3.10	3.02	2.93	2.75	
	.001	16.1	11.0	9.01	7.94	7.27	6.80	6.46	62.0	5.98	5.81	5.55	5.27	4.99	4.85	4.70	4.54	4.39	4.06	
17	.05	4.45	3.59	3.20	2.96	2.81	2.70	2.61	2.55	2.49	2.45	2.38	2.31	2.23	2.19	2.15	2.10	2.06	1.96	17
	.01	8.40	6.11	5.18	4.67	4.34	4.10	3.93	3.79	3.68	3.59	3.46	3.31	3.16	3.08	3.00	2.92	2.83	2.65	
	.001	15.7	10.7	8.73	7.68	7.02	6.56	6.22	5.96	5.75	5.58	5.32	5.05	4.78	4.63	4.48	4.33	4.18	3.85	
18	.05	4.41	3.55	3.16	2.93	2.77	2.66	2.58	2.51	2.46	2.41	2.34	2.27	2.19	2.15	2.11	2.06	2.02	1.92	18
	.01	8.29	6.01	5.09	4.58	4.25	4.01	3.84	3.71	3.60	3.51	3.37	3.23	3.08	3.00	2.92	2.84	2.75	2.57	
	.001	15.4	10.4	8.49	7.46	6.81	6.35	6.02	5.76	5.56	5.39	5.13	4.87	4.59	4.45	4.30	4.15	4.00	3.67	

(Columns 1–∞ are df for numerator.)

df for denominator	α	df for numerator																		df for denominator
		1	2	3	4	5	6	7	8	9	10	12	15	20	24	30	40	60	∞	
19	.05	4.38	3.52	3.13	2.90	2.74	2.63	2.54	2.48	2.42	2.38	2.31	2.23	2.16	2.11	2.07	2.03	1.98	1.88	19
	.01	8.18	5.93	5.01	4.50	4.17	3.94	3.77	3.63	3.52	3.43	3.30	3.15	3.00	2.92	2.84	2.76	2.67	2.49	
	.001	15.1	10.2	8.28	7.27	6.62	6.18	5.85	5.59	5.39	5.22	4.97	4.70	4.43	4.29	4.14	3.99	3.84	3.51	
20	.05	4.35	3.49	3.10	2.87	2.71	2.60	2.51	2.45	2.39	2.35	2.28	2.20	2.12	2.08	2.04	1.99	1.95	1.84	20
	.01	8.10	5.85	4.94	4.43	4.10	3.87	3.70	3.56	3.46	3.37	3.23	3.09	2.94	2.86	2.78	2.69	2.61	2.42	
	.001	14.8	9.95	8.10	7.10	6.46	6.02	5.69	5.44	5.24	5.08	4.82	4.56	4.29	4.15	4.00	3.86	3.70	3.38	
21	.05	4.32	3.47	3.07	2.84	2.68	2.57	2.49	2.42	2.37	2.32	2.25	2.18	2.10	2.05	2.01	1.96	1.92	1.81	21
	.01	8.02	5.78	4.87	4.37	4.04	3.81	3.64	3.51	3.40	3.31	3.17	3.03	2.88	2.80	2.72	2.64	2.55	2.36	
	.001	14.6	9.77	7.94	6.95	6.32	5.88	5.56	5.31	5.11	4.95	4.70	4.44	4.17	4.03	3.88	3.74	3.58	3.26	
22	.05	4.30	3.44	3.05	2.82	2.66	2.55	2.46	2.40	2.34	2.30	2.23	2.15	2.07	2.03	1.98	1.94	1.89	1.78	22
	.01	7.95	5.72	4.82	4.31	3.99	3.76	3.59	3.45	3.35	3.26	3.12	2.98	2.83	2.75	2.67	2.58	2.50	2.31	
	.001	14.4	9.61	7.80	6.81	6.19	5.76	5.44	5.19	4.99	4.83	4.58	4.33	4.06	3.92	3.78	3.63	3.48	3.15	
23	.05	4.28	3.42	3.03	2.80	2.64	2.53	2.44	2.37	2.32	2.27	2.20	2.13	2.05	2.01	1.96	1.91	1.86	1.76	23
	.01	7.88	5.66	4.76	4.26	3.94	3.71	3.54	3.41	3.30	3.21	3.07	2.93	2.78	2.70	2.62	2.54	2.45	2.26	
	.001	14.2	9.47	7.67	6.70	6.08	5.65	5.33	5.09	4.89	4.73	4.48	4.23	3.96	3.82	3.68	3.53	3.38	3.05	
24	.05	4.26	3.40	3.01	2.78	2.62	2.51	2.42	2.36	2.30	2.25	2.18	2.11	2.03	1.98	1.94	1.89	1.84	1.73	24
	.01	7.82	5.61	4.72	4.22	3.90	3.67	3.50	3.36	3.26	3.17	3.03	2.89	2.74	2.66	2.58	2.49	2.40	2.21	
	.001	14.0	9.34	7.55	6.59	5.98	5.55	5.23	4.99	4.80	4.64	4.39	4.14	3.87	3.74	3.59	3.45	3.29	2.97	
25	.05	4.24	3.39	2.99	2.76	2.60	2.49	2.40	2.34	2.28	2.24	2.16	2.09	2.01	1.96	1.92	1.87	1.82	1.71	25
	.01	7.77	5.57	4.68	4.18	3.86	3.63	3.46	3.32	3.22	3.13	2.99	2.85	2.70	2.62	2.54	2.45	2.36	2.17	
	.001	13.9	9.22	7.45	6.49	5.89	5.46	5.15	4.91	4.71	4.56	4.31	4.06	3.79	3.66	3.52	3.37	3.22	2.89	
26	.05	4.23	3.37	2.98	2.74	2.59	2.47	2.39	2.32	2.27	2.22	2.15	2.07	1.99	1.95	1.90	1.85	1.80	1.69	26
	.01	7.72	5.53	4.64	4.14	3.82	3.59	3.42	3.29	3.18	3.09	2.96	2.82	2.66	2.58	2.50	2.42	2.33	2.13	
	.001	13.7	9.12	7.36	6.41	5.80	5.38	5.07	4.83	4.64	4.48	4.24	3.99	3.72	3.59	3.44	3.30	3.15	2.82	

Table A-6 *Continued*

df for denominator	α	df for numerator 1	2	3	4	5	6	7	8	9	10	12	15	20	24	30	40	60	∞	df for denominator
27	.05	4.21	3.35	2.96	2.73	2.57	2.46	2.37	2.31	2.25	2.20	2.13	2.06	1.97	1.93	1.88	1.84	1.79	1.67	**27**
	.01	7.68	5.49	4.60	4.11	3.78	3.56	3.39	3.26	3.15	3.06	2.93	2.78	2.63	2.55	2.47	2.38	2.29	2.10	
	.001	13.6	9.02	7.27	6.33	5.73	5.31	5.00	4.76	4.57	4.41	4.17	3.92	3.66	3.52	3.38	3.23	3.08	2.75	
28	.05	4.20	3.34	2.95	2.71	2.56	2.45	2.36	2.29	2.24	2.19	2.12	2.04	1.96	1.91	1.87	1.82	1.77	1.65	**28**
	.01	7.64	5.45	4.57	4.07	3.75	3.53	3.36	3.23	3.12	3.03	2.90	2.75	2.60	2.52	2.44	2.35	2.26	2.06	
	.001	13.5	8.93	7.19	6.25	5.66	5.24	4.93	4.69	4.50	4.35	4.11	3.86	3.60	3.46	3.32	3.18	3.02	2.69	
29	.05	4.18	3.33	2.93	2.70	2.55	2.43	2.35	2.28	2.22	2.18	2.10	2.03	1.94	1.90	1.85	1.81	1.75	1.64	**29**
	.01	7.60	5.42	4.54	4.04	3.73	3.50	3.33	3.20	3.09	3.00	2.87	2.73	2.57	2.49	2.41	2.33	2.23	2.03	
	.001	13.4	8.85	7.12	6.19	5.59	5.18	4.87	4.64	4.45	4.29	4.05	3.80	3.54	3.41	3.27	3.12	2.97	2.64	
30	.05	4.17	3.32	2.92	2.69	2.53	2.42	2.33	2.27	2.21	2.16	2.09	2.01	1.93	1.89	1.84	1.79	1.74	1.62	**30**
	.01	7.56	5.39	4.51	4.02	3.70	3.47	3.30	3.17	3.07	2.98	2.84	2.70	2.55	2.47	2.39	2.30	2.21	2.01	
	.001	13.3	8.77	7.05	6.12	5.53	5.12	4.82	4.58	4.39	4.24	4.00	3.75	3.49	3.36	3.22	3.07	2.92	2.59	
40	.05	4.08	3.23	2.84	2.61	2.45	2.34	2.25	2.18	2.12	2.08	2.00	1.92	1.84	1.79	1.74	1.69	1.64	1.51	**40**
	.01	7.31	5.18	4.31	3.83	3.51	3.29	3.12	2.99	2.89	2.80	2.66	2.52	2.37	2.29	2.20	2.11	2.02	1.80	
	.001	12.6	8.25	6.59	5.70	5.13	4.74	4.44	4.21	4.02	3.87	3.64	3.40	3.15	3.01	2.87	2.73	2.57	2.23	
60	.05	4.00	3.15	2.76	2.53	2.37	2.25	2.18	2.10	2.04	1.99	1.92	1.84	1.75	1.70	1.65	1.59	1.53	1.39	**60**
	.01	7.08	4.98	4.13	3.65	3.34	3.12	2.95	2.82	2.72	2.63	2.50	2.35	2.20	2.12	2.03	1.94	1.84	1.60	
	.001	12.0	7.76	6.17	5.31	4.76	4.37	4.09	3.86	3.69	3.54	3.32	3.08	2.83	2.69	2.55	2.41	2.25	1.89	
120	.05	3.92	3.07	2.68	2.45	2.29	2.18	2.09	2.02	1.96	1.91	1.83	1.75	1.66	1.61	1.55	1.50	1.43	1.25	**120**
	.01	6.85	4.79	3.95	3.48	3.17	2.96	2.79	2.66	2.56	2.47	2.34	2.19	2.03	1.95	1.86	1.76	1.66	1.38	
	.001	11.4	7.32	5.78	4.95	4.42	4.04	3.77	3.55	3.38	3.24	3.02	2.78	2.53	2.40	2.26	2.11	1.95	1.54	
∞	.05	3.84	3.00	2.60	2.37	2.21	2.10	2.01	1.94	1.88	1.83	1.75	1.67	1.57	1.52	1.46	1.39	1.32	1.00	∞
	.01	6.63	4.61	3.78	3.32	3.02	2.80	2.64	2.51	2.41	2.32	2.18	2.04	1.88	1.79	1.70	1.59	1.47	1.00	
	.001	10.8	6.91	5.42	4.62	4.10	3.74	3.47	3.27	3.10	2.96	2.74	2.51	2.27	2.13	1.99	1.84	1.66	1.00	

Table A-7 Critical Values of χ^2

	Level of Significance for One-Tailed Test					
	0.10	0.05	0.025	0.01	0.005	0.0005
	Level of Significance for Two-Tailed Test					
df	0.20	0.10	0.05	0.02	0.01	0.001
1	1.64	2.71	3.84	5.41	6.64	10.83
2	3.22	4.60	5.99	7.82	9.21	13.82
3	4.64	6.25	7.82	9.84	11.34	16.27
4	5.99	7.78	9.49	11.67	13.28	18.47
5	7.29	9.24	11.07	13.39	15.09	20.52
6	8.56	10.64	12.59	15.03	16.81	22.46
7	9.80	12.02	14.07	16.62	18.48	24.32
8	11.03	13.36	15.51	18.17	20.09	26.12
9	12.24	14.68	16.92	19.68	21.67	27.88
10	13.44	15.99	18.31	21.16	23.21	29.59
11	14.63	17.28	19.68	22.62	24.72	31.26
12	15.81	18.55	21.03	24.05	26.22	32.91
13	16.98	19.81	22.36	25.47	27.69	34.53
14	18.15	21.06	23.68	26.87	29.14	36.12
15	19.31	22.31	25.00	28.26	30.58	37.70
16	20.46	23.54	26.30	29.63	32.00	39.25
17	21.62	24.77	27.59	31.00	33.41	40.79
18	22.76	25.99	28.87	32.35	34.80	42.31
19	23.90	27.20	30.14	33.69	36.19	43.82
20	25.04	28.41	31.41	35.02	37.57	45.32
21	26.17	29.62	32.67	36.34	38.93	46.80
22	27.30	30.81	33.92	37.66	40.29	48.27
23	28.43	32.01	35.17	38.97	41.64	49.73
24	29.55	33.20	36.42	40.27	42.98	51.18
25	30.68	34.38	37.65	41.57	44.31	52.62
26	31.80	35.56	38.88	42.86	45.64	54.05
27	32.91	36.74	40.11	44.14	46.96	55.48
28	34.03	37.92	41.34	45.42	48.28	56.89
29	35.14	39.09	42.56	46.69	49.59	58.30
30	36.25	40.26	43.77	47.96	50.89	59.70
40	47.27	51.80	55.76	60.44	63.69	73.40
50	58.16	63.17	67.50	72.61	76.15	86.66
60	68.97	74.40	79.08	84.58	88.38	99.61
70	79.72	85.53	90.53	96.39	100.42	112.32

Table A-8 Critical Values of U for the Mann-Whitney Test for 0.05 (First Value) and 0.01 (Second Value) Significance Levels for Two-Tailed Test and for 0.025 and 0.005 Levels for One-Tailed Test[a]

N_1 / N_2	1	2	3	4	5	6	7	8	9	10	11	12	13	14	15	16	17	18	19	20
1	—	—	—	—	—	—	—	—	—	—	—	—	—	—	—	—	—	—	—	—
	—	—	—	—	—	—	—	—	—	—	—	—	—	—	—	—	—	—	—	—
2	—	—	—	—	—	—	—	0	0	0	0	1	1	1	1	1	2	2	2	2
	—	—	—	—	—	—	—	—	—	—	—	—	—	—	—	—	—	—	0	0
3	—	—	—	—	0	1	1	2	2	3	3	4	4	5	5	6	6	7	7	8
	—	—	—	—	—	—	—	—	0	0	0	1	1	1	2	2	2	2	3	3
4	—	—	—	0	1	2	3	4	4	5	6	7	8	9	10	11	11	12	13	14
	—	—	—	—	—	0	0	1	1	2	2	3	3	4	5	5	6	6	7	8
5	—	—	0	1	2	3	5	6	7	8	9	11	12	13	14	15	17	18	19	20
	—	—	—	—	0	1	1	2	3	4	5	6	7	7	8	9	10	11	12	13
6	—	—	1	2	3	5	6	8	10	11	13	14	16	17	19	21	22	24	25	27
	—	—	—	0	1	2	3	4	5	6	7	9	10	11	12	13	15	16	17	18
7	—	—	1	3	5	6	8	10	12	14	16	18	20	22	24	26	28	30	32	34
	—	—	—	0	1	3	4	6	7	9	10	12	13	15	16	18	19	21	22	24
8	—	0	2	4	6	8	10	13	15	17	19	22	24	26	29	31	34	36	38	41
	—	—	—	1	2	4	6	7	9	11	13	15	17	18	20	22	24	26	28	30
9	—	0	2	4	7	10	12	15	17	20	23	26	28	31	34	37	39	42	45	48
	—	—	0	1	3	5	7	9	11	13	16	18	20	22	24	27	29	31	33	36
10	—	0	3	5	8	11	14	17	20	23	26	29	33	36	39	42	45	48	52	55
	—	—	0	2	4	6	9	11	13	16	18	21	24	26	29	31	34	37	39	42
11	—	0	3	6	9	13	16	19	23	26	30	33	37	40	44	47	51	55	58	62
	—	—	0	2	5	7	10	13	16	18	21	24	27	30	33	36	39	42	45	48
12	—	1	4	7	11	14	18	22	26	29	33	37	41	45	49	53	57	61	65	69
	—	—	1	3	6	9	12	15	18	21	24	27	31	34	37	41	44	47	51	54
13	—	1	4	8	12	16	20	24	28	33	37	41	45	50	54	59	63	67	72	76
	—	—	1	3	7	10	13	17	20	24	27	31	34	38	42	45	49	53	57	60
14	—	1	5	9	13	17	22	26	31	36	40	45	50	55	59	64	69	74	78	83
	—	—	1	4	7	11	15	18	22	26	30	34	38	42	46	50	54	58	63	67
15	—	1	5	10	14	19	24	29	34	39	44	49	54	59	64	70	75	80	85	90
	—	—	2	5	8	12	16	20	24	29	33	37	42	46	51	55	60	64	69	73
16	—	1	6	11	15	21	26	31	37	42	47	53	59	64	70	75	81	86	92	98
	—	—	2	5	9	13	18	22	27	31	36	41	45	50	55	60	65	70	74	79
17	—	2	6	11	17	22	28	34	39	45	51	57	63	69	75	81	87	93	99	105
	—	—	2	6	10	15	19	24	29	34	39	44	49	54	60	65	70	75	81	86
18	—	2	7	12	18	24	30	36	42	48	55	61	67	74	80	86	93	99	106	112
	—	—	2	6	11	16	21	26	31	37	42	47	53	58	64	70	75	81	87	92
19	—	2	7	13	19	25	32	38	45	52	58	65	72	78	85	92	99	106	113	119
	—	0	3	7	12	17	22	28	33	39	45	51	57	63	69	74	81	87	93	99
20	—	2	8	14	20	27	34	41	48	55	62	69	76	83	90	98	105	112	119	127
	—	0	3	8	13	18	24	30	36	42	48	54	60	67	73	79	86	92	99	105

[a] U must be equal to or *less than* the stated value. Dashes indicate there is no value of U small enough for significance.

Table A-9 Critical Values of *r* for the Sign Test

	Level of Significance for One-Tailed Test						
	0.10	0.05	0.025	0.01	0.005	0.001	0.0005
	Level of Significance for Two-Tailed Test						
N	0.20	0.10	0.05	0.02	0.01	0.002	0.001
5	0	0	—	—	—	—	—
6	0	0	0	—	—	—	—
7	1	0	0	0	—	—	—
8	1	1	0	0	0	—	—
9	2	1	1	0	0	—	—
10	2	1	1	0	0	0	—
11	2	2	1	1	0	0	0
12	3	2	2	1	1	0	0
13	3	3	2	1	1	0	0
14	4	3	2	2	1	1	0
15	4	3	3	2	2	1	1
16	4	4	3	2	2	1	1
17	5	4	4	3	2	1	1
18	5	5	4	3	3	2	1
19	6	5	4	4	3	2	2
20	6	5	5	4	3	2	2
21	7	6	5	4	4	3	2
22	7	6	5	5	4	3	3
23	7	7	6	5	4	3	3
24	8	7	6	5	5	4	3
25	8	7	7	6	5	4	4
26	9	8	7	6	6	4	4
27	9	8	7	7	6	5	4
28	10	9	8	7	6	5	5
29	10	9	8	7	7	5	5
30	10	10	9	8	7	6	5
31	11	10	9	8	7	6	6
32	11	10	9	8	8	6	6
33	12	11	10	9	8	7	6
34	12	11	10	9	9	7	7
35	13	12	11	10	9	8	7

Dashes indicate there is no value of *r* small enough for significance

Table A-10 Critical Values of T for the Wilcoxon Signed Ranks Test

	Level of Significance for One-Tailed Test					Level of Significance for One-Tailed Test			
	0.05	0.025	0.01	0.005		0.05	0.025	0.01	0.005
	Level of Significance for Two-Tailed Test					Level of Significance for Two-Tailed Test			
N	0.10	0.05	0.02	0.01	N	0.10	0.05	0.02	0.01
5	0	—	—	—	**28**	130	116	101	91
6	2	0	—	—	**29**	140	126	110	100
7	3	2	0	—	**30**	151	137	120	109
8	5	3	1	0	**31**	163	147	130	118
9	8	5	3	1	**32**	175	159	140	128
10	10	8	5	3	**33**	187	170	151	138
11	13	10	7	5	**34**	200	182	162	148
12	17	13	9	7	**35**	213	195	173	159
13	21	17	12	9	**36**	227	208	185	171
14	25	21	15	12	**37**	241	221	198	182
15	30	25	19	15	**38**	256	235	211	194
16	35	29	23	19	**39**	271	249	224	207
17	41	34	27	23	**40**	286	264	238	220
18	47	40	32	27	**41**	302	279	252	233
19	53	46	37	32	**42**	319	294	266	247
20	60	52	43	37	**43**	336	310	281	261
21	67	58	49	42	**44**	353	327	296	276
22	75	65	55	48	**45**	371	343	312	291
23	83	73	62	54	**46**	389	361	328	307
24	91	81	69	61	**47**	407	378	345	322
25	100	89	76	68	**48**	426	396	362	339
26	110	98	84	75	**49**	446	415	379	355
27	119	107	92	83	**50**	466	434	397	373

Table A-11 Critical Values of χ_r^2 for the Friedman Test

N	$k = 3$		$k = 4$	
	$\alpha = 0.05$	$\alpha = 0.01$	$\alpha = 0.05$	$\alpha = 0.01$
2	—	—	6.000	—
3	6.000	—	7.400	9.000
4	6.500	8.000	7.800	9.600
5	6.400	8.400		
6	7.000	9.000		
7	7.143	8.857		
8	6.250	9.000		
9	6.222	8.667		

Appendix B
The Application of Signal Detection Theory to Recognition Memory

In a typical recognition memory experiment, a subject is shown a set of old items to learn, in the study phase of the experiment, and then is shown the same set of old items along with some new or distractor items, in the test phase of the experiment. Items may be presented singly, in which case the subject's task may be simply to classify a particular item as old or new, in the yes/no procedure, or may be asked to rate his or her degree of certainty about whether an item is old or new, in the rating scale procedure. Alternatively, an old item may be presented with one or more new items, and the subject's task is to decide which among the items presented on a trial is the old item in a forced choice procedure.

Here we consider how signal detection theory and methodology may be applied to the single item presentation in which the subject either makes a yes/no decision ("Yes, it's old," or "No, it's not") or rates his or her degree of confidence about the oldness or newness of the item.

The signal detection model for recognition memory proposes that items presented for testing in a recognition memory task lie along a continuum of familiarity or memory strength. Some old items will have high familiarity, some will have medium familiarity, and some will have low familiarity. Similarly, some new items will have high familiarity, some will have medium familiarity, and some will have low familiarity, and the distributions of familiarity values of old and new items will overlap. The distribution of familiarity values for old items corresponds to the signal plus noise distribution of signal detection theory, and the distribution for new items corresponds to the noise alone distribution.

Naturally, we expect the average familiarity of old items to be higher than the average familiarity of new items. If, additionally, we assume that the familiarity values are normally distributed, then the theoretical distribution of familiarity values of old and new items will look something like that shown in Figure B-1.

Signal detection models for recognition memory have been proposed and reviewed by various authors (Banks, 1970; Egan, 1958; Lockhart & Murdock, 1970; Wickelgren & Norman, 1966). They assume that, just as in a sensory experiment, subjects will be intrinsically uncertain about whether a particular item is old or new, will evaluate their decision on the basis of the degree of familiarity an item has, and will differ from one another on the degree to which they are willing to classify an item as old or new. If this model of memory is correct, then the methods of signal detection theory are appropriate for analyzing recognition memory data.

As we showed in Chapter 4, a way of evaluating the applicability of signal detection theory to data from sensory experiments is by determining whether or not data obtained from such studies follow the characteristic shape of the receiver operating characteristic (ROC) curve predicted

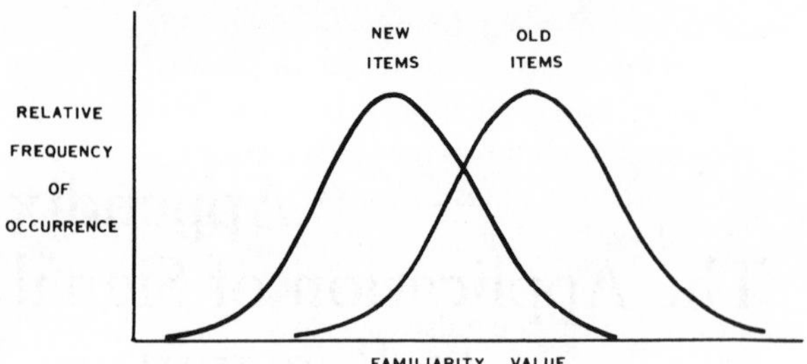

Fig. B-1 Theoretical distribution of familiarity values for old and new items predicted by signal detection theory.

by signal detection theory. This is done by plotting hit rates against false alarm rates obtained in several different sessions in which response bias has been manipulated by signal probabilities or payoffs. Similar curves may be constructed from recognition memory data (in this context they are called memory operating characteristic, or MOC curves) and similar curved shapes are obtained. For recognition memory data, a hit is defined as correctly classifying an old item as OLD and a false alarm is defined as incorrectly classifying a new item as OLD.

Because it is difficult to run the same subject repeatedly in a memory experiment, MOC curves are usually obtained from confidence rating data rather than

Fig. B-2 Cumulative conditional probabilities of ratings R_j or stricter for *A-B* and *A-X* presentations. (From "Signal-Detection Theory and Short-Term Memory," by B. B. Murdock, Jr. In *Journal of Experimental Psychology*, 1965, 70, 443–447. Copyright 1965 by the American Psychological Association. Reprinted by permission.)

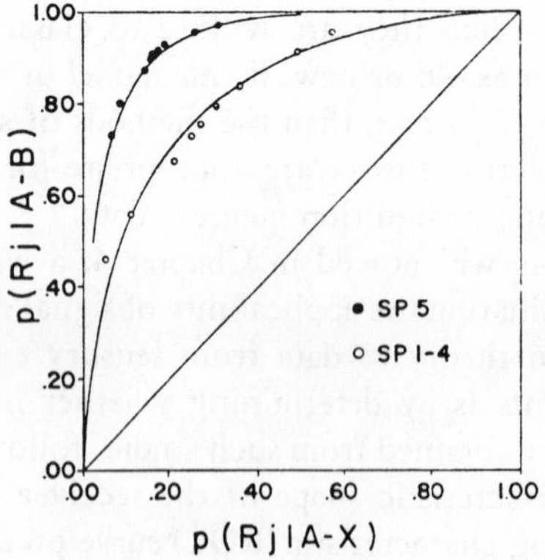

from a series of YES/NO sessions in which probabilities or payoffs are varied. Additionally, data are usually combined across subjects rather than plotted for individual subjects. One such plot, from a recognition memory experiment of Murdock (1965), is shown in Figure B-2.

In Murdock's experiment, subjects were shown a sequence of six paired words (in Figure B-2 these are called the A–B pairs) and, at the end of each list, were tested for recognition of a single pair drawn from one of the six serial positions. For half of the test trials, the pair presented was old—that is, it had been presented as a pair during the study trial. An old pair is denoted A–B, and the subject's correct response to this pair is YES. For the other half of the trials, the pair was new in the sense that the first word of the pair was re-paired with a different second member that had appeared somewhere in the list of the six pairs just seen. This new pair is denoted A–X, and a correct response to it is NO. In addition, subjects rated their confidence in their YES or NO responses on a five-point confidence scale, thereby producing ten possible responses to each A–B and A–X pair.

Figure B-2 shows a plot of confidence ratings for serial positions 1 through 4 (SP 1–4), which are combined because they did not differ from one another, and a separate plot for serial position 5 (SP 5). Although the data are combined across subjects, the data points form the type of curved MOC curve that would be predicted by signal detection theory, and hence support the signal detection model of memory.

If signal detection theory is an appropriate model for how familiarity values of old and new items are distributed, then it is necessary to use an appropriate measure of recognition memory that takes into account the subject's bias toward responding OLD or NEW. That is, only the hit rate (the probability of correctly saying YES to an old item) or the false alarm rate (the probability of incorrectly saying YES to a new item) is not sufficient, because subjects who have a bias toward saying YES will have a high hit rate but also a high false alarm rate, whereas subjects who have a bias toward saying NO will have a low hit rate but also a low false alarm rate.

The classic method for correcting such differences in bias, as described in Woodworth (1938), was to subtract the false alarm rate (FA) from the hit rate (H). We can describe this correction by the following formula:

$$\text{Corrected recognition score} = H - FA$$

However, as Egan (1958) has shown, this correction for guessing implies a model of recognition memory that is different from that implied by signal detection theory.

Specifically, the correction is based on a *two-high-threshold* theory of recognition memory, in which there is a high threshold that an old item will cross an old item threshold, and a high threshold that a new item will cross a new item threshold. The term *high threshold* means that only an item appropriate to the threshold is capable of crossing it. Thus, only an old item is capable of crossing the old item threshold, and only a new item is capable of crossing the new item threshold. When an old item crosses its threshold, the subject will respond YES correctly, and when a new item crosses its threshold, the subject will respond NO correctly. When neither threshold is crossed by an old or new item, the subject will guess according to his bias towards YES or NO responses. The correction given above is based on the assumption that the old and new item thresholds, measured by the probability that their corresponding items will cross them, are equal.

However, if memory strengths are continuously distributed, as SDT implies, then a different measure of recognition memory should be used. If subjects respond only with the two responses, "Yes, it's old" or "No, it's new," then the resulting hit and false alarm rates can be used to compute the signal detection measure of sensitivity, d', as described in Chapter 4.

The problem with d', however, is that because we are generally limited in the number of recognition trials given to individual subjects, some subjects may produce a false alarm rate of 0, a hit rate of 1.0, or both, in which case d' is not computable. An alternative measure, first proposed by Pollack (Pollack, 1970; Pollack & Norman, 1964), is a nonparametric analog to d' called A'. A' is the area under a kind of "average" MOC curve, which includes that predicted from signal detection theory. In addition, A' has been shown to be highly correlated with d' in a recognition memory experiment (Snodgrass, Volvovitz, & Walfish, 1972). It has the advantage of being calculable no matter what the hit and false alarm rates are, and thus can be used to calculate recognition memory performance for individual subjects.

A' is calculated by the following formulas, where H = hit rate, FA = false alarm rate.

1. If $H > FA$, $A' = .5 + \dfrac{(H - FA)(1 + H - FA)}{4H(1 - FA)}$
2. If $H = FA$, $A' = .5$
3. If $H < FA$, $A' = .5 - \dfrac{(FA - H)(1 + FA - H)}{4FA(1 - H)}$

The area under the MOC curve has been shown to be theoretically equivalent to the probability of a correct response in a two-alternative, forced-choice experiment (Green & Swets, 1974). If the hit rate is greater than the false alarm rate, as in Equation 1, the subject's performance lies on an MOC curve above the chance diagonal, and the area below it is greater than .5. If the hit rate is equal to the false alarm

Table B-1 *A′* Values for Selected Hit and False Alarm Rates

Hit rate (*H*)	False alarm rate (*F*)	*A′*
1.00	.00	1.000
1.00	.90	.775
.90	.05	.960
.90	.85	.597
.80	.05	.932
.80	.70	.615
.70	.05	.903
.70	.30	.786
.70	.65	.554
.60	.10	.847
.60	.50	.592
.50	.00	.875
.50	.05	.843
.50	.25	.708
.50	.50	.500
.50	.60	.408

Note. A′ is computed as follows:

1. For $H > FA$, $A' = .5 + \dfrac{(H - FA)(1 + H - FA)}{4H(1 - FA)}$
2. For $H = FA$, $A' = .5$
3. For $H < FA$, $A' = .5 - \dfrac{(FA - H)(1 + FA - H)}{4FA(1 - H)}$

rate, as in equation 2, the subject's performance is on the chance diagonal of the MOC (that is, she or he is doing no better than chance), and the area below the MOC is .5. If the hit rate is less than the false alarm rate, as in equation 3, the subject's performance is on an MOC curve below the chance diagonal, so the area will be less than .5. Performance below chance reflects the operation of sampling error—if subjects remember nothing at all, the theoretical expected value of their performance in terms of *A′* is .5, but some subjects will have *A′* values greater than .5 and some will have *A′* values less than .5 because of sampling error. Table B-1 shows *A′* values calculated for some selected hit and false alarm rates and can be used by the student to check his or her understanding of the computational procedures.

When subjects grade their responses into more than the two categories OLD and NEW by providing confidence ratings, it is also possible to use the area under the entire MOC curve, which is produced by cumulating confidence ratings.

Table B-2 shows some hypothetical data from an experiment in which subjects responded with a six-category confidence scale—three levels of confidence for OLD responses and three for NEW responses—in which a 3 represents the highest level of confidence and a 1, the lowest.

To plot this as an MOC curve, we cumulate the frequencies from the right as shown in matrix b, and then we convert the cumulated frequencies into probabilties, as shown in matrix c, by dividing each cumulated frequency by the total number of old and new stimulus presentations (60 in each case).

Table B-2 Hypothetical Data from a Six-Category Rating Scale Procedure for Recognition Memory

(a) Uncumulated frequency matrix

	Response						
	NEW			OLD			
Stimulus	3	2	1	1	2	3	Σ
Old	3	7	5	5	13	27	60
New	25	13	5	4	10	3	60

(b) Cumulated frequency matrix

Stimulus						
Old	60	57	50	45	40	27
New	60	35	22	17	13	3

(c) Cumulated probability matrix

Stimulus						
Old	1.00	.95	.83	.75	.67	.45
New	1.00	.58	.37	.28	.22	.05

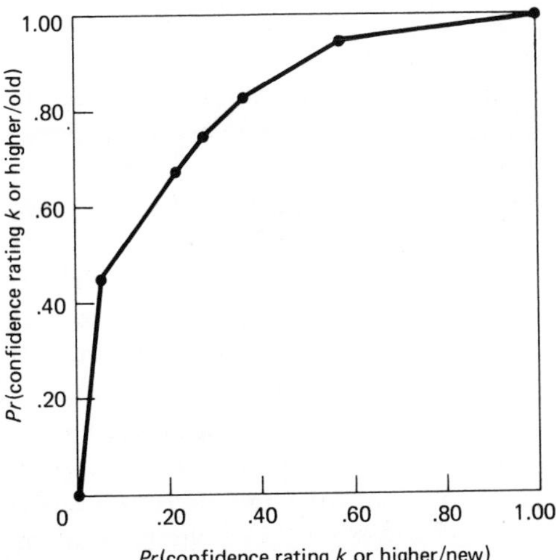

Fig. B-3 MOC function constructed from the data in Table B-2 by plotting the cumulated probabilities of ratings for old items along the ordinate against the cumulated probabilities of ratings for new items along the abscissa.

Note that when the frequencies are cumulated and converted into probabilities, the last set of probabilities for hits and false alarms always equals 1.00. Thus, an n-category rating scale produces an MOC curve with $n - 1$ points. In this case, our MOC plot will have five points because we used a six-category rating scale. The first pair of hit and false alarm rates, .45 and .05, represent the subject's most stringent criterion placement—she or he responds OLD-3 only when very sure that the item is old. As we move to the left through the cumulated probability matrix, we encounter more and more liberal criteria. As described in Chapter 4, the use of the confidence rating procedure assumes that subjects set up $n - 1$ criterion placements and respond according to where along the familiarity continuum the item appears to lie. The plotted MOC curve is shown in Figure B-3, where we connected the points with straight lines.

Table B-3 Procedure for Computing the Area under the MOC Curve from Confidence Ratings Using the Trapezoidal Rule

	Uncumulated frequency matrix Response						
	NEW			OLD			
Stimulus	3	2	1	1	2	3	
Old	O_1	O_2	O_3	O_4	O_5	O_6	$O = \sum_{i=1}^{6} O_i$
New	N_1	N_2	N_3	N_4	N_5	N_6	$N = \sum_{i=1}^{6} N_i$

$$\text{Area} = \frac{O_6\left(\sum_{i=1}^{5} N_i\right) + O_5\left(\sum_{i=1}^{4} N_i\right) + O_4\left(\sum_{i=1}^{3} N_i\right) + O_3\left(\sum_{i=1}^{2} N_i\right) + O_2(N_1)}{O \times N}$$

Example from Table B-2(a)

$$\frac{27(25 + 13 + 5 + 4 + 10) + 13(25 + 13 + 5 + 4) + 5(25 + 13 + 5) + 5(25 + 13) + 7(25)}{60 \times 60}$$

$$\text{Area} = \frac{2730}{3600} = .758$$

It is possible from the plot of such an MOC curve to find the empirical area under the MOC curve using the trapezoidal rule (Brown, 1974, has provided a rationale for this procedure). However, there is a very simple rule for computing the area from the uncumulated frequency matrix itself, which bypasses the steps of cumulating the frequencies, converting the frequencies to proportions, and plotting the proportions as we have done in Figure B-3. The method for using the trapezoidal rule with raw frequencies is presented symbolically in Table B-3 and used with the data from Table B-2 to illustrate the method.

In Table B-3, we have renumbered the old and new responses so that O_6 and N_6 refer to the frequencies of a confident old (OLD-3) response to old and new stimuli respectively, whereas O_1 and N_1 refer to the frequencies of a confident new response (NEW-3) to old and new stimuli, respectively. The formula for the area is shown in Table B-3, first symbolically, using the new notation, and then with an example from Table B-2.

In summary, considerable evidence exists that memory traces, like sensory experiences, are distributed continuously rather than in an all-or-none fashion, and thus that the data from a recognition memory experiment should be analyzed using the tools of signal detection theory. Snodgrass (1983) reviews the topic of recognition memory measurement in more detail and compares the efficiency of various measures against several sets of empirical data.

References

Abramson, L. Y., Seligman, M. E. P., & Teasdale, J. D. (1978). Learned helplessness in humans: Critique and reformulation. *Journal of Abnormal Psychology, 87*, 49–74.

Adair, J. G. (1973). *The human subject: The social psychology of the psychological experiment.* Boston: Little, Brown.

Adamson, R. E. (1952). Functional fixedness as related to problem solving: A repetition of three experiments. *Journal of Experimental Psychology, 44*, 288–291.

Allen, L. R., & Garton, R. F. (1968). The influence of word-knowledge on the word-frequency effect in recognition memory. *Psychonomic Science, 10*, 401–402.

Allen, L. R., & Garton, R. F. (1969). Detection and criterion change associated with different test contexts in recognition memory. *Perception & Psychophysics, 6*, 1–4.

Alloy, L. B., & Abramson, L. Y. (1979). Judgment of contingency in depressed and nondepressed students: Sadder but wiser? *Journal of Experimental Psychology: General, 108*, 441–485.

Alloy, L. B., & Seligman, M. E. P. (1979). On the cognitive component of learned helplessness. In G. H. Bower (Ed.), *The psychology of learning and motivation* (Vol. 13, pp. 219–276). New York: Academic Press.

American Psychiatric Association. (1980). *Diagnostic and statistical manual* (DSM-III) (3rd ed.). Washington, DC: Author.

American Psychological Association. (1983). *Publication manual of the American Psychological Association* (3rd ed.). Washington, DC: Author.

Amsel, A. (1958). The role of frustrative nonreward in noncontinuous reward situations. *Psychological Bulletin, 55*, 102–119.

Amsel, A. (1962). Frustrative nonreward in partial reinforcement and discrimination learning: Some recent history and a theoretical extension. *Psychological Review, 69*, 306–328.

Anderson, B. F. (1971). *The psychology experiment* (2nd ed.). Belmont, CA: Brooks/Cole.

Anderson J. R., & Bower, G. H. (1973). *Human associative memory.* Washington, DC: Winston.

Anderson, J. R., & Bower, G. H. (1974). A propositional theory of recognition memory. *Memory & Cognition, 2*, 406–412.

Argyle, M. (1953). The relay assembly test room in retrospect. *Occupational Psychology, 27*, 98–103.

Arkes, H. R., & Clark, P. (1975). Effects of task difficulty on subsequent preference for visual complexity. *Perceptual and Motor Skills, 41*, 395–399.

Armstrong, S. L., Gleitman, L. R., & Gleitman, H. (1983). What some concepts might not be. *Cognition, 13*, 263–308.

Asch, S. E. (1951). Effects of group pressure upon the modification and distortion of judgments. In H. Guetzkow (Ed.), *Groups, leadership and men* (pp. 177–190). Pittsburgh: Carnegie Press.

Asch, S. E. (1955, November). Opinions and social pressure. *Scientific American, 193*, 31–35.

Asch, S. E. (1956). Studies of independence and conformity: I. A minority of one against a unanimous majority. *Psychological Monographs, 70* (Whole No. 416).

Atkinson, J., & Egeth, H. (1973). Right hemisphere superiority in visual orientation matching. *Canadian Journal of Psychology, 27*, 152–158.

Atkinson, R. C., & Juola, J. F. (1973). Factors influencing speed and accuracy of word recognition. In S. Kornblum (Ed.), *Attention and performance IV* (pp. 583–612). New York: Academic Press.

Atkinson, R. C., & Shiffrin, R. M. (1968). Human memory: A proposed system and its control processes. In K. W. Spence & J. T. Spence (Eds.) *The psychology of learning and motivation.* (Vol. 2, pp. 89–195). New York: Academic Press.

Attneave, F. (1955). Symmetry, information, and memory for patterns. *American Journal of Psychology, 68,* 209–222.

Attneave, F. (1957). Physical determinants of the judged complexity of shapes. *Journal of Experimental Psychology, 53,* 221–227.

Attneave, F., & Arnoult, M. D. (1956). The quantitative study of shape and pattern perception. *Psychological Bulletin, 53,* 452–471.

Averbach, I., & Coriell, A. S. (1961). Short-term memory in vision. *Bell System Technical Journal, 40,* 309–328.

Baddeley, A. D. (1966a). The influence of acoustic and semantic similarity on long-term memory for word sequences. *Quarterly Journal of Experimental Psychology, 18,* 302–309.

Baddeley, A. D. (1966b). Short-term memory for word sequences as a function of acoustic, semantic and formal similarity. *Quarterly Journal of Experimental Psychology, 18,* 362–365.

Baddeley, A. D. (1978). The trouble with levels: A reexamination of Craik and Lockhart's framework for memory research. *Psychological Review, 85,* 139–152.

Baddeley, A. D., & Hitch, G. (1974). Working memory. In G. H. Bower (Ed.), *The psychology of learning and motivation* (Vol. 8, pp. 47–89). New York: Academic Press.

Badia, P., Rosenberg, B. G., & Langer, J. (1965). Representational value, meaningfulness, and pronounceability in serial learning. *Psychological Reports, 13* (3), 997–1000.

Baird, J. C., & Noma, E. (1978). *Fundamentals of scaling and psychophysics.* New York: Wiley.

Banks, W. P. (1970). Signal detection theory and human memory. *Psychological Bulletin, 74,* 81–99.

Barton, M. I., Goodglass, H., & Shai, A. (1965). Differential recognition of tachistoscopically presented English and Hebrew words in right and left visual fields. *Perceptual and Motor Skills, 21,* 431–437.

Battig, W. F., & Montague, W. E. (1969). Category norms for verbal items in 56 categories: A replication and extension of the Connecticut category norms. *Journal of Experimental Psychology Monograph, 80* (3, Pt. 2).

Beck, A. T. (1967). *Depression: Clinical, experimental, and theoretical aspects.* New York: Harper & Row.

Belvedere, E. & Foulkes, D. (1971). Telepathy and dreams: A failure to replicate. *Perceptual and Motor Skills, 33,* 783–789.

Benitez, J. T. (1970). Eye-tracking and optokinetic tests: Diagnostic significance in peripheral and central vestibular disorders. *Laryngoscope, 80,* 834–848.

Bergin, A. E., & Lambert, M. J. (1978). The evaluation of therapeutic outcomes. In S. L. Garfield & A. E. Bergin (Eds.), *Handbook of psychotherapy and behavior change* (pp. 139–190). New York: Wiley.

Berlin, B. & Kay, P. (1969). *Basic color terms: Their universality and evolution.* Berkeley, CA: University of California Press.

Berlyne, D. (1960). *Conflict, arousal, and curiosity.* New York: McGraw-Hill.

Bernstein, T. M. (1971). *Miss Thistlebottom's hobgoblins.* New York: Farrar, Straus & Giroux.

Bever, T. G., & Chiarello, R. J. (1974). Cerebral dominance in musicians and nonmusicians. *Science, 185,* 537–539.

Bexton, W. H., Heron, W., & Scott, T. H. (1954). Effects of decreased variation in the sensory environment. *Canadian Journal of Psychology, 8,* 70–76.

Biederman, I., Glass, A. L., & Stacy, E. W., Jr. (1973). On searching for objects in real-world scenes. *Journal of Experimental Psychology, 97,* 22–27.

Boakes, R. A., & Ismail, R. B. (1971). *An effect similar to sensory preconditioning in autoshaping of key pecking in pigeons.* Unpublished manuscript. (University of Sussex, Brighton, England.)

Bolles, R. C. (1975). *Theory of motivation.* New York: Harper & Row.

Boring, E. G. (1957). CP speaks . . . *Contemporary Psychology, 2,* 279.

Bourne, L. E., Jr. & Restle, F. (1959). Mathematical theory of concept identification. *Psychological Review, 66,* 278–296.

Bousfield, A. K., & Bousfield, W. A. (1966). Measurement of clustering and of sequential constancies in repeated free recall. *Psychological Reports, 19,* 935–942.

Bousfield, W. A., Esterson, J., & Whitmarsh, G.

A. (1957). The effects of concomitant colored and uncolored pictorial representations on the learning of stimulus words. *Journal of Applied Psychology, 41,* 165–168.

Bower, G. H. (1972). A selective review of organizational factors in memory. In E. Tulving & W. Donaldson (Eds.), *Organization of memory* (pp. 93–137). New York: Academic Press.

Bower, G., H., & Trabasso, T. (1964). Concept identification. In R. C. Atkinson (Ed.), *Studies in mathematical psychology* (pp. 32–94). Stanford, CA: Stanford University Press.

Bower, T. G. R. (1971, October). The object in the world of the infant. *Scientific American, 225,* 30–38.

Bower, T. G. R. (1972). Object perception in infants. *Perception, 1,* 15–30.

Brabyn, L. B., & McGuinness, D. (1979). Gender differences in response to spatial frequency and stimulation orientation. *Perception & Psychophysics, 26,* 319–324.

Bradshaw, J. L., & Nettleton, N. C. (1981). The nature of hemispheric specialization in man. *The Behavioral and Brain Sciences, 4,* 51–91.

Bramel, D., & Friend, R. (1981). Hawthorne, the myth of the docile worker, and class bias in psychology. *American Psychologist, 36,* 867–878.

Bransford, J. D., & Franks, J. J. (1971). The abstraction of linguistic ideas. *Cognitive Psychology, 2,* 331–350.

Broadbent, D. E. (1958). *Perception and communication.* London: Pergamon.

Brown, A. S. (1976). Catalog of scaled verbal material. *Memory & Cognition, 4,* (1B), 1S–45S.

Brown, J. (1974). Recognition assessed by rating and ranking. *British Journal of Psychology, 65,* 13–22.

Brown, J. A. (1948). Some tests of the decay theory of immediate memory. *Quarterly Journal of Experimental Psychology, 10,* 12–21.

Brown, J. S. (1942). The generalization of approach responses as a function of stimulus intensity and strength of motivation. *Journal of Comparative Psychology, 33,* 209–226.

Brown, R. W., & Lenneberg, E. H. (1954). A study in language and cognition. *Journal of Abnormal and Social Psychology, 49,* 454–462.

Bruner, J. S., Goodnow, J. J., & Austin, G. A. (1956). *A study of thinking.* New York: Wiley.

Bryan, W. L., & Harter, N. (1897). Studies in the physiology and psychology of telegraphic language. *Psychological Review, 4,* 27–53.

Bryan, W. L., & Harter, N. (1899). Studies on the telegraphic language: The acquisition of a hierarchy of habits. *Psychological Review, 6,* 345–375.

Bryden, M. P. (1976). Response bias and hemispheric differences in dot localization. *Perception & Psychophysics, 19,* 23–28.

Burton, M. (Ed.). (1980). *The new Laurousse encyclopedia of animal life.* New York: Bonanza Books.

Cannon, W. B. (1932). *The wisdom of the body.* New York: Norton.

Carey, A. (1967). The Hawthorne studies: A radical criticism. *American Sociological Review, 32,* 403–416.

Carmichael, L., Hogan, H. P., & Walter, A. A. (1932). An experimental study of the effect of language on the reproduction of visually perceived form. *Journal of Experimental Psychology, 55,* 73–86.

Carroll, J. B. (1964). Words, meanings and concepts. *Harvard Educational Review, 34,* 179–202.

Carroll, J. B., & Casagrande, J. B. (1958). The function of language classifications in behavior. In E. E. Maccoby, T. M. Newcomb, & E. L. Hartley (Eds.), *Readings in social psychology* (pp. 18–31). New York: Holt, Rinehart, & Winston.

Carroll, J. B., & White, M. N. (1973a). Word frequency and age of acquisition as determiners of picture-naming latency. *Quarterly Journal of Experimental Psychology, 25,* 85–95.

Carroll, J. B., & White, M. N. (1973b). Age-of-acquisition norms for 220 picturable nouns. *Journal of Verbal Learning and Verbal Behavior, 12,* 563–576.

Cattell, J. M. (1893). On errors of observation. *American Journal of Psychology, 5,* 285–293.

Chapman, L. J., & Chapman, J. P. (1959). Atmosphere effect re-examined. *Journal of Experimental Psychology, 58,* 220–226.

Cherry, E. C. (1953). Some experiments on the recognition of speech, with one and with two ears. *Journal of the Acoustical Society of America, 25,* 975–979.

Clark, H. H. (1969). Linguistic processes in deductive reasoning. *Psychological Review, 76,* 387–404.

Clark, H. H. (1973). The language-as-fixed-effect fallacy: A critique of language statistics in psychological research. *Journal of Verbal*

Learning and Verbal Behavior, 12, 335–359.

Clark, W. C. (1966). The *Psyche* in psychophysics: A sensory-decision theory analysis of the effect of instructions on flicker sensitivity and response bias. *Psychological Bulletin, 65,* 358–366.

Clark, W. C., Brown, J. C., & Rutschmann, J. (1967). Flicker sensitivity and response bias in psychiatric patients and normal subjects. *Journal of Abnormal Psychology, 72,* 35–42.

Cohen, J. (1977). *Statistical power analysis for the behavioral sciences* (rev. ed.). New York: Academic Press.

Collins, A. M., & Loftus, E. F. (1975). A spreading-activation theory of semantic processing. *Psychological Review, 82,* 407–428.

Collins, A. M., & Quillian, M. R. (1969). Retrieval time from semantic memory. *Journal of Verbal Learning and Verbal Behavior, 8,* 240–247.

Conrad, C. (1972). Cognitive economy in semantic memory. *Journal of Experimental Psychology, 92,* 149–154.

Conrad, R. (1964). Acoustic confusions in immediate memory. *British Journal of Psychology, 55,* 75–84.

Conrad, R., & Hull, A. J. (1964). Information, acoustic confusion and memory span. *British Journal of Psychology, 55,* 429–432.

Craik, F. I. M., & Lockart, R. S. (1972) Levels of processing: A framework for memory research. *Journal of Verbal Learning and Verbal Behavior, 11,* 671–684.

Craik, F. I. M., & Tulving, E. (1975). Depth of processing and the retention of words in episodic memory. *Journal of Experimental Psychology: General, 104,* 268–294.

Cross, J. F., Cross, J. , & Daly, J. (1971). Sex, race, age, and beauty as factors in recognition of faces. *Perception & Psychophysics, 10,* 393–396.

Deci, E. L. (1972). Intrinsic motivation, extrinsic reinforcement, and inequity. *Journal of Personality and Social Psychology, 22,* 113–120.

Deregowski, J. B. (1972). Pictorial perception and culture. *Scientific American, 227,* 82–88.

Deregowski, J. B. (1980). Perception. In H. C. Triandis & W. Lonner (Eds.), *Handbook of cross-cultural psychology: Basic processes* (Vol. 3, pp. 21–115). Boston, MA: Allyn & Bacon.

DeSoto, C. B., London, M., & Handel, S. (1965). Social reasoning and spatial paralogic. *Journal of Personality and Social Psychology, 2,* 513–521.

Deutsch, J. A., & Deutsch, D. (1963). Attention: Some theoretical considerations. *Psychological Review, 70,* 80–90.

Dixon, W. J. (1953). Processing data for outliers. *Biometrics, 9,* 89.

Dixon, W. J., & Massey, F. J., Jr. (1969). *Introduction to statistical analysis* (3rd ed.). New York: McGraw-Hill.

Dixon, W. J., & Tukey, J. W. (1968). Approximate behaviour of the distribution of Winsorized t (Trimming/Winsorization z). *Technometrics, 10,* 83–98.

Dollard, J., Doob, L., Miller, N. E., Mowrer, O. H., & Sears, R. R. (1939). *Frustration and aggression.* New Haven, CT: Yale University Press.

Dollard, J., & Miller, N. E. (1950). *Personality and psychotherapy: An analysis in terms of learning, thinking and culture.* New York: McGraw-Hill.

Donders, F. C. (1969). On the speed of mental processes. In W. G. Koster (Ed. and Trans.), *Attention and performance II* (pp. 412–431). Amsterdam: North-Holland. (Reprinted from *Acta Psychologica,* 1969, *30,* 412–431). (Original work published 1868.)

Dukes, W. F. (1965). $N = 1$. *Psychological Bulletin, 64,* 74–79.

Durso, F. T., & Johnson, M. K. (1979). Facilitation in naming and categorizing repeated pictures and words. *Journal of Experimental Psychology: Human Learning and Memory, 5,* 449–459.

Ebbinghaus, H. (1964). *Memory: A contribution to experimental psychology.* (H. A. Ruger & C. E. Bussenius, Trans.) New York: Dover. (Original work published 1885.)

Edmonds, E. M., Evans, S. H., & Mueller, M. R. (1966). Learning how to learn schemata. *Psychonomic Science, 6,* 177–178.

Egan, J. P. (1958). Recognition memory and the operating characteristic. Indiana University Hearing and Communication Laboratory, AFCRC-TN-58-51, AD-152650, June 15.

Egeth, H., Jonides, J., & Wall, S. (1972). Parallel processing of multielement displays. *Cognitive Psychology, 3,* 674–698.

Elkins, R., Rapoport, J., Zahn, T., Buchsbaum, M., Weingartner, H., Kopin, I., Langer, D., & Johnson, C. (1981). Acute effects of caffeine in normal prepubertal boys. In S. A. Miller (Ed.), *Nutrition & behavior.* Philadelphia: Franklin Institute Press.

Elliott, E. S., Wills, E. J., & Goldstein, A. G. (1973). The effects of discrimination training on the recognition of white and oriental faces. *Bulletin of the Psychonomic Society, 2,* 71–73.

Epstein, S. (1967). Toward a unified theory of anxiety. In B. A. Maher (Ed.), *Progress in experimental personality research* (Vol. 4, pp. 2–89). New York: Academic Press.

Epstein, S., & Levitt, H. (1962). The influence of hunger on the learning and recall of food-related words. *Journal of Abnormal and Social Psychology, 64,* 130–135.

Erdelyi, M. H. (1974). A new look at the new look: Perceptual defense and vigilance. *Psychological Review, 81,* 1–25.

Estes, W. K., & Skinner, B. F. (1941). Some quantitative properties of anxiety. *Journal of Experimental Psychology, 29,* 390–400.

Evans, S. H. (1967). A brief statement of schema theory. *Psychonomic Science, 8,* 87–88.

Eysenck, H. J. (1952). The effects of psychotherapy: An evaluation. *Journal of Consulting Psychology, 16,* 319–324.

Farber, I. E. & Spence, K. W. (1953). Complex learning and conditioning as a function of anxiety. *Journal of Experimental Psychology, 45,* 120–125.

Fechner, G. T. (1860). *Elemente der Psychophysik.* Leipzig, Germany: Breitkopf und Hürtel. (Translated by H. Adler, New York: Holt, Rinehart & Winston, 1966).

Federer, W. T. (1955). *Experimental design.* New York: Macmillan.

Fehrer, E. V. (1935). An investigation of the learning of visually perceived forms. *American Journal of Psychology, 47,* 187–221.

Ferster, C. B., & Skinner, B. F. (1957). *Schedules of reinforcement.* New York: Appleton-Century-Crofts.

Festinger, L. (1957). *A theory of cognitive dissonance.* Stanford, CA: Stanford University Press.

Festinger, L. (1958). The motivating effect of cognitive dissonance. In G. Lindzey (Ed.), *Assessment of human motives* (pp. 65–86). New York: Holt, Rinehart & Winston.

Fisher, R. A. (1951). *The design of experiments* (6th ed.). Edinburgh: Oliver & Boyd.

Fisher, S., & Greenberg, R. P. (1977). *The scientific credibility of Freud's theories and therapy.* New York: Basic Books.

Fishman, J. A. (1960). A systematization of the Whorfian hypothesis. *Behavioral Science, 5,* 323–339.

Fisk, A. D., & Schneider, W. (1983). Category and word search: Generalizing search principles to complex processing. *Journal of Experimental Psychology: Learning, Memory, and Cognition, 9,* 177–195.

Flexser, A. J., & Tulving, E. (1978). Retrieval independence in recognition and recall. *Psychological Review, 85,* 153–171.

Fodor, J. A., Bever, T. G., & Garrett, M. F. (1974). *The psychology of language.* New York: McGraw-Hill.

Fowler, H. (1965). *Curiosity and exploratory behavior.* New York: Macmillan.

Franke, R. H. (1979). The Hawthorne experiments: Re-view. *American Sociological Review, 44,* 861–867.

Franke, R. H., & Kaul, J. D. (1978). The Hawthorne experiments: First statistical interpretation. *American Sociological Review, 43,* 623–643.

Franken, R. E., & Davis, J. (1975). Predicting memory for pictures from rankings of interestingness, pleasingness, complexity, figure-ground and clarity. *Perceptual and Motor Skills, 41,* 243–247.

Franks, J. J., & Bransford, J. D. (1971). Abstraction of visual patterns. *Journal of Experimental Psychology, 90,* 65–74.

French, R. S. (1954). Identification of dot patterns from memory as a function of complexity. *Journal of Experimental Psychology, 47,* 22–26.

Friedman, M. (1969). *Pathogenesis of coronary artery disease.* New York: McGraw-Hill.

Friedman, M., & Rosenman, R. H. (1959, March). Association of specific overt behavior pattern with blood and cardiovascular findings. *Journal of the American Medical Association, 169,* 1286–1296.

Gardner, H. (1982). What we know (and do not know) about the two halves of the brain. In H. Gardner, *Art, mind, and brain* (pp. 278–285). New York: Basic Books.

Garner, W. R., Hake, H. W., & Eriksen, C. W. (1956). Operationism and the concept of perception. *Psychological Review, 63,* 149–159.

Gazzaniga, M. S. (1970). *The bisected brain.* New York: Appleton-Century-Crofts.

Gescheider, G. A. (1976). *Psychophysics: Method and theory.* Hillsdale, NJ: Erlbaum.

Gibson, E. J., Bishop, C. H., Schiff, W., & Smith, J. (1964). Comparisons of meaningfulness and pronounceability as grouping principles in the perception and retention of verbal material. *Journal of Experimental Psychology, 67,* 173–182.

Gibson, E. J., Pick, A., Osser, H., & Hammond,

M. (1962). The role of grapheme-phoneme correspondence in the perception of words. *American Journal of Psychology, 75,* 554–570.

Gibson, E. J., & Walk, R. D. (1960, April). The "visual cliff." *Scientific American, 202,* 64–71.

Glanzer, M. (1972). Storage mechanisms in recall. In G. H. Bower (Ed.), *The Psychology of Learning and Motivation.* (Vol. 5, pp. 129–193). New York: Academic Press.

Glanzer, M., & Clark, W. H. (1963a). Accuracy of perceptual recall: An analysis of organization. *Journal of Verbal Learning and Verbal Behavior, 1,* 289–299.

Glanzer, M., & Clark, W. H. (1963b). The verbal loop hypothesis: Binary numbers. *Journal of Verbal Learning and Verbal Behavior, 2,* 301–309.

Glanzer, M., & Cunitz, A. R. (1966). Two storage mechanisms in free recall. *Journal of Verbal Learning and Verbal Behavior, 5,* 351–360.

Gleitman, H. (1981). *Psychology.* New York: Norton.

Glucksberg, S., & Weisberg, R. W. (1966). Verbal behavior and problem solving: Some effects of labeling in a functional fixedness problem. *Journal of Experimental Psychology, 71,* 659–664.

Gorman, A. M. (1961). Recognition memory for nouns as a function of abstractness and frequency. *Journal of Experimental Psychology, 61,* 23–29.

Gormezano, I., & Hiller, G. W. (1972). Omission training of the jaw-movement response of the rabbit to a water US. *Psychonomic Science, 29,* 276–278.

Goss, A. E., & Nodine, C. F. (1965). *Paired-associates learning: The role of meaningfulness, familiarity and familiarization.* New York: Academic Press.

Gosset, W. S. (1971). ("Student"), The Lanarkshire milk experiment. In J. A. Steger (Ed.), *Readings in statistics for the behavioral scientist* (pp. 159–168). New York: Holt, Rinehart & Winston.

Grant, D. A., & Berg, E. A. (1948). A behavioral analysis of degree of reinforcement and ease of shifting to new responses in a Weigl-type card-sorting problem. *Journal of Experimental Psychology, 38,* 404–411.

Grant, D. A., & Cost, J. R. (1954). Continuities and discontinuities in conceptual behavior in a card sorting problem. *Journal of General Psychology, 50,* 237–244.

Gray, J. A., & Wedderburn, A. A. I. (1960). Grouping strategies with simultaneous stimuli. *Quarterly Journal of Experimental Psychology, 12,* 180–184.

Green, D. M., & Swets, J. A. (1974). *Signal detection theory and psychophysics.* Huntington, NY: Krieger.

Greenwald, A. G. (1976). Within-subjects designs: To use or not to use? *Psychological Bulletin, 83,* 314–320.

Grether, W. F., & Baker, C. A. (1972). Visual presentation of information. In H. P. van Cott & R. G. Kinkade (Eds.), *Human engineering guide to equipment design* (pp. 41–121). Washington, DC: U.S. Government Printing Office.

Gruenberg, B. C. (1929). *The story of evolution.* New York: Van Nostrand.

Gumbel, E. J. (1958). *Statistics of extremes.* New York and London: Columbia University Press.

Haber, R. N. (1958). Discrepancy from adaptation level as a source of affect. *Journal of Experimental Psychology, 56,* 370–375.

Haber, R. N., & Hershenson, M. (1980). *The psychology of visual perception* (2nd ed.). New York: Holt, Rinehart, and Winston.

Hagen, M. A. (1978). An outline of an investigation into the special character of pictures. In H. I. Pick, Jr., & E. Saltzman (Eds.), *Modes of perceiving and processing information* (pp. 23–38). Hillsdale, NJ: Erlbaum.

Hagen, M. A., & Elliott, H. B. (1976). An investigation of the relationship between viewing condition and preference for true and modified liner perspective with adults. *Journal of Experimental Psychology: Human Perception and Performance, 2,* 479–490.

Hall, J. F. (1954). Learning as a function of word-frequency. *American Journal of Psychology, 67,* 138–140.

Haner, C. F. & Brown, P. A. (1955). Clarification of the instigation to action concept in the frustration-aggression hypothesis. *Journal of Abnormal and Social Psychology, 51,* 204–206.

Harlow, H. F. (1962). Fundamental principles for preparing psychology journal articles. *Journal of Comparative and Physiological Psychology, 55,* 893–896.

Havens, L. L., & Foote, W. E. (1963). The effect of competition on visual duration threshold and its independence of stimulus frequency. *Journal of Experimental Psychology, 65,* 6–11.

Hayden, B. S. & Loud, L. (1969). Some norms

for the pronounceability of nonsense syllables. *Psychological Reports, 25* (2), 415–418.

Hayes-Roth, B., & Hayes-Roth, F. (1977). Concept learning and the recognition and classification of exemplars. *Journal of Verbal Learning and Verbal Behavior, 16,* 321–338.

Hebb, D. O. (1955). Drives and the C.N.S. (conceptual nervous system). *Psychological Review, 62,* 243–254.

Hebb, D. O. (1966). *A textbook of psychology* (2nd ed.). Philadelphia: W. B. Saunders.

Hecht, S., Shlaer, S., & Pirenne, M. H. (1942). Energy, quanta, and vision. *Journal of General Physiology, 25,* 819–840.

Heider, E. R. (1971). "Focal" color areas and the development of color names. *Developmental Psychology, 4,* 447–455.

Heider, E. R. (1972). Universals in color naming and memory. *Journal of Experimental Psychology, 93,* 10–20.

Heider, F. (1958). *The psychology of interpersonal relations.* New York: Wiley.

Henle, M. (1962). On the relation between logic and thinking. *Psychological Review, 69,* 366–378.

Henley, N. M. (1969). A psychological study of the semantics of animal terms. *Journal of Verbal Learning and Verbal Behavior, 8,* 176–184.

Herrnstein, R. J. (1970). On the law of effect. *Journal of the Experimental Analysis of Behavior, 13,* 243–266.

Hintzman, D. L. (1976). Repetition and memory. In G. L. Bower (Ed.), *The psychology of learning and motivation* (Vol. 10). New York: Academic Press.

Hochberg, J., & Brooks, V. (1962). Pictorial recognition as an unlearned ability. *American Journal of Psychology, 75,* 624–628.

Holzman, P. S., Levy, D. L., & Proctor, L. R. (1976). Smooth pursuit eye movements, attention and schizophrenia. *Archives of General Psychiatry, 33,* 1415–1420.

Holzman, P. S., Proctor, L. R., Levy, D. L., Yasillo, N. J., Meltzer, H. Y., & Hurt, S. W. (1974). Eye-tracking dysfunctions in schizophrenic patients and their relatives. *Archives of General Psychiatry, 31,* 143–151.

Horner, M. S. (1972). Toward an understanding of achievement-related conflicts in women. *Journal of Social Issues, 28,* 157–175.

Hosch, H. M., & Cooper, D. S. (1982). Victimization as a determinant of eyewitness accuracy. *Journal of Applied Psychology, 67,* 649–652.

Howells, T. H. (1938). A study of the ability to recognize faces. *Journal of Abnormal and Social Psychology, 33,* 124–127.

Howes, D. H., & Solomon, R. L. (1951). Visual duration threshold as a function of word-probability. *Journal of Experimental Psychology, 41,* 401–410.

Huck, S. W., & Sandler, H. M. (1979). *Rival hypotheses.* New York: Harper & Row.

Hudson, W. (1960). Pictorial depth perception in sub-cultural groups in Africa. *Journal of Social Psychology, 52,* 183–208.

Hudson, W. (1967). The study of the problem of pictorial perception among unacculturated groups. *International Journal of Psychology, 2,* 89–107.

Hull, C. L. (1920). Quantitative aspects of the evolution of concepts. *Psychological Monographs* (Whole No. 123).

Hull, C. L. (1943). *Principles of behavior.* New York: Appleton-Century-Crofts.

Hunt, E. B. (1962). *Concept learning, an information processing problem.* New York: Wiley.

Hunter, I. M. L. (1957). The solving of three-term series problems. *British Journal of Psychology, 48,* 286–298.

Hursh, S. R. (1978). The economics of daily consumption controlling food- and water-reinforced responding. *Journal of the Experimental Analysis of Behavior, 29,* 475–491.

Hursh, S. R., & Natelson, B. H. (1981). Electrical brain stimulation and food reinforcement dissociated by demand elasticity. *Physiology and Behavior, 26,* 509–515.

Huttenlocher, J. (1968). Constructing spatial images: A strategy in reasoning. *Psychological Review, 75,* 550–560.

Huttenlocher, J., Eisenberg, K., & Strauss, S. (1968). Comprehension: Relation between perceived actor and logical subject. *Journal of Verbal Learning and Verbal Behavior, 7,* 527–530.

James, W. (1890). *The principles of psychology* (Vol. 1). New York: Holt.

Jastrow, J. A. (1888). A critique of psychophysic methods. *American Journal of Psychology, 1,* 271–309.

Javornisky, G. (1979). Task content and sex differences in conformity. *Journal of Social Psychology, 108,* 213–220.

Jenkins, C. D. (1975). The coronary-prone personality. In W. D. Gentry & R. B. Williams (Eds.), *Psychological aspects of myocardial infarction and coronary care.* St. Louis, MO: Mosby.

Jennings, J., Geis, F. L., & Brown, V. (1980). Influence of television commercials on women's self-confidence and independent judgment. *Journal of Personality and Social Psychology, 38,* 203–210.

Jevons, W. S. (1871). The power of numerical discrimination. *Nature, 3,* 281–282.

Johnson, E., Smith, S., & Myers, T. I. (1968). Vigilance throughout seven days of sensory deprivation. *Proceedings of the 76th Annual American Psychological Association Convention,* 627–628.

Johnson-Laird, P. N. (1972). The three-term series problem. *Cognition, 1,* 57–82.

Johnston, W. A., & Heinz, S. P. (1978). Flexibility and capacity demands of attention. *Journal of Experimental Psychology: General, 107,* 420–435.

Julesz, B. (1971). *Foundations of cyclopean perception.* Chicago: University of Chicago Press.

Kahneman, D. (1973). *Attention and effort.* Englewood Cliffs, NJ: Prentice-Hall.

Kahneman, D., & Tversky, A. (1973). On the psychology of prediction. *Psychological Review, 80,* 237–251.

Kamin, L. J. (1974). *The science and politics of IQ.* Hillsdale, NJ: Erlbaum.

Karlin, L. (1959). Reaction time as a function of foreperiod duration and variability. *Journal of Experimental Psychology, 58,* 185–191.

Kaufman, L. (1974). *Sight and mind.* New York: Oxford University Press.

Kaufman, L. (1979). *Perception: The world transformed.* New York: Oxford University Press.

Kennedy, J. M. (1974). *A psychology of picture perception.* San Francisco: Jossey-Bass.

Kent, G. H., & Rosanoff, A. J. (1910). A study of association in insanity. *American Journal of Insanity, 67,* 317–390.

Keppel, G. (1973). *Design and analysis: A researcher's handbook.* Englewood Cliffs, NJ: Prentice-Hall.

Kimura, D. (1967). Functional asymmetry of the brain in dichotic listening. *Cortex, 3,* 163–178.

Kimura, D., & Durnford, M. (1974). Normal studies on the function of the right hemisphere in vision. In M. Kinsbourne (Ed.), *Hemisphere function in the human brain* (pp. 25–47). New York: Elek Science.

Kintsch, W. (1970). Models for free recall and recognition. In D. A. Norman (Ed.). *Models of human memory.* New York: Academic Press.

Kintsch, W. (1974). *The representation of meaning in memory.* Hillsdale, NJ: Erlbaum.

Kintsch, W. (1980). Semantic memory. A tutorial. In R. S. Nickerson (Ed.), *Attention and performance VIII.* Hillsdale, NJ: Erlbaum.

Kintsch, W., & Keenan, J. (1973). Reading rate and retention as a function of the number of propositions in the base structure of sentences. *Cognitive Psychology, 5,* 257–274.

Kintsch, W., & Monk, D. (1972). Storage of complex information in memory: Some implications of the speed with which inferences can be made. *Journal of Experimental Psychology, 94,* 25–32.

Kirk, R. E. (1968). *Experimental design: Procedures for the behavioral sciences.* Belmont, CA: Brooks/Cole.

Klatzky, R. L. (1975). *Human memory: Structures and processes.* San Francisco: Freeman.

Klein, D. F., & Fink, M. (1962). Psychiatric reaction patterns to imipramine. *American Journal of Psychiatry, 119,* 432–438.

Klein, D. F., Zitrin, C. M., & Woerner, M. (1978). Antidepressants, anxiety, panic, and phobia. In M. A. Lipton, A. DiMascio, & K. F. Killam (Eds.), *Psychopharmacology: A generation of progress* (pp. 1401–1410). New York: Raven Press.

Köhler, W. (1927). *The mentality of apes* (trans. from 2nd ed.). New York: Harcourt, Brace.

Kraepelin, E. (1899, 1909–1915). [Psychiatrie. *Ein Lehrbuch für Studiereude und Arzte* (ed. 5, ed. 6, ed. 8)]. Leipzig: Barth.

Krippner, S., & Ullman, M. (1970). Telepathy and dreams: A controlled experiment with electroencephalogram-electro-oculogram monitoring. *The Journal of Nervous and Mental Disease, 151,* 394–403.

Kruskal, J. B. & Wish, M. (1978). *Multidimensional scaling.* Sage University Paper series on Quantitative Applications in the Social Sciences, Series No. 07-011. Beverly Hills and London: Sage Publications.

Kučera, H., & Francis, W. N. (1967). *Computational analysis of present-day American English.* Providence, RI: Brown University Press.

Labov, W. (1973). The boundaries of words and their meanings. In C. J. N. Bailey & R. W. Shuy (Eds.), *New ways of analyzing variation in English.* Washington, DC: Georgetown University Press.

Lachman, R., Lachman, J. L., & Butterfield, E. C. (1979). *Cognitive psychology and information processing: An introduction.* Hillsdale, NJ: Erlbaum.

Lakoff, G. (1975). Hedges: A study in meaning criteria and the logic of fuzzy concepts. In D. Hockney, W. Harper, & B. Freed (Eds.), *Contemporary research in philosophical logic and linguistic semantics* (pp. 221–271). Boston: Reidel.

Landauer, T. K. (1962). Rate of implicit speech. *Perceptual & Motor Skills, 15,* 646.

Landauer, T. K., & Streeter, L. A. (1973). Structural differences between common and rare words: Failure of equivalence assumptions for theories of word recognition. *Journal of Verbal Learning and Verbal Behavior, 12,* 119–131.

Larson, R. S., & Stroup, D. F. (1976). *Statistics in the real world.* New York: Macmillan.

LeDoux, J. E., Wilson, D. H., & Gazzaniga, M. S. (1977). Manipulo-spatial aspects of cerebral lateralization: Clues to the origin of lateralization. *Neuropsychologia, 15,* 743–750.

Leippe, M., Wells, G. L., & Ostrom, T. (1978). Crime seriousness as a determinant of accuracy in eyewitness identification. *Journal of Applied Psychology, 63,* 345–351.

Lenneberg, E. H. (1967). *Biological foundations of language.* New York: Wiley.

Lenneberg, E. H., & Roberts, J. M. (1953). The denotata of color terms. Paper read at the Linguistic Society of America, Bloomington, Indiana.

Lepper, M. R., Greene, D., & Nisbett, R. E. (1973). Undermining children's intrinsic interest with extrinsic reward. *Journal of Personality and Social Psychology, 28,* 129–137.

Lewin, K. (1938). *The conceptual representation and the measurement of psychological forces.* Durham, NC: Duke University Press.

Light, L. L., & Carter-Sobell, L. (1970). Effects of changed semantic context on recognition memory. *Journal of Verbal Learning and Verbal Behavior, 9,* 1–11.

Lipton, J. P. (1977). On the psychology of eyewitness testimony. *Journal of Applied Psychology, 62,* 90–95.

Lockhart, R. S., & Murdock, B. B., Jr. (1970). Memory and the theory of signal detection. *Psychological Bulletin, 74,* 100–109.

Loftus, E. F. (1983a). Silence is not golden. *American Psychologist, 38,* 564–572.

Loftus, E. F. (1983b). Whose shadow is crooked? *American Psychologist, 38,* 576–577.

Loftus, E. F., Altman, D., & Geballe, R. (1975). Effects of questioning upon a witness' later recollections. *Journal of Police Science and Administration, 3,* 162–165.

Loftus, E. F., Miller, D. G., & Burns, H. J. (1978). Semantic integration of verbal information into a visual memory. *Journal of Experimental Psychology: Human Learning and Memory, 4,* 19–31.

Loftus, E. F., & Palmer, J. C. (1974). Reconstruction of automobile destruction: An example of the interaction between language and memory. *Journal of Verbal Learning and Verbal Behavior, 13,* 585–589.

Loftus, G. R. (1972). Eye fixations and recognition memory for pictures. *Cognitive Psychology, 3,* 525–551.

Luce, T. S. (1974, November). Blacks, whites and yellows: They all look alike to me. *Psychology Today,* 105–108.

Luchins, A. S. (1942). Mechanization in problem solving. *Psychological Monographs, 54* (No. 6.).

MacDougall, C. D. (1940). *Hoaxes.* New York: Macmillan.

MacKay, D. G. (1973). Aspects of the theory of comprehension, memory and attention. *Quarterly Journal of Experimental Psychology, 25,* 22–40.

Maier, N. F. R. (1931). Reasoning in humans. II. The solution of a problem and its appearance in consciousness. *Journal of Comparative Psychology, 12,* 181–194.

Malinowski, B. (1927). *Sex and repression in savage society.* New York: Harcourt, Brace.

Malpass, R. S., & Kravitz, J. (1969). Recognition for faces of own and other race. *Journal of Personality and Social Psychology, 13,* 330–334.

Maltzman, I., Simon, S., Raskin, D., & Licht, L. (1960). Experimental studies in the training of originality. *Psychological Monographs, 74,* 6 (Whole No. 493).

Mandler, G. (1967). Organization and memory. In K. W. Spence & J. T. Spence (Eds.), *The psychology of learning and motivation* (Vol. 1, pp. 327–372). New York: Academic Press.

Marquis, K. H., Marshall, J., & Oskamp, S. (1972). Testimony validity as a function of question form, atmosphere, and item difficulty. *Journal of Applied Social Psychology, 2,* 167–186.

Marshall, J. (1966). *Law and psychology in conflict.* New York: Doubleday.

Martin, E. (1975). Generation-recognition theory and the encoding specificity principle. *Psychological Review, 82,* 150–153.

Massaro, D. W. (1975). *Experimental psychology and information processing.* Chicago: Rand McNally.

Matlin, M. W., & Stang, D. J. (1978). *The Pollyanna principle: Selectivity in language, memory, and thought.* Cambridge, MA: Schenkman.

Mayo, E. (1933). *The human problems of an industrial civilization.* Cambridge, MA: Harvard University Press.

Mayzner, M. S., & Tresselt, M. E. (1958). Anagram solution times: A function of letter order and word frequency. *Journal of Experimental Psychology, 56,* 376–379.

Mayzner, M. S., & Tresselt, M. E. (1965). Tables of single-letter and digram frequency counts for various word-length and letter-position combinations. *Psychonomic Monograph Supplements, 1* (Whole No. 2), 13–32.

Mayzner, M. S., Tresselt, M. E., & Wolin, B. R. (1965a). Tables of trigram frequency counts for various word-length and letter-position combinations. *Psychonomic Monograph Supplements, 1* (Whole No. 3), 33–78.

Mayzner, M. S., Tresselt, M. E., & Wolin, B. R. (1965b). Tables of tetragram frequency counts for various word-length and letter-position combinations. *Psychonomic Monograph Supplements, 1* (Whole No. 4), 79–143.

Mayzner, M. S., Tresselt, M. E., & Wolin, B. R. (1965c). Tables of pentagram frequency counts for various word-length and letter-position combinations. *Psychonomic Monograph Supplements, 1* (Whole No. 5), 145–185.

McClelland, D. C., Atkinson, J. W., Clark, R. A., & Lowell, E. L. (1953). *The achievement motive.* New York: Appleton-Century-Crofts.

McClelland, J. L., & Rumelhart, D. E. (1981). An interactive activation model of context effects in letter perception: Part 1. An account of basic findings. *Psychological Review, 88,* 375–407.

McCloskey, M., & Egeth, H. (1983a). Eyewitness identification. What can a psychologist tell a jury. *American Psychologist, 38,* 550–563.

McCloskey, M., & Egeth, H. (1983b). A time to speak or a time to keep silence? *American Psychologist, 38,* 573–575.

McCloskey, M. E., & Glucksberg, S. (1978). Natural categories: Well defined or fuzzy sets? *Memory & Cognition, 6,* 462–472.

McCormack, P. D., & Swenson, A. L. (1972). Recognition memory for common and rare words. *Journal of Experimental Psychology, 95,* 72–77.

McDougall, R. (1904). Recognition and recall. *Journal of Philosophical Psychology and Scientific Methods, 1,* 229–233.

McDowell, J. J. (1981). On the validity and utility of Herrnstein's hyperbola in applied behavior analysis. In C. M. Bradshaw, E. Szabadi, & C. F. Lowe (Eds.), *Quantification of steady-state operant behaviour.* Amsterdam: Elsevier.

McGhie, A., & Chapman, J. (1961). Disorders of attention and perception in early schizophrenia. *British Journal of Medical Psychology, 34,* 103–116.

McGinnies, E. (1949). Emotionality and perceptual defense. *Psychological Review, 56,* 244–251.

McGlone, J. (1980). Sex differences in human brain asymmetry: A critical survey. *The Behavioral and Brain Sciences, 3,* 215–263.

McGuinness, D. (1976). Away from a unisex psychology: Individual differences in visual sensory and perceptual processes. *Perception, 5,* 279–294.

Medin, D. L., & Schaffer, M. M. (1978). Context theory of classification learning. *Psychological Review, 85,* 207–238.

Meehl, P. E. (1950). On the circularity of the law of effect. *Psychological Bulletin, 47,* 52–75.

Meehl, P. E. (1978). Theoretical risks and tabular asterisks: Sir Karl, Sir Ronald, and the slow progress of soft psychology. *Journal of Consulting and Clinical Psychology, 46,* 806–834.

Melton, A. W. (1963). Implications of short-term memory for a general theory of memory. *Journal of Verbal Learning and Verbal Behavior, 2,* 1–21.

Mervis, C. B., Catlin, J., & Rosch, E. (1976). Relationships among goodness-of-example, category norms, and word frequency. *Bulletin of the Psychonomic Society, 7,* 283–284.

Meyer, D. E., & Schvaneveldt, R. W. (1971). Facilitation in recognizing pairs of words: Evidence of a dependence between retrieval operations. *Journal of Experimental Psychology, 90,* 227–234.

Milgram, S. (1963). Behavioral study of obedience. *Journal of Abnormal and Social Psychology, 67,* 371–378.

Milgram, S. (1972). The lost-letter technique. In L. Bickman & T. Henchy (Eds.), *Beyond the laboratory: Field research in social psychology.* New York: McGraw-Hill.

Milgram, S. (1973). *Obedience to authority.* New York: Harper & Row.

Milgram, S., Bickman, L., & Berkowitz, L. (1969). Note on the drawing power of crowds of different size. *Journal of Personality and Social Psychology, 13,* 79–82.

Miller, G. A. (1956). The magical number seven, plus or minus two: Some limits on our capacity for processing information. *Psychological Review, 63,* 81–97.

Miller, G. A. (1962). Decision units in the perception of speech. *IRE Transactions on Information Theory, IT-8,* 81–83.

Miller, G. A. (1981). *Language and speech.* San Francisco: Freeman.

Miller, G. A., Bruner, J. S., & Postman, L. (1954). Familiarity of letter sequences and tachistoscopic identification. *Journal of General Psychology, 50,* 129–139.

Miller, G. A., Galanter, E., & Pribram, K. H. (1960). *Plans and the structure of behavior.* New York: Holt, Rinehart, & Winston.

Miller, N. E. (1944/1972). Experimental studies of conflict. In J. McV. Hunt (Ed.), *Personality and the behavior disorders.* New York: Ronald Press.

Miller, N. E. (1951a). Comments on theoretical models illustrated by the devleopment of a theory of conflict behavior. *Journal of Personality, 20,* 82–100.

Miller, N. E. (1951b). Learnable drives and rewards. In S. S. Stevens (Ed.), *Handbook of experimental psychology* (pp. 435–472). New York: Wiley.

Milner, B., Taylor, L., & Sperry, R. W. (1968). Lateralized suppression of dichotically presented digits after commissural section in man. *Science, 161,* 184–185.

Mishkin, M., & Forgays, D. G. (1952). Word recognition as a function of retinal locus. *Journal of Experimental Psychology, 43,* 43–48.

Moray, N. (1959). Attention in dichotic listening: Affective cues and the influence of instructions. *Quarterly Journal of Experimental Psychology, 11,* 56–60.

Mowrer, O. H. (1947). On the dual nature of learning: A reinterpretation of "conditioning" and "problem-solving." *Harvard Educational Review, 17,* 102–148.

Mowrer, O. H., & Lamoreaux, R. R. (1942). Avoidance conditioning and signal duration—a study of secondary motivation and reward. *Psychological Monographs, 54,* No. 247.

Mowrer, O. H., & Lamoreaux, R. R. (1946). Fear as an intervening variable in avoidance conditioning. *Journal of Comparative and Physiological Psychology, 39,* 29–50.

Murdock, B. B., Jr. (1961). The retention of individual items. *Journal of Experimental Psychology, 62,* 618–625.

Murdock, B. B., Jr. (1965). Signal-detection theory and short-term memory. *Journal of Experimental Psychology, 70,* 443–447.

Neisser, U. (1963). Decision time without reaction time: Experiments in visual scanning. *American Journal of Psychology, 76,* 376–385.

Neisser, U. (1967). *Cognitive psychology.* New York: Appleton-Century-Crofts.

Neisser, U., & Becklen, R. (1975). Selective looking: Attending to visually-specified events. *Cognitive Psychology, 7,* 480–494.

Neisser, U., Novick, R., & Lazar, R. (1963). Searching for ten targets simultaneously. *Perceptual and Motor Skills, 17,* 955–961.

Nelson, D. L., Reed, V. S., & McEvoy, C. L. (1977). Learning to order pictures and words: A model of sensory and semantic encoding. *Journal of Experimental Psychology: Human Learning and Memory, 3,* 485–497.

Nelson, D. L., Reed, V. S., & Walling, J. R. (1976). Pictorial superiority effect. *Journal of Experimental Psychology: Human Learning and Memory, 2,* 523–528.

Nelson, T. O., & Rothbart, R. (1972). Acoustic savings for items forgotten from long-term memory. *Journal of Experimental Psychology, 93,* 357–360.

Neumann, P. G. (1974). An attribute frequency model for the abstraction of prototypes. *Memory & Cognition, 2,* 241–248.

Newbigging, P. L. (1961). The perceptual redintegration of frequent and infrequent words. *Canadian Journal of Psychology, 15,* 123–132.

Newell, A., Ernst, G., & Simon, H. A. (1957, February). Empirical explorations with the logic theory machine. *Proceedings of the Western Joint Computer Conference,* 218–230.

Newell, A., Shaw, J. C., & Simon, H. A. (1959, 1965). Report on a general problem-solving program. Proceedings of International Conference on Information Processing. Reprinted in R. D. Luce, R. Bush, & E. Galanter (Eds.), *Readings in mathematical psychology* (Vol. II, pp. 41–57). New York: Wiley.

Newell, A., & Simon, H. A. (1961). Computer simulation of human thinking. *Science, 134,* 2011–2017.

Nickerson, R. S. (1965). Short-term memory for

complex meaningful visual configurations: A demonstration of capacity. *Canadian Journal of Psychology, 19,* 155–160.

Noble, C. E. (1963). Meaningfulness and familiarity. In C. N. Cofer & B. S. Musgrave (Eds.), *Verbal behavior and learning* (pp. 76–119). New York: McGraw-Hill.

Noble, C. E. (1967). Comparative pronounceability ratings (*p*) of 100 CVCs in two college populations. *Psychonomic Science, 8,* 433–434.

Norman, D. A. (1968). Toward a theory of memory and attention. *Psychological Review, 75,* 522–536.

Norman, D. A. (1976). *Memory and attention* (2nd ed.). New York: Wiley.

Norman, D. A., & Bobrow, D. G. (1975). On data-limited and resource-limited processes. *Cognitive Psychology, 7,* 44–64.

O'Brien, C. P., Testa, T., O'Brien, T. J., Brady, J. P., & Wells, B. (1977). Conditioned narcotic withdrawal in humans. *Science, 195,* 1000–1002.

O'Connor, N., & Hermelin, B. (1961). Like and cross-modality recognition in subnormal children. *Quarterly Journal of Experimental Psychology, 13,* 48–52.

Olds, J., & Milner, P. (1954). Positive reinforcement produced by electrical stimulation of septal area and other regions of rat brain. *Journal of Comparative and Physiological Psychology, 47,* 419–427.

Orne, M. T. (1962). On the social psychology of the psychological experiment: With particular reference to demand characteristics and their implications. *American Psychologist, 17,* 776–783.

Ornstein, R. (1977). *The psychology of consciousness* (2nd ed.). New York: Harcourt, Brace, Jovanovich.

Pachella, R. G. (1974). The interpretation of reaction time in information-processing research. In B. H. Kantowitz (Ed.), *Human information processing: Tutorials in performance and cognition* (pp. 41–82). Hillsdale, NJ: Erlbaum.

Paivio, A. (1971). *Imagery and verbal processes.* New York: Holt, Rinehart, & Winston.

Paivio, A., & Csapo, K. (1973). Picture superiority in free recall: Imagery or dual coding? *Cognitive Psychology, 5,* 176–206.

Paivio, A., Rogers, T. B., & Smythe, P. C. (1968). Why are pictures easier to recall than words? *Psychonomic Science, 11,* 137–138.

Paivio, A., & Simpson, H. M. (1966). The effect of word abstractions and pleasantness on pupil size during an imagery task. *Psychonomic Science, 5,* 55–56.

Paivio, A., Yuille, J. C., & Madigan, S. (1968). Concreteness, imagery, and meaningfulness values for 925 nouns. *Journal of Experimental Psychology, 76* (Monograph Suppl.), No. 1, Pt. 2.

Palmer, S. E. (1975a). The effects of contextual scenes on the identification of objects. *Memory & Cognition, 3,* 519–526.

Palmer, S. E. (1975b). Visual perception and world knowledge. In D. A. Norman, D. E. Rumelhart, & the LNR Research Group, *Explorations in cognition.* San Francisco: Freeman.

Patterson, K., & Bradshaw, J. L. (1975). Differential hemispheric mediation of nonverbal visual stimuli. *Journal of Experimental Psychology: Human Perception and Performance, 1,* 246–252.

Pavlov, I. P. (1927). *Conditioned reflexes.* Oxford, England: Oxford University Press.

Payne, R. W., & Caird, W. K. (1967). Reaction time, distractability, and over-inclusive thinking in psychotics. *Journal of Abnormal Psychology, 72,* 112–121.

Peterson, L. R., & Peterson, M. J. (1959). Short-term retention of individual verbal items. *Journal of Experimental Psychology, 58,* 193–198.

Pfungst, O. von (1911). [*Clever Hans (the horse of Mr. von Osten): A contribution to experimental, animal, and human psychology*] (C. L. Rahn, trans.). New York: Holt.

Pierrel, R. & Sherman, J. (1963, February), Train your pet the Barnabus way. *Brown Alumni Monthly,* 8–14.

Pirenne, M. H. (1970). *Optics, painting, and photography.* Cambridge, England: Cambridge University Press.

Pollack, I. (1970). A nonparametric procedure for evaluation of true and false positives. *Behavior Research Methods and Instrumentation, 2,* 155–156.

Pollack, I., & Norman, D. A. (1964). A nonparametric analysis of recognition experiments. *Psychonomic Science, 1,* 125–126.

Pollio, H. R., Kasschau, R. A., & DeNise, H. E. (1968). Associative structure and the temporal characteristics of free recall. *Journal of Experimental Psychology, 76,* 190–197.

Posner, M. I. (1969). Abstraction and the process of recognition. In G. H. Bower & J. T. Spence (Eds.), *The psychology of learning and motivation* (Vol. 3, pp. 43–100). New York: Academic Press.

Posner, M. I., Boies, S. J., Eichelman, W. H., & Taylor, R. L. (1969). Retention of visual and name codes of single letters. *Journal of Experimental Psychology, 79* (Monograph Suppl. 1), 1–16.

Posner, M. I., Goldsmith, R., & Welton, K. E., Jr. (1967). Perceived distance and the classification of distorted patterns. *Journal of Experimental Psychology, 73,* 28–38.

Posner, M. I., & Keele, S. W. (1968). On the genesis of abstract ideas. *Journal of Experimental Psychology, 77,* 353–363.

Posner, M. I., & Mitchell, R. F. (1967). Chronometric analysis of classification. *Psychological Review, 74,* 393–409.

Postman, L., Bronson, W. C., & Gropper, G. L. (1953). Is there a mechanism of perceptual defense? *Journal of Abnormal and Social Psychology, 48,* 215–224.

Postman, L., & Keppel, G. (Eds.). (1970). *Norms of word association.* New York: Academic Press.

Poulton, E. C. (1973). Unwanted range effects from using within-subject experimental designs. *Psychological Bulletin, 80,* 113–121.

Pylyshyn, Z. W. (1973). What the mind's eye tells the mind's brain: A critique of mental imagery. *Psychological Bulletin, 80,* 1–24.

Quillian, M. R. (1968). Semantic memory. In M. Minsky (Ed.), *Semantic information processing.* Cambridge, MA: MIT Press.

Quillian, M. R. (1969). The teachable language comprehender: A simulation program and theory of language. *Communications of the ACM, 12,* 459–476.

Rachlin, H., & Green, L. (1972). Commitment, choice and self-control. *Journal of the Experimental Analysis of Behavior, 17,* 15–22.

Ratliff, F. (1976). On the psychophysiological bases of universal color terms. *Proceedings of the American Philosophical Society, 120,* 311–330.

Reder, L. M., Anderson, J. R., & Bjork, R. A. (1974). A semantic interpretation of encoding specificity. *Journal of Experimental Psychology, 102,* 648–656.

Reed, S. K. (1972). Pattern recognition and categorization. *Cognitive Psychology, 3,* 382–407.

Reed, S. K., & Friedman, M. P. (1973). Perceptual vs. conceptual categorization. *Memory & Cognition, 1,* 157–163.

Reicher, G. M. (1969). Perceptual recognition as a function of meaningfulness of stimulus material. *Journal of Experimental Psychology, 81,* 275–280.

Reitman, W. R. (1965). *Cognition and thought.* New York: Wiley.

Rescorla, R. A. (1966). Predictability and number of pairings in Pavlovian fear conditioning. *Psychonomic Science, 4,* 383–384.

Rescorla, R. A. (1967). Pavlovian conditioning and its proper control procedures. *Psychological Review, 74,* 71–80.

Rescorla, R. A. (1968). Probability of shock in the presence and absence of CS in fear conditioning. *Journal of Comparative and Physiological Psychology, 66,* 1–5.

Restle, F. (1962). The selection of strategies in cue learning. *Psychological Review, 69,* 329–343.

Riess, B. F. (1940). Semantic conditioning. *Journal of Experimental Psychology, 26,* 238–240.

Rips, L. J., Shoben, E. J., & Smith, E. E. (1973). Semantic distance and the verification of semantic relations. *Journal of Verbal Learning and Verbal Behavior, 12,* 1–20.

Rizzolatti, G., Umilta, C., & Berlucchi, G. (1971). Opposite superiorities of the right and left cerebral hemispheres in discriminative reaction time to physiognomical and alphabetical material. *Brain, 94,* 431–442.

Roethlisberger, F. J., & Dickson, W. J. (1939). *Management and the worker.* Cambridge, MA: Harvard University Press.

Rosch, E. H. (1973). Natural categories. *Cognitive Psychology, 4,* 328–350.

Rosch, E. H. (1975). Cognitive representations of semantic categories. *Journal of Experimental Psychology, 104,* 192–233.

Rosch, E. H. (1977). Human categorization. In N. Warren (Ed.), *Studies in cross-cultural psychology* (Vol. 1, pp. 1–49). New York: Academic Press.

Rosch, E. (1978). Principles of categorization. In E. Rosch & B. B. Lloyd (Eds.), *Cognition and categorization* (pp. 28–49). Hillsdale, NJ: Erlbaum.

Rosch, E. H., & Mervis, C. B. (1975). Family resemblances: Studies in the internal structure of categories. *Cognitive Psychology, 7,* 573–605.

Rosch, E. H., Mervis, C. B., Gray, W. D., Johnson, D. M., & Boyes-Braem, P. (1976). Basic objects in natural categories. *Cognitive Psychology, 8,* 382–439.

Rosenthal,. R. (1976). *Experimenter effects in behavioral research.* New York: Irvington Publishers (Wiley, distributor).

Rosenthal, R., & Fode, K. L. (1963). The effect of experimenter bias on the performance of the albino rat. *Behavioral Science, 8,* 183–189.

Ross, E. D. (1982, February). The divided self. *The Sciences, 22,* 8–12.

Roth, S., & Kubal, L. (1975). Effects of noncontingent reinforcement on tasks of differing importance: Facilitation and learned helplessness. *Journal of Personality and Social Psychology, 32,* 680–691.

Rozeboom, W. W. (1960). The fallacy of the null-hypothesis significance test. *Psychological Bulletin, 57,* 416–428.

Rumelhart, D. E., & McClelland, J. L. (1982). An interactive activation model of context effects in letter perception: Part 2. The contextual enhancement effect and some tests and extensions of the model. *Psychological Review, 89,* 60–94.

Sattath, S., & Tversky, A. (1977). Additive similarity trees. *Psychometrika, 42,* 319–345.

Savage, C. W. (1966). Introspectionist and behaviorist interpretations of ratio scales of perceptual magnitudes. *Psychological Monographs, 80* (19, Whole No. 627).

Schachter, S., & Singer, J. E. (1962). Cognitive, social, and physiological determinants of emotional state. *Psychological Review, 69,* 379–399.

Schneider, W., & Shiffrin, R. M. (1977). Controlled and automatic human information processing: I. Detection, search, and attention. *Psychological Review, 84,* 1–66.

Schulman, A. I. (1967). Word length and rarity in recognition memory. *Psychonomic Science, 9,* 211–212.

Schwabacher, S. (1972). Male versus female representation in psychological research: An examination of the Journal of Personality and Social Psychology, 1970, 1971. *JSAS Catalog of Selected Documents in Psychology, 2,* 20 (Ms. No. 82).

Schwartz, B., & Williams, D. R. (1972). The role of the response-reinforcer contingency in negative automaintenance. *Journal of the Experimental Analysis of Behavior, 17,* 351–357.

Segall, M. H., Campbell, D. T., & Herskovits, M. J. (1966). *The influence of culture on visual perception.* Indianapolis: Bobbs-Merrill.

Seligman, M. E. P. (1974). *Helplessness.* San Francisco: Freeman.

Seligman, M. E. P., Abramson, L. Y., Semmel, A., & von Baeyer, C. (1979). Depressive attributional style. *Journal of Abnormal Psychology, 88,* 242–247.

Seligman, M. E. P., & Maier, S. F. (1967). Failure to escape traumatic shock. *Journal of Experimental Psychology, 74,* 1–9.

Seligman, M. E. P., Maier, S. F., & Solomon, R. L. (1971). Unpredictable and uncontrollable aversive events. In F. R. Brush (Ed.), *Aversive conditioning and learning.* New York: Academic Press.

Shagass, C., Roemer, R. A., & Amadeo, M. (1976). Eye tracking performance and engagement of attention. *Archives of General Psychiatry, 33,* 121–125.

Shakow, D. (1977). Segmental set: The adaptive process in schizophrenia. *American Psychologist, 32,* 129–139.

Shannon, C. E., & Weaver, W. (1949). *The mathematical theory of communication.* Urbana, IL: University of Illinois Press.

Shepard, R. N. (1967). Recognition memory for words, sentences, and pictures. *Journal of Verbal Learning and Verbal Behavior, 6,* 156–163.

Shepard, R. N., Romney, A. K., & Nerlove, S. B. (Eds.). (1972). *Multidimensional scaling: Theory and applications in the behavioral sciences.* New York: Seminar Press.

Shepard, R. N., & Teghtsoonian, M. (1961). Retention of information under conditions approaching a steady state. *Journal of Experimental Psychology, 62,* 302–309.

Shulman, H. G. (1971). Similarity effects in short-term memory. *Psychological Bulletin, 75,* 399–415.

Sidman, M. (1960). *Tactics of scientific research.* New York: Basic Books.

Siegel, S. (1956). *Nonparametric statistics for the behavioral sciences.* New York: McGraw-Hill.

Siegel, S., Hearst, E., George, N., & O'Neal, E. (1968). Generalization gradients obtained from individual subjects following classical conditioning. *Journal of Experimental Psychology, 78,* 171–174.

Silverman, J. (1967). Variations in cognitive control and psychophysiological defense in the schizophrenias. *Psychosomatic Medicine, 29,* 225–251.

Simon, H. A. (1974). How big is a chunk? *Science, 183,* 482–488.

Simon, H. A., & Feigenbaum, E. A. (1964). An information-processing theory of some effects of similarity, familiarization, and meaningfulness in verbal learning. *Journal of Ver-*

bal Learning and Verbal Behavior, 3, 385–396.

Skinner, B. F. (1937). Two types of conditioned reflex: A reply to Konorski and Miller. *Journal of General Psychology, 16,* 272–279.

Skinner, B. F. (1938). *The behavior of organisms.* New York: Appleton-Century-Crofts.

Skinner, B. F. (1956). A case history in scientific method. *American Psychologist, 11,* 221–233.

Skinner, B. F. (1961, November). Teaching machines. *Scientific American, 205,* 90–102.

Smith, E. E., & Medin, D. L. (1981). *Categories and concepts.* Cambridge, MA: Harvard University Press.

Smith, E. E., Shoben, E. J., & Rips, L. J. (1974). Structure and process in semantic memory: A featural model for semantic decisions. *Psychological Review, 81,* 214–241.

Smith, O. W., Badia, P., & Rosenberg, B. G. (1968). Pronounceability ratings of some CVCs: Their reliability and relationship to *m'*. *Psychological Reports, 23,* 691–694.

Smith, O. W., Badia, P., & Rosenberg, B. G. (1969). Are pronounceability and effort ratings psychologically equivalent? *Psychological Reports, 24,* 95–99.

Smith, S., & Myers, T. I. (1966). Stimulation seeking during sensory deprivation. *Perceptual and Motor Skills, 23,* 1151–1163.

Snodgrass, J. G. (1969). Foreperiod effects in simple reaction time: Anticipation or expectancy? *Journal of Experimental Psychology Monograph, 79* (No. 3, Pt. 2).

Snodgrass, J. G. (1971). Objective and subjective complexity measures for a new population of patterns. *Perception & Psychophysics, 10,* 217–224.

Snodgrass, J. G. (1975). Psychophysics. In B. Scharf (Ed.), *Experimental sensory psychology* (pp. 16–67). (Glenview, IL: Scott, Foresman.

Snodgrass, J. G. (1977). *The numbers game: Statistics for psychology.* New York: Oxford University Press.

Snodgrass, J. G. (1980). Toward a model for picture and word processing. In P. A. Kolers, M. E. Wrolstad, & H. Bouma (Eds.), *Processing of visible language 2.* New York: Plenum.

Snodgrass, J. G. (1983). The pragmatics of measuring recognition memory performance. Paper presented at the meetings of the Psychonomic Society, San Antonio, TX.

Snodgrass, J. G., & Antone, G. (1974). Parallel versus sequential processing of pictures and words. *Journal of Experimental Psychology, 103,* 139–144.

Snodgrass, J. G., & Jarvella, R. J. (1972). Some linguistic determinants of word classification times. *Psychonomic Science, 27,* 220–222.

Snodgrass, J. G., Luce, R. D., & Galanter, E. (1967). Some experiments on simple and choice reaction time. *Journal of Experimental Psychology, 75,* 1–17.

Snodgrass, J. G., & McClure, P. (1975). Storage and retrieval properties of dual codes for pictures and words in recognition memory. *Journal of Experimental Psychology: Human Learning and Memory, 1,* 521–529.

Snodgrass, J. G., & Townsend, J. T. (1980). Comparing parallel and serial models: Theory and implementation. *Journal of Experimental Psychology: Human Perception and Performance, 6,* 330–354.

Snodgrass, J. G., & Vanderwart, M. (1980). A standardized set of 260 pictures: Norms for name agreement, image agreement, familiarity, and visual complexity. *Journal of Experimental Psychology: Human Learning and Memory, 6,* 174–215.

Snodgrass, J. G., Volvovitz, R., & Walfish, E. R. (1972). Recognition memory for words, pictures, and words + pictures. *Psychonomic Science, 27,* 345–347.

Solomon, R. L., & Corbit, J. D. (1974). An opponent-process theory of motivation: I. Temporal dynamics of affect. *Psychological Review, 81,* 119–145.

Solomon, R. L. & Corbit, J. D. (1975). An opponent-process theory of motivation. In F. M. Levine (Ed.), *Theoretical readings in motivation.* Chicago: Rand-McNally.

Solomon, R. L., & Wynne, L. C. (1954). Traumatic avoidance learning: The principles of anxiety conservation and partial irreversibility. *Psychological Review, 61,* 353–385.

Solomons, L., & Stein, G. (1896). Normal motor automatism. *Psychological Review, 3,* 492–512.

Spelke, E., Hirst, W., & Neisser, U. (1976). Skills of divided attention. *Cognition, 4,* 215–230.

Spence, K. W. (1936). The nature of discrimination learning in animals. *Psychological Review, 43,* 427–449.

Spence, K. W. (1942). The basis of solution by chimpanzees of the intermediate size problem. *Journal of Experimental Psychology, 31,* 257–271.

Spence, K. W. (1958). A theory of emotionally

based drive (D) and its relation to performance in simple learning situations. *American Psychologist, 13,* 131–141.

Spence, K. W., Farber, I. E., & McFann, H. H. (1956). The relation of anxiety (drive) level to performance in competitonal and non-competitional paired-associates learning. *Journal of Experimental Psychology, 52,* 296–305.

Sperling, G. (1960). The information available in brief visual presentations. *Psychological Monographs, 74,* No. 11.

Sperry, R. W. (1968). Hemisphere deconnection and unity in conscious awareness. *American Psychologist, 23,* 723–733.

Spooner, A., & Kellogg, W. N. (1947). The backward conditioning curve. *American Journal of Psychology, 60,* 321–334.

Springer, S. P., & Deutsch, G. (1981). *Left brain, right brain.* San Francisco: Freeman.

Standing, L., Conezio, J., & Haber, R. N. (1970). Perception and memory for pictures: Single-trial learning of 2,560 visual stimuli. *Psychonomic Science, 19,* 73–74.

Stedman's medical dictionary (24th ed.). (1982). Baltimore, MD: Williams & Wilkins.

Steger, J. A. (Ed.). (1971). *Readings in statistics for the behavioral scientist.* New York: Holt, Rinehart, & Winston.

Sternberg, S. (1966). High-speed scanning in human memory. *Science, 153,* 652–654.

Sternberg, S. (1967). Two operations in character recognition: Some evidence from reaction-time measurements. *Perception & Psychophysics, 2,* 45–53.

Sternberg, S. (1969a). The discovery of processing stages: Extensions of Donders' method. In W. G. Koster (Ed.), *Attention and performance II* (pp. 276–315). Amsterdam: North-Holland Publishing Company. (Reprinted from *Acta Psychologica,* 1969, *30,* 276–315.)

Sternberg, S. (1969b). Memory-scanning: Mental processes revealed by reaction-time experiments. *American Scientist, 57,* 421–457.

Sternberg, S. (1975). Memory scanning: New findings and current controversies. *Quarterly Journal of Experimental Psychology, 27,* 1–32.

Stevens, S. S. (1961a). The psychophysics of sensory function. In W. A. Rosenblith (Ed.), *Sensory Communication* (pp. 1–33). Cambridge, MA: MIT Press.

Stevens, S. S. (1961b). To honor Fechner and repeal his law. *Science, 133,* 80–86.

Stevens, S. S. (1975). *Psychophysics: Introduction to its perceptual, neural, and social prospects.* New York: Wiley.

Stevens, S. S., & Galanter, E. (1957). Ratio scales and category scales for a dozen perceptual continua. *Journal of Experimental Psychology, 54,* 377–411.

Stroop, J. R. (1935). Studies of interference in serial verbal reactions. *Journal of Experimental Psychology, 18,* 643–662.

Strunk, W., Jr., & White, E. B. (1979). *The elements of style* (3rd ed.). New York: Macmillan.

Studdert-Kennedy, M., & Shankweiler, D. (1970). Hemispheric specialization for speech perception. *Journal of the Acoustical Society of America, 48,* 579–594.

Suedfeld, P., & Landon, P. B. (1970). Motivational arousal and task complexity. *Journal of Experimental Psychology, 83,* 329–330.

Sumby, W. H. (1963). Word frequency and serial position effects. *Journal of Verbal Learning and Verbal Behavior, 1,* 443–450.

Tajfel, H. (1982). Social psychology of intergroup relations. *Annual Review of Psychology, 33,* 1–39.

Taylor, J. A. (1956). Drive theory and manifest anxiety. *Psychological Bulletin, 53,* 303–320.

Terrace, H. S. (1979). *Nim.* New York: Knopf.

Terrace, H. S., Petitto, L. A., Sanders, R. J., & Bever, T. G. (1979). Can an ape create a sentence? *Science, 206,* 891–902.

Teuber, M. L. (1974, July). Sources of ambiguity in the prints of Maurits C. Escher, *Scientific American,* 90–104.

Theios, J., Smith, P. G., Haviland, S. E., Traupmann, J., & Moy, M. C. (1973). Memory scanning as a serial self-terminating process. *Journal of Experimental Psychology, 97,* 323–336.

Thorndike, E. L. (1898). Animal intelligence: An experimental study of the associative processes in animals. *Psychological Monographs* 2 (No. 8).

Thorndike, E. L. (1911). *Animal intelligence: Experimental studies.* New York: Macmillan.

Thorndike, E. L., & Lorge, I. (1944). *The teacher's word book of 30,000 words.* New York: Columbia University, Teacher's College.

Tolman, E. C. (1948). Cognitive maps in rats and men. *Psychological Review, 55,* 189–208.

Tolman, E. C. (1951). *Purposive behavior in animals and men.* Los Angeles: University of California.

Trapold, M. A. (1970). Are expectancies based upon different positive reinforcing events discriminably different? *Learning and Motivation, 1,* 129–140.

Treisman, A. M. (1964). Verbal cues, language and meaning in selective attention. *American Journal of Psychology, 77,* 206–219.

Treisman, A. M., & Geffen, G. (1967). Selective attention: Perception or response. *Quarterly Journal of Experimental Psychology, 19,* 1–17.

Tukey, J. W. (1977). *Exploratory data analysis.* Reading, MA: Addison-Wesley.

Tulving, E. (1962). Subjective organization in free recall of "unrelated" words. *Psychological Review, 69,* 344–354.

Tulving, E. (1972). Episodic and semantic memory. In E. Tulving & W. Donaldson (Eds.), *Organization of memory.* (pp. 381–403). New York: Academic Press.

Tulving, E., & Thomson, D. M. (1971). Retrieval processes in recognition memory: Effects of associative context. *Journal of Experimental Psychology, 87,* 116–124.

Tulving, E., & Thomson, D. M. (1973). Encoding specificity and retrieval processes in episodic memory. *Psychological Review, 80,* 352–373.

Ullman, M., Krippner, S., & Feldstein, S. (1966). Experimentally-induced telepathic dreams: Two studies using EEG-REM monitoring technique. *International Journal of Neuropsychiatry, 2,* 420–437.

Underwood, B. J., & Schulz, R. W. (1960). *Meaningfulness and verbal learning.* Chicago: Lippincott.

Urban, F. M. (1910). The method of constant stimuli and its generalizations. *Psychological Review, 17,* 229–259.

Valins, S. (1966). Cognitive effects of false heart-rate feedback. *Journal of Personality and Social Psychology, 4,* 400–408.

Vanderplas, J. M., Sanderson, W. R., & Vanderplas, J. N. (1965). Statistical and associational characteristics of 1,100 random shapes. *Perceptual and Motor Skills, 21,* 339–348.

Very, P. S. (1967). Differential factor structures in mathematical ability. *Genetic Psychology Monographs, 75,* 169–207.

Wade, N. (1980). Does man alone have language? Apes reply in riddles, and a horse says neigh. *Science, 208,* 1349–1351.

Wardwell, W. I. (1979). Critique of a recent professional put-down of the Hawthorne researchers. *American Sociological Review, 44,* 858–867.

Warner, L., & Clark, C. C. (1938). A survey of psychological opinion on ESP. *Journal of Parapsychology, 2,* 296–301.

Warren, R. M. (1970). Perceptual restoration of missing speech sounds. *Science, 167,* 392–393.

Warren, R. M., & Warren, R. P. (1970, December). Auditory illusions and confusions. *Scientific American,* 30–36.

Wason, P. C. (1960). On the failure to eliminate hypotheses in a conceptual task. *Quarterly Journal of Experimental Psychology, 12,* 129–140.

Wason, P. C. (1968a). On th failure to eliminate hypotheses—a second look. In P. C. Wason, & P. N. Johnson-Laird (Eds.), *Thinking and reasoning* (pp. 165–174). Harmondsworth, England: Penguin Books.

Wason, P. C. (1968b). Reasoning about a rule. *Quarterly Journal of Experimental Psychology, 20,* 273–281.

Watkins, M. J., & Tulving, E. (1974). Episodic memory: When recognition fails. *Journal of Experimental Psychology, 104,* 5–29.

Waugh, N. C., & Norman, D. A. (1965). Primary memory. *Psychological Review, 72,* 89–104.

Webb, E. J., Campbell, D. T., Schwartz, R. D., & Sechrest, L. (1966). *Unobtrusive measures: Nonreactive research in the social sciences.* Chicago: Rand McNally.

Weigel, R. G., Weigel, V. M., & Hebert, J. A. (1971). Non-volunteer subjects: Temporal effects. *Psychological Reports, 28,* 191–192.

Weiner, B., Russell, D., & Lerman, D. (1978). Affective consequences of causal ascriptions. In J. H. Harvey et al. (Eds.), *New directions in attribution research* (Vol. 2, pp. 59–90). Hillsdale, NJ: Erlbaum.

Welkowitz, J., Ewen, R., & Cohen, J. (1982). *Introductory statistics for the behavioral sciences.* New York: Academic Press.

Wells, G. L. (1978). Applied eyewitness-testimony research: System variables and estimator variables. *Journal of Personality and Social Psychology, 36,* 1546–1557.

Wells, J. E. (1972). Encoding and memory for verbal and pictorial stimuli. *Quarterly Journal of Experimental Psychology, 24,* 242–252.

Wertheimer, M. (1959). *Productive thinking* (enlarged ed.). New York: Harper (first published, 1945).

Wheeler, D. D. (1970). Processes in word recognition. *Cognitive Psychology, 1,* 59–85.

Whorf, B. L. (1956). *Language, thought, and reality.* New York: Wiley.

Wickelgren, W. A. (1965). Acoustic similarity and intrusion errors in short-term memory.

Journal of Experimental Psychology, 70, 102–108.

Wickelgren, W. A., & Norman, D. A. (1966). Strength models and serial position in short-term recognition memory. *Journal of Mathematical Psychology, 3,* 316–347.

Wickens, D. D. (1973). Some characteristics of word encoding. *Memory & Cognition, 1,* 485–490.

Wike, E. L. (1971). *Data analysis: A statistical primer for psychology students.* Chicago: Aldine.

Winer, B. J. (1971). *Statistical principles in experimental design* (2nd ed.). New York: McGraw-Hill.

Wittgenstein, L. (1953). *Philosophical investigations.* New York: MacMillan.

Wolpe, J. (1958). *Psychotherapy by reciprocal inhibition.* Stanford, CA: Stanford University Press.

Woodford, F. P. (1967). Sounder thinking through clearer writing. *Science, 156,* 743–745.

Woodrow, H. (1914). The measurement of attention. *Psychological Monographs, 17,* (5, Whole No. 76).

Woodworth, R. S. (1938). *Experimental psychology.* New York: Holt.

Woodworth, R. S., & Sells, S. B. (1935). An atmosphere effect in formal syllogistic reasoning. *Journal of Experimental Psychology, 18,* 451–460.

Yeaton, W. H., & Sechrest, L. (1981). Meaningful measures of effect. *Journal of Consulting and Clinical Psychology, 49,* 766–767.

Yerkes, R. M., & Dodson, J. D. (1908). The relation of strength of stimulus to rapidity of habit-formation. *Journal of Comparative Neurology and Psychology, 18,* 459–482.

Yerkes, R. M. & Morgulis, S. (1909). Method of Pavlov in animal psychology. *Psychological Bulletin, 6,* 257–273.

Young, R. K. (1959). Digit span as a function of the personality of the experimenter. *American Psychologist, 14,* 375.

Yuen, K. K. (1974). The two sample trimmed *t* for unequal population variances. *Biometrika, 61,* 165–170.

Yuen, K. K., & Dixon, W. (1973). The approximate behaviour and performance of the two-sample trimmed *t*. *Biometrika, 60,* 369–374.

Zajonc, R. B. (1962). The effects of feedback and probability of group success on individual and group performance. *Human Relations, 15,* 149–161.

Zubek, J. P. (1969). *Sensory deprivation: 15 years of research.* New York: Appleton-Century-Crofts.

Subject Index

Name Index